Walter Goffart

CW00538440

AFTER ROME'S FALL
NARRATORS AND SOURCES OF EARLY MEDIEVAL HISTORY

EDITED BY ALEXANDER CALLANDER MURRAY

After Rome's Fall

Narrators and Sources
of Early Medieval History
Essays presented to Walter Goffart

UNIVERSITY OF TORONTO PRESS
Toronto Buffalo London

© University of Toronto Press Incorporated 1998
Toronto Buffalo London
Printed in Canada

ISBN 0-8020-0779-1

Printed on acid-free paper

Canadian Cataloguing in Publication Data

Main entry under title:

After Rome's fall : narrators and sources of early medieval history

ISBN 0-8020-0779-1

1. Europe – History – 392–814 – Historiography.   2. Franks – History – To 768 –
Historiography.   3. Franks – History – 768–814 – Historiography.   I. Murray,
Alexander C., 1946–   .   II. Goffart, Walter, 1934–   .

D116.A37 1998   940.1′072   C98-930205-9

University of Toronto Press acknowledges the financial assistance to its publishing
program of the Canada Council for the Arts and the Ontario Arts Council

Contents

Map and Figures

Preface

The essays in this volume were gathered together as a Festschrift for Walter Goffart. They are all intended to be read as self-contained contributions and were written independently of one another. There has been no attempt to harmonize the viewpoints they espouse; attentive readers may in fact detect differences of opinion on various issues among the contributors.

Originally there was no requirement that there be a unifying perspective, other than a connection with the historical developments of the early Middle Ages. Even so broad a focus reflects only one side of Walter Goffart's interests; he called his own collection of essays *Rome's Fall and After*. It seemed appropriate to call the present collection *After Rome's Fall*, as almost all the contributions are concerned with the history of the new kingdoms that replaced the political edifice of the Roman Empire, especially in Gaul and Italy.

Walter Goffart's writings have ranged widely over political and institutional history and historiography. This compass is again only in part reflected in the essays in this volume. The political and social underpinnings of the early medieval period are subjects that could hardly be passed over in a book of essays by more than a dozen historians of the early Middle Ages, but the individual choice of the contributors determined that the present collection would, in large measure, be about the writing of early medieval history, both in the past and in the present. Modern historiography of particular subjects as well as of broad approaches to the period looms large in the following pages – perhaps the promise of being provided with footnotes encouraged contributors to share with readers the rich and detailed contexts of their comments. The sources of the period, especially the historical writing, constitute the subject of two-thirds of the contributions. This book, as it turns out, is largely about reading the sources and interpreting their narrators, both medieval and modern. A direction of this kind was not simply a result of the coincidental historical self-consciousness of the contributors, but was felt by many to be a fitting way to pay tribute to some-one who has himself been prominent in modern historiographical debates and who has expanded our understanding of the subtle and purposeful designs of narrators in all ages.

Walter Goffart takes almost as much delight in editing as he does in scholar-ship, and it has often seemed to me that he would enjoy editing his own Fest-schrift. Without this resource at my disposal, I have had to rely on others to help bring this project to completion. Heartfelt thanks are due to my wife for edito-rial assistance, Roberta Frank for supplying me with information on Walter's early years, the Press for recognizing the value of the essays, and its readers for enthusiastic and helpful responses to the arguments they present. I especially want to thank the contributors. Located as they are from North Bay to Sydney and from Chicago to Paris, my communication with them has relied on e-mail, fax, and telephone and in some cases the modern equivalent of the *cursus cla-bularis*. That co-ordinating this volume turned out to be a pleasant and reward-ing experience is due largely to their patience, good will, and generous participation.

ALEXANDER CALLANDER MURRAY
ORTON, SPRING, 1998

Abbreviations

Aistulf	Laws of Aistulf in *Leges Langobardorum, 643–866*, ed. F. Beyerle (Witzenhausen, 1962)
AMP	*Annales Mettenses priores*, ed. B. von Simson, MGH SRG [10] (1905)
AN	Archives nationales, Paris
Anec. Hold.	*Anecdoton Holderi*, in MGH AA 12 (1894), v–vi
ARF	*Annales regni Francorum inde ab a. 741 usque ad a. 829*, ed. Friedrich Kurze, MGH SRG (1895)
BnF	Bibliothèque nationale de France, Paris
Cass. *Variae*	Cassiodorus Senator, *Variae*, ed. Theodor Mommsen, MGH AA 12 (1894)
CCSL	Corpus Christianorum. Series Latina
CCSL 96	*Variarum libri XII*, ed. Å.J. Fridh, CCSL 96 (Turnhout, 1973)
CDL I, II, III	*Codice diplomatico longobardo*, I and II, ed. L. Schiaperelli (Rome, 1929–33); III, ed. C.R. Brühl (Rome, 1973)
CM	*Chronica Minora Saec. IV, V, VI, VII*, ed. Th. Mommsen, 3 vols., MGH AA 9, 11, 13 (1892–8)
CSEL	Corpus Scriptorum Ecclesiasticorum Latinorum (Vienna)
DTR	Bede, *De temporum ratione*, CCSL 123B
ep., epp.	epistula, epistulae
Fred. [*Chron.*]	*Fredegarii quae dicuntur Chronicarum libri IV*, ed. Bruno Krusch, MGH SRM 2 (1888), 18–168
Gregory, *Hist.*	Gregory of Tours, *Historiarum libri X*, ed. Bruno Krusch and Wilhelm Levison, MGH SRM I/1, 2d. ed. (1937–51)
HL	*Pauli Diaconi Historia Langobardorum*, ed. L. Bethmann and G. Waitz, MGH SS Rerum Langobardicarum et Italicarum (1878), 12–187
Liutprand	Laws of Liutprand in *Leges Langobardorum, 643–866*, ed. F. Beyerle (Witzenhausen, 1962)
mag. off.	*magister officiorum*

MDL V   *Memorie e documenti per servire all'istoria del ducato di Lucca* V, ed.
                 D. Barsocchini (Lucca, 1837–44)

MGH   Monumenta Germaniae Historica. Date of publication follows in
                 parentheses after series title.
    AA   Auctores Antiquissimi
    DD   Diplomata
    LL   Leges
    SS   Scriptores
    SRG NS   Scriptores Rerum Germanicarum, Nova Series
    SRG   Scriptores Rerum Germanicarum in Usum Scholarum Separatim Editi
    SRM   Scriptores Rerum Merovingicarum

PL   *Patrologiae cursus completus. Series latina*, ed. J.-P. Migne, 221 vols.
                 (Paris, 1841–64)

PLRE   *The Prosopography of the Later Roman Empire*, ed. A.H.M. Jones,
                 J.R. Martindale, and J. Morris, 3 vols. (Cambridge, 1971–92)

PPO   *praefectus praetorio*

Ratchis   Laws of Ratchis in *Leges Langobardorum, 643–866*, ed. F. Beyerle
                 (Witzenhausen, 1962)

RB   *La règle de Saint Benoit*, introduction, translation, and notes by Adal-
                 bert de Vogüé, text edited by Jean Neuville, 6 vols., Sources chréti-
                 ennes 181-6, Série des Textes Monastiques d'Occident 34–9 (Paris,
                 1971)

RE   *Realencyclopädie der classischen Altertumswissenschaften*[2], ed. A.F.
                 von Pauly, G. Wissowa (Stuttgart and Munich, 1893–1978)

Rev.   Revised version of *ARF*

RGA   *Reallexikon der germanischen Altertumskunde*, 2d edition, ed. Herbert
                 Jankun (Berlin, 1967–)

Schanz-Hosius   *Geschichte der römischer Litteratur bis zum Gesetzgebungswerk des
                 Kaiser Justinians*, ed. Martin Schanz, Carl Hosius, and Gustav Krüger,
                 4 vols. (Munich, 1914–35)

Settimane   *Settimane del Centro italiano di studi sull'alto medioevo*

VC   Jonas of Bobbio, *Vita Columbani*, ed. B. Krusch, MGH SRM 4 (1902)

VK   *Einhardi Vita Karoli Magni*, ed. O. Holder-Egger, MGH SRG (1911)

AFTER ROME'S FALL

Introduction:
Walter André Goffart

ALEXANDER CALLANDER MURRAY

The plans for this book were set in motion, perhaps not untypically, by a departmental memorandum. At the beginning of each fall term, a list circulates among the History faculty at the University of Toronto, outlining the upcoming leaves and retirements; I usually read it in anticipation of reminding myself how near (or how far) my leave might be. In 1992, with uncharacteristic thoroughness, the list reached all the way to the millennium. In the roster of retirees under the date 1999, my eye caught the name Walter Goffart. That Walter Goffart's retirement could be on the horizon came as a surprise; its near accord with the millennium I put down to mere coincidence. It was difficult to imagine History or Medieval Studies at Toronto without Walter Goffart and even more difficult to imagine the profession without his critical direction. On the last score, there was clearly no need for alarm. Walter's most recent book, *The Narrators of Barbarian History* (1988), was riding on a wave of congratulatory acclamation; and Walter was involved in placing the Goffartian stamp on a new field of endeavour a little removed from his usual haunts.

Elementary arithmetic told me Walter's birth date, but I knew nothing of his early years, which, though probably not extraordinary for those born in his time and place, turned out to be more exciting than he had let on; whether they have any bearing on his historical perspective, I leave others to decide. Walter Goffart was born on 22 February 1934, a dismal year marked by the death of Hindenburg, the election of Hitler as Führer, and a string of political murders in central Europe. The cohort of that year included the Dionne quintuplets, a source of amazement to the world's press, born a few hundred kilometres north of Walter's eventual home in Toronto, and Sophia Loren, whose fame was reserved until maturity, born in poverty in Naples. Walter's circumstances were somewhat better. He was born in Berlin, close to the great political events of the time. His mother was of French and Romanian extraction, and his father a Belgian diplomat serving in the mission trying to deal with the new German chancellor. Diplomatic life soon brought Walter to Belgrade, where he received his early schooling. The outbreak of war separated Walter's father from the rest of the family, which was forced to undertake a trek eastward. From Belgrade they caught the last train of the Orient Express taking enemy nationals to neutral Turkey, and then moved on briefly to Beirut, Jerusalem, and then Cairo, the birthplace of Walter's mother. (It seems safe to suggest that a permanent result of these years may be Walter's propensity for lunching with friends on Middle Eastern cuisine in a small Toronto bistro inaptly named Kensington Kitchen.) The *Walterswanderung* did not end there, however. A two-and-a-half-month trip eventually brought the family to New York, and then to Montreal, where Walter began to learn his third language, English. In 1943, his father, still serving the Belgian government-in-exile, was reunited with the family in New York. Walter had arrived to stay in North America. His undergraduate years were spent at Harvard (1951–5), where his interest in theatre and radio fortunately did not get in the way of his love of history. In 1961 he earned his PhD at Harvard for a thesis on the ninth-century Le Mans Forgeries. The previous year, Walter had taken up the post of Lecturer in the Department of History, University of Toronto.

His publishing career had begun even earlier than that, with a piece, perhaps not surprising from the son of a diplomat, on Byzantine policy in the West in the late sixth century. One can already see in his early publications, especially *The Le Mans Forgeries* (1967), Walter's real forte – combining the technicalities of diplomatics, law, and institutional history with a keen interest in authorial purpose and technique. His outstanding contribution to historiography began as early as 1963, with a seminal study of the chronicle of Fredegar, the implications of which are only now beginning to be worked out.

Walter's early work had been on the Carolingian and Merovingian periods. By the late 1960s his interests were focused on the late Roman Empire with an eye to how ancient and modern historiography had defined the period and how institutional changes were worked out through the early Middle Ages. In *'Caput' and Colonate* (1974), he tackled the problem of the evolution of Roman tax administration and the impact of public law on the social tranformations of late Roman society. In *Barbarians and Romans* (1981), he applied this understanding to one of the great questions of early medieval history, the barbarian settlements, and succeeded in overthrowing more than a century of consensus on how the barbarians were integrated into the social and rural fabric of the successor kingdoms.

In the 1980s, Walter was still clarifying the intricacies of the evolution from Roman to medieval fiscality – what in *Barbarians and Romans* he had called the 'devolution of Roman taxation' – and continued to refine his view of the transition from ancient to medieval Europe, but his thoughts had turned increasingly to understanding the principal historians of early medieval historiography as authors with deliberate agendas, employing rhetorical and narrative conventions of exposition. In *The Narrators of Barbarian History* (1988), this interest, which had always been a leitmotif of Walter's work, was enriched with concepts of genre drawn from literary criticism and applied in a concentrated fashion to Jordanes, Gregory of Tours, Bede, and Paul the Deacon. The Haskins Medal of the Medieval Academy of America, awarded in 1991, was only part of the acclaim that greeted the book's publication, and now seems superfluous to highlight. In the year *Narrators* was published, there appeared a sign of the future: Walter revealed his cartographic interests in an article appropriately concerned with the standard adjunct of modern histories of the early medieval period – maps of the barbarian invasions.

Walter Goffart is not someone who will need to say, with Horace Walpole, 'It is charming to totter into vogue.' For over a decade and a half, the terms of discourse on some of the most innovative undertakings in early medieval history have been established by Walter. His unrivalled position among contemporary historians of late antiquity and the early Middle Ages will one day invite detailed acknowledgment, but not yet. His ideas have hardly begun to run their course; the owl of Minerva spreads its wings only at dusk, and Walter's recent observations on the absence of the heroic motif in the earliest Middle Ages is ample confirmation, if any were needed, that we cannot be sure what surprises he still has in store for us. Still, there are some obvious, and perhaps not so obvious, aspects to his approach to scholarship that I think are worth noting.

The breadth of Walter's knowledge is evident to any reader of his books, but only those who work in the period will have a real sense of how deep Walter's views cut through the various areas of early medieval history. I am not the only contributor to this volume to have the experience of exploring what seemed at first to be regions not recently travelled only to find undeniable signs that Walter had already passed that way. His mark has not been limited to the specialist's terrain. All of Walter's books have combined ideas of general and genuinely original significance with detailed expositions of sources. It is a result of his penetrating criticism of modern and ancient historiography, for example, that we use the standard scholarly categories – barbarian invasions, migration period, fall of the Roman Empire – with an embarrassed sense of how inadequately they convey the complicated reality of the age. Walter's handling of the big picture in fact has rather left us all in the lurch when we look for simple and conventionally recognizable markers for the period – a hazard from which the title of Walter's own collection of essays, and the present one, has not escaped entirely unscathed.

The devil is in the details, and Walter is a master of the details. His fearsome reputation in some quarters may have suggested to some that the devil is dispensing the details. Walter's standards are high. But there is another side to his criticism: patience, generosity, and a real delight in debate. This side of Walter is my first memory of him, when I was an undergraduate in History in the early years of Walter's tenure at Toronto. I never took a course from him; I never quite knew why that was so until, in tracking his whereabouts during those years for this introduction, I realized that he was not always in Toronto at this time. He was present the year my interest in the early Middle Ages took a serious turn, because I remember being directed to visit his office and discuss my plans with him. When I arrived, I was invited in and, after a few pleasantries, there began a long debate. How long, I am not sure, but the subject I remember quite distinctly: feud in early medieval society. It was an invigorating and delightful experience. I would probably still stick by the position I took that day, but I recognize now that behind his remarks was the gentle prodding that in later years opened up to me the potential of late antique sources for studying the early Middle Ages.

The value of such an approach is commonplace in many quarters today, but at the time it distinguished Walter from most of his contemporaries. Walter has often been labelled a Romanist. Whether he would approve of that label, I do not know. It recalls the terms of old debates. And one has to reconcile it with Walter's own assertion from time to time that this or that Romanist idea should be rejected and with his demolishing of Romanist doctrine in favour of locating novel and inventive adaptations of ancient institutions. The term is appropriate in the sense that Walter regards the social and institutional history of the early Middle Ages as devolving in large measure from mutations of late Roman forms. But he has never been one to transpose mechanically some enduring *Romanitas* onto the early Middle Ages. What he has done with unrivalled precision is chart in detail, and with nuances that often escape critics and synthesizers, the step-by-step transformation of the antique to the medieval. Walter's antiquity is no ideal construct but multivalent (and multi-ethnic), bound to particular times and contexts, subject to constant change, yet still part of a continuum of historical development. It is inevitable that this approach would run up against certain prevalent Germanist assumptions, and Walter has not been shy in applying the same critical standards to sources, whether or not they have been claimed as material suitable for the study of Germanic antiquity.

Walter Goffart's work is distinguished from much current writing by the historical character of its discourse, which addresses not just contemporary audiences, but also its own past; Walter takes history seriously, and that includes its scholarship. In his pages, scholarship abides, and is engaged, not because it bears a recent publication date, but because it is pertinent to our understanding of the past and the historian's craft. To recognize the importance of past scholarship enriches historical enterprise and helps reveal historical process. In Walter's case, it clearly does not detract from the immediate relevancy of his work, for no one who reads him will miss the contemporary sound of the heartbeat animating his concerns or the currency of the perspective brought to bear on their resolution.

Walter's ideas have not been designed with an aim to please, but with the power to demand response. The term *eigenwillig*, applied to him by German reviewers, is one reflection of this effect. So, too, is the conference that met in Austria in 1986 to discuss his interpretation of barbarian settlement. The proceedings of other conferences on other subjects have begun by acknowledging his views, even as they have sought to establish contrary positions. Images of his role suggest themselves. His absence from a recent conference on historiography was noted, while the presence of his ideas was acknowleged by means of a metaphor of the spider and its web: the spider, constantly in attendance, ready to drop onto the unsuspecting participant who dared ignore the problems of interpreting narrative sources; the web, entangling the efforts to derive history from historiography. The gathering might equally have suggested the image of the cat among the pigeons; Walter's work, like all important scholarship, elicits praise and criticism, but also consternation. 'Hat Goffart recht und warum nicht' is supposed to be part of a set of satirical examination questions, but the joke catches the insistent power of Walter's ideas to challenge the assumptions of contemporary scholarship.

Among the group whose work is gathered within these pages there would no doubt be disagreement about what issues Goffart has been right or wrong about, but there will be no consternation. As former students and colleagues, we celebrate his friendship and the incomparable impact his work has had upon a generation of historians.

Walter Goffart:
Bibliography, 1957–[1997]

1957

'Byzantine Policy in the West under Tiberius II and Maurice: The Pretenders Hermenegild and Gundovald (579–585).' *Traditio* 13 (1957): 73–118.

1959

Review: J.P. Bodmer, *Der Krieger der Merowingerzeit* (Zurich, 1957). *Speculum* 34 (1959): 450.

Review: H.M. Rochais, ed., *Defensoris liber scintillarum aliaeque* (Turnhout, 1957). *Speculum* 34 (1959): 502–6.

1961

'The Privilege of Nicholas I for St. Calais: A New Theory.' *Revue Bénédictine* 71 (1961): 287–337.

Review: J.M. Wallace–Hadrill, ed. and tr., *The Fourth Book of the Chronicle of Fredegar and Its Continuations* (London, 1960). *Speculum* 36 (1961): 692–5.

1963

'The Fredegar Problem Reconsidered.' *Speculum* 38 (1963): 206–41; *Rome's Fall and After*, 319–54.

Review: Marc Bloch, *Feudal Society*, tr. L.A. Manyon (London, 1961). *Canadian Historical Review* 44 (1963): 65–6.

1964

Review: J.M. Wallace-Hadrill, *The Long-Haired Kings and Other Studies in Frankish History* (London, 1960). *Speculum* 39 (1964): 571–4.

Review: Heinz Quirin, *Einführung in das Studium der mittelalterlichen Geschichte*, 2d ed. (Brunswick, 1961). *Canadian Historical Review* 45 (1964): 53.

Review: Joseph Balon, *Études franques* (Namur, 1963). *Speculum* 39 (1964): 481–2.

1966

'Gregory IV for Aldric of Le Mans (833): A Genuine or Spurious Decretal?' *Mediaeval Studies* 28 (1966): 22–38.

Review: Alexandre Vidier, *L'historiographie à Saint-Benoît-sur-Loire et les miracles de Saint Benoît* (Paris, 1965). *Speculum* 41 (1966): 379–80.

1967

The Le Mans Forgeries: A Chapter from the History of Church Property in the Ninth Century. Harvard Historical Studies 76. Cambridge, Mass.: Harvard University Press, 1966 [1967]. Pp. xv + 382.

'Le Mans, St. Scholastica, and the Literary Tradition of the Translation of St. Benedict.' *Revue Bénédictine* 77 (1967): 107–41.

Review: *The Cambridge Medieval History.* IV. *The Byzantine Empire*, part 1, 2d ed. (Cambridge, 1966). *Canadian Historical Review* 48 (1967): 78–9.

Review: Karl Friedrich Stroheker, *Germanentum und Spätantike* (Zurich and Stuttgart, 1965). *Speculum* 42 (1967): 411–13.

Review: Lynn White, Jr, ed., *The Transformation of the Roman World: Gibbon's Problem after Two Centuries* (Berkeley–Los Angeles, 1966). *Canadian Historical Review* 48 (1967): 182–3.

1969

'The Literary Adventures of St. Liborius: A Postscript to the Le Mans Forgeries.' *Analecta Bollandiana* 87 (1969): 5–62.

1970

'Did Julian Combat Venal *Suffragium*? A Note on *CTh* 2. 29. 1.' *Classical Philology* 65 (1970): 145–51.

Review: R.I. Frank, *Scholae palatinae: The Palace Guards of the Later Roman Empire* (Rome, 1969). *Phoenix* 24 (1970): 361–3.

Review: F.-L. Ganshof, *Frankish Institutions under Charlemagne*, tr. B. and M. Lyon (Providence, R.I., 1968). *Speculum* 45 (1970): 129–30.

Review: E.A. Thompson, *The Goths in Spain* (Oxford, 1969). *Canadian Historical Review* 51 (1970): 213–14.

1971

'Zosimus, the First Historian of Rome's Fall.' *American Historical Review* 76 (1971): 412–41; *Rome's Fall and After*, 81–110.

Review: Averil Cameron, *Agathias* (Oxford, 1970). *American Historical Review* 76 (1971): 767.

Review: Dietrich Lohrmann, *Das Register Papst Johannes' VIII* (Tübingen, 1968). *Speculum* 46 (1971): 164–6.

1972

'Le problème des *Translationes s. Liborii* (tr. R. de Ransart).' *La Province du Maine* 73 (1972): 125–37.

'From Roman Taxation to Mediaeval Seigneurie: Three Notes.' *Speculum* 47 (1972): 165–87, 373–94; *Rome's Fall and After*, 167–211.

Review: Erich Zöllner, *Geschichte der Franken bis zur Mitte des sechsten Jahrhunderts* (Munich, 1970). *Speculum* 47 (1972): 578–9.

1974

'Caput' and Colonate: Towards a History of Late Roman Taxation. Phoenix Supplementary Volume 12. Toronto: University of Toronto Press, 1974. Pp. ix + 165.

Review: Bernard S. Bachrach, *A History of the Alans in the West* (Minneapolis, 1973). *Catholic Historical Review* 60 (1974): 472–3.

1975

Review: Georges Duby, *The Early Growth of the European Economy*, tr. H.B. Clark (London, 1974). *Canadian Historical Review* 56 (1975): 235–6.

Review: Robert Folz et al., *De l'Antiquité au monde médiéval* (Paris, 1972). *Speculum* 50 (1975): 489–91.

1976

Review: Geoffrey Barraclough, *The Crucible of Europe* (London, 1976). *Canadian Journal of History* 11 (1976): 366–7.

Review: A.H.M. Jones, *The Roman Economy* (Totowa, N.J., 1974). *Classical World* 69 (1976): 366 7.

Review: John Matthews, *Western Aristocracies and Imperial Court, A.D. 364–425* (Oxford, 1975). *English Historical Review* 91 (1976): 351–4.

1977

'The Date and Purpose of Vegetius' *De re militari.' Traditio* 33 (1977): 65–100; *Rome's Fall and After*, 45–80.

Review: François Paschoud, *Cinq études sur Zosime* (Paris, 1975). *Classical World* 70 (1977): 464.

1978

Translator with Marshall Baldwin. Carl Erdmann, *The Origin of the Idea of Crusade.* Princeton: Princeton University Press, 1978. Pp. xxx + 446.
Review: May Vieillard–Troiekouroff, *Les monuments religieux de la Gaule d'après les oeuvres de Grégoire de Tours* (Paris, 1976). *Speculum* 53 (1978): 870-1.

1979

Review: Jean Devisse, *Hincmar, archévêque de Reims*, 3 vols. (Geneva, 1975–6). *Speculum* 56 (1979): 793–6.
Review: Patrick J. Geary, *Furta Sacra* (Princeton, 1978). *Catholic Historical Review* 65 (1979): 356–7.
Review: Jeremy Richards, *The Popes and the Papacy, 476–752* (London, 1979). *International History Review* 1 (1979): 588–9.

1980

Review: Martin Heinzelmann, *Bischofsherrschaft in Gallien* (Munich, 1976). *Speculum* 55 (1980): 127–8.
Review: Peter R. McKeon, *Hincmar of Laon and Carolingian Politics* (Urbana, Ill., 1978). *Catholic Historical Review* 66 (1980): 602–3.

1981

Barbarians and Romans, A.D. 418–584: The Techniques of Accommodation. Princeton: Princeton University Press, 1980 [1981]. Pp. xv + 278. (See also 1987.)
'*Hetware* and *Hugas*: Datable Anachronisms in *Beowulf.*' In *The Dating of 'Beowulf.'* Toronto Old English Series 7, ed. Colin Chase, 83–100. Toronto: University of Toronto Press, 1981.
'Rome, Constantinople, and the Barbarians.' *American Historical Review* 86 (1981): 275–306; *Rome's Fall and After*, 1–32.
Review: James J. O'Donnell, *Cassiodorus* (Berkeley–Los Angeles, 1979). *English Historical Review* 96 (1981): 900.
Review: Michel Rouche, *L'Aquitaine des Wisigoths aux Arabes* (Paris, 1979). *Speculum* 56 (1981): 652–6.

1982

'Foreigners in the *Histories* of Gregory of Tours.' *Florilegium* 4 (1982): 80–99; *Rome's Fall and After*, 275–91.

'Merovingian Polyptychs: Reflections on Two Recent Publications.' *Francia* 9 (1982): 57–77; *Rome's Fall and After*, 233–53.

'Old and New in Merovingian Taxation.' *Past and Present* no. 96 (August 1982): 3–21; *Rome's Fall and After*, 213–31.

'The Subdivisions of Trevet's *Cronicles* in Bodleian Library MS Fairfax 10.' *Scriptorium* 36 (1982): 96–8.

Review: Herwig Wolfram, *Geschichte der Goten*, 2d ed. (Munich, 1980). *Speculum* 57 (1982): 444–7.

1983

'The Supposedly "Frankish" Table of Nations: An Edition and Study.' *Frühmittelalterliche Studien* 17 (1983): 98–130; *Rome's Fall and After*, 133–65.

1984

Review: Jill N. Claster, *The Medieval Experience: 300–1400* (New York, 1982). *Speculum* 59 (1984): 470–1.

Review: K.L. Noethlichs, *Beamtentum und Dienstvergehen: Zur Staatsverwaltung in der Spätantike* (Wiesbaden, 1981). *Speculum* 59 (1984): 192–4.

Review: Justine Davis Randers-Pehrson, *Barbarians and Romans: The Birth Struggles of Europe, A.D. 400–700* (Norman, Okla., 1983). *Gnomon* 55 (1984): 564–5.

Review: Warren T. Treadgold, *Byzantine State Finances in the Eighth and Ninth Centuries* (Boulder, Colo., 1982). *American Historical Review* 89 (1984): 110.

1985

'The Conversions of Avitus of Clermont and Similar Passages in Gregory of Tours.' In *'To See Ourselves as Others See Us.' Christians, Jews, 'Others' in Late Antiquity*, ed. J. Neusner and E.S. Frerichs, 473–97. Chico, Calif.: Scholars' Press, 1985; *Rome's Fall and After*, 293–317.

Review: Thomas S. Burns, *A History of the Ostrogoths* (Bloomington, 1983). *American Historical Review* 90 (1985): 914–15.

Review: C.W. Fornara, *The Nature of History in Ancient Greece and Rome* (Berkeley–Los Angeles, 1984). *Canadian Journal of History* 20 (1985): 102–3.

Review: Stefan Krautschick, *Cassiodor und die Politik seiner Zeit* (Bonn, 1983). *Speculum* 60 (1985): 969–71.

1986

Review: Luce Pietri, *La ville de Tours du IVe au VIe siècle* (Paris, 1983). *Speculum* 61 (1986): 988–91.

Review: E.A. Thompson, *Saint Germanus of Auxerre and the End of Roman Britain* (Woodbridge, Suffolk, 1984). *Speculum* 61 (1986): 213–14.

1987

Barbarians and Romans: The Techniques of Accommodation (see 1981). Limited paperback edition, 1987.

'From Historiae to Historia Francorum and Back Again: Aspects of the Textual History of Gregory of Tours.' In *Religion, Culture, and Society in the Early Middle Ages: Studies in Honor of Richard E. Sullivan*, ed. Thomas F.X. Noble and John J. Contreni, 55–76. Studies in Medieval Culture 23, Kalamazoo, 1987; *Rome's Fall and After*, 255–74.

1988

The Narrators of Barbarian History (A.D. 550–800): Jordanes, Gregory of Tours, Bede, and Paul the Deacon. Princeton: Princeton University Press, 1988. Pp. xv + 491. (Awarded the Haskins Medal, Medieval Academy of America, 1991.)

'After the Zwettl Conference: Comments on the "Techniques of Accommodation." ' In *Anerkennung und Integration. Zu den wirtschaftlichen Grundlagen der Völkerwanderungszeit,400–600*, ed. Herwig Wolfram and Andreas Schwarcz, 73–85. Österreichische Akademie der Wissenschaften, Denkschriften, philos.-hist. Klasse 193. Vienna, 1988.

'The Map of the Barbarian Invasions: A Preliminary Report.' *Nottingham Medieval Studies* 32 (1988): 49–64 (with 1 map).

'Paul the Deacon's *Gesta episcoporum Mettensium* and the Early Design of Charlemagne's Succession.' *Traditio* 42 (1986 [1988]): 59–93.

Review: Michael McCormick, *Eternal Victory: Triumphal Rulership in Late Antiquity, Byzantium and the Early Medieval West* (Cambridge and Paris, 1986 [1987]). *Canadian Journal of History* 23 (1988): 96–7.

1989

Rome's Fall and After. London and Ronceverte: Hambledon Press, 1989. Pp. viii + 371.

'An Empire Unmade: Rome, A.D. 300–600.' *Rome's Fall and After*, 33–44.

'Private Life: From Rome to Byzantium' (concerning *A History of Private Life, From Pagan Rome to Byzantium*, ed. Paul Veyne, tr. Arthur Goldhammer [*A History of Pri-*

vate Life, ed. Philippe Ariès and Georges Duby, I; Cambridge, Mass., and London, 1987]). *University of Toronto Quarterly*, 58 (1989): 409–11.

'The Theme of "*The* Barbarian Invasions" in Late Antique and Modern Historiography.' In *Das Reich und die Barbaren*, ed. Evangelos K. Chrysos and Andreas Schwarcz, 87–107. Veröffentlichungen des Instituts für österreichische Geschichtsforschung 29. Vienna and Cologne, 1989; *Rome's Fall and After*, 111–32.

Review: G.R. Evans, *The Thought of Gregory the Great* (Cambridge, 1986). *English Historical Review* 104 (1989): 448.

Review: Patrick Geary, *Before France and Germany* (New York and Oxford, 1987). *Canadian Journal of History* 24 (1989): 94–5.

1990

With David Ganz. 'Charters Earlier than A.D. 800 from French Collections.' *Speculum* 65 (1990): 906–32.

'The Historia ecclesiastica: Bede's Agenda and Ours.' *Haskins Society Journal: Studies in Medieval History* 2 (1990): 29–45.

Review: Christopher Harper-Bill, Christopher Holdsworth, and Janet L. Nelson eds., *Studies in Medieval History presented to R. Allen Brown* (Woodbridge, Suffolk, 1989). *Notes and Queries* 235 (1990): 319–20.

Review: Ralph W. Mathisen, *Ecclesiastical Factionalism and Religious Controversy in Fifth-Century Gaul* (Washington, D.C., 1989). *Catholic Historical Review* 76 (1990): 5848–85.

Review: J.M. Wallace-Hadrill, Thomas Charles-Edwards, Patrick Wormald, and others, eds., *Bede's* Ecclesiastical History of the English People. *A Historical Commentary* (Oxford, 1988). *Journal of Ecclesiastical History* 41 (1990): 83–5.

1991

Review: Bernhard Bischoff, *Latin Palaeography: Antiquity and the Middle Ages*, tr. Daibhi O Croinin and David Ganz (Cambridge, 1990). *Canadian Journal of History* 26 (1991): 293–4.

Review: Rosamond McKitterick, ed., *The Uses of Literacy in Early Medieval Europe* (Cambridge, 1990). *Canadian Journal of History* 26 (1991): 294–6.

Review: Joachím Martínez Pizarro, *A Rhetoric of the Scene: Scenic Narrative in the Early Middle Ages* (Toronto, 1989). *Journal of Medieval Latin* 1 (1991): 189–93.

1992

Review: Jean Durliat, *Les finances publiques de Dioclétien aux Carolingiens, 284–889* (Sigmaringen, 1990). *English Historical Review* 107 (1992): 675–6.

Review: Edward James, *The Franks*. The Peoples of Europe, ed. J. Campbell and B. Cunliffe (Oxford, 1988). *English Historical Review* 107 (1992): 161–2.

Review: Robin Macpherson, *Rome in Involution: Cassiodorus's Variae in Their Literary and Historical Setting* (Poznan, 1989). *American Historical Review* 97 (1992): 174.

1993

'The Map of the Barbarian Invasions: A Longer Look.' In *The Culture of Christendom: Essays in Medieval History in Commemoration of Denis L. T. Bethell*, ed. Marc A. Meyer, 1–27. London: Hambledon Press, 1993.

Review: Peter Heather, *Goths and Romans, 332–489*. Oxford Historical Monographs (Oxford, 1992). *American Historical Review* 98 (1993): 1580–1.

1994

'Storytelling and Fraud in Some Early Medieval Historians.' *South African Journal of Medieval and Renaissance Studies* 4/1 (1994): 21–49. Also in *'Tis all in peeces, all cohaerence gone': Change and Medieval and Renaissance Studies* (UMA/SAS-MARS Journal), ed. Rosemary Gray and Estelle Maré, Miscellanea Congregalia 47, 67–84. Pretoria: University of South Africa, 1995.

Review: D.A. Bullough, *Carolingian Renewal: Sources and Heritage* (New York, 1991). *Speculum* 69 (1994): 285.

Review: John Moorhead, *Theoderic in Italy* (Oxford, 1992). *American Historical Review* 99 (1994): 1995–6.

Review: Marc van Uytfanghe and Roland Demeulenaere, eds., Aevum inter utrumque: *Mélanges offerts à Gabriel Sanders*. Instrumenta patristica 23 (Steenbrugge, 1991). *Journal of Medieval Latin* 4 (1994): 188–92.

1995

'Breaking the Ortelian Pattern: Historical Atlases with a New Program, 1747–1830.' In *Editing Early and Historical Atlases*. Papers Given at the Twenty-Ninth Conference on Editorial Problems, University of Toronto, 5–6 November 1993, ed. Joan Winearls, 49–81. Toronto: University of Toronto Press, 1995.

'Conspicuous by Absence: Heroism in the Early Frankish Era (6th–7th Cent.).' In *La funzione dell'eroe germanici: Storicità, metafora, paradigma*. Atti del Convegno internazionale di studio, Rome, 6–8 May 1993, ed. Teresa Pároli, 41-56. Rome, 1995.

'Two Notes on Germanic Antiquity Today.' *Traditio* 50 (1995): 9–30.

Review: Francesco Giunta and Antonino Grillone, eds., Iordanis *De origine actibusque Getarum*. Istituto storico italiano per il medio evo, Fonti per la storia d'Italia 117 (Rome, 1991). *Gnomon* 67/3 (1995): 227–9.

1996

'What's Wrong with the Map of the Barbarian Invasions?' In *Minorities and Barbarians in Medieval Life and Thought*, ed. Susan J. Ridyard and Robert G. Benson, Sewanee Medieval Studies, no. 7, 159–77. Sewanee, Tenn.: University of the South, 1996.

Review: Ian Wood, *The Merovingian Kingdoms, 450–751* (London and New York, 1994), *English Historical Review* 111 (1996): 661.

Review: Jill Harries, *Sidonius Apollinaris and the Fall of Rome AD 407–485* (Oxford, 1994), *The Historian* 58 (1996): 435.

1997

'The First Venture into "Medieval Geography": Lambarde's Map of the Saxon Heptarchy (1568).' In *Alfred the Wise, Studies in Honour of Janet Bately*, ed. Jane Roberts and Janet L. Nelson, 53–60. Woodbridge, Suffolk, 1997.

Review: Michael Richter, *The Formation of the Medieval West. Studies in the Oral Culture of the Barbarians* (New York, 1994), *American Historical Review* 102 (Feb. 1997), 95–6

Forthcoming, 1998–9

'Christian Pessimism in the Vatican Galleria delle carte geografiche: The Historical Vignettes Interpreted.' Forthcoming in *Renaissance Quarterly*, autumn 1998.

'The Genesis of John Speed's "Battles" Maps.' Forthcoming in *Imago mundi*, 1999.

Review: Stefano Maria Cingolani, *Le Storie dei Longobardi. Dall'Origine a Paolo Diacono* (Rome, 1995). Forthcoming in *Speculum*.

Review: Robert Fossier, ed., *The Cambridge Illustrated History of the Middle Ages*, 3 vols. (Cambridge, 1997). Forthcoming in *Notes and Queries*.

1

Our Forefathers?
Tribes, Peoples, and Nations in the
Historiography of the Age of Migrations

SUSAN REYNOLDS

It would be folly for someone who has only a nodding acquaintance with sources before the seventh century to write an essay on the barbarian migrations, invasions, and settlements for Walter Goffart to read. This essay, therefore, is concerned, not with the evidence of the events themselves – whatever they were – but with the ideas about human collectivities that lie behind what historians have written about them since the time of Jordanes. Even here, of course, I am treading in Walter's footsteps. A good deal of what I say will merely amplify his remarks about, for instance, 'the wellspring of ... piety' that demands a worthy and continuous history for the Germanic peoples, or the way that hindsight 'simplified muddled events and gave them a definite direction.'[1] I start, not from the evidence, or even the modern works devoted to it, of all of which Walter is a master, but from some of our ideas – or, rather, some of our assumptions – and address them more directly and in more detail than he has done in his published work. Both the events that Walter objects to our calling *'the* barbarian invasions'* and the arguments about them may be easier to understand if we start from a consideration of the point from which we observe them. One way of doing this is to examine some of the words we use – 'peoples,' 'nations,' 'tribes,' 'races' – and the notions that seem to lie behind these words in their current use. Once we have cleared that out of the way, we shall have more hope of understanding the notions or concepts that may have lain behind the words (and the Latin words from which we translate them) at different periods of the past. Much of what I say may seem commonplace to many early medievalists, but, if I am right in suspecting that old and untenable assumptions

---

1 Walter Goffart, 'The Theme of *"The* Barbarian Invasions,"' in Later Antique and Modern Historiography,' in *Rome's Fall and After* (London and Ronceverte, 1989), 120; and 'Barbarians in Late Antiquity,' in *Barbarians and Romans, A.D. 418–584: The Techniques of Accommodation* (Princeton, 1980), 22.

still lurk in the background of discourse about the Age of Migrations, it may still be worth bringing them out for inspection.[2]

The idea of the nation is fundamental to the history of Europe as it has been written over the past two hundred years. Much history is what is called 'national history,' while historiographical traditions tend to follow what are called 'national lines.' Though medieval historians generally write about barbarian 'tribes' rather than 'nations,' and some now prefer 'ethnic groups' or the apparently noncommittal 'peoples,' the barbarians generally occupy an important place at or near the beginning of most 'national histories.' Long tradition sees them as something like the founding fathers, or at least grandfathers, of medieval kingdoms, and ultimately of the nation-states of modern Europe. The word 'nation' is often used as a synonym for 'state' (as in the United Nations or nationalization) but, as the use of 'nation-state' suggests, two distinct notions or concepts can be detected behind some ways that each word is used.[3] The idea of the nation seems to be that of some kind of natural community which exists whether or not it is embodied in the governmental fact of a state. The nation is the community that forms – or has the right to form – a state and will live on even if the state is conquered. It is, in Rupert Emerson's words, 'the body which legitimizes the state,'[4] so that the nation-state enjoys a degree of cohesion and a kind of legitimacy that other kinds of states do not. Even if one does not think of oneself as a nationalist, it is difficult today to get away from the belief or assumption that lies at the heart of modern nationalism: namely, that nations by their very existence have some kind of right to some kind of self-government and independence.[5] Tribes are also seen as cohesive natural communities that may to some eyes – such as those of anthropologists or sentimental conservatives – enjoy a certain legitimacy, but their government is not generally dignified with the label 'state.' The distinction seems to be that tribes are generally seen as smaller, less organized or more 'primitive,' and more closely based on kinship than are nations. They may become, or join

2 Edward James, 'The Origins of Barbarian Kingdoms,' in *The Origins of Anglo-Saxon Kingdoms*, ed. Steven Bassett (Leicester, 1989), 40–52, expresses the same suspicion.
3 I discuss the problems of defining states, with particular reference to the Middle Ages, in 'The Historiography of the Medieval State,' in *The Writing of History*, ed. Michael Bentley (London, 1997), 117–38.
4 Rupert Emerson, *From Empire to Nation* (Cambridge, Mass., 1960), 96.
5 Ernest Gellner, *Nations and Nationalism* (Oxford, 1983), 1; Eric Hobsbawm, *Nations and Nationalism since 1780* (Cambridge, 1990), 9; Anthony D. Smith, *Nationalism* (= *Current Sociology* 21/3 [1973]), 10. The literature on nationalism is now vast. James G. Kellas, *The Politics of Nationalism and Ethnicity* (London, 1991), and John Hutchinson, *Modern Nationalism* (London, 1994), seem to me useful recent surveys.

together to become, nations as they grow up and form proper kingdoms, and even, eventually, states.[6]

The problems raised by envisaging nations as natural, given units into which human beings are naturally divided, however they are governed, start as soon as one tries to identify them. Most people, including a good many historians, seem to start by assuming that what they call the 'nation-states' of today form the basic stock of nations. They then add to the list a few collectivities which are not independent states but which have members who consider them to be nations and think that they ought to have at least some degree of political independence. The difficulty arises in deciding which groups count as nations and where their boundaries lie. Some people in the states from which members of non-state nations want to liberate themselves deny the separate nationhood of the would-be seceders. Definitions by ethnicity or culture do not help. The concept of ethnicity has developed only in the late twentieth century and is as liable to carry anachronistic connotations as any other concept.[7] It is a slippery concept that sometimes seems to cover the possession both of a common culture and of a common descent, but sometimes relates only to the former.[8] The

6 Aidan W. Southall, 'The Illusion of Tribe,' *Journal of Asian and African Studies* 5 (1970): 28–50; Walker Connor, 'From Tribe to Nation?' *History of European Ideas* 13 (1991): 5–18; Patricia Crone, 'The Tribe and the State,' in *States in History*, ed. John A. Hall (Oxford, 1986), 48–77; Hugh Seton-Watson, *Nations and States* (London, 1977), 4–5; Martin Thom, 'Tribes within Nations,' in *Nations and Narration*, ed. Homi K. Bhaba (London and New York, 1990), 23–43. On German usage: Josef Fleckenstein, 'Grundlagen und Beginn der deutschen Geschichte,' in *Deutsche Geschichte*, vol. 1, ed. Josef Fleckenstein et al. (Göttingen, 1985), 3–181, at 13–20 (the English translation, *Early Medieval Germany* [Amsterdam, 1978], distorts Fleckenstein's distinctions by translating *Reich* as 'nation'); Carlrichard Brühl, *Deutschland – Frankreich: Die Geburt zweier Völker* (Cologne and Vienna, 1990), 7, 243–67; cf. František Graus, *Die Nationenbildung der Westslawen*, Nationes vol. 3 (Sigmaringen, 1980), 11–16. On the medieval use of *tribus*: Benedykt Zientara, 'Populus – gens – natio,' in *Nationalismus in vorindustrieller Zeit*, ed. Otto Dann (Munich, 1986), 11–20, at 17.
7 Eugeen Roosens, *Creating Ethnicity* (London and New Delhi, 1989), 12–13; Malcolm Chapman, 'Introduction,' in *Social and Biological Aspects of Ethnicity*, ed. Malcolm Chapman (Oxford, 1993), 1–46. On the suggestion of 'ethnic group' as a substitute for 'race' in Julian Huxley and Alfred Haddon, *We Europeans* (London, 1935), see Elazar Barkan, *The Retreat from Scientific Racism* (Cambridge, 1992), 297, 300–2. On German usage: Herwig Wolfram, 'Einleitung,' in *Typen der Ethnogenese unter besonderer Berücksichtigung der Bayern*, ed. Herwig Wolfram and Walter Pohl, 2 vols. (Vienna, 1990), 1: 20.
8 Chapman, *Social and Biological Aspects*, esp. 14–22; Walker Connor, 'A Nation is a Nation, is a State, is an Ethnic Group, is a ...,' *Ethnic and Racial Studies* 1 (1978): 377–400; Anthony D. Smith, *The Ethnic Origins of Nations* (Oxford, 1986), 13–16; Kellas, *Politics of Nationalism and Ethnicity*, 4–5; Hutchinson, *Modern Nationalism*, 7; Hobsbawm, *Nations and Nationalism*, 63–4.

boundaries of cultures are hard to determine. Customs, traditions, religion, and even language are not always homogeneous within groups that claim to be nations, nor do they always differ from those of other nations. Cultures change: those who look for a continuous traditional culture in the past of their own nation will probably find it, but, though some elements in any culture may be old and cherished, a sceptic may doubt whether the people in the past would recognize the link if they could see the present culture as a whole. Traditionally, European nationalists have thought of language as an important defining characteristic of a nation, but even in Europe that works imperfectly: arbitrary lines have to be drawn between dialects and languages. Sometimes religion is important, but sometimes not: the boundaries of supposed nations do not always alter when people change their religion. It seems to be impossible to define nations except by saying that they are the communities which people think are nations. Opinions about their identity will vary. That does not mean the bonds and hostilities created by belief will be any less strong than if nations had unambiguous, objective reality. What it does mean is that we can best make sense of nations if we start from the *idea* that nations exist, and look at it as an idea – an idea that has done much to shape our world and that is very difficult to get out of our heads.

This applies to the heads of historians too, even when they accept in principle that nations are creations of history rather than eternal realities. Some medieval historians, warned off nationalism by modernists, are as wary of referring to nations as they are of referring to states. Most, nevertheless, use 'national' without a qualm and assume that the late medieval 'national monarchies' were the polities that were already destined to last. A good deal of the 'national history' that European historians write assumes not only the solidarity that the inhabitants of modern states feel today, but also their solidarity with the past of their assumed nation. It is the story of the way that 'we' – whichever nation 'we' are – either achieved our predestined nation-state or survived as a nation even when deprived of it. This feeling is quite often expressed, though perhaps most often by non-professional historians, by talking in quasi-genealogical terms of ancestors, forefathers, and so on, as if the reason 'we' feel solidarity with our fellow-citizens is that 'we' are all of common descent. But that is often untrue. The children or grandchildren of immigrants may feel just as much solidarity, while not even noticing the implications of talking about their forefathers. Most people do not know about their distant ancestors anyway. What counts is not the physical fact, but the vague idea that common descent matters. Historians may be more affected by these ideas in the air around us than we notice or admit.

II

Most of those who write about nationalism say or assume that the belief in naturally distinct peoples or nations with an inherent right to separate government dates from the late eighteenth century. Some put its origins as far back as the sixteenth, while medievalists tend to trace its origins to the 'national monarchies' of France, England, Spain, and – if they know about them – Scotland, Bohemia, Poland, and Hungary.[9] As this suggests, discussion of nationalism seems to invite teleology, so that historians look most readily for symptoms of nationalism in the polities that look most like the nation-states of today.[10] It also seems to be often assumed that ethnic or national consciousness developed first, and that true political nationalism came later, when ideas of popular government brought nations, like Sleeping Beauties, to vibrant life.[11] What is striking about all this is the confident assumption that earlier governments did not rely on feelings of solidarity among their subjects and that such ethnic consciousness as then existed lacked a political dimension. The most confident statements about the starting-point of nationalism seem to be based on the greatest ignorance of previous history, combined with a narrow understanding of what is included in politics, and sometimes with a naïve attitude towards the relation between words (like 'nation' or 'nationalism') and what they denote.[12]

9 E.g. Benedict Anderson, *Imagined Communities* (London, 1983), 16, 40; John A. Armstrong, *Nations before Nationalism* (Chapel Hill, 1982), 4–5; Dann, ed., *Nationalismus*, 8–9; Gellner, *Nations*, 39–40, 55, 94; Liah Greenfeld, *Nationalism* (Cambridge, Mass., 1992), 14; Graus, *Nationenbildung*, 138–47; Bernard Guenée, *States and Rulers in Later Medieval Europe*, trans. J. Vale (London, 1985), 49–65, 216–20; Eric Hobsbawm, 'Some Reflections on Nationalism,' in *Imagination and Precision in the Social Sciences*, ed. Thomas J. Nossiter (London, 1972), 385–406, at 388, 390, and *Nations and Nationalism*, 9–10; Eugen Lemberg, *Nationalismus,* 2 vols. (Munich, 1964), 1: 36–40; Seton-Watson, *Nations and States*, 6, 17; Smith, *Ethnic Origins*, 10–12; Jenő Szűcs, *Nation und Geschichte* (Budapest, 1974), 24–8, 79–94, 161–244.

10 Even those who admit that nations come and go seem, ever since Renan (Ernest Renan, *Oeuvres complètes*, ed. H. Psichari, 10 vols. [Paris, 1947–61], 1: 905), to be drawn to studying those now recognized as such. Karl F. Werner, 'Les nations et le sentiment national dans l'Europe médiévale,' *Revue historique* 244 (1970): 285–304, is a notable exception. Also, despite the theme of the book: Brühl, *Geburt*, 272–3.

11 The image is Emerson's: *Empire to Nation*, 91. Cf. Smith, *Ethnic Origins*; for a standard summary: *Brockhaus Enzyklopädie* 13 (17th ed. 1971), 217.

12 Many seem to rely on old textbooks. Hans Kohn, *The Idea of Nationalism* (New York, 1945), expounding ideas about the Middle Ages that seem to be based primarily on nineteenth-century textbook versions of German history, is still sometimes regarded as authoritative. On words, even if fewer now maintain that *natio* was rarely used in the Middle Ages, nearly all modernists remain confident that it was not used in anything like its modern sense.

I have argued elsewhere that medieval ideas of units of government, and especially kingdoms, as comprising peoples of common descent, custom, and law, are very like the modern nationalist's idea of nations.[13] Medieval kingdoms and city-states seem to have been perceived as political communities and to have developed an ethnic consciousness that transcended local differences of custom and sometimes ignored differences of language. Many of them developed myths of the common origin of their inhabitants that paid scant attention to conquered populations or such immigrants as did not impose their own name on the whole.[14] There was little argument either about the myths or about the nature of the political communities to which they related: it seems to have simply been assumed that kingdoms, lordships, or city-states were natural, given communities. Even Dante, when he argued for a supreme Empire, assumed that nations, kingdoms, and cities had differing characteristics that required them to be ruled by different laws.[15] The Latin words *gentes, nationes*, and *populi* could be used interchangeably for all of them, though *gentes* seems to have been the most common term.[16]

Medieval government was supposed to involve, and generally did involve, a good deal of consultation with its subjects, or at least the more substantial of them, who were supposed to represent the whole community. It was not 'popular government' in the modern sense, but it was in its own way representative and participatory, all the more because so much collective activity and voluntary submission were required to carry it out. Medieval ideas of hierarchy and custom allowed for layers of political authority and community. Just as lords at every level had rights against their superiors, so each lord's subjects could envisage themselves as a community with its own rights and customs within the wider community of the kingdom. People owed loyalties at each level, so that conflicts could arise, just as they can arise today, between those owed to king-

---

13 *Kingdoms and Communities* (Oxford, 1984), 250–61 and passim.
14 Susan Reynolds, 'Medieval *origines gentium* and the Community of the Realm,' *History* 68 (1983): 375–90, reprinted with corrections in *Ideas and Solidarities of the Medieval Laity* (London, 1995); Gyorgy Györffy, 'Formation des états au ixe siècle suivant les "Gesta Hungarorum,"' *Nouvelles études historiques* (Budapest, 1965), 27–53. The suggestion of Richard C. Hoffmann, 'Outsiders by Birth and Blood,' *Studies in Medieval and Renaissance History* n.s. 6 (1983): 1–34, that 'racist' ideas were especially found on peripheral areas of European culture seems to ignore the stories told elsewhere.
15 *De Monarchia*, c. 14, in *Tutte le opere di Dante Alighieri*, ed. Edward Moore and Paget Toynbee (Oxford, 1924), 349, and cf. 344 (c. 7).
16 Some writers distinguished them, but the distinctions are not consistent. All three words could be used for political communities and in other ways: Reynolds, *Kingdoms and Communities*, 255–6; Brühl, *Geburt*, 243–67. On the non-collective use of *natio* to indicate an individual's origin: Karl F. Werner, 'Volk, Nation III–V,' in *Geschichtliche Grundbegriffe*, ed. Otto Brunner et al., vol. 7 (Stuttgart, 1992), 171–281, at 214–23.

doms and those owed to the other communities to which people belonged.[17] To assert that medieval evidence casts doubt on the model in which ethnic and national consciousness preceded political nationalism is not to deny that similarities of religion, language, and custom made it easier for rulers to foster collective solidarities. Circumstances varied, and cause and effect are often hard to disentangle.[18]

What the medieval evidence suggests is the fallacy of assuming that 'imagined communities' of a distinctly political kind can have appeared only along with modern forms of popular government. The ideas of political community that I have described seem, moreover, to have been neither new in the Middle Ages nor peculiar to Europe. Throughout a good deal of human history, many units of government have been small and have depended heavily on social solidarity. Some of them have been the kind of units that are called 'tribes' and enjoy the unbureaucratic kind of government that is called 'tribal.' Others, like the city-states of the ancient world, are dignified by being called 'states.' Both kinds of polity, whether or not totally independent, often seem to claim some sort of corporate autonomy which appears to be associated, however vaguely, with myths of common descent and of distinctive, shared laws and customs. However different their society, their government, and their ideas may be from those associated with modern nationalism, they think of themselves as natural collective units of culture and descent in much the same way as do many modern nationalists.[19]

Modern writers seem reluctant to acknowledge that these small polities could have evoked the kind of solidarities they call 'national,' but their chief reason, apart from the *a priori* assumption that the ideas associated with political nationalism are modern, seems to be that they were too small. If true nations are to be defined by size, however, then it is hard to know just where to draw the line. No doubt the general modern view would put it somewhere between,

17 E.g. Benedykt Zientara, 'Nationale Strukturen des Mittelalters,' *Saeculum* 32 (1981): 301–16; Linda Colley, *Britons* (New Haven and London, 1992); David M. Potter, 'The Historian's Use of Nationalism,' in *Generalization in Historical Writing*, ed. Alexander V. Riasanovsky and Barnes Riznick (Philadelpia, 1963), 114–66; Kellas, *Politics of Nationalism and Ethnicity*, 2–3, 16–19.

18 E.g. Thomas N. Bisson, 'L'Essor de la Catalognc,' *Annales ESC* 39 (1984): 454–79; Paul Freedman, 'Cowardice, Heroism and the Legendary Origins of Catalonia,' *Past & Present* 121 (1988): 3–28; Graus, *Nationenbildung*.

19 Apart from the obvious example of the biblical Jews, see e.g. Elias Bickerman, '*Origines gentium,*' *Classical Philology* 47 (1952): 65–81; cf. Moses Finley, *The Use and Abuse of History* (London, 1975), 13, 23–6, 124; Isaac Schapera, 'The Political Organization of the Ngwato,' in *African Political Systems*, ed. Meyer Fortes and E. Edward Evans-Pritchard (Oxford, 1940), 56–82; Sally Falk Moore, *Law as Process* (London and Boston, 1978), 149–63; Southall, 'Illusion of Tribe'; Crone, 'Tribe and State.'

say, ancient Athens and modern Greece, though where to put Macedonia would be controversial.[20] That is mere presentism: the most important difference between these past solidarities and those of modern nations may be that modern communications make it possible to foster togetherness over much wider areas. There is very little difference in the underlying ideas about the bonds of custom and descent. My argument is not that the idea of natural political communities of common descent and culture is an ineradicable part of human nature: great empires sometimes obliterated them pretty successfully, and many powerful political and social theories have ignored them. They nevertheless seem to have been common enough to suggest that the ideas that underlie political national-ism were not themselves the product of modern political theories, modern industrialization, or modern communications. Whether or not myths of descent were widely known or believed, whether or not laws and cultures were really as distinctive as people thought, is hardly significant. What is significant is that the ideas of political community which they embody have long been both widespread and seldom argued-about. They used to be taken for granted.

The societies of northern Europe that Greeks and Romans saw as barbarian may have formed political communities of this kind. The difficulty is that we know so little about them, and what we know from archaeology, philology, and rare references in classical sources does not fit together very well.[21] Given the conditions of society and politics on the boundaries of the Roman Empire, com-munities there may not have been stable or permanent.[22] It would, moreover, be rash to assume that every name mentioned by authors writing about peoples they did not know at first hand represented a real community. All the same, the use of collective names – what Tacitus calls *gentis appellationes*[23] – below the level of *Germani* or Celts may sometimes imply some sort of political commu-nity. If so, it is likely that such solidarity as the group achieved profited from the ideas of common descent and law that I have suggested are usual in small polities. That, however, remains little more than a possibility: adding heavy glosses from later sources to Tacitus' information does not strengthen it much.

20 Emerson, *Empire to Nation*, 99. Florence, as opposed to Italy, is not normally considered an appropriate object of nationalism, but see Reynolds, *Kingdoms and Communities*, 213.
21 Rolf Hachmann, *The Germanic Peoples*, trans. J. Hogarth (London, 1971); Malcolm Todd, *The Northern Barbarians* (Oxford, 1987), 5–9; Barry Cunliffe, *Greeks, Romans and Barbar-ians* (London, 1988), 116.
22 Christian Courtois, *Les Vandales et l'Afrique* (Paris, 1955), 26–7; Reinhard Wenskus, *Stammesbildung und Verfassung* (Cologne, 1961), 76, 374–409; Cunliffe, *Greeks, Romans and Barbarians*, 114–17, 14–92; Peter Heather, 'The Huns and the End of the Roman Empire in the West,' *English Historical Review* 110 (1995): 4–41.
23 Tacitus, *Germania*, c. 2. For his contrasting use, just after, of *gens* and *natio*: Fritz Gschnitzer, 'Volk, Nation II,' in *Geschichtliche Grundbegriffe*, vol. 7 (Stuttgart, 1992): 169.

The problem with the glosses is not only that they rely on later sources written in different conditions, but that so many of those sources were written with a particular purpose and started from a particular premise. The purpose was to trace the history of later peoples or nations back to Tacitus' *Germani*, and the premise was that those peoples, like Tacitus' tribes, were communities of both custom and descent.

What needs to be stressed about the premise is that it does not distinguish between biological inheritance and cultural transmission. For the biblical Jews, for the citizens of Greek city-states, and for the subjects of medieval kingdoms, as for Tacitus, common descent, common customs, and (where it fitted) language were simply assumed to go together. The Latin word *gentes*, which was often used in medieval texts for whole peoples as well as for smaller groups more obviously connected by kinship, covered all of what might now be distinguished as nations, racial or ethnic groups, and lineages or families. The lack of distinction went beyond words to concepts. Until the late nineteenth century, no one seems to have felt the need to try to distinguish between these features that we see as physically inherited and those features that we call cultural.[24] They were assumed to go together. To some extent they probably did. People living in one country and under one government are likely to share some customs, perhaps to speak one language (though they surprisingly often manage without), and to marry together more than they marry outsiders. If they are few enough and isolated enough, they may in the long run develop physical peculiarities that mark them off from people in other societies. In other words, cultural groups may correspond roughly to what human biologists call 'populations.' In many parts of Europe, however, differences of class, status, language, and religion within political units, together with contact between them, have long made the correspondence so rough as to be insignificant. Whatever they believe, the inhabitants of nation-states or those who wish to form a nation-state, at least in Europe, are not races in the sense of being groups that share physical characteristics which distinguish them from other groups.[25]

Like the inhabitants of later kingdoms or nation-states in Europe, the barbarians who invaded and settled in the Roman Empire in the fourth and fifth centuries are not likely to have formed the solid, separate groups implied by the long arrows on maps to which Walter Goffart so rightly objects.[26] The way that

24 This is discussed further below.

25 E.g. Francis J.G. Ebling, *Racial Variation in Man* (London, 1975), esp. the essays of E. Sunderland and E.R. Leach; Joseph B. Birdsell, *Human Evolution* (Boston, 1981), 345–76; Helen Macbeth, 'Ethnicity and Human Biology,' in Chapman, *Social and Biological Aspects*, 47–91; J.M. Smith, 'Natural Selection of Culture,' *New York Review of Books*, 6 Nov. 1986, 11–12.

26 Goffart, 'Rome, Constantinople, and the Barbarians,' in *Rome's Fall and After*, 9–10, and

collective names appear and disappear suggests a good deal of mixing. Barbarians who served in Roman armies or independent guerrilla groups presumably sometimes took up with women from other groups or from the settled populations where they served or travelled. Culturally, barbarians may have been indistinguishable to Romans and like enough to one another for individuals or small groups to be fairly easily assimilated into larger groups that they joined. Barbarian groups were quite often called *gentes* in Latin sources. Scholars living before this century, who did not distinguish biological descent from cultural transmission, normally translated *gens* as 'race,' though they sometimes used 'tribe' or 'nation.' For them there was no significant difference. Today the situation is different – or ought to be. Unfortunately some historians still use the words 'race' and 'racial' in a way which suggests that they continue to conflate biological and cultural inheritance. This makes for confusion. The differences between barbarian groups, and between them and the population of the Empire, were surely not biological, but cultural and, above all, political. As such, they were liable to vary and change much more quickly than if they had been biological.[27] As for the relation between particular categories within the populations of different parts of Europe in the fourth and fifth centuries and within the populations of the same areas five, let alone fifteen, centuries later, it is surely misleading to stress any significant biological continuity. Cultural continuity, moreover, would be better established by comparing the societies of different periods and different countries rather than connecting it by implication with some supposed biological continuity.

III

Most medieval myths of origin related to collective groups which corresponded to political units at the time the stories were being told. There does not seem to have been any concern at first to distinguish rulers and nobles from the rest: the genealogies of kings and great nobles might be given mythical beginnings, but, if these mentioned the stories about the whole community of their subjects, they followed the same lines. The myths about whole peoples or nations were about political unity, not about the justification of inequality and subordination, which was taken for granted. While this kind of myth continued to be told, a new kind appeared in the course of the Middle Ages which proposed separate

'What's Wrong with the Map of the Barbarian Invasions,' in *Minorities and Barbarians in Medieval Life and Thought*, ed. S.J. Ridyard and R.G. Benson (Chapel Hill, 1996), 159–77.
27 Ian Wood, 'The Channel from the 4th–7th Centuries AD,' in *Maritime Celts, Frisians and Saxons*, ed. S. McGrail, CBA Research Report 71 (London, 1990), 93–7.

origins for the free and unfree. In twelfth-century France, stories were told of how Charlemagne had either rewarded with liberty those who served in his armies or penalized with servitude the descendants of those who did not. Similar justifications of inherited servitude are found in Hungary from the late thirteenth century, and in Catalonia at about the same time or a little later.[28] By the fifteenth century, the Catalan stories were used to resist servitude as well as to justify it. Sometimes the ancestors of the oppressed were conquered Muslims who, having been converted, ought in justice to have been freed.[29]

The reasons for this development look fairly straightforward. By the thirteenth century, economic and demographic growth had exacerbated divisions and conflicts between rich and poor. At the same time, associated social changes, including more widespread education, made more powerful and professional government possible. At first this seems to have lent new force to the old cohesive myths, producing the evidence that has often been interpreted as marking the beginning of nationalism in France and England.[30] One product of the new government, however, was the division into separate estates of the earlier medieval assemblies in which greater subjects had represented the lesser. This, combined with the disappearance of formal unfreedom but the emergence of increasingly hard class divisions in general, may have helped to turn the myths about the separate origins of free and unfree into myths about the separate origins of nobles and peasants. By the seventeenth century, the difference between French nobles and peasants was being explained by their respective descent from conquering Franks and conquered Gauls.[31] The older ideas, however, never entirely disappeared. Emphasis on the restricted and exclusive character of the 'political nation,' or *Adelsnation*, and the very use of the words, may risk anachronism. Believing that a nation is a natural political unit need not

28 Freedman, 'Cowardice, Heroism' and 'Sainteté et sauvagerie: Deux images du paysan au Moyen Age,' *Annales ESC* 47 (1992): 539–60, at 550.
29 Paul Freedman, *The Origins of Peasant Servitude in Medieval Catalonia* (Cambridge, 1991), 189–202; the suspicion of surviving non-Christian beliefs complicated the links between descent and culture implied in later Spanish ideas about purity of Christian blood: Jocelyn N. Hillgarth, *The Spanish Kingdoms, 1250–1516*, 2 vols. (Oxford, 1976–8), 2: 465–83.
30 Joseph R. Strayer, 'The Historical Experience of Nation-building in Europe,' in *Medieval Statecraft and the Perspectives of History* (Princeton, 1971), 341–8; Guenée, *States and Rulers*, 216–20.
31 André Devyver, *Le sang épuré* (Brussels, 1973). Although the English nobility was occasionally seen as descended from those who 'came over with the Conqueror,' the myth of the 'Norman yoke' focused much more on Anglo-Saxon law and Norman tyranny than on descent: Christopher Hill, *Puritanism and Revolution* (London, 1958), 50–122. The sources cited by Thorlac Turville-Petre, 'Politics and Poetry in the Early Fourteenth Century,' *Review of English Studies* 39 (1988): 1–28, do not suggest to me that either king or nobles were generally seen after 1066 as Norman.

involve believing that all its inhabitants should share equally in governing it. Before theories of equal political rights were propagated, the exclusion of the lower classes from political activity needed little more justification than the exclusion of women. Both exclusions continued in many countries well into the period in which real political nationalism is allowed to have existed. Early modern peasants were not always regarded as unambiguously outside the nation.[32] Myths of their separate origin, or of the loss by their cowardly ancestors of rights that they should have shared with nobles of the same origin, suggest that things were more complicated than that. What stimulated the development of the new myths was the need to overcome the *a priori* assumption of the common descent of any people or nation under one government.

Meanwhile, the discovery of Tacitus' *Germania* in the fifteenth century stimulated new interest in the ancient Germans and in differences between Roman and Germanic culture, thus giving the old myths a new lease of life. This influenced the later forms of the French myths about noble and peasant origins, but the impact was far wider and more lasting than that. Medieval stories of Trojan and biblical descent seem to have been intended for the delectation of the peoples they concerned. The combination of Tacitean ethnography with humanist philology and law, on the other hand, provided scholars with new lines along which they could organize the general history of Europe. To search for origins in the forests of Germany – or, from the seventeenth century, in Scandinavia – is still generally regarded as more scholarly than to search for them in Troy, in Scythia, or on Mount Ararat. If a German or Scandinavian origin seems more probable, however, it is not, as Walter Goffart has pointed out, based on anything that would normally be called reliable evidence.[33] It presupposes the same premises about the long continuity of peoples as communities both of descent and of culture.[34]

From the eighteenth century, German scholarship led the way in emphasizing language as the supreme distinguishing mark of a people or nation: those who spoke German must, despite their division into many small states, nevertheless form a true nation – a nation which Caesar, Tacitus, and the medieval

32 Rainer C. Schwinges, '"Primäre" und "secundäre" Nation: Nationalbewusstsein und sozialer Wandel im mittelalterlichen Böhmen,' in *Europa Slavica – Europa Orientalis: Festschrift für H. Ludat*, ed. Klaus-Detlev Grothusen and Klaus Zernak (Berlin, 1980), 490–532, at 505, 530; Zientara, 'Nationale Strukturen.'

33 *Barbarians and Romans*, 8–30.

34 Klaus von See, *Deutsche Germanen-Ideologie* (Frankfurt, 1970), 9–33; Jacques Ridé, *L'image du Germain dans la pensée et la littérature allemandes de la redécouverte de Tacite à la fin du xvie siècle* (Lille and Paris, 1977), 129–40, 1057–94, 1193–1209; Donald R. Kelley, 'Tacitus noster,' in *Tacitus and the Tacitean Tradition*, ed. Torrey J. Luce and Anthony J. Woodman (Princeton, 1993), 152–67.

Empire showed to have been as ancient and noble as any other. The fact that Herder, for instance, did not want the existing states of Germany to be abolished may seem at first sight to support the contention that his nationalism, like that of the eighteenth century in general, was merely 'cultural.' That is surely to allow his conservatism about existing institutions to distract attention from his more general ideas. Both he and Ranke after him clearly thought of Germany as some sort of political community, even if they did not want it to be a conventionally centralized nation-state.[35] Meanwhile, though the political situation of Germany provoked Germans into developing new arguments, Germanist ideas have never been the prerogative of Germans: Montesquieu, for instance, cited Tacitus to demonstrate that the English derived their system of government from the ancient Germans, who were also 'nos pères.'[36] By the nineteenth century, such ideas were propagated or assumed by a great many writers of national histories as well as by politicians and publicists of many persuasions.[37] Basing ideas of nations on an assumed link between language and descent allowed information about one group of Germanic-speakers to be used to fill in gaps elsewhere: relatively late Anglo-Saxon laws or Norse sagas could be used to illustrate the characteristics of all Germanic societies.

Although the fundamental ideas about nations that were subsumed in the new philological nationalism were not new, they were turned into something significantly different by being combined with other sets of ideas of quite separate and more recent origin.[38] First, there were ideas of popular or democratic government of a genuinely new and different kind, based not on old ideas of custom, law, and community, but on the Rights of Man – individual natural rights. The origin of these ideas falls well outside the scope of this essay, but something about the climate in which they appeared is relevant to the historiography of nationalism. As the development of bureaucracy since the later Middle Ages had begun to drive a wedge between governments and people, so there

---

35 Frederick M. Barnard, *Herder's Social and Political Thought* (Oxford, 1965), 54–76, 120–2, 153–67; Georg G. Iggers, *The German Conception of History* (Middletown, 1968), 65–89.
36 *Oeuvres complètes*, ed. R. Caillois, 2 vols. (Paris, 1949–51), 2: 407, 474–89, 329 (*L'esprit des lois*, XI 6, XIV passim, esp. 14).
37 For nineteenth-century Germanism: Heinz Gollwitzer, 'Zum politischen Germanismus des 19. Jahrhunderts,' *Festschrift für H. Heimpel*, 3 vols. (Göttingen, 1971), 1: 281–356; Reginald Horsman, *Race and Manifest Destiny* (Cambridge, Mass., 1981); Hugh A. MacDougall, *Racial Myth in English History* (Hanover, N.H., 1982). Though see e.g. Numa D. Fustel de Coulanges, *L'invasion germanique* (Paris, 1891), 285–326, 521–59. A late example: Carlo Guido Mor, 'Gouvernés et gouvernants en Italie du vi[e] au xie siècle,' *Recueils de la Société Jean Bodin* 23 (1968): 395–420, at 395–6.
38 This point has been made, e.g., by Denis W. Brogan, *French Personalities and Problems* (London, 1946), 42–4, and Potter, 'Historian's Use of Nationalism,' 137–40.

had come with it a new theory of absolutism, which emphasized rulers at the expense of their subjects. By the seventeenth century, it was possible for governments – and some intellectuals – to envisage a kingdom as merely the territory that its ruler ruled, with no identity or community apart from him. Their claims, together with the polemic of the French Revolution against them, have led historians of modern nationalism to believe that ideas of political community were foreign to earlier centuries. That seems to explain why they suppose that political nationalism was born in the eighteenth century.

Popular government of the kind advocated by the opponents of absolutism needed cohesive units in which to work. If one is going to make decisions by finding a majority of equal individuals, one needs a collectivity in which votes can be counted. It must then be strong enough to hold together when opinions differ and the votes have been counted. Those who took up the new ideas found the collective units they needed in the naturally cohesive peoples or nations that had long been assumed to form the basis of European polities. The new nationalism was, however, different from the old because it was articulated and rationalized in a way that the old assumptions had never been. The result was a conscious ideology of nationalism that, instead of merely validating existing states, became a program for creating new ones.

All the anomalies hidden in the old assumptions about nations as political communities of descent and culture were thus much more likely to be revealed and to fuel conflicts: disagreements about who formed a nation, about the boundaries of nations, all mattered much more when nations were thought of as composed of equal individuals with equal rights to share in their governments. New forms of government profited from the ideas of collective identity and habits of collective activity that survived from the days when collective privileges had been granted to all sorts of groups. At the same time, the old ideas posed problems in an age when rights were thought to belong either to the whole nation or to single individuals within it. Increasingly, whatever the reality of local or regional government and loyalties, politicians and journalists tended to stress the unique and overriding claims of the state that was supposed to embody the whole nation. New ideas of legal personality had to be worked out to control collective action by groups that stood between individuals and the supreme collectivity of the state.[39] Particular problems arose where medieval immigrant groups, like the Germans of the kingdom of Hungary, had secured collective privileges that had helped them preserve their distinctive language and culture over the centuries.[40] Jewish communities had been kept as outsiders

39 Susan Reynolds, 'The History of the Idea of Incorporation or Legal Personality,' in *Ideas and Solidarities of the Medieval Laity.*
40 Schwinges, '"Primäre" und "secundäre" Nation,' 505–12; cf. on Belgium: Roosens, *Creating Ethnicity*, 128–9.

within the states they had long inhabited by collective disabilities that had once been as much taken for granted as collective privileges. Both kinds of groups were difficult to accommodate within a framework of states whose claim to be nations rested on the old ideas of common descent and culture.

Growing knowledge of peoples outside Europe, new study of philology and archaeology, and new ideas of evolution did not at first threaten these old ideas. Nineteenth-century Europeans became more interested in physical differences as they learned more about the rest of the world, but that did not mean that they needed to rethink their old assumptions. Ideas of evolution gave them new force. Black or brown people seemed to be culturally and intellectually less advanced as well as physically different. As abhorrent as the idea of a hierarchy of races may seem now, it was not merely self-serving to believe that Indians or Africans – or Jews, or Slavs, or even the lower classes – inherited their intellectual and moral inferiority along with their physical characteristics. Historians of nineteenth-century ideas sometimes refer to the way that race and culture were confused, but they do not always make clear that the confusions were not new. Nor do they generally explain that what they see as loose uses of the word 'race' were matters not merely of terminology, but of thought.[41] The distinction between cultural transmission and physical inheritance was not obvious before it had been drawn. Some scholars in the later nineteenth century began to worry about the difference between biological and cultural transmission, but they did not have the information to make much sense of it.[42] Only after the rediscovery of Mendel in 1900 did biologists begin to discover how complicated genetic variation is and how poorly it can be fitted to cultural variation.

What Franz Boas began to tell anthropologists in the early years of this century took some time to percolate through to historians, including historians of early medieval Europe.[43] Many, of course, understand that the inhabitants of Europe have never been divisible into separate and homogeneous populations in the biological sense, and that the kind of continuity implied by talking of

41 Marvin Harris, *The Rise of Anthropological Theory* (London, 1969), 80–1, 130–3; Werner Conze, 'Rasse,' in *Geschichtliche Grundbegriffe*, vol. 5 (1984): 135–78, at 137–58; Michael Banton, *Racial Theories* (Cambridge, 1987), xix, 30–1; Hobsbawm, *Nations and Nationalism*, 108. George W. Stocking, *Race, Culture, and Evolution* (Chicago, 1982), 35–41, 65, 245–68, and *Victorian Anthropology* (New York, 1987), 63, 106, 138–46, suggests a more than semantic confusion, but one deriving only from Romanticism. Nancy Stepan, *The Idea of Race in Science: Great Britain, 1800–1960* (London, 1982), ix, x, xvii, and passim.

42 Stocking, *Race, Culture*, 65, 133–94, and *Victorian Anthropology*, 56–69, 145–7; MacDougall, *Racial Myth*, 119–28; also e.g. Johannes Voigt, *Max Mueller* (Calcutta, 1981), 5–11, 89; John Beddoe, *Races of Britain* (Bristol, 1885), 68, 75, 261, 269.

43 Barkan, *Retreat of Scientific Racism*, implies that arguments about race were less concerned with its relation to *different* cultures than with the superiority or inferiority of individuals within American or British society, though see e.g. 55–7, 76–90, 296–301.

'our' descent from 'our forefathers' is problematical. Others, however much they have grasped it in theory, continue to talk of the medieval inhabitants of their countries as 'We' and 'Us' in a way that may mislead their readers. Many think they must not use the word 'race,' because it sounds racist, but use 'ethnic' as what may be little more than a euphemism, while continuing to refer to 'tribe' and 'nation' (or at least 'national') without thinking much about them. Some, especially perhaps the British, still refer to the Celtic race, the Germanic race or races, and racial differences between Goths and Romans or Anglo-Saxons and Normans. Often, with a fine empiricist disregard for mere semantic quibbles, they are simply lifting the word 'race' from pre–twentieth-century works, just as they lift *gens* from medieval sources. Using either word without explanation implies, at best, a failure to explain the intellectual context of past usage and, at worst, a failure to understand how the intellectual context has changed. All this makes it difficult to disentangle modern interpretations of archaeological, philological, and documentary sources about early medieval peoples from all the accumulations of myths about them and from the work of past scholars who started from premises about human societies that can no longer be assumed.

IV

It would be nice to conclude by hoping that this or any other look at the old agenda lurking behind past discussions of the *Völkerwanderung* would make it possible to discard what we no longer need. It is not as easy as that. We cannot abolish the desire for origins and continuity. As the author of the Icelandic *Landnámabók* said: 'of course all wise peoples want to know about the beginnings of their settlement and of their own families.'[44] It is, moreover, hard to separate the real advances in knowledge and understanding that old controversies provoked from the intellectual context in which they were made. Sometimes the very effort to examine old myths in the light of modern knowledge has the paradoxical effect of drawing attention to issues that mattered only in the context of the myths. In order to overcome deep-rooted traditions that now look wrong, Wenskus and other German historians since the 1960s have stressed the discontinuities of German history and the political, rather than 'ethnic,' basis of both the 'tribal duchies' and the kingdom of the East Franks or Germans. The result may make the discontinuities and disunities of German history look more significant, more continuous, and, above all, more excep-

---

44 Jesse L. Byock, *Medieval Iceland* (Berkeley and London, 1988), 14, trans. from Landnámabók, in *Islandingabók, Landnámabók*, ed. J. Benediktsson (Reykjavík, 1986), 336 *n.*

tional than they look to an outsider. In spite of that, the early history of other countries could do with some of the deliberate consideration of assumptions about nations and national identity that German historians have lavished on the subject.[45] It is probably pointless to hope that historians of each European country will stop thinking that their country's history is special, but it may be more stimulating to worry about the peculiarity of one's national history than to glory in it – especially if the glorying takes the form of a quiet complacency that evades explicit argument.

Apart from any question of our relation to the barbarians of the Age of Migrations, and their relation to Tacitus' *Germani*, there is one old assumption that is still sufficiently prevalent to be worth questioning. It is revealed in the tendency to lump all the barbarian groups together by using the same word – whether 'tribe' or *Stamm*, 'ethnic group,' or 'people' – to denote all the named collectivities we find in the historical sources or the archaeological record. If it is right that no human groups above the immediate family are natural in the sense that still-surviving traditional ideas of races, nations, and ethnic groups imply, then the particular word we use does not much matter. What is misleading is the use of different words to suggest, without further definition or argument, that at some point after the fall of Rome European tribes or ethnic groups turned into nations. The names of some of the polities that emerged in the tenth century are more or less the same as those of modern states, while their territories could be regarded as very roughly similar, but neither characteristic in itself qualifies them for membership – if not yet full membership – in a new category. Groups that are now perceived as the founders of modern nations were not always more cohesive than those whose names have disappeared.

Do we need to put all barbarian groups in the same category? Many of the barbarians with whom we are concerned spoke – probably – fairly similar languages and shared – probably – a good deal of their general culture, but that does not mean that groups whose names happen to be recorded had the same political or social character. The long tradition of using information about any one group to fill gaps in information about others would surely be wrong even if the interpolated material were better attested in the first place than it generally is. Perhaps some of the 'peoples' or 'tribes' who are named in the sources were little more than names – and names that they themselves may never have used. Their names may have identified them as guerrilla groups or alliances of gangs that might become the nucleus of something more but had not done so

45 E.g. Wenskus, *Stammesbildung*; Brühl, *Geburt*; J. Fried, *Der Weg in die Geschichte: Die Ursprünge Deutschlands bis 1024* (Berlin, 1994), 9–27; survey by Joachim Ehlers, *Die Entstehung des deutschen Reiches* (Munich, 1994), 70–3.

yet. Some groups were large enough to demand and receive apparently significant amounts of grain, land, or shares of tax. That does not mean that all were. Some may already have formed relatively well-established polities moving with women and children, as, according to Caesar, the Helvetii had done hundreds of years before.[46] Groups like that are surely unlikely to have moved very far without losing some members and picking up others. The size and homogeneity of the groups that crossed the sea to Britain are still much contested: both numbers and relations with the pre-existing population raise problems of reconciling archaeological and linguistic evidence which are still not fully recognized, let alone solved.[47]

The change of language and the apparent loss of Christianity make England a special case, though one that cries out for comparison on the linguistic side. Whatever the answer in England, some at least of what are seen elsewhere as migrations of peoples may have been more like military invasions, though by armies that probably had a fair number of women, captives, and other camp-followers in train. Recent opinion on the Visigothic settlement of 418 seems to be divided on this.[48] Some of the 'waves of migration' may have been no more a motion of peoples than what future archaeologists may see as the spread throughout the world by 1950 of the 'Coca-Cola bottle people,' who were then 'displaced and massacred by the Coca-Cola can people by 1990.'[49] If we have doubts about migration, we should perhaps also have them about settlement. This need not have quite the same implication of large numbers, but it may tend to imply new villages ('settlements') and even new clearance of land when evidence for either is slight. Even if we cannot avoid the words 'migration' and 'settlement,' and even if all their implications are justified in some cases, it is worth wondering whether many more people moved round Europe at this time than at others. There seems to have been a good deal of movement, chiefly but not entirely over shortish distances, at many periods of European history.[50]

46 *De Bello Gallico* I 2–4, 28–9.
47 Most recent archaeological surveys seem to ignore the problem: e.g. Barbara Yorke, *Kings and Kingdoms in Early Anglo-Saxon England* (London, 1990), 7; David Kirby, *The Earliest English Kings* (London, 1991), 12–14; though see Martin Welch, *English Heritage Book of Anglo-Saxon England* (London, 1992), 103–7, and the interesting discussion in Nicholas Higham, *Rome, Britain and the Anglo-Saxons* (London, 1992), 189–208. I discussed Anglo-Saxon/English national identity in 'What Do We Mean by Anglo-Saxon and Anglo-Saxons?' *Journal of British Studies* 24 (1985): 395–414 (repr. in *Ideas and Solidarities of the Medieval Laity*).
48 John Drinkwater and Hugh Elton, 'Introduction' in *Fifth-Century Gaul: A Crisis of Identity*, ed. Drinkwater and Elton (Cambridge, 1992), esp. 50–1, and the contributions of C.E.V. Nixon and J.H.W.G. Liebeschuetz.
49 Malcolm Chapman, *The Celts* (London, 1992), 43.
50 Goffart, *Barbarians and Romans*, 26–7 and especially n. 42.

If mild scepticism about the old concept of the migration of peoples is in order, so it may be about two new ones. The ideas of a nucleus or core of tradition (*Traditionskern*) and of ethnogenesis both seem to represent attempts to save something from old historiographic traditions that we have now formally discarded. Wenskus postulated a nucleus of old traditions handed on as one element of continuity in tribes that were not really the communities of common descent that later historians, and perhaps they themselves, claimed.[51] Wolfram thinks that, though Theoderic's army was mainly composed of Ostrogoths, the fifth-century Gothic army had a 'fundamental polyethnic character.' Wood suggests that those who were called Burgundians in their early sixth-century laws were not a single ethnic group, but covered any non-Roman followers of Gundobad and Sigismund.[52] Some of the leaders of Goths or Burgundians may have been descended from long-distant ancestors somewhere round the Baltic. Maybe, but everyone has a lot of ancestors, and some of theirs may well have have come from elsewhere. There is, as Walter Goffart has repeatedly argued, little reason to believe that sixth-century or later references to what look like names for Scandinavia, or for places in it, mean that traditions from those particular ancestors had been handed on through thick and thin. We may guess at the kind of values barbarian leaders are likely to have had, and may suspect that they encouraged their followers to feel the kind of loyalty and solidarity that was often symbolized in myths of common descent and law. We also know from other societies and periods that traditions can be invented, changed, lost, and borrowed by one group from another. That makes them, if anything, more, rather than less, interesting historically. They tell us about beliefs and ideas current at the time they were told.

As for 'ethnogenesis,' it may be a fair enough word to decribe the appearance of new societies or polities in and around what had been the western Empire, so long as too much is not read into it.[53] Just as this may not have been

---

51 *Stammesbildung und Verfassung*, 54–82, 138 n. 108, 462–5 (and index, s.v. Tradition). Cf. František Graus' review in *Historica* 7 (1963): 185–91; Goffart, *Barbarians and Romans*, 18.

52 Herwig Wolfram, *History of the Goths*, trans. T.J. Dunlap (Berkeley and London, 1988), 300; Ian Wood, 'Ethnicity and Ethnogenesis of the Burgundians,' in Wolfram, *Typen der Ethnogenese*, 53–69, at 61–3. Wolfram seems to maintain the possibility of a real Scandinavian origin behind Gothic traditions: 'L'itinéraire des Goths de la Scandinavie à la Crimée,' in *Sur les traces de Busbecq et du Gothique*, ed. André Rousseau (Lille, 1991), 135–41, and 'Origo et religio,' *Early Medieval Europe* 3 (1994): 19–38; Thomas Anderson, 'Roman Military Colonies in Gaul, Salian Ethnogenesis and the Forgotten Meaning of Pactus Legis Salicae 59.5,' *Early Medieval Europe* 4 (1995): 129–44. Cf. Patrick Amory, *People and Identity in Ostrogothic Italy* (Cambridge, 1997), 33-9, 300, 306-17, and on 'barbarian' or 'Germanic culture': 307-13, 326-31, 338-47.

53 Wenskus used the word in *Stammesbildung*, 246; cf. Wolfram in *Typen der Ethnogenese*, 20. *Oxford English Dictionary*, 20 vols. (2d ed. 1989), 5: 424, gives the first English use in 1962.

a period of exceptionally large and long migrations, it was not the only period of ethnogenesis in Europe. Europeans seem to be rather good at creating new nations to suit their new states, whether in Europe or outside.[54] Ethnic groups nowadays, moreover, are generally taken to be units of culture and descent, rather than of government.[55] The *gentes*, peoples, or nations that lasted in western Europe, although they believed in their common descent and culture, were in reality defined primarily by their political allegiance.

Questions about the numbers of the barbarian groups; about their cultural homogeneity and stability; and about whether any or most of them were more like armies (with followers and captives) or migrating groups of families: all these are intrinsically interesting to historians of the period. Some of them are probably unanswerable, but they are still worth investigation and thought. I suggest that our thought about them will be clarified by remembering the reasons why they exercised our predecessors and why, much as we profit from the learning of those predecessors and the discoveries they made, we cannot start from the same premises as they did.

54 E.g., for the Middle Ages: Fulcher of Chartres, *Historia Hierosolymitana*, ed. H. Hagenmeyer (Heidelberg, 1913), 748–9 (III. 37).
55 Above, n. 7.

2

The Purposes of Cassiodorus' *Variae*

ANDREW GILLETT

The *Variae* of Cassiodorus is one of the most important sources for our knowledge of government in the late Roman Empire and its successor states in the west. A selection of the official correspondence drafted by Cassiodorus between the 500s and 530s on behalf of Theoderic, Ostrogothic king of Italy from 493 to 526, and his successors, the *Variae* stands with the *Theodosian Code* and the *Notitia dignitatum* as one of a small number of extant documentary texts illustrating public administration and other aspects of social and economic life in late antiquity.[1] It is a work difficult to categorize into existing

Earlier versions of this essay have benefited from the comments of Walter Goffart, Timothy Barnes, Alexander C. Murray, Jocelyn Hillgarth, and Walter Kaegi. I am most grateful to the Australian Academy for the Humanities and the Canadian Association for Graduate Studies for generous assistance towards the completion of this essay.

1 Editions: Cassiodorus Senator, *Variae*, ed. Theodor Mommsen MGH AA 12 (1894) [hereinafter Cass. *Variae*]; *Variarum libri XII*, ed. Åke J. Fridh, CCSL 96 (Turnhout, 1973) [hereinafter CCSL 96]. Mommsen's edition, which has indispensable indices, is used here. Translations: *The Letters of Cassiodorus*, tr. Thomas Hodgkin (London, 1886), offers an abridged translation; *Cassiodorus: Variae*, tr. S.J.B. Barnish, Translated Texts for Historians 12 (Liverpool, 1992), contains a selection of the letters. Both have been consulted, but the translations offered here are my own. On the *Variae*: B. Hasenstab, *Studien zur Variensammlung des Cassiodor Senator: Ein Beitrag zur Geschichte der Ostgothenherrschaft in Italien* (Munich, 1883); Mommsen, Prooemium to Cass. *Variae*, v–xxxix; Åke J. Fridh, *Terminologie et formules dans les* Variae *de Cassiodore: Études sur le développement du style administratif aux derniers siècles de l'antiquité*, Studia graeca et latina Gothoburgensia 2 (Stockholm, 1956); Odo John Zimmermann, *The Late Latin Vocabulary of the* Variae *of Cassiodorus, with Special Advertance to the Technical Terminology of Administration* (Washington, D.C., 1944; repr. Hildersheim, 1967); James J. O'Donnell, *Cassiodorus* (Berkeley, 1979), 55–102; Stefan Krautschick, *Cassiodor und die Politik seiner Zeit* (Bonn, 1983), 41–117; Robin Macpherson, *Rome in Involution: Cassiodorus'* Variae *in Their Literary and Historical Setting* (Poznan, 1989); P.S. Barnwell, *Emperor, Prefects, and Kings: The Roman West, 395–565* (London, 1992), 166–9; John Moorhead, *Theoderic in Italy* (Oxford, 1992), 1–3.

genres: unlike other letter collections by individual authors, the *Variae* consists of only official, not private, letters; unlike the *Theodosian Code* and other collections of imperial edicts and rescripts, the *Variae* has no pretence to be a legal reference work.

Why did Cassiodorus gather together and publish a selection of the letters he had written while in public office? The question needs to be answered, for interpretations of the intent of the collection, in particular those which see it as a work of propaganda on behalf of the Ostrogothic regime, affect the perceived reliability of the individual letters as sources; a recent critic has called into question the genuineness of all the letters, and even of Cassiodorus' career.[2] Such views arise from too concerted an effort to locate the *Variae* in the context of events at the time of publication – namely the early years of Justinian's war against the Ostrogoths in Italy – and to assign clear political agenda to the work. Cassiodorus himself states his purposes in publishing his letters: to demonstrate his literary and administrative talents to admiring friends, at their request, and to provide models of letter-writing for successors to imitate. Though a commonplace, Cassiodorus' evocation of a literary circle need not be disingenuous or fictitious. Many features of the *Variae* are most readily explained in the context of the traditional use of literary artefacts in aristocratic *amicitia*, here restricted to a circle of senior civil servants. The work is the product of a quasi-professional bureaucratic culture, not of government propaganda.

Fl. Magnus Aurelius Cassiodorus Senator was a descendant of an important family which had served first the imperial, then the royal, courts of Ravenna since the mid-fifth century.[3] Cassiodorus himself held posts at court three

---

2 Barnwell, *Emperor, Prefects, and Kings,* 168–9.

3 Cass. *Variae*, 1.3 and 4, 9.24 and 25; *Anecdoton Holderi* (*Ordo generis Cassiodorum*) [hereinafter *Anec. Hold.*] in Mommsen, Prooemium to Cass. *Variae*, v–vi, also CSEL 96, v–vi, and Alain Galonnier, 'Anecdoton Holderi ou Ordo generis Cassiodorum: Introduction, édition, traduction et commentaire,' *Antiquité Tardive* 4 (1996): 299–312. On Cassiodorus: L. Hartmann, 'Cassiodorus 1–4,' *RE* 3.2: 1671–6; J. Sundwall, *Abhandlungen zur Geschichte des ausgehenden Römertums* (Helsinki, 1919), 154–6; Schanz-Hosius 4.2: 92–109 (*Variae*: 97–9); A. van de Vyver, 'Cassiodor et son oeuvre,' *Speculum* 6 (1931): 244–92; Arnaldo Momigliano, 'Cassiodorus and the Italian Culture of His Time,' in his *Studies in Historiography* (London, 1966), 181–210; O'Donnell, *Cassiodrus*; *PLRE* 2, 'Cassiodorus 1–3,' 263–5 (ancestors), 'Fl. Magnus Aurelius Cassiodorus Senator 4,' 265–9; John Matthews, 'Anicius Manlius Severinus Boethius,' in *Boethius: His Life, Thought and Influence*, ed. Margaret Gibson (Oxford, 1981), 25–31; Krautschick, *Cassiodor und die Politik seiner Zeit.*

Cassiodorus' career is compared with that of a contemporary Eastern officeholder, John Lydus, in T.F. Carney, *Bureaucracy in Traditional Society: Romano-Byzantine Bureaucracy Viewed from Within* (Lawrence, Kans., 1971), Book 2, Part 2, 97–153, and Michael Maas, *John Lydus and the Roman Past: Antiquarianism and Politics in the Age of Justinian* (London

times, each for about four years, throughout three decades. The letters included in the *Variae* were written in his capacity of *quaestor palatii*, an office he held *ca* 506/7–11. Later, when in office as *magister officiorum* (*mag. off.*), 523–7, and *praefectus praetorio* (PPO) *Italiae,* 533–7, he again wrote on behalf of the Gothic rulers, lending his literary talents to the current incumbents of the quaestorship.[4] In addition, Cassiodorus wrote letters and edicts for his own signature during his period as PPO. Letters from each of these periods in office are included in the collection.[5] Cassiodorus indicates that he assembled the collection while still in office as PPO.[6] Between his periods of office, he was appointed consul, in 514, and *patricius*, at an unknown date.

Throughout his secular career, Cassiodorus produced a number of writings and orations undoubtedly supportive of the Ostrogothic regime. His first appointment as a palatine officer was precipitated by the delivery, while still *iuvenis*, of a panegyric on Theoderic. Subsequently he presented orations on other Gothic leaders, including Theoderic's nominated successor, the king's son-in-law Eutharic, in honour of whose consulship in 519 Cassiodorus also prepared a lightly annotated list of Roman consuls. Most famously, he completed his now lost *historia Gothica*, allegedly at the request of Theoderic, in which *originem Gothicam historiam fecit esse Romanam*.[7]

Cassiodorus was clearly an individual whose literary talents the royal court was keen to exploit. Even so, the list of his overtly political writings is not an adequate basis for presuming either that Cassiodorus was personally partisan to Theoderic and his successors, or that all his extant writings prior to his retirement into monastic leisure at Vivarium should be read as propaganda. Entry and promotion in governmental office in recognition of rhetorical skills, demonstrated by the delivery of panegyrics on public figures, was a typical career pattern in late Roman public administration. The use of panegyrists to reinforce claims to authority and justify policies was the common coin of political life. Theoderic received panegyrics from other contemporaries also, among

and New York, 1992), chap. 2, 'Portrait of a Bureaucrat,' 28–37. Lydus, however, was a professional, middle-level bureaucrat, whereas Cassiodorus, like other members of the senatorial class, held senior posts intermittently between stretches of *otium*.

4 Cass. *Variae*, *Praef.* 7; 9.24.6 and 25.8.

5 The distribution of Cassiodorus' letters throughout his career is tabulated by Krautschick, *Cassiodor und die Politik seiner Zeit*, 48.

6 Mommsen, Prooemium to Cass. *Variae*, xxx–xxxi.

7 Panegyric to Theoderic: *Anec. Hold.* ll. 17–18; to Eutharic: Cass. *Variae* 9.25.3; fragments of this work and a panegyric delivered for the marriage of Vitiges and Mathesuentha appear in MGH AA 12, 457–84. Consular list: Cass. *Chronicon*, ed. Theodor Mommsen, MGH AA 11, 109–61. On the *Gothic History* of Cassiodorus: Walter Goffart, *The Narrators of Barbarian History (A.D. 550–800): Jordanes, Gregory of Tours, Bede, and Paul the Deacon* (Princeton, 1988), esp. 23–42; quote from Cass. *Variae* 9.25.5.

them Ennodius, then deacon of Milan, and Boethius, on the occasion of the entry into the consulship of his two sons in 522; neither is regarded as a fervent partisan of the Ostrogothic regime.[8] The political exploitation of Cassiodorus' literary talents in politically oriented genres shows him, at most, as a dedicated servant of the state, a role he performed in quite conventional ways. Conflating the explicitly propagandistic functions of his panegyrical and historical works with the aims of the publication of the *Variae* is an easy but superficial assumption.

Close examination of the letter collection suggests less ambitious aims than participation in high politics. Though conventionally described as a work in twelve books, the *Variae* in fact circulated in thirteen parts. The initial preface introduces Books 1 to 12, the collection of official correspondence. Books 1 to 5 consist of letters written in the name of King Theoderic. In Books 6 and 7, Cassiodorus assembled *formulae*, model letters for appointments to palatine office and for other regular court functions, to be used on short demand in lieu of personalized letters such as appear in the other books of letters. Correspondence written in the name of Theoderic's successors, the Gothic monarchs Athalaric, Amalasuintha, Theodahad, and Gudeliva, comprises the next three books. Books 11 and 12 contain only letters written in Cassiodorus' own name as PPO, and are introduced by a separate preface in Book 11. After completing this collection of official correspondence, but before its publication, Cassiodorus wrote a theological treatise on the nature of the soul, the *De anima*, at the request of friends.[9] This work, despite the radical difference in subject-matter from the letters, did not circulate independently but was appended to the other twelve books, to be published together. About a decade after publication, Cassiodorus referred to the *De anima* as the thirteenth book of the *Variae*.[10] The published *Variae* consisted of the twelve books of letters and *formulae* and the one theological book. Mommsen did not include the *De anima* in his influential 1894 edition of the *Variae*, an omission which has led to the *Variae* being viewed as a more thematically unified collection than it truly is.[11]

8 On panegyric and public careers: Alan Cameron, 'Wandering Poets: A Literary Movement in Byzantine Egypt,' *Historia* 14 (1965): 470–509. Ennodius: in *Opera*, ed. F. Vogel, MGH AA 7; Boethius: *Anec. Hold.* ll. 10–11.

9 Cassiodorus, *De anima*, ed. James W. Halporn, in CCSL 96, 501–75; see especially 'Introduction,' 505–6, and *De anima*, c. 1; *Variae*, 11, *Praef.* 7.

10 Cassiodorus, *Expositio psalmorum*, ed. M. Adriaen, 2 vols., CCSL 97–8 (Turnhout, 1958), 145.30, cf. 38.187, 123.87 (though cf. *Anec. Hold.*, cited n. 30, below); dated 548, CSEL 96, xi. Date of composition of the *De anima*: CSEL 96, 504–6 and n. 14

11 The *De anima* has been restored to the twelve books of letters in CSEL 96. The work appears both independently and with the *Variae* in manuscript; Halporn in CSEL 96, 521–7.

All the letters of the first ten books, including those drafted when Cassiodorus held the posts of *magister officiorum* and PPO, were written in the capacity of *quaestor*. Athalaric's letter appointing Cassiodorus as PPO in 533, drafted by the appointee himself, states that 'when in the office [of *mag. off.*], you were always at hand for the *quaestores*. For when there was need of clarified eloquence, the case was immediately entrusted to your talents.'[12] The letters of Book 10 written by Cassiodorus as PPO in the name of the last Gothic rulers presumably represent similar assistance to the current incumbents of the quaestorship; most of this book is diplomatic correspondence. The office of *quaestor* in the late Empire served primarily as the spokesman of the emperor, 'the man appointed to communicate the emperor's decisions,' as Zosimos put it.[13] By the fifth and sixth centuries, the office had acquired an important role in legislation, primarily in legal drafting, but also in legal advice to the emperor and in law reform; the compilations of the *Theodosian Code* and the *Corpus iuris* of Justinian were made by *quaestores*.[14] These legal duties, however, were an extension of the original function of the office as confidant and publicist of the emperor, the framing of laws being only one use of the *quaestor*'s eloquence to present his ruler's wishes. Other imperial pronouncements, too, were drafted by the *quaestor*, but the first ten books of the *Variae* are the only extensive example extant of the *quaestor*'s duties as spokesman, other than legal sources.

The *quaestor*'s services were highly valued. In Ostrogothic Italy, the *quaestor* was the third-highest-ranking official, following the PPO and Prefect of Rome, having supplanted the *magister officiorum*.[15] The Italian *quaestores*

---

12 Cass. *Variae* 9.24.6: 'quo loco [sc. magistri] positus semper quaestoribus affuisti. Nam cum opus esset eloquio defaecato, causa tuo protinus credebatur ingenio'; cf. 25.8 and *Praef.* 7. Theodor Mommsen, 'Ostgotische Studien,' *Neues Archiv der Gesellschaft für ältere deutsche Geschichtskunde* 14 (1889): 455–7 = his *Gesammelte Schriften* (Berlin, 1910), 6: 390–1.

13 On the quaestorship: *Notitia dignitatum*, ed. Otto Seeck (Berlin, 1876) [hereinafter *Not. dig.*], *Or.* 12, *Oc.* 10; Cass. *Variae* 6.5 (*formula*), 5.3–4, 8.13–14, 18–19, 10.6–7 (letters of appointment for *quaestores*), 9.24.3; Mommsen, 'Ostgothische Studien,' 387–94; Wilhelm Ensslin, *Theoderich der Grosse* (Munich, 1949), 167–9; Jill Harries, 'The Roman Imperial Quaestor from Constantine to Theodosius II,' *Journal of Roman Studies* 78 (1988): 148–72; Barnish, xli–xliv. Quote: Zosimos, *Historia Nova*, 5.32.6, cited in Harries, 'Roman Imperial Quaestor,' 153.

14 Tony Honoré, *Tribonian* (London, 1978), 8–9; idem, 'The Making of the *Theodosian Code*,' *Zeitschrift der Savigny-Stiftung für Rechtsgeschichte. Romanistiche Abteilung* 103 (1986): 139–56, 189–216 (on the role of *quaestores* in individual imperial *constitutiones*), 173–5, 183–9 (on the role of the *quaestor* Antiochus in the compilation of the *Code*); idem, 'Some Quaestors of the Reign of Theodosius II,' in *The Theodosian Code*, ed. Jill Harries and Ian Wood (New York, 1973), 68–94; Harries, 'Roman Imperial Quaestor,' 148.

15 Cass. *Variae* 6 *capitula*, arranged in rank order. In the *Not. dig.*, the *magister officiorum* ranks

presumably did not draft laws, as the Ostrogothic kings did not usurp the imperial prerogative of legislation; the duties of drafting edicts and rescripts remained, however, and many of the *quaestores* of the Ostrogothic period are previously attested as *advocati*.[16] But eloquence and its political uses were regarded as the main purpose of the *quaestor* by Cassiodorus. A letter of appointment *ca* 526 for a *quaestor* under Athalaric, Ambrosius, is a clear statement of the duty of the position as publicist:

It is tactless to praise the talents of eloquence in a *quaestor*, since he is judged to have done well in his office specifically when he graces the reputation of our times with the quality of his speech. For to some magistrates in the provinces taxation is committed, to others is delegated the care of royal finances; here, however, are stored the outward signs of the fame of the palace, and from here the popular reputation of the court is extolled throughout the whole world.[17]

Views of the *Variae* as 'a self-confessed work of propaganda' overlook the fact that the deployment of rhetorical skills to enhance public perceptions of the imperial or royal court was the fundamental duty of the *quaestor*'s office, just as it is of many public-relations positions in modern governments and corporations.[18] Cassiodorus' generally convoluted style was characteristic of much quaestorial and other official palatine writings.[19] The element of governmental

above the *quaestor*; *Not. dig.*, *Or. Index*; *Oc. Index*. The order in which individuals in Ostrogothic Italy held these two offices, however, seems to have been interchangeable. Cassiodorus held the quaestorship before his appointment as *mag. off.*, as did Eugenes (*PLRE* 2, 414–16), but Faustus Niger was *mag. off.* before his appointment as *quaestor* (*PLRE* 2, 'Faustus 9,' 454–6). Faustus, Eugenes, and Cassiodorus seem to have succeeded one another to the quaestorship, all holding the office between 503 and 511.

16 Restriction of legislation: Mommsen, 'Ostgothische Studien,' 410–11; Jan Prostko-Prostynski, *Utraeque res publicae: The Emperor Anastasius I's Gothic Policy (491–518)*, tr. Przemyslaw Znaniecki, Publikacje Instytutu Historii UAM 1 (Poznan, 1994), 185–8. *Quaestores* as former *advocati*: five of the eight attested *quaestores* for the Ostrogothic period listed in the *fasti* of *PLRE* 2: 1259 (Eugenes, Decoratus 1, Honoratus 2, Ambrosius 3, Fidelis).

17 Cass. *Variae* 8.14.4: 'Eloquentiae vero bona ineptum est in quaestore praedicare, cum ad hoc specialiter probetur adscitus, ut opinionem temporum commendet qualitate dictorum. Aliis enim iudicibus provinciarum committatur exactio, aliis privati aerarii custodia delegata: hic autem aulicae famae insignia reponuntur, unde per totum mundum opinio vulgata laudetur.' Cf. 1.12.2, 1.13.2 (on the literary learning of Eugenes, probably Cassiodorus' immediate predecessor as *quaestor*), 6.5 (*formula*), 9.25.1 (on Cassiodorus as *quaestor*); Ennodius, *Vita Epiphanii*, c. 135, ed. F. Vogel, MGH AA 7 (1885) (on the *eloquentia* displayed by the *quaestor* Vrbicus in his duties).

18 Quote from Barnwell, *Emperor, Prefects, and Kings*, 167.

19 Hermann Peter, *Der Brief in der römischen Literatur* (Leipzig, 1901; repr. Hildersheim, 1965), 199–201; Macpherson, *Rome in Involution*, chap. 1; Gunhild Vidéu, *The Roman*

propaganda evident in the *Variae* is a residue of the original letters, intended to have effect at the time of their dissemination between the 500s and 530s. The later assembly of the letter collection, Cassiodorus' professional portfolio, needs to be clearly differentiated, and the motivating purpose behind it should not conflated with those of the individual and ageing letters.

Similarly, Cassiodorus' career path is not that of the propagandist for the Ostrogothic regime he is sometimes claimed to have been. He held office for only some twelve years in a thirty-year period, interrupted by conventional periods of *otium*, and all his letters were written during his periods of office and as part of his duties. The only apparent irregularity in his career is his occasional performance of the *quaestor*'s function of letter-composition while holding the offices of *mag. off.* and PPO. But the informal adoption of the duties of a second office, including that of the quaestorship, is attested for other servants of Theoderic's court, while in imperial government it was not unprecedented for individuals to hold several senior positions simultaneously.[20]

In two prefaces, one at the head of the collection, the other at the beginning of Book 11, Cassiodorus describes the motivation and purpose behind publishing the official letters he had written.[21] His justification for publication is literary: to collect the writings which he had produced while in office, in order to demonstrate his labours on behalf of the state and record some of the benefits conferred on individuals advanced in office by royal favour, 'so that future generations may recognize both the weightiness of my labours, undertaken for the common good, and the unsuborned behaviour of a clear conscience.'[22] Primarily, however, these official letters would display the literary art which Cassiodorus brought to his offices and maintained despite the burden of duties: 'it all the more advances the vote of praise for you, if among so many and so great public duties you succeeded in producing works fit to read' (the speakers are Cassiodorus' literary friends, demanding publication).[23] Cassiodorus presents

Chancery Tradition: Studies in the Language of the Codex Theodosianus *and Cassiodorus's* Variae, Studia graeca et latina Gothoburgensia 46 (Gothenburg, 1984).

20 Theoderic's court: Ambrosius, *comes rei privatae* under Theoderic before 526, simultaneously undertook the duties of the quaestorship, Cass. *Variae* 8.13; Senarius was holder of several unspecified positions at court, Cass. *Variae* 4.3.2, 4.4.3. Imperial offices: e.g. Cyrus of Panopolis, praefect of Constantinople and PPO *Orientis*, 439–41, *PLRE* 2, 'Cyrus 7,' 336–9; Anastasius, *mag. off.* and *quaestor* in Constantinople, 565/6, *PLRE* 3, 'Anastasius 14,' 64–6.

21 Cass. *Variae*, *Praef.*; 11. *Praef.* The *De anima*, mentioned in 11. *Praef.* 7, also has its own preface: *De anima*, c. 1. On the following: Fridh, *Terminologie et formules*, 1–4.

22 Cass. *Variae*, *Praef.* 1: 'ut ventura posteritas et laborum meorum molestias, quas pro generalitatis commodo sustinebam, et sinceris conscientiae inemptam dinosceret actionem.' Benefits to individuals: *Praef.* 9.

23 Cass. *Variae*, *Praef.* 2–8, quote at 8: 'Verum hoc magis tibi ad suffragium laudis potest proficere, si inter tanta et talia valueris legenda proferre.' On the convention of publication

the collection as a monument to his career and literary talent, an act of self-aggrandizement not at all uncharacteristic of the traditional Roman nobility.

As an extensive collection of correspondence on diverse topics and in rhetorical style, the *Variae* resembles in genre the *Letters* of Pliny the Younger and his imitators.[24] There are, however, significant differences. Pliny assembled nine books of private letters, displaying 'people in their daily pursuits or confronting the important events of upper and middle class life.' Only after his death was a tenth book added to the collection, which contained Pliny's correspondence with the emperor Trajan, mostly written while Pliny held public office.[25] This structure, nine books of private correspondence and a tenth of official letters, was adopted by Pliny's imitators, including, in the fourth century, the editor of the letters of Aurelius Symmachus. Ambrose also followed Pliny in collecting his letters into ten books, the tenth reserved for letters concerning public affairs.[26] In the fifth century, too, Pliny's work was recognized as the model for the collected letters of Sidonius Apollinaris, although Sidonius did not attach a tenth book of official correspondence to his nine of private letters.[27] Cassiodorus' collection does not follow Pliny's in either subject or structure. The collection is exclusively of official, not private, letters, most written in

prompted by friendly demands: Tore Janson, *Latin Prose Prefaces: Studies in Literary Conventions*, Studia Latina Stockholmiensia 13 (Stockholm, 1964), 116–24.

24   C. Plinius Caecilius secundus, *Epistularum libri decem*, ed. R.A.B. Mynors (Oxford, 1963).

25   Ronald Syme, *Tacitus*, vol. 1 (Oxford, 1958), 95–9, quote at 96; A.N. Sherwin-White, *The Letters of Pliny the Younger: A Historical and Social Commentary* (Oxford, 1966), 525–55, esp. 535; Betty Radice, 'The *Letters* of Pliny,' in *Empire and Aftermath: Silver Latin II*, ed. T.A. Dorey (London, 1975), 119, 126–7.

26   Q. Aurelius Symmachus, *Quae supersunt*, ed. Otto Seeck, MGH AA 6/1 (1883); Ambrose, *Epistularum libri I-X*, ed. Otto Faller and Michael Zelzer, 3 vols., CSEL 83, parts 1–3 (Vienna, 1968, 1990, 1982); see *Prolegomena* to part 3, xx–xxi. Alan Cameron, 'The Fate of Pliny's *Letters* in the Late Empire,' *Classical Quarterly* n.s. 15 (1965): 295–6; John Matthews, 'The *Letters* of Symmachus,' in *Latin Literature of the Fourth Century*, ed. J.W. Binns (London, 1976), 66; *Text and Transmission: A Survey of the Latin Classics*, ed. L.D. Reynolds (Oxford, 1983), 316–17.

27   Sidonius Apollinaris, ep. 9.1.1, and cf. 1.1.1, *Poèmes et lettres*, ed. and tr. André Loyen, vol. 3, Budé (Paris, 1970). It is possible, but not certain, that the tenth books of Pliny and Symmachus circulated as independent works: Cameron, 'Fate of Pliny's *Letters*,' 292, 296–7. If so, Sidonius may not have seen Pliny's or Symmachus' tenth books; at the opening of his ninth book of letters, Sidonius states that 'Pliny completed his collection of letters with an equal number of books [paribus titulis opus epistulare determinet].' Even if Sidonius were familiar with the books of official letters, however, he may not have wished, when assembling his letter collections in the 470s, and especially after his ordination as bishop, to emphasize his public career, which included imperial service under Avitus, Majorian, and Anthemius; cf. C.E. Stevens, *Sidonius Apollinaris and His Age* (Oxford, 1933), 61–2; Cameron, 'Fate of Pliny's *Letters*,' 296–7; Jill Harries, *Sidonius Apollinaris and the Fall of Rome* (Oxord 1994), 7–19, noting, however, the pervasive theme of public service in the first book of Sidonius' *Letters*.

the *personae* of the Ostrogothic rulers. Structurally, the choice of twelve books, ten of letters interrupted by the two of *formulae*, does not reflect Pliny's model; twelve books may have been a preferred structure for Cassiodorus, whose *Gothic History* also consisted of that number of volumes.[28]

Despite similarity in rhetorical style, there are significant differences in audience and intent between the genre of Latin epistolary collections exemplified by Pliny and the *Variae*. Though Pliny's collection was imitated by later authors and collectors of letters, it was not Pliny's aim to provide epistolary models. Cassiodorus, however, explicitly states that one aim of his collection is to provide models for his bureaucratic successors (the speakers are again his demanding friends): 'your labour may also gently teach untrained men who need preparation in conscious eloquence for public service, and the skills which you practised when already hurled among the dangers of disputants, they may more happily acquire in tranquillity.'[29] He offers the *Variae*, not to a general audience or a circle of close friends and relatives, as Sidonius does, but specifically to fellow and future bureaucrats, to provide rhetorical models to follow. In the *Ordo generis Cassiodorum* (or *Anecdoton Holderi*), a brief account of the careers and writings of Boethius, his father-in-law Symmachus, and Cassiodorus, apparently written by Cassiodorus himself, he describes the *Variae* as 'models of composition, which he arranged in twelve books and entitled *Variae*.'[30] To this end, Cassiodorus includes the two books of *formulae* as templates for standardized letters.[31] In the other books of letters, specific items of

---

28 *Anec. Hold.* in CSEL 96, vi, ll. 28–30.

29 Cass. *Variae, Praef.* 8: 'rudes viros et ad rem publicam conscia facundia praeparatos [praeparandos Traube] labor tuus sine aliqua offensione poterit edocere, et usum, quem tu inter altercantium pericula iactatus exerces, illos, qui sunt in tranquillitate positi, contingit felicius adipisci.'

30 *Anec. Hold.*, vi, ll. 26–8: 'formulas dictionum, quas in duodecim libris ordinauit et Variarum titulum superposuit.' O'Donnell, *Cassiodorus*, 263–5, suggests that this reference to the *Variae* is a later interpolation, because the opening lines of the *Anec. Hold.* do not refer to Cassiodorus' tenure as PPO; Cassiodorus' original letter, from which the *Anec. Hold.* was excerpted, must therefore have been written before publication of the *Variae*, and the *formulae* mentioned must be the actual letters he composed after his formal tenure as *quaestor*, not his later collection. This is not sound: the opening lines of the *Anec. Hold.* are themselves clearly an interpolation (so Mommsen, MGH AA 12, v), and are not a firm basis for rejecting other parts of the received text. The entries for Symmachus and Boethius in the *Anec. Hold.* follow a clear order: brief outline of public offices and titles; public orations; published works. The entry for Cassiodorus follows the same pattern; the *formula* collected in the *Variae*, together with the *Gothic History*, are listed as Cassiodorus' publications, not as part of his governmental career. On the crux in the MS of this passage: F. Dolbeau, 'Un nouveau témoin fragmentaire de l'*Anecdoton Holderi*,' *Revue d'histoire des textes* 12–13 (1982–3): 398.

31 Cass. *Variae, Praef.* 14.

information, such as the names of envoys and individuals other than the
addressees of the letters, are often omitted and replaced with *ille*, one means of
making even letters written for specific occasions timeless and suitable for imitation.[32] Antiquity offers comparisons but no exact precedent of one individual's letters written in public office, edited for use by fellow civil servants.[33] It
is this consciousness of a professional culture which reveals the true aim of the
Variae.

Notwithstanding Cassiodorus' prefaces, moderns have often assumed a
political motive behind the publication of the *Variae*, related to the circumstances in Italy at the probable time of publication, *ca* 537/8. By then, the
Byzantine war against the Goths had already lasted some two years, with considerable success for the east.[34] Modern scholars have generally concluded that
the motive behind the publication of Cassiodorus' official letters was tied to the
ongoing war, assuming it to be a sophisticated form of propaganda justifying
Ostrogothic rule or Cassiodorus' own service to the barbarians.[35] The text

---

32 Cf. L. Traube's *Index rerum et verborum* to Cass. *Variae*, s.v. *ille*, 546–7, classified under
    names, times, places, and other items. On *ille* as part of the formulaic nature of the *Variae*:
    Mommsen, Prooemium to Cass. *Variae*, xxiii–xxiv; followed by Fridh, *Terminologie et for-
    mules* 2; O'Donnell, *Cassiodorus*, 93; Barnish, xviii. The substitution of *ille* for details fea-
    tures in other late antique letter collections, e.g., the *Registrum* of Pope Gregory I; Dag
    Norberg, *In registrum Gregorii Magni studia critica*, vol. 2 (Upsala, 1939), 6 n.3. There is no
    evidence to support the suggestion of Peter, *Der Brief*, 205–6 (followed by Krautschick, *Cas-
    siodor und die Politik seiner Zeit*, 43), that the use of *ille* indicates that Cassiodorus compiled
    his collection from personal draft copies, written before the envoys were appointed.
      The letters of Books 1 to 5 and 8 to 10 were understood as *formulae* by the scribes of several
    twelfth-century manuscripts of the work, who gave the title as *Variae formulae*, rather than the
    more common *Variae epistolae*; CCSL 96 3, 9, 55, 96 (incipits to MS X), 499 (explicits to
    MSS B and M). None of these manuscripts contains *Variae* 6–7, the *formulae* proper.
33 Peter, *Der Brief*, 201; Fridh, *Terminologie et formules*, 4–5. The tenth books of Pliny and
    Symmachus, if they did circulate separately (cf. n. 27 above), would be comparable collec-
    tions. An earlier, though much briefer, Greek collection of stylistic models of letters for offi-
    cials is Pseudo-Demetrius, *Epistolary Types*, tr. in Abraham J. Malherbe, *Ancient Epistolary
    Theorists*, Sources for Biblical Study 19 (Atlanta, 1988), 4, 31–41; unfortunately, the work
    cannot be dated more accurately than between the second century B.C. and the third century
    A.D. In the third century A.D., Philostratus of Lemnos wrote a work on government servants'
    letter-writing: Stanley K. Stowers, *Letter Writing in Greco-Roman Antiquity* (Philadelphia,
    1986), 34.
      The use of a highly rhetorical style in official letters, which characterizes the *Variae*, was no
    novelty; see the advice on the inclusion of historical and learned digressions in official letters
    by Julius Victor, *The Art of Rhetoric*, c. 77, 'On Letter Writing,' tr. in Malherbe, 63.
34 J.B. Bury, *History of the Later Roman Empire: From the Death of Theodosius I to the Death
    of Justinian*, 2 vols. (London, 1923; repr. New York, 1958), 2: 168–95; Ernst Stein, *Histoire
    du Bas-Empire*, tr. J.-R. Palanque, 2 vols. (Paris, 1959), 2: 339–55.
35 E.g., O'Donnell, *Cassiodorus*, 85, 100; Krautschick, *Cassiodor und die Politik seiner Zeit*,

itself, however, gives no direct support for this view, and the nature of the connection, if any, between the publication of the *Variae* and the political circumstances of the time is difficult to discern. To be sure, the inclusion of certain individual letters must have struck a chord in 537/8: for example, the very first letter, from Theoderic to Anastasius, seeking peace between *utraeque res publicae*, or the two letters of Theoderic reprimanding Theodahad, whose later, ill-fated rule was to see the outbreak of the Byzantine attack. The last letters of Book 10, written in the name of Vitigis, directly address the current war.[36] Moreover, the arrangement of the books reflects the reigns of the Gothic monarchs, Theoderic's letters occupying the first five books (set off from the letters of the later rulers by the two books of *formulae*), Athalaric's the eighth and ninth, and those of Amalasuintha, Theodahad, and Vitigis the tenth. This structuring device is reminiscent of the common division of *historiae* and *breviaria* into books according to emperors.

Despite these echoes of the circumstances of the *Variae*'s publication, it is difficult to understand in what real way the *Variae* could have functioned as propaganda. A functional context is required for any form of propaganda to have effect; mere praise is not the same as political suasion.[37] The named audience of the *Variae*, senior civil servants in Italy, may have formed a constituency whose opinion a government propagandist would court, but is the *Variae* a suitable medium for propaganda, and do the contents of the work convey a coherent message capable of moulding the outlook of its sophisticated audience? Cassiodorus' earlier two historical works, his *Chronicle* and the *Gothic History*, were, like his panegyrics of Theoderic and Eutharic, highly flattering to the ruling Amal dynasty. But the *Variae* cannot be assimilated to this historical propaganda.[38] It is certainly not a record of events of the Gothic monarchs' rule. The collection contains only a selection of letters from Cassiodorus' twelve or so years in office over three decades.[39] Though the letters

41–2; Barnwell, *Emperor, Prefects, and Kings*, 166–9; John Moorhead, '*Libertas* and *Nomen Romanorum* in Ostrogothic Italy,' *Latomus* 46 (1987): 161–8. Cf. Mommsen, Prooemium to Cass. *Variae*, xxiii–xxiv, and Hartmann, 'Cassiodorus 1–4,' 1673–4, who suggest that the *Variae* may have been published on the assumption that a Byzantine victory in the war in Italy was close, and that Cassiodorus wished to demonstrate to an Eastern audience his *lack* of partisanship for the Goths.

36 Cass. *Variae* 1.1 (Anastasius); 4.39, 5.12 (Theodahad); 10.32–5 (Vitigis).

37 Cf. the discussion on panegyric and propaganda in C.E.V. Nixon, 'Latin Panegyrics in the Tetrarchic and Constantinian Periods,' in *History and Historians in Late Antiquity*, ed. Brian Croke and Alanna M. Emmett (Rushcutters Bay, 1983), 88–99.

38 There is no evidence that the *Variae* circulated with the *Chronicle* (written twenty years earlier) or the *Gothic History* (begun before Theoderic's death in 525), or was meant to be read in association with them, *contra* Barnwell, *Emperor, Prefects, and Kings*, 166.

39 Hasenstab, *Studien zur Variensammlung*, 30–4.

give insight into civil administration and certain individual events, the periods they cover are too inconsecutive to constitute a history of the Gothic regime. Furthermore, all protocol and subscriptions, and therefore dates, have been deleted from the texts of the individual letters as preserved in the collection, and so have certain other important data. These deletions, customary signs of preparation for literary publication, further inhibit the use of the collection as a chronicle of the deeds of the Ostrogothic monarchs.[40]

The letters demonstrate ideals of just rule and the continuity of imperial administrative practice. Such themes, of considerable interest to modern students of late Roman government, were commonplaces to contemporaries, stemming from a tradition of official rhetoric employed by imperial *quaestores.* Similar themes are evident in prefatory remarks to individual *constitutiones* in the *Theodosian Code.* The element of propaganda in the letters is a remnant of the time of original composition of the letters, rather than of the compilation of the *Variae.* It would require the greatest optimism to hope that this lengthy and diffuse work could affect political decisions when Byzantine soldiers already held Rome and Milan. Cassiodorus named his publication *Variae* to reflect the diversity of rhetorical styles employed throughout; such diversity does not lend itself to a political tract.[41]

The literary motives expressed in Cassiodorus' prefaces should be taken seriously rather than dismissed.[42] The political circumstances at the time of publication are not irrelevant to an assessment of the *Variae,* but they need not be seen as motivating Cassiodorus' decision to publish. The allusions to the Byzantine war may merely reflect the obvious topicality of the conflict, not

40 Fridh, *Terminologie et formules,* 2, 10; cf. at n. 32 above. Nor is the *Variae* a record of Cassiodorus' time in office. Though his transition from *quaestor* to *magister officiorum* is marked by the division of Books 4 and 5, there is no corresponding demarcation of his change in circumstances from *mag. off.* to PPO; letters of both offices appear in Book 9. The letters of his appointment as PPO are included (Cass. *Variae* 9.24–5), but not those of his appointments as *quaestor* or *mag. off.,* nor of his elevation to the consulate. The chronology of his career must be reconstructed from the internal evidence of the letters; Krautschick, *Cassiodor und die Politik seiner Zeit,* 41–9.

41 Cass. *Variae, Praef.* 15–18. Variety, though of subject rather than rhetorical style, was also a guiding principle of Pliny's selection of letters: Sherwin-White, *Letters of Pliny the Younger,* 42–50, esp. 46. Cassiodorus explains the work's title by the diversity of subject-matter (*Praef.* 13), style, recipient, and quality of the letters, but curiously he does not cite the variety of nominal authors of the letters, i.e., the five Ostrogothic monarchs, himself as PPO, and the Senate of Rome (*Variae,* 11.13). The range of nominal authors, reflected in the division of books by ruler, is one feature of the collection which would be obvious to a contemporary reader. In advanced rhetorical training, letter-writing served as an exercise in *prosopopoeia,* characterization in different *personae*; Malherbe, *Ancient Epistolary Theorists,* 7. Cassiodorus refers to classical precepts for writing in *personae* in *Variae* 11. *Praef.* 2.

42 Hasenstab, *Studien zur Variensammlung,* 7–9; Fridh, *Terminologie et formules,* 1–2.

underlying political agenda, and present an opportunity for Cassiodorus to display his continuing involvement in diplomatic correspondence, a distinctive category emphasized by his arrangement of letters. Cassiodorus saw no inconsistency in publishing the theological tract *De anima* with the official letters, and for the same reason – to satisfy the urging of his friends and peers, with whom Cassiodorus shared a culture embracing professional, literary, and philosophical and theological interests.[43] No claim for a political purpose behind the *Variae* has accounted for this inclusion.

Cassiodorus appears to have been still in office as PPO when he collected his letters for publication, and this, rather than the current war, may explain the date of publication. Literary publication while holding public office was a demonstration of virtuosity. Boethius published the second book of his commentary on Aristotle's *Categories* when consul in 510 and drew attention to the fact: 'Although the duties of the consular office prevent us from spending all our leisure and the whole of our effort in these studies, yet this seems to be part of a certain duty to the state – to instruct its citizens in the teaching of subjects over which we have laboured at night.'[44] Cassiodorus had no qualms about using his collection as a monument to his career, a literary alternative to a public inscription. He places praise for his professional skills in the mouths of friends in the fictitious dialogue which comprises most of the preface of the *Variae*; more subtly, he sets the clearest outlines of his career, Athalaric's letters appointing him PPO and notifying the Senate, as the last letters of Book 9. The placement of first and last letters in each book is deliberate; most are diplomatic correspondence addressed to eastern emperors or western kings.[45] Not only

43 Momigliano, 'Cassiodrus and the Italian Culture of His Time'; Pierre Courcelle, *Latin Writers and Their Greek Sources*, tr. Harry E. Wedeck (Cambridge, Mass., 1969), 273–409; Helen Kirkby, 'The Scholar and His Public,' in *Boethius*, ed. Gibson (as at n. 3), 44–69.

44 Boethius, *In categorias Aristotelis libri quatuor*, PL 64: 201B: 'Etsi nos curae officii consularis impediunt quominus in his studiis omne otium plenamque operam consumimus, pertinere tamen videtur hoc ad aliquam reipublicae curam, elucubratae rei doctrina cives instruere.' Cf. Schanz-Hosius 4.2, 154–5. Fl. Turcius Rufius Apronianus Asterius, consul for 494, edited Virgil's *Bucolics* during his consular year, advertising the fact in a sixteen-line elegy in which he asked the reader to 'kindly spare me / if a less leisured mind has omitted anything' while engaged in the busy preparations of his consular games ('parcasque benignus / si qua minus uacuus praeteriit animus ...'); Virgil, *Bucoliques*, ed. and tr. E. de Saint-Denis, 2d ed. (Paris, 1978), xxiv–xxv.

45 Of the sixteen first and last letters in Books 1 to 5 and 8 to 10, twelve are addressed to emperors or kings, or directly relate to preceding letters to an emperor; Mommsen, Prooemium to Cass. *Variae*, xxvii; Peter, *Der Brief*, 209; Fridh, *Terminologie et formules*, 9; Moorhead, *Theoderic in Italy*, 145. Another instance of placement of letters aggrandizing Cassiodorus is *Variae* 1.3–4, the letters announcing the appointment of Cassiodorus' father as *patricius*, placed immediately after correspondence with imperial themes, the opening letter to Anastasius and a letter to the officer in charge of producing imperial purple dye for the Ostrogothic court.

Cassiodorus but also his peers were commemorated in the *Variae*, as Cassiodorus has them state in the preface: 'you assumed the task of describing [those who received high offices] with truthful praise and, at least to some extent, of painting them with the colours of history. If you pass them on to future generations as figures deserving fame, then, following the practice of our ancestors, you will have taken oblivion away from those who died honourably.'[46] The inclusion of individualized letters of appointment for high officials in the collection preserved and published the eulogistic praises of their careers.[47] The prefatory remarks to the various books of Sidonius' *Letters* show that literary publication of an epistolary collection could be an extension of the *amicitia* served by the original exchange of letters.[48]

The proper context for viewing Cassiodorus is not the military conflict of the Goths and Byzantium, but the high administrative milieu which characterizes his family background and public career. The urging of friends to publish both a selection of Cassiodorus' letters and his treatise on the soul, though a literary convention, may nevertheless have been real; the publication of Cassiodorus' letters may have been of as much interest to the aristocratic bureaucrats named therein as private letters were within a circle of correspondents. The collection has every sign of serving the practical purpose of providing models of epistolary eloquence for subsequent *quaestores*. The *Variae* is a monument to its author and his peers rather than their masters, an extension of the cultivation of eloquence as part of public administration.[49]

---

46 Cass. *Variae*, *Praef.* 9: 'Tu enim illos assumpsisti vera laude describere et quodam modo historico colore depingere. Quos si celebrandos posteris tradas, abstulisti, consuetudine maiorum, morientibus decenter interitum.'

47 The officials addressed by the letters in the *Variae* are listed in Mommsen, Prooemium to Cass. *Variae*, xxviii–xxx.

48 E.g. Sidonius, epp. 1.1, 7.18, 8.1, 8.16, 9.1, 9,15.1, 9.16.

49 Hasenstab, *Studien zur Variensammlung*, 7–9; Fridh, *Terminologie et formules*, 1–2; cf. Ernst Robert Curtius, *European Literature and the Latin Middle Ages*, tr. Willard R. Trask (New York, 1953), 74–5, 76; Nicholas Purcell, 'The Arts of Government,' in *The Oxford History of the Classical World*, ed. John Boardman, Jasper Griffin, and Oswyn Murray (Oxford, 1986), 589.

3

Gregory of Tours and the Franks

EDWARD JAMES

Gregory of Tours lived towards the end of what we have come to call the *Völker-wanderungszeit*, the Migration Period, whose ethnic complexities are recalled on those twentieth-century maps in which numerous barbarian tribes move from side to side and up and down, 'whirling furiously over the plains of Europe,'[1] following the arrows on gaily coloured ribbons, for all the world as if they were playing some cosmic game of snakes and ladders. This is a world which seems to pullulate with different peoples and tribes, each with their own language, customs, laws, and, perhaps, dress. The process of migration may have confused the ethnic map, but, as the initial chaos settled, new tribes or peoples were formed: the Angles became the East Angles and the Middle Angles and the Humbrians and the Northumbrians, not to mention the Hwicce and the Pecsæten and all those tribes in the Tribal Hidage; the Saxons became the South Saxons, the East Saxons, the West Saxons, and the Middle Saxons; and so on. If the Chamavi and the Bructeri and others were all regarded by Romans as Franks as early as the third century, then they themselves may well have preserved their identity as Chamavi and Bructeri at least until the eighth century; and the Franks, as they settled west of the Rhine, themselves split into the Salians and the Ripuarians. Ethnic difference, whether created by or itself

---

1 Walter Goffart, 'The Map of the Barbarian Invasions: A Preliminary Report,' *Nottingham Medieval Studies* 32 (1988): 49–64, at 49. Goffart refers specifically to *The Times Atlas of World History*, ed. G. Barraclough, rev. ed. (London, 1984), 98–9, but a choice example can also be found in J. Hubert, J. Porcher, and W.F. Volbach, *Europe in the Dark Ages* (London, 1969), fig. 355. A further critique of the standard model of the Migration Period can be found in Walter Goffart, 'The Theme of "The Barbarian Invasions" in Late Antique and Modern Historiography,' in *Das Reich und die Barbaren*, ed. Evangelos K. Chrysos and Andreas Schwarz, Veröffentlichen des Instituts für österreichische Geschichtsforschung 29 (Vienna, 1989), 87–107; repr. in Walter Goffart, *Rome's Fall and After* (London, 1989), 111–32.

creating political difference, seems to be a significant fact of life in the post-Roman world.

For a long time, historians and archaeologists operated within this model, derived from the documentary sources, in which ethnicity is extremely important and ethnic groups figure as crucial protagonists in the events. The discussion of this question among historians and archaeologists used to be couched in the discreetly scholarly language of racism. Nineteenth-century rivalries between French and Prussian, between Saxon and Celt, between Latin and Nordic, which were perfectly normally seen in biological and racial terms, played themselves out in the migration period, as anthropologists measured skulls, and historians spoke wisely of miscegenation and the social and political effects of intermarriage between vital Germanic warriors and degenerate Roman aristocrats, or between civilized and advanced Romans and primitive barbaric Germans. The assumption was always that the ethnic groups mentioned by the historical sources were, as those groups often portrayed themselves, genetically linked biological races.

The debate on ethnogenesis – the birth of new ethnic entities – over the last three decades has overturned many old assumptions.[2] Nowadays it is recognized that we are probably not dealing with large-scale popular migrations; nor are we dealing with fixed and easily defined ethnic groups, but with fluid and ever-changing political groupings which our sources are inclined to treat as if they were ethnic groups. We can no longer take for granted that our Latin texts reflect in any way the social and political reality of what is going on in Germanic societies. Our problem, or one of our many problems, is knowing how people identified *themselves*; all too often our evidence comes from outsiders. We cannot assume that outsiders saw people as they saw themselves; we cannot assume that people had only *one* label for themselves, or only one type of identity.

It is somewhat of a shock to turn from all the discussions of ethnicity and ethnogenesis to look at the writings of Gregory of Tours. Gregory, of course, is best known for doing something that he did not do: write an ethnic history, the *History of the Franks*.[3] Later generations became so familiar with ethnic histo-

---

2 A good recent discussion of the problem can be found in Patrick Amory, 'The Meaning and Purpose of Ethnic Terminology in the Burgundian Laws,' *Early Medieval Europe* 2 (1992): 1–28.

3 For a conclusive discussion of the question of the title, see W. Goffart, 'From *Historiae* to *Historia Francorum* and Back Again: Aspects of the Textual History of Gregory of Tours,' in *Religion, Culture and Society in the Early Middle Ages*, ed. T.F.X. Noble and J.J. Contreni (Kalamazoo, 1987), 55–76, reprt. in *Rome's Fall and After*, 255–74; and W. Goffart, *The Narrators of Barbarian History (A.D. 550–800): Jordanes, Gregory of Tours, Bede, and Paul the Deacon* (Princeton, 1988), 119–27.

ries (the *History of the Goths* by Jordanes, the *History of the Lombards* by Paul the Deacon, the *Ecclesiastical History of the English* by Bede) that it became perfectly natural to think of Gregory as the author of the *History of the Franks*, particularly when Gregory's work was often known in an abbreviated edition which emphasized the narrative of the Frankish kingdom and diminished the importance of the Gallic church. In all the 537 pages of what Gregory called his *Ten Books of Histories*, in the Monumenta Germaniae Historica edition, there are in fact only forty-eight passages in which Gregory mentions the word 'Frank' or 'Franks'; many of those occurrences of *Francus* are in the form *Francorum*, in formulae such as *reges Francorum* and *regnum Francorum*, that is, in a title or standard phrase rather than in a reference to an individual Frank or to a recognizable group of Franks. One could compare that infrequency of mention with what we find in a rather more recent history of the Franks, which was published by Blackwell's in 1988, which appears to use it on average four or five times per page.[4] In Gregory's other writings, in particular his *Glory of the Martyrs*, his *Glory of the Confessors*, his *Miracles of St Martin*, and his *Life of the Fathers*, he used the word 'Frank' precisely three times: three times in 427 printed pages. The twentieth century, perhaps, has been rather more obsessed with ethnic identity than, apparently, the sixth was.

The above figures are somewhat of a simplification, as it happens. *Francus* sometimes appears disguised as *barbarus*, for instance, though, as we shall see, in very particular circumstances. And *Francus* itself is used only in particular contexts and circumstances. In this essay I shall be looking at those contexts, and coming to some conclusions about Gregory's view of the world around him. I am treading a path which has been trodden before me by various distinguished scholars: I shall refer above all to studies by Godefroid Kurth, by Michel Rouche, and by Walter Goffart. Kurth published 'Francia et Francus' in his collected essays *Études franques*, in 1919; Rouche published 'Francs et gallo-romains chez Grégoire de Tours' in 1977, in the proceedings of an Italian conference on Gregory; and Goffart, his 'Foreigners in the *Histories* of Gregory of Tours' in 1982. Although I have done my own trawl and my own analysis of Gregory's works in order to write this essay, I obviously owe a great debt to my predecessors, even if I do not necessarily agree with them.[5]

---

4 See Edward James, *The Franks* (Oxford, 1988).
5 G. Kurth, '*Francia et francus,*' in Kurth, *Études franques*, 2 vols (Paris and Brussels, 1919), 1: 68–137; M. Rouche, 'Francs et gallo-romains chez Grégoire de Tours,' in *Gregorio di Tours*, ed. R. Morghen, Convegno del Centro di Studi sulla Spiritualità Medievale XII, 10–13 October 1971 (Todi, 1977), 143–69; Walter Goffart, 'Foreigners in the *Histories* of Gregory of Tours,' *Florilegium* 4 (1982): 80–99, cited here from *Rome's Fall and After*, 275–91.

A word or two about their conclusions. Kurth looked at the use of the terms *Francus* and *Francia* right through the early medieval period, but he did have particular thoughts on Gregory's use of the terms. He saw a slow development in usage. In the time of the fifth-century Frankish king Clodio, there was in Gaul, as in other areas of the Empire, a clear ethnic distinction: 'Francs et Romains formaient donc, dans le royaume de Clodion, deux groups entière-ment distincts au point de vue juridique et politique ... Si cette situation avait duré, nul doute qu'il se fût bientôt formé deux classes héréditaires, comprenant l'une les indigènes, l'autre les étrangers ... On les aurait distingués les uns des autres à la religion, à la langue, à la condition sociale, à la constitution physique.'[6] But a change came, argues Kurth, with the arrival of Clovis, and with the emergence of a kingdom in Gaul in which both Frank and Gallo-Roman could take part with some degree of equality. He distinguishes, some-what unnecessarily, between two parts of Clovis's reign. The second phase, before the conquest of the southern Gallic kingdom of the Visigoths, he calls the *premier royaume de Clovis*. In that stage, 'Frank' came to mean any free inhabitant of the kingdom of the Franks, whether Frank or Gallo-Roman. In the final stage, the *seconde royaume de Clovis*, after the conquest of the Visigoths, he concluded that Gregory meant by 'Frank' an inhabitant of Gaul who was a free subject of the king of the Franks, whether he was of Roman origin or descended from any other Germanic immigrants into the former Roman Empire. This was confirmed, in Kurth's mind, by other writers of the sixth cen-tury, such as Venantius Fortunatus and the authors of the *Vita* of Caesarius of Arles. The differences that Kurth found in the *Chronicle* of Fredegar are explained by the fact that Fredegar was writing from a Burgundian point of view, and that *Francus*, for Fredegar, designated all the inhabitants of the king-dom of the Franks *outside* the former territory of the kingdom of the Burgundi-ans.[7]

Kurth's opinions were quite contrary to accepted position in the nineteenth century, which tended to oppose Roman and German, and to imagine that the 'fusion' of the two into one French 'race' was a development that occurred long after the time of Clovis. Indeed, archaeologists long ignored Kurth, and believed that they could distinguish 'Roman' and 'Frank' in the ground, partic-ularly in their graves, well into the late twentieth century.[8]

---

6 Kurth, '*Francia*,' 97.

7 Ibid., 112.

8 This is discussed in Edward James, 'Cemeteries and the Problem of Frankish Settlement in Gaul,' in *Names, Words and Graves: Early Medieval Settlement*, ed. P.H. Sawyer (Leeds, 1979), 55–89.

To a large extent Michel Rouche accepted Kurth's conclusions: the three chronological distinctions that Kurth made (the narrow, medium, and broad interpretations of the word 'Frank') 'restent à mon avis totalement fondés et n'ont pas remis en question depuis le début du XXe siècle.'[9] Nevertheless, he does not follow Kurth totally. He argues that Gregory does not use *barbarus* exclusively as 'soldier,' but uses it also in other pejorative contexts; and also argues that 'Roman' stands for something which Gregory values above 'Frank.' In other words, Rouche emphasizes that the impression of ethnic indifference and ethnic tolerance which Kurth sees in the sources is not the whole story. Gregory still displays something of the traditional Roman hostility to the Frank as barbarian: Gregory still has a hierarchy of values which he expresses in his use of terms such as *Francus*, *barbarus*, and *Romanus*. 'Romain et chrétien, telle est la composante principale du tranquille complex de supériorité qui anime Grégoire de Tours devant les Francs.'[10]

Our third commentator on this question is Walter Goffart (who either does not know Rouche's paper or, more plausibly, does not consider it worth citing). He, too, concludes in somewhat different tones from Kurth's classic study. Ethnic distinctions are unimportant for a bishop like Gregory; he lived at a time and place when ethnic distinctions seemed to be dissolving. Rouche assumed that Gregory thought of himself as a Roman, as opposed to 'Frank' or 'barbarian': Goffart points out, in the concluding words of his article, that Gregory in fact did *not* refer to himself as a Roman.

Among all the labels he uses, the conspicuous absentee is the most natural one, the one that ought automatically to accompany the senatorial title that Gregory willingly assumes. Senatorial, yes; Roman, no. Gregory speaks for his place and time precisely by refusing to espouse the ethnic identity that he had the most historic reason to assume. No longer a Roman but not yet a Frank, he found in his faith and its principles of conduct a position that was adequate for a portrayal of his surroundings – a world in which all men were neither insiders nor outsiders but merely potential citizens in God's kingdom.[11]

What I want to draw attention to in my addition to the debate is the context of Gregory's use of words such as *Francus*, *barbarus*, and *Romanus*: not only the context within Gregory's Latin, but also the chronological context within Gregory's works, most notably within the *Histories*. I reproduce three diagrams to assist with the visualization of the chronological framework, two to situate

9 Rouche, 'Francs et gallo-romains,' 144. He thus appears to accept Kurth's distinction between the 'moyen' and the 'large' senses, despite the fact that they are semantically identical.
10 Ibid., 169.
11 Goffart, 'Foreigners,' 291.

Gregory's *Histories* in an historical context, and one to help to plot the use of the word *Francus*, in its various forms, across the time-span of Gregory's *Histories*. These diagrams show the chronological structure of the *Histories* in two different ways. The first (fig. 1a) shows the chronological span of each of the books, demonstrating very clearly, I hope, the way in which the focus narrows dramatically from Book V on to the end. The figures are only simplifications, of course; there is some overlap and some rounding up. The second diagram (fig. 1b) represents the same figures in a different way, showing how most of the history of Gaul, and of the Franks, in the fifth and sixth centuries is in fact to be found in Book II alone. Against this diagram might be plotted Gregory's own life. He was born two-thirds of the way through the events described in Book III, becomes bishop of Tours towards the end of the events described in Book IV, and is witness and often participant of the events described in the last six books. Most of his own political career came in the twenty years following the assassination of Sigibert in 575, during the period of internal strife in which Childebert II, Sigibert's baby son, came to adulthood and to supremacy within the Merovingian kingdom.

The third diagram (fig. 2) plots the occurrence of the word *Francus* in its relationship to the structure of the *Histories*. Each circle indicates a passage in which the word *Francus* is used (perhaps in more than one instance). The distinction between the dark and open circles, the two usages of *Francus*, is a significant one. The dark circles in effect indicate occurrences of the word *Francorum* in a number of fairly set phrases: above all, *rex* or *reges Francorum* and *regnum Francorum*, but also phrases such as *potestas Francorum* (one occurrence), *gens Francorum* (two occurrences), and, less significantly perhaps, *mos* or *ritum Francorum* (one occurrence each).[12] The open circles indicate single occurrences, or passages, in which an individual Frank or a specific group of Franks appear as protagonists: that is, of course, not every mention of a known Frank, such as Clovis or Chilperic, but every time the ethnic term is used. It has often been noted that while Gregory will often explain the ethnic origin of someone from outside Gaul – a Saxon, a Lombard, a Taifal – he very rarely bothers to identify or single out a Frank. The sixth-century kings themselves, for instance, are called 'kings of the Franks,' but are never themselves called Franks. The attempts of modern historians to divide up the characters in Gregory's *Histories* into Franks and Gallo-Romans is based largely on the lin-

---

12 'Nam semper Brittani sub Francorum potestatem post obitum regis Chlodovechi fuerunt': *Hist.* IV 4, p. 137; 'Francorum gentem et regnum': *Hist.* V, preface, p. 193; Chilperic's salver: 'ego haec ad exornandum atque nobilitandum Francorum gentem feci': *Hist.* VI 2, p. 266; 'legatos ... cum virgus consecratis iuxta ritum Francorum': *Hist.* VII 32, p. 352; 'ablata mensa, sicut mos Francorum est': *Hist.* X 27, p. 520.

Figure 1 Gregory of Tours' *Histories*

a. The time-span of each book

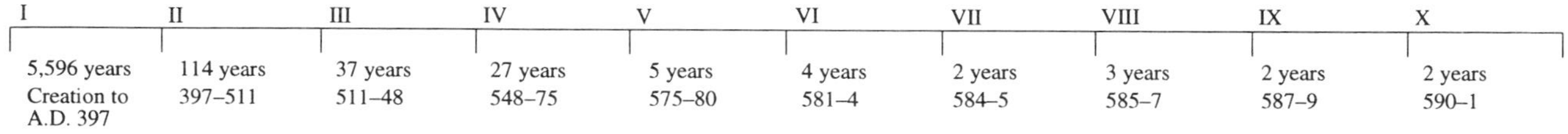

I	II	III	IV	V	VI	VII	VIII	IX	X
5,596 years Creation to A.D. 397	114 years 397–511	37 years 511–48	27 years 548–75	5 years 575–80	4 years 581–4	2 years 584–5	3 years 585–7	2 years 587–9	2 years 590–1

b. The coverage of each book

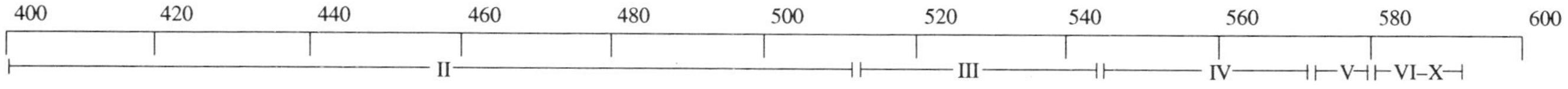

400   420   440   460   480   500   520   540   560   580   600

II ——————————————
III ——————
IV ————————————————————
V ⊢⊣ VI ⊢⊣ VII ⊢⊣ VIII ⊢⊣ IX ⊢—V—⊢—VI–X—⊣

Figure 2 *Francus* in Gregory of Tours' *Histories*

O = *Franci* as protagonists   ● = *Francus* in combinations such as *rex Francorum, regnum Francorum, mos Francorum*

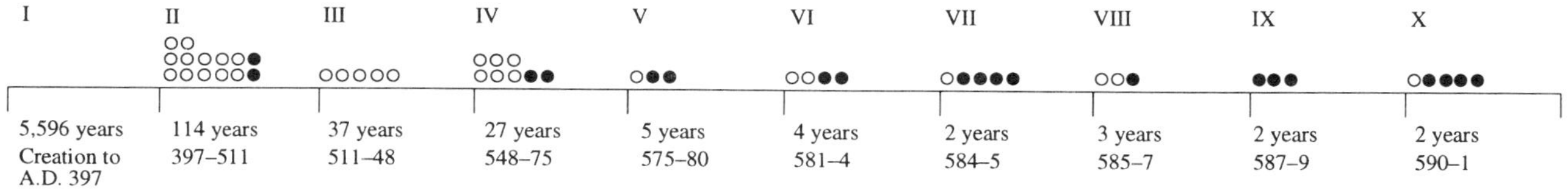

I	II	III	IV	V	VI	VII	VIII	IX	X
5,596 years Creation to A.D. 397	114 years 397–511	37 years 511–48	27 years 548–75	5 years 575–80	4 years 581–4	2 years 584–5	3 years 585–7	2 years 587–9	2 years 590–1

guistic origin of names, and all we can say about that is that Franks rarely seem to have taken Roman names, while Romans quite often took Germanic ones. Duke Gundulf, Gregory's mother's uncle, is the classic case, and Kurth has listed others.[13]

A number of perhaps fairly obvious conclusions can be drawn from figure 2. It can be seen that the Franks are referred to quite frequently in the course of the events of the fifth century, described in Book II: it is worth noting that quite a high proportion of these references come from written sources that Gregory used and quoted, such as the Roman historians Sulpicius Alexander and Renatus Profuturus Frigeridus, or the so-called *Annales Andecavenses* (the hypothetical source of the sketchy list of events cited in chapters 18 and 19 of Book II). And one can see that the references to individual Franks or to the activities of specified groups of Franks broadly diminish as time goes on. In Book VII, for instance, the only specific reference to individual Franks are to those many whom Audo and the prefect Mummolus unjustly taxed; in Book VIII, there is an interesting reference to 'all the citizens of Rouen and especially the Frankish leaders in that place' and a mention of the son of a noble Frank who was cured by Saint Martin; in Book X, only a reference to some Franks in Tournai.[14] Gregory himself is using the word less and less frequently the closer he gets to his own times, a trend which figure 2 actually disguises to some extent. The only two occurrences of *Franci* as protagonists from Book IX, for instance, are in the text of the Treaty of Andelot, which Gregory cites in full, while two of the occurences of the *Francorum* formula in Book X occur in the section in the last chapter which recapitulates the history of the bishops of Tours and refers to events very much earlier in the sixth century. A high proportion of the straight references to Franks indeed do not occur in Gregory's own words, but in those passages where he is using other, written, sources. What Gregory did not know, but which we may suspect, is that for Roman writers of the fourth or early fifth century 'Frank' was a convenient short-hand term for the various peoples living at the far north of the Rhine frontier, a term used by Romans but not necessarily by the 'Franks' themselves. There is actually no evidence to suggest that Bructeri, Chamavi, or Tubantes thought of themselves as 'Franks' in the Roman period; nor did they and the other 'Frankish' peoples invariably act as a political entity. The Franks were welded together as a people by Childeric and his

---

13 Gundulf appears in the *Histories* at VI 11, p. 281; see Kurth, '*Francia*,' 126.

14 '[Audo] cum Mummolo praefecto multos de Francis, qui tempore Childeberthi regis seniores ingenui fuerunt, publico tributo subegit': *Hist.*VII 15, p. 337; 'Magnus tunc omnes Rothomagensis cives et praesertim seniores loci illius Francos meror obsedit': *Hist.* VIII 31, p. 398; 'Franci cuiusdam et nobilissimi in gente sua viri filius mutus surdusque erat': *Hist.* VIII 16, p. 383; 'Inter Tornacensis quoque Francos non mediocris disceptatio est orta': *Hist.* X 27, p. 519.

son Clovis; their name and their sense of ethnic identity may, in part, have been imposed upon them by those Romans among whom they lived. This was not, of course, a process which Gregory himself understood, any more than twentieth-century historians have; and part of our problem may have been Gregory inevitably viewing the past, to some extent, from the perspective of the late sixth century.

Kurth's conclusion about the chronological development of the word *Francus*, not just in Gregory, but in all our Frankish sources, is that there were three main stages: the Frank as the barbarian in the fifth century; the Frank as the free citizen of Clovis' kingdom in northern Gaul, whatever his ethnic background; and, after the Frankish conquest of southern Gaul, the free inhabitant of the whole of Frankish Gaul. Kurth suggests that there are problems with understanding Gregory's own usage: in particular, that he seems to be using the word in more than one way. Sometimes, says Kurth, Gregory clearly included Gallo-Romans in the category. At *Hist.* III 27, for instance, Gregory tells us that the Franks were irritated because King Theudebert would not marry his Lombard fiancée: Kurth says that could not be just the Germanic Franks, but the entire free population, since politically there was no difference between the two. At *Hist.* IV 22, Chilperic seeks out the *Francos utiliores*, the more important Franks of the kingdom, in order to bribe them; again Kurth says that he would not have singled out Germanic Franks while ignoring all the influential Gallo-Romans. At *Hist.* VI 45, Chilperic calls together *melioribus Francis reliquisque fidelibus*, the more important Franks, and the rest of his faithful subjects, and Kurth argues that 'the rest' cannot be the Gallo-Romans, since it must include also the 'less important' Franks.[15] But such subtle arguments are making assumptions about the political realities of the sixth century: rejecting, for instance, the possibility that the political élite was precisely made up of Franks as opposed to Gallo-Romans. But this also begs the question of the definition of 'Frank' in the sixth century: we can no longer assume that 'Franks' were all of Germanic descent in the late sixth century, let alone that they all belonged to one biologically linked group of Germans. Close association with the king of the Franks may have meant that Romans would begin to identify themselves as Franks, and to be seen as Franks by others. *Franci* often seems to be used of those people who were politically active: certainly not all the free subjects in the kingdom, but those at the king's court or assembled in the army. There are, however, passages that do seem to support Kurth's argument rather more con-

15 '... coniuncti Franci contra eum valde scandalizabantur ...' *Hist.* III 27, p. 124; 'Chilpericus vero post patris funera thesaurus ... accepit et ad Francos utiliores petiit ipsusque muneribus mollitus sibi subdidit': *Hist.* IV 22, p. 154; '... convocatis melioribus Francis reliquisque fidelibus, nuptias celebravit filiae suae': *Hist* VI 45, p. 318.

vincingly. Commenting on Gregory's preface to Book V, Kurth points to Gregory's despair at the civil wars which have ravaged 'Francorum gentem et regnum,' and justly remarks that this must be a broad use of the term, to encompass all the subjects of the Frankish kings. In the text, after all, Gregory primarily bewails the fate of the indigenous, Gallo-Roman, population of central Gaul at the hands of the warring armies of the various Frankish kings; it is that portion of the *gens Francorum* which must have suffered most.

There are, however, also texts which seem to exhibit a much narrower and more conventionally ethnic use of the term. At *Hist.* IV 40, an embassy consisting of *Warmarium Francum et Firminum Arvernum*, Warmarius a Frank and Firminus an Arvernian, goes to Constantinople,[16] and at *Hist.* X 2, another embassy is made up of *Bodigyselus, filius Mummolini Sessionici, et Evantius, filius Dinami Arelatensi, et hic Gripo genere Francus*: Bodigyselus, son of Mummolinus of Soissons; Evantius, son of Dinamus of Arles; and Gripo, by birth a Frank.[17] Kurth argued that Warmarius, by his name, could be a Roman, but he was from northern Gaul, and hence was called a Frank. The second passage refers to a man from Soissons, in northern Gaul, who is not a Frank in Gregory's mind, and is the son of someone with an apparently Roman name: Mummolinus. In these passages he seems to be relating the origins of the people he mentions: for Romans it means mentioning the name of their *civitas*, which in most cases commemorates the name of the ethnic group, the Gallic tribe, that lived in that area before the Romans; for Franks the only identifer he knows is 'Frank.' Thus 'Frank' and 'Arvernian' (inhabitant of the Auvergne, Gregory's own *civitas*) are treated as if they were equivalent ethnic terms. But it is equally significant that, in the case of Bodigyselus and Evantius, he also identifies them by the name of their father, while he does not mention, or know, the name of Gripo's father. Perhaps this is not so much of an ethnic distinction as a class distinction: a difference between those who have parents of note and those who do not.

The other category of apparently ethnic-specific references contains our only two references to specifically Frankish customs: the carrying of consecrated rods by envoys, and the removal of tables after a meal.[18] Both these customs may well be Frankish customs which had, by Gregory's day, become generally accepted in Gaul: Gregory may therefore be identifying the *origins* of customs rather than ethnically identifying the actors. Certainly there is nothing

16 'Denique Sigyberthus rex legatus ad Iustinum imperatorem misit, pacem patens, id est War-
    marium Francum et Firminum Arvernum': *Hist.* IV 40, p. 172.

17 'Erat enim ibi tunc, ut diximus, legati Bodigysilus, filius Mummolini Sessionici, et Euantius,
    filius Dinami Arelatensis, et hic Gripo genere Francus ...': *Hist.* X 2, p. 482.

18 References in n. 11.

to suggest that those whom Gundovald sent out with consecrated rods were Germanic Franks: that custom was presumably associated with the Frankish kingship by the 580s. In the other case, however, the protagonists involved were described as *Tornacensis Francos*, 'Franks from Tournai,' which suggests an identifiable group of people within the general population of Tournai. The incident itself – involving drinking and multiple assassination by axes – certainly fits in well with traditional images of the barbarian Frank, but this is hardly conclusive.

If one looks at Gregory's use of *barbarus*, other patterns appear. In the *Histories*, the word *barbarus* appears in the singular only in one chapter: III 15. It is an exceptionally long anecdote in the context of Book III, which is mostly made up of relatively short passages, illustrating, above all, that Gregory did not know very much about the political history of Gaul between 511 and 544, under the sons of Clovis. The long anecdote is about Attalus, a nephew of Bishop Gregory of Langres, and thus a member, if a distant one, of Gregory's own family. Two of the sons of Clovis make an agreement, and hand over the sons of senators as hostages and as guarantees for this agreement. When the agreement collapsed, many of these hostages, including Attalus, were enslaved. Attalus' owner was a barbarian, living in the region of Trier. We may assume that he was a Frank, but Gregory never says so. In the whole passage in which the escape of Attalus is described, the word *Francus* is not used, but *barbarus* appears five times. The word *barbaries* also appears, in an aside in which Gregory explains that the barbarian for the Lord's day, *dies dominicus*, is *dies solis*, or Sunday.[19] Such is the exceptional nature of this passage in terms of its vocabulary that we may assume that Gregory is here drawing from a prior written account in the possession of his family. Again, these are not, in a sense, Gregory's own words, and this passage does not therefore necessarily reflect Gregory's own preferred vocabulary.

Gregory used *barbarus* only here in the *Histories*; *barbari*, in the plural, appears hardly more often in that text, at least in Gregory's own mouth. He writes of Eufrasius, hoping for the bishopric of Clermont, plying the barbarians with drink (IV 35), for instance.[20] And, famously, he writes of one of the leaders of the Frankish community in Reims – *seniores loci illius Francos* – who goes to Queen Fredegund to berate her for the murder of Bishop Praetextatus, and who is rash enough to accept a drink from her: he drank *absentium, cum vini et melle mictum, ut mos barbarorum habet*, 'wormwood (absinthe), mixed

19 'Et ille: "Ecce enim dies solis adest" – sic enim barbaries vocitare diem dominecum consueta est – "in hac die vicini atque parentes mei invitabuntur in domo mea ..."': *Hist.* III 15, p. 113.
20 'Erat quidem elegans in conversatione, sed non erat castus in opere, et plerum inebriebat barbaros, sed rare reficiebat egenos': *Hist.* IV 35, p. 167.

with wine and honey, as is the custom of barbarians.' He should have realized
that the bitter wormwood was a good disguise for the taste of poison.[21] Here
Gregory is saying that a Frank was following a barbarian habit, but he is not
necessarily equating 'Frank' with 'barbarian': he may, rather, be using 'barbarian' to mean, as we commonly do, 'uncivilized.' In other passages he puts the
word in the mouths of others: thus, King Gundobad of the Burgundians, in
speech with Aredius, talks of the impending arrival of the barbarians, that is,
the Franks,[22] while the monks of Latte warn off the troops who are about to
invade Saint Martin's property and address them as *o barbari*.[23] Most interestingly of all, the clearly Roman messenger of King Guntram, called Claudius, is
shown going to Tours and looking out for omens, 'ut consuetudo est barbarorum,' following the custom of barbarians.[24] In the latter case, the word barbarian is as likely to mean 'pagan' or 'unChristian' as 'uncivilized'; it can hardly
be a synonym for 'Frank.' But the two earlier cases are more difficult. Both
occurences of the word 'barbarian' are in reported speech. It is possible that
Kurth is right, and that 'barbarian' here means 'soldier,' with a particular pejorative tone. But it may be that this is the word Gregory found in his own source;
or that Gregory is using that word because he thinks that Gundobad or the
monks of Latte would have used that word. It is certainly no clear indication of
his own understanding of the term.

It is rather different in Gregory's other works, his hagiographical works,
where, as we have seen, the word 'Frank' is used very sparingly, and 'barbarian' appears much more clearly as a synonym for 'Frank.' There are only three
passages in which *Francus* appears. One refers to Quintianus of Rodez hoping
for the Frankish 'liberation' of his part of Gaul: here 'Frank' has to be used,
because the Goths are mentioned in the same paragraph, and the term *barbari*
would thus be confusing. The second, also in the *Life of the Fathers* (the most
'historical' of Gregory's hagiographical works), refers to a vision that Saint
Nicetius of Trier had about the Frankish kings: a vision that recalls nothing so
much as the vision revealed to Macbeth by the three witches. And the final reference is in the *Glory of the Confessors*, where a priest with the apparently

21 'Magnus tunc omnes Rothomagensis cives et praesertim seniores loci illius Francos meror
   obsedit': *Hist.* VIII 31, p. 398; 'Quo expectante, accepto poculo, bibit absentium cum vino et
   melle mixtum, ut mos barbarorum habet; sed hoc potum venenum inbutum erat': *Hist.* VIII 31,
   p. 399.
22 '"Vallant me undique angustiae, et quid faciam ignoro, quia venerunt hi barbari super nos, ut,
   nobis interemptis, regionam totam evertant"': *Hist.* II 32, p. 79.
23 'Clamaverunt monachi dicentes: "Nolite, o barbari, nolite huc transire; beati enim Martini
   istud est monasteriu"': *Hist.* IV 48, p. 185.
24 'Et cum iter ageret, ut consuetudo est barbarorum, auspicia intendere coepit ac dicere sibi esse
   contraria ...': *Hist.* VII 29, p. 347.

Frankish name of Arboast had a dispute, in the presence of King Theudebert, 'cum Franco quidam.'[25] The word *Francus* appears twice in this passage, once in the reported speech of the priest; and the same man is then referred to twice as a *barbarus*. The Frank was formerly sceptical, but the fate of the priest who perjured himself at Saint Maximin's tomb convinced him of the power of the saint. This is unlike any passage in the *Histories*, where we never see a man referred to as a Frank and a barbarian in the same passage, but it may be that the change of terminology is significant. When the man is involved in legal dealings, he is a *Francus*; when he is denying the power of the saint, he is a *barbarus*. Significantly also, perhaps, it does relate to the diocese of Trier, to which in several instances in Gregory's writings *barbari* specifically refers. It is in Trier that the young Saint Gallus, Gregory's uncle, sees a temple where barbarians used to make offerings and gorge themselves with meat and wine until they vomited; it is in the area of Trier that Attalus, also Gregory's relative, is kept as a slave by a *barbarus*.[26] Is it that Gregory knows these Franks in the Trier region to be pagans? In the *Miracles of St Julian*, where Gregory is referring to a church in the diocese of Tours in which perjurors are frequently uncovered, he mentions swearing by the 'barbarorum cruda rusticitas,' the crude rusticity of barbarians. Again 'barbarians' are associated with paganism, or at least an unacceptably low level of Christian practice, for that is what is implied by the word *rusticitas*.[27]

There are other, less highly charged, appearances of *barbari* in Gregory's hagiographical works. The Franks attacked the Auvergne in around 525, according to Ian Wood: an episode to which Gregory makes several references

---

25 'Non post multum vero tempus, orto inter cives et episcopum scandalo, Gothos, qui tunc in antedictam urbem morabantur, suspicio attigit, quod se villit episcopus Francorum ditionibus subdere ...': *Liber Vitae Patrum* IV 1, MGH SRM 1, 1st ed., 674; 'Sed nec hoc silere putavi, quod eidem de regibus Francorum a Domino sit ostensum': *Vitae Patrum* XVII 5, p. 732; 'Tempore enim Theodoberthi regis Arboastis quidam presbiter cum Franco quodam intendebat, rego praesente ... dixit: "Huius sancti virtute oppraemar, si aliquid falsi loquor de his quae prosecutio mea contra hunc Francum insistit." Fremente autem barbaro et quasi contra sanctum Dei furibundo, egressi sunt de basilica. ... Laudavitque deinceps barbarus virtutem sancti, cui prius detraxerat ...': *Liber in Gloria Confessorum*, 91, p. 806.

26 'Erat autem ibi fanum quoddam diversis ornamentis refertum in quo barbaries proxima libamina exhibens, usque ad vomitum cibo potuque replebatur': *Vitae Patrum* VI 2, p. 681; for Attalus, see above, n. 17.

27 'Non tamen causam remanere inultam, martyr prorsus indulget, sed nec inibi tam ausu temerario periurat barbarorum cruda rusticitas': *Liber de Virtutibus S. Iuliani* 40, p. 580. For a subtle discussion of Gregory's use of *rusticitas*, see P.R.L. Brown, *Relics and Social Status in the Age of Gregory of Tours*, Stenton Lecture 1976 (Reading, 1977), 8–10, reprt. in Peter Brown, *Society and the Holy in Late Antiquity* (London, 1982), 230–3.

in his works, and in the *Miracles of St Julian*, Gregory refers to it as an attack by *barbari*.[28] *Barbari* try to steal a cross from above an altar;[29] *barbari* attack the city of Nantes at the time of Clovis;[30] and *barbari* are twice referred to as the purchasers or owners of slaves.[31]

One might think of reasons why *barbarus* should appear in hagiographical texts in contexts where, in the *Histories*, the word *Francus* might be more obvious. On the whole, hagiographical texts wish to elide over specifically historical references, in order to emphasize the timeless significance of the saint. And specific identification – remarking that the *barbari* who attack Nantes may be Saxons, for instance – may cloud the issue: Gregory is, normally, portraying *barbari* as enemies of the saint, and hostile to the peace and stability of the church. *Francus* might actually have appeared to Gregory as a much more positive word, which would be seen by Gregory as inappropriate in the context of his hagiography: the king of the Franks was, after all, the protector of the church in Gaul, and the enemy of the heretics abroad. It is clear that Gregory despises *barbari*; it is not at all clear, *pace* Rouche, that he despises *Franci*.

Gregory does not, as historians have become accustomed to do in the historiography of the late Roman and early medieval period, use 'barbarian' as if it meant the opposite of 'Roman.' Indeed, Gregory's use of *Romanus* is just as interesting as his use of *Francus* or *barbarus*. Where Gregory uses the word *Romanus* in its various forms in the *Histories*, it refers almost exclusively to the city of Rome or to Roman authorities in Gaul in the fifth century: he calls Syagrius *rex Romanorum*, for instance, and refers to the mildness of the Burgundian laws, which did not oppress their Roman subjects.[32] But the word is not used after *Hist.* II 33: it is not, therefore, used in any sixth-century context. In Gregory's hagiographical works, the word either is put into other people's mouths, as *barbarus* was, or again has a very specific context. He has

---

28 'Et quia saepius commemoravi, quale excidium Arvernae regioni rex Theodoricus intulerit, cum neque maioribus neque minoribus natu aliquid de rebus propriis est relictum praeter terram vacuam, quam secum barbari ferre non poterant': *De Virtutibus S. Iuliani* 23, p. 574. For the date, see Edward James, *Gregory of Tours: Life of the Fathers*, 2d ed. (Liverpool, 1991), 23–4, and Ian Wood, *The Merovingian Kingdoms, 450–751* (London, 1994), 53.

29 'Advenientibus vero barbaris, a quodam esse aurea aestimata direpta est et sinu recondita': *De Virtutibus S. Iuliani* 44, p. 581.

30 'Igitur cum supra dicta civitas tempore Chlodovechi regis barbarica vallaretur obsidione ...': *Liber in Gloria Martyrum* 59, p. 529.

31 'Hic enim servus fertur fuisse ciuisdam barbari': *Vitae Patrum* V 1, p. 677; 'Simile est huic et illud, quod mulier post emeritam libertatem rursum a patroni filiis barbaris venundatur': *Libri de Virtutibus S. Martini* II 59, p. 629.

32 'Siacrius Romanorum rex, Egidi filius': *Hist.* II 27, p. 71; 'Burgundionibus leges mitiores instituit, ne Romanos obpraemerent': *Hist.* II 33, p. 81.

Theudegisel, the Visigothic king of Spain, talk about Romans, and explains that 'they [that is, Arian heretics] call men of our religion Romans';[33] he has the Visigothic count of Agde talk to his servants about 'these Romans,' again meaning Catholics;[34] he refers to a specific clause in *lex Romana*, the Roman law; and he explains that at the time of Martin, in the late fourth century, the senators of Clermont took pride in their Roman pedigree, 'Romanae nobilitatis.'[35] It is significant that when he refers to the pedigree of Gallic senators in sixth-century contexts, including his own pedigree, he does not use the word 'Roman'; he talks in terms of 'those of noble ancestry,' or similar phrases.

It is difficult to draw any conclusions about ethnicity in the sixth century from the study of one man's vocabulary. It would be tempting to suggest that the apparent fluidity of ethnic terms in this one author demonstrates that ethnicity was not actually as important as many historians have thought. This might, for instance, support those who now cast doubt on the idea that ethnicity was an essential element of the legal system in the sixth century, under the regime of the 'personality of the laws.'[36] But Gregory's writings, primarily and above all, exist to tell us what Gregory thought and what Gregory wanted us to know about the past. We might conclude that Gregory was confused, and that he does not always think hard about the words he uses, and one might compare this confusion with the haphazard way in which people in the United Kingdom, and those outside the United Kingdom, use the words 'British' and 'English.' But Gregory was not, on the whole, careless with words. One only has to look at the care with which he investigates the words used by his sources Sulpicius Alexander and Renatus Profuturus Frigeridus for the Frankish leaders of the late fourth and early fifth centuries (*History*, II 9). It is more plausible to suggest that Gregory was using ethnic words according to context – again, as we use them. If he was referring to origins and birth, he might use one word; if referring to political allegiance, he might use another. But it is worthwhile here to recall figure 2. It is clearly significant that Gregory's use of *Francus* diminished considerably the closer he got to his own time, and that, as we have seen,

33 'Theodigiselus huius rex regionis ... cogitavit intra se, dicens, quia: "Ingenium est Romanorum" – Romanos enim vocitant nostrae homines relegionis – "ut ita accedat, et non est Dei virtus"': *Gloria Martyrum* 24, p. 502.

34 '... ait suis: "Quid putatis, quid isti nunc Romani dicant?"' *Gloria Martyrum* 78, p. 541.

35 'Audientes autem senatores urbis, qui tunc in loco illo nobilitatis Romanae stimmati refulgebant ...': *Gloria Confessorum* 5, p. 751.

36 Amory argues that, since the personality of the law is attested only from Carolingian times, we can by no means assume that it goes back as far as the sixth century: against, e.g., S.L. Guterman, *From Personal to Territorial Law* (Metuchan, N. J., 1972), and E. James, *The Origins of France: From Clovis to the Capetians, A.D. 500–1000* (London, 1982), 39–41.

many of the occasions on which he uses *Francus* are where he is quoting from a written source. I think that we are forced to conclude that recent commentators on Gregory's usage have not really got it right. Gregory was not a Roman looking down his nose at the Franks, as Rouche said; to begin with, his use of *Romanus* demonstrates that he did not think of himself as a Roman at all. Figure 2 might be seen to support Goffart's view, that Gregory thought of himself as neither Frank nor Roman, and wanted to stress more than anything that he was Christian. But it is not that Gregory is reluctant to use the word 'Frank' of himself – he never identifies himself as anything, except, indirectly, as 'Arvernian' – it is that he rarely uses the word at all, except in those standard formulae such as *rex Francorum*. As we have seen, there are very few occasions on which he identifies an individual as a Frank; but this is because he is not at all concerned, as so many modern historians have been, to distinguish Gallo-Romans from the Germanic Franks. When he does identify people ethnically they are foreigners: Goths, Lombards, Saxons, Taifals. It is not that he wishes to eradicate ethnic difference in favour of a religious characterization: it is ethnic difference *within the Frankish kingdom* that Gregory is eradicating. Gregory, writing within the *regnum Francorum*, sees its inhabitants, including himself, as fellow-subjects of the 'kings of the Franks.' He does not distinguish them, as modern historians have tried to do, on racial or ethnic lines; he was writing from inside, needing only to distinguish those who were outsiders. Historians of England, after all, do not constantly refer to the individuals who people their pages as 'English' (although they may note the appearance of someone from Scotland or Wales). The evidence suggests to me that we should to go back to Kurth's position: that by Gregory's day most Gauls who were subjects of the Frankish kings thought of themselves as Franks, if they were thinking in political terms. Gregory may have been an Arvernian by birth, but, as a bishop, a politician, and a writer, he was a Frank.

4

Heresy in Books I and II of Gregory of Tours' *Historiae*

MARTIN HEINZELMANN

Gregory was no more superstitious
than Augustine had been.

Walter Goffart, *The Narrators of Barbarian History*, 142

It is quite astonishing to see how, at the end of the twentieth century, the
'national celebrations' of Clovis' baptism can still arouse media excitement.[1]
As far as the scholarship of the subject is concerned, it is equally astonishing to
see arising once again in this context the old problems bearing on the events of
481–511 – problems once fully considered by Bruno Krusch, Ferdinand Lot,
André van de Vyver, and Wolfram von den Steinen, among others.[2] Our aston-
ishment has, finally, a third aspect: despite some effort to expand the subject,
most often there is recourse to the portrait that Gregory of Tours has left us of
the king; the procedure here is quite simple and consists of extracting from the
Histories the material on Clovis chapter by chapter and subjecting it to classic,

A warm thanks to Sandy Murray for his translation. Naturally the responsibility for the final text
remains my own.

1 For a glimpse of the year's 'festivités': *Célébrations nationales 1996*, published by the French
   Ministry of Culture (Direction des archives de France, 1996): 10–13, with a presentation,
   'Baptême de Clovis 496,' by Karl Ferdinand Werner, 7 f. Among numerous articles in the
   media, I will mention only 'A propos de Clovis' by Suzanne Citron (*Le Monde*, 28 Feb.,
   1996): she deplores, not without reason, the resurgence of the school catechism – 'd'origine à
   la fois royaliste et républicaine' – of an eternal France already present in the history of Clovis
   and rarely misses a chance to demystify national myths.
2 For a good treatment of the question and bibliography: Mark Spencer, 'Dating the Baptism of
   Clovis, 1886–1993,' *Early Medieval Europe* 3/2 (1994): 97–116. See also the wise restriction
   to contemporary sources by William W. Daly, 'Clovis: How Barbaric, How Pagan,' *Speculum*
   69 (1994): 619–64.

critical analysis.[3] In other words, by following chapters 27 to 43 of Gregory's work, an attempt is made to create the illusion of a portrait of Clovis, based apparently on the set chronological order of historical facts.[4] This approach persists despite the fact that, in the latest work on Gregory, real doubt has been cast upon the innocence usually detected in his *Histories* – a re-evaluation that Walter Goffart has had a hand in;[5] and still another year of 'célébration nationale' – this time in 1994, commemorating the fourteenth centenary of the death of the bishop of Tours – has provided further impetus for correcting the traditional image of the historian.[6]

In this re-evaluation, little remains of the old view of Gregory as the historian of Frankish national history, faithfully rendering his historical environment just as it was. On the contrary, Gregory's work has proven to be characterized to a considerable degree by principles of deliberate selection and purposeful composition.[7] In this context, Book II certainly deserves a more thorough analysis in view of its importance for the beginnings of Frankish history and, even more, for contemporary history: in one of his programmatic prologues, the bishop of Tours could actually propose the reign of Clovis as a reference point with respect to the kings of his own day.[8]

3 See e.g. Claude Carozzi, 'Le Clovis de Grégoire de Tours,' *Le Moyen Âge* 98 (1992): 169–85. This piece nevertheless has the considerable merit of trying to understand the structure of Gregory's narrative, even if it starts from three interpolations added to the Gregorian corpus by two editors of the seventh and eighth centuries; cf. M. Heinzelmann, 'Clovis dans le discours hagiographique du VIe au IXe siècle,' *Bibliothèque de l'Ecole des chartes* 154 (1996): 87–112, at 89, n. 11.

4 Hereinafter I refer to the standard edition of Bruno Krusch (assisted by W. Levison and W. Holtzmann), MGH SRM 1/1, 2d. ed. (1937–51). For the 'hagiographical' portrait of Clovis according to Gregory and his successors, see my article cited in n. 3, 'Clovis dans le discours hagiographique.'

5 Walter Goffart, *The Narrators of Barbarian History (A.D. 550–800): Jordanes, Gregory of Tours, Bede, and Paul the Deacon* (Princeton, 1988). In my *Gregor von Tours (538–594): 'Zehn Bücher Geschichte': Historiographie und Gesellschaftskonzept im 6. Jahrhundert* (Darmstadt, 1994), I had the opportunity to stress the value of Walter Goffart's work for my own research.

6 See Pascale Bourgain, 'Grégoire de Tours en 1994,' *Revue Mabillon*, n.s. 6 [= 67] (1995): 295–8, dealing with the two monographs mentioned in n. 5; *Grégoire de Tours et l'espace gaulois*, Actes du congrès international, Tours, 3–5 November 1994, ed. Nancy Gauthier and Henri Galinié, 13e Supplément à la Revue Archéologique du Centre de la France (Tours, 1997); and Adriaan H.B. Breukelaar, *Historiography and Episcopal Authority in Sixth-Century Gaul: The Histories of Gregory of Tours Interpreted in Their Historical Context* (Göttingen, 1994), for which see my revue in *Jahrbuch für Antike und Christentum* 38 (1995): 201–5.

7 'The high level of selectivity' of Gregory is well documented in Goffart, *Narrators*, 164 and passim; for its composition, see Heinzelmann, *Gregor*, passim.

8 *Hist.* V prol., pp. 193 f.: 'Remember [*scil.* kings contemporary with Gregory] what Clovis, the author of your victories, did, Clovis who killed the kings that opposed him, who crushed the

Such a reference could in fact be understood if Clovis were being presented as the model of a Christian prince, basing his rule on the principles of justice and prosperity for all. But this is clearly not the case. The hagiographical Life composed by Gregory looks very different. First, the bishop announces the birth of Clovis with the same words the evangelist Luke had used for that of the Saviour in order next to allude to the good inclinations of the still-pagan king and to his later baptism.[9] Cleansed of his previous sins at the time of baptism and becoming in that way part of the church of Christ,[10] Clovis is finally ready for what appears to be his true historic calling: with the assistance of several prestigious saints, principally Saint Martin and Saint Hilary, he strikes the heretic kings, Gundobad and, especially, Alaric the Visigoth. Having fulfilled his messianic role, he is fully rewarded by God, who gives him victory over all his enemies.[11]

While it is true that at a later stage, from the Carolingian period onwards, the baptism of Clovis indisputably became the chief element in the portrait of the

nations causing harm and conquered their homelands, thus leaving you his kingdom whole and intact'; cf. Goffart, *Narrators*, 171, 205, 219, and Heinzelmann, *Gregor*, 42, 125, and passim.

9 *Hist.* II 12, p. 119: 'Quae concipiens [*scil.* the mother of Clovis] peperit filium vocavitque nomen eius Chlodovechum. Hic fuit magnus et pugnator egregius.' The resemblance with Luke 1: 31 was noted by Franz Brunhölzl. The sanctity of Clovis is not, however, an invention of Gregory, who found it already in the letter of Avitus of Vienne to Clovis: 'et quicquid felicitas usque hic praestiterat, addet hic sanctitas'; see Jean-Pierre Brunterc'h, *Le Moyen Âge* (*V^e–XIe siècle*) (Paris, 1994), 112, 114. The identification with Christ, who is the typos of all the saints, is equally suggested by the epithet *pugnator*, applied regularly to God in the Scriptures (see Heinzelmann, 'Discours hagiographique,' n. 16); by the typological association of Clovis with David, who is himself a figure of Christ (cf. Isidore of Seville, *Allegoriae quaedam sacrae Scripturae* 89, *PL* 83: 112: 'David filii Dei et Salvatoris nostri expressit imaginem, sive quod insectatione Judaeorum injustam persecutionem sustinuit [theme of persecution – *heresis*!], sive quia Christus ex eius stirpe carnem assumpsit') in the prologues to *Hist.* II and III; and finally by anointing at the time of baptism (cf. *Sancti Eucherii Lugdunensis instructionum libri duo* I, ed. C. Wotke, CSEL 2/1, 140: 'Messias unctus, id est Christus').

10 For the baptism, stress has been laid particularly on the model of the *Actus s. Silvestri* on the basis of the formula 'procedit novus Constantinus ad lavacrum, deleturus leprae veteris morbum sordentesque maculas gestas antiquitus recenti latice deleturus' (*Hist.* II 31, p. 77), but in the end all that remains is the pair Constantine/Silvester, and perhaps leprosy (*lepra elephantiae* in the *Actus*), which, however, has more general significance; see Eucherius, *Formulae spiritalis intelligentiae* VIII, CSEL as in n. 9, 49 (s.v. *mundare*) and 51: 'Lepra [est] peccatorum contaminatio'; and now, Pascale Bourgain and Martin Heinzelmann, '"Courbe-toi, fier Sicambre, adore ce que tu as brûlé": À propos de Grégoire de Tours, *Hist.* II 31,' *Bibliothèque de l'École des chartes* 154 (1996): 591–606, 593, n. 8. The typology of the *novus Constantinus* is restricted to this chapter alone, 'Clovis the first king baptised.' Taking into account the critical picture of Constantine in *Hist.* I 36, Goffart, *Narrators*, 219, even considers it an expression of Gregory's irony.

11 *Hist.* II 40–2; for the biblical model, see Heinzelmann, 'Discours hagiographique,' n. 22.

king,[12] for Gregory, on the contrary, the most important feature was the action of the baptized king against the heretics. The stress upon the military side of the event is found also, as we have seen, in Gregory's exhortation to the kings of his own day, recalling the times of Clovis,[13] and it is strongly expressed as well in the programmatic prologues to Books II and III: just as David – *quem Fortem manu dicunt* – had crushed the heretic (*alophilus*) Goliath, and just as the sacrilegious priest Phineas had perished under the prophet Samuel the Just, in modern times (*nostra tempora*) Clovis, as an image of the first model king of the Israelites, crushed the heretic Alaric, and Saint Hilary (of Poitiers) recovered his see, while Arius had to perish miserably.[14]

It is natural to conclude just from the approach favoured by the two prologues that the predominant issue in the eyes of the bishop of Tours was the commitment to oppose heresy. This finding is all the more significant as there were no longer real political powers supporting Arianism in Gaul at the time of the composition of the *Histories*.[15] As, moreover, no real danger of a revival of 'the iniquitous sect' was in sight, we are compelled to look for other meanings for the major theme of heresy in the *Histories,* unless we suppose that the work was already lacking reality at the moment of its composition.[16]

To get the real measure of the impact of heresy, it is necessary as a first step to return to Book II as a whole, although the career of Clovis, the victor over heresy in a context of heretical barbarian kings, is the subject of only several chapters of the second part.[17] The prologue's typological figures, which have already been touched upon, put us on the track of Gregory's intentions: even before the antithetical pairing of the *kings*, the historian-exegete had established a contrasting pair, the *priest* Samuel 'the Just' and the sacrilegious *priest*.[18]

12 Heinzelmann, 'Discours hagiographique,' passim. What for Gregory was just a sign of Clovis' new Christian identity becomes a ritual royal anointing.
13 Cf. above, n. 8.
14 Heinzelmann, *Gregor*, 110.
15 Goffart, *Narrators*, 213 f.; see *Hist.* IX 20, with Gregory's own words in 588 to his king, Guntramn: 'Aeclesiae fides periculo ullo non quatitur; heresis nova non surgit.'
16 In an interesting and stimulating fashion, Kathleen Mitchell, 'History and Christian Society in Sixth-Century Gaul: An Historiographical Analysis of Gregory of Tours' Decem libri Historiarum' (Phil. diss., Michigan State University, East Lansing, 1983), 78–90, 114 f., explains the hostility of Gregory towards Arianism by identifying the heresy with a materialist viewpoint. It is true that the Arian point of view considerably narrows the perspectives offered by a christological definition of society in the manner of Augustine and Gregory of Tours (see below).
17 *Hist.* II 27–43.
18 The choice of Samuel as a typological figure is far from innocent. As the last judge of Israel, it was the servant of God Samuel who had invested the first two kings of Israel, Saul, not approved by God, and David; in the programme of Gregory, Samuel represents a figure of the bishop and of the saint of Christ through the epithet 'just' (*Liber in gloria martyrum* 3, Christ

Book II of the *Histories* in fact treats bishops as being just as responsible for Christian society as kings. The role of bishops, represented in all parts of Book II, and even extensively beyond it, proves itself, moreover, to be even more central to our author's preoccupations than the part attributed to kings. This episcopal role is revealed in three areas, the first of which is the representation of the universal church and its continuity. Thus, in the sequence of chapters, our author regularly introduces a chapter called 'De episcopatu N.' or even 'De N. episcopo,' concerning, in particular, the sequence of bishops of Tours and of the Auvergne in the fifth century.[19] These choice morsels in Book II are presented as veritable manifestations of the church of Christ, signifying its continuity in the face of persecutions by barbarian kings. Other historians preceded Gregory on this path. In his *Ecclesiastical History*, Eusebius had already conveyed the universality of the church by means of episcopal lists of Jerusalem, Antioch, Alexandria, and Rome,[20] and, in *The City of God*, Saint Augustine referred to the example of the seven churches signifying the *plenitudo* of the church of Christ;[21] this last instance clearly recalls the 'seven' sent to Gaul according to the *Histories*, among which *septem viri missi* were the first bishops of Tours and the Auvergne – the seven messengers being figures of the apostles or the founders of the church.[22]

The second area of episcopal participation in the plan of Book II concerns the role of bishops with respect to kings. The *sacerdotes Domini* take part in royal government – namely, by opposing heretic kings and guiding the (only) faithful king on the right road. Thus the Vandal Huniric had his challenger in Eugenius of Carthage, *virum enarrabili sanctitate* (c. 3); the Burgundian Gundobad had at hand 'his' sainted bishop in the person of Avitus of Vienne (c. 34);

---

himself designated as *Iustus*). In choosing next the *alophilus* Goliath – and not Saul – as antitype to David, Gregory emphasized once again the importance of the theme of heresy! In *Hist.* I 12, Gregory notes that the Israelites had entreated God through Samuel as intermediary to give them kings, 'sicut reliquae gentes habent,' and they received Saul, then David.

19 See the chapter titles of *Hist.* II: 1, 5, 13, 14, 16, 21, 22, 23, 26, 36, 39 (pp. 34–6); these chapters were, moreover, regularly removed from *Histories* by the editor of the B-manuscripts at the time of the seventh-century edition. See M. Heinzelmann, 'Grégoire de Tours "père de l'histoire de France"?,' in *Histoires de France, historiens de la France: Actes du colloque international*, Reims, 14–15 May 1993, ed. Y.-M. Bercé and Ph. Contamine (Paris, 1994), 19–45, esp. 24–6.

20 Cf. Harald Zimmermann, *Ecclesia als Objekt der Historiographie*, Österreich. Akad. der Wiss. Phil.-hist. Kl., Sitzungsberichte 235/4 (Vienna, 1960), 19 f.

21 *De civitate Dei* XVII 4, ed. B. Dombart and A. Kalb, *Sancti Aurelii Augustini episcopi De civitate Dei libri XXII*, 2 vols., 5th ed., CSEL (Stuttgart, 1981), 2: 206: 'Propter quod et Iohannes apostolus ad septem scribit ecclesias, eo modo se ostendens ad unius plenitudinem scribere.'

22 *Hist.* I 30, title: 'De septem viris in Galleis ad praedicandum missis.' Cf. Heinzelmann, *Gregor*, 143.

and Clovis was assisted by 'his' Saint Remigius (chap. 31) – Constantine and Saint Silvester prefiguring the couple. Clovis was a king with whom bishop saints, such as Martin of Tours and Hilary of Poitiers, associated themselves after his entrance into the church through baptism. No doubt royal government was highly dependent on episcopal participation.

The third aspect of the role of bishops in Book II appears to be even more important and brings us nearer the subject of heresy. It concerns the role of prelates in their city, that is, to put it simply, the governance of Christian society.[23] The theme, which is at the centre of Gregory's interests, is developed significantly in the first chapter and in another in the middle of the book; a similar structure is found, moreover, in other books of the *Histories*.[24] The first chapter deals with Saint Brice, the bishop designated by Saint Martin to be his successor. Falsely accused by the people of Tours, Saint Brice vividly demonstrates his sanctity by performing a miracle, but the people of Tours, *in sua malitia perdurantes*, still replace him, saying, 'You shall no longer rule ['dominaberis'] us under the false name of pastor'; the two bishops elected in his place die, each one *iudicio Dei percussus*, and Brice eventually recovers his former position, which he holds happily for seven years, until his death.[25]

The thematic significance of this introductory episode[26] is evident only if we consider an incident with the same structure in a chapter featuring Sidonius Apollinaris, bishop of Clermont and eminent saint, according to Gregory.[27] Two priests of Clermont had succeeded in taking away the bishop's discretionary power over church property, but soon after the coup one of them died in the privy. Gregory's comment on this follows in a fashion as explicit as it is unrelenting: 'There is also no question but that this man was guilty of a crime no less than that of Arius, who likewise emptied his entrails into a latrine

---

23 The city as a symbol of Christian society already comes from the title of Augustine's monumental work *De civitate Dei*; in 'Die Franken und die fränkische Geschichte in der Perspektive der Historiographie Gregors von Tours,' in *Historiographie im frühen Mittelalter*, ed. A. Scharer and G. Scheibelreiter (Vienna and Munich, 1994), 326–44, I have shown that the relation of the people (*populus*) of a city to its bishop is exactly on the same level as that of a *gens* to its king. See also Cass. *Var.* 9.2, ed. Th. Mommsen, MGH AA 12, 269: 'Unicuique civi urbs sua res publica est.'

24 Heinzelmann, *Gregor*, 113 f. and 131 f. and passim.

25 *Hist.* II 1. In the full list of the bishops of Tours in *Hist.* X 31, Gregory does not attribute official positions to Brice's two replacements, Iustinianus and Armentius, who are mentioned only in the notice on Brice.

26 See also cc. 5 and 6: divine punishment of the people of Tongres and Metz 'pro dilictis populi,' despite intervention by the bishop or local saint; in c. 7, the *populus* of Orléans is obedient to its bishop, Saint Aignan, and is saved; see Heinzelmann, 'Franken,' 239 ff.

27 In *Hist.* II, Sidonius occupies the entire middle part of the book (cc. 21–5); cf. especially c. 23 'De sanctitate Sidonii episcopi, et de iniuriis eius ultione divina moderatis' (p. 35).

through his hind quarters, because it cannot be accepted without heresy that in the church one may disobey God's bishop, who has been entrusted with the task of pasturing the sheep, and that power may be usurped there by a man who has been entrusted with nothing by either God or man.'[28] Now, without it being necessary to comment on it at greater length, this phrase contains the whole essence of the book. Its importance is stressed again by the reference to Arius, the undisputed prince of heretics; in the programmatic prologue to Book III, it will be Arius who stands for the archetype of modern heresies.[29]

The phenomenon of *heresis* is therefore neither a political argument for distancing himself from the neighbouring Visigoths,[30] nor chiefly a question of dogma reserved only to ecclesiastics: it concerns the structures of society as a whole, from the people to the king, through the members of the clergy. In a Christian society the bishop is the supreme spiritual guide, chosen by God himself, and all disobedience and, even more, all persecution with respect to him are crimes against God.[31] The breach in this principle of divine order is what Gregory calls *heresis*. To flesh out this subject of the primordial role of the bishop as leader of Christian society, it is enough to have a close look at the *Regula pastoralis* of Gregory the Great[32] and once again at the twenty-two

28 *Hist.* II 23, p. 68: 'Unde indubitatum est, non minoris criminis hunc reum esse quam Arrium illum ... quia nec istud sine heresi potest accipi, ut in ecclesiam non obaudiatur sacerdos Dei.' Translations such as 'dans une église' (Robert Latouche) or 'in his own church' (Lewis Thorpe) for *in ecclesiam* reveal misunderstanding about the intentions of Gregory; but cf. O.M. Dalton, 'in the Church.'

29 In the antithetical configuration with Saint Hilary of Poitiers, Arius represents heresy of the modern period, the pair prefigured by Samuel/Phineas in the prologue to Book II. The first mention of heresy (*Hist.* I 28) concerns Marcion (second century), with important consequences for christology.

30 For the openly hostile attitude of Gregory to the Visigoths of his time, see Hans Messmer, *Hispania-Idee und Gotenmythos*, Geist und Werk der Zeiten 5 (Zürich, 1960), 64 f. and 73 f.; in his view Gregory would have been party to a quasi-official polemic against the neighbours of the Frankish kingdom. But since, as concerns the *Histories,* this propaganda purpose can be excluded, we must take into account that old prejudices, in part of a religious nature, preserved their hold on the bishop of Tours. See also n. 77, below.

31 See e.g. *Hist.* II 4, p. 45: 'Multae enim heresis eo tempore Dei ecclesias inpugnabant, de quibus plerumque ultio divina data est. Nam et Athanaricus Gothorum rex magnam excitavit persecutionem'; here persecution is clearly counted as a 'heresy': see also Isidore, above, n. 9.

32 The manual of Gregory I does not otherwise foresee a real opposition to the *rectores* of the church, that is, Christian society: the term *haeresis* does not appear there (*hereticus,* once, in III 24, in the sense of those who 'sacrae legis uerba non recte intellegunt'). See, on the other hand, the description of the social situation (I 1) around the same time as the bishop of Tours' *Histories* were composed: 'Now that all the grandeur of the present age, God willing, bows with respect before religion, within the holy church are people who under the guise of governing aspire to the splendour of office': *Règle pastorale*, ed. F. Rommel, trans. C. Morel, vol. 1, Sources chrétiennes 381 (Paris, 1992), 131.

books of Augustine's *De civitate Dei*, a work sharing with Gregory of Tours' *Histories* an equal interest in dealing with history and with the structure and foundations of Christian society. Indeed, in developing his point of view on the governing of society, Augustine cites only the single example of episcopal action, the major purpose of which is 'eam salutem subditorum, quae secundum Deum est'; recommending complete distrust with regard to the *honor* and *potentia* accompanying the office, he nevertheless judges them acceptable when they serve a just and beneficial governance.[33]

II

With this meaning of *heresis* relating to the hierarchy of society, we are still far from having exhausted the subject – all the more because in this period the social is intimately tied to a theological conception. In fact, scrutinizing the structures of Book I of the *Histories* reveals this conception fully, and one very quickly realizes its impact on the philosophy and historiography of our author.

This first book, which neither Fredegar nor others using the *Histories* knew how to incorporate into their own presentations of history, proves to be the indispensable key to comprehending Gregorian intentions.[34] Let us summarize briefly the main points of this part of the work, beginning with the prologue containing a *definition* of the faith of the bishop – and not simply a 'confession of faith,' a creed. The chief feature of the definition is without doubt the key portion dedicated to Christ, who appears as such a fundamental element of the creation, and thus of history, from its beginning. With the phrase, 'I renounce those and declare them excluded from the church who say "there was a time when he did not yet exist," '[35] Gregory joins the grand theology of the fifth century and takes as his own the definition of heresy used, among other places, in the chronicle of Sulpicius Severus.[36]

33 *De civitate Dei* XIX 19, 2: 388: 'In actione vero non amandus est honor in hac vita sive potentia ... sed opus ipsum, quod per eundem honorem vel potentiam fit, si recte atque utiliter fit, id est, ut valeat ad eam salutem subditorum, quae secundum Deum est.' See also ibid.: 'locus vero superior, sine quo regi populus non potest, etsi ita teneatur atque administretur ut decet, tamen indecenter appetitur.' The actual application of this thinking can be seen for example in a letter to a high functionary, the *spectabilis* Marcellinus, *PL* 133: 509–10: 'quoniam christiano loquor [i.c., Bishop Augustine to Marcellinus] ... non arroganter dixerim, audire te episcopum convenit jubentem.'
34 Heinzelmann, *Gregor*, 114–18, 131 f., 179 f.
35 *Hist.* I prol., p. 4 l : 'Illos vero, qui dicunt: "Erat quando non erat," execrabiliter rennuo et ab ecclesia segregare contestor.' See also ibid., n. 3, for the formula in Cassiodorus (*Hist. Tripart.* 2.9) and in the Nicene Creed.
36 *Sulpicii Severi chronicorum libri duo* II 35, *PL* 20: 148, '[Arians maintaining] fuisse autem tempus quo filius non fuisset.'

In a book clearly structured in two principal parts, the middle is concerned with a series of chapters dealing with the deeds of Christ on earth, exemplary deeds, even in their detail, for all the saints who are his imitators. As for the Creation, with which the book quite logically opens, Gregory already attributes it to Christ, for he is 'the beginning and the principle (*principium*) of all things' by which everything is made.[37] At the very moment of the creation of the first man Adam – who represents the 'type' of Christ (*tipum Redemptoris domini*) – and his wife, Eve, the church appears immaculate, which is none other than the relation established by Christ between himself and mankind.[38]

At the end of Book I (c. 47), a paradigmatic chapter corroborates the theme of the 'immaculate church' as far as the whole book is concerned. At first sight, the content of the chapter looks extremely banal and would be extremely difficult for us to decipher if the same episode were not related differently in the hagiographical work on confessors.[39] Now, it is by his own references to the briefer hagiographic text, telling the story of the two young lovers living chastely to the end of their lives (on the model of the couple Adam and Eve, before the Fall), that Gregory the exegete was able to express himself:[40] while in the hagiographic tale (*Glory of the Confessors*, 31) the name of the Saviour is not mentioned once, it is introduced nine times in the long commentaries put in the mouth of the young woman in the *Histories* (I 47); in addition, the virgin, a figure of the immaculate church, speaks at length of her *sponsus Iesus Christus*, employing the kind of vocabulary proper to ecclesiology[41] and, above all, she

---

37 *Hist.* I 1, p. 5: '*Principio* Dominus caelum terramque in christo suo, qui est omnium *principium*, id est in Filio suo, furmavit.' Cf. Eucherius, *Instructionum libri duo* I (as at n. 9), 66–7: 'In principio, hoc est, in filio, quia per filium fecit deus pater caelum et terram ... Omnia enim per filium operatus est, quia omnia per ipsum facta sunt ...; and Quodvultdeus, *Sermo* 5.7 (CPL 405), PL 40, 684: 'fuit aliquod tempus quando Pater fuit sine Verbo, aut fuit aliquod principium ante ipsum principium, quoniam ipse Filius dixit se esse principium?' (commenting on John 1: 1–3).

38 *Hist.* I 1, pp. 5 f.: 'quod hic primus homo Adam, antequam peccaret, tipum Redemptoris domini praetulisset. Ipse enim in passionis sopore obdormiens, de latere suo dum aquam cruoremque producit, virginem inmaculatamque eclesiam sibi exhibuit, redemptam sanguine, latice emundatam, non habentem maculam aut rugam'; for the meaning of *exhibuit*, and for the beginning of the church at the Creation, see Heinzelmann, 'Grégoire,' 31 and n. 42 f.

39 *Hist.* I 47, and *Liber in gloria confessorum* 31, ed. B. Krusch, MGH SRM 1/2, 317.

40 For Gregory's commentary in the form of speeches that he attributes to his characters, see F. Thürlemann, *Der historische Diskurs bei Gregor von Tours: Topoi und Wirklichkeit*, Geist und Werk der Zeiten 39 (Bern and Frankfurt, 1974).

41 Cf. Eucherius, *Formulae* V, p. 31: 'Sponsus Christus ideo quod a patre ab initio sit promissus ... Sponsa ecclesia, quae utique diuinis sponsionibus sit promissa.' See also Isidore, *Allegoriae* 233, p. 127: 'Sponsus Christus est, cuius nuptiae cum Ecclesia celebrantur.'

three times returns to the key-word *immaculatus* of the first chapter (on the Creation and the beginnings of the church), a word not found in any other book of the *Histories*.[42]

It is easy to see that Gregory requires a certain knowledge of patristic theology on the part of his audience. This is likewise the case when he wants to explain the content and essence of this 'church' in the series of chapters chosen for their paradigmatic value. Our author presents two types of humans, best characterized with the words of Augustine, 'duo genera sunt [generis humani] ... unum eorum qui secundum hominem, alterum eorum, qui secundum Deum vivunt';[43] Gregory develops in two of his prologues an analogous contrast between the saints and *miseri* as the material of his historiography and its point of departure.[44]

The *miseri* are Cain and his ilk, the church's aggressors and persecutors, with a place of honour for Herod and the dismal series of Roman emperors.[45] But the real subjects of the book are the others, those who represent the church, the patriarchs, prophets, bishops, and other *sancti* and *iusti*.[46] They all have one thing in common: they represent in their fashion Christ, who is the beginning

42 *Hist.* I 47, p. 30, line 18: 'ut corpusculum meum inmaculatum Christo a virili tactu servarem'; p. 31, lines 15, 23; apart from c. 1, *inmaculatus* appears again only one other time: *Hist.* I 10, p. 12, on baptism, 'renati per baptismum, inmaculati ab omni inquinamentum carnis.' Neither *sponsus* nor *inmaculatus* is found in the hagiographical version, which totally lacks the ecclesiological signification of the historiographic chapter.

43 *De civitate Dei* XV 1, p. 58: 'quas etiam mystice appellamus civitates duas, hoc est duas societates hominum.'

44 *Hist.* II prol., p. 36: 'Non enim inrationabiliter accipi puto, se filicem beatorum vitam inter miserorum memoremus excidia'; and ibid.: 'mixte confusaeque tam virtutes sanctorum quam strages gentium memoramus.' *Hist.* I prol., opening with 'Scripturus bella regum cum gentibus adversis, martyrum cum paganis, eclesiarum cum hereticis.'

45 *Hist.* I 2, without citing the names of the children of the original couple, the names being cited in the chapter title; and cf. c. 3: 'Exhinc cunctum genus in facinus exsecrabile ruit praeter Enoch iustum, qui ambalans in viis Dei.' For the negative image of the emperors, with the exception of Theodosius, see Goffart, *Narrators*, 165, 208, and passim; also Heinzelmann, 'Die Franken,' 335. One can add to this profile Gregory's clever handling of chronology: he has Maximinus (portrayed very negatively, contrary to Orosius who nevertheless furnished the model) close the list in an appropriate fashion, and not, as required by chronology, Theodosius, the sole positive note in the series.

46 See the definition of 'the church' in Nicetas of Remesiana, *Explanatio symboli*, from the beginning of the fifth century (*PL* 52, 871): 'Ecclesia quid aliud, quam sanctorum omnium congregatio? Ab exordio enim saeculi, sive patriarchae, sive Abraham, Isaac, et Jacob, sive prophetae, sive apostoli, sive martyres, sive caeteri iusti qui fuerunt, qui sunt, qui erunt, una Ecclesia sunt, quia una fide et conversatione sanctificati, uno spiritu signati, unum corpus effecti sunt: cuius corporis caput Christus, sicut perhibetur et scriptum est.'

and head of his church.[47] Thus Enoch the Just (c. 3), the image of all saints,[48] or Noah representing the 'type' of Christ, as the ark stands for that of the church.[49] Thus Abraham, the *initium fidei nostrae*, to whom Christ revealed himself in a vision,[50] and Jacob and Joseph, who also 'signify' him, the Redeemer.[51] Thus even Joshua, David, Solomon, Zorobabel ('id est Christus'), or the other Joseph.[52] As figures of Christ, this long series of 'saints' confirms the presence of Christ and of his church a long time *before* his arrival on earth; to testify to this indisputable reality, Gregory calls to the witness box once again Abraham, Moses, Aaron, David, and others, in the prologue to his third book of *Histories*.[53]

47 For *principium*, see n. 37. For Christ as the head of his church, and thus of the body composed of the saints, see *inter alia*, the following note (Augustine), and as far as Gregory is concerned, esp. *Hist.* V, prol., p. 194: 'tu liber capite tuo, id est Christo, servias'; and *Explanatio de titulis psalmorum*, p. 424: 'retributionem sanctorum sive ecclesiae, quae est corpus Christi.'

48 See Augustinus, *De civitate Dei* XV, 19, p. 98: 'Sed huius Enoch translatio nostrae dedicationis est praefigurata dilatio. Quae quidem iam facta est in Christo capite nostro, qui sic resurrexit, ut non moriatur ulterius, sed etiam ipse translatus est; restat autem altera dedicatio universae domus, cuius ipse Christus est fundamentum [*scil.* the church], quae difertur in finem, quando erit omnium resurrectio non moriturorum amplius. Sive autem domus Dei dicatur sive templum Dei sive civitas Dei, id ipsum est.' See also Isidore, *Allegoriae* 11, p. 102: 'Henoch ... significat septimam requiem futurae resurrectionis, quando transferentur sancti in vitam perpetuae immortalitatis.'

49 *Hist.* I 4, p. 6: 'Noe fidelissimum ac peculiarem sibi suique tipus speciem praeferentem'; and ibid.: 'nec hoc ambigo, quod species illa arcae tipum matris gessisset aeclesiae.' Cf. also Isidore, *Allegoriae* 12.

50 *Hist.* I 7, p. 9; ibid., n. 3, for reference to *Liber de promiss. et praedict. Dei* I, 17, *PL* 51: 747.

51 Ibid., 9, p. 10: 'Ioseph ... tipum praeferens Redemptoris'; see also Isidore, *Allegoriae* 26, col. 105: 'Jacob autem Christum demonstrat'; ibid., 45, col. 107, for Joseph.

52 See *Hist.* I 11, 12, 13, 21, and cf. Isidore, *Allegoriae* 72, col. 111 ('Jesu Nave [Joshua] imaginem Salvatoris expressit'); 89, col. 112 ('David filii Dei et Salvatoris nostri expressit imaginem'); 91, col. 113 ('Salomon Christi praenuntiat figuram'); 121, col. 116 ('Zorobabel typus est Domini Salvatoris'); 138, col. 117 ('Joseph typice Christi gestavit speciem qui ad custodiam sanctae Ecclesiae deputatus est, quae non habet maculam aut rugam'). In the *Histories* (I 10), a typology of the church is tied to the explanation of baptism, prefigured by the crossing of the Red Sea, and (*Hist.* I 15) to delivery from the Babylonian captivity (signifying the state of the sinful soul) by Zorobabel, 'id est Christus': see Heinzelmann, *Gregor*, 115.

53 *Hist.* III, prol., p. 96: 'I wish to compare the successes of the Christians who confess the Trinity and the disasters of the heretics who divide it. Let us refrain from recalling how Abraham venerated it at the oak, how Jacob preached it in his benediction, how Moses saw it in a bush etc.'; and further, 'there is a great miracle in the fact that the spirit that the heretics regarded as lesser a prophetic voice has called principal.' A comparable series of Old Testament witnesses is found in *Hist.* V 43 – a series with which Gregory in the end associates Saint Martin: see also the following note.

In the second part of the book, divided in two by the Ascension of the Redeemer (c. 24), Gregory brings together those who followed the patriarchs and prophets in the footsteps of Christ, that is, the apostles and especially the martyrs.[54] The first of them is Saint Stephen, crowned with martyrdom 'pro Christi nomine': in a repetitive fashion, this phrase will recur regularly as a leitmotiv in seven chapters.[55] Next, in the same vein, Saint Martin – whose birth miraculously coincides with the discovery of the true cross[56] – is stylized as the most perfect figure of Christ; like him, he appears at the time of his *adventum* as a light to the world,[57] his deeds are patterned on those of Christ, and his death is a journey to Christ ('migrare ad Christum'), occurring on the very day of the Lord (Sunday).[58]

III

It is not my intention to show here what Walter Goffart has already expressed perfectly as 'Gregory's determination to multiply the holy.'[59] The purpose of my analysis of the first book of the *Histories* is only to reveal the distinct structures bestowed on sanctity by the bishop of Tours in order to better grasp the significance of the phenomenon of heresy in his work. These structures concentrate in an extraordinary manner on the person of Christ and the life that he proposed to those who would emulate him, that is to say, to real Christians: thus, in Gregory's view, to speak precisely requires one to say '*a* Life of the saints,' and not '*the* Lives of the saints,' 'for a single life of the body,' which is that of the church and of Christ 'sustains all these saints no matter what their different merits.'[60]

54 *Hist.* I 26, p. 20: 'Primus tamen omnium hanc viam levita Stefanus martyr intravit'; cf. Gregory, *Liber de virt. s. Juliani* prol., p. 113: 'Per hanc enim viam Abel iustus sucipitur, Enoch beatus adsumitur [etc.] ... Per hanc viam apostoli diriguntur, martyres beati glorificantur.' For the apostles, see the prologue of a life of Saints Ursus and Leobatius by Gregory, *Liber vitae patrum* XVIII, prol., p. 283: 'Hii enim apostoli merito pro tota accipiuntur eclesia; quae non habens rugam aut maculam, inpolluta subsistit.'

55 *Hist.* I 26 (here Gregory's words are added to the text of Saint Jerome and Rufinus!), 27 (addition by Gregory), 28, 29 (item), 30 (added to the text of Jerome: 'ob dominici nominis confessionem'), 31, 35.

56 *Hist.* I 36, title, p. 2: 'De nativitate sancti Martini et crucis inventione.'

57 *Hist.* I 39, title, p. 3: 'De adventum sancti Martini'; p. 27: 'lumen nostrum exoritur'; cf. Heinzelmann, *Gregor*, 222 n. 77.

58 For the deeds of Martin (*Hist.* I 39) compared to those of Christ (*Hist.* I 20), see Heinzelmann, *Gregor*, 148, with n. 50 f; for the death of Martin, *Hist.* I 48, Heinzelmann, 131 ff.

59 Goffart, *Narrators*, 135.

60 *Liber vitae patrum*, general prologue, 212: 'Unde manifestum est, melius dici *vitam* patrum quam *vitas*, quia, cum sit diversitas meritorum virtutumque, una tamen omnes vita corporis alit in mundo'; see Heinzelmann, *Gregor*, 151 f. For the different merits, see esp. *Hist.* I 10, 15.

Obviously this person of Christ represents more than a theological idea for Gregory of Tours, but rather quite simply the principle inherent in the history that he depicts, in the Christian society whose outline he traces, and in the historiography he uses to present this ensemble to Christians. The phrases 'noster vero finis ipse Christus est' and '[Christus] qui est omnium principium,' used in a programmatic fashion in the prologue to the first book and in the first chapter of the work, are the eloquent witnesses of this.[61]

Now in Christian historiography before Gregory, there is only one author who made use of Christ in almost the same way for the object as well as the method of his writing, and this author is clearly Augustine.[62] In the work of the bishop of Hippo, we actually find the same kind of structural contrast between the earthly city (of the *miseri*) and the heavenly city of the saints, two cities belonging to the single *ecclesia* or kingdom of God (that is to say, of Christ), a church that is distinct, however, during its sojourn on earth before Judgment: to Augustinian *permixtio*, Gregory responds with the pell-mell of the saints and the others (*mixte confusaeque*).[63] Also, in Augustine we find the schematic plan of history, with *exortus*, *excursus*, and *finis cuius nullus est finis*, that I think can be roughly found again in the *Histories*.[64] If the bishop of Tours was able to integrate perfectly the continual deeds of the saints – long-dead saints as well as contemporary ones – into the run of general history, Augustine had already dealt substantially in the eschatological part of his history (Books XIX–XXII) with the governance exercised by the saints in association with

61 *Hist.* I, prol., and *Hist.* I 1, p. 5. The phrase '*finis* ipse Christus est, qui nobis vitam aeternam ... praestabit,' evidently recalls the meaning given *finis* by Augustine, e.g. *De civitate Dei* XVIII 54, p. 345: 'et percipiat unaquaeque [scil. *civitatum*, heavenly and earthly] suum finem, cuius nullus est finis.'

62 For Augustine, in the Creation stage (*exortus* of his history) it is more the role of the Trinity that is stressed, while Gregory emphasizes in an extreme fashion the sole person of Christ.

63 For Gregory, see n. 44. Among the numerous examples of Augustinian *permixtio*, see esp. *De civitate Dei* XI 1, 1: 461 f., the first chapter of what will be the history, properly speaking, of the two cities, that is to say, in a way the counterpart of Gregory's *Histories*: 'Nunc vero ... de duarum civitatum, terrenae scilicet et caelestis, quas in hoc interim saeculo perplexas quodam modo diximus *invicemque permixtas*, exortu et excursu et debitis finibus ... [disputare aggrediar].' For a more detailed interpretation of Augustine's work (with bibliography), especially from the social vantage point, see now my 'Adel und *societas sanctorum*: Soziale Ordnungen und christliches Weltbild von Augustinus bis zu Gregor von Tours,' in *Nobilitas, Funktion und Repräsentation des Adels in Alteuropa*, Akten des Kolloquiums Schloß Ringberg, 20–3 Feb. 1994, ed. O.G. Oexle and W. Paravicini (Göttingen, 1997), 216–56.

64 Heinzelmann, *Gregor*, 84 f. (chap. 3). Gregory gives his first book the theme of the 'immaculate church,' and his last book that of 'eschatological occurrences,' but all his chapters, from *Hist.* I 1 to *Hist.* X 30, correspond to the Augustinian *excursus* (XV–XVIII, from the beginnings of the two cities with Cain and Abel). Augustine had reserved four books each for the *exortus* and *finis* (XI–XIV and XIX–XXII).

Christ in historical times before the Last Judgment.[65] Again it was the author of *The City of God* who set out to 'prove' the reality of Christ's resurrection on the basis of about twenty reports of saintly miracles in the longest chapter of his work,[66] one that paved the way for countless works of medieval hagiography.

It is true that Gregory made greater and more systematic use of miracles like this, and of the supernatural in general, than did the African bishop; on this precise point, doubtless he gave way to the same literary and religious tastes to which his famous namesake, the bishop of Rome, also wished to devote himself. But just as for Augustine, the chief purpose of Gregory of Tours was to demonstrate the historical presence of Christ and, through this reality, a 'society of the saints,' taken in the literal sense.[67] As for this society, we already know that it was supposed to be led by bishops and directed according to Christian principles, which no one, not even the king, can avoid. The contribution of Gregory as far as the formation of this society in the image of the perfect society of the saints is concerned,[68] is founded chiefly on his writing of 'edification.'[69] Along with a commentary on the psalter that brings to mind in a repetitive and sustained fashion the omnipresence of Christ, matching the very reality of all human existence,[70] and a treatise that institutionalizes the regular reading of the

---

65 *De civitate Dei* XX 9, 2: 427 f.: 'sancti regnant cum Christo etiam ipsi mille annis ... id est isto iam tempore prioris eius adventus'; ibid., p. 429: 'Ergo et nunc ecclesia regnum Christi est regnumque caelorum. Regnant itaque cum illo etiam nunc sancti eius, aliter quidem, quam tunc regnabunt'; and ibid., p. 430: 'Regnat itaque cum Christo nunc primum ecclesia in vivis et mortuis.' Also ibid., XX 13, p. 437: 'Sed certe animae victrices gloriosissimarum martyrum ... postea quam mortalia membra posuerunt, cum Christo utique regnaverunt et regnant.'

66 *De civitate Dei* XXII 8, 2: 566–81. See also c. 9, 2: 582, for the meaning of the miracles: 'Cui, nisi huic fidei adtestantur ista miracula, in qua praedicatur Christus resurrexisse in carne.'

67 In *De civitate Dei*, the expression *societas* or *regnum sanctorum* appears esp. in XIV 28 (end of book), XV 1, XX 13 (5 times), and XX 23: 2: 57, 59 ('Superna est enim sanctorum civitas, quamvis hic pariat cives, in quibus peregrinatur, donec regni eius tempus adveniat'), 436–8, 463. In the other works of Augustine, the references are very frequent. For equivalent notions, see e.g. *Ennaratio in psalmum C, PL* 37: 1293: 'Ut dispergantur de civitate Domini, de societate Jerusalem, de societate sanctorum, de societate Ecclesiae.' Gregory only uses the term *eclesia* (or *corpus Christi*): see Heinzelmann, *Gregor*, 145–52; Gregory in his hagiographical writings depicts the same phenomenon in a way different from that of Augustine by fully presenting this society (with Christ, the apostles, martys, old and new confessors).

68 Knowledge that this perfect society of the saints is only sojourning on earth (see previous note for citation of Augustine) establishes the *Histories'* real rhythm, perhaps even the irony that Walter Goffart revealed so magisterially in *Narrators* (see esp. III 6, 'Miracles and Slaughters').

69 For the term and its significance for Christian literature, see Heinzelmann, *Gregor*, 150 f.

70 Gregory, *Explanatio de titulis psalmorum*, p. 424: 'Illi autem [*scil.* psalmi] qui *In finem* inscribuntur perfectionem bonorum operum ostendunt, quia hic finis dissimilis est aliis finibus, cum illi habent terminum, hic replimentum: Finis enim legis est Christus.' Part of the work edited

psalms,[71] this writing comprises ten books of history dealing with the contrast between the two societies (or 'cities') from the beginning of time and eight hagiographical books intended to emphasize only the society of the saints and illustrated by their miracles performed in the name of Christ.[72]

This astonishingly coherent body of writing cannot be founded on the simple belief in a paternal God, or indeed one impersonal and distant. On the contrary, the Gregorian corpus depends on an image of the Dominus Iesus Christus who, by his very historical existence, signifies the hope of a perfect society, the only one that would be able to last until the end of time. If Christ is 'less than the Father,' as the Arians maintain, according to the bishop of Tours, who often enjoys disclosing this heretical claim,[73] the society of the saints, the body of Christ, would lose its assurance of a future life and its way towards constructing the true Christian society. For this reason, Gregory devotes all his scholarly activity to the beginning (*principium*) and the finality (*finis*), which is Christ.[74] It is thus the 'Christ principle,'[75] and the social values it stands for, that guide

by Krusch in MGH SRM 1/2 is composed of an exegesis of the psalms from the point of view of their meaning for Christ and his church; another part is composed of 89 (of the 150) *tituli psalmorum* or *Diapsalmae*, that is to say, a full register of titles (or summaries) for each psalm, a kind of table of contents regularly accompanying the psalter 'for directing prayer': see Pierre Salmon, *Les 'tituli psalmorum' des manuscrits latins*, Études liturgiques 3 (Paris, 1959), esp. 135–48, who edits six series of texts, of which the fifth series corresponds to that in the edition of Gregory's *Explanatio*. As the series could be prior to Gregory, there has been a mistaken effort to withdraw attribution of the whole text from him; cf. Heinzelmann, *Gregor*, 139. As far as the *Diapsalmae* are concerned, if they are not from the very pen of Gregory, their character corresponds perfectly nevertheless to the text of the commentary; perhaps they were selected as a kind of supplement conforming with the bishop's intent: we have here the only series which relates *all* the psalms to the person of Christ!

71 Gregory, *De cursu stellarum ratio* 36, p. 420: 'si signum moveatur ad matutinus, quinque psalmis in Dei laude concinere in antyphanis potest'; cf. Heinzelmann, *Gregor*, 140–1.

72 Significantly in the prologue of his first hagiographic work, the *Liber in gloria martyrum*, Gregory deals with John 1: 1–3: 'In principio erat Verbum, et Verbum erat apud Deum, et Deus erat Verbum. Hoc erat in principio apud Deum. Omnia per ipsum facta sunt, et sine ipso factum est nihil.' For *principium*, cf. above, n. 37.

73 See *Hist.* I, prol. (3 times), *Hist.* III, prol. ('quem heretici asserunt minorem, principalem vox prophetica nuntiavit'), *Hist.* V 43 (5 times: Gregory's discussion with a heretic), *Hist.* VI 5 (to convert a Jew, Chilperic correctly presents the characteristics of Christ: 'filium non potestati minori'; in *Hist.* V 44, because of his definition of the Trinity, Chilperic is accused of heresy by Gregory), *Hist.* IX 15 (2 times, at the time of the conversion of King Reccared in 587). *Hist.* V 43, 44 and VI 5 (and 40) are used in part by a Carolingian tradition in several MSS of the canonical collection of Saint Maur: see Heinzelmann, *Gregor*, 138–9.

74 See nn. 37, 61, 70. Note the double meaning of both terms which refer to the limits of historical (Christian) time and the principle inherent in all Christian existence.

75 See n. 73, with Christ who is *principalis* in the Trinity!

the pen of Gregory; every breach of this principle, whether it pertains to the theological or social order, necessarily signifies for him the presence of heresy.

Epilogue: In a chapter of the ninth book of the *Histories*, Gregory relates the circumstances of the conversion of the Visigothic king Reccared in 587, marking the end of Arianism, at least in Gaul.[76] According to Gregory, the king would have gathered the Arian and Catholic bishops, the former having set forth their heretical propositions 'as we have already reported so often'; afterward, the Catholic bishops answered with their own arguments, often presented by Gregory in his earlier books. To this discussion, the king, it seems, applies the decisive criterion: according to him, no Arian bishop was ever distinguished by effecting a sick cure. Thus grasping the truth, he submits to the Catholic faith, 'credidit Iesum Christum, filium Dei, aequalem Patri cum Spiritu sancto.'[77] The miracle being, since Augustine, the visible sign of belonging to the society of the saints, which appears more and more to be the only admissible model of society, the king's decision reported by the bishop is thus fully in accord with the logic set in motion by the *City of God*.

---

76 *Hist.* IX 15. See Jacques Fontaine, 'Conversion et culture chez les Wisigoths d'Espagne,' *Settimane* 14 (1967) 1: 87–147, esp. 114–15.

77 According to Fontaine, Gregory 'est anti-arienne beaucoup plus qu'anti-gothique,' which is true, even if the two points of view doubtless intermingle. The phenomenon of heresy always goes well beyond the actions of mere Visigoths, or even mere Arians (this is why the conversion of the Visigoths holds only a modest place in the *Histories*, in strong contrast to the importance of heresy in the prologues of Books I and III of the same work). According to Fontaine, Gregory's point of view would always be more religious than political, and more doctrinal than pragmatic: on this point I would have reservations, for it was not Gregorian intentions to separate social and religious, or the dogmatic framework of Christian society from its political and social workings.

5

War, Warlords, and Christian Historians from the Fifth to the Seventh Century

STEVEN MUHLBERGER

A feature of the Middle Ages well known to moderns is the idea of holy war or crusade. This idea is one aspect of a more general phenomenon in which the medieval church not only preached war against the infidel, but blessed the knight's sword and prayed for the king's army, even when he went to battle Christian neighbours. The paradox of the church of Christ, who told his disciples to love their enemies, endorsing warfare is a topic of perennial interest, and one that has been described and analysed often before. It is also well known that the Latin church in late antiquity was seldom so anxious to bless the arms of the warrior. Gibbon's characterization is famous: 'The clergy successfully preached the doctrines of patience and pusillanimity: the active virtues of society were discouraged; and the last remains of military spirit were buried in the cloister.'[1] Gibbon's judgment can be disputed or qualified, but one must agree that the earliest Christians were unwarlike; even long after the conversion of the emperors, during the great crisis of the fifth century A.D., there is little trace of clerical support for the defence of Rome in the name of true religion.

The transition from the earlier attitude to the later has been the subject of long and detailed studies, and involves more issues than can be dealt with in a single essay.[2] I would simply like to draw attention to a stage in that transition, when the evaluation by western clerics of war and warmakers began to change. At the turn of the seventh century, we find a Latin Christian literature that takes a positive view of military virtue. We can identify three Christian chroniclers and historians – two of them clerics, and all of them working in the ecclesiasti-

---

1 Edward Gibbon, *The Decline and Fall of the Roman Empire*, ed. J.B. Bury, 3 vols. (New York, 1946), 1221.

2 For instance, Friedrich Prinz, *Klerus und Krieg im früheren Mittelalter* (Stuttgart, 1971), and Carl Erdmann, *The Origin of the Idea of Crusade,* tr. M.W. Baldwin and W. Goffart (Princeton, 1977).

cal-chronicle tradition – who valued forthrightly rulers for their victories and justified war even against other believers. Comparing these three with earlier Christian historians throws an interesting light on the development of western Christian attitudes towards war, and is the purpose of this essay. The focus here is on professedly Christian historians and chroniclers writing in Latin in the western provinces of the Roman Empire. Historians have been chosen to represent Christian thought on this subject because it is among them that we can expect to find a concern with judging politics and war from a Christian perspective.

II

The early church, east and west, did not feel itself obliged to concern itself with the Roman Empire or its defence. The Empire was the enemy, a pagan enterprise, unjust, unholy, the active persecutor of the truth. War was the vocation of men of blood. In their private persons, Christians were sometimes grateful for the protection that the emperors and their armies provided them from external enemies; sometimes this down-to-earth view is evident in the writings of church fathers.[3] But a specifically Christian evaluation of events could not rate such matters very highly. The Christian was concerned with eternal things, not with the passing fortunes of rulers and kingdoms. Christian writers before the time of Eusebius, the late third and early fourth centuries, wrote no history, even of the church; the earliest moves in that direction were chronographies focused on dating the end of the present world.

The conversion of the emperors meant some change in Christian attitudes. Few doubted that the advent of Constantine and his victories over his enemies were divinely ordained. Hostility to military service by Christians declined, while it became possible to exploit imperial victories for their apologetic value. In some specific situations, such as on the hotly contested Persian frontier, an identification of the Christian cause and the fortune of imperial arms might seem very appropriate.[4] Generally, however, there is little sign that Christian thinkers rethought their position on warfare in any systematic way. War still was the business of men of blood, while the military defence of the Empire was not a high priority for most Christians, who generally remained secure from outside threat. The most important challenges facing the church in the minds of its articulate members had little to do with the military skill of emperors or the success of their armies. Issues of doctrine and ecclesiastical discipline loomed

3 W.H.C. Frend, *The Rise of Christianity* (London, 1984), 420.
4 Ibid., 533.

so large that very few Christian writers found the time to write history in the fourth century. Those who did, such as Eusebius and his Latin continuators, Jerome and Rufinus, concentrated on the struggles of the church.[5]

In the early and mid-fifth century, the military preparedness of the Empire and the competence of its rulers became an issue impossible to ignore in the western provinces. Political and military events became compelling enough that some Latin Christians did take up the pen to write history. It is in this period that Jerome's *Chronicle* received its first western continuations, in Gaul, Italy, and Spain. Despite the setbacks of the Empire and the victories of barbarian armies, the dominant attitude of Christian writers towards military affairs remained rather ambivalent. The point may be made best by looking first at two chroniclers who did identify the fortunes of the Empire with the safety of the church, and then comparing them with others who did not.

The earlier of the two exceptional writers was the Gallic Chronicler of 452. This now-anonymous writer lived in the south of Gaul and composed his brief account of recent history in the immediate aftermath of Attila's invasion.[6] Attila had been turned back, but the chronicler was not reassured, and for good reason: the Huns were now in Italy and the outcome of this incursion was not yet known.[7] The chronicler saw the bleakness of the current situation as of a piece with the rest of recent history. For years now, barbarian success had been practically uninterrupted. Large parts of the Empire had been lost to them, and his own region was now directly threatened.[8] A pious man, he was very disturbed by the religious consequences of barbarian power. Arianism, a heresy that had apparently been defeated generations ago, was now creeping back into the Empire under barbarian protection.[9]

The Gallic Chronicler had a keen appreciation of the price paid by the church for the Empire's military weakness. Fear of barbarian rule and barbarian sponsorship of heresy led him to idealize strong rulers of the past. His special

---

5 Jerome continued Eusebius' *Chronicle,* Rufinus his *Ecclesiastical History.* Each included and commented on major political and military events.

6 *Chronica a. CCCCLII,* ed. Th. Mommsen, in *Chronica Gallica,* CM 1: 516–666. The most recent detailed discussion is my own *The Fifth-Century Chroniclers: Prosper, Hydatius and the Gallic Chronicler of 452* (Leeds, 1990), 136–92.

7 *Chron. CCCCLII* c. 141.

8 The chronicler's view of his own time is succinctly given in *Chron. CCCCLII* c. 138. The chronicle provides two impressive lists of disasters: one for Honorius' reign (A.D. 395–423), in cc. 61–5; another for the imperial defeats of the 440s, in cc. 124, 126–33. For his special concern with barbarian settlements in the south of Gaul, see cc. 124, 127, 128, and Muhlberger, *Fifth-Century Chroniclers,* 176–7.

9 The connection between imperial weakness and the growth of Arianism is directly stated in *Chron. CCCCLII* c. 138. Earlier entries on Arianism and its defeat: cc. 8, 13, 22, 51.

favourites were the emperor Theodosius I, a champion, in the chronicler's view, of both orthodoxy and imperial power, and the usurper Magnus Maximus, whose efforts on behalf of both church and state almost excused his illegitimate seizure of power.[10]

Another chronicler with a similar view was Hydatius. Hydatius was bishop of Chaves in the remote province of Gallaecia (present-day northwestern Spain and northern Portugal), an area that had effectively been lost to the Roman government as early as 409.[11] Hydatius, who became bishop in 427, spent his life struggling to maintain Roman standards of order and religious orthodoxy in what had become a wild frontier.[12] By the time he wrote his historical account, in the 460s, he knew that barbarians and heretics had defeated him. The discord of life in Gallaecia encouraged Hydatius, who could still recall the undivided, orthodox Empire of his youth, to idealize those far-off figures who symbolized for him legitimate effective authority. Hydatius, like the Gallic Chronicler, looked back with fondness to the days of Theodosius I, and remembered more recent generals, Aetius, Aegidius, and Majorian, not only as defenders of the Roman Empire, but as men who were doing God's will on earth.[13]

In each of these cases, a retrospective look at the disintegration of the old Roman system inspired a Christian historian – each of them among the earliest Christian historians writing in Latin – to abandon the older detachment from political and military concerns. Historians begin with the idea that time and change matter. Time and change had taught Hydatius and the Gallic Chronicler that military strength in the right hands might make a tremendous difference. Its failure at a crucial time had exposed the church – at least in their own vulnerable regions – to heretical rulers whose triumph endangered true religion. In both men's works, we see an identification of Roman order with orthodoxy, and heresy or unbelief with barbarism, that would not seem out of place in later

---

10 Theodosius' reign as a period of victories for the faith: *Chron. CCCCLII*, cc. 20, 22, 28, 30 (where he defeats a usurper through 'the open favour of God'). Maximus, cc. 7 (as victorious general) and 12 (zealous enemy of heresy). On the Chronicler's ambiguous view of Maximus and its parallel in other sources, see Muhlberger, *Fifth-Century Chroniclers*, 190–1.

11 Hydatius of Lemica, *Continuatio chronicorum Hieronymianorum ad a. CCCCLXVIII* [hereinafter *Chron.*], ed. Th. Mommsen, in CM 2: 1–36. Hydatius has recently been re-edited and translated: *The Chronicle of Hydatius and the Consularia Constantinopolitana*, ed. and tr. Richard Burgess (Oxford, 1993). See also Muhlberger, *Fifth-Century Chroniclers*, 193–266.

12 Hydatius, like the Chronicler of 452, saw heresy and imperial weakness as closely related: *Chron. praef.* 7. His own activities as supporter of imperial authority: cc. 96, 98, 201, 207; as opponent of heresy: c. 130; Suevic and Gothic support for Arianism in Gallaecia: c. 232.

13 Hydatius clearly believed that God supported Roman order and its champions. See, for example, *Chron.*, cc. 154, 218, 234, and Muhlberger, *Fifth-Century Chroniclers*, 230–4.

Byzantine works. It is noteworthy, however, that each chronicler took this stance only when ultimate disaster seemed inevitable.[14]

These views were not those of the dominant clerical voices of the fifth-century west. The traditional detachment from military matters and mundane political responsibility seems to have been much stronger. Among those Christians who attempted to explain current history from a theological standpoint, Augustine is the dominant figure. Augustine's famous analysis in the *City of God* is so comprehensively worked out, and so influential for later generations, that any summary is oversimplification. Let it suffice to say here that Augustine, like most of his predecessors, refused to identify the church with any earthly polity, even a Christian Roman Empire. The defeats of the Empire, however distressing, were not the defeats of the church, of the people of God. The battle they fought was a different one, not to be won or lost in any one generation; nor was it to be decided by human effort.

Two of Augustine's early fifth-century disciples attempted to apply this analysis to the recent history of the western Empire. The more famous of them is Orosius, who in A.D. 417 wrote his *History against the Pagans*, to demonstrate that the defeats of the Empire could not be fixed, as pagan critics claimed, on the abandonment of the old gods by Christian Rome.[15] To answer the charge, he wrote a huge compendium of world history, in which he demonstrated that defeats and catastrophes of Christian times were nothing compared with those suffered in the pagan past; in fact, they were blessings in disguise, and would in the end advance the cause of Christ. Orosius' apology, however, was heavy-handed, and would, in its own time, have required a very sympathetic reader indeed.

A more subtle history in the Augustinian vein was written by Prosper of Aquitaine, whose *Epitoma chronicon* was written in several editions, in southern Gaul and Rome, between 433 and 455.[16] Prosper's chronicle was originally written as part of a theological propaganda campaign, to promote Augustine's still-controversial theology of grace and show that it had received the blessing of the Roman church. It was thus written for a theologically aware readership,

---

14 The depiction of Anthemius' great naval expedition in Hydatius, *Chron.*, c. 247, may seem to argue for the possibility of hope, and I took this position in *Fifth-Century Chroniclers*, 234. Richard Burgess, 'Hydatius and the Final Frontier: The Fall of the Roman Empire and the End of the World,' in *Shifting Frontiers in Late Antiquity*, ed. R.W. Mathisen and H. Sivan (Aldershot, 1996), 319–30, has since explored the depth of apocalyptic beliefs, and argued convincingly that Hydatius thought the end of time imminent.

15 Paulus Orosius, *Historiarum adversum paganos libri VII*, ed. K. Zangemeister, CSEL 5 (Vienna, 1882).

16 Prosper of Aquitaine, *Epitoma chronicon*, ed. Th. Mommsen in CM 1: 341–499. See the discussion in Muhlberger, *Fifth-Century Chroniclers*, 48–135.

one committed to Augustinian thought, or at least sympathetic to it. For such an audience, it was possible to present the crisis of the Empire as a failure of moral leadership. Generals and their mistakes are prominent in his brief account, but their sins even more so. Generals and usurpers are shown as jealous, treacherous, murderous, and oppressors of the church to boot.[17]

Prosper opposed the faults of the all-too-worldly guardians of the Roman state to the prudence and fidelity of the clergy and other true Christians, especially that of the Roman pontiffs. The fruit of their virtues was victory. The chronicle shows the authority of the Roman church crushing the Pelagian heresy that Prosper hated even in distant Britain and Ireland, where Rome had sent missionaries to crush Pelagianism and to plant the true faith.[18]

The vanity of earthly power and the effectiveness of the efforts of the saints is emphasized most strongly in the final version of Prosper's chronicle, issued in 455. Prosper was looking back over very dramatic events, ending with the sack of Rome by the Vandals, a catastrophe that Prosper probably witnessed. The merely human efforts of generals and emperors had been ineffective; it was the leadership of Pope Leo the Great 'relying on God's help, which is never missing from the labours of the pious,'[19] that had saved Rome from Attila and mitigated the sack of the city at the hand of Geiseric when all other expedients failed.

It is hard to say how convincing the average Christian of the mid-fifth century found the argument that the pure leadership of the orthodox clergy would show the way, and that spiritual victories compensated for imperial defeats. We know, however, that Prosper was not alone in presenting such an interpretation. Leo himself, with whom Prosper was probably associated in his later life, presented a similar view in his sermons on several occasions.[20] Furthermore, a number of other fifth- and early sixth-century clerical writers, hagiographers interpreting recent events for their readers, took a similar attitude. Constantius

---

17 Prosper's open criticism of the dead generalissimos Castinus and Felix can be found in *Epitoma chronicon,* cc. 1278, 1282, 1292, 1294, 1303. In regard to other warlords, especially the powerful Aëtius, Prosper was more subtle. In later editions (those of 445 and 455), Prosper emphasized that the limited foresight of human leaders obtained only transient victories. See cc. 1324, 1335 (Litorius wins one victory through strategem, then overreaches himself), 1339 (Aëtius, successful against the Goths in Gaul, is quickly outwitted by the Vandal Geiseric), 1364, 1367 (Aëtius defeats Attila in Gaul through foresight, which then fails him).

18 The entire structure of Prosper's edition of 433, a chaotic year in western politics, contrasts imperial defeats to the spiritual victories of the church over heresy and unbelief. Such victories are described in *Epitoma chronicon,* cc. 1204, 1252, 1261, 1265 (the overcoming of persecution), 1266, 1297, 1301, 1307, 1309 (cf. the civil war of c. 1310). The same contrast can be seen in the later editions.

19 Prosper, *Epitoma chronicon,* c. 1367. Leo's intervention with Geiseric, c. 1375.

20 Leo, *Sermones* 39, 40.2, 49.3, 88.4 (*PL* 54: 263–7, 268–9, 303, 442–3).

of Lyon's Life of Germanus of Auxerre (written *ca* 480), Ennodius of Pavia's Life of Epiphanius of Pavia (*ca* 503), and Eugippius' Life of Severinus of Noricum (*ca* 510) all demonstrate a distaste for warriors and war, and show the spiritual power of holy men to be far more efficacious than the exercise of normal military virtue.[21]

What explains this continued detachment? The old clerical disdain for the rough and disorderly men who commanded armies, whether the armies of Rome or of Rome's enemies, clearly continued to be important. The opportunistic generals of the disintegrating Empire were an uninspiring lot, as one might expect of warlords in a chaotic political situation. Furthermore, most were either barbarians and Arian heretics, or Romans whose power depended on their ability to lead and deal with barbarians and heretics.[22] These were not men who could be expected to take a principled stand against heresy, even had they wanted to. We can easily imagine that many dedicated churchmen would have been revolted by those who supposedly led the Christian Empire, and seen them as unstable, bloody-handed representatives of everything Christians were supposed to abhor.[23]

Had impressive and pious emperors dramatically restored a healthy and orthodox Empire through their military efforts, the clerical attitude might have been different.[24] But defeat was one of the chief facts to be explained, and, given that, a continued detachment from the woes of a now-failed Empire had something to offer that nostalgia for past Roman victories and good, old-fashioned Roman discipline did not. Those who believed that spiritual victories were possible in the ruins of earthly glory had a message for the future. Those

21 Constantius of Lyon, *Vie de St. Germaine d' Auxerre*, ed. R. Borius, Sources chrétiennes 112 (Paris, 1965); Sr Genevieve Cook, *The Life of St. Epiphanius by Ennodius: A Translation with an Introduction and a Commentary*, Catholic University of America Studies in Medieval and Renaissance Latin Language and Literature 14 (Washington, D.C., 1942); Eugippius, *Das Leben des Heiligen Severin*, ed. Rudolf Noll (Berlin, 1963); see commentary in Muhlberger, *Fifth-Century Chroniclers,* 131–5. On Eugippius and Ennodius, see Steven Muhlberger, 'Eugippius and the Life of St. Severinus,' *Medieval Prosopography* 17 (1996): 107–24.

22 An interesting case is provided by Augustine's relationship with the general Boniface, whom the bishop initially regarded as an unusually pious and worthwhile military leader. Augustine was subsequently disappointed by Boniface's ambitious behaviour and his willingness to marry an Arian. Augustine, *Epistolae* 185, 185a, 189, 220 (CSEL 52: 1–44, 131–7, 431–41); Muhlberger, *Fifth-Century Chroniclers,* 99–101.

23 An example of what might be said of a ranking general (put here in the mouth of an emperor) is provided by Cook, *Life of St. Epiphanius by Ennodius*, cc. 67–9.

24 Ennodius' extravagant praise of King Theodoric of Italy, which ignores his heretical allegiance, hints at the possibilities, though Theodoric is not praised for his warlike deeds: Cook, *Life of St. Epiphanius by Ennodius,* cc. 142–6. See also the comments of Marc Reydellet, *La royauté dans la littérature latine de Sidoine Apollinaire à Isidore de Séville* (Rome, 1981), 161.

who knew, as Augustine had taught so fervently, that man without God was helpless, but that with God all things were possible, at least had hope.

So in the late fifth and early sixth centuries, a pacifistic attitude, or at least a certain aloofness from the struggles of earthly rulers, continued to make sense to the pious. Clerics who had had their reservations about Roman emperors and their often turbulent generals did not embrace the heretical warlords who ruled most western provinces after the Empire's collapse. War was a competition between alien kings; the religious leaders of the conquered Romans had no stake in war, and everything to gain from peace.[25] Roman Christians who lived under Catholic dynasties likewise showed little enthusiasm for the military virtues and those who might be expected to display them. Gildas, the obscure sermonizer who gives us what little we know about the last days of sixth-century Roman Britain, may have looked back with nostalgia to the discipline and order of the Roman days; however, he knew that the kings of his time were guilty of every sin, targets for God's retribution. Gildas' *De excidio Britonum* is not a call to arms, but a call to repentance.[26] Gregory of Tours' famous portrait of the victorious and orthodox Clovis may seem to show him as yearning for a true Christian champion; however, his detailed account of his own times reveals Gregory as a man deeply unenthusiastic about military adventures, even against dangerous enemies like the Bretons or the Goths. Recent wars near-to-hand Gregory uniformly portrayed as expensive, futile, even farcical. They were undertaken for the worst possible reasons, and never worked out as they were meant to. Among contemporary rulers, Gregory admired those who were generous, merciful, and as much like bishops as possible.[27]

III

This quick and incomplete survey shows that the traditional detachment of the Christian clergy from any deep commitment to the politics of this world, and the basic distaste for war and warmakers, continued in the western provinces

---

25 Eugippius on the essential irrelevance of warlike rulers: *Das Leben des Heiligen Severin*, c. 31 (p. 98).

26 Gildas, *De excidio Britonum*, ed. and tr. Michael Winterbottom (London, 1978). Some of the best recent commentary on Gildas is found in *Gildas, New Approaches*, ed. Michael Lapidge and David N. Dumville (Woodbridge, Suffolk, 1984); see also Robert Hanning, *The Vision of History in Early Britain: From Gildas to Geoffrey of Monmouth* (New York, 1966).

27 Gregory on Clovis: *Hist.* II, prol., 27–42, and V, prol.; a typically unheroic warlike episode from Gregory's own time: VIII 30; extraordinary royal virtue displayed by Tiberius II and Guntram: V 19, IX 21 (Tiberius, a distant symbol of perfection, earns the military victories denied to the Frankish kings Gregory criticized: V 30). Walter Goffart has recently discussed Gregory's attitudes towards war and warmakers: *The Narrators of Barbarian History (A.D.*

long after the conversion of the emperors. Even those who had an interest in recounting in historical form the slow collapse of imperial power, the threat of barbarian invasion and occupation, and the growth of heresy under alien kings were usually not enthusiastic for war; they found it difficult to identify Christians champions, at least in the present. The most that can be said is that, in explaining the troubles of their own time, they might refer to such champions in the past.

It is not until shortly before the year 600 – about the time that Gregory of Tours put down his pen – that we encounter ecclesiastics who speak in a somewhat different language about war. Three writers of this period are worthy of notice: John of Biclar, Isidore of Seville, and the so-called Copenhagen Continuator of Prosper – two Spaniards and an Italian, all of them historians in the Christian-chronicle tradition. I do not want to give the impression that these men, two of them bishops, were bellicose men; they were not. All preferred peace to war. But where their predecessors saw only the destruction and futility of war, they were more appreciative of what strong military leadership might accomplish. Indeed, the utility of military virtue was for them so compelling that it seemed to them a necessary component of any legitimate secular power.

The oldest of these Christian historians is John of Biclar.[28] Although practically unknown to all but students of Visigothic Spain, John is a chronicler of more than usual interest, and not merely because he preserves much unique information. John was both a Goth and a Catholic in an era when most of his people were Arians. Catholic and Roman sympathies may have run in his family – about the year 558, at an early age, he went or was sent to Constantinople to obtain an education in both Greek and Latin. One suspects that he had already entered the church at this point.

John spent seventeen years in the Byzantine capital, and the experience made a deep and favourable impression on him. As his chronicle reveals, John the Goth became and remained a great fan of all things Byzantine.

In 575 John returned to his native Spain, and immediately became embroiled in religious controversy. King Leovigild, the most powerful Gothic ruler in a century, had restored the fortunes of his people by reconquering most of the

550–800): Jordanes, Gregory of Tours, Bede, and Paul the Deacon (Princeton: 1988), 216–27, and 'Conspicuous by Absence: Heroism in the Early Frankish Era (6th–7th Cent.),' in *La funzione dell'eroe germanici: Storicità, metafora, paradigma,* ed. Teresa Pároli (Rome, 1995), 41–56.

28 For details of John's career and the text of his chronicle, see John of Biclar, *Chronica a. DLXVII–DXC,* CM 2: 207–20, and Julio Campos, *Juan de Biclaro, Obispo de Gerona: su vida y su obra* (Madrid, 1960). John's chronicle has been recently translated into English and commented upon by Kenneth Baxter Wolf, *Conquerors and Chroniclers of Early Medieval Spain,* Translated Texts for Historians 9 (Liverpool, 1990), 61–80.

Iberian peninsula; he was also determined to protect the position of the Gothic Arian church. John's stubborn adherence to the Roman religion earned him the king's enmity, and he spent ten years in exile in Barcelona. The death of the Arian king not only released John, but ushered in a new day for all Spanish Catholics. Recarred, Leovigild's son and successor, opted to achieve religious unity by converting his own people to the religion of the majority. The conversion of the Goths took place in 587, and the unification of the Spanish church under royal auspices was confirmed at the Council of Toledo of 590.

John of Biclar wrote his chronicle, a continuation of earlier works going back to Jerome and Eusebius, in that same year, 590, in the light of that epochal conversion. The chronicle, of course, is constructed with that dramatic conclusion in mind.[29] But the route that John takes and the sights that he shows his readers along the way are very interesting, and on occasion surprising.

John's chronicle begins in the year 565, with the death of Justinian. At that time and for some years after, John was living in Constantinople, and as a result imperial affairs take centre stage for the first half of his work. John's picture of the Empire is a very friendly one; indeed, a native-born Byzantine historian could hardly have praised it more. The aggressive ecclesiastical policy pursued by Justinian in his later years had alienated much of the western church; John explicitly brushed away all doubts of Byzantine orthodoxy at the beginning of his chronicle.[30] For him the Empire was pre-eminently a Christian state working to propagate the true religion throughout the world. He shows us barbarian peoples being converted to Christianity and allying themselves to the Empire simultaneously; conversion and alliance are two sides of a single phenomenon. Further, John tells the reader that the ongoing war with Persia began because the impious Persian king tried to force the Armenians and the Iberi to worship idols. The Gothic chronicler reports Roman successes against the Persians and their other enemies with great satisfaction, and minimizes such Roman defeats as the Lombard invasion of Italy.[31]

---

29 J.N. Hillgarth, one of the few writers in English to pay any attention to the chronicle, states that John began writing while still in Constantinople. Yet as Hillgarth himself recognizes, the work includes later judgments on earlier events. Such judgments probably belong to the time at which he finished the chronicle, i.e., 590 or shortly thereafter. J.N. Hillgarth, 'Historiography in Visigothic Spain,' *Settimane* 17/1 (1970): 267, 269.

30 John of Biclar, *Chronica* s.a. 567, 2.

31 Ibid., 569, 1 (The Garamantes associate themselves with the Roman *res publica* and the Christian faith simultaneously); 567, 3 (Persian persecution causes their Christian subjects to defect to Rome, causing war); 575, 1 (a crushing Roman victory over the Persians); 572, 1; 573, 1 (two incidents that show Roman superiority to the Lombards). The actual Lombard invasion of Italy is not described. See also Hillgarth, 'Historiography,' 267–9.

John's discussion of his own homeland seems at first a strange contrast to the foregoing. The earliest Spanish material is devoted to an appreciative account of Leovigild's victories and success in 'marvelously restoring the Gothic kingdom to its original boundaries.' Leovigild's efforts to make Arianism more attractive to Roman Catholics are described in a single entry;[32] but his progress in defeating rebels, rustics, usurpers, even the Byzantines, is thoroughly documented.[33] That Leovigild's rebellious son died a Catholic is ignored; for John, the prince was a usurper and a rebel, rightly put down by his father.[34]

At first John's admiration for Leovigild, the man who exiled him for his beliefs, seems odd – until one remembers the sequel. John praises the old king's work because it was inherited by Reccared, the new Constantine who rescued the Goths from their centuries-old enslavement to heresy.

John's picture of King Reccared is sheer panegyric. To describe it in detail is not possible. But an important element is the emphasis John puts on Reccared's military success, which acts as a guarantee of his position and a sign of divine approval for his policy. Not only was the new king his father's equal in putting down rebels – in his case, Arian rebels intent on resurrecting heresy – he won a victory of unprecedented proportions over foreign enemies.[35] His general Claudius, fortified by the king's Catholic faith and divine help, had defeated 40,000 Franks with 300 Goths, equalling the biblical victory of Gideon over the Midianites, who also, John reminds us, attacked the people of God. The incident has its Byzantine equivalent – John reports in the next and last year of his chronicle a false story that the king of the Persians has converted and made peace with Byzantium.[36] John ended his work with the feeling that all was right in the world; the peculiarity of equating the Catholic Franks with the pagan Persians, not to mention the Midianites of old, escaped him.

John of Biclar combined a pragmatic appreciation of the benefits of victory for Spain and the Goths with a certain providential view of recent history. He believed that God had worked marvels in his lifetime, not the least of them being the restoration of the power of the Goths through the military virtue of the

---

32 John, *Chronica* s.a. 580, 2.

33 Ibid., 569, 4; 570, 2; 571, 3; 572, 2; 573, 5; 574, 2; 575, 2; 576, 3; 577, *I Tib.* 2; 578, 4.

34 John's attitude towards the rebel is best seen in *Chronica* s.a. 579, 3; 582, 3. The lack of
    enthusiasm of prominent Catholics has been much discussed by modern historians. See for
    instance Hillgarth, 'Coins and Chronicles: Propaganda in Sixth-Century Spain and Its Byzan-
    tine Background,' *Historia* 15 (1966): 483–508; Roger Collins, 'Mérida and Toledo:
    550–585,' in *Visigothic Spain: New Approaches*, ed. Edward James (Oxford, 1980), 215–18.

35 Rebels put down: John, *Chronica* s.a. 588, 1; 589, 2; 590, 3. Victory over foreign enemies: s.a.
    589, 2.

36 Ibid., 590, 2.

heretic Leovigild. Leovigild had made his people a great power once again, so that they lacked only conversion to be compared to the Byzantines as effective champions of true religion.[37]

John's message was read and appreciated by his younger contemporary Isidore of Seville. Isidore, the most important Spanish thinker of the next generation, used John's chronicle in the course of his own historical writing – namely, the *History of the Goths* (composed about A.D. 619) and his own chronicle (first edition, A.D. 615).[38] Isidore was a wider and subtler political thinker than John; one cannot do justice to his variety in a short space.[39] Yet there are important points of similarity between the two men. Isidore shared John's devotion to the Gothic monarchy as the mainstay of Spanish Catholicism, his hostility to the enemies of that monarchy, and a propensity to measure Gothic achievements against the standard set by Byzantium. But where John was always a friend of the Empire, Isidore manifested a certain hostility to it. John showed Spain emulating a wholly admirable orthodox Empire; Isidore scorned the Empire and presented the Goths as surpassing the Romans of his day.

Reasons for Isidore's unfriendly attitude to the Empire can easily be found: the Byzantine province was the only part of Spain not under Gothic domination. The kings of Toledo, Isidore's patrons, were unwilling to tolerate this imperfection in their rule. Further, Isidore's family seems to have had a history of opposition to Byzantine rule in Spain.[40] At the same time, Isidore took a much dimmer view of Byzantine orthodoxy than John of Biclar had.[41] More interesting than the factors behind Isidore's hostility to the Empire, however, is the way in which he compared the rival powers, and the reasons he cited for preferring the Goths. These are most easily seen in the *History of the Goths*, where he states that the chief virtue of that people is strength. Their very name, says Isidore, connotes strength, 'and with truth,' he continues, 'for there has not been any nation in the world that has harassed Roman power so much.'[42] Isidore mentions many Gothic victories from the far past – especially their sack of Rome in 410 – but it is clear that their conquest of Spain was the climax of

---

37 John symbolically equates the Gothic kings from Leovigild with the Byzantine emperors by using Gothic regnal as well as imperial regnal years to date events. He is the first western chronicler to give this dignity to a non-Roman dynasty.

38 Isidore of Seville, *Chronica maiora*, ed. Th. Mommsen, CM 2: 391–488; *Historia Gothorum Wandalorum Sueborum*, ed. Th. Mommsen, CM 2: 241–303. The latter has recently been translated into English: *Chroniclers and Conquerors*, 81–110.

39 For a recent treatment see Marc Reydellet, *La royauté,* 505–606.

40 E.A. Thompson, *The Goths in Spain* (Oxford, 1969), 320–34.

41 Hillgarth, 'Historiography,' 297.

42 *Hist. Goth.* c. 2.

them all. Isidore's famous prologue makes this point clear. In former days, the old Romans desired and betrothed themselves to Spain with Romulean virtue; latterly, however, the Goths have seized and now enjoy that most blessed of lands as a reward for their many victories.[43]

The comparison between Gothic strength and Roman weakness is repeated in the summary: Many nations, says the historian, are scarcely permitted to reign by means of prayers and gifts; for the Goths, freedom is the result of battle.[44] The reference is obscure today, but was crystal clear to contemporaries. The Empire was in the midst of a grave crisis. It was threatened on the west by the Avars and the east by the Persians; the latter had occupied Egypt, Syria, and most of Asia Minor, while the Avars threatened Constantinople. At the time Isidore wrote the *History of the Goths*, the Roman military response had been pathetic. The emperor Heraclius had been forced to pay the Avars tribute and, after years of delay, had yet to take the field against the Persians.

Bribery of inconvenient barbarian enemies was a centuries-old Roman technique, as was the avoidance of battle. Yet to the bishop of Seville, they were signs of weakness; the Romans, by falling back on tribute, put themselves in the same category as the insignificant Sueves, who had ruled northwestern Spain with 'indolent sluggishness' until the more vigorous Goths had taken it away from them.[45]

It might be objected that a work so clearly designed as a panegyric of the ruling race of Spain is a bad place to look for Isidore's true opinions on war, peace, and the place of military virtue in the life of a Christian nation. Yet his *Chronicle*, written as a summary of universal history on a Christian plan, shows us essentially the same picture. In its later parts, the rise of the Goths in military strength and true piety is counterposed to imperial heresy and weakness. Romans are shown fighting civil wars, suffering defeats, and turning back enemies with gold instead of steel, while Spain enjoys the rule of kings whose justice and piety is supported by their military power.[46] Indeed, later editions of both the *Chronicle* and the *History of the Goths* gloat over the victories of Suinthila, who finally conquered the Romans and 'acquired absolute rule over the whole of Spain.'[47] This was the way of the world: as Isidore said in his *Ety-*

---

43 Ibid., prologue, 4.
44 Ibid., c. 69.
45 Ibid., c. 68.
46 Gothic progress: *Chronica maiora*, cc. 403, 407 (Leovigild), 408, 415, 416, 416a, 416b.
    Roman defeats: 404a, 409, 409a, 411, 412, 413, 414a (cf. the more favourable 414b, added
    after Heraclius' dramatic victories).
47 *Hist. Goth.* c. 62; cf. *Chronica maiora*, c. 416b.

mologies, 'Every kingdom of this world is obtained by war and extended by victories,' and this included Christian kingdoms.[48]

We know that Isidore's picture of a declining Empire and the rise of new and more militarily capable peoples struck a responsive chord in one of his earliest overseas readers. About 625, the second edition of Isidore's chronicle fell into the hands of an Italian who used it in the construction of a continuation of Prosper's chronicle. He, like Isidore, judged that he was seeing the final decline of the Roman Empire, in the world at large, and specifically in his native Italy.

Little is known about this writer – usually called the 'Copenhagen' Continuator, from the location of the single extant manuscript – except that he was from northern Italy and was a steadfast opponent of Arianism.[49] His work is a compilation, cobbled together from diverse sources, some of them unknown. Nevertheless, a consistent theme emerges from it.

The world of the Copenhagen Continuator is one where military virtue is an absolutely necessary attribute for a ruler. The history of Italy, as he saw it, demonstrated that only a strong ruler made prosperity possible; weak or divided leadership spelled ruin for a country.[50] Both his reading and his own experience taught the Copenhagen Continuator that the Romans had for a very long time failed to provide such leadership. Like Isidore, he scorned the emperors of his time for their ruinous civil wars and their preference for paying tribute to fighting. Recent disasters had convinced him that nothing more could be expected from them.[51]

The Continuator believed that the Lombards were now the true defenders of Italy. We are accustomed to think of the early Lombards as Gregory the Great saw them – as pitiless barbarians. A generation after Gregory, the Copenhagen Continuator regarded them and their captains as the only force strong enough to preserve internal peace and protect his country against hostile outsiders – notably the Franks. Indeed, in the face of Roman incapacity, he thought it inevitable that the Lombards would eventually rule all of Italy.[52]

The situation of the Copenhagen Continuator differed in one important respect from those of John and Isidore – in praising military success, they were directly or indirectly supporting a Catholic establishment. In 625, the Lombard

48 *Etymologiae* XVIII ii 1, as cited and discussed by Reydellet, *La royauté,* 514. Isidore was quoting from Tertullian. As Reydellet points out in n. 30, Tertullian was condemning war and victory; Isidore saw victory, rather, as the reward of virtue.
49 On the Copenhagen Continuator, see the edition *Continuatio Havniensis Prosperi,* in *Consularia Italica,* ed. Th. Mommsen, CM 1: 249–339, and my 'Heroic Kings and Unruly Generals: The "Copenhagen" Continuation of Prosper Reconsidered,' *Florilegium* 6 (1984): 50–70.
50 See esp. *Cont. Havn. Prosp.,* p. 337, nos 1, 2, 4.
51 Ibid., p. 338, nos 10, 11, 13; p. 339, nos 19, 20. Cf. Isidore, *Chronica maiora* cc. 409, 413.
52 *Cont. Havn. Prosp.,* p. 338, no. 8; p. 339, no. 21.

kings were yet Arians, and the Continuator could only hope for their conversion. Thus, while he blasted the Arians of the past in his account, he was discreetly silent about heresy among the Lombards – and full of praise for the pro-Catholic queen Theudelinda.[53]

The Continuator's regard for yet-unconverted heretics is very remarkable; he is, of our three authors, the strongest believer in the necessity of military might. He lived in a land divided into two hostile camps, a land where only strength could bring security. He dreamed of a united Italy, but had no hope that this would be achieved by an imperial revival. Rather, he looked to a new, more vigorous people, and hoped for the best.

Are these three writers, with their more positive attitude to military virtue, indicative of an important shift? I think so. The contrast between John of Biclar, Isidore, and the Copenhagen Continuator, on the one hand, and the Christian historians of the earlier period is striking. I am unaware of anything quite comparable to their attitude in earlier histories and chronicles – even those of the atypical chronicles of the Gaul of 452 and Hydatius. In the fifth and sixth centuries, as before, clerics had sought to insulate themselves from warfare. The worldly battles being fought around them were less important than the theological conflicts raging within the worldwide community of Christian Romans that extended beyond the area controlled by any earthly sovereign. This orientation influenced even those most interested in the changeable affairs of the world, the historians and chroniclers.

If the later chroniclers do not deceive us, the men of the seventh century seem to have felt more keenly the claims of their own countries. Religious conflicts between east and west, the precipitous decline of imperial influence and prestige, and the long disunity of the Latin world made the links between one former Roman province and another very tenuous. One could now be a Christian without being a Roman, and the descendants of Romans were ceasing to value that proud and ancient name.[54] In an increasingly fragmented world, both danger and opportunity pressed churchmen to accommodate themselves to the powers that were. Thus the enthusiasm of John and Isidore for Gothic kings; thus the hope of the Copenhagen Continuator for a strong king of his own.

If the alliance with warrior kings had its advantages for the church, it also had a darker side. Once orthodoxy and secular security were as seen as dependent on the local ruler, those who obeyed another were enemies. People who in

---

53 Anti-Arian anecdotes (derived from Isidore): *Cont. Havn. Prosp.*, p. 269, nos 23, 24. Theudelinda: ibid., p. 338, no. 9; p. 339, nos 15, 24.

54 See the remarks of Walter Goffart, 'Rome, Constantinople, and the Barbarians,' *American Historical Review*, 86 (1981), esp. 301; repr., with addenda, in *Rome's Fall and After* (London and Ronceverte, 1989), 1–32.

a former generation had been brothers were now considered foreigners, perhaps even a threat to the church. The way was open, for those who wished to take it, for Christian to fight Christian and for the church to bless them with something approaching a clear conscience.

6

Jonas, the Merovingians, and Pope Honorius: *Diplomata* and the *Vita Columbani*

IAN WOOD

The narrators of early medieval history never simply recorded events. Always writing, as they did, with a purpose, they were interpreters rather than mere record-keepers.[1] They made conscious choices in determining what to include and what to exclude from their narratives. They also made unconscious choices, hemmed in, as they were, like all historians, by received knowledge and literary forms. What holds true for the narrators of history is equally applicable to the narrators of hagiography.

It is one thing to note that historical writers and hagiographers in the early Middle Ages were interpreters. It is another to identify their deliberate intentions and their unconscious standpoints. Here the deconstruction of a text involves the construction of a context, and sometimes – indeed, often in the early Middle Ages – a single source provides the material for both exercises.[2] It is rare that enough early medieval sources overlap for it to be possible to keep the source to be deconstructed out of the initial construction. The dearth of material is such that there will always be argument as to whether a context is accurately specified. Moreover interpretations are open to endless revision, as new contexts are perceived and as old ones are rejected or modified.[3] What is

Versions of this paper were delivered at Kalamazoo and to the group which meets regularly at Bucknell under the aegis of Wendy Davies. The final version owes much to discussions with Walter Pohl.

1 See the seminal work of Walter Goffart, *The Narrators of Barbarian History (A.D. 550–800): Jordanes, Gregory of Tours, Bede, and Paul the Deacon* (Princeton, 1988).
2 See P. Fouracre, 'Merovingian History and Merovingian Hagiography,' *Past & Present* 127 (1990): 3–38. Fouracre may seem less optimistic about the possibility of deconstructing an early medieval text than I do, but it should be noted that I use the term 'deconstruction' in a broader sense than he does.
3 Fouracre, 'Merovingian History and Merovingian Hagiography,' 3. For an earlier attempt at interpreting Jonas' *Vita Columbani* – and one that is not necessarily incompatible with the pre-

important is the recognition of the author as an intelligent individual with a message or messages, however much, in reconstructing a context, one fails, necessarily, to give due weight to the integrity of all the sources used.

An enhanced recognition of the authors of our source material has been one of Walter Goffart's many contributions to historical work. It is no longer enough to reconstruct a narrative, accepting what is deemed to be accurate and discarding what is seen as inaccurate. Indeed, in trying to understand our sources, it is, ironically, often the case that the recording of a factual error by an early medieval author is more useful for the identification of that author's perspective than is any supposedly accurate recitation of 'fact.' Identifiable dislocations between event and record can provide a starting-point from which one may study an author's intentions. Certainly this approach may be argued for Jonas of Bobbio's *Vita Columbani*. So slight is the additional material available, both for reconstructing the events covered in the work and for understanding the context in which Jonas was writing, that his identifiable errors are a vital clue to what he was doing. Fortunately visible weak points, occurring at a number of important moments in the narrative, allow the historian to get behind the façade of the text.

This is not the place to attempt a wholesale deconstruction of Jonas' *magnum opus*, though it is necessary to sketch out the hagiographer's scheme and indicate some of the problems. In Book I, the Life of Columbanus himself, Jonas constructs his narrative to cover a series of themes: birth, entry into asceticism, *peregrinatio* to Gaul, entry into the desert, establishment of Luxeuil, re-entry into the secular community after exile from Luxeuil, and efforts to convert the heathen at Bregenz; he creates narrative closure with the foundation of Bobbio and the saint's death. The logic of this progression is, on the whole, echoed by the types of miracles described: life is made to seem more basic at Annegray and more cultivated at Luxeuil. This is more than simple hagiography: it is a carefully ordered thematic deployment of material. Moreover, it triumphantly bypasses the problems of Columbanus' theological failings, which included support for the Celtic Easter and probably for the Tricapitoline schismatics.[4] Further, the themes are all set against a political history that for the most part carries conviction, though marred by some obvious mistakes, such as the identi-

---

sent essay – see I.N. Wood, 'The *Vita Columbani* and Merovingian Hagiography,' *Peritia* 1 (1982): 63–80. What follows is a return to some of the ideas expressed in 1982, as well as a justification of the assertions to be found in I.N. Wood, *The Merovingian Kingdoms, 450–751* (London, 1994), 195. For a literary perspective on the *Vita Columbani*, see W. Berschin, *Biographie und Epochenstil im lateinischen Mittelalter* II, *Merowingische Biographie, Italien, Spanien und die Inseln im frühen Mittelalter*, Quellen und Untersuchungen zur lateinischen Philologie des Mittelalters Band IX (Stuttgart, 1988), 26–52.

4 I. Müller, 'Die älteste Gallus-vita,' *Zeitschrift für Schweizerische Kirchengeschichte* 66 (1972): 249.

fication of the ruling monarch at the time of Columbanus' arrival in Gaul.[5] Getting beyond these mistakes is not easy, since Jonas is by far the most important source for Frankish history in the first decade of the seventh century. What is one to make of his claim that Paris was in the hands of Theudebert in *ca* 610,[6] when, according to Fredegar, it was in the hands of Theuderic in 603/4?[7] Does this imply a takeover by Theudebert? Or is Jonas attempting to associate the aristocracy of Theuderic with his less obnoxious brother?[8]

Book II of the *Vita Columbani* cannot be analysed in the same way as Book I, not least because it was Krusch who combined the various chapters on the subsequent histories of Luxeuil, Bobbio, and Faremoutiers, all which have separate manuscript traditions, into a single whole: whether this was Jonas' intention is unclear.[9] Nevertheless, the various sections of the text provide opportunities for analysing Jonas' work, because of a series of cruces, some of them, at least, caused by monastic and theological developments after Columbanus' death. The account of Agrestius' opposition to Eustasius, for example, makes possible an exploration of some of the contradictions within early Columbanian spirituality and theology.[10] Agrestius' support for the Aquileian schismatics may well have been closer to the position of Columbanus, who criticised Vigilius' collapse before Byzantine pressure, than was that of Eustasius and Athala, Columbanus' successors, who supported the papal position.[11] The

---

5 On this, see below.

6 *VC* I 25.

7 Fred., IV 26.

8 One might note, by contrast, that the wicked Agrestius is said to have been 'Theuderici regis notarius': *VC* II 9.

9 Berschin, *Merowingische Biographie*, 26, demonstrates clearly that Book II is essentially Krusch's reconstruction. On the varying textual tradition of Book II, see also C. Rohr, 'Hagiographie als historische Quelle: Ereignisgeschichte und Wunderberichte in der Vita Columbani des Ionas von Bobbio,' *Mitteilungen des Instituts für Österreichische Geschichtsforschung* 103 (1995): 243–4. The individual sections on Bobbio under Athala, Luxeuil under Eustasius, and Faremoutiers under Burgundofara require separate analysis.

10 *VC* II 9–10; cf. Wood, *Merovingian Kingdoms*, 196–7.

11 Columbanus, ep. 5. 5, in *Sancti Columbani Opera*, ed. G.S.M. Walker, Scriptores Latini Hiberniae 2 (Dublin, 1970). Columbanus' stance is not as clear as it might have been, and Walker (p. xxxviii) notes internal discrepancies in the letter. Nor is Columbanus' stance helped by the tendency in the sixth-century West to regard Eutyches and Nestorius as closely associated (e.g., Columbanus, ep. 5. 10, 16: compare Nicetius of Trier in *Epistolae Austrasiacae* 7, ed. W. Gundlach, MGH Epistolae Merowingici et Karolini Aevi 1 [1892]). It is clear that Columbanus was seeking above all for clarification (ep. 5. 9–10, 13), but it is equally clear that he thought that the papacy had to defend itself against charges of heresy (ep. 5. 10–11), and that the Fifth (Ecumenical) Council (i.e., Constantinople) was, if rightly reported, in error (ep. 5. 10, 13).

probability that Agrestius reflected Columbanus' position more accurately than
did subsequent abbots of Luxeuil and Bobbio is, inevitably, ignored by Jonas,
who here, as elsewhere, attempted to imply that the Columbanian tradition was
unchanging.

To return to Book I, the descriptions of the arrival of Columbanus in Francia
and the subsequent foundations of Annegray and Luxeuil offer reasonable
opportunities for analysis. These passages deserve close attention, as they raise
a host of issues relating to the origins of the monasteries and to Jonas' description of those origins. With regard to the rights granted to Luxeuil after 613 and
to the foundation of Bobbio and the privilege that it later received, the charter
evidence, both Frankish and papal, fortunately provides some additional han-
dles, which will be grasped in due course.

In Book I of the *Vita Columbani*, Jonas of Bobbio records the foundation of
three monasteries by the Irish saint Columbanus: two of them, Annegray and
Luxeuil, were in Burgundy, and the third, Bobbio, in the Lombard kingdom.
According to Jonas, some while after his arrival in Gaul (we do not know how
long), Columbanus went to King Sigibert and the following debate took place
between the king and the saint:

Then the king began to ask him to stay inside the frontiers of Gaul and not leave them,
crossing to other peoples; he said he would prepare everything which he wanted. Then
he said to the king that he would not be enriched by the wealth of others, but would follow the herald of the Gospel, in so far as the weakness of the flesh did not get in the way:
'If any man,' he said, 'will come after me, let him deny himself, take up his cross and
follow me.' The king responded thus to such arguments: 'If you wish to take up the cross
of Christ and follow him, pursue the silence of a better wilderness, but do not leave the
soil of our jurisdiction to pass over to neighbouring peoples; rather add to your own
rewards and provide things useful for our salvation.' Having been given this choice, he
yielded to the king's persuasions, and sought the wilderness. There was at that time a
vast wilderness called the Vosges, in which there was a fortress which had been
destroyed long ago. It was called, according to ancient tradition, Anagrates. When the
holy man came there, although the place was harsh from the vastness of the solitude and
from the presence of rocks, he settled with his followers, content with slight consolation
of food, remembering the words that man should not live by bread alone, but, satisfied
by the word of Life, should luxuriate in the rich feast, as a result of which whoever tasted
it never knew hunger.[12]

---

12 *VC* I 6: 'Coepit tandem ab eo rex querere ut intra terminos Galliarum resederet nec eos ad
    alias gentes transiens se relinqueret: omnia quae eius voluntas poposcisset se paraturum. Tunc
    ille rege ait, non se aliorum opum fore ditaturum, sed evangelici praeconii, in quantum fragili-
    tas non obstat, sectaturum exemplum: "Qui vult," inquid, "post me venire, abnegat semet

The foundation of Luxeuil followed a little while later:

As he was already hemmed in by the presence of many monks, he began to consider whether he might discover a suitable place in the same wilderness where he might found a monastery, and he discovered a fortress which had once been protected with the strongest of fortifications, approximately eight miles from the aforementioned place. Earlier times had called it Luxovium. There hot baths [lit. waters] had been built with considerable care; there a large number of stone images filled the neighbouring woodland: these, ancient pagan times had honoured with miserable ritual and profane rites, and for them they performed execrable ceremonies; the place was frequented only by wild animals and beasts, a multitude of bears, wolves, and buffalo.[13]

Some twenty years later, having left the Merovingian kingdom, Columbanus reached the Lombard court:

Having been given the option of deciding where he wanted to live in Italy, it happened, by God's decision that, while he was living in the city of Milan, he wanted to destroy and burn away, with the caustic of scripture, the deceit of the heretics, that is, the perfidy of the Arians. Against them he wrote a book, full of learning. Meanwhile a certain man called Iocundus came to the king, and told him that he knew of a basilica of the blessed Peter, prince of the Apostles, in the solitude of the Appenine countryside. There he knew miracles happened: it was a place rich in fruitfulness, irrigated with waters, and well endowed with fish. They called the place, according to ancient tradition, Bobium, on account of a stream of the same name which flowed through the place; there was another called the Trivea. There Hannibal had once wintered, and had suffered great losses of

---

ipsum sibi, tollat crucem suam et sequatur me." Cui talia obicienti rex praebet responsa: "Si Christi crucem tollere et ipsum sequi desideras, potioris heremi sectare quietem, tantum ne, nostrae ditionis solo relicto, ad vicinas pertranseas nationes, ut tui praemii augmentum et nostrae salutis provideas oportuna." Data itaque obtione, obtemperavit regis persuasionibus, heremum petiit. Erat tunc vasta heremus Vosacus nomine, in qua castrum dirutum olim, quem antiquorum traditio Anagrates nuncupabant. Ad quem vir sanctus cum venisset, licet aspera vastitate solitudinis et scopulorum interpositione loca, ibi cum suis resedit, parvo alimentorum solamine contentus, memor illius verbi, non in solo pane hominem vivere, sed verbo vite satiatus, adfluenti dape habundare, quam quisquis sumptam esuriem nesciat in evum.'

13 *VC* I 10: 'Cum iam multorum monachorum societate densaretur, coepit cogitare, ut potioris loci in eodem heremo quereret, quo monasterium construxisset, invenitque castrum firmissimo olim fuisse munimine cultum, a supradicto loco distantem plus minus octo milibus, quem Luxovium prisca tempora nuncupabant. Ibi aquae calidae cultu eximio constructae habebantur; ibi imaginum lapidearum densitas vicina saltus densabant, quas cultu miserabili ritoque profano vetusta paganorum tempora honorabant, quibusque execrabiles ceremonias litabant; solae ibi ferae ac bestiae, ursorum, bubalorum, luporum multitudo frequentabant.'

men, horses, and elephants. When he came there, finding the basilica semi-ruined, he restored it with enormous effort, returning it to its original state.[14]

There is a fourth passage which is related to these three foundation stories. It concerns Columbanus' choice of the site of Bregenz as a base:

Theudebert promised to find him pleasant places inside his territories offering every opportunity to the holy man, and having neighbouring nations on all sides to be preached to. To these words the holy man said: 'If you offer the support of your promise, and if the harm of falsehood does not get in the way of your recognizance, let me be allowed to stay there a little and see what may be done, sowing faith into the hearts of the neighbouring people.' The king allowed him to stay wherever he wanted, and he sought out a place for the experiment, which was pleasing to him and his followers; and they found a place of which everybody approved, within the boundaries of Germania, but close to the Rhine, an *oppidum*, which had once been ruined, and which was called Bregenz.[15]

Unlike Annegray, Luxeuil, and Bobbio, however, Bregenz did not appeal to Columbanus as a site for a monastery.

Jonas himself seems to invite comparison of the three foundation stories, and resemblances in vocabulary (for instance, the recurrent *nuncupabant*) and theme suggest comparison with the description of Bregenz. Each place had a past: Annegray its fort, Luxeuil its baths, Bregenz its *oppidum*, and Bobbio its association with Hannibal. These earlier histories were well and truly finished: they were part of an old and failed world. The fort at Annegray was ruined, as

---

14 *VC* I 30: 'Qui, largita optione, ut intra Italiam, quocumque in loco voluisset, habitaret, ibi Dei consultu actum est, dum ille poenes Mediolanium urbem moraretur et hereseorum fraudes, id est Arriane perfidie scripturarum cauterio discerpi et desecrari vellet, contra quos etiam libellum florenti scientia ededit, vir quidem nomine Iocundus ad regem venit, qui regi indicat se in solitudine ruribus Appenninis basilicam beati Petri apostolorum principis scire, in quam virtutes expertus sit fieri, loca ubertate fecunda, aquis inrigua, piscium copia. Quem locum veterum traditio Bobium nuncupabant ob rivum in eo loco hoc nomine fluentem amnemque alium profluentem nomine Triveam; super quem olim Hannibal hiemans, hominum, aequorum, elefantorum atrocissime damna sensit. Ubi cum venisset, omni cum intentione basilicam inibi semirutam repperiens, prisco decori renovans reddidit.'

15 *VC* I 27: 'Pollicitusque est Theudebertus se repperire intra suos terminos loca venusta et famuli Dei ad omni oportunitate congrua proximasque ad predicandum nationes undique haberi. Ad haec: "Si," inquit vir Dei, "pollicitationis tuae adminiculum preberis, et vademonio falsitatis noxa non opponeretur, quantisper se moraturum ac probaturum, si in cordibus gentium vicinarum fidem serere valeat." Dedit ergo rex optionem, quacumque in partem voluisset, experimento quereret locum, qui sibi et suis placuisset; inquisitumque locum, quem favor omnium reddebat laudabilem, intra Germaniae terminos, Reno tamen vicina, oppidum olim dirutum quem Bricantias nuncupabant.'

were the baths of Luxeuil and the *oppidum* at Bregenz. Hannibal had lost men, horses, and elephants at Bobbio. Perhaps the long-vanished elephants were meant to contrast with the wild animals still present at Luxeuil when Columbanus arrived: bears, buffalo (or perhaps *bubalus* should be translated even more exotically as 'African gazelle,' in keeping with Hannibal's elephants), and wolves. There can be no doubt that Bobbio is intended to come off best from these comparisons, for it also had a Christian past: the site could already boast a church of Saint Peter, which was only *semiruta*: there *virtutes* happened. The topography of the place is sketched in a less general way, with two streams being named, perhaps reflecting Jonas' personal association with the Italian monastery.[16] In its precision, Jonas' description of Bobbio is almost comparable to Eigil's deliberate description of the site of Fulda, in his Life of Sturm, Boniface's disciple.[17] Like Jonas,[18] Eigil was a monk of the monastery whose site he was describing.

Unlike the foundations of Annegray and Luxeuil, that of Bobbio is accurately described and dated: Jonas ascribes this to the reign of King Agilulf. This is confirmed by a fundamentally authentic, but possibly interpolated, charter issued on 24 July, probably 613.[19] By contrast, the narration of the foundation of Annegray is almost certainly inaccurate. Jonas is probably correct in saying that Columbanus, after his arrival, went to the king. As a foreigner he would unquestionably have had to get official permission to remain in the kingdom.[20] Jonas dates the arrival, however, to the reign of Sigibert I, that is, before 575.[21] On the whole, historians have preferred to follow the implications of a comment made by Columbanus himself in a letter written to the Frankish bishops, apparently in 603, stating that he had been in Gaul for twelve years.[22] It seems, therefore, that Columbanus arrived in Gaul *ca* 591, a date which can be supported by another passage of the *Vita Columbani*, where Jonas places Columbanus' exile – an event which can be dated to 610[23] – twenty years after his entry into the Gallic wilderness.[24] By 591, Sigibert had been dead for fifteen years.[25] One

16 Compare the description of the land round the Trivea in *VC* II 3.
17 Eigil, *Vita Sturmi*, 7–9, ed. P. Engelbert, *Die Vita Sturmi des Eigil von Fulda*, Veröffentlichungen der Historischen Kommission für Hessen und Waldeck 29 (Marburg, 1968).
18 *VC* II 5.
19 *CDL* III 3–7, n. 1.
20 For the evidence of Anglo-Saxons passing through Merovingian Gaul, see I.N. Wood, 'Northumbrians and Franks in the Age of Wilfrid,' *Northern History* 31 (1995): 10–21.
21 *VC* I 6.
22 Columbanus, ep. 2, 6: for the date, Walker, ed. *Sancti Columbani Opera*, x–xi, n. 7.
23 Walker, *Sancti Columbani Opera*, x–xi. On the chronology of Columbanus see now Rohr, 'Hagiographie als historische Quelle,' 250–6.
24 *VC* I 20.
25 Gregory of Tours, *Hist.* IV 5.

might guess, therefore, that the king who received him was Sigibert's brother, Guntram, who died in 593.[26] His kingdom of Orléans unquestionably stretched as far as the Vosges,[27] and if the later kingdom of Theuderic II can be taken as having the same eastern border as that of his great-uncle, then Annegray must have been in territory that belonged to Guntram.[28] On the other hand, one might accept the subsequent testimony of the *Vita Agili* and conclude that Columbanus waited two or more years in Gaul before approaching Sigibert's son, Childebert II, who succeeded to the kingdom of Burgundy on Guntram's death.[29]

Jonas' account of the foundation of Annegray implies royal involvement, in that the king is determined that the saint should not leave his kingdom,[30] just as Theudebert will later be concerned that Columbanus should remain within Austrasia.[31] Yet, in stating that Columbanus refused any endowment from Sigibert ('non se aliorum opum fore ditaturum') in order to follow the Gospel precept of Luke 9: 23, Jonas appears to deny the possibility that the monastery itself was a royal foundation. His account of the discovery of Luxeuil suggests even more clearly that the saint himself was the only agent involved in the creation of his second monastery.[32] The idea of founding a monastery in a wilderness is, of course, a topos, and one that was propagated by a text that Jonas knew well, Athanasius' *Life of Anthony*, in which a disused fortress also features.[33] It is, moreover, unlikely that a walled *castrum* in Merovingian Gaul had no owner. In Anglo-Saxon England, at least, such sites seem to have been in royal hands.[34] In all probability the *castrum* of Luxeuil belonged to the king. It follows, therefore, that the monastery is likely to have been founded with royal support. Such was the belief of the author of the *Vita Sadalberga*, which states that Columbanus built Luxeuil *ex munificentia Childberti regis*,[35] and also of the author of the *Vita Agili*.[36] Unfortunately the *Vita Sadalbergae*, although in origin a text of the

26 Fred., IV 14.

27 Gregory, *Hist.* X 10.

28 Rohr, 'Hagiographie als historische Quelle,' 255, seems unnecessarily tentative on this point.

29 *Vita Agili* I 2.3, *Acta Sanctorum*, August VI (30th). One should perhaps note that one MS of the *VC*, A3, does emend Sigibert to Childebert in I 6.

30 *VC* I 6.

31 *VC* I 27.

32 *VC* II 10.

33 Athanasius, *Vita Antonii*, 12, PG 26, col. 862. That Jonas read the *Vita Antonii* is clear from *VC* I, *pref.* See also Berschin, *Merowingische Biographie*, 29.

34 Compare the grant of Burgh Castle to Fursey, Bede, *Historia Ecclesiastica*, III 19, ed. B. Colgrave and R.A.B. Mynors (Oxford, 1969).

35 *Vita Sadalbergae*, 1, ed. B. Krusch, MGH SRM 5 (Hanover, 1910). See Rohr, 'Hagiographie als historische Quelle,' 253.

36 *Vita Agili*, I 3. See Rohr, 'Hagiographie als historische Quelle,' 253. Rohr assumes, perhaps rightly, that the *Vita Agili* refers to the foundation of Annegray, though I tend to think Luxeuil.

seventh century, survives only in a reworked form,[37] while the *Vita Agili* is a late text.[38] It is necessary, therefore, to look more closely at the early evidence for Luxeuil to be certain of its royal origins.

There are, indeed, seventh-century indications that Luxeuil was a royal monastery.[39] By the last quarter of the century, it was used as a high-status prison: thus, both Leodegar of Autun and Ebroin were imprisoned there in the crisis of 675.[40] Other monasteries, like St-Calais,[41] which were used as prisons for the highest classes of prisoner, were very closely associated with the Merovingian family. The association between Luxeuil and the Merovingians might, of course, have post-dated its foundation. Chlothar II deliberately supported the house after Columbanus had left for Italy.[42] There are, however, yet earlier indications of a close association with the Frankish crown. Thus, Columbanus' Rule refers to prayers for the concord of kings,[43] a practice that he may have brought over from Ireland,[44] but which nevertheless shows the concern of his continental foundations for the Merovingian and Lombard monarchies. That Columbanus himself was expected to act as holy man for the Merovingian house might also be implied by the speech given by Jonas to Sigibert: 'add to your own rewards and provide things useful for our salvation.'[45] Further, even in Jonas' account, the assumption made by Theuderic and his grandmother Brunhild, that the saint would bless the king's bastards, implies that the Merovingians perceived Columbanus as being dependant on royal favour.[46] Such dependency is made clear by Jonas in the dialogue he gives Theuderic and Columbanus, when the king forced his way into the refectory at Luxeuil:

To this the king said: 'If you want the gifts of our generosity and the support of our supplies, you will allow everyone access everywhere.' The man of God replied: 'If you attempt to violate what has up to now been regulated by the reins of regular discipline, I

---

37 Berschin, *Merowingische Biographie*, 25.
38 Rohr, 'Hagiographie als historische Quelle,' 253.
39 Wood, 'The *Vita Columbani* and Merovingian Hagiography,' 76–8.
40 *Passio Leodegarii I*, 12–14, ed. B. Krusch, MGH SRM 5 (Hanover, 1910).
41 Gregory, *Hist.* V 14: Wood, *Merovingian Kingdoms*, 185.
42 *VC* I 30.
43 Columbanus, *Regula Monachorum*, VII, ed. Walker.
44 C.f. *Antiphonary of Bangor*, 40–56, ed. F.E. Warren, Henry Bradshaw Society (1893–5). For Merovingian prayers for the king in hagiographic sources, see M. Van Uytfanghe, *Stylisation biblique et condition humaine dans l'hagiographie mérovingienne [600–750]* (Brussels, 1987), 207–8: there is also a tradition of such prayers in Gallic church councils, starting with the council of Agde.
45 *VC* I 6.
46 *VC* I 19, also 18.

will not be supported by your gifts and subsidies from now on. And if you have come to this place in order to tear down the monastery of the servants of God and to undermine regular discipline, your kingdom will soon fall to its foundations and will be over-whelmed with the whole royal race.'[47]

Thus, the probability is that the Merovingians had some involvement in the foundation of Luxeuil, providing its founding abbot with land, as they did a host of seventh-century monasteries.[48]

Since the foundation of Luxeuil followed some while after that of Annegray, it is likely that it was supported either by his Childebert II or, if the foundation occurred after 596, by Childebert's son, Theuderic II.[49] The *Life of Sadalberga* associates the foundation of Luxeuil directly with Childebert,[50] while that of Agilus remarks more generally on Childebert's provision of a site for the foun-dation of a monastery.[51] Moreover, Jonas himself may provide an indication that Columbanus was associated at some point with Childebert. In describing the saint's arrival in Gaul, he says that Columbanus approached the king (iden-tified by Jonas as Sigibert), who ruled over two Frankish kingdoms, that of the Austrasians and that of the Burgundians:[52] the only king between Chlothar I and Chlothar II who can be so described is Childebert.[53] While Guntram may pos-sibly have founded Annegray, Childebert has at least as strong a claim to have done so and is likely to have been the founder of Luxeuil. There may also have been another agent involved in the foundation of this second monastery – Brun-hild, mother of Childebert and grandmother of Theuderic. She was known for her piety and was active in founding monasteries at Autun and in securing papal help for her foundations.[54] Moreover, the *Vita Agili*, albeit a later text, explicitly

47   VC I 19: 'Ad haec rex: "Si," inquid, "largitatis nostrae munera et solaminis supplimentum capere cupis, omnibus in locis omnium patebit introitus." Vir Dei respondit: "Si, quod nunc usque sub regularis disciplinae abenis constrictum fuit violare conaris, nec tuis muneribus nec quibusque subsidiis me fore a te sustentaturum. Et si hanc ob causam tu hoc in loco venisti, ut servorum Dei caenubia distruas et regularem disciplinam macules, cito tuum regnum funditus ruiturum et cum omni propagine regia dimersurum".'
48   F. Prinz, *Frühes Mönchtum im Frankenreich*, 2d ed. (Munich, 1988), 152–85: Wood, *Merovingian Kingdoms*, 184, 192–3: Wood, '*Vita Columbani* and Merovingian Hagiography,' 76–8.
49   Fred., IV 16.
50   *Vita Sadalbergae*, 1.
51   *Vita Agili*, I 3.
52   VC I 6. On the grammar of the passage see W. Fritze, *Untersuchungen zur frühslawischen und frühfränkischen Geschichte bis ins 7. Jahrhundert* (Frankfurt am Main, 1994), 263–4.
53   Rohr, 'Hagiographie als historische Quelle,' 252–3.
54   Gregory the Great, *Register*, XIII 7, 11, 12, 13, ed. P. Ewald and L.M. Hartmann, MGH Epis-tolae 2 (1892–9).

refers to concessions made to Luxeuil by Brunhild and Theuderic after Columbanus had left the monastery.[55]

Jonas' silence over royal involvement in the foundation of Luxeuil, and his error in identifying the king involved at Annegray, is remarkable. That Childebert founded Luxeuil was known later in the century at Sadalberga's Laon, and later still at Agilus' Rebais. Moreover, Jonas rightly named the Lombard king Agilulf as being responsible for the foundation of Bobbio, even though he was almost certainly an Arian at the time of the monastery's establishment, whether or not he was subsequently converted.[56] Heresy was a major concern for Columbanus, as is apparent in his letters. It was also a concern for his successor, Athala, who refused the offer of gifts from the Arian *dux* Ariowald.[57] Whatever their faults, heresy was not one of the failings of the descendants of Sigibert.

The problems of Jonas' accounts of the foundations of Annegray and Luxeuil cannot simply be ascribed to a lack of available information. Certainly, having been brought up at Bobbio,[58] and having been put in charge of the preservation of at least some of the community's archives,[59] Jonas is likely to have been more familiar with the history of Columbanus' Italian foundation than with that of Luxeuil or of Annegray. On the other hand, he was capable of providing a perfectly reasonable account of the death of Sigibert and the succession, first of Childebert, and then of Childebert's sons.[60] He himself tells us that he learnt much from Eustasius, Columbanus' successor at Luxeuil, and from other members of the Frankish church.[61] Moreover, the *Vita Columbani* was addressed to the abbots of Luxeuil and Bobbio, Waldebert and Bobolenus.[62] It would not have been difficult for the monks of Luxeuil to have provided Jonas with more accurate and more specific information on the foundation of their

55 *Vita Agili,* II 11.
56 Paul the Deacon, *HL* IV 6, claims that he was converted, and was then a benefactor of churches and restorer of bishops. This is denied by N. Christie, *The Lombards* (Oxford, 1995), 186, n. 2. That Agilulf had been Arian is clear from Paul's earlier comments and from the implications of Gregory the Great's letter on the baptism of Adaloald: *Register,* XIV 12. There is nothing, however, to disprove a conversion late in the reign: Columbanus, ep. 5, 17, suggests that the king was considering conversion to Catholicism, and 5, 8, makes no distinction between Agilulf's position and that of the unquestionably Catholic Theudelinda and Adaloald. See also 5, 14.
57 *VC* II 24: 'nam munera impii hac heretici hominis numquam in perpetuum suscipere respondit.' One should, however, contrast the relatively favourable account of Ariowald, when he refused to adjudicate between Bishop Probus of Tortona and Abbot Bertulf: *VC* II 23.
58 *VC* II 5.
59 Thus Athala hands Agrestius' letter to Jonas for safe keeping, *VC* I 9.
60 *VC* I 18.
61 *VC epistula,* I 11, 15, 17, 27, II 12: Müller, 'Die älteste Gallus-vita,' 248.
62 *VC epistula*: Rohr, 'Hagiographie als historische Quelle,' 230–3.

monastery, had they so wanted. That they did influence Jonas in certain ways is implied by the non-Neustrian tone of the *Vita Columbani*: thus Austrasians and Burgundians are singled out as being the most renowned peoples in Gaul.[63] Yet more interesting, in the light of the community's attachment to Chlothar II, Jonas specifically ascribes the murder of Sigibert I to the hand of Chlothar's father, Chilperic.[64] Whether or not the errors in the *Vita Columbani* were accidental, the fact that they were not corrected implies a connivance on the part of the monks of Luxeuil in the promulgation of an inaccurate version of Columbanus' first years in Francia.

Jonas, therefore, misdates the arrival of Columbanus in Francia, placing it in the reign of Sigibert I, whereas it is practically certain that it fell in that of Guntram. He implies royal acquiescence, but denies actual involvement in Annegray. He ascribes the foundation of Luxeuil to Columbanus alone, although it is more than probable that the monastery was royal. In all this he, or perhaps Luxeuil tradition, seems to have been intent on belittling the involvement of certain members of the Merovingian family in Columbanus' Frankish foundations: more precisely, while he is prepared to acknowledge, wrongly as it so happens, Sigibert's involvement in Columbanus' foundation of Annegray, he allows no room for Sigibert's brother, Guntram; ignores the work of his successor, Childebert II, at Luxeuil; and concentrates on the worst aspects of Theuderic II's relations with that monastery.

The treatment of the last of these kings is easy enough to understand. It was Theuderic's bastards whom Columbanus refused to bless when asked to do so by Brunhild, and it was Theuderic who drove Columbanus out of Luxeuil.[65] Brunhild was the victim of a massive *damnatio memoriae* directed against her by Chlothar II after Theuderic's death in 613.[66] The impact of this onslaught is most visible in the depiction of Brunhild presented *ca* 660 by Fredegar, himself a reader of Jonas' *Vita Columbani*.[67] Further, Luxeuil itself is likely to have been one of the epicentres of this *damnatio memoriae*, to judge by Chlothar's deliberate backing for the monastery, in the immediate aftermath of Brunhild's fall.[68]

---

63 *VC* I 6.
64 *VC* I 18. Jonas does not try to hide the relationsip between Chilperic and Chlothar, *VC* I 24.
65 *VC* I 19, 20.
66 I.N. Wood, 'Forgery in Merovingian Hagiography,' in *Fälschungen im Mittelalter*, MGH Schriften 33 (1988) 5: 374–5: see also J. Fontaine, 'King Sisebut's *Vita Desiderii* and the Political Function of Visigothic Hagiography,' in *Visigothic Spain: New Approaches*, ed. E. James (Oxford, 1980), 93–129.
67 For the date of Fredegar, W. Goffart, 'The Fredegar Problem Reconsidered,' *Speculum* 38 (1963): 206–41, repr. in *Rome's Fall and After* (London, 1989), 319–54.
68 *VC* I 30.

Jonas' failure to associate Childebert in any way with Columbanus is also worth noting:[69] At Luxeuil, prayers may well have been offered for the royal founder. That Brunhild and her descendents did encourage such prayers for their blood relations, though not necessarily at Luxeuil, may be indicated by the list of names scratched on the back of the Barberini diptych: arguably the names refer to Brunhild's relatives, and the list may have been made for liturgical commemoration.[70] Yet, although Childebert is nowhere depicted as an enemy of the saint, he is mentioned only to fill in the gap between the death of Sigibert and the accessions of Theudebert and Theuderic.[71] He was, however, the son of Brunhild, who was active with her grandson, Theuderic, in persecuting Columbanus after his failure to support the dynasty: it may well be that his descent from Brunhild made him *persona non grata* in Luxeuil tradition.

Jonas' coverage of Brunhild and Theuderic is possibly easier to explain than his silence over Guntram, a monarch highly regarded by Gregory of Tours for his piety,[72] and also the founder of one of the great monasteries of Burgundy, St-Marcel at Chalon[73] – a monastery, it should be noted, whose rights would often be cited in tandem with those of Luxeuil in later charters.[74] This silence over Guntram might be explained if one assumes either that Jonas had little hard knowledge about the community at Annegray or that Guntram was indeed dead by the time that the monastery was founded. Perhaps the silence, more than anything else, confirms the claim of the *Vita Agili* that Childebert was the king whom Columbanus initially approached.

Whatever the explanation for excluding Childebert and Guntram from the historical record, Sigibert was unimpeachable. Although he was the husband of Brunhild, he was not of her blood: Chlothar explicitly referred to him as a predecessor in his legislation.[75] He does not seem to have been regarded as responsible for Brunhild's actions: indeed, he was seen in or after 613, quite absurdly, as her first murder victim.[76] It was, thus, acceptable to ascribe the arrival of

---

69 Childebert's reign is, however, mentioned in *VC* I 18.

70 Wood, *Merovingian Kingdoms*, 135.

71 *VC* I 18.

72 On Gregory's view of Guntram, see Goffart, *Narrators*, 224–6; also M. Heinzelmann, *Gregor von Tours (538–94) 'Zehn Bücher Geschichte'* (Darmstadt, 1994), 49–69.

73 Fred., IV 1.

74 Cf. two documents from Rebais: *Diplomata Regum Francorum e Stirpe Merowingica*, ed. K.A.F. Pertz, MGH Diplomata (1872), no. 15; *Diplomata, Chartae, Epistolae, Leges Aliasque Instrumenta ad Res Gallo-Francicas Spectantia*, ed. J.-M. Pardessus, 2 vols (Paris, 1843–9), no. cclxxv. For a discussion of these documents, see below.

75 Chlothar II, *Edictum*, 14, in *Capitularia Regum Francorum* 1, ed. A. Boretius, MGH Capitularia (1883).

76 Fred., IV 22.

Columbanus in Francia to his reign. Indeed, to do so was acceptable in a very specific way: it coincided with Chlothar's own view of the limits of what could be recognized in his uncle's family.

There may have been another factor in placing Columbanus' arrival in Gaul in Sigibert's reign. According to Jonas, the saint arrived in Gaul at a moment 'when the strength of religion had almost been destroyed by the pressure of foreign enemies and the negligence of bishops.'[77] Jonas wished to depict Gaul as being in a state of military and religious collapse on Columbanus' arrival. Military collapse could scarcely be claimed for the 590s. If anything the danger of outside pressure was something that Jonas introduced from his own day, when Dagobert I was defeated by the Slavs under Samo in the early 630s[78] and Sigibert III failed to crush a revolt in Thuringia in 639,[79] that is, shortly before the composition of the Vita Columbani.[80] Yet, at least in the 560s, Sigibert had been under considerable pressure, having to buy off the Avars.[81] Whether or not this is a factor, Jonas' factual errors in ascribing Columbanus' arrival to the reign of Sigibert, and in ignoring royal involvement in the foundation of Luxeuil, are probably a reflection of the impact of propaganda launched against Brunhild and her offspring after 613, rather than an indication that Jonas had no sources for Columbanus' early years in Francia.

There is one further piece of evidence to suggest that seventh-century politics determined part of what Luxeuil chose to remember about its past. According to Jonas, Columbanus prophesied the success of Chlothar;[82] indeed, prophecies about Chlothar are one of the organizing principles of the Vita Columbani.[83] When the prophesy was fulfilled, Chlothar sent Eustasius to ask Columbanus, who was already installed at Bobbio, to visit him. The saint refused, but wrote to Chlothar, making certain criticisms of the king and certain demands. According to Jonas,

the king received the most pleasant gift rejoicing as if it were a pledge of agreement with the man of God; nor did he ignore the request with the evil of forgetfulness. He was zealous in protecting the aforesaid monastery with every assistance, he enriched it with

---

77 VC I 5: 'ubi tunc vel ob frequentia hostium externorum vel neglegentia praesulum religionis virtus pene abolita habebatur.'

78 Fred., IV 48, 68.

79 Ibid., 87.

80 Berschin, Merowingische Biographie, 27: Rohr, 'Hagiographie als historische Quelle,' 233.

81 Gregory of Tours, Hist. IV 23, 29: Menander, fragment 8, ed. R.C. Blockley, The History of Menander the Guardsman (Liverpool, 1985). The story was known later in Italy, Paul the Deacon, HL II 10.

82 VC I 20, 24, 29.

83 VC I 19, 20, 28, 29: Wood, 'Vita Columbani and Merovingian Hagiography,' 71.

annual income, increased its bounds on all sides, following the wish of the venerable Eustasius, and he was active to the best of his ability in helping those living there, out of love for the man of God.[84]

Jonas is much more forthcoming on Chlothar's support for the monastery than he is over its original foundation. And his comment on the increase of the monastic bounds might be seen as confirming the notion that Luxeuil was, from the start, a monastery founded on royal land. Nevertheless, the exact nature of the king's concessions are not specified. We may guess that they were similar to those spelled out in Chlothar's edict (the very edict, it should be noted, which acknowleged Sigibert's legislation), where the king stated that church property was to be defended by public agents, who were, however, not to violate earlier immunities.[85] Ecclesiastical rights are also mentioned in the *Praeceptio* of the same king, where, despite the vagueness of the text, it is clear that they involved the exclusion of fiscal agents from ecclesiastical property.[86]

Chlothar did not found Luxeuil, but he emerges in Book I of the *Vita Columbani* as the monastery's main secular benefactor: the work of Childebert or Theuderic is studiously ignored. So, too, is that of Brunhild. Yet to judge from the evidence of her correspondence with Gregory the Great, from whom she sought letters of privilege for her foundations at Autun, the dowager queen is likely to have ensured favourable treatment for any monastery with which she was involved. At Autun, her *xenodochium* and monastery of St Martin, together with Syagrius' nunnery of St Mary, received papal privileges at her request.[87] The privileges protected the possessions of the three foundations; placed the appointment of abbot or abbess in the hands of the king, who was to act in concert with the community in question; and forbade payment to king or bishop for any services. In addition, a case against an abbot or priest of the *xenodochium* was to be heard by the bishop of Autun and six episcopal colleagues; no abbot

---

84 *VC* I 30: 'Gratissimum munus rex velut pignus foederis viri Dei ovans recepit nec eius petitioni oblivionis noxam preponit. Omni presidio supradictum monasterium munire studet, annuis censibus ditat, terminos undique, prout voluntas venerabilis Eusthasii erat, auget omnique conatu ad auxilium inibi habitantium ob viri Dei amorem intendit.' This passage should be compared with *VC* I 24.

85 Chlothar II, *Edictum*, 14. On the context of the edict, A.C. Murray, 'Immunity, Nobility and the Edict of Paris,' *Speculum* 69 (1994): 18–39. On immunities, E. Ewig, 'Beobachtungen zur Klosterprivilegien des 7. und frühen 8. Jahrhunderts,' in Ewig, *Spätantikes und fränkisches Gallien* 2 (Munich, 1979), 411-26: W. Goffart, 'Old and New in Merovingian Taxation,' *Past & Present* 96 (1982): 11. See most recently P. Fouracre, 'Eternal Light and Earthly Needs: Practical Aspects of the Development of Frankish Immunities,' in *Property and Power in the Early Middle Ages,* ed. W. Davies and P. Fouracre (Cambridge, 1995), 53–81.

86 Chlothar, *Praeceptio*, 11–13, in *Capitularia Regum Francorum* 1, ed. A. Boretius.

87 Gregory I, *Register*, XIII 11, 12, 13.

or priest was to be removed from the institution to become a bishop; and nothing was to be taken from the poor. These immunities may give an indication of
the rights which were originally granted to Luxeuil, especially since Columbanus' monastery seems to have been a foundation of Brunhild's son. The
appointment of the abbot of Autun by king and community may seem particularly significant in the light of Theuderic's treatment of Columbanus: was
Columbanus any less of a royal abbot than his counterpart in Autun? Brunhild
wanted her family to keep an interest in her foundations. Yet this royal interest
did not mean that the monastic standards of the foundations were lax. Further,
the communities in Autun were well protected by Gregory the Great at her insistence. Not that a link between Brunhild and Gregory would have cut much ice
with Columbanian communities, who may have harboured some hostility
towards the pope, because of his treatment of their founding figure.[88] Gregory's
privileges for the communities at Autun do, however, suggest that Chlothar's
grants may not have been as significant an improvement in Luxeuil's position as
Jonas would have us believe. Even under Brunhild and Theuderic, Luxeuil may
have been well looked after, and this is indeed implied by the *Vita Agili*.[89]
Chlothar's edict of 614, moreover, shows the king protecting immunities which
had already been conferred, rather than conferring new ones.

It is nevertheless possible that Chlothar did improve the position of Luxeuil,
but what evidence there is for Luxeuil's rights is such that it is impossible to
determine what was granted by Brunhild and Theuderic, what by Chlothar, and
what by his son Dagobert I. Any reconstruction of Luxeuil's rights depends
entirely on analogy. The best analogy might be the royal immunity supposedly
granted by Dagobert I to Rebais in 635 or 636.[90] As it stands, this document
may be a forgery, although it certainly conforms to a type of immunity issued in
the course of the seventh century, and thus may indicate something of the rights
of a Columbanian foundation.[91] Rebais itself was founded by a disciple of
Columbanus, Audoin/Dado, for another disciple, Agilus, on royal land given by
Dagobert for his salvation. The king then supposedly granted an immunity for
the peace of the monks. The document claimed to uphold canonical authority
and granted a 'privilege of liberty' (*privilegium libertatis*) of the sort to be
found at Agaune, Lérins, Luxeuil and St Marcel, Chalon, 'following the consti-

---

88 See the explanation offered by Berschin, *Merowingische Biographie*, 30, to explain the
    absence of Gregory among the models cited by Jonas.
89 *Vita Agili* II 11.
90 Pertz, *Diplomata*, no.15; also Pardessus, *Diplomata*, no. cclxx .
91 Fouracre, 'Eternal Light and Earthly Needs,' 57, n. 7. For an example of such an immunity,
    Marculf, *Formulae* I 3, in *Formulae Merowingici et Karolini Aevi*, ed. K. Zeumer, MGH Formulae (Hanover, 1886).

tutions of bishops and according to royal sanction' (*iuxta constitutiones pontifi-cum, per regalem sanctionem*). This immunity protected all property granted by the king, or indeed anyone else, from the action of bishops or others. No one was to have power over, or to expect payment of gifts from, the monastery. No bishop could enter except to pray. On the death of an abbot, the monks were to elect his successor. No one, not even a judge, was to defraud the monastery or take anything from it. Those who did so would be fined. Judges could not even enter to hear cases or raise fines. Any income which the king might have expected from the community's holdings was to be used to light the monastery.[92]

Whether or not the Rebais immunity of 635/6 is a forgery, the essentials of Dagobert's grant were confirmed the following year, at the royal court at Clichy, by Bishop Burgundofaro, who claimed to be following the example of Bishop Canderic of Lyons and the documents (*litteras*) of Dagobert.[93] By this exemp-tion the holdings of the monastery were confirmed inviolate; a new abbot was to be elected by the congregation of monks; the community could choose whichever bishop it wanted to bless altars, consecrate chrism, and convey holy orders; no bishop or archdeacon of Meaux was to have power over the monastery's property, or of ordination, nor were they to expect gifts for any ser-vices; no bishop should enter the monastic enclosure without being invited, and, if he was invited, he should leave as soon as he had done what was required of him. Monks, meanwhile, should pray for the state of the church and the safety of king and country, a requirement which may be compared with the prayers for the concord of kings specified in Columbanus' Rule.[94] The abbot should correct the monks according to the Rule of Benedict and Columbanus.

Although the exemption for Rebais is the earliest of its sort to survive, it clearly drew on rights established elsewhere, not least at Luxeuil. As Burgundo-faro's exemption states: 'And let episcopal posterity not think that we have decreed this as a result of our own thought, since it has been ordered already under the norm of this constitution, at the site of Agaune, the monasteries of Lérins, and Luxeuil, and the basilica of the Lord Marcellus, both as regards the liberty of the inhabitants and of anything given to them.'[95] Clearly Agaune,

---

92 Fouracre, 'Eternal light and earthly needs,' 68–78.
93 *Diplomata,* cclxxv, ed. Pardessus; E. Ewig, 'Das Formular von Rebais und die Bischofsprivi-legien der Merowingerzeit,' in *Spätantikes und fränkisches Gallien* 2: 456–84.
94 Columbanus, *Regula Monachorum,* VII.
95 *Diplomata,* cclxxv, ed. Pardessus: 'Et ne hoc nos propriis deliberationis instinctu sacerdotalis posteritas aestimet decrevisse, quum etiam sub huius constitutionis norma Agaunensium locum, imoque et monasteria Lirinensium, Luxoviensium, vel basilica domini Marcelli, tam de inhabitatoribus libertatem, quam a quibuscumque ibidem aliquid delegatum, eatenus fuit sancitum.'

Lérins, Luxeuil, and St Marcel at Châlon-sur-Saône already had some, if not all, of the privileges in question.[96] The exemption of 636/7, therefore, is a clue to the rights held by Luxeuil during Dagobert's reign, and possibly earlier.

Whether or not Burgundofaro's exemption sheds light on the status of Luxeuil in or after 613, Rebais and a number of individuals associated with its exemption appear in the *Vita Columbani*, and help to define the audience of the work. Audoin's foundation of the monastery in the aftermath of Columbanus' ejection from Luxeuil is itself described: Dado 'built a monastery in the territory of Brie on the stream Resbacis following the Rule of the aforesaid man.'[97] Jonas also records Eustasius' cure of Agilus, who was abbot of Rebais at the time of Burgundofaro's grant in 636/7.[98] More important, the donor of the exemption, Burgundofaro, is present as a witness to a miracle in Book II of the *Vita Columbani*.[99] His sister, Burgundofara, appears in Book I and her presence looms over much of the second book,[100] even though she herself is largely absent from the narrative. This absence, however, is itself significant: since she was still living Jonas was almost certainly concerned not to give her any cause for pride.[101] He probably, therefore, regarded her and her brother as part of the audience of the *Vita Columbani*. Among the signatories to the exemption were Donatus of Besançon, Acharius of Noyon, and Amandus. Donatus appears in Jonas as Columbanus' godson, and as bishop and founder of the monastery called Palatium.[102] Acharius is cited as one of the many pupils of Eustasius who became a bishop.[103] Amandus does not appear in the main body of Jonas' text, but in the prefatory letter to Waldelenus and Bobolenus the hagiographer relates how he worked for three years with Amandus in the regions of the Scarpe, the Scheldt, and Elno.[104] Amandus was also the founder of the monastery of St-Amand-les-Eaux: a monastery which claimed to have a papal privilege, although the surviving privilege, said to have been granted by Pope John IV in

96 Prinz, *Frühes Mönchtum im Frankenreich*, 85–7: on the early development of the Mero-vingian immunity see B.H. Rosenwein, 'Inaccessible Cloisters: Gregory of Tours and Epis-copal Exemption,' (forthcoming).

97 *VC* I 26.

98 *VC* II 8.

99 *VC* II 21.

100 *VC* I 29; II 7, 10, 11-22.

101 Wood, '*Vita Columbani* and Merovingian Hagiography,' 67. See the comments of Jonas in *Vita Columbani*, *epistola* to Waldebert and Bobolenus, and in II 2, 16 on pride, and II 25 on its avoidance by Leubardus and Meroveus.

102 *VC* I 24.

103 *VC* II 8.

104 *VC epistola*.

642, is known to be a forgery.[105] At all costs the signatories to Burgundofaro's exemption and the audience of the *Vita Columbani* are likely to have overlapped substantially.[106]

Luxeuil and the pro-Columbanian clerics of the Merovingian kingdom were not, however, the only audience of the *Vita Columbani*. Equally important was Bobbio. To judge by the contrasting foundation stories of Annegray, Luxeuil, and Bobbio, the last held pride of place in Jonas' affections. Certainly its legal status was of greater concern to Jonas than was that of Luxeuil. Jonas balances his account of Chlothar's grants to Luxeuil in Book I with an account of the grant of a privilege to Bobbio by Pope Honorius in Book II. It is an account which is rendered all the more eye-catching in that the chapter which covers the issue, the so-called *Vita Bertulfi abbatis*,[107] is anything but a traditional *vita*: half of it is concerned simply with the acquisition of the papal privilege. Further, Bertulf's life, and thus presumably his success in gaining the privilege, is explicitly set up as a model for succeeding generations:

Therefore what is now known to have happened in our times, we ought in no way to pass over because we are overcome by the silent sleep of negligence, so that just as the examples of our predecessors generate a richer zeal for religion among us, so afterwards the profitable deeds of our times may be fruitful for posterity, and while we set out things worthy of imitation for others, we may more often set out things worthy of commemoration for ourselves.[108]

In his dispute over episcopal jurisdiction with Bishop Probus of Tortona, Bertulf, abbot of Bobbio, appealed to the Lombard king Ariowald. The king insisted that the issue had to be decided by the church, and he was prepared to allow and make provision for an appeal to the pope.[109] Ariowald was unquestionably an Arian, and he had previously caused trouble for the monks of Bobbio.[110] His support for Bertulf, however slight, provides a contrast to the harassment of the monastery at the hands of a Catholic bishop, just as the

---

105 *Diplomata*, cccii, ed. Pardessus: H.H. Anton, *Studien zu den Klosterprivilegien der Päpste im frühen Mittelalter* (Berlin, 1975), 71, n. 74.
106 Berschin, *Merowingische Biographie*, 41, is optimistic about the early readership of the *Vita Columbani*, because he does not distinguish between seventh-century and later *vitae*.
107 *VC* II 23.
108 *VC* II 23: 'Quae ergo nunc nostris noscuntur patrata temporibus, nequaquam silendo negligentiae somno torpentes pretermittere debemus, ut sicut nobis precendentium exempla uberius religionis studia generant, ita postmodum posteritate nostrorum temporum acta augmenta pariant; dum aliis imitanda propagamus, nobis sepius memoranda opponimus.'
109 *VC* II 23.
110 *VC* II 24: although later in Krusch's text, this event antedates Ariowald's accession.

actions of Chlothar and Agilulf stand as criticism of Brunhild and Theuderic. Bertulf's appeal was to result in the surviving privilege granted by Pope Honorius to Bobbio in 628.[111] By this, the pope took Bobbio directly under his jurisdiction, excluding all other ecclesiastical power. No bishop should extend his authority over the monastery and, unless invited by the prior, should not even celebrate mass there. The prior was to be responsible for his monks, following the rules of paternal tradition. Jonas describes Bertulf's meeting with Honorius and the concession of the privilege clearly, if concisely: at the end of their discussions, Honorius 'granted the gift which had been hoped for: he conferred the privilege of the apostolic see, by which no bishop was to try to dominate the aforesaid monastery in any way.'[112]

The precision with which Jonas describes the granting of the privilege is sharper than that used in the account of Chlothar's reaction to Columbanus' demands. It also contrasts markedly with the absence of any clear reference to the original grants which had instituted Columbanus' foundations in Francia. In part the contrast can be attributed to Jonas' own involvement in securing the privilege. He accompanied Bertulf to Rome. The visit to the pope must have been memorable. So, too, though for less pleasant reasons, was the return journey. Bertulf came close to dying of fever, and was cured only after seeing a vision of Saint Peter.[113] The impact of the journey on Jonas could easily be thought to explain the attention given to it in the *Vita Columbani*. Nevertheless, a purely personal explanation is probably not wholly satisfactory for the emphasis placed on the privilege. Literary questions may also have impinged: whereas a hagiographer had an abundance of 'topoi' relating to the wilderness when describing the founding of a monastery, Jonas had no obvious model when it came to describing the acquisition of a papal privilege: if the subject was going to be covered, it had to be set out in full. Arguably more important, as his account of Chlothar II's concessions to Luxeuil shows, Jonas was as interested in the development of a monastery's rights as in its original foundation, which, in the case of Luxeuil, he or his sources seem to have been concerned to misinterpret.

Bobbio received its papal privilege in 628. Luxeuil may have received one at approximately the time that Jonas wrote the *Vita Columbani*. Book I appears to have been completed in 641, and Book II a year or so later.[114] It is certainly pos-

111 C. Cipolla, *Codice diplomatico del monastero di S Columbani di Bobbio*, Fonti per la storia d'Italia 52 (Rome, 1918), 1: 100–3, n. 10.
112 *VC* II 23: 'praebuit optatum munus, privilegia sedis apostolicae largitus est, quatenus nullus episcoporum in praefato caenubio quolibet iure dominare conaretur.'
113 *VC* II 23.
114 Berschin, *Merowingische Biographie*, 27. On the date of the *Vita Columbani* see also Rohr, 'Hagiographie als historische Quelle,' 233.

sible that Pope John granted a privilege to the monastery in 641: the surviving privilege is a forgery, although it may have an authentic core.[115] If, at the time that Jonas was writing, Luxeuil received a privilege similar to that granted by Honorius to Bobbio,[116] this might further explain his emphasis on the 628 grant and his insistence on Bertulf's Life being a model to be followed. We may guess that the Bobbio privilege of 628 was known in Luxeuil before the latter monastery was itself the recipient of a privilege, probably in 641,[117] and it is likely that Bobbio inspired Luxeuil to seek a papal charter for itself.

One might, however, ask if there is any relationship between Luxeuil's apparently earlier independence from a bishop, as suggested by the Rebais exemption, and Bertulf's determination to appeal against Bishop Probus of Tortona. Certainly there are parallels in Burgundofaro's charter and Honorius' privilege in excluding bishops from the monasteries and setting the prior/abbot up as being responsible for monastic standards, but there are no clear verbal similarities.[118] Moreover, Honorius' privilege differs in one crucial respect from that granted by Burgundofaro: seventh-century episcopal exemptions and royal immunities free the monastery from intervention by the grantor or his agents, while papal privileges exempt the monastery from the local bishop but arrogate the *dictio* to the papacy:[119] in Jonas' words, Honorius 'conferred the privilege of the apostolic see, by which no bishop was to try to dominate the aforesaid monastery in any way.'[120] Nevertheless, despite these differences, papal and episcopal concessions of the mid-seventh century represent a growing concern about monastic liberty, in both Italy and Francia, which impinged on Jonas as he constructed the *Vita Columbani*.

Bertulf's concerns are likely to have influenced Jonas in his attitudes towards monastic rights in general. Further, it was he who had originally asked Jonas to

---

115 *Diplomata* ccxcix, ed. Pardessus; Anton, *Studien zu den Klosterprivilegien*, 59, with n. 57. On the early privileges for Columbanian houses see also E. Ewig, 'Bemerkungen zu zwei merowingischen Bischofsprivilegien und einem Papstprivileg des 7. Jahrhunderts für merowingische Klöster,' *Vorträge und Forschungen* 20, ed. A. Borst, *Mönchtum, Episkopat und Adel zur Gründungzeit des Klosters Reichenau* (Sigmaringen, 1974), 214–49, where an attempt is made to reconstruct the papal privileges granted to Columbanian houses in 641 and 643.

116 Although Anton, *Studien zu den Klosterprivilegien*, 55–92, points to the significance of the Honorius privilege as a model for subsequent privileges, the surviving evidence of the interpolated 641 privilege of John IV for Luxeuil suggests that a different model was followed at Luxeuil: Ewig, 'Bemerkungen zu zwei merowingischen Bischofsprivilegien,' 232–45.

117 Ewig, 'Bemerkungen zu zwei merowingischen Bischofsprivilegien,' 243.

118 Ewig, ibid. 232–41, considers the similarities between the (altered) John IV privilege of 641 and Burgundofaro's exemption for Rebais.

119 I am indebted to Professor Barbara Rosenwein for discussion of this topic.

120 *VC* II 23.

write the Life of Columbanus. The *Vita Columbani* and the papal privilege for Bobbio can usefully be seen as casting light on each other. That Jonas was interested in Merovingian monastic immunities is not directly apparent from his text. Simple prosopography, however, suggests that the *Vita Columbani* and episcopal immunities were being discussed by one and the same group of individuals. Like the Honorius privilege, Frankish immunities are likely to have weighed on Jonas as he wrote. This influence could have been a factor, along with the *damnatio memoriae* of Brunhild and her descendants,[121] and with the changing spirituality of Luxeuil, in Jonas' presentation of Columbanus' Merovingian foundations.

In the *Vita Columbani*, Jonas describes three monastic foundations,[122] and two subsequent concessions of rights: one by Chlothar II to Eustasius, following a request by Columbanus, and the other by Honorius in his privilege for Bobbio. In the foundation stories, Jonas seems to downgrade the role of the descendants of Brunhild, most especially Theuderic II, though whether he did so consciously, of his own accord, or as the heir to Luxeuil tradition, is open to question. To judge by Brunhild's work at Autun, Chlothar's grants to Luxeuil may not have greatly improved the monastery's standing. In caring for her foundations at Autun, indeed, Brunhild had already involved the papacy. Nevertheless, Chlothar may have enhanced the position of Luxeuil. The concessions he made to Columbanus, at least according to Jonas, are paralleled, and indeed trumped, in Book II by Pope Honorius, who removed Bobbio from episcopal jurisdiction. Honorius' privilege eclipsed anything Brunhild had secured for Autun, and anything she or her descendants might have granted to Luxeuil, despite the fact that Bertulf's appeal to the papacy may have been inspired by what he knew of the rights of Columbanus' Gallic foundation.

Although Columbanus was Jonas' prime subject, partly as a result of the politics of 613, partly for personal reasons, and partly reflecting the ecclesiastical concerns of his own generation, the hagiographer described the immunities obtained by Luxeuil after the saint's departure, and by Bobbio after the saint's death, with more precision and accuracy than he described the original foundation of the monasteries in question. Yet by trying to understand the original foundations, and so by seeing the extent to which Jonas misrepresented the late sixth century, the modern historian can be more specific in defining which issues affected Jonas at the time of writing. The interpretation of the *Vita Columbani*, like that of any early medieval text, shows just how far construction and deconstruction are symbiotically connected for the early medievalist.

---

121 Wood, '*Vita Columbani* and Merovingian Hagiography,' 70–1.
122 He also mentions other foundations in passing: e.g., Besançon, *VC* I 14: Faremoutiers, *VC* II 7.

7

Post vocantur Merohingii:
Fredegar, Merovech, and 'Sacral Kingship'

ALEXANDER CALLANDER MURRAY

Lord! said my mother, what is all this story about?
– A Cock and a Bull, said Yorick.

Tristram Shandy, IX , ch. 33

To judge from surveys of Frankish history, modern scholarship has embraced the idea that the Merovingian kings believed themselves to be descended from the gods, specifically a divine sea creature.[1] As scholarly notions go, this idea is not a trifle; nor is it new, having been around since the mid-nineteenth century. In its modern form, it tends to be associated with a particular understanding of the Frankish state; religion, in this view, is the true foundation of primitive social and political organization, and divine descent, as an essential component in the

I am very grateful to Edward James, Roger Collins, and the dedicatee of this volume for advice on a variety of points. A version of the piece was presented to the conference 'Culture and the Creation of Identity in the Early Medieval West,' Centre for Medieval Studies, University of Toronto, 2 November 1996.

1 Herwig Wolfram, *Das Reich und die Germanen: zwischen Antike und Mittelalter* (Berlin, 1990), 298 f.; now translated by Thomas Dunlap, *The Roman Empire and Its Germanic Peoples* (Berkley and Los Angeles, 1997), 208 f. Eugen Ewig, *Die Merowinger und das Frankenreich* (Stuttgart, 1988), 77 f. Hans K. Schulze, *Vom Reich der Franken zum Land der Deutschen: Merowinger und Karolinger* (Berlin,1987), 76–80. E. Zöllner, *Geschichte der Franken bis zum Mitte des sechsten Jahrhunderts* (Munich, 1970), 5, 178. As the following notes will show, the idea has particularly strong roots in German scholarship. In English-language scholarship, see Patrick J. Geary, *Before France and Germany: The Creation and Transformation of the Merovingian World* (New York and Oxford, 1988), 85, 89, and cf. 94 ('almost magical force of Merovingian blood'); and Ian Wood, *The Merovingian Kingdoms, 450–751* (London and New York, 1994), 37 f., 40, 44; cf. his 'Gregory of Tours and Clovis,' *Revue Belge de philologie et d'histoire* 63 (1985): 267 n. Wood's views may better be associated with older approaches rather than the recent perspective of German scholarship. The latter seems influential in a sur-

'charisma' of Merovingian kings, shows that Frankish kingship rested to a significant degree upon the 'sacral' roots of an archaic type of Germanic kingship.[2]

Primitive religious beliefs are commonly thought to be expressed through myth. The divine descent of the Merovingian kings, too, is said to be accompanied by a myth, propagated by the royal house itself; the myth is supposed to appear in the *Chronicle* of Fredegar, written about 660, where it is associated with the conception and birth of Merovech, a mid-fifth-century king, and founder of the Merovingian house.[3] In epitomizing Gregory of Tours' account of the reign of Chlodio, Fredegar adds a story about a strange encounter on the seashore between Chlodio's wife and a creature from the sea.

Fertur, super litore maris aestatis tempore Chlodeo cum uxore resedens, meridiae uxor ad mare labandum vadens, bistea Neptuni quinotauri [= Minotauri] similis eam adpetisset. Cumque in continuo aut a bistea aut a viro fuisset concepta, peperit filium nomen Meroveum, per co regis Francorum post vocantur Merohingii.[4]

It is said that, when Chlodio was staying with his wife on the seashore in the summer, his wife went to the sea around noon to bathe and a beast of Neptune resembling the *quinotaur* [= Minotaur] sought her out. Right away she conceived by either the beast or her husband and afterwards gave birth to a son called Merovech, after whom the kings of the Franks were later called Merovingians.

The modern account of Merovech's conception as an expression of Germanic myth begins with Karl Hauck.[5] Hauck was the creator of an exegetical framework designed to detect and explain fragments of Germanic myth and religious practice embedded in the sources of antiquity and the early Middle

vey of a different kind: Michael Richter, *The Formation of the Medieval West: Studies in the Oral Culture of the Barbarians* (New York, 1994), 20. Edward James, *The Franks* (Oxford, 1988), 163, on the other hand, explicitly rejects Germanic myth as the origin of the Merovech tale.

2 For the intellectual foundations of sacral kingship theory see Eve Picard, *Germanisches Sakralkönigtum: Quellenkritische Studien zur Germania des Tacitus and zur altnordischen Überlieferung* (Heidelberg, 1991). For comments and literature on some of the broader problems, of which sacral kingship is only a part, see Walter Goffart, 'Two Notes on Germanic Antiquity Today,' *Traditio* 50 (1995): 9–30.

3 Since Walter Goffart, 'The Fredegar Problem Reconsidered,' *Speculum* 38 (1963): 206–41 (repr. in his *Rome's Fall and After* [London, 1989], 319–54), and A. Erikson, 'The Problem of Authorship in the Chronicle of Fredegar,' *Eranos* 63 (1965): 47–76, theories of multiple authorship of the *Chronicle* have largely been abandoned. See also Andreas Kusternig, trans., 'Die vier Bücher der Chroniken des sogennanten Fredegar,' in *Quellen zur Geschichte des 7. und 8. Jahrhunderts*, ed. Herwig Wolfram (Darmstadt, 1982), 9–13; and now Roger Collins, *Fredegar*, Authors of the Middle Ages 13 (Aldershort, Hunts., and Brookfield, Vermont, 1997).

4 Fred. *Chron.* III 9.

5 'Lebensnormen und Kultmythen in germanischen Stammes- und Herrschergenealogien,' *Saeculum* 6 (1955): 186–223.

Ages. Hauck's conceptual models depended heavily on products of the comparative study of religion; he expanded the scope for applying this material by using terminology that he derived from the Latin sources by wrenching terms from their original contexts, redefining them, and generalizing them into genres, types, and models of mythic discourse and cultic practice. In Hauck's scheme, the circumstances surrounding Merovech's birth constitute an *origo*, an old cult myth of the Franks explaining the origin of the people and their royal house. The *origo* describes the begetting of the royal lineage by the chief god of the Franks through the *primus rex*, their first king. The god in question, Hauck believes, was the OHG Frô, the equivalent of Freyr of Scandinavian sources, a representative of the Vanic powers of fertility; the myth alludes to a process of temporary divinization by which Chlodio became the god, who took the form of a divine sea creature, half man and half bull. This theriomorphic divinization is demonstrated by the fact that Merovech's conception is said to be effected 'aut a bistea aut a viro,' a phrase Hauck reads to mean 'by both the beast and the husband.' The *origo* myth, Hauck argues, is also linked to *usus*, cult practice, repeatable acts celebrated as part of the state cult of the Franks. Here he discovered one of the cherished motifs of comparative religion, the holy marriage between representatives of divine powers. Details of the cult can also be detected in the bathing, which represents the purificatory preparation of the bride; in the season, the time of a midsummer festival; and in the location, the beach as the meeting zone of the elements. In Hauck's reconstruction, the myth and the cult practice associated with it represent the beginnings of the lineage (*primus rex*) and the people it leads. To meet the objection that such *primordia* should lie in the dim past and can hardly be applied to a fifth-century king such as Chlodio, Hauck argues that primordial myths could be transferred to heroes of more recent vintage, who were glorified as representatives of the original divine ancestor (*Stammvater*); Fredegar's text, in calling the dynasty *Merohingii*, presupposes such an ancestor with the name *Mero*. Despite its association with Chlodio, the Merovingian *origo* is, in Hauck's view, one of the true old cult myths of the pre-Christian state religion of the Germanic peoples.

Hauck's reading can be traced in many recent accounts of the Fredegar passage.[6] It is now generally claimed, for example, that the eponymous hero of the Merovingian dynasty was not Merovech, the historical king, but a mythical Mero; Merovech appears in Fredegar's version as a result of contamination.

6 O. Höfler, 'Abstammungstraditionen,' § 15, RGA 1: 26 f.; R. Wenskus, 'Bemerkungen zum Thunginus der Lex Salica,' in *Festschrift Ernst Percy Schramm zu seinem siebzigsten Geburtstag*, ed. P. Classen and P. Scheibert (Wiesbaden, 1964), 1: 234–6; and 'Chlodio,' RGA 4: 477; H.H. Anton, svv. 'Merowech' and 'Merowinger,' *Lexikon des Mittelalters*, vol. 6 (Munich, 1993), 542 f.; H. Moisl, 'Anglo-Saxon Royal Genealogies and Germanic Oral Tradition,' *Journal of Medieval History* 7 (1981): 223–6; and cf. his 'Kingship and Orally Trans-

The divine progenitor of the Merovingians is supposed to be Frô, in the form of a bull deity. Even the legendary and real sexual practices of the Merovingians are interpreted as an extension of their role as agents of Vanic fertility. The Merovingians of historical times are said to have continued to hedge their kingship with ideology, symbols, and ritual derived from pagan times, prime exhibits from the early Middle Ages of an ancient form of sacral kingship.

Those who champion these ideas also claim to find support for them outside Fredegar. In particular, two interesting, but rather minor, objects in the archaeological record of the Franks have taken on a disproportionate role in substantiating the association of the Merovingians with a bull deity.[7]

The first of these is a small bull head found among the grave goods of Clovis' father, Childeric, discovered in Tournai in 1653, subsequently stolen, and for the most part lost in 1831.[8] Moderns have been rather quick to impute symbolic significance to the various objects in the grave, though with varying perceptions. Almost immediately the large number of insect-shaped fittings, the so-called *apes*, bees, were interpreted as marks of rulership, and their imputed connection to the later lilies of France became a minor point of dispute in the Bourbon-Habsburg rivalry of the period. Napoleon, too, passed over the significance of the bull's head, but had the cloak he wore at his imperial coronation decorated with 'bees' like those found in the grave, believing them to be an

---

mitted *Stammestradition* among the Lombards and Franks,' in *Die Bayern und ihre Nachbarn*, ed. Herwig Wolfram and Andreas Schwarcz (Vienna, 1985), 111–19; Georg Scheibelreiter, 'Vom Mythos zur Geschichte: Überlegungen zu den Formen der Bewahrung von Vergangenheit im Frühmittelalter,' *Historiographie im frühen Mittelalter*, ed. A. Scharer and G. Scheibelreiter, Veröffentlichungen des Instituts für Österreichische Geschichtsforschung 32 (Vienna and Munich, 1994), 33–6. Shorn of details, Hauck seems influential in J.M. Wallace-Hadrill, *Early Germanic Kingship in England and on the Continent* (Oxford, 1971), 16–20; cf. his earlier *The Long-Haired Kings and Other Studies in Frankish History* (London, 1962), 84, 220.

7   On representations of bulls in the Merovingian period, Edouard Salin commented: 'il semble bien que cette figuration animale, fort en honneur auprès de civilisations antérieures, n'ait pas été pratiquement retenue par la civilisation mérovingienne.' He gives two examples with confidence, both fifth century – the bull head from Childeric's grave and another from a Gallo-Roman fibula: *La civilisation mérovingienne*, part 4 (Paris, 1959), 166–9.

8   We depend on J.-J. Chiflet's *Anastasis Childerici I. Francorum regis, sive thesaurus sepulchralis Tornaci Nerviorum effosus et commentario illustratus* (Anvers, 1655) not only for the circumstances of the find, but also for illustrations of some of the furnishings, including the bull head. His illustrations can be found in the citations that follow but have also been reproduced innumerable times in other modern works. The furnishings are discussed in detail by K. Böhner, 'Childerich von Tournai,' sec. III, RGA 4: 441 f., 457; and Michel Kazanski and Patrick Périn, 'Le mobilier funéraire de la tombe de Childeric Ier: État de la question et perspectves,' *Revue archéologique de Picardie* 3/4 (1988): 13–38. For the results of the most recent excavation in the area of the original find, and especially the horse interments near Childeric's burial, see Raymond Brulet et al., *Les fouilles du quartier Saint-Brice à Tournai*, Collection d'archéologie Joseph Mertens 3 (Louvain-la-Neuve, 1990–1), 2 vols.

ancient symbol of French royalty.[9] Modern scholars, looking for the religious foundation of Germanic kingship, have taken a different tack: not only do they detect the god Frô behind the bull head, but they also claim to find Wodan in the spear included among the grave furnishings.[10] However, only those disposed to find a bull god in the past of the Merovingians will find the significance of the bull head in Childeric's grave impressive, for bull figures, with or without religious associations, are a common-enough motif in ancient art. Chiflet, who described the find in 1655, called the bull head the *idolum regis*, and Hauck and others have been quick to seize on this term.[11] But it is a small item, belonging, along with the 'bees,' to the harness of the king's horse, the bull head ornamenting the animal's brow.[12] Though well made, like everything else in the grave, the bull head may not be of Frankish manufacture, and forms only a minor part of impressive furnishings that have broad geographical associations. Harness with bull-head- and insect-shaped ornaments seems to have had a long history in the lower Danube and Black Sea region, and fittings of this kind have associations in much earlier Greek art.[13] The bull head of Childeric's grave tells us about art and fashion, not religion.

The significance of the second piece is even less impressive. Two bull heads have been detected on a belt buckle found in a well-furnished female grave uncovered at St Denis in 1959. Because a ring found on the body is inscribed with the name Arnegund, the woman has commonly been identified as Aregund, Chilperic's mother, and her death placed at around 570 on the basis of the skeletal remains; serious questions nevertheless remain unanswered about the attribution and date of the furnishings.[14] The report describing the restoration

9 K. Böhner, 'Childerich von Tournai,' 441 f., 457.
10 And in the characteristic long hair of Merovingian kings: Ewig, *Die Merowinger*, 78, is an example.
11 'Lebensnormen und Kultmythen,' 198; Ewig, *Die Merowinger*, 78. Hauck, nevertheless, accepts that the bull head belongs to the horse harness (199 n.). Modern notions of the proper location for religious significance seem to determine the common view that the bull head was the personal amulet of the king and stems from Abbé Cochet in 1859, despite the clear evidence that it was 'e capistro' and 'ex equi regii fronte'; cf. J. Werner in Brulet, *Les fouilles,* 2: 15.
12 The identification of the insect-shaped fittings as bees has been conventional since Chiflet, though they are sometimes identified as cicadas, probably on the basis of Eastern examples. Inasmuch as the specimens from Childeric's grave resemble any insects in particular, the resemblance is to flies. Perhaps such an identification is never made because the thought of the king's horse (or, as some would have it, the king himself) covered in flies is not quite the image we think appropriate.
13 K. Böhner, 'Childerich von Tournai,' 457.
14 James, *Franks*, 155–7; the most recent consideration of the question by Patrick Périn ('Pour une révision de la datation de la tombe d'Arégonde, épouse de Clotaire I, découverte en 1959 dans la basilique de Saint-Denis,' *Archéologie médiévale* 21 [1991]: 21–50) retains identifica-

of the objects detected within the pattern of the cast frames of the buckle plates two 'strongly stylized' bull heads, sympathetically facing each other, one on each plate.[15] Lineally arranged niello points decorate the frame, and the identification of a bull image within the frames seems to owe much to interpreting two of these niello inserts on one of the plates as the eyes of the animal; the other plate, at least in the condition we possess it, lacks the two corresponding inserts, and indeed any clear shape that suggests a bull head at all. In fact, the bull heads – if such they are – are less 'strongly stylized' than weakly suggested. For the frames of the buckle plates do contain genuine highly stylized animal figures – snake- or dragon-like animal heads, confidently presented to the viewer, unmistakable in their form, with clearly delineated eyes and features. The 'bull heads,' on the other hand, are small, flat featureless planes with indefinite outlines, intended to help tie together the abstract framework of the buckle plates. It seems to me unlikely that they were meant to be construed as bulls at all.

The effort to place a bull divinity at the centre of Germanic paganism extends well beyond the Frankish material. Cattle in general, and bulls in particular, were certainly objects of sacrifice among the Germanic peoples, but the hypothesis that the bull was an important subject of cult – that tauromorphic divinities were prominent among the denizens of Germanic paganism – has yet to be demonstrated. Jacob Grimm, who may have been the first to interpret the conceiving of Merovech as a reflection of Germanic myth, thought, like modern scholars, that he saw the Vanic powers of Freyr behind Fredegar's sea beast, but his understanding of Germanic philology, history, and folklore led him to suppose the beast must have taken the form of a sea pig, because of the important role of the boar in the cult of the Vanir.[16] More recent scholarship has

tion of the body as 'Aregund' on the basis of the ring. As the grave furnishings suggest a seventh-century date, however, he places her death at the earliest possible point consonant with the furnishings – in the last decade of the sixth century, when the queen would have been in her seventies or eighties – and suggests that a re-examination of the bones is needed.

15 A. France-Lanord and M. Fleury, 'Das Grab der Arnegundis,' *Germania* 40 (1962): 357, which includes photographs. A good colour photograph can also be found in Jean Hubert et al., *Europe of the Invasions* (New York, 1969), 234. Those who like 'Where's Waldo' may prefer to find the bulls themselves, but, if in need of guidance, look to the spandrels between the half-circles of the fields formed like kite-shaped shields. Only the spandrels on the ends of the belt plates farthest from the buckle clasp are thought to contain bull heads, and only one of these is suggestive. Their mates in the spandrels next to the clasp are clearly not intended to be bull heads.

16 *Teutonic Mythology*, trans. (from the 4th ed.) by James Steven Stallybrass (New York, 1966), 1: 391. This interpretation, Grimm believes, explains the Byzantine reference to the 'crested' Merovingians: Theophanes (d. *ca* 818), claims the Merovingians were called *kristatai*, 'which means "those with hair down their backs," for they had hair growing along their backs like swine' (s.a. 6216 [723–4], trans. Harry Turtledove, *The Chronicle of Theophanes* [Philadel-

enrolled philology and the archaeological record from the Bronze Age to the early Middle Ages to demonstrate Germanic bull cults analogous to those of the Near East. Even with so wide a net, the catch should not be seen as encouraging. A charitable interpretation of the claims made for philology suggests that they are unlikely to prove convincing on the subject; and, as for archaeology, the standard interpretation of so many bull objects as products of foreign importation, especially from the Celtic world, seems in itself to defeat the argument of a highly developed autochthonous bull cult.[17] The Celtic cast to much of this evidence points to a curious lapse on the part of those who see the effect of myth and religion on Fredegar. For, as a product of Gaul, with a Gallic setting, the story – if it is myth – is arguably a reflection of the Gallic milieu in which the evidence for divine bulls, not just the occasional bull image, is not hard to come by.[18]

Perhaps those sticking to Germanic tracks in tracing the mythic origins of Fredegar's tale feel justified in doing so because of their reliance on two other texts that are supposed to demonstrate the notion of sacral kingship among the Franks; if it could be demonstrated that the Merovingians and their followers believed in a divine or supernatural origin for the royal house, would this not justify us in supposing a Germanic, pagan mythic background to Fredegar's account of Merovech's conception? It would help, but reliance on these two texts is misplaced. Like the Fredegar text itself, neither is an unequivocal statement of divine descent or sacral ideology, nor is there anything particularly puzzling about their meaning or context.

In his letter to Clovis on the occasion of his baptism, Avitus refers to the king as 'de toto priscae originis stemmate sola nobilitate contentus.' This phrase has

phia, 1982]). The comment is commonly understood to be related to the long hair of the Merovingians as a mark of kingship. William A. Chaney finds theriomorphic divinization here, taking Theophanes' reference as a 'reminiscence of the primitive ritual battle in which the king slew his predecessor, impersonating the god during the struggle in the guise of the deity's sacred animal' – in this case, the boar (*The Cult of Kingship in Anglo-Saxon England* [Berkeley–Los Angeles, 1970],126).

17 Gert Esterle, *Die Boviden in der Germania*, Wiener Arbeiten zur germanischen Altertumskunde und Philologie 2 (Vienna, 1974), is a very interesting compendium of these efforts. My conclusions are not the ones the author draws.

18 This is also the context for the brazen bull of the Cimbri (Plutarch, *Marius* XXIII), no matter what one makes of the ethnicity of the Cimbri themselves. For the most recent discussion of the Cimbri, assuming a Danish origin, see Dieter Timpe, 'Kimberntradition und Kimbernmythos,' in *Germani in Italia*, ed. Barbara and Piergiuseppe Scardigli (Rome, 1994), 23–60, esp. 50 f. for 'Celtic' characteristcs; these are also stressed by, among others, Jan De Vries, 'Kimbern und Teutonen: ein Kapitel aus den Beziehungen zwischen Kelten und Germanen,' *Zur germanischen Stammeskunde: Aufsätze zum neuen Forschungsstand*, ed. Ernst Schwarz, Wege der Forschung 249 (Darmstadt, 1972), 104–22.

commonly been interpreted to mean that Clovis was now satisfied to derive only noble birth from his ancestors and had, therefore, given up any claim to divine descent with his conversion to Christianity.[19] Avitus' letter is renowned for its obscurities, but at least as far as it concerns our problem the meaning seems sufficiently clear, when the context of the phrase is looked at as a whole.

In this same issue [of conversion], a great many people – if by the exhortation of priests or at the prompting of associates they are moved to seek out the sanity of believing – are accustomed to adduce [as an impediment] the customs [they inherit with] birth and ancestral practices; thus harmfully preferring reverence to salvation, they reveal that they do not know how to choose anything, while preserving, as prisoners of unbelief, useless veneration for their parents. Let harmful shame give up this pretext after the miracle of such a deed. From the entire garland of ancient descent, you are content simply with nobility and have tried to draw from yourself whatever can adorn in its entirety the summit of nobility of your own descendants. You have authors of good deeds [in your descent]; you have wished to be the author of better ones. You answer to your ancestors by reigning in the world; for the sake of posterity, you make provision to reign in heaven.[20]

The theme of the passage is a cliché of conversion: the duty due to one's ancestors versus the rejection of tradition required by genuine Christian conversion. This is not an issue unique to Clovis, according to Avitus, who begins by classing the dilemma as a problem faced by many converts ('Solent plerique ... consuetudinem generis et ritum paternae observantiae obponere'). The traditions that hold back converts are *consuetudo generis, ritus paternae observantiae*, and *parentibus reverentia*. These broadly imply the pious obligation to follow the religion of one's ancestors, the faith of one's fathers, but also, more specifically, the religious duty to venerate one's ancestors. Clovis as a genuine con-

---

19 W. Junghans, *Histoire critique des règnes de Childeric et de Clovis*, trans. Gabriel Monod, Bibliotheque de l'École des Hautes Études 37 (Paris, 1879; first published, Göttingen, 1856), 63 n, 123, seems to have been the first to make this point.

20 Epist. 46, *Opera quae supersunt,* ed. R. Peiper, MGH AA 6/2: 'Solent plerique in hac eadem causa, si pro expetenda sanitate credendi aut sacerdotum hortatu aut quorumcumque sodalium ad suggestionem moveantur, consuetudinem generis et ritum paternae observationis obponere; ita saluti nocenter verecundiam praeferentes, dum parentibus in incredulitatis custodia futilem reverentiam servant, confitentur, se quodammodo nescire, quid eligant. Discedat igitur ab hac excusatione post talis facti miraculum noxius pudor. Vos de toto priscae originis stemmate sola nobilitate contentus, quicquid omne potest fastigium generositatis ornare prosapiae vestrae a vobis voluistis exurgere. Habetis bonorum auctores, voluistis esse meliorum. Respondetis proavis, quod regnatis in saeculo; instituistis posteris, ut regnetis in caelo.' I have removed the editor's comma after 'ornare'; even if 'prosapiae vestrae' are datives, the meaning of the sentence is not substantially changed. The *miraculum* referred to is the conversion itself.

vert, says Avitus, has recognized the need to reject traditional religious obligations of his past. Thus from the various elements constituting ancestral observance ('de toto ... stemmate'), he retains only nobility.[21] Clovis knows, according to Avitus, that by his conversion his own great deeds as a Christian king will discharge the obligation to achieve wordly renown owed his noble ancestors, while the same accomplishments will adorn the Christian lineage that will now stem from him, bringing to it the promise of salvation.

Avitus' terms have nothing to do with divine descent.[22] Clovis' dilemma is a general phenomenon, and his rejection of the past follows the pattern of all genuine conversion. It may be even more surprising to note, as well, that the terms Avitus uses to describe the past really have nothing much to do with Germanic paganism at all. The language alludes to the hindrance caused by the moral imperatives of Roman paganism, resting originally on a foundation of public and domestic cult; the image evoked is that of the ancestral portraits of the senatorial nobility, hung with garlands.[23] The point of the cliché depends on the duty that ancient religion laid upon its adherents, especially the aristocracy, to venerate their ancestors and to continue the practices of traditional religion. The relevance such a sentiment had for Clovis' particular situation may be doubted. Avitus has used the motif to depict the passage of a great aristocrat from paganism to Christianity; he was not clothing some special knowledge about Clovis in antique garb.

The second text is Einhard's famous description of the last Merovingians, eclipsed by the mayors of the palace and travelling about placidly by ox-drawn wagon in their empty role as kings:

The wealth and power of the kingdom was held by the palace prefects, called mayors of the palace, to whom ultimate authority belonged. Nothing was left to the king but to sit on the throne, with his flowing hair and long beard, and pretend to rule, satisfied only

---

21 *Stemma* means garland, and, in particular, a garland hung on an ancestral image, hence genealogy, pedigree, nobility (Lewis and Short, s.v.). There seems to be a play on words with 'fastigium generositatis ornare prosapiae vestrae.'

22 Cf. the doubts by Marc Reydellet, *La royauté dans la littérature latine de Sidoine Apollinaire à Isidore de Séville*, Bibliothèque des Écoles Françaises d'Athènes et de Rome 243. (Rome, 1981), 106–7. Nikolaus Staubach, 'Germanisches Königtum und lateinisches Literatur vom fünften bis zum siebten Jahrhundert,' *Frühmittelalterliche Studien* 17 (1983): 29–31, draws a comparison with the language in Leo the Great's Christmas sermon, but his interpretation owes more to the terminological invention of Karl Hauck than to the Latin of Avitus. His reading of Avitus *and* Leo through Tacitus and Hauck seems rather odd.

23 The *imagines* of ancestors were still a common sight in the late fifth century, to judge from Sidonius Apollinaris' letter to Eutropius ("qui cotidie trabeatis proavorum imaginibus ingeritur"), usually dated to around 467: Ep. 1.6, ed. W.B. Anderson, *Poems and Letters,* Loeb Classical Library (Cambridge, Mass., 1936) 1: 362.

with the royal name: he would receive ambassadors who came from all over and, when they departed, provide them as if on his own authority with replies that he had been directed or even commanded to give. And except for the empty title of king and the precarious living-allowance that the prefect of the palace at his discretion provided for him, he possessed nothing of his own but one estate – and even that produced a very small income. He obtained lodging there along with a small number of servants to tend to his needs and to provide him with service. Wherever he had to travel, he went by wagon, drawn by yoked oxen and driven by a teamster in country fashion. In this way he used to go to the palace, or to the public assembly of his people that convened every year for the sake of the well-being of the kingdom, and in this way he used to return home. The prefect of the palace took care of the administration of the kingdom and provided for the execution and planning of everything that had to be done inside the palace or out.[24]

One would have thought that Henri Pirenne's discussion almost seventy years ago would have laid to rest this relic of nineteenth-century *Germanistik*.[25] But we are still solemnly assured that the ox cart of the Merovingians was no simple mode of transport, but a *Kultwagen*, re-enacting a ritual reminiscent of the yearly circuit of Nerthus, 'terra mater,' as described by Tacitus, and linked to fertility cults of the Vanir.[26] A few obvious observations show just how distant such an interpretation lies from the sense of Einhard's words.

Einhard does not tell us that the ox cart was traditional to the Merovingians, as is frequently alleged, but restricts his remarks to the last representatives of the house. In all of the sources of Merovingian history prior to Einhard, there is no reference to kings being conveyed in this manner. Nor does Einhard include the ox cart among the marks of Merovingian kingship – these he identifies with

---

24 *VK* I: 'Nam et opes et potentia regni penes palatii praefectos, qui majores domus dicebantur, et ad quos summa imperii pertinebat, tenebantur. Neque regi aliud relinquebatur, quam ut regio tantum nomine contentus crine profuso, barba summissa, solio resideret ac speciem dominantis effingeret, legatos undecumque venientes audiret eisque abeuntibus responsa, quae erat edoctus vel etiam jussus, ex sua velut potestate redderet; cum praeter inutile regis nomen et praecarium vitae stipendium, quod ei praefectus aulae prout videbatur exhibebat, nihil alius proprii possideret quam unam et eam praeparvi reditus villam, in qua domum et ex qua famulos sibi necessaria ministrantes atque obsequium exhibentes paucae numerositatis habebat. Quocumque eundum erat, carpento ibat, quod bubus junctis et bubulco rustico more agente trahebatur. Sic ad palatium, sic ad publicum populi sui conventum, qui annuatim ob regni utilitatm celebrabatur, ire, sic domum redire solebat. Ad regni administrationem et omnia quae vel domi vel foris agenda ac disponenda erant praefectus aulae procurabat.'

25 'Le Char à boeufs des derniers Mérovingiens: note sur un passage d'Eginhard,' *Mélanges Paul Thomas* (Bruges, 1930), 555–60: 'La méprise est comparable à celle que commettra peut-être un érudit de l'avenir si, étudiant une caricature de Louis-Philippe, il s'avise de connaître le sceptre des Capétiens dans le parapluie du roi.'

26 Ewig, *Die Merowinger*, 78. Translators of Einhard rarely fail to comment on a connection with paganism.

the Merovingian name, long hair, beard, and public role. He introduces travel by wagon to exemplify the reduced circumstances of the last Merovingians and their ludicrous position in the state; far from having ritual or kingly significance, travel by ox cart is associated with rusticity and poverty. The penury of the late Merovingians is, of course, completely relative, and Einhard's account, obviously tendentious, is unlikely to be free of exaggeration or misrepresentation. But it is difficult to see what purpose would be served in disguising pagan associations, and difficult to imagine who indeed in the ninth century would be in a position to recognize such a peculiar form of irony.[27]

Wallace-Hadrill saw in Einhard's description a connection with late imperial governors doing their rounds using *angariae*, the heavy ox wagons of the imperial slow post, the *cursus clabularis*.[28] It is true that such wagons were used by the imperial post for conveying not only all kinds of freight, but occasionally personnel.[29] The problem with the evidence of the Roman post is that it does not establish that high-ranking officials normally rode in ox carts, though it does show that such wagons accompanied their peregrinations, no doubt conveying baggage, and possibly providing comfort and shelter. The suggestion, nevertheless, does have the merit of stressing the point that ox-drawn vehicles *were* standard modes of transport – Einhard does not limit their use by the Merovingians to state occasions, as is often implied.[30] Despite his tone, ox wagons were not really a mode of transport to be despised; they moved at the rate an army could march, were no doubt the most spacious and comfortable vehicle available, and were particularly useful where the roads were bad.[31]

And, of course, references to ox-drawn vehicles in the *cursus publicus* are only a faint reflection of their widespread use in society as a whole. A good Merovingian example of the ox cart's role as a general mode of travel for the

27 'Einhard ironisiert offenbar ein Ritual, das zum heidnischen Königsmythos gehörte'(Ewig, *Die Merowinger*, 78). Many commentators seem to imagine that Einhard was unaware of the ritual significance of the ox transport; this hardly saves the situation and is an acknowledgment that there is no direct evidence of paganism in the passage at all.

28 J.M. Wallace-Hadrill, 'Gregory of Tours and Bede: Their Views on the Personal Qualities of Kings,' *Early Medieval History* (Oxford, 1975), 98. Despite adopting notions of sacral kingship in *Early Germanic Kingship in England and on the Continent* (Oxford, 1971), Wallace-Hadrill treated the principal sources for it with circumspection.

29 The best example is *Novella Majoriani* 7.1.13, a. 458 (in *Codex Theodosianus*, ed. Th. Mommsen = CT) where Majorian tried to limit governors to requisitioning only one heavy ox-wagon for themselves and one for their *officia*, along with four riding horses, as they moved from one *civitas* to another. Cf. also Ammianus Marcellinus 20. 4. 11 (heavy wagons put at the disposal of *familiae* of soldiers being reassigned); CT 8. 5. 11 (military units alloted two wagons for the sick); CT 8. 5. 66 (wagons accompanying *duces* and their *officia*). See A.H.M. Jones, *The Later Roman Empire* (Oxford, 1964), 2: 830–4 and nn.

30 'Quocumque eundum erat, carpento ibat.'

31 K.D. White, *Greek and Roman Technology* (London, 1984), 127–40.

well-to-do is recorded in a famous sixth- or seventh-century donation in which a certain Erminthrude bequeathed 'the wagon in which I customarily ride, with oxen (*boves*) and furnishings (*lectaria*), along with all its harness (*stratura*).'[32] Moderns might be less inclined to allege archaic, religious significance to explain their own puzzlement with Einhard's description, if, along with evidence like this, they remembered that even in quite recent times continents have been traversed expeditiously by the steady pull of ox teams. Still, despite its relative comfort and utility, the ox cart could hardly project the vigour or splendour expected of a Carolingian king. Though we have not yet reached the absurdity of *Le chevalier à la charette*, Einhard has seized on the ox cart as a symbol of ignoble weakness demonstrating his contention that the Merovingians had ended up as do-nothing kings turned minor gentry, peacefully navigating the tracks of country life.

II

Neither Avitus nor Einhard gives us grounds for believing in sacral kingship among the Merovingians; nor does either source substantiate the existence of alleged bull deities among the Franks. Interpretations of Merovech's conception cannot begin with dubious theories about archaic kingship or Germanic paganism. If notions of divine descent and bull cults are to be considered pertinent, they have to be sustained by the context of the story itself and, most importantly, must be shown to be the best categories available for interpreting the peculiarities of the tale. Closer examination shows there are other categories that better account for the distinctive features of Fredegar's portrayal of the encounter on the beach between Chlodio's wife and the beast from the sea.

The description of the conceiving of Merovech in Fredegar's *Chronicle* occurs in Book III, a condensation of Gregory of Tours' *Histories* into which Fredegar has inserted material of his own, much of it concerning the Trojan origin of the Franks. The passage in the *Histories* relevant to Fredegar's Merovech interpolation concerns Chlodio, the first king of the Franks, about whom Gregory knows very little; it ends with Gregory's comments regarding the uncertain relationship between Chlodio and Merovech. Then, calling attention to the paganism of the Franks at the time, Gregory enters into a long-winded refutation of pagan belief. In the corresponding passage, Fredegar follows Gregory's

---

32 *Chartae Latinae Antiquiores XIV: France,* ed. Hartmut Atsma and Jean Vezin (Dietikon-Zurich, 1982), no. 592: 'basilicae s(an)c(t)i Sinfuriani ... carruca in qua sedere consueui, cum boues et lectaria, cum omni stratura sua, pro deuocione mea ... dari praecipio ...' A second cart with oxen and harness goes to another church. Cf. also the death of Deuteria's daughter in Gregory, *Hist.* III 26.

account of Chlodio, interpolating his own material on the connections among
the early kings of the Franks; he retains Gregory's allusion to the paganism of
the Franks, but leaves out the refutation of paganism and inserts his story of
Merovech's birth.[33] In a process that often seems to reverse the relation of the
epitomizer to his subject, many interpreters have been quick to suggest that
Gregory must have known the Merovech story, suppressed it, and replaced it
with a sermon on the falseness of paganism.[34] This view may be correct; it cannot be demonstrated or refuted. It is worth stressing that reading Gregory in this
way does not require that the Merovech tale be associated with Germanic,
pagan myth. As will be discussed below, Fredegar's story may be related to the
revival of the name under Chilperic and succeeding kings. Gregory was a contemporary of this revival, and his comments on Merovech can better be read as
commentary on current speculation about the founder of the dynasty than as a
critique of oral tradition. Moreover, the distinction between Roman and Germanic paganism, though important to moderns, is not one he would have recognized as significant at all; if antique rhetorical motifs with pagan associations
accompanied the revival of the name, he is not likely to have been pleased and
would have regarded them as no less pagan and no less objectionable than any
tale that might have descended from the salty shores of the Rhine mouth. In any
case, there are no clear signs that Gregory was suppressing an indecent tale of
sexual misadventure: his refutation of paganism cannot be tied to specific items
of Frankish belief that he might have decided to challenge by means of a
homily rather than include in his narrative; nor is there a clear connection in the
refutation to material Fredegar associates with Merovech's birth. Gregory's
refutation is composed of commonplaces from the Bible and general Christian

33 In the phrase Gregory uses to introduce his homily, 'haec generatio fanaticis semper cultibus
    visa est obsequium praebuisse' *(Hist.* II 10), *generatio* is best taken to mean the Franks. The
    phrase is rendered in Fredegar's epitome as 'haec generacio fanaticis usibus culta est.' Ignor-
    ing Gregory's model, Wolfram (n. 1 above, Engl. trans., 209) translates Fredegar as follows:
    'This race [the Merovingians] was celebrated in pagan feasts.' This translation will not with-
    stand examination. Fredegar's words, as the assignment of fonts in Krusch's edition has long
    made clear, are an epitome of Gregory's not an independent interpolation. The *Mittellatein-
    isches Wörterbuch* glosses *cultus* in the Fredegarian passage with *deditus-ergeben*, giving the
    verb an active meaning. In a Fredegarian context, there is no peculiarity here. A reversal of
    standard active and passive usage happens to be one of the occasional quirks of Fredegar's
    style. For example, immediately following 'culta est' with an active sense ('were devoted to'),
    Fredegar uses the passive form of the verb *concipio* ('fuisset concepta,' above p. 122) to mean
    the king's wife 'conceived,' though standard usage would require an active form of the verb
    here as well. In this case, Wolfram translates the passive form in the active voice. Incidentally,
    had Fredegar taken *generatio* to mean family, the family in question would have been the
    genus Priami.
34 Godefroid Kurth, *Histoire poétique des Mérovingiens* (Paris, 1893), 151–3; most recently
    Wood, *Frankish Kingdoms,* 37.

critiques of paganism. We should proceed on the assumption that Fredegar is the epitomizer, adding fresh information, not restoring some original narrative that Gregory has deceptively distorted.

Nevertheless, the positioning of Fredegar's story next to Gregory's comment on the paganism of the period could be considered suggestive, and as such is the only real evidence that Fredegar thought he might be dealing in pagan myth. It is hardly conclusive. If Fredegar did associate the story with paganism, it is more likely to be the paganism of Greek and Roman history, fitting not only the internal references of his story, but also the Trojan origin of the Franks and their leading dynasty, descended, in Fredegar's view, from Priam. But whether Fredegar expected his story to be associated with paganism is, given his way of working, questionable. In Gregory's *Histories*, the reference to paganism is found following his discussion of the times of Chlodio and Merovech, and introduces a homily against paganism. In condensing his model, Fredegar may simply have included the reference, relevant enough to an early history of the Franks, while rejecting the homily, which was not. Having finished excerpting Gregory's section on Chlodio and Merovech, he then added his own story about Merovech's birth, without intending this to be read as a gloss on Frankish paganism. No doubt, if he had included Gregory's reference to paganism in the times of Chlodio and Merovech only after his addition of Merovech's conception, moderns, given their interests, would still be inclined to read the two together. In condensing Gregory's text just as it lay to hand – which is Fredegar's method – the juxtaposition of Gregory's comment on paganism with the interpolation on the birth of Merovech was unavoidable.

Fredegar introduces his story about the conceiving of Merovech with the expression *fertur*, 'it is said.' This has often been taken as an unequivocal sign of a source in Germanic, oral tradition, and an argument for its subject-matter being pagan and mythical. This view of *fertur*, unfortunately, fails to take into consideration Fredegar's use of the expression. He uses it some thirteen other times.[35] Eight of the thirteen times are in Book IV, in reference to relatively recent events of Frankish, Gothic, or Byzantine provenance.[36] Of the five other references from the earlier books, one is to a geographical feature, that is, a current reference, though the setting is fifth century;[37] one pertains to the early Lombards in a context that many believe derives from ancient Lombard legend, though extracted by Fredegar from a written source;[38] and one other concerns a

---

35 Analogous expressions, *ferunt, traditur* and the like, are not used.
36 Bk IV 38, 66, 67, 81, 82 (2X), 85, 87.
37 Bk II 60.
38 Bk III 65.

reported vision drawn from the dialogues of Gregory the Great.[39] The two remaining instances concern the Trojan legend of Frankish origins and pertain to Francio, Aeneas, and Frigas, ancestors of the Franks and Romans.[40] None of the usages conforms to the modern understanding of Frankish or Germanic oral tradition. *Fertur* cannot be tied exclusively to oral or written sources, and the common presumption that the phrase tags Germanic oral tradition is clearly wrong.

Fredegar tells us that from Merovech – Meroveus is simply the Latin contraction of the name – the Frankish kings derive their dynastic name of Merovingians (*Merohingii*). Godefroid Kurth some time ago clearly confronted the implications of Merovingian genealogy for theories of divine descent. Kurth held to the view that belief in the divine descent of kings was characteristic of primitive peoples, and that the Merovech story attested to such a belief among the Franks, but he also recognized the historical character of Merovech, the father of Childeric, and the shallow depth of the Merovingian genealogy above Clovis. He proposed, simply enough, that Merovingian kingship was of relatively recent vintage; the tale told by Fredegar was a late mythological tradition, fixed at an early stage in its development by the victory of Christianity.[41]

One of the peculiar features of recent arguments for divine descent is to spot in the Merovech story an unattested, mythical ancestor of the Merovingians, called Mero. This notion is not new, but goes back to the mid-nineteenth century and the views of Karl Müllenhoff, who hoped thereby to connect the dynastic name of the Merovingians with the Merwe, a river at the mouth of the Rhine.[42] As the survival of this view cannot have anything to do with the merits of his argument, which has long been shown to be inadequate,[43] it is instructive to clarify the function the invention of Mero serves in modern sacral theory. Recent scholarship would find views like those of Kurth insufficient for establishing Frankish kingship as an archaic model of early rulership; the

39 Bk II 59.
40 Bk II 5, 8. Hauck used *fertur*, his mark of Germanic oral tradition, to exclude any connection with Trojan tales (supposedly learned) and written sources ('Lebensnormen und Kultmythen,' 22). An express appeal to oral tradition is one of his four criteria for detecting Germanic myth, in the case of Merovech's birth hinging completely on *fertur*. According to Moisl, 'Kingship,' oral *Stammestradition* is 'certified' by *fertur*.
41 Kurth, *Histoire poétique*, 147–59.
42 Karl Müllenhof, 'Die Merovingische Stammesage,' *Zeitschrift für deutsches Alterthum* 6 (1848): 431.
43 On the linguistic side, see below, n. 81. The derivation from the Merwe had already been suggested by Leo, but Müllenhoff provided linguistic arguments. The claim that, if Merovingian was derived from Merovech, we should expect *Merovechingi* was dealt with by Kurth in *Histoire poétique*, 155.

Merovingians, if they are to be portrayed as sacral kings, must trace their dynastic roots into the distant past of Frankish political and religious history. The complete lack of evidence for such an interpretation is an inconvenience that the putative Mero is designed to overcome. The antiquity of the Merovingian house, for example, cannot otherwise be demonstrated from the names of Frankish leaders of the late Empire, despite the inclination to make the evidence carry burdens it cannot possibly bear.[44] Even Hauck's far-fetched theory of the (recurrent) *primus rex* and theriomorphic divination pertains to Chlodio, not Merovech, and reduces Merovech to an historical and mythological irrelevancy.[45] Whence came the Merovingian name and its distant, archaic sacral associations, then, if there was only Merovech and no Mero?

There is no Mero, of course, nor is there the slightest reason to suppose contamination in Fredegar's reference to Merovech and the descent of the Frankish kings. Gregory of Tours is the first source to mention Merovech.[46] He identifies him as a king and as the father of Childeric, but is uncertain of his relation to Chlodio; Clovis' victories seem to him, nevertheless, to confirm the lineage's connection to the first family of the Franks from which they chose their kings – an argument that clearly shows Gregory was not loath to connect Merovech to Chlodio, and would have done so if any evidence of kinship had been available. Gregory does not apply the term 'Merovingian' to the Frankish kings. It may seem surprising that the *gens Merovingorum* appears rather late in Frankish sources and is a rare occurrence, but there are few occasions in the sources we have that might call for a reference to the family name of the Frankish kings. Rarity does not call into question the term Merovingian or the descent of the Frankish kings from Merovech; it does make it difficult to determine when the dynastic name was adopted. Though Gregory does not use it, he was surely aware of the term, because he derives the descent of the present royal family from Merovech and is uncertain of the nature of the connections beyond him. The currency of the term is also suggested by the circumstance that, about the same time Gregory was writing, the name Merovech had been revived as a king's name in a fashion that speaks for its connection with the dynastic name of the royal house.[47]

The first source we have that uses the term 'Merovingian' is not Fredegar, but Jonas of Bobbio, writing about 640: he uses it in the singular (*Mervengus*)

44 Eugen Ewig, 'Die Namegebung bei den ältesten Frankenkönigen und im merovingischen Königshaus,' *Francia* 18. 1 (1991): 21–69. Germanic name-giving practices do not permit the reconstruction of lineage structures.
45 See above, pp. 122–4.
46 *Hist.* II 9
47 See below, p. 145.

and in a context that shows it was a term commonly understood for Frankish kings.[48] Next Fredegar uses it *(Merohingii)* around 660, and only once, in the story under consideration. Thereafter, we have to wait for eighth-century sources, especially the *Liber historiae Francorum*, where we are again told that the Frankish kings are called Merovingians *(Merovingi)*, after Merovech.[49] Typically enough for the period, the orthography of the name is erratic, but then it is equally erratic for the name Merovech itself, Fredegar alone, with the help of sundry scribes, giving us the variants Meroveus, Meroheus, Meroeus, Maeroeus, Maeroveus, and Merveus.[50] There is no reason to reject the testimony of the sources since they are consistent with a patronymic form derived from Merovechus/Meroveus. The Merovingians derived their name from Merovech, an historical king of the mid-fifth century, not a distant, mythical ancestor.

The most striking feature of Fredegar's account is his description of the encounter of Chlodio's wife with a sea beast and the conception of Merovech by either the beast or Chlodio. Fredegar connects the beast to Neptune and compares it with the Minotaur, *quinotaur* universally being taken to be an error on the part of a copyist or Fredegar. As we have seen, the Minotaur reference (along with the bull in Childeric's grave) has frequently led modern commentators to imagine a figure half man and half bull, representing a bull divinity, though no such creature from Frankish, or even Germanic, paganism appears to have any bearing on the story. As Neptune and the Minotaur are derived from classical traditions, Latin literature and Latin learning are areas that at least promise some help in defining Fredegar's frame of reference.

Latin literature had absorbed from Greek a series of tales, conceptualized as myths in modern scholarship, concerning the Cretan king Minos and his difficult relations with the god Neptune.[51] In the common version of the story, Minos, himself the product of a union between Jupiter in the form of a bull and Europa in the form of a cow, prays to Neptune for a bull to sacrifice and is rewarded with a dazzlingly white bull that appears from the sea. But Minos fails to sacrifice the bull, offending Neptune, who causes Minos' wife, Pasiphaë, to fall in love with the bull. She has Daedalus construct a hollow form

---

48 *Vita Columbani,* I 28, ed. Bruno Krusch, MGH SRM 4 (1904): 'Quod et regi et omnibus circumadstantibus ridiculum excitat, aientes, se numquam audisse, Mervengum, in regno sublimatum, voluntarium clericum fuisse.'

49 *Liber Historiae Francorum* 5, ed. Bruno Krusch, MGH SRM 2 (1888): 'Ab ipso Merovecho rege utile reges Francorum Merovingi sunt appellati.'

50 Fred. *Chron.* III 9, 11, 60, 74, 78.

51 For the early sources: Timothy Gantz, *Early Greek Myth: A Guide to Literary and Artistic Sources* (Baltimore and London, 1993), 259–70; for the late antique and early medieval tradition, nn. 56–63, below.

in the shape of a cow, inserts herself into it, and successfully mates with the bull. The union results in the birth of the Minotaur, Minos' bull, half man and half beast, which the king shuts up in the labyrinth. The story became a commonplace of Latin culture: Virgil alludes to it several times; Ovid treats it, along with other stories of river gods capable of metamorphosing into bulls; and Apuleius explores its pornographic possibilities in a contemporary setting.[52] These literary appearances were just signs of a much wider popular currency for the story: minotaurs were among the images decorating the standards of Republican legions, and Nero had the mating of Pasiphaë and Neptune's bull re-enacted in the amphitheatre.[53] Characters in the story were also appropriated for genealogical speculation: Galba, when he became emperor, claimed descent from Jupiter on the paternal side and Pasiphaë on the maternal.[54] It is difficult to say if the popularity of the story ever really faded. Among historians, Orosius in the early fifth century accepted the Minotaur as a real character in the history of early Greece.[55] In the late fifth century, Sidonius Apollinaris regarded minotaurs as a type of beast that symbolized voraciousness, and the tale was obviously still current in the early sixth century, when Ennodius of Pavia, inspired by images on the tableware of an acquaintance, took up the subject in his epigrams.[56] In the early Middle Ages, its elements in one form or another continued to be an adjunct to the study of the literary and pseudo-historical monuments of antiquity. Their association with Virgil's *Aeneid*, if nothing else, guaranteed their survival, as did their inclusion in the mythographic tradition, which also dealt with the Trojan War and its aftermath.[57] The story of the Minotaur was, as a consequence, a small part of pseudo-historical material that someone interested in the Trojan background to European history was likely to

---

52 Virgil, *Aeneid* , esp. VI 24–6; Ovid, *Metamorphoses* VIII (Minos); VIII 1090, IX (Achelous, the river god); Apuleius, *Metamorphoses* X 19–35.

53 Pliny, *Natural History* X 5 (16) (Minotaur standards). Suetonius, *Nero* XII; though the re-enactment was part of a *munus gladiatorium,* Suetonius introduces the section with the comment 'neminem occidit, ne noxiorum quidem.' There was a temple of Pasiphaë in Sparta.

54 Suetonius, *Galba* II. Minos is identified only as Pasiphaë's husband, not as progenitor. Who, then, was thought to be her mate?

55 *Historiae* I 13.2, ed. Marie-Pierre Arnaud-Lindet (Paris, 1990), 1: 61.

56 Sidonius: Ep. 5.7.4, ed. W.B. Anderson, *Poems and Letters*, 2: 190. Ennodius: *Magni Felicis Ennodi Opera*, nos. 133, 136, ed. Fridericus Vogel, MGH AA 7 (1885); the subject appears again (no. 232) alongside other epigrams (nos. 232, 232a) concerned with the sexual exploits of Jove pictured, once more, on dishes.

57 *Servii grammatici qui feruntur in Virgilii carmina commentarii,* VI 14, 24–6, ed. G. Thilo and H. Hagen (Hildesheim, 1961), vol. 2. Hyginus, *Fabulae*, xl, xli, xlii, i.a., ed. H.I. Rose, 2d ed. (Leiden, 1963). Mythographus Vaticanus, I 43, 47, 120, 121, 126, and III 11.7; and cf. I 94, 148: *Scriptores rerum mythicarum latini tres Romae nuper reperti,* Georg Heinrich Bode (Hildesheim, 1968; reprint of 1834 ed.).

meet with in some form. Latin literary tradition is, therefore, suggestive for understanding Fredegar's story, but the fit is rather imperfect: Neptune's bull is the bull that came from the sea, as presumably does Fredegar's beast; but, according to its name, the Minotaur is Minos' bull, the product of the union between the queen and the bull of Neptune, and it is kept in the labyrinth. Fredegar, though, is not recounting the Minotaur story as such – we can never be sure exactly how he understood it – but only drawing upon some of its elements by way of comparison: the association with Neptune and the resemblance to a bull-like creature.

Latin learning of the age casts a slightly different light on the Merovech story.[58] Two aspects seem particularly important. The first is the interest in strange beasts and monstrous births, natural phenomena often interpreted as portentous indicators of the future. A section on portents in the *Etymologiae* of Isidore of Seville (d. 636), for instance, considers the Minotaur twice: the first instance includes it among the serious categories of portentous creations as a special type with human and animal parts;[59] the second instance appears to be an attempt to rationalize the Minotaur story itself, on the basis of a false etymology from *homo* and *taurus*.[60] The Minotaur appears as a real creature not only in Orosius, but also in the *Enigmata* of Aldhelm (d. 709), a collection of riddles about the natural world.[61] The author of the *Liber monstrorum*, celebrated because he depicts the bones of Higlacus (the Hygelac of *Beowulf*) attracting tourists on an island at the mouth of the Rhine, includes among his human monsters the Minotaur, though with a certain hostility towards the veracity of the Greek tales with which it was associated.[62] In the fabulous account of Aethicus Ister, minotaurs were depicted as a race of creatures, independent of the accidents of birth or Greek fables; near the Caspian gates, in a

58 Of the works cited below, only those of Isidore and Aldhelm can be dated with any precision.

59 *Etymologiae* XI iii 9, *Isidori Hispalensis episcopi etymologiarum sive originum libri XX*, ed. W.M. Lindsay (Oxford, 1911), 1: 'Alia [portenta], quae in parte transfigurantur, sicut qui leonis habent vultum vel canis, vel taurinum caput aut corpus, ut ex Pasiphaë memorant genitum Minotaurum; quod Graeci *heteromorphîan* vocant.'

60 Ibid., 38: 'Minotaurum nomen sumpsisse ex tauro et homine, qualem bestiam fabulose in Labyryntho inclusam fuisse.' Only the inclusion of the creature in the labyrinth is being doubted here.

61 Orosius, as in n. 55. Aldhelm, *Engimata* XVIII, dependent, at least in part, on Isidore. *Aldhelmi Opera*, ed. R. Ehwald, MGH AA XV; English translation by Michael Lapidge and James L. Rosier: Aldhelm, *The Poetic Works* (Cambridge, 1985), 75.

62 Bk. I 2 (Higlacus); I 50 (Minotaurus): *Liber Monstrorum: Introduzione, edizione, versione e commento*, ed. Franco Porsia (Bari, 1976). An English translation can now be found in Andy Orchard, *Pride and Prodigies: Studies in the Monsters of the* Beowulf-*Manuscript* (Cambridge, 1995).

region associated with the exploits of Alexander, the author claims, young minotaurs were to be found that could be trained to war.[63]

Although Fredegar made use of Isidore and Orosius, there is no question of any of the works mentioned above being linked directly to his account of Merovech's birth.[64] Yet they do tell us something about the Minotaur in the imagination of the early Middle Ages. The Minotaur remained an exotic beast through its connection with the world of the Greek gods, though these could be interpreted through Euhemerism, a process that brought them and their associations within the realm of historical speculation. In addition, the Minotaur could be conceptualized as a type of creature and an element in the category of the monstrous and portentous creations of nature. The Minotaur, or rather, we should say, creatures of that ilk, were potentially imaginable attendants on past events.

A second aspect of Latin learning fundamental to the Merovech story is etymology. Sometimes a playful or scurrilous source of amusement, etymology was also a serious category of explanation, with roots in biblical, classical, and patristic tradition.[65] The character of individuals, peoples or, indeed, almost any subject, could be explained through the name (*causa nominis*); for matters dealing with *origines, causa nominis* was an interpretative tool of the first order. *Origo* in fact came to mean not only 'origin' in its usual senses of beginning, birth, or descent, but also 'etymology' itself.

The most influential early medieval proponent of etymology as a road to understanding was Isidore of Seville in his *Etymologiae*. By no means all Isidore's etymologies are negligible, but the desire to provide a *causa nominis* at any cost is particularly noticeable in his treatment of the names of peoples in Book IX, which also conveys something of the method of seventh-century etymological explanation.[66] Some names are derived rather unexcitingly from topographical features, especially rivers. Many are derived from royal or princely founders, occasionally recognized as the offspring of gods.[67] The method here typically proceeds in a direction completely opposite to that of the

---

63 *Cosmographia* VII 68: *Die Kosmographie des Aethicus*, ed. Otto Prinz (Munich, 1993).

64 There is a faint echo in an addition to Servius' commentary on the *Aeneid* VI 14 ('vaccam ligneam ... quam maxime taurus adpetebat'), but not enough to preclude coincidence.

65 Ernst Robert Curtius, *European Literature and the Latin Middle Ages*, trans. Willard R. Trask (New York, 1953), Appendix XIV, 495–500. Separating the playful and the serious is difficult: Matthew 16:18 is good case in point. See also Isidore's own description of etymology, *Etymologiae* I xxix: 'Omnis enim rei inspectio etymologia cognita planior est.'

66 For a French translation and commentary, *Étymologies: Livre IX*, ed. Marc Reydellet (Paris, 1984).

67 E.g. the Dorians, from Dorus son of Neptune and Ellepsis: *Etymologiae* IX ii 80, but cf. Reydellet, *Étymologies*, 83.

explanation, the founder's name in reality being fashioned in retrospect from the name of the people; for example, Isidore tells us that the Franks were named after a *dux* of theirs, obviously the Francio of Fredegar's *Chronicle*.[68] Many other explanations attempt to link names to cultural characteristics. Some people suspect, we are told, that the Britons are called that in Latin because they are stupid (*bruti*); the Gepids (*Gipedes*) derive their name from their preference for foot combat (*pedestre proelium*), the Sarmatians (*Sarmatae*) from their enthusiasm for war (*studium armorum*).[69] Physical characteristics are invoked as well: the *Germani* are so called because of their hugeness – in the size of their bodies and in the numbers making up the various peoples (*inmania corpora inmanesque nationes*); the Gauls get their name from the whiteness of their bodies, for milk, in Greek, is called *gála*.[70] Isidore recognizes the role of languages other than Latin and Greek, though he was rarely in a position to make use of them.[71] In his etymology of the Britons, for instance, he seems to recognize the existence of a non-Latin derivation, and he mistakenly believes that the name of the Scotti in their own language is derived from the practice of tattooing;[72] one of his etymologies for the name Franks may be based on a Frankish word.[73]

Ancient and early medieval etymological speculation, needless to say, was not based upon scientific linguistics. Casual and even remote resemblances between words and word elements were sufficient to establish explanatory connections. Derivations could come from Latin, Greek, and other languages, though sometimes without much discrimination. As far as the present subject is concerned, this kind of etymology is important because, when its presuppositions and methodology are taken into account, the prospect that the Merovech story was tied to contemporary etymological theory becomes an attractive possibility. The tale seems designed to clarify the derivation of the name Merovingian from Merovech ('per co regis Francorum post vocantur Merohingii').

68 'Franci a quodam proprio duce vocari putantur.' *Etymologiae* IX ii 101.
69 Ibid., 102, 92, 93
70 Ibid., 97, 104
71 Except for Hebrew in biblically based etymologies; cf. ibid., I xix: 'Multa [vocabula] etiam e diversarum gentium sermone vocantur. Unde et origo eorum vix cernitur. Sunt enim pleraque barbara nomina et incognita Latinis et Graecis.'
72 Ibid., IX ii 103. There is a confusion here with the Picti, but whether as a result of a false etymology yet again is another story.
73 Or not. 'Alii [cf. n. 68] eos a feritate morum nuncupatos existimant' (ibid., 101). *Feritas* is often taken in modern scholarship as referring to a Frankish word related to ON *frekkr*. Isidore's readership, at any rate, is likely to have been satisfied with the Latin etymology from *feritas*; it is no worse than many others. Cf. the derivation of the Thracians from *trux* (ibid, 82). Isidore is not alone, incidentally, in giving more than one explanation. Readers could pick what pleased them: 'Hic quoque mensis habet dubias in nomine causas, / quae placeant, positis omnibus, ipse leges' (Ovid, *Fasti* VI 1–2).

Viewed in this light, the conceiving of Merovech would be an *origo* – not in Hauck's sense, as a type of authentic myth of primitive origins, but in the contemporary sense of a *causa nominis*, an explanatory tale cast in the mode of sixth- or seventh-century etymological speculation. How is the story related to the etymology of Merovech?

For some time modern philology has pursued the etymology of Merovech in its own way. Though it is armed with the achievements of scientific linguistics, its goals have often been very similar to those of its ancient and medieval predecessors: to explain origins by etymology, to find in the name a key to original circumstances and conditions. Thus, Müllenhoff some time ago proposed that behind Merovech stood a god, Merwe, the name for an arm of the sea at the mouth of the Scheldt. More recent philology, starting with a completely different etymology for Merovech, has been enlisted, not very successfully, to aid the current claims for bull-worshipping Franks.[74] These modern efforts have been hampered, however, by the nineteenth-century association of philology, mythology, and history of religion, and by the conviction that the correct etymology of Merovech, if only it could be determined, would unlock some of the religious secrets of Frankish paganism.

Earlier generations, untutored by modern philology and unfamiliar with the concerns of comparative religion, saw more clearly the role of unscientific, contemporary etymology in the story of Merovech's conception. Johannes Georg von Eckhart, in the early eighteenth century, for example, proposed simply that the story derived from Meroveus' name. *Mer* signified *mare*, sea; *veus*, the equivalent of a German *veh* or *vieh,* meant beast (*bestia*). The elements of the name Meroveus together were thus the equivalents of *animal marinum* or *bestia Neptuni*.[75]

Such an interpretation still needed to be seriously addressed by nineteenth-century scholarship. Waitz considered an etymologizing explanation a possibility.[76] Müllenhoff argued, to the contrary, that the Frankish word for 'sea' was

---

74 Franz Rolf Schröder, 'Merowech,' *Beiträge zur Geschichte der deutschen Sprache und Literatur* 96 (1974): 241–5, deriving the first element, Mero, from a word meaning 'ruminant.' In Gregory's story of Ragnachar and Farro (*Hist.* II 42), Wenskus ('Bemerkungen zum Thunginus,' 236) claims to find the meaning 'bull' in the latter's name, and confirmation of sexual rituals connected with Frankish kingship. The story actually depends on a pun between Farro and *fara*, Ragnachar's retinue: A.C. Murray, *Germanic Kinship Structure: Studies in Law and Society in Antiquity and the Early Middle Ages* [Toronto, 1983], 93–4.

75 *Commentarii de rebus Franciae Orientalis* (Würzburg, 1729), I: 29; quoted in Kurth, *Histoire poétique*, 153 n, and cf. p. 9. His interpretation of the story as an allegory, with Meroveus as Chlodio's stepson by a previous marriage, is not likely to find a sympathetic modern reading.

76 Georg Waitz, *Deutsche Verfassungsgeschichte* (Kiel, 1847), 2: 37. Scheibelreiter (as in n. 6) accepts the likelihood that the '(Burgondo-) Roman' Fredegar saw the etymology 'sea' in Merovech's name, but in doing so confounded genuine Frankish tradition.

mari, and that a vowel change of the 'a' to 'e' was improbable in the fifth and sixth centuries.[77] But this kind of argument is to miss the point that the only linguistic criterion for association was similitude.[78] The first element of Merovech could readily be interpreted as Frankish for 'sea' by Frankish, Latin, Burgundian, or even Gothic speakers; sound and appearance were close enough to satisfy the not very exacting standards of sixth- or seventh-century etymologizers. We have already seen the variations that orthography could produce.[79] The same considerations apply to the second element, *vechus/veus*, which readily suggests common Germanic words for cattle (from a Germanic *fehu*). Kurth acknowledged, but rejected, an etymologizing interpretation because, he argued, fifth-century Franks would not have had a scholar capable of undertaking the task.[80] Again, this poorly represents the implications of an etymologizing interpretation. An etymological fable built upon Merovech's name would hardly have been a product of the fifth century in the first place; the sixth and seventh, on the other hand, would have been rife with scholars, and possibly wags, of varying ethnicities, happy to apply the etymological arts to a distant, poorly attested, king of the Franks.

The possibility of an etymologizing tale was increasingly passed over as scholarship vainly pursued its goal of determining the true etymology and its connection to primitive myth.[81] While nineteenth-century scholarship grudgingly acknowledged a contemporary etymologizing interpretation, we should recognize that the rejection of it was largely due to commitment in the scholarly discourse of the day to thoroughly different modes of explanation, focused on mythology and the oral transmission of primitive religious notions.[82] These modes are still very much in evidence in recent scholarship, where, adapted to

---

77 'Die Merovingische Stammesage,' 431. Müllenhoff's argument is made again by Otto Höfler (as in n. 6). But cf. Ewig's argument ('Die Namengbung,' 29) that the name of Maroveus, bishop of Poitiers, is actually the royal name Meroveus, and presupposes kinship with the royal house. One awaits explanation for the wool-worker's daughter Merofled.

78 See Isidore on the Goths: 'Goti a Magog filio Iafeth nominati putantur de similitudine ultimae sillibae' (*Etymologiae* IX ii 89). Similitude served etymologizers well for the next millennium.

79 Above, at n. 50.

80 *Histoire poétique*, 154: the next argument, one suspects, is the real reason for his rejection: 'et la légende a un caractère trop archaïque pour cela.'

81 The failure is clear from the handbooks and the reviews of literature: M. Schönfeld, *Wörterbuch der Altgermanischen Personen- und Völkernamen nach der Überlieferung des klassischen Altertums*, 2d ed. (Heidelberg, 1965; first published 1911), s. vv. Chlodavichus, Merobaudes, Meroveus; Franz Jostes, *Sonnenwende: Forschungen zur germanischen Religions- und Sagengeschichte* (Munster, 1926), 1: 199–200; Franz Rolf Schröder, 'Merowech,' 242 f.

82 Not endorsed everywhere, of course; see, for example, Henry Bosley Woolf, *The Old Germanic Principles of Name-Giving* (Baltimore, 1939), 179–80, who in passing explains the story of Merovech's birth as 'the result, doubtless, of an attempt to explain the meaning of the name.'

current theories about the social and political constructs of Germanic society, they have acquired a new lease on life.

Etymologizing is common in Fredegar's *Chronicle*. We are told, for example, that the Franks were called after Francio, the Turks after Torquatus or Turcoth, the Latins after Latinus, and that Friga ruled over Phrygia.[83] Etymologizing can also involve brief narrative explanations. Following Orosius, Fredegar derives the name of the Burgundians, for example, from their establishment of fortresses (*burgi*) on the Rhine.[84] The town of Daras is built on the spot where the Emperor Justinian supposedly told the Persian emperor, 'You shall give back' the towns and provinces of the Roman Empire.[85] The account of the relation between the Avar and Slav battlelines is based on a false explanation of the term *befulci*.[86] The early Franks are said to have built a city named after Troy (Xanten, that is, Colonia Traiana?);[87] indeed, the legend of the Trojan origin of the Franks probably depended on a series of false linguistic associations. A good example of etymologizing word play is a fable of the stag and lion: the emperor Leo is represented by, naturally, the lion.[88] To this list should be added Fredegar's account of the conception of Merovech and the derivation of the Merovingian name.

III

The argument presented here is that Merovech's name, Mero-vechus, would have easily lent itself to being interpreted as *Neptuni bestia*, Neptune's beast, or, more specifically, Neptune's bull. The story connected with the name was thus intended to answer the common query *cur et unde*: How did this name first arise?[89] If a typical line of reasoning was followed closely connected with explaining the name elements (*causa nominis*), the name Merovech would have

83 Fred. *Chron.* II 5; II 6; III 2; II 9.

84 Ibid., II 46.

85 Ibid., II 62, and see notes by Krusch in his edition of Fredegar; Kusternig, 'Fredegar' (as in note 3); and comments by Wallace-Hadrill, *Long-Haired Kings*, 91.

86 Fred. *Chron.* IV 48, and see the notes by Krusch, Kusternig, and Wallace-Hadrill. Krusch suggested *vexilla* for *vestila* in the phrase 'vestila priliae facientes.' *Tela* seems to me more likely; cf. 'telam priliae ... preparatam' (IV 64) and 'tela priliae construens' (IV 90).

87 Fred. *Chron.* III 2.

88 Ibid., II 57.

89 A good example appears in Suetonius' report of etymological speculation surrounding the name Galba: 'Qui primus Sulpiciorum cognomen Galbae tulit cur aut unde traxerit, ambigitur. Quidam putant, quod oppidum Hispaniae frustra diu oppugnatum inlitis demum galbano facibus succenderit; alii, quod in diuturna valitudine galbeo, id est remediis lana involutis, assidue uteretur; nonulli, quod praepinguis fuerit visus, quem galbam Galli vocent; vel contra, quod tam exilis, quam sunt animalia quae in aesculis nascuntur appellanturque galbae.' (It is

suggested that the first king bearing it must have been the product of a brutish coupling of his mother with a bull of Neptune. The best-known creatures of this kind were the beasts associated with Neptune in stories concerning Pasiphaë and the Minotaur, which has accordingly been invoked by way of analogy. We ourselves also need to ask *cur et unde* with respect to the etymology itself and the character of the tale accompanying it. The following discussion considers whether it is possible to locate the circumstances behind the etymological invention. If the investigation reveals a veritable *embarras de richesse*, and thus a definite context remains elusive, the effort to find it shows how readily an etymologizing explanation fits the content of the tale and conditions of the sixth- and seventh-century Merovingian kingdom.

The frequency of the name Merovech in the Merovingian house could suggest a context for the origin of the story. Scholars have long noted that the name was revived for the first time under Chilperic and enjoyed a short-lived popularity as a king's name until the early seventh century. To his children by Audovera, Chilperic gave names meant to recall the founders of the dynasty: Merovech and Clovis, to two of his sons; and Basina, the name of Childeric's queen, to a daughter. The Merovech in question failed to outlive his father, being killed in 577 after an ill-considered marriage to Sigibert's widow, Brunhild.[90] Clothar II, another son of Chilperic, and his successor, used 'Merovech' again for his own first-born son, who died in some way as a result of his defeat and subsequent captivity at the hands of Theuderic II in 604.[91] A short time later, the Austrasian and Burgundian houses adopted the name: first, Theuderic II in 607 named his fourth-born son Merovech, and arranged for the child to have Clothar II as his godfather;[92] and Theudebert II had a son Merovech who was still a child in 613.[93] Both Merovechs fell victim to the troubles of that year: according to Fredegar, Theudebert's son was picked up by the foot and his head smashed against a rock at the command of his victorious uncle; Theuderic's son had his life spared by his godfather, Clothar II, after the latter's vic-

---

uncertain why the first of the Sulpicii who bore the surname Galba assumed the name, and whence it was derived. Some think that it was because after having for a long time unsuccessfully besieged a town in Spain, he at last set fire to it by torches smeared with *galbanum*; others because during a long illness he made constant use of *galbeum*, that is to say remedies wrapped in wool; still others, because he was a very fat man, such as the Gauls term *galba*, or because he was, on the contrary, as slender as the insects called *galbae*, which breed in oak trees): *Galba* III, trans. J.C. Rolfe, Loeb Classical Library (Cambridge, Mass., and London, 1914).

90 Gregory, *Hist.* IV 28; V 2; 18.
91 Fred. *Chron.* IV 25, 26.
92 An arrangement surely meant to offset the death of Clothar's Merovech.
93 Fred. *Chron.* IV 29, 38.

tory, and was removed from political life, though he lived for many years after.[94] The name was never used again in the Merovingian house. If the revival of the name Merovech by Chilperic after four generations suggests an occasion for the etymologizing story, still more fundamental – no matter when the tale might have arisen – is the question of the purpose of the story. This inquiry takes us in two main directions.

In the first, the story might be understood to be favourable to the Merovingians and a product of the court or its supporters. Eugen Ewig has argued that in Chilperic's name-giving there is an initiative on the king's part to emphasize the mythic implications of the dynasty's origins, such implications being, in Ewig's view, the pagan, Germanic, and sacral traditions associated with the Merovingian house.[95] Chilperic *is* the best candidate for the type of ruler who may have been inclined to associate remarkable circumstances with the foundation of his dynasty, but the character of his antiquarianism points to the contemporary world of Latin letters grounded in ecclesiastical and secular models of antiquity. Poet, reformer of the alphabet, composer of hymns, and dabbler in theological questions, Chilperic is the one Merovingian with a claim to learning; his efforts to refurbish the amphitheatres in Paris and Soissons in order to provide their citizens with shows (*spectaculum*) is a testament to the depth of his desire to imitate the ancient secular traditions of Roman rulership.[96] The 'mythic' and 'sacral' elements we know to have been available to him or any other Merovingian ruler of Gaul in the sixth century were not Germanic, but antique, and pagan only in the unreal and conventionalized form of late Roman rhetoric. Viewed from this perspective, the type of antiquarian associations that could be expected can be seen in the panegyric for the emperor Anthemius delivered by Sidonius Apollinaris in 468, about a year before he became bishop of Clermont. Sidonius, whose name evoked respect in the sixth century, develops the antique theme of the sympathetic fecundity of nature that accompanies the hero's birth (in this instance, Anthemius), but also the miraculous intervention of the gods; in the latter case, Sidonius not surprisingly reserves his more remarkable illustrations for long-dead heroes. Thus, he invokes the cases of Alexander the Great and Augustus, the mother of each of whom was considered to have conceived by a serpent god, representing Apollo and Jove, respectively.[97] As Merovech's name suggests a related, remote fic-

---

94 Ibid., IV 38, 40, 42.
95 Ewig, 'Die Namengebung bei den ältesten Frankenkönigen,' 33, 43.
96 Gregory, *Hist.* V 17, V 44, VI 46, and James, *Franks,* 165–8.
97 *Carmina* 2. 94–133, ed. W.B. Anderson, 2: 15–19, esp. 'venisse beatos / sic loquitur natura deos ... / magnus Alexander nec non Augustus habentur / concepti serpente deo Phoebumque Iovemque / divisere sibi ...' The stories are told more fully in Plutarch, *Alexander* 2, 3, and Suetonius, *Augustus* 94.

tion, Fredegar's story could originally have been presented in a similar setting, and found a sympathetic Merovingian audience pleased to hear that the founding of its own house was comparable to the allegedly wondrous conceptions of the great historical figures Alexander and Augustus.[98]

Especially if the Merovech story is a relatively late invention, then a slightly different perspective on this imaginary setting is possible. By Fredegar's time at least, the Macedonians, Romans, and Franks were all deemed to be descendants of the Trojans.[99] To someone learned in the rhetorical and pseudo-historical tradition of antiquity, a pleasing fiction, according to which the founder of the Merovingian house was conceived by a creature of Neptune, might be thought to complete a series of triads: the three great peoples of Trojan descent (Macedonians, Romans, and Franks); the wondrous conception of three, distant heroes (Alexander, Augustus, and Merovech); and their descent from the three principal gods of antiquity (Apollo, Jove, and Neptune). Such a simulated antique fantasy might have been a pleasing diversion, but to maintain that one like it was ever created and left its mark on Fredegar's *Chronicle* exceeds the evidence available to us.

In more general terms, the antique portrayal of the births of Alexander and Augustus has a bearing on the ambiguous description of Merovech's conception. In Fredegar's story the king is said to have been conceived 'aut a bistea aut a viro.' Hauck saw temporary divinization in this phrase, interpreting it in a possible, if unusual, manner ('by both the beast and the husband'). The standard meaning ('by either the beast or the husband') has, with somewhat more reason, suggested to others the effect of a bowdlerizing Christian interpretation of a real animistic Germanic myth in which, originally, only a divine beast was believed to have engendered the king. It might have been noticed above that, in Sidonius' reference to the births of Alexander and Augustus, the soon-to-be bishop chooses his words with care: their conceptions, he says, are regarded as supernatural, but he does not affirm that they were. We should avoid the temptation simply to see Christian sensibilities at work here: neither Fredegar nor Sidonius was altering traditional material owing to his Christian beliefs. Ancient historiography shows the same reticence. Though the births of Alexander and Augustus are surrounded with portents and omens, conception is not presented unequivocally as divine. Plutarch on Alexander and Suetonius on Augustus present the supernatural origins of their subjects as versions for readers to consider; while detailing the mysterious and intimate relations between the mothers and creatures sacred to the gods, as recounted by other sources, they avoid committing themselves to the view that such relations demonstrate

98 Cf. Fred. *Chron.* II 4, 8, 27, 28, 33.
99 Ibid., II 4, 6, 8.

sexual intercourse and divine impregnation, though readers were free to draw more definite conclusions.[100] Ambiguity is a motif in the conception stories of classical heroes. The account of Merovech's conception follows the same pattern even in its very restricted compass, presenting the possibility that either the beast or Chlodio engendered the king. The motif, it seems likely, was present in Fredegar's source.

The model of the antique hero presents its subject in a laudatory fashion. Another line of inquiry takes a different direction, starting from the premise that Fredegar's story is unfavourable to the Merovingians.[101] Byzantine parallels are helpful in showing how hatred generated by contemporary political life could be expressed in defamatory tales that might seem suggestive for understanding the treatment of Merovech as founder of the Merovingian house. In the *Secret History*, a catalogue of seething invective against Justinian and Theodora (among others), Procopius attributes the emperor's conception – by the admission of Justinian's own mother – to intercourse with a demon. Anxious to prove that Justinian himself, as a consequence, was a demon, he alleges eyewitness accounts of the emperor's appearance undergoing grotesque, supernatural changes late at night in the palace. Theodora, too, Procopius tells us, was a consort of demons even before her union with Justinian; former lovers were sure they had been driven from her presence by a demon desiring to spend the night with her.[102] A society that readily saw the divine at work in the fortunate outcome of human affairs was also inclined to perceive the demonic behind life's reverses and failures. In the *Secret History*, the natural marriage of the demonic and the pornographic, prevalent in contemporary thought, found a congenial home in invective. Though it would hardly be surprising if those suffering at the hands of the Merovingians or critical of their rule were tempted to find in the name of the dynasty's founder demonstration of the fiendish, unnatural origins of the regime, Fredegar's account, as brief as it is, on balance weighs against reading its elements as pornographic and demonic. The ambivalent treatment of the impregnation of Merovech's mother, as discussed above, points rather to a heroic model for the tale.[103] Invective, as Procopius' unconstrained remarks show, does not equivocate.

100 Plutarch, *Alexander* II, III and Suetonius, *Augustus* XCIV.
101 Cf. Kusternig, 'Fredegar,' 12, 89, who regards the Merovech and Basina stories (III 12, and below, p. 150) as anti-Merovingian, but is reluctant to reject interpretation of the former as myth.
102 *SH* 12; and see Averil Cameron, *Procopius and the Sixth Century* (Berkeley and Los Angeles, 1985), 49–66
103 Anti-Merovingians familiar with Fredegar's story might have found confirmation of their views in Aulus Gellius' comment: 'poetae ... ferocissimos et inmanes et alienos ab omni humanitate, tamquam e mari genitos, Neptuni filios dixerunt.' The comparison is with the *praestantissimi virtute filii Iovis. NA* XV xxi.

The insertion of the story in Fredegar's *Chronicle* itself also requires another approach to interpreting the story's contents: does the point of view of Fredegar's work as a whole imply a purpose for the interpolation? We have to consider the possibility of two contexts for the Merovech story, each one distinct from the other: the original context for which the tale was first invented, and a later adaptation of the tale by Fredegar and his use of it in the *Chronicle*. Since the recognition of the *Chronicle* as the work of one author, conventionally called Fredegar, we are in a better position to consider the second context, but our understanding of Fredegar as an author is still undeveloped. In particular, his approach to sources and his method of condensing, paraphrasing, and interpolating in the first three books are in need of more consideration from the perspective of the work as a whole than they have received to date. What are offered here are brief and tentative observations.

To begin with, the elements of the Merovech story, it should be observed, echo other interests of Fredegar. For instance, references to animals abound in the *Chronicle*, almost always used as fables, prodigies, and didactic analogies.[104] The portentous character of some of these references is part of a broader category of Fredegarian interests concerned with monitory and prophetic signs. He employs the standard litany of these topoi, derived from classical and biblical traditions and part of the intellectual climate of the day: dreams, prophecies – Sybilline, supposedly, and contemporary – and portents drawn from the celestial, natural, and animal worlds.[105] It is worth considering, therefore, whether the Minotaur-like sea beast in the Merovech story was supposed to be seen as part of this category of interpretation.[106] Isidore had classified creatures resembling the Minotaur among portents established for future significations, just like the dreams and oracles by which God forewarned individuals and peoples of future misfortune (*clades*).[107]

The *Neptuni bestia* of the Merovech story also recalls the most famous oracular presentation of Fredegar's *Chronicle*: the visions (*visiones*) of Merovech's

---

104 Fred. *Chron.* II 57 (horses in the false dream of Lilia; fable of the lion and the stag); II 60 (wild-animal guide and the invasion of Africa); II 62 (eagle and Justinian); III 12 (various *bestiae* in Childeric's visions); IV 38 (fable of the wolf and its cubs); IV 68 (Wends as the dogs of God).

105 Dreams (II 57, III 12); prophecies and signs (II 56, 60, 62; III 58, 59, 71; IV 11, 13, 15, 18, 20, 32, 36, 56, 65).

106 That the animal (*fera*) that Fredegar very self-consciously has accompany the Vandal crossing to Africa (*Chron.* II 60) was supposed to be a sea beast is doubtful.

107 *Etymologiae* XI iii 4: 'Quaedam autem portentorum creationes in significationibus futuris constituta videntur. Vult enim deus interdum ventura significare per aliqua nascentium noxia, sicut et per somnos et per oracula, qua praemoneat et significet quibusdam vel gentibus hominibus futuram cladem.'

son, Childeric.[108] On his wedding night, Childeric is instructed by his bride, Basina, to go outside the palace and report to her what he sees. He does so three times, and each time sees beasts in the likeness of various kinds of animals. The first time, the creatures appear as lions, unicorns, and leopards; the second time, they appear in the likeness of bears and wolves; the third time, they appear as dogs and lesser creatures, dragging one another down and tumbling about.[109] Basina explains the significance of each vision by relating it to the history of the Merovingian house: the lion stands for the son soon to be born (Clovis), the unicorns and leopards for his sons; the bears and wolves represent the kings that come after; the dogs stand for those who will rule when the kingdom falls apart; and the lesser creatures, the people at the time who will rend one another without the fear of princes. It has long been recognized that this story rests on knowledge of the four beasts (*bestiae*) in the Book of Daniel (c. 7) – the lioness, bear, leopard, and the final *bestia terribilis* with ten horns – representing the four *regna*, the great empires of antiquity. In Fredegar, the elements of Daniel's *visio* are handled very freely, however, and harmonized with the particular conditions of the Merovingian kingdom.[110] The freedom with which the biblical material is recycled – it serves less as a model than as a stimulus for a good, and pointed, story – should warn us against assuming that the original perspective of a source was transferred when its elements were adapted to new conditions or inserted in the *Chronicle*. Moreover, how much, if any, of the story should be attributed to Fredegar himself is a question, for the sequence of generations, as usually interpreted, seems to point to a period of composition early in the seventh century or before. Yet, Childeric's visions give us reason to wonder if Fredegar should be regarded as a particular friend of the Merovingians.[111]

The relation of Childeric's dream to the Book of Daniel draws us back again to the etymological interpretation of the name Merovech. Daniel's vision brings the beasts from the sea: 'Et quattuor bestiae grandes ascendebant de mari.' Fredegar elsewhere displays interest in the prophecies of Daniel.[112] It is therefore difficult to imagine that the author who inserted both the visions of Childeric and the Merovech story in his *Chronicle* almost side by side did so without noticing reminiscence of Daniel's beasts, but, if so, how he understood the conjunction is quite another question. Did Fredegar harbour the notion that the

---

108 Fred. *Chron.* III 12.
109 The concept here seems to be related to the 'bestias ... nocturnas, et non tam bestias quam dira prodigia, quod nequequam in luce sed in umbris cernuntur nocturnis,' of the *Liber Monstrorum*, II 20, though the fit is not quite perfect.
110 See Krusch's note to Fred. *Chron.* III 12.
111 Cf. n. 108, above.
112 Chron. II 27: the context is the capture of Jerusalem (Dan. 9).

Merovingian dynasty may have had its origins in an unwholesome event of portentous significance, denoting the temporary success of dynasties? There must surely have been those in Gaul who viewed the Merovingians by the mid-seventh century as a dismal interlude in the long history of the Franks going back to the days of Priam. Or did the sea beast of the Merovingians simply signify the new kingdom arising in Gaul under the hegemony of the Franks and their royal family? By identifying the fourth *regnum* of Daniel as Rome, Orosius, an author known to Fredegar, had already altered the original assignment of the kingdoms and rendered innocuous the apocalyptic significance.[113] A *bestia Neptuni* may have seemed a suitable sign marking the rise of the kingdom of the Franks, like that of the Macedonians and the Romans, the creation of Trojan exiles.

To sum up: Sacral kingship among the Franks is a hypothetical construct of modern historiography founded on the exegesis of nineteenth-century *Germanistik* as adapted to recent theories about the nature of early Germanic society. No source gives unequivocal testimony to the existence of such an institution. The centre-piece of the evidence, the story of Merovech's conception in the seventh-century *Chronicle* of Fredegar, has commonly been interpreted as an archaic myth underpinning the sacral ideology of Merovingian kingship. The common assumption that only archaic myth could produce the peculiar features of the Merovech story is clearly mistaken, if the historical setting and the literary and intellectual context of the tale are examined. The story is better understood as an etymologizing fable conforming to sixth- and seventh-century interest in *origines*. By the mid-sixth century, the figure of the ancestral Merovech, about whom nothing very definite was known, was distant enough to lend his name to speculation on the origins of the royal house. Etymological examination, a primary tool in investigating the origins of the past, readily suggested a derivation from terms meaning 'sea' and 'beast,' or, more specifically, 'bull,' giving the meaning *Neptuni bestia*. To match this etymology, a tale in which a sea creature might have copulated with Merovech's mother seemed an appropriate explanation for the name; events of this kind had analogues in pseudo-historical tales of Alexander and Augustus, and especially in stories associated with Minos and the bull of Neptune.

It is hard to determine with precision the circumstances in which such a tale may have arisen. The revival of the name Merovech in the half-century or so after Chilperic reintroduced it into the dynasty is a likely moment for an ety-

---

113 *Hist.* II 1. On Orosius' treatment of the *regna*, see edition by Marie-Pierre Arnaud-Lindet, XLV–LXVI.

mologizing account of origins to be devised, but other contexts, about which we are uninformed, could have occasioned the tale. The brevity of the passage in the *Chronicle* makes it difficult to establish with certainty the original perspective of the story on the basis simply of the contents before us, which can be construed *in bono* or *in malo*, as favourable or unfavourable to the Merovingians. The ambivalent treatment of the queen's impregnation, however, speaks in favour of the former perspective, and points to the tale being modelled on the ambiguous tales told about the conception of antique heroes. Such a reading fits the tale having its origins among those close to the court and being intended to model the origins of the Merovingian house upon ancient heroes, especially those of the Macedonians and the Romans, who by the mid-seventh century at least were understood to be related to the Franks through common Trojan origins. It is also conceivable that the tale was developed by someone with a neutral outlook on Merovingian politics, but curious about the reappearance of the name Merovech as a principal name of the Frankish house in the late sixth and early seventh centuries.

The inclusion of the tale in Fredegar's *Chronicle* presents a slightly different set of problems. The tale certainly fits Fredegar's interest in animal tales and portentous events. It is unlikely this conjunction makes Fredegar the author, but it does help explain his selection of an existing story, and possibly his adaptation of it to his own understanding of Frankish history. He may also have been attracted by the resemblance between the beast from the sea and the beasts in the Book of Daniel, which helped inspire the neighbouring tale of the visions of Childeric, Merovech's son. Difficulty arises in determining the meaning he attributed to these correspondences. Whether Fredegar's reflections on the course of Merovingian politics prompted him to consider the origin of the present dynasty with a certain degree of dismay or whether he simply saw the *bestia Neptuni* as marking the debut of Frankish hegemony, the Book of Daniel was surely no source of rigorous, and learned, apocalyptic, but inspiration for entertaining and prophetic tales.

8

Aristocratic Power in
Eighth-Century Lombard Italy

CHRIS WICKHAM

In August 714, Ambrosius *inluster maioredomus* arrived in Arezzo, sent by the
Lombard king Liutprand (712-44) to resolve a boundary dispute between the
dioceses of Siena and Arezzo; his judgment was in favour of Arezzo, and, the
following March, Liutprand ratified it. The bishop of Siena presumably appealed at once, for in June 715 a second royal emissary (*missus*), Guntheram
notarius, arrived in Siena to reopen the case; in July, he and four bishops judged
again for Arezzo, and, in October, Liutprand in a formal hearing confirmed
their judgment. The case is famous, in part because it went on being reopened
fairly regularly until after 1200, with the bishop of Siena nearly always losing,
but never giving in; and in part because Guntheram's inquisition of local priests
and laymen survives, offering us a rich slice of life at an unusually early date. I
cite it here, however, for a different reason: it also sheds an unusually early
shaft of light on judicial routine. The case was certainly a serious one, involving
local leaders with entrenched positions, but it seems to have been normal that
they should appeal to the Lombard king or seek his ratification in the capital at
Pavia, 350 kilometres away, four times in little over a year; and equally normal
that the king should twice send judicial emissaries to judge on the spot by
means of systematic inquisition.[1]

I am grateful to Steven Bassett, Leslie Brubaker, and Wendy Davies for criticizing this text.

1 Documents in *CDL* I 4, 17, 19, 20; III 12, 13. Both Ambrosius and Guntheram are called *missi*
in the body of the texts. In I 19 (p. 62), there is reference to Ambrosius' previous inquest. The
dispute blew up because the civil territory of Siena extended some way into the diocese of
Arezzo, and the bishops of Siena, with the active support of the gastalds of Siena, laid claim to
the whole civil territory of their city as their diocese. The cases have been treated many times;
a good recent example is S. Gasparri, 'Il regno longobardo in Italia,' in *Langobardia*, ed. P.
Cammarosaro and S. Gasparri (Udine, 1990), 237–305, at 241–9. For the long term, see J.-P.
Delumeau, *Arezzo: Espace et sociétés, 715–1230* (Paris, 1996), 475–85.

This impression of routine administrative intervention by Lombard kings throughout their kingdom of northern Italy and Tuscany (I exclude the still largely autonomous southern duchies of Spoleto and Benevento) is not atypical.[2] There is evidence of other formal appeals to kings and their central court in Pavia across the sixty years of the reigns of Liutprand and his successors, the last independent Lombard kings; some is found in court cases, some in royal legislation.[3] This does not mean that more local, city, procedures were not effective; documents for disputes show that local courts were entirely standard – indeed, so much so that the major local government officials, dukes and gastalds, who ran the armies of each city territory and also local royal estates, are increasingly referred to in royal legislation just as *iudices*: in the king's mind, their judicial function stood for the rest.[4] But appeal to Pavia was already normal; people indeed went to Pavia, or more specifically to the king, to ratify even uncontentious documentation. And when the king decided, they listened; cases were reopened and judges reversed their judgments. Royal legislation is even occasionally cited in private land transactions, as it never was in contemporary Francia.[5] The impact of central government on the local society of the Lombard kingdom was, by the eighth century, consistent, capillary, and, as far as can be seen, widely accepted.

Why this was so, and how the system worked politically, are the problems I wish to raise here; for there are a number of reasons why the conditions of the Lombard kingdom could be seen as surprising. However we deal with the endless debate over the crisis and transformation of the western Roman Empire, few disagree that the Roman fiscal system finally crumbled in the early seventh century at the very latest. Eighth-century Lombard kings did not tax. Their resources rested almost exclusively on their extensive landowning; but so,

2 For the purposes of this essay, I also stop with the Frankish conquest in 774. Spoleto and Benevento were probably structurally similar; however, their terrain was mountainous (and therefore communications were poorer), and their urban infrastructure was almost certainly weaker. But they are ill documented as yet, except for the Spoleto–Rome border area, around the monastery of Farfa.

3 *CDL* II 163, 255; Liutprand 135, 136, etc., Ratchis 10.

4 *Iudices*: see Liutprand, Ratchis, Aistulf passim. For local administration, the best survey is Gasparri, 'Regno longobardo.' On power as jurisdiction, see P. Delogu, 'Lombard and Carolingian Italy,' in *New Cambridge Medieval History*, ed. R. McKitterick (Cambridge, 1995), 2: 290–319, at 290–3. In the more numerous court-case records of the Carolingian period, courts were also held overwhelmingly in cities: see H. Keller, ' Der Gerichtsort in oberitalienischen und toskanischen Städten,' *Quellen und Forschungen* 49 (1969): 1–72; F. Bougard, *La justice dans le royaume d'Italie* (Rome, 1995), 209–18.

5 Ratification: e.g., *CDL* II 137, 163, 170. Judges reversing judgments: *CDL* II 255. Royal legislation cited in *CDL* I 81, 96, etc.

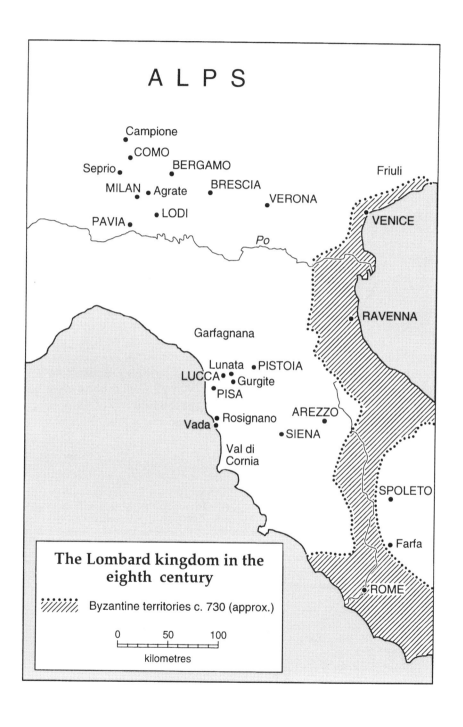

ALPS

Campione
COMO
Seprio
BERGAMO
MILAN • Agrate
BRESCIA
VERONA
LODI
PAVIA
Po
Friuli
VENICE

RAVENNA

Garfagnana

Lunata • PISTOIA
LUCCA • • Gurgite
• PISA
Vada • • Rosignano
AREZZO
• SIENA
Val di
Cornia

SPOLETO

• Farfa

ROME

The Lombard kingdom in the
eighth century

Byzantine territories c. 730 (approx.)

0   50   100

kilometres

therefore, did their capacity to reward the loyal.[6] This offered the usual medieval risks: the more generous kings were, the less they might have in the future; and an infrastructure of local checks and balances became hard to fund. If a local *iudex* was unjust or domineering, it was not easy to see how kings could correct or replace him, except by force. In Francia, only the unusually coherent and directed government of Charlemagne's reign was able to institute administrative measures, such as the *missaticum*, to get around problems such as these, and they did not last out a century; but Lombard Italy had had *missi* like Ambrosius and Guntheram, perhaps sent *ad hoc* but at least acting routinely, from 674 at least, and probably from the 620s.[7] Furthermore, Lombard kings seem to have managed to maintain their power without extensive gifts to dependants; such gifts are, at any rate, rarely mentioned in our sources.[8]

Another reason for possible surprise is that the Lombard aristocracy should not be seen as any easier to deal with than was the aristocracy of other parts of early medieval Europe. They appear in the pages of Paul the Deacon as proud, militaristic, and quick to anger, sometimes to an almost comic degree.[9] And they were certainly not on a personal level all subservient to kings; as the royal dynasty changed, in 744 and 757, and at other times as well, aristocrats came in and out of favour somewhat abruptly, and the unlucky sometimes fled, usually to the Franks. It is not necessary to see the final Lombard failures before Frankish armies in 754, 755, and 773–4 as signs of the structural weakness of the kingdom, given the extent of Frankish military success against nearly everyone else in the period; but Frankish power in itself made it hard to coerce aristocrats who might simply flee north over the Alps, and sometimes did.[10] Faced with

6 Walter Goffart, 'Old and New in Merovingian Taxation,' *Past & Present* 96 (1982): 3–21; Gasparri, 'Regno longobardo,' 262–8.

7 *CDL* III 4 (626x36), 6 (674).

8 *CDL* III 15 and pp. 267–312 lists all known royal gifts to the laity: there are sixteen, mostly small-scale (and also several confirmations of property, which count rather as ratifications, as above, n. 5). *CDL* II 293, the lengthy will of Taido of Bergamo, a royal *gasindius* (retainer), does not show him disposing of any royal gifts. I have discussed this issue in *Early Medieval Italy* (London, 1981), 132–6; see also below, n. 12.

9 Paul, *HL*, e.g. VI 24, 51; see Walter Goffart, *The Narrators of Barbarian History (A.D. 550–800): Jordanes, Gregory of Tours, Bede, and Paul the Deacon* (Princeton, 1988), 378–431. The Beneventan principalities inherited this cultural style (as well as Paul's way of narrating touchy and treasonable behaviour): see for example *Chronicon Salernitanum*, cc. 38–80, ed. U. Westerbergh (Lund, 1956).

10 The classic survey of the mounting problems of the Lombard kingdom in its last two decades is still K. Schmid, 'Zur Ablösung der Langobardenherrschaft durch die Franken,' *Quellen und Forschungen* 52 (1972): 1–35, though he is more catastrophist than others would be (e.g., Wickham, *Early Medieval Italy*, 45–7; Delogu, 'Lombard and Carolingian Italy,' 301–3; D. Harrison, *The Early State and the Towns* [Lund, 1993], 223–32); I would also read his analysis of monastic foundations differently.

these objective problems, one might expect to find at least occasional reference to public power being thwarted, or to kings recognizing the political impossibility of moving too forcefully against powerful opponents; we certainly do in the tenth century in Italy, and in Francia almost continuously. Not among the Lombards in our period, however: at the administrative level I began with, local officials (themselves nearly all aristocrats) continued to do the king's bidding right up to 773 and, apparently, for unusually little reward.[11]

If we want to understand this process better, we need to leave the administrative level, however, and look at how aristocrats themselves dealt in practice with kings, with their peers, and with their inferiors. In the space at my disposal, I will focus in particular on aristocrats in cities, on aristocratic resources, and, finally, on clienteles as guides to aristocratic political action on the local level. This last aspect is perhaps the most neglected up to now; but all are necessary if we want to understand how aristocratic power in general worked, and how it fitted with the image of the state I have just delineated.

II

First, briefly, aristocrats and kings. The signs we have for Lombard Italy, as for other early medieval kingdoms, point clearly towards the conclusion that aristocrats were very interested in royal service. Exactly what an 'aristocrat' is in the eighth-century context is not, it must be said, clear; no word for the category then existed. Paul the Deacon said in a poem that *nobilitas* was, in effect, the opposite of *aegestas*, 'poverty'; this is little more than an epigram, but we have no more precise definitions. Giovanni Tabacco showed in 1972 that the great landowners of the Lombard kingdom were the social group from which royal servants were systematically drawn: private wealth was the basis of (public) political power.[12] My rule-of-thumb definition of 'aristocrats' will in fact be: 'those who were rich enough to have access to royal/public political power.' I will come back in a moment to how rich this actually was; here, however, it must be stressed that such power was pretty systematically sought. Our documents are almost all private, but those for the relatively rich nearly all make reference to relationships with the king, whether titles, offices, relations of personal dependence (the *gasindi regis*), or – as with the family of Gisulf *stra-*

---

11 Though one must never underestimate the capacity of officials simply to amass wealth corruptly; see e.g. Ratchis 10, and, before that, Liutprand, *Notitia de actoribus regis,* 5.

12 Paul, *Poetae Latini Aevi Carolini* (I), ed. E. Dümmler, MGH Poetae Latini Medii Aevi 1 (1881), 48; G. Tabacco, ' La connessione fra potere e possesso nel regno franco e nel regno longobardo,' *Settimane* 20 (1972): 133–68; see also S. Gasparri, 'Grandi proprietari e sovrani nell'Italia longobarda dell'VIII secolo,' *Atti del 6° Congresso di studi sull'alto Medioevo* (Spoleto, 1980), 429–42.

tor of Lodi in the 760s – all of these at once. Sometimes these relationships were achieved by groups of notables, as with the striking arrays of royal dependants and officials who witness in two Brescia documents, of 769 and 771: these may well have simply been the Brescia city élite who transferred to royal offices *en bloc* when their duke became King Desiderius (757–74).[13] I think we can be fairly sure that what the Germans call *Königsnähe* was a normal aspiration for the Lombard landowning élite except in cases of political opposition.

On the other hand, even more immediate on a day-to-day basis was attachment to a city. The Lombard aristocracy seem above all to have been city-based and city-orientated. They are called *cives*, or they state in documents that their *casa habitationis* is in a city or its immediate suburbs, or they privilege urban churches in their pious gifts. Of the thirteen richest families documented in Lucca and its territory in the late Lombard period (Lucca being far and away the best-documented city in Italy, then and later), only two or three seem to have lived in the countryside, and this pattern repeats itself across most of the kingdom.[14] The origins of this urban identity seem to go back to the very start of the Lombard kingdom, and thus, genealogically, to the Roman world before it. But in the eighth-century context we are looking at, consequences are more relevant than origins; urban society in this period had a clear political form. As at the national level, power at the level of the city was closely linked to landowning. The five bishops of Lucca between 713 and 818 were all from the landowning élite just mentioned, and again there are many parallels to this elsewhere; on the secular side, to take just one example, Walpert, the father of Bishop Walprand of Lucca (737–54), had earlier been the city's duke (713–36). Each city, with its local government and local tribunals, and its episcopal structures as well, was the focus of the immediate political activity of most of the landed élite of its territory. It was also the focus of local military identity (as with the *exercitus Senensium civitatis* in a document of 730 from Siena); and there were indeed possibilities for collective urban political activity in the national arena, as with the shifting allegiances of the *nobiles* of Brescia in the 680s, narrated by Paul the Deacon.[15]

---

13 Gisulf's family: *CDL* II 137, 155, 226. Bresciani: *CDL* II 228, 257.

14 In turn, *CDL* I 28, II, 154, 161 (with *MDL* V 170, a. 778); I 30, 70; I 48, 73; I 80, 88, 102, 106, II 179 (this figure, *Crispinus negudians*, may have lived in the countryside, but his profession was presumably urban); I 89, 111 (with *MDL* V 231); I 90 (location uncertain); I 105, 118, 114; II 148 (a rural figure); II 178; II 214; II 250; II 287; and the substantial set of texts for Gunduald of Campori in the mountains of the Garfagnana, for which see below, n. 34. For Lucca and its aristocratic power structure, see in general H.M. Schwarzmaier, *Lucca und das Reich bis zum Ende des II. Jhts* (Tübingen, 1972). Cf. the Bresciani, above n. 13, who show similar patterns.

15 For Walprand, see especially his will, *CDL* I 114; his father is active in *CDL* I 16, 21, 30, 40,

Why does this focus on the city matter? One reason is simply that the infrastructure of the Lombard kingdom was much more concentrated than that of many parts of the early medieval west: everything was essentially in the same place, army and law courts and local élites and local political action, all together inside (or immediately outside) the walls of each town, and each, as a result, much easier to reach. Cities were also major points of reference even for country-dwellers. The 715 Siena–Arezzo inquest, for example, makes it clear that the small and medium owners of the contested territories, some of them living deep in the countryside of southern Tuscany, cared where the boundaries of the diocese of Arezzo lay; and they looked politically to the gastald of Siena, in an apparently systematic manner, even while disagreeing with his attempt to make them subject to the bishop of Siena. All this in itself must have greatly facilitated the administrative routine I began with.[16] And the city focus of local politics also made the maintenance of checks and balances far easier; cities were dominated, not by one family, but many, and one local official could relatively easily be counterposed to another, potentially from a rival family. We do not have precise documentation of city rivalries and factions in our period, but they must have existed; there were certainly fewer major civic offices in a place like Lucca than there were families to fill them, and the resultant struggles probably made Italian cities look very much like the highly factious Clermont of the Merovingian period chronicled by Gregory of Tours and recently analysed by Ian Wood.[17] These patterns, too, would have helped the local affirmation of royal authority.

Italian cities, then, were strong political and social foci for the upper classes. In strictly material terms, however, they were, as archaeologists have shown in the last fifteen years, by no means impressive. The, at times, violent debate over whether early medieval *civitates* in Italy were urban at all according to economic definitions has recently receded; it is increasingly recognized that a certain density of settlement and a relative complexity of economic activity did indeed characterize most of the surviving Roman towns of the Lombard kingdom. But in this debate even the most 'optimistic' scholars (a category that has certainly included me) must recognize that the urban fabric of even the major Lombard cities was in a state of crisis.[18] Brescia, one of the main political cen-

56. See further Schwarzmaier, *Lucca*, 74–8; B. Andreolli, *Uomini nel Medioevo* (Bologna, 1983), 19–32. For Siena, *CDL* I 50; for Brescia in the 680s, Paul, *HL* V 36, 38–9.

16 The major current discussions of these issues are Harrison, *Early State*, which also has a substantial and valuable bibliography, and Gasparri, ' Regno longobardo,' 279–92. For the gastald of Siena in the countryside, see *CDL* I 19 (pp. 63, 67, 71, 74).

17 I.N. Wood, 'The Ecclesiastical Politics of Merovingian Clermont,' in *Ideal and Reality in Frankish and Anglo-Saxon Society*, ed. C.P. Wormald (Oxford, 1983), 34–57.

18 For discussions of this debate, including full bibliographies, see C. Wickham, *Land and Power*

tres of the kingdom and currently the city most systematically studied by archaeologists, saw most of the eastern third of the Roman town razed to the ground and turned into fields, and the monumental buildings north of the Forum given over to squatter settlement in wooden huts; the *cives* and *nobiles* of the city may have been restricted to its western fringe, around the cathedral and the *curtis ducalis*, before King Desiderius built his prestigious royal nunnery, S. Salvatore, on the eastern side in the 750s. Even after that, there may have been in effect two Brescias, not one, subsisting as islands of urbanization inside the old Roman walls. This image of 'città ad isole,' as the Brescian archaeologist Gianpietro Brogiolo (among others) calls them, can be generalized; it has recently been argued that Lucca itself, notwithstanding its active urban families, its dozens of new eighth-century churches, and its nearly perfect Roman street plan, experienced a similar (if rather milder) destructuring process.[19] Simple buildings made out of poor materials, substantial open spaces, the decay and collapse of earlier monumental buildings – these are the features that characterized eighth-century cities, alongside the occasional well-built prestige church with, in some cases, startlingly fine furnishings, and maybe one or two quality town houses and secular public buildings.[20]

We must conclude from this sketch, not that there was a lack of urbanization in Lombard Italy, but that Lombard Italy, including its urban centres, was poor – measured by the standards of late Rome, of the eleventh century, and even of contemporary Francia. Indeed, one of the paradoxes that has emerged from the archaeology of recent years is that Lombard aristocrats were both more urbanized and materially poorer than Frankish aristocrats. The distribution and sophistication of fine pottery, for example, one of the basic archaeological indi-

(London, 1994), 108–11, 117–18; C. Wickham, 'Considerazioni conclusive,' in *La storia dell'alto Medioevo italiano (VI–X secolo) alla luce dell'archeologia,* ed. R. Francovich and G. Noyé (Florence, 1994), 742–7.

19 For all this, see the important new survey of Brescia by G.P. Brogiolo, *Brescia altomedievale* (Mantua, 1993), 85–96; 117 for 'città ad isole.' For Lucca, see I. Belli Barsali, 'La topografia di Lucca nei secoli VIII–XI,' *Atti del 5° Congresso internazionale di studi sull'alto Medioevo* (Spoleto, 1973), 461–554; and now A. De Conno, 'L'insediamento longobardo a Lucca,' in *Pisa e la Toscana occidentale nel Medioevo* (Pisa, 1991) 1: 59–127. De Conno's comments on destructuration (122–7) are measured and fairly convincing; they are to be read in preference to the more radical argument implied by his map (90–1).

20 For the wealth and scale of S. Salvatore in Brescia, see Brogiolo, *Brescia*, 98–107; for a classic, small prestige church with dramatic furnishings, see H. L'Orange and H. Thorp, *Il tempietto di Cividale* (Rome, 1977). The first clear examples in Italy of quality stone-built town houses, dating to shortly after 800, were found in Rome in early 1996: see R. Santangeli Valenzani, 'Edilizia residenziale e aristocrazia urbana a Roma nell'altomedioevo,' in *I Congresso nazionale di archeologia medievale* (Florance, 1997), 64–70. Rome was of course atypical, but how much so?

cators of the complexity of economic life, was far more developed in Francia than in the Lombard kingdom in our period; indeed, Lombard market networks seem barely to have focussed on pottery at all – the rich perhaps preferred metal, and the less rich actually used stone, the *pietra ollare* from the Alps that is found throughout the Po plain.[21] This material weakness is, furthermore, not restricted to the ceramic record and to urban archaeology; it can be inferred from our private charters, too. This is where we return to the wealth of Lombard aristocrats, in fact, for their landowning does not seem to have been particularly extensive. King Aistulf in 750 used the phrase *maiores et potentes* for soldiers with the equivalent of seven tenant-houses: this is not a large number. Did seven tenant-houses really make one an 'aristocrat'? It is hard to tell; but if we were to restrict the definition of aristocracy further, say, to people in our documents with more than five *curtes* (estates) each, which is not an ambitious criterion for wealth even in the early Middle Ages, then only half a dozen 'aristocrats' would be documented in the nearly 300 charters for the Lombard period. None of this last group has much more land than that, either, even though they are *viri magnifici*, *gasindi*, royal officials or bishops.[22] Compare men like Bertram of Le Mans (d. after 616) and Abbo of Maurienne (d. after 739) in Francia, whose property lists in their wills amount to dozens of pages in the modern editions! Even the greatest Lombard aristocrats could not compete with men like this, and they might have been outclassed by middling Frankish *nobiles*. It seems fairly clear, in fact, that the effective Lombard aristocracy regularly operated on a pretty small scale: five *curtes* would be closer to a maximum than to a minimum. Rotpert *vir magnificus* of Agrate, northeast of Milan, left four estates, two or more tenant-houses, and two fields to his female heirs and his favourite churches in 745; the bequest is atypical only in that Rotpert apparently listed all his property – the scale of the document is widely parallelled elsewhere.[23] Four or five estates is, of course, enough to live very comfortably from; but it is not much if one wants to buy enough to maintain a

---

21 See references in Wickham, 'Considerazioni conclusive,' 749–52; for Francia, e.g., *Travaux du groupe de recherches et d'études sur la céramique dans le Nord-Pas-de-Calais* (Arras, 1993).

22 Aistulf 2, 3; an approximate list of the five absolutely richest documented landowners might be Walfrid of Pisa (*CDL* I 116), Erfo of Friuli (II 162), Gaidoald of Pistoia (II 203), Taido of Bergamo (II 293), Peredeus of Lucca (II 154, 161, *MDL* V. 170). None of these can be shown to be from a ducal family; men like Aistulf and Desiderius, before they became kings, must be added to the list. See Gasparri, 'Grandi proprietari,' for general comments.

23 The Frankish wills are edited in M. Weidemann, *Das Testament des Bischofs Berthramn von Le Mans vom 27. März 616* (Mainz, 1986); P.J. Geary, *Aristocracy in Provence* (Philadelphia, 1985), 38–78. It is not as yet clear how far this scale of possession can be extended to the whole of Francia, which was highly diverse at the regional level, as Ian Wood reminds me. For Rotpert, *CDL* I 82.

complex interregional exchange system, to maintain a powerful armed entourage, or to fund a rich urban church, at the same time as endowing one's heirs properly. Nor could kings (who certainly were hugely rich) underwrite an entire exchange economy on their own. On the economic level, Lombard Italy, however urban, looks decidedly modest.

The stratum of society that does seem to be more prosperous than in Francia – and is certainly better documented – is that of small and medium landowners, owner-cultivators, and small-scale rentiers, most of them with less than the seven tenants stressed by Aistulf. In Francia, the evidence for them is so fleeting in some areas that scholars have doubted their existence. Such a doubt is misplaced, but no one who works on Italy has ever had it. Modest landholders dominate our documentation; some of them are even city-dwelling, though of course most lived in the countryside. Their lands were scattered across the territories of every city, intercutting with lands of the rich that were themselves highly scattered. They formed the Lombard army as its *exercitales*, and often used military titles, such as *vir devotus*, though they were probably mostly seldom called up and of doubtful use when they were. Their existence in such large numbers is an essential explanation for the relatively small scale of aristocratic landowning: it is likely that a rather larger percentage of the land area of the Lombard kingdom was in the hands of modest landholders than would have been the case in much of Francia, particularly its Seine–Rhine heartlands.[24]

III

Up to now, I have largely been dealing with material familiar to scholars of the period. The parts of the picture I have drawn seem to fit reasonably well together: a relatively poor aristocracy, with little negotiating power, set against a king who was extremely rich (even if that wealth came from land, not tax). This aristocracy was more likely to play the political game by royal rules and hope at best to siphon off some of the wealth of public office into family coffers while it could. Furthermore, the urban focus of both government and aristocracy greatly facilitated a functioning administration. By early medieval standards, the Lombard kingdom, with a city network at its core, was run unusually tightly. Much of the problem I posed at the start could already be said to be solved.

But not all of it. We are used to discussing medieval political systems in terms of the narrow relationships between kings and aristocrats (lay and eccle-

24 For Francia, see e.g. F. Staab, *Untersuchungen zur Gesellschaft am Mittelrhein in der Karolingerzeit* (Wiesbaden, 1975), 261–80, and below, n. 26. For Italy, see e.g. G. Tabacco, 'Dai possessori dell'età carolingia agli esercitali dell'età longobarda,' *Studi medievali* 10 (1969): 221–68.

siastical), for these are often the only real political actors. But in a region like the Lombard kingdom, where there were so many smaller landowners, holding in toto as much as, or more than, the aristocracy, we have to ask more complex questions. How did small owners relate to the aristocracy? Did aristocrats have any influence on them, whether as dominators or patrons? Or did the small free look only to the king (and maybe his local dukes and gastalds) as the makers of the Lombard laws – like their Carolingian successors – undoubtedly assumed or hoped?[25] If we want to answer these questions, we will have to look at local realities, for the answers are likely to have varied from place to place; a variety of conditions have to be faced if we want to understand how (or if) aristocratic *local* power functioned.

I would like to sharpen this set of questions more by means of another Frankish contrast. One of the reasons why the existence of the small free has been doubted by German historians is that they do not figure to any great extent in the best documentation we have for the period, the cartularies for fast-rising new monasteries such as Fulda and Lorsch. But if one looks in detail at well-documented Rhineland villages in the eighth century, one can find that small landowners are indeed there – not as donors of land to monasteries, it is true, but as witnesses. It can be argued that village élites in effect chose to stay out of the aristocratic patronage networks that funnelled land to the monasteries.[26] Aristocrats in the Rhineland were certainly rich, and locally powerful; villagers might well have felt at risk from them. Further work is needed to tease out what the relationship between the rich and the middling actually was in the Frankish heartlands. But it is interesting that one can hypothesize a significant social separation between them already in the eighth century, since a sharp distinction between *milites/nobiles* and *rustici* – aristocrats in a full sense and the rest – certainly characterized Frankish society from the tenth century onwards. In Italy, this divide, though it certainly came to exist, was always incomplete; there were always in-between groups, and often patron–client relationships between *milites* and their non-military neighbours, into the eleventh and twelfth centuries.[27] One can thus wonder how far back these relationships go in Italy:

25 For the king and the free, the classics are G. Tabacco, 'Dai possessori,' and idem, *I liberi del re nell'Italia carolingia e postcarolingia* (Spoleto, 1966).

26 For Dienheim south of Mainz seen through this optic, see C. Wickham, 'Rural Society in Carolingian Europe,' in *New Cambridge Medieval History* 2: 510–37, at 519–23; cf. 523–6 for references to clienteles in Carolingian Lombardy. I have hypothesized some of the subsequent argument before, without proving it, e.g., in *Land and Power*, 208–11. In what follows, I am building on several arguments I have previously made; hence a certain amount of self-citation, which I regret.

27 See C. Wickham, *The Mountains and the City* (Oxford, 1988), 285–92; H. Keller, *Adelsherrschaft und städtische Gesellschaft in Oberitalien (9. bis 12. Jht)* (Tübingen, 1979), 342–79.

whether indeed patronage networks stretching down into the strata of small and medium owners can be found as early as the Lombard period; whether this might help to explain the fact that such owners are documented at all in our charter collections, which in Italy as elsewhere are dominated by the interests of churches; and whether such patterns, if found, might not help to fill out the picture of relative social and institutional stability sketched in the preceding pages.

One thing is certain: Lombard aristocrats (and kings) could have close military dependents, *gasindi* and others – retainers, perhaps already making up what were in effect private armies. The issue has been much discussed, most notably (and most recently) by Stefano Gasparri. But, for all the militarism of Paul the Deacon's late eighth-century narratives, or of the laws, or of prevailing terminology such as *exercitalis* or *vir devotus*, one may ask how often the lesser landowners of Lombard Italy really identified with military affairs. As Gasparri notes, we actually have three wills from the 750s and 760s made by men about to go to war, apparently worried whether they would ever return (probably with reason, given that the wills survive), 'quoniam incerti sumus omnis de Dei iudicio,' as one of them gloomily remarks, in a phrase taken, remarkably, from Liutprand's law critiquing the justice of judicial duels.[28] These were not the type of men who annually turned up at the Carolingian Marchfield, wondering which Frankish borderland they would invade this year; they remind us that military activity was not a universal or even a regular preoccupation of the Lombard state and its subjects. If we want to look for more 'civilian' clienteles, however, we will have to look in different directions.

The church of S. Colombano in the southern extramural suburbs of Lucca was founded in 730 by three *gasindi regis* and Sichimund *archipresbiter*, brother of Bishop Talesperianus, with the latter's consent. It was later remembered as the bishop's own foundation, and it is probable that all the founders were from his family. By the 760s, it was in the hands of the cathedral, and was rebuilt and reconsecrated by Bishop Peredeus (755–79), himself from a major local aristocratic family.[29] In that context, gifts to the church suddenly begin to appear in our Lucchese documentation. In 766, Deusdona from Montenonni in the Val di Cornia (a dependency of Lucca some 120 kilometres to the south, down the Tuscan coast) gave a plot of land to S. Colombano, 'which the lord

---

28 S. Gasparri, 'Strutture militari e legami di dipendenza in Italia in età longobarda e carolingia,' *Rivista storica italiana* 98 (1986), 664–726; 681–3 for the wills, which are *CDL* I 114, 117, II 230. See II 230 for the quote, and cf. Liutprand 118.

29 *CDL* I 48; for Peredeus, see Schwarzmaier, *Lucca*, 78–85; L. Bertini, 'Peredeo vescovo di Lucca,' *Studi storici in onore di O. Bertolini* (Pisa, 1972), 21–45; for S. Colombano, see Belli Barsali, 'Topografia,' 533.

Bishop Peredeus consecrated' (one of the witnesses was a cleric promoted by the bishop in the same year). In 768 Anacard, the city owner of the church of S. Pietro di Castiglione in the Garfagnana, 60 kilometres into the mountains north of Lucca, gave his church to S. Colombano, this time 'built' by Peredeus (the mountain church had already passed from hand to hand three times since its foundation in the 720s, between urban aristocrats and city artisans). In the same year, Gausfrid and his wife, Gausperga, of Vada Volterrana, the centre of marine salt production for early medieval Tuscany, gave a land-plot to the church, following the precedent of Gausperga's dead brother Praetextatus; a Praetextatus (the name is very rare in this period) is also recorded as a neighbour of Peredeus' lands in the diocese of Pisa in the years before 762, and Gausfrid's own charter is witnessed by Peredeus' nephew and grand-nephew. In 772, Lucifrid, a small landowner, gave his own house just south of Lucca to the nearby church, receiving it back for rent. In 773, another landowner, Serbulo, made S. Colombano his executor (and thus in practice beneficiary) of his properties. And finally in this sequence, at some point in this same time-span Andreas of Salisciamo left property to the church, as we know because his probable kinsman Prandulus of Griciano unsuccessfully contested the gift in December 774. After this, we have only two more gifts, one by Peredeus himself in his will of 778, and one in 799 by Periprand, a cathedral cleric of Peredeus' time, and possibly his kinsman; the church then virtually drops out of the documentary record again.[30]

This flurry of gifts is evidently very restricted in time; all except the last two date from an eight-year period, between 766 (perhaps shortly after Peredeus' rebuilding) and the fall of the Lombard kingdom. Peredeus was in fact exiled or imprisoned in Francia in 774–7; gifts to S. Colombano stop abruptly, that is to say, when he left Lucca, and it may not be chance that immediately after this an enterprising landowner sought to take one of the gifts back. The gifts seem, then, in large part to reflect the prestige of the bishop; after his departure, the pious patronized different foundations. This pattern is matched by the experience of S. Salvatore, the prestige foundation of Peredeus' successor, John I (779–801), which was generously endowed with gifts in John's lifetime and never again later.[31] But in S. Colombano's case, we can say more. Gifts from the Garfagnana in the north to the Val di Cornia in the south show a considerable territorial range; Peredeus' own family lands are, however, attested in

---

30 *CDL* II 195 (202 for the cleric), 219, 221 (161 for Praetextatus), 276, 281; *MDL* V 154, 170, 276. All the donations seem to be genuinely pious gifts from independent landowners. For Castiglione, see Wickham, *Mountains*, 57–8.

31 Peredeus' exile: Schwarzmaier, *Lucca*, 78–9. S. Salvatore: *MDL* V 261, 262, 264, 265, 267, 271, 288, 292.

both. His family also owned a large estate at Rosignano, about halfway between Lucca and the Val di Cornia, and very near Vada;[32] and his own relatives made a rare appearance as witnesses to the Vada gift. The S. Colombano donors as a group, therefore, correlate closely with Peredeus' family's interests and activities. What better proof of loyalty to a family would there be than the direction of pious donations by clients specifically to the church refounded by the family's major representative? I would argue that these donors were indeed members of Peredeus' family clientele, in the various localities where the family had influence.

Clientage is a fairly broad concept. At its core, there is little more than the notion of the exchange of favours between the powerful and the less powerful; it certainly does not have to involve oaths or any ceremonial, as with *gasindi* and (later, in the Frankish period) vassals. Peredeus' family clients may have had little in common except a desire to keep in with the family and gain unspecified benefits from it (land, employment, preferment, favourable treatment, succour and assistance – the possible list is long).[33] But I think that what the pattern of gifts to S. Colombano does show, at a minimum, is that this family connection was sufficiently strong to get a wide variety of owners to give land to Peredeus' church. Exactly what status these owners had is not easy to tell. Lucifrid, the only one who was certainly an owner-cultivator or the equivalent, may simply have ceded his property to the nearest church, regardless of clientship relations. The richest, Anacard, was the brother of a city goldsmith. The others were rural owners of indeterminate wealth. These latter do show, however, that patron–client relationships could extend some way out into the countryside, just as the official power of the gastald of Siena did at the beginning of the century.

A second pattern of patron–client relationships can be seen in the more-or-less contemporary gifts of two men to different bishops: Gundualid of Campori to Bishops Peredeus and John of Lucca in 773 and 780, and Toto of Campione to Archbishop Thomas of Milan in 777. The two gifts in fact make a very interesting pair, even if the fact that they are contemporaneous is certainly chance: in both cases a childless, medium-level rural landowner, dominant in his own small upland village, donates his whole property to the bishop and his church. We actually know quite a lot about both families, for the church in each case absorbed their archives. Gundualid (fl. 740–84) was a local entrepreneur and church founder; Toto's family also founded the local church, S. Zeno, and kept documents for transactions involving its own slaves going back to the 720s – a

32 *CDL* I 28, II 154, 161; *MDL* V 170.
33 A rare example of land being given in a document in return for 'faithful service' is *CDL* I 124.

rare practice. In neither case did the gifts extinguish the local activity of the family; Toto carried on negotiating, buying property in the area on behalf of his own estate for the next thirty years; and Gundualdʼs heirs continued to hold their church and estate from the bishop for nearly two centuries.[34] Both cessions can, in fact, be seen in a double light: as pious gifts to the church, but also as the acquisition of episcopal support for local political strategies that carried on without a break. Gunduald and Toto were actually seeking patrons, and regarded the loss of full ownership as a price worth paying for episcopal patronage (including *defensio*, legal protection). And in each case it is significant that the donors came from some distance away. Campori is in the Garfagnana, in which Lucchese bishops did have an interest, for, despite the distance, it was in the diocese of Lucca, and Bishop Peredeus, as we have just seen, had land there. Campione, however, was in the diocese of Como and the secular territory of Seprio; Toto must have made a very conscious choice when he looked to Milan in the plains 60 kilometres to the south. Totoʼs family had had prior dealings in the plains; they were perhaps well enough known to be interesting clients for a Milanese prelate. In any case, the political networks of both bishops, however we explain them, could extend a long way into the countryside, just as that of Peredeusʼ own family could.

We cannot here pursue and unpick every possible patronage relationship in Lombard documents. I am arguing that there are patterns of gift-giving to churches in our period (as in other places and periods)[35] that make best sense if they are seen as signs of patron–client relationships; although I would not claim that all such gifts can be read in that way, we ought in principle to look at all the nearly 200 alienations to churches surviving from the period in this light to see if they fit the argument. Such a task would be immense, and, given the high frequency of context-less single gifts, would run a high risk of circularity of argument. Here, I would rather stand back from the detail and, instead, comment on some of its implications. I will again take Lucca as my field of reference, since the documentation for that city is relatively good (and that for most others quite fragmentary).

Luccaʼs archive in the eighth century is that of the bishop and his churches. Even the private transactions between laymen and the foundations of propri-

---

34 The main texts are, respectively, *CDL* II 285 with *MDL* V 179, for Gunduald; *Codex diplomaticus Langobardiae* 56, ed. G. Porro Lambertenghi (Turin, 1873), for Toto. For discussions and other texts, see Wickham, *Mountains*, 40–51, for Campori; G. Rossetti, ʻ I ceti proprietari e professionali,ʼ *Atti del 10° Congresso internazionale di studi sullʼalto Medioevo* (Spoleto, 1986), 165–207, at 182–207, and R. Balzaretti, ʻThe Lands of Saint Ambrose,ʼ (PhD dissertation, London University, 1989), 205–9, for Campione.

35 Cf. Wickham, *Mountains*, 190–7, 210–15, 256–68.

etary churches that survive there do so because the land or the churches concerned came into the hands of the bishop, usually before 850. A standard pattern is one like that for Campori (we find it again, for example, in the affairs of Crispinus *negudians*, founder of S. Martino di Lunata, just east of the city, in 764): country dwellers sell land to a local or city notable, who founds a local or city church and later gives it to the bishop.[36] At other times, rural owners of all kinds give lands to urban or rural churches under the bishop's control. It is striking that in the immediate hinterland of Lucca a high percentage of the settlements of the area are documented by this means. The network of pious gift-giving extended all over the lands nearest the city, and also (as we have indeed seen) rather farther afield.

I would argue that this network is at least sometimes, and maybe usually, a guide to more secular patron–client relations too. It is a guide to the relationships of the bishop; but in some cases (as with S. Colombano) it seems also to derive from the secular status of the bishop's family, and we might conclude that other major non-episcopal families could have been at the centre of similar networks, maybe linked to gift-giving to their own churches, as well as to more strictly secular (and thus less-documented) relationships. Put like this, I would suppose that few historians would find these proposals very surprising. But the capillarity of these relationships across the core lands of the Lucchesia is perhaps more striking, and goes some way to allowing one to claim that patronage relations structured a good proportion of free society in this period. For example, Lunata, 5 kilometres east of Lucca, where, as just noted, Crispinus, a substantial (probably urban) owner, had founded his church, was on the main roads east and south of the city; its leading inhabitants had property scattered in all directions, some of which they, too, gave to the bishop and to Lunata's other, episcopal, church. Lunata's village élite were thus easily integrated into the episcopal political network.[37] It is probable that there were gaps, however. Gurgite (the modern Pieve S. Paolo), for example, was a little to the south of Lunata, and off the road; its closely knit inhabitants seem in surviving documents to have had very little link to the city, even though it was so close, until, that is, Gurgite's leading owner, Saximund, gave to the cathedral his portions of two of the settlement's three churches in 793.[38] Saximund may have felt the need for city clientelar links, unlike his neighbours; but many of them were

---

36 For Crispinus, see above, n. 14, with *MDL* V 373; for commentary, Andreolli, *Uomini nel Medioevo*, 33–8.

37 See, in addition to references in n. 14: *CDL* II 211, 232, 279; *MDL* V 152, 228, 232, 235, 333, 373, 395, 401, 432.

38 See *CDL* II 125, 126, 157, 280; *MDL* V 229, 240 (Saximund's gift), 250, 269, 272, 323, 388, 390, 504, 573. After 793 Gurgite's links with other areas of the diocese steadily increase.

linked to him and his family, and the city could thus reach them second-hand. Before 793, however, Gurgite was outside the network; had it not been for Saximund, it might have stayed that way, and its charters would not have survived. Such patterns show that the political networks spreading outward and downward from the city's élites were by no means complete. But they were substantial, for all that; and they included landowners of all levels, even peasant owners, as demonstrably with some of the lesser associates of Gumprand of Campori, or of Saximund of Gurgite and his brothers. Political clienteles of one form or another tied Lucchese society together from top to bottom.

This picture is essentially based on Lucchese material; all that can be said by way of generalizing it is that the picture, drawn in broader brush-strokes, for Milan, Brescia, Pisa, or Siena does not contradict it. It is a picture that lends support to the argument for the essential stability of the Lombard political system, for now we see that not only the city aristocracy could be brought into it, but, through them, most of the rest of free society could as well. It cannot be said whether the latter's informal links to the aristocracy were more important than their direct responsibility to the king and his local officials; it may be that it would have been hard to disentangle the two, and it is certain that it would have varied from place to place (as between Lunata and Gurgite). It is quite likely, in fact, that private relationships shadowed nearly all public ones in Lombard society, rendering them more corrupt, very likely, but not necessarily weakening them; indeed, connections of this kind survived for centuries into the communal world of the twelfth century. The pattern was something that the Franks would not disturb in the decades after 774; and it is one major cause of the considerable continuities in Italian society and politics even after kings dramatically lost their authority in the tenth century.[39] Aristocrats in the eighth-century Lombard kingdom did not have the wealth (and thus power) to dominate their neighbours, still less to expropriate them, any more than they had the wealth and power to contest the royal domination of the national political structure. But they did, at least sometimes, have patronage links with their poorer neighbours, as we have just seen, and they were a stable part of the royal political system too, through which they gained power: they were central to both national and local politics. The political centrality enjoyed by collectivities of urban landowners is what defined the parameters of aristocratic power in our period.

---

39 In general, see the arguments in Wickham, *Land and Power*, 208–11 (which contrasts Italy and Catalonia), and in Wickham, 'Property Ownership and Signorial Power in Twelfth-century Tuscany,' in *Property and Power in the Early Middle Ages*, ed. W. Davies and P. Fouracre (Cambridge, 1995), 221–44.

A final point brings us back to the small landowners of the Lucchesia. I have argued elsewhere that the relative absence of aristocrats in the societies of several areas of Europe in this period (parts of Catalonia and Brittany are most visible in our documents), or their social separation from the small free (as in parts of the Rhineland), allowed the stabilization of social and economic patterns dominated by peasants themselves.[40] These did not last anywhere in mainland Europe; it may well be that the Carolingian period itself saw their final collapse in many areas. Eighth-century northern Italian aristocrats were not rich, and not politically dominant, but the small free did in this part of Europe very often look to them as patrons. Inside the landowning strata, the rich were socially close to the poor in parts of Lombard Italy, rather more than in many other places. I would conclude from this that aristocratic values and practices were more likely to have been socially hegemonic in much of the Lombard kingdom than they were in some other parts of Europe: by 700 at the latest, the Lombard aristocracy, however economically modest, controlled more of the rules of the game at a local level than did many of their Frankish (not to speak of Visigothic or Breton) counterparts. In this respect, too, we can talk of aristocratic power: without being able to be the violent oppressors of the Frankish world, but also not having to be, the Lombard aristocracy controlled the parameters of rural social life more surely than any of their counterparts.

40 Wickham, *Land and Power*, 212–25, with references; see further W. Davies, *Small Worlds* (London, 1988), esp. 146–60.

9

Making a Difference
in Eighth-Century Politics:
The Daughters of Desiderius

JANET L. NELSON

Maps of Charlemagne's Empire, from the first one, made in the early seventeenth century and dedicated to Louis XIII, to late twentieth-century ones designed for a remade Europe, powerfully convey an impression of Charlemagne's control over his world: he was monarch of all he surveyed.[1] Add dates, and you get a sense of inexorable expansion, following geographical logic as the Frankish war-machine rolled through peripheral principalities and *exterae gentes*. Genealogies provide another powerful visual display of unity and continuity. Patrilines wonderfully renew themselves over the generations – wonderfully, not least because they often seem to be all-male achievements. In either case, the vision is Carolingian-centred.

That is true, too, of the historiography. Pierre Riché called his recent book *Les Carolingiens: Une famille qui fit l'Europe*.[2] Fundamental here is a dynasty's rise, the re-establishment of Frankish monarchy, and Charlemagne's expanding of its power. The story, for the eighth century at least, is coherent. It was told with particularly compelling clarity by the author of the *Annales Mettenses priores* in ca 805.[3] It was retold, with acknowledgments to those annals,

I should like to thank Paul Fouracre, Sandy Murray, Geoff West, and especially Julia Smith for their helpful criticisms of drafts of this paper, and the University of London 'Age of Charlemagne' Special Subject class of 1995–6 for thought-provoking comments on many contentious points.

1 The seventeenth-century map of Charlemagne's Empire has been identified and its significance illuminated by Walter Goffart in a forthcoming paper. My contribution to this Festschrift acknowledges gratefully, but inadequately, long-standing debts to Walter's multifarious scholarly inspiration and personal kindness.

2 (Paris 1983), now translated as *The Carolingians: A Family that Forged Europe* (London, 1994). Cf. the reprint of my review article of the original French work, in my collection of papers, *The Frankish World* (London, 1996), ch. 10.

3 B. von Simson, ed., MGH SRG (1905); cf. Nelson, *Frankish World*, 191–4.

by K.-F. Werner in his influential paper on peripheral principalities.[4] Nothing succeeds like success. The combination of Carolingian leadership and Frankish military prowess seems to explain everything.

Or does it? Mysteries still surround such politically key issues as the solidity of 'the' Carolingian family, or the chronology of Charlemagne's campaigns and the motivation behind them. Look closely at the centre of the Carolingian Empire, and you will detect seams pulling apart.[5] Look closely at the fringes, and you will detect fraying. The where and why of that may explain the regime's persistent insecurity: not just the single crisis in 778 diagnosed by F.L. Ganshof,[6] but, frankly, one goddamn crisis after another.

It makes a difference, of course, where you look from: what is your vantage point. I am going to shift it from a teleologically determined, Charlemagne-centred, male-monopolized one. First of all I am going to take my vantage point among Lombards rather than Franks, starting in the valley of the Po rather than the Meuse or the Rhine. Adding the women to the genealogies makes a further difference. But putting royal women back in the political picture, where they do absolutely belong, means examining what is specific to their activities and importance, seeing just what difference gender makes. The point of these exercises is not to indulge in some entertaining speculation at the margins, but to throw light on one or two central mysteries of the later eighth century.

Desiderius, king of the Lombards, and his wife, Ansa, had (so far as we know) four daughters.[7] The destiny of three of them was what, according to Einhard, you would have expected in the case of Charlemagne's daughters: that is, to be married either to one of their father's own men or to a man from among the *exteri*.[8] Most of the rest of this essay is about those three daughters. But I want to start with the one whom the sources record earliest, so, perhaps, the

4 'Les principautés périphériques,' in his collected papers, *Structures politiques du monde franc* (London, 1979), ch. 2.

5 On nephews and uncles, see the continuing problems posed for Pippin by Drogo in the early 750s: M. Becher, "Drogo und die Königserhebung Pippins," *Frühmittelalterliche Studien* 23 (1989): 131-53. For another Carolingian with a hitherto unsuspected long political life, Theudoald, son of Grimoald II, see R. Collins, "Deception and Misrepresentation in Early Eighth Century Frankish Historiography," in *Karl Martell in seiner Zeit,* ed. J. Jarnut, U. Nonn, and M. Richter (Sigmaringen, 1994), 227–47, at 229–35. Collins links Theudoald's death in 741 with the succession problems of the sons of Charles Martel. More generally, see R. Schieffer, 'Väter und Söhne im Karolingerhause,' in *Beiträge zur Geschichte des Regnum Francorum,* Beihefte der Francia 22 (Paris, 1990), 149–64.

6 Ganshof, *The Carolingians and the Frankish Monarchy* (London, 1971), 18–19.

7 See the article 'Desiderio,' by P. Delogu, *Dizionario biografico degli Italiani* 39 (Rome, 1991), 373–81. Cf. also the article 'Ansa,' by H. Helbling, ibid. 3 (1961), 360–1.

8 Einhard, *VK* c. 19, ed. O. Holder-Egger, MGH SRG (1911), 25.

Descendants of Desiderius, King of the Lombards (757–774), and Ansa

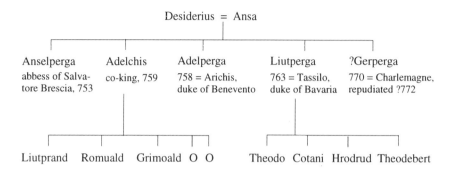

oldest of them. Before Desiderius and Ansa became king and queen of the Lombards in February 757, their daughter Anselperga became abbess of San Salvatore, Brescia.[9] This large convent was their foundation, probably in 753, and it was exceptionally well endowed, not just by Desiderius, but more especially by Ansa from lands inherited from her own father and brothers.[10] Now there is nothing gender-specific about monasticism or about monastic founding. Nor was this foundation unique in Lombardy in the early 750s: in fact, it was part of a rash of foundations, which have been explained, not entirely convincingly, as the Lombard aristocracy's insurance policy against possible Frankish conquest in those years.[11] But the way San Salvatore developed, I should like to explain (along lines suggested by Karl Leyser for places like Quedlinburg in tenth-century Saxony) as the construction of a female-run palladium: a centre

9 C.-R. Brühl, *CDL* III 41, p. 240, suggests that the 'abbess Oriperga' uniquely attested in this charter is Anselperga under another name. See also below, nn. 10, 13.

10 *CDL* III 31, 33, 36–42, 44, at pp. 187–91, 203–8, 221–45, 251–60 (no. 38, p. 231, gives details of Ansa's family). S. Wemple, 'S. Salvatore/S. Giulia: A Case Study in the Endowment and Patronage of a Major Female Monastery in Northern Italy,' in *Women of the Medieval World,* ed. J. Kirshner and S. Wemple (Oxford, 1985), 85–102, has useful information on the endowment of San Salvatore, though there are some slips (Ansa was not 'queen' before 757; and the man killed by Cunimond [*CDL* III 36, p. 233] was Ansa's *gasindus*, not 'her husband's'), and the references given are all to the edition of 1873 rather than to Brühl's. See also, *S. Giulia de Brescia: Archeologia, arte, storia di un monasterio regio dai Longobardi al Barbarossa,* ed. C. Stella and G. Brentegani (Brescia, 1992), and N. Christie, *The Lombards* (Oxford, 1995).

11 K. Schmid, 'Zur Ablösung der langobardischen Herrschaft durch die Franken,' *Quellen und Forschungen aus italienischen Archiven und Bibliotheken* 52 (1972): 13–36; for the broader context of Frankish contacts with Lombardy, see G. Tabacco, 'L'avvento dei Carolingi nel regno dei Longobardi,' in *Langobardia,* ed. S. Gasparri and P. Cammarosano (Udine, 1993), 375–423, esp. 379–85.

of prayer and commemoration for the dynasty Desiderius and Ansa planned to found and so, eventually, for the stability of the Lombard realm they worked hard to re-create.[12] Both king and queen made exceptionally lavish donations to San Salvatore; and associated their son, Adelchis, with them in these gifts. The relevant charters all mentioned the relationship of the donors to the abbess: daughter or sister. Anselperga's own charters show her energetically buying and exchanging property, commissioning iron doors for the convent church, and constructing a hydraulic system probably to supply the convent's bath. Bryan Ward-Perkins has stressed the combination of purposes in such eighth- and ninth-century hydraulic works undertaken by and for Italian churches: charitable care of the poor and sick, ritual performance, as well as the cleanliness and sheer enjoyment of the inmates.[13] Ward-Perkins stresses in the case of earlier Ostrogothic and Lombard rulers that, when royal sponsorship was involved, there was also a conscious evocation of the classical past. This, I suggest, also became true of Desiderius and Ansa and their abbess-daughter, women's patronage of public works being a well-documented feature of late antique and earlier medieval Italy.

The world in which Anselperga grew up had changed dramatically in 751 with the fall of Byzantine Ravenna to Desiderius's predecessor, Aistulf, and the *de facto* collapse of eastern imperial power in northeastern Italy. The Lombard kingdom now resumed the inheritance of Galla Placidia and Justinian. True, the Franks had intervened in northern Italy in (probably) 755 and 756, and King Pippin had extracted nominal concessions of extensive territories to papal lordship.[14] But the transfers had never taken place; and Desiderius in the 760s reasserted his claims to the Pentapolis, and eventually, in 772, intervened in the territory of Ravenna too.[15] Ravenna evokes not the late antique imperial past, but the realm of Theoderic, about which Desiderius might well have known through the kind of oral traditions that surfaced in Paul the Deacon's *History*,[16]

12 K.J. Leyser, *Rule and Conflict in an Early Medieval Society: Ottonian Saxony* (London, 1979), 49–74; cf. now P. Geary, *Phantoms of Remembrance: Memory and Oblivion at the End of the First Millennium* (Princeton, 1994), 48–80.

13 *From Classical Antiquity to the Middle Ages: Urban Public Building in Northern and Central Italy, AD 300–850* (Oxford, 1984), ch. 7, esp. 136–7.

14 *Vita Stephani II*, cc. 33–7, 43–7, ed. L. Duchesne, *Le Liber Pontificalis: Texte, introduction et commentaire*, reissued C. Vogel, 3 vols (Paris, 1955–7), 1: 449–54; trans. R. Davis, *The Lives of the Eighth-Century Popes* (Liverpool, 1992), 67–8, 70–3.

15 *Vita Stephani III*, c. 25; trans. Davis, *Lives*, 101.

16 See D. Bullough, 'Ethnic History and the Carolingians. An Alternative Reading of Paul the Deacon's *Historia Langobardorum*,' in *The Inheritance of Historiography*, ed. C. Holdsworth and T. Wiseman (Exeter, 1986), 85–105; cf. W. Goffart, *The Narrators of Barbarian History (A.D. 550–800): Jordanes, Gregory of Tours, Bede, and Paul the Deacon* (Princeton, 1988),

or through Cassiodorus' *Variae*.[17] Desiderius apparently made Pavia something of a centre of learning;[18] and a scholar-courtier could have suggested attractive historical models. Theoderic's policy of dynastic marriage might well have impressed the Lombard king. Direct imitation on Desiderius' part is unprovable, however, and perhaps improbable. Similarity of circumstances provides sufficient explanation for familial strategies: a ruler with hegemonial aspirations was likely to deploy available daughters as diplomatic counters.[19] Theoderic had married his daughters to Sigismund, king of the Burgundians, and Alaric, king of the Visigoths; his sister to Thrasamund, king of the Vandals; his niece to the king of the Thuringians.[20] The meaning of these marriages was clear in the letters Cassiodorus wrote on the king's behalf: the married-out daughter was a cultural emissary, civilizing the barbarians and asserting her uncle's hegemony.[21] This, surely, was just what was being attempted from the late 750s by Desiderius. Evidence that he did indeed conceive such a project , and even that Ansa may have played a key role in conceiving it (as well as the daughters), may be found in Ansa's epitaph, written by Paul the Deacon:

> The fatherland that was wounded by wars and now falling into ruin
> Along with her great spouse, she made firm and augmented, raising it up.

427; also the comments of W. Pohl, 'Paulus Diaconus und die "Historia Langobardorum,'" in *Historiographie im frühen Mittelalter*, ed. A. Scharer and G. Scheibelreiter (Vienna, 1994), 375–405, esp. 382–8.

17 The earliest manuscript evidence for the *Variae* points back to Charlemagne's court, not Desiderius', however: see S. Barnish, *Cassiodorus: Variae* (Liverpool, 1992), xxxiii and n. 68.

18 For Peter of Pisa at his court, disputing with the Jew Lullus about theology, see Alcuin, Ep. 172, *Epistolae Karolini Aevi*, ed. E. Dümmler, MGH Epistolae 4 (1895), 285, recalling what he heard at Pavia as an *adolescens en route* to Rome.

19 For the family tree of Desiderius, see above, 173. Diplomatic marriages were a familiar feature of barbarian, and not least Lombard, history (see J. Jarnut, 'Beiträge zu den fränkisch-bayerisch-langobardischen Beziehungen im 7. und 8. Jhdt.,' *Zeitschrift für Bayerische Landesgeschichte* 49 [1976]: 331–52), but few rulers had so many women to deploy as did Theoderic and Desiderius.

20 See J. Moorhead, *Theoderic in Italy* (Oxford, 1993), 67–8, 108–9, 193. For knowledge of Theoderic in the earlier Middle Ages, see H. Löwe, 'Vom Theodoric dem Grossen zu Karl dem Grossen,' *Deutsches Archiv* 9 (1952): 353–401, and D. Bullough, *Carolingian Renewal* (Manchester, 1991), 61–2. For Charlemagne's transporting of a statue of Theoderic from Ravenna to Aachen, see F. Thürlemann, 'Die Bedeutung der Aachener Theoderich-Statue für Karl der Grosse,' *Archiv für Kulturgeschichte* 59 (1977): 25–65.

21 Cass. *Variae* 4.1, ed. T. Mommsen, 114 (trans. Barnish, 74): 'mittimus ad vos ornatum aulicae domus, augmenta generis, solacia fidelis consilii, dulcedinem suavissimam conjugalem ... Habebit Thoringia quod nutrivit Italia, litteris doctam, moribus eruditam, decorem non solum genere quantum et feminea dignitate, ut non minus patria vestra splendeat moribus quam suis triumphis.'

She gave birth for us to one who would hold the sceptres of the realm,
Great Adelgis, mighty in body and mind,
In whom, through Christ, the greatest hope of the Lombards remained.
She joined the strong breasts of her daughters in marriages,
Embracing men divided, whom the swift river Ofanto borders,
And binding in love of peace those whom Rhine and Danube gird.
A share of hers also remained for the eternal King,
Shining in virginal splendour, dedicated to these temples.
For the cult of the High-throned how many churches she has founded!
The needy flock [is] there, and their lofty reputation spreads everywhere.
Whether you seek the heights of revered Peter
Or Monte Gargano of the cave to be venerated,
Made safe by her help, you will not fear the weapons of brigands
Nor cold nor cloud under the dark night:
She has prepared ample shelter for you, and supper as well.[22]

Ofanto, Rhine, and Danube stand for the three husbands of the daughters of Desiderius.[23] I consider each in turn. First, Ofanto: the river is the frontier of the Lombard principality of Benevento. The installation of the Friulan noble Arichis as duke of Benevento in 758 was a major political coup for Desiderius, for he thus brought an outlying region as securely as it had ever been within the orbit of royal control from Pavia.[24] Soon after this, Arichis was given Adalperga, the daughter of Desiderius and Ansa, as his bride. Southwards with her from Lombardy perhaps travelled Paul the Deacon, also from Friuli, probably born in Cividale, and quite possibly a kinsman of Arichis'.[25] His main

---

22 *Die Gedichte des Paulus Diaconus: Kritische und erklarende Ausgabe*, ed. K. Neff, Quellen und Untersuchungen zur lateinische Philologie des Mittelalters, ed. L. Traube, 3, fasc. 4 (Munich, 1908), no. 9, pp. 47–8. Paul's authorship of the epitaph is generally accepted. The date of writing is controversial and problematic: Ansa was still alive when Charlemagne conquered the Lombard kingdom in 774, and her daughter's marriage to Charlemagne had ended. Either Paul composed the epitaph some years later for the Beneventan court of Ansa's daughter, evoking as it were the spirit of 770, or he wrote in 770–1, hence during Ansa's lifetime. See Goffart, *Narrators*, 343–4, n. 53. For local Brescian tradition of Ansa either remaining in or returning to Brescia, see Wemple, 'S. Salvatore,' 89, n. 25

23 Desiderius also sought a marriage-alliance between his son Adelchis and Gisela, sister of the Frankish kings Charles and Carloman: *Codex Carolinus*, 45, ed. W. Gundlach, *Epistolae Merowingici et Karolini Aevi*, MGH Epistolae 3 (1892), 561. Cf. below, p. 181.

24 S. Gasparri, *I duchi longobardi* (Rome, 1978), 98 (Arichis) and cf. 82 (for similar tactics in Spoleto); see also Delogu, 'Il regno longobardo,' in *Storia d'Italia*, ed. G. Galasso, 1 (Turin, 1980), 180–1.

25 Goffart, *Narrators*, 334–5. The context is neatly sketched by J. Jarnut, *Geschichte der Langobarden* (Stuttgart, 1982), 116–20, 131, with further references. Coincidentally, there

patron thereafter was to be Adalperga, however; and he may have been her tutor before her marriage. In 763, when she was the mother of one child, he dedicated to her a poem on the ages of the world, beginning with the Creation and ending with the contemporary new golden age of peace established by Desiderius, Arichis, and Adelperga.[26] Dedicating to her, probably about 773 (by this time she had three children) his *Historia Romana*, an amplified version of Eutropius' *Summary of Roman History*, Paul acclaimed his patroness as the 'emulator' of her husband: he was 'almost the only prince of our age to hold the palm of wisdom,' she the admired 'lover of philosophy and poetry, history and exegesis.'[27] All that may have been conventional froth; but Paul's account of his *History*'s genesis rings true as evidence of Adalperga's genuine interest: 'You read through the work of Eutropius eagerly, as you always do, but what displeased you about it, in addition to its unsuitable brevity, was that he, as a pagan, had omitted all reference to divine history and our religion; so Your Excellency asked me to expand it somewhat by reference to Holy Writ, so that the chronology of his narrative would become clearer.' Among his additions were a number of stories about women, mostly (though not all) bad ones, like Cleopatra,[28] which may have been intended to appeal to Adalperga's known tastes, or what Paul considered her needs – namely, warnings against feminine folly. Paul continued what was essentially an Italian history beyond Eutropius, down to the age of Justinian, whom he depicted as a restorer of the state.[29] Perhaps it was no coincidence that Arichis and Adalperga built at Benevento a church dedicated to Holy Wisdom, in evident imitation of Justinian's great Hagia Sophia.[30] Small in scale though it is, this is an impressive church, inspired in part, surely, by Adalperga's love of 'divine history and our religion.'

It is time to quit the Ofanto for the Danube. On its banks was Regensburg, main residence of Duke Tassilo.[31] He had married Desiderius' and Ansa's daughter Liutperga, probably in 763, the year after he had allegedly withdrawn, pleading illness, from campaigning with his uncle King Pippin against the

---

survives at Cividale a beautiful stucco frieze of female martyrs who happen to be depicted as Lombard princesses and abbesses; see Bullough, *The Age of Charlemagne* (London, 1965), 37, plate 7.

26 Neff, *Gedichte*, no. 2, pp. 9–10.

27 *Historia Romana*, ed. A. Crivellucci, Fonti per la Storia d'Italia 51 (Rome, 1913), 3–4.

28 Goffart, *Narrators*, 351, comments that 'female initiatives meet with unfailing disapproval,' suggesting that the taste for such material may have been Paul's as much as Adalperga's; cf. idem, 354, for the virtuous Digna.

29 *Historia Romana* XVI, c. 11, p. 231.

30 H. Belting, 'Studien zum beneventanische Hof im 8. Jhdt.,' *Dumbarton Oaks Papers* 16 (1962): 175 ff.

31 H. Wolfram, *Die Geburt Mitteleuropas* (Vienna, 1987), 100–6.

Aquitanians.[32] While the later *Royal Frankish Annals* depict Tassilo as a subordinate of Pippin, the contemporary story of the 760s was of reasserted Bavarian autonomy now that Tassilo had attained adulthood.[33] The Lombard marriage was part of this. Soon after Pippin's death in September 768, Tassilo went to Italy, and almost certainly to Rome, where he presumably forged bonds of *amicitia* with Pope Stephen III.[34] In September 770, Tassilo held an assembly at Freising attended by large numbers of Bavarian nobles.[35] This may well have been the occasion when the Frankish dowager-queen Bertrada, herself *en route* to Rome, met Tassilo along with his leading men. In 772, Theodo, Tassilo's and Liutperga's eldest son, was sent to Desiderius, and thence to Rome, to be baptised by Pope Hadrian at Whitsun.[36] Desiderius' ambit embraced the Danube.

The fourth of his daughters had been destined for the Rhine – in other words, for Charlemagne. In the words of Einhard, 'after his father's death, ... Charles with his mother's encouragement married the daughter of Desiderius king of the Lombards.'[37] Given that Desiderius in *ca* 770 is generally thought to have

32 For the date of the marriage, see J. Jahn, *Ducatus Baiuvariorum: Das bairische Herzogtum der Agilolfinger* (Stuttgart, 1991), 374. For Tassilo's abandonment of his uncle, see *Annales regni Francorum* [hereinafter *ARF*] , a. 763 (revised), ed. F. Kurze, MGH SRG (1895), 23. But for some long-overdue cautions about the *ARF*'s account, see M. Becher, *Eid und Herrschaft: Untersuchungen zum Herrscherethos Karls des Grossen* (Sigmaringen, 1993), 45–51. This is a book with far-reaching implications about the 'reading' of medieval texts.

33 Documents in the Freising archive from 763, and consistently from 767, were dated no longer by the reign-years of Pippin as well as of Tassilo, but only by Tassilo's: T. Bitterauf, *Die Traditionen des Hochstifts Freising*, vol. 1 (Munich, 1905), nos. 19 and 21, and from no. 24 on.

34 Jahn, *Ducatus Baiuvariorum*, 390–5, on the evidence of the *Vita Corbiniani*, c. 41, ed. B. Krusch, MGH SRG (1920), 150, and Bitterauf, *Traditionen des Hochstifts Freising*, vol. 1, no. 34, p. 62: 'Tassilone ... rediente de Italia anno ducatus eius XXII.'

35 Bitterauf, *Traditionen des Hochstifts Freising*, vol. 1, no. 39, pp. 66–8. See Jahn, *Ducatus Baiuvariorum*, 394–8; and below, 180. Jarnut, 'Genealogie und politische Bedeutung der agilolfingeschen Herzöge,' *Mitteilungen des Instituts für österreichische Geschichtsforschung* 99 (1991): 1–22, argues convincingly that Abbot Sturm of Fulda's mediation between Tassilo and Charlemagne occurred after Carloman's death; cf. *Vita Sturmi*, c. 22, ed. G.H. Pertz, MGH SS (in folio) 2 (1829), 375–6, English translation, P.D. King, *Charlemagne: Translated Sources* (Kendal, 1987), 332.

36 E. Klebel, 'Eine neuaufgefundene Salzburger Geschichtsquelle,' *Mitteilungen des Gesellschaft für Salzburger Landeskunde* 61 (1921): 33–54, at 34 (a. 772); S. Riezler, 'Ein verlorene bairisches Geschichtswerk des achten Jhdts.,' *Sitzungsberichte der königlichen bayerischen Akademie der Wissenschaften*, hist. Kl. 1 (Munich, 1881), 255. See further Becher, *Eid*, 50. There is an English translation of this part of Riezler's 'lost source' in King, *Charlemagne*, 341 (as 'Crantz'). Jahn, *Ducatus Baiuvariorum*, 469–70, suggests that Tassilo now acted as a middleman between his father-in-law and the new pope, Hadrian. For Desiderius' wider plans in early 772, see below, 183.

37 Einhard, *VK* c. 18, p. 22.

posed a huge threat to the papacy's territorial interests, and the Franks are supposed to have adopted the role of papal protectors, the story of this marriage has long been 'one of the most mysterious problems of Charlemagne's reign.'[38] The very fact that the young woman's name is unrecorded in any contemporary source has added to the aura of mystery surrounding her.[39] The problem has remained mysterious, despite an enormous amount of ink spilled about it, largely because of the tantalizing evidence of a letter of Pope Stephen III which reveals both strong hostility to the idea of a Franco-Lombard marriage, and curious ignorance over *which* Frankish king – there were two in 770 – was planning to marry Desiderius' daughter.[40] Scholarly attention has focused on the papacy's interest in preventing the Lombard marriage, but I think the strength and consistency of papal policy has been overestimated, particularly since the publication of Thomas Noble's *The Republic of St Peter*, which highlighted precisely those alleged traits.[41] Similar assumptions about strong and consistent Franklish policy have been fairly pervasive, too, and I think equally misleading.

38 So E. Delaruelle, 'Charlemagne, Carloman, Didier et la politique du mariage franco-lombard (770–771),' *Revue Historique* 170 (1932): 213–24, at 213; cf. now the fine study of Jarnut, 'Ein Bruderkampf und seine Folgen: die Krise des Frankenreiches (768–771),' in *Herrschaft, Kirche, Kultur: Beiträge zur Geschichte des Mittelalters. Festschrift für Friedrich Prinz zu seinem 65. Geburtstag*, ed. G. Jenal and S. Haarländer (Stuttgart, 1993), 165–76.

39 The idea (still accepted in some recent historiography) that she was called Desiderata rests on a misreading of *Vita Adalardi*, c. 7, *PL* 120, col. 1511: a reference to Desiderius's sending *desideratam filiam* — 'the desired daughter.' See B. Kasten, *Adalhard von Corbie: Die Biographie eines karolingischen Politikers und Klostervorstehers* (Düsseldorf, 1986), 24, n. 42, rightly pointing out that the capital D is a nineteenth-century editorial addition (by Pertz, MGH SS [in folio] 2, 525), and that Desiderata is undocumented as a personal name. For a suggestion as to what the bride's name really was, see below, 183.

40 *Codex Carolinus*, 45, p. 561 (English translation, King, *Charlemagne*, 271). Their father, Pippin, had arranged for both Charles and Carloman marriages with 'lovely wives (*coniuges*) from the most noble people of the Franks,' according to the pope.

41 T.F.X. Noble, *The Republic of St Peter: The Birth of the Papal State, 680–825* (Philadelphia, 1984). My reservations attest (if back-handedly) the force of Noble's thesis. For accounts of papal policy between *ca* 750 and *ca* 774 that seem to rest on monochrome readings of papal sources, see D. Miller, 'Papal-Lombard Relations during the Pontificate of Pope Paul I,' *Catholic Historical Review* 55 (1969): 358–76; J.T. Hallenbeck, 'Instance of Peace in Eighth-Century Lombard-Papal Relations,' *Archivum Historiae Pontificiae* 18 (1980): 41–56; M.V. Ary, 'The Politics of the Frankish-Lombard Marriage Alliance,' *Archivum Historiae Pontificiae* 19 (1981): 7–26. Although the commentary of Davis, *Lives of the Eighth-Century Popes*, follows Noble very closely, the translated texts themselves (together with King's translations of many of the letters in the *Codex Carolinus*) reveal the extent to which swings of papal 'policy' were determined by faction.

Between 768 and the end of 771, that is, for some three years, 'Frankish policy' cannot be said to have existed, because of the very uneasy *co*existence of Charlemagne and his brother Carloman.[42] The *Royal Frankish Annals* say that their mother, Bertrada, visited Carloman at Seltz in the summer of 770, before journeying 'to Italy by way of Bavaria.'[43] Neither the *Royal Frankish Annals* nor the *Liber Pontificalis* mention Charlemagne's Lombard marriage. The contemporary *Moselle Annals* say: 'Queen Bertrada was in Italy for a meeting with King Desiderius; and numerous cities were given back to St Peter, and Bertrada brought Desiderius's daughter to Francia.'[44] There has been a slightly romanticized tendency to credit Charlemagne's mother, Bertrada, with the role of international peacemaker. According to Delaruelle, Bertrada had a grander vision than the pope himself. 'Elle revait d'inaugurer un équilibre général en occident ... [d'une] réconciliation européenne.'[45] This smacks more of the peace efforts of the early 1930s than of Carolingian family politics. While not underestimating Bertrada's role as middleman, I think two factors conditioned it: first, the bitter rivalry between Charlemagne and Carloman, and, second, the preponderance of Desiderius' influence in 770. Bertrada had to pass through Carloman's kingdom *en route* to Bavaria. What she and Carloman said to each other at Seltz is unrecorded. Perhaps the mother misled her younger son, since it seems that Charlemagne was her favourite. It is only the revised version of the *Royal Frankish Annals* that asserts that Bertha's journey to Seltz was 'in the cause of peace,' and goes on to imply that she returned to 'her sons' rather than to Charlemagne alone.[46] Yet it is clear from a letter of Pope Stephen III of (probably) late 770 that Bertha was then living in Charlemagne's household.[47] In

42 Jarnut, 'Bruderkampf,' 165–6, ascribes the absence of Frankish campaigns in 770 and 771 to fraternal hostility, and stresses (p. 168) the aggressive implications of Carloman's naming of his new-born son, Pippin, in 770: clearly a riposte to Charles's naming of *his* eldest son. Jarnut is perhaps too keen to stress the danger arising from the 'fact' that Charles's son was 'a hunchback': the earliest evidence to this effect is Einhard, *VK* c. 20, p. 25: 'gibbo deformis.' Charles's treatment of his son down to 792 gives no clear hint that he was regarded as unthroneworthy: see P. Classen, 'Karl der Grosse und die Thronfolge im Frankenreich,' in his *Ausgewählte Aufsätze*, ed. J. Fleckenstein (Sigmaringen, 1983), 205–29. But see also W. Goffart, 'Paul the Deacon's *Gesta Episcoporum Mettensium* and the Early Design for Charlemagne's Succession,' *Traditio* 42 (1986): 53–87.
43 *ARF*, 30 (trans. King, *Charlemagne*, 75). For evidence that she did not go without military support, see below, nn. 47, 51.
44 *Annales Mosellani*, a. 770, ed. C. Lappenberg, MGH SS (in folio) 16 (1859), 496, trans. King, *Charlemagne*, 132.
45 Delaruelle, 'Charlemagne, Carloman,' 215.
46 *ARF* (Rev.), 31, trans. King, *Charlemagne*, 109.
47 *Codex Carolinus*, 46, p. 564, trans. King, *Charlemagne*, 274–5: to Bertrada and Charles, in that order. This letter also shows that Hitherius, *fidelis vester*, was active with *concomites* (a warband?) on the borders of Benevento, enforcing the return of some disputed lands to the

view of the evidence for severe tension between the two brothers,[48] it seems more than likely that Charlemagne's Lombard marriage was directed against Carloman. The object of Bertrada's Grand Tour was to draw closer the ties around the royal family at Pavia, and to effect Charlemagne's entrée into the circle. In so doing, Bertrada, and Charlemagne, acknowledged Desiderius' centrality, as well as his usefulness in their isolating of Carloman. The Lombard alliance was the best defence they could construct. The double bond of a parallel marriage between Charlemagne's sister Gisela with Adelchis, son of Desiderius and Ansa, might, had it materialized, have strengthened that bond still further.[49] Meanwhile, however, what did strengthen the bond of alliance were oaths sworn by Frankish leading men, including Charlemagne's cousin Adalard, to underwrite the marriage agreement.[50] Carloman, by the end of 770, was effectively encircled. It has been argued that a Lombard alliance went against the grain of Frankish policy in the reign of Pippin: yet Charlemagne was not bound to continue that policy; and what, anyway, did that policy amount to? Not direct intervention in Italy; not consistent unequivocal support for papal territorial claims; not the displacement of the Lombard ruling family. In 770, everything suggests that Desiderius' position appeared strong. It was Charlemagne who needed support – though he was also anxious to retain some freedom of manoeuvre, intervening in Ravenna to persuade Desiderius to accept the papal nominee as archbishop.[51]

papacy. The pope's *vester* is likely to include Bertrada: Hitherius had been the leading notary of her late husband since 753 (see D. Bullough, 'Aula Renovata: The Court before the Aachen Palace,' in his collected essays, Carolingian Renewal [Manchester, 1991], 126–7), and he became Charles's notary from 768: the absence of any charters of Charles between March 770 and April 771 is therefore likely to mean that Hitherius had gone with Bertrada to Italy and stayed there when she returned to Francia.

48 In addition to Einhard's explicit statement, VK c. 3, p. 6, there is Cathwulf's letter of 774, ed. E. Dümmler, MGH Epistolae 4, 502, which mentions the insidiae, 'plots,' 'ambushes,' laid by Carloman for his brother. The fate of Tilpin of Rheims, in whose church Carloman was buried, is significant: according to Flodoard, Historia Remensis Ecclesiae II 17, ed. J. Heller and G. Waitz, MGH SS (in folio) 13, 464, Tilpin received from Charlemagne confirmation of immunities granted by Carloman for Rheims estates, but he is never otherwise recorded in relation to Charlemagne. For Autchar, one of Carloman's leading men known to have gone to Italy with the widow of his lord, see Vita Hadriani, cc. 9, 23, 25, 31, 34, Liber Pontificalis 1: 488, 493–6, trans. Davis, Lives, 126, 133–4, 136, 138. The only evidence for his being forgiven by Charlemagne is the later medieval epic 'Ogier le Danois': Becher, Eid, 150.

49 In Codex Carolinus, 45, p. 561, trans. King, Charlemagne, 273, Pope Stephen III mentioned this only to express his strong opposition. Jahn, Ducatus Baiuvariorum, 391, suggests that Desiderius may have made this proposal some years earlier.

50 These oaths must be inferred from Vita Adalardi c. 7, PL 120, col. 1511, where Adalard is said to have denounced nonnulli Francorum who subsequently perjured themselves by accepting Charlemagne's repudiation of the agreement: see Kasten, Adalhard von Corbie, 24–5.

51 Vita Stephani III, c. 26, Liber Pontificalis 1: 477–8, trans. Davis, Lives, 102, shows Charles'

To grasp Charlemagne's motives in marrying Desiderius' daughter is to become more than half-aware of the reasons why the marriage was short-lived. There is no strictly contemporary evidence for the timing of Charlemagne's decision to reject his Lombard bride. Einhard says that Charlemagne repudiated her *post annum*, 'after a year,' or 'when the year was out,' and 'married a Swabian of outstanding nobility called Hildegard.'[52] I think the key event was Carloman's death on 4 December 771,[53] followed by Charlemagne's evident determination to disregard the claims of Carloman's young sons, and to take over his late brother's kingdom himself. It looks as if the area where Charlemagne foresaw most need to build up support was Alemannia, the only part of Carloman's kingdom located east of the Rhine:[54] hence the wisdom of the marriage with Hildegard – and the prerequisite of repudiating the Lombard wife, in effect sending her home. (The accusation that she was barren is made only in the late ninth century:[55] a mere twelve months of married life was hardly long enough to make it sound plausible.) Once that had happened, the flight of Carloman's widow, Gerberga, and her sons to King Desiderius was a logical conse-

missi, presumably with a military retinue, in Ravenna in 770 (though cf. the curious subsequent papal memory-lapse on this episode, *Codex Carolinus*, 85, p. 621, trans. King, *Charlemagne*, 304): was this intervention, too, connected with Bertrada's visit, i.e., were these *missi*, like Hitherius and his men, left in Italy after the queen's departure? And was this intervention on behalf of Stephen's nominee the price of papal agreement to Charles's Lombard marriage (cf. Jarnut, 'Bruderkampf,' 171–2)?

52 Einhard, *VK* c. 18, p. 22.

53 *ARF* a. 771, 32, trans. King, *Charlemagne*, 75. No contemporary source clarifies the chronology, and modern historians have disagreed. Kasten, *Adalhard von Corbie*, 20–2 and n. 34, gives full references, and thinks, as I do, that the repudiation immediately post–dated Carloman's death. Jahn, *Ducatus Baiuvariorum*, 466, sits on the fence.

54 *ARF* a. 771, 32, trans. King, *Charlemagne*, 75: the naming of Abbot Fulrad, who had extensive interests in Alemannia, Warin, *administrator Alamanniae*, Kasten, 204–5, and Adalard, an Aleman count, as present at the Corbény meeting within three weeks of Carloman's death, when some of Carloman's *primates* acknowledged Charles' overlordship, reveals Alemannia as a priority. In the first judgment extant from his reign, *Die Urkunden Pippins, Karlmanns und Karls des Grossen*, ed. E. Mühlbacher, MGH DD Karolinorum 1 (1906), no. 65, pp. 94–5, datable to early 772, Charles decided against the claims to Lorsch of Heimeric son of Cancor, another powerful man in Alemannia: see Bullough, '*Albuinus deliciosus Karoli regis*: Alcuin of York and the Shaping of the Early Carolingian Court,' in *Institutionen, Kultur und Gesellschaft im Mittelalter: Festschrift für Josef Fleckenstein zu seinem 65. Geburtstag*, ed. L. Fenske, W. Rösener, and T. Zotz, (Sigmaringen 1984), 73–92, at 87 ff. A. Stoclet, *Autour de Fulrad de Saint-Denis (v.710–784)* (Geneva, 1993), esp. 219–21, 434–42, offers further insights, some of them debatable, into Charles' interventions in aristocratic factions in Alemannia.

55 Notker, *Gesta Karoli* II 17, ed. H. Haefele, MGH SRG NS 12 (1959), 82. Cf. Einhard, below, n. 57.

quence.[56] Significantly, Einhard is economical with the truth on both counts: of the repudiation he says, 'the reason is uncertain' (*incertum qua de causa*); of the widow's flight, he says, 'there were no reasons for this' (*nullis existentibus causis*).[57] The widow's choice of refuge was yet further testimony to Desiderius' power; the wife's expulsion seemed to point in the opposite direction, yet was in fact merely an epiphenomenon of Charlemagne's urgent need to reunite the Franks and establish his *monarchia*. The Lombard princess was the fall-guy. That is one reason why she suffered a kind of *damnatio memoriae*. Only one source, the *Vita Adalhardi*, claims that the pious hero Adalard objected to her repudiation, and protested by withdrawing from the court and from secular life.[58]

The similarity, indeed close association, between the plights of the two queens might have led to confusion – compounded, I suggest, by a coincidence. I think Desiderius's youngest daughter was named Gerperga. That was almost certainly the name given her in a ninth-century manuscript of Andrew of Bergamo's *Little History*.[59] Further, it fits with the names of the other daughters of Desiderius, all of them with the same second element.[60] It helps explain why Stephen III was unsure which of the brothers was marrying the Lombard princess. It helps to explain the otherwise bizarre confusion of the *Annals of Lobbes*, which stated that 'Carloman's wife fled to her father, King Desiderius.'[61]

Charlemagne's repudiation of Gerperga definitely broke his entente with the Lombards. From now on, Desiderius was an enemy, The flight of Charlemagne's sister-in-law and, more especially, of his nephews, and the taking up of their cause by Desiderius, meant that Charlemagne was drawn, against his original instincts and calculations, into deep and permanent involvement in Italy. Reluctantly still, though: he first campaigned in Saxony, in 772, and moved southwards towards the Alpine passes only, in what the *Royal Frankish Annals*

56 *Annales Mettenses priores*, a. 771, 58, trans. King, *Charlemagne*, 150, is the only source to name her. Cf. above, n. 40, for her being noble and Frankish. Nothing seems to be known about her family, and the two name-elements Ger- and -berga (-burga) are fairly common.

57 Einhard, *VK* c. 18, p. 22 (note that he does not allege sterility); c. 3, p. 6.

58 *Vita Adalardi*, c. 7, *PL* 120, col. 1511; cf. Kasten, *Adalhard von Corbie*, 24–35; Nelson, *Frankish World*, 233–4.

59 Andrew, *Historia*, c. 3, MGH SS Rerum Langobardicarum et Italicarum (1878), 224 and n. (a). For this work, see W. Pohl, 'Paulus Diaconus und die "Historia Langobardorum",' 393–4. See further R. Balzaretti, 'Charlemagne in Italy,' *History Today* 46 (1996), 33–4.

60 See family tree, above, 173. The element *-perga* was rendered *-berga* by Frankish writers: see below, 185, on Liutberga in the *ARF*.

61 *Annales Laubacenses*, MGH SS II, 195. These annals were apparently written up in the tenth century.

presents as a response to urgent papal appeals, in summer 773. As late as November, he twice offered Desiderius the huge sum of 'gold and silver to the amount of 14,000 gold solidi,' perhaps not, or not only, to conciliate the papacy and avert war, but as the price of two princes.[62] Desiderius refused. Do you negotiate with the man who has repudiated your daughter? When Pavia fell, finally, to the Frankish besiegers in early June 774, 'Desiderius and his wife and the/a daughter' – who must surely be Gerperga – were carried off to Francia.[63] The parents were consigned to monastic imprisonment.[64] The daughter is never heard of again.

What of her sisters? First, let us consider Liutperga (Liutpirc). There is some Bavarian evidence for her political activity. First, a Freising charter of 804 recalled that Bishop Arbeo (764–83) had 'lost many churches because he had aroused the wrath of Tassilo and Liutperc against him because he was truer to the Franks than to them.'[65] Then, the Confraternity Book of Salzburg, compiled under the auspices of Bishop Virgil in 784, has the names of Desiderius and Ansa, and Adelchis, and also those of Tassilo, Liutpirc [*sic*] and Theodo, Cotani and Hrodrud (implying that the younger son, Theodebert, was not yet born),[66] while a later hand[67] in the Confraternity Book adds the name of Liutpirc to a list of dead dukes and their wives.[68] Third, a scholar named Dobdegrecus (Dubdá-Crích) in the entourage of Virgil is documented as having two special patrons: Tassilo and Liutperga.[69] Fourth, and and most impressive, is the Tassilo chalice. This fine object was apparently made by an insular craftsman or someone with insular training, and can be dated to *ca* 770x788.[70] The upper

62 *Vita Hadriani*, cc. 28, 30, *Liber Pontificalis* 1: 494, 495, trans. Davis, *Lives*, 135 with n. 39, 136. Was this in part recycled Saxon loot? cf. *ARF* a. 772, 34: 'ipsum fanum [i.e., Ermensul] destruxit et aurum vel argentum quod ibi repperit abstulit.' Though no royal wergeld is given in extant Frankish codes, early Anglo-Saxon kings' wergelds seem to have been fixed at 7,500 shillings: see G.N. Garmonsway's comment on the 694 annal in his translation of *The Anglo-Saxon Chronicle* (London, 1972), 40, n. 1.
63 *ARF* a. 774, 38, adding 'cum omni thesauro eius palatii.' *Vita Hadriani*, c. 44, *Liber Pontificalis* 1: 499, records the parents' fate but does not mention the daughter.
64 At Corbie, according to *Annales Sangallenses maiores*, MGH SS 1 (1826), 75.
65 Bitterauf, *Traditionen des Hochstifts Freising*, vol. 1, no. 193b, p. 183 (13 January 804).
66 *Liber Confraternitatum S. Petri Salisburgensis Vetustior*, ed. S. Herzberg-Fränkel, MGH Necrologia Germaniae 2 (1904), 12. See Wolfram, *Geburt*, 106 and 490, n. 48.
67 Wolfram, *Geburt*, 135, 192, suggests that Liutperga died before 794, because she is not mentioned in the Capitulary of Frankfurt, below n. 79, hence the 'later hand' would have been working in the decade after 784.
68 *Liber Confraternitatum*, 27. Note that the Bavarian rendering of the name Liutperga stays close to the Lombard form. Cf. Jahn, *Ducatus Baiuvariorum*, 26–8.
69 Wolfram, 'Virgil als Abt,' in *Virgil von Salzburg*, ed. H. Dopsch and R. Juffinger (Salzburg, 1985), 342–56, at 347–8.
70 David Wilson and L. Webster, in *The Making of England: Anglo-Saxon Art and Culture, AD*

ring of images shows Christ, with the Greek characters alpha and omega and 'i' and 's' for *ihesus soter*, and the evangelists. Around the bottom are the words: '+ Tassilo Dux fortis + Liutpirc virga regalis' – not a misprint for *virgo*, but meaning 'the royal rod' or 'branch.' Below are saints: John the Baptist, Maria Theotokos, Pantaleon Thaumaturgos, and Theodoros Martyr. These point to Kremsmünster, consecrated on 9 November, the day of St Theodore. Wolfram suggests a link, linguistically 'wrong' but understandable, between *Theod*ore and *Theoto*, the son of Tassilo and Liutperga:[71] perhaps the saint was the child's special patron, and the chalice was made to mark the occasion of Theodo's baptism, in 772. Perhaps the 'Greek' scholar had some influence on the chalice's design.[72] It is still at Kremsmünster, and may have been given to the monastery by Tassilo and Liutperga themselves, or by Liutperga alone after Tassilo's fall in 788. Frankish sources are equally emphatic on Liutperga's political influence. According to the *Annales Mettenses priores* for 787, 'Tassilo following the advice of his wicked wife contumaciously scorned to come to the king [Charles].'[73] The original version of the *Royal Frankish Annals* has two references to this 'wicked' woman under the year 788: 'Tassilo incited by his wife Liutberga [*sic*] had not maintained his faith ...'; and then, of the attacks of the Avars, 'all this had been treacherously plotted by the above-mentioned duke Tassilo and his malevolent wife Liutperga hateful to God.'[74] The revised version of the *Royal Frankish Annals* puts more stress on the Avars and on Liutperga's role: '[Bavarians alleged that Tassilo] at the urging of his wife Liutberga who was the daughter of Desiderius king of the Lombards, and had been constant and extreme in her enmity of the Franks since her father's exile, incited the people of the Huns to hostility against the king and to undertake a war against the Franks.'[75]

600–900, ed. L. Webster and J. Backhouse (London 1991), 168; and, esp. for what follows, Wolfram, *Geburt*, 139–40. The *terminus post quem* need not be set by the date of Kremsmünster's consecration (a. 777): the link with Theodore could already have been supplied by Theodo. This does, however, seem to preclude the chalice's having been commissioned to mark the wedding of Tassilo and Liutperga.

71 The boy's name, Theoto, derives from the Germanic element *theod*-, 'of the people'; Theodore, from Greek *theos* + *doron*, means 'gift of God.'

72 Cf. n. 69 above. The scholar was an Irishman who knew Greek.

73 *Annales Mettenses priores*, 75, trans. King, *Charlemagne*, 156. The entry continues: 'but ... seeing himself surrounded on all sides surrendered himself *in vassaticum* to Charles ... and gave his son Theodo as a hostage.'

74 *ARF* a. 788, 80, 82 (trans. King, *Charlemagne*, 86–7): '... malivola uxor eius Liutberga Deo odibilis ...' Manuscript variants are 'Luitberga' and 'Liudberga.' No manuscript shifts 'b' to 'p,' however.

75 *ARF* (Rev.) a. 787, 81, trans. King, *Charlemagne*, 121. Manuscript variants of the name are 'Liuthburga,' 'Leutberga.'

This may be scapegoating, but such annalistic misogyny has a wider import: it defames not only Liutperga, but also Tassilo, as a husband who failed to maintain control of his wife, and thus by implication reaffirms the rectitude of Frankish authority, political and ideological.[76] Further, that allegation rings true as an explanation of Liutperga's motives. The fall of Tassilo in 788 necessarily brought hers too. The envoys sent by Charlemagne to Bavaria to fetch Liutperga and her children to Francia 'carried out their orders with zeal and effectiveness: they brought all of them, together with their treasures and their very numerous household ['familia eorum copiosa valde'].'[77] While Tassilo and Theodo were tonsured, Liutperga's daughters, Cotani and Hrodrud, were carted off by Abbot Hunric of Mondsee to captivity in West Frankia, where one of them ended up at Chelles.[78] Liutperga's fate is unknown. In 794, when Tassilo was brought before the Council of Frankfurt and his offspring definitively disinherited, Liutperga was unmentioned.[79] Perhaps she was already dead.

The Bavarians were not Charlemagne's only headache in the 780s. The Beneventans were equally worrisome, intriguing with Constantinople to secure the return of Adelchis, the *spes Bardorum*.[80] The loyalty of the abbot of San Vincenzo became suspect, and Charlemagne reacted sharply.[81] Charlemagne visited Italy in the autumn of 786, and early the following year reached Rome. There he put pressure on Benevento. Duke Arichis sent one son, Romuald, with gifts, then his younger son, Grimoald, was chosen as a hostage by Charlemagne.[82] At this point, Tassilo's envoys, Bishop Arn of Salzburg and Abbot Hunric of Mondsee, were also in Rome, seeking papal mediation. The *Royal Frankish Annals* say no more, simply recording the departure of Tassilo's envoys and Charlemagne's return to Francia.[83] Can we surmise some concerted

---

76 Cf. the penetrating comments of J. Smith, 'Gender and Ideology in the Earlier Middle Ages,' *Studies in Church History* 34 (1998), forthcoming.

77 *Annales Nazariani* 788, ed. G. Pertz, MGH SS (in folio) (1826), 1: 43.

78 She took with her apparently the Mondsee Psalter, MS Montpellier 409. See Stoclet, 'Gisèle, Kisyla, Chelles, Benediktbeuren et Kochel: Scriptoria, bibliothèques et politique à l'époque carolingienne: Une mise au point,' *Revue Bénédictine* 96 (1986): 250–70; McKitterick, *The Carolingians and the Written Word* (Cambridge, 1989), 253–5.

79 *Capitularia Regum Francorum* 2: 74, no. 28, c. 3, ed. A. Boretius and V. Krause, MGH LL Capitularia 2 (1890–7). Cf. above, n. 67.

80 Cf. Ansa's epitaph, with laudatory reference to her son Adalgis [*sic*], cited above, 175 f.

81 *Codex Carolinus*, 66, 67, pp. 593–7, trans. King, *Charlemagne*, 292. C. Wickham, 'Monastic Lands and Monastic Patrons,' in *San Vincenzo al Volturno*, 2, ed. R. Hodges, British School at Rome (London, 1995), 138–52, at 146, gives the wider context.

82 *ARF* a. 787, 74, *ARF* (Rev.) a. 786, 75, trans. King, *Charlemagne*, 84, 120; cf. Einhard, *VK* c. 10, p. 13.

83 Ibid.

diplomacy involving not only Bavaria and Benevento, but the two sisters, Liutperga and Adalperga? Virilocal their marriages were, but their political concerns were very far from local. It seems entirely conceivable that in 787 they contributed for their own reasons to the concerting of action against their common enemy, the Frankish king who had destroyed their father and dishonoured their sister.

Papal sources reveal at this point that Arichis had sought help from Byzantium, asking for his brother-in-law (Adelperga's brother) Adelchis to be sent back to southern Italy with a powerful force.[84] When Arichis died, in the summer of 787 – and at about the same time his son Romuald also died[85] – it was Adelperga who took command (her only surviving son, Grimoald, was a hostage in Charlemagne's hands), and conducted negotiations with Greek envoys. A unique, remarkable survival, a report of Charlemagne's *missus* Maginar, sent back in January 788, reveals that Adelperga was in charge in Benevento, along with Beneventan *primates*.[86] A letter (also preserved in the original) from Pope Hadrian to Maginar and his colleagues confirms that Adelperga was recognized to be running affairs in Benevento: Capuan envoys had asked the pope to write to Adelperga to secure their protection.[87] A papal letter to Charlemagne confirms this: 'Adelperga and the Beneventans are constantly engaged in wicked and hostile deeds towards you and us.'[88] Soon after, yet another papal letter reported that Adelchis had arrived in Campania. Hadrian warned Charlemagne not to allow Grimoald to return to Benevento: 'if you do, it will be quite impossible for you to hold Italy without trouble ... We say this because Bishop Leo has secretly informed us that Adelperga, widow of Arichis, has a scheme whereby as soon as Grimoald her son crosses the Beneventan frontier she intends deviously to take her two daughters with her and travel as if with prayer in mind to Sant'Angelo in Gargano and from there, since it is only 80 miles distant, to Taranto where she also has her treasures

---

84 *Codex Carolinus*, 80, 83, 84, pp. 611–13, 616–20, trans. King, *Charlemagne*, 299–303. For continuing Byzantine interests in Benevento, which was seen at Constantinople as still part of the empire, see J. Herrin, *The Formation of Christendom* (Princeton, 1986), 424–6.

85 *Codex Carolinus*, 83, p. 618, trans. King, *Charlemagne*, 299; *Chronicon Salernitanum*, cc. 20, 21, ed. U. Westerbergh (Stockholm, 1956), 24–5, 26–7, dating the deaths to 26 August (Arichis), and 21 July (Romuald); cf. Alcuin, Ep. 211 (early 801), p. 352, trans. King, *Charlemagne*, 326.

86 *Codex Carolinus*, Appendix, 2 (*ca* 22 January 788), pp. 655–7 (trans. King, *Charlemagne*, 295–7), is a surviving papyrus original, preserved at St-Denis, where Maginar was abbot from 784 until his death in 793. (There is a new edition by H. Atsma and J. Vezin, with facsimile, in *ChLA* 16 (1986), no. 629, pp. 59–65.)

87 *Codex Carolinus*, Appendix, 1, 564–5, trans. King, *Charlemagne*, 298.

88 *Codex Carolinus*, 82 (February 788), 615–16; trans. King, *Charlemagne*, 297.

stored ...'[89] Notice the combination of Adelperga's resources and resourceful-ness. The alleged destination of herself and her daughters, St Michael's on Monte Gargano, was perfectly sited to permit a link-up with Byzantine forces arriving across the Adriatic. It was also the great traditional shrine of the Lombard realm,[90] where these women's prayers might be hoped to achieve maximum effect in keeping Lombard hopes alive; and to these spiritual weapons Adelperga added wordly ones in the form of treasure, with which her brother's armies could be sustained.

The Beneventans retained their independence. The very price against which Hadrian warned was the one Charlemagne decided to pay: he sent Grimoald back, choosing negotiation rather than retaliation, perhaps because he realized that he simply lacked the military power to defeat the Beneventans, but, more importantly, driving a wedge between them and Byzantium.[91] *De facto*, the Beneventans therefore kept their autonomy. Right at the end of Charlemagne's reign, in 810, the year when his son King Pippin of Italy died, and a terrible cattle-plague also ravaged Francia, rumours spread that the cause was men with magic poison dust who had been sent to Francia by the duke of Benevento 'because he was the enemy of the most Christian Emperor Charles.'[92]

I return, finally, to the daughter of Desiderius with whom I began, Anselperga, Abbess of Brescia. She is never heard of again after her father's downfall in 774. In 775–6 there was a very serious Lombard revolt based in Friuli.[93] Was Anselperga implicated, or had she already been removed from office? Charlemagne gave no favours to San Salvatore until 781, when the revolt was well over and his son was being installed as sub-king of Italy. The

89 *Codex Carolinus*, 80, pp. 610–14, February/April 788, King, *Charlemagne*, 301–2. (Gundlach, MGH Epistolae 3: 611, dated this letter to late 787/early 788, but King's dating is preferable).

90 D. Harrison, 'The Duke and the Archangel: A Hypothetical Model of Early State Integration in Southern Italy through the Cult of Saints,' *Collegium Medievale* 6 (1993), 5–33.

91 *ARF* (Rev.) a. 788, 83, says that Constantine VI, 'angered at being refused the king's daughter' [that is, Charlemagne's daughter Rotrude, betrothed to the young emperor since the early 780s], ordered the governor of Sicily to attack the Beneventans. 'Grimoald and Hildebrand duke of Spoleto attacked [the Greeks] in Calabria ... and killed an immense multitude of them.'

92 Agobard, *De Grandine et Tonitruis*, c. 16, ed. L. van Acker, *Agobardi Opera omnia*, Corpus Christianorum, Continuatio Medievalis 52 (Turnhout, 1981), 14–15, with the comment, 'What was truly amazing: the men, when arrested, confessed. *Tanta stultitia oppressit miserum mundum.*' For the text and its context, see now P.E. Dutton, 'Thunder and Hail over the Carolingian Countryside,' in *Agriculture in the Middle Ages*, ed. D. Sweeney (Philadelphia, 1995), 111–37.

93 H. Krahwinkler, *Friaul im Frühmittelalter* (Vienna 1992), 119–43.

recipient of the favour was a new abbess, Radoara, perhaps a Frank.[94] From the early ninth century, certainly, the convent became the Carolingians' bastion in Lombardy, under a series of their own royal women.[95]

What light does all this throw on Charlemagne's reign? In broad comparative terms, it invites reconsideration of the ways in which the early Carolingians from Charles Martel onwards, and especially Charlemagne himself, kept their daughters out of the internal and (after some havering) external marriage markets.[96] After all, the decision to forgo such alliances was abnormal enough for Einhard to offer explanation, even apology. In a Frankish kingdom with exceptionally long-standing dynastic continuity before 751, *not* to marry off royal daughters, but instead to place them in convents, may have reflected the insecurity of parvenus and their need to assert a new kind of inviolability. Charlemagne's domestic arrangements in his later years were *sui generis*.[97] Desiderius's strategy, by contrast, can be seen as the badge of a Lombard kingship with its own traditions, its own brand of security. If this is right, then a reassessment of the years around 770 is overdue. Hindsight knowledge of the dénouement of 774 has made historians underestimate Desiderius' strength before that date; it has engendered neglect of the Theodorician scale, hence the implications, of Desiderius' marriage strategy. Consideration of the women involved offers a rather different perspective on the scene in the early 770s. Lombard kingship need not appear doomed, nor does Charlemagne yet have to be seen as the central controlling figure. Opening up space around Desiderius allows his daughters' political power to be appreciated. Though connections between these women are barely documented, and only in 787 is there even a hint of concerted policy, it seems at least possible that Liutperga and Adelperga maintained contacts with each other alongside other likely diplomatic ties between their husbands' regimes. Though Liutperga failed, Adelperga succeeded in avenging, in some sense, her father's defeat and her sister's humiliation. Benevento, embodiment of Lombard continuity, was Charlemagne's Waterloo. And it was so, not least, because Adelperga perhaps perceived herself as embodying Lombard identity, just as her sister Liutperga seems to have seen *her*self as continuing the Lombard royal line. Even on a conservative estimate,

94 MGH DD Karolinorum 1: 185–6, no. 135.
95 H. Becher, 'Das königliche Frauenkloster San Salvatore/Santa Giulia in Brescia im Spiegel seiner Memorialüberlieferung,' *Frühmittelalterliche Studien* 17 (1983): 299–392.
96 R. Schieffer, 'Karolingische Töchter,' in *Herrschaft, Kirche, Kultur,* ed. Henal and Haarländer, 125–39, esp. 127–8, 138, offers characteristically thoughtful observations.
97 Cf. J.L. Nelson, 'La cour impériale de Charlemagne,' in *Élites et royauté au neuvième siècle,* ed. R. Le Jan et al. (Lille 1998), forthcoming.

these women played key political roles, keeping opposition going, keeping their own royalty alive as a rival to that of the Carolingians. For these women, married out into other families and other courts, also remained what they had been born – the daughters of Desiderius. From the 760s to the 780s, just that made a difference, reminding contemporaries of the fragility of Frankish power, reminding Charles the Great of his own limitations, reminding modern historians of the particular, gendered, contingencies of political histories that were also familial histories with women, necessarily, at their heart.

10

The 'Reviser' Revisited: Another Look at the Alternative Version of the *Annales Regni Francorum*

ROGER COLLINS

The small late ninth- early tenth-century Asturian *Chronicle of Alfonso III*, a text of some brevity without much of a medieval manuscript transmission, has recently been the beneficiary of three new critical editions in the course of a single decade. It may seem surprising, therefore, that the *Annales regni Francorum* (hereinafter *ARF*) still has to be consulted in the 1845 edition of Georg Pertz, as revised by Frederick Kurze and published in 1895.[1] The number of times a work has been edited reflects its importance no more than age alone prejudices the quality of the edition. Nevertheless, the three editions of the *Chronicle of Alfonso III*, though strikingly different in editorial conceptions and in their respective strengths and weaknesses, taken together offer a vast amount of erudition on the work, its manuscript tradition, and the period with which it is concerned. Can Carolingian scholars say as much for *ARF*? Kurze's edition has no commentary and is based upon assessments of manuscripts and sources that in some cases seem in need of serious revision.[2] Useful as it has been, and

Although this is just a small beginning of a large undertaking, if but a reflection of the true Goffartian refusal to be bound by the dead hand of received wisdom be found in this article, it will have served its purpose and acknowledged a great debt. I am most grateful to Timothy Reuter for invaluable comments and corrections.

1 *Die Chronik Alfons' III*, ed. Jan Prelog (Frankfurt, Bern, and Cirencester, 1980); *Crónicas asturianas*, ed. J. Gil, J.L. Moralejo, and J.L. Ruiz de la Peña (Oviedo, 1985); *Chroniques asturiennes*, ed. Yves Bonnaz (Paris, 1987). Kurze's edition of *ARF* and *Rev.: Annales regni Francorum inde ab a. 741 usque ad a. 829*, MGH SRG (1895).

2 For examples of manuscripts that have been redated: MS Vatican Reginensis lat. 213 (Kurze's B3) is now regarded as ninth century rather than tenth, while MS Vienna Österreichische Nationalbibliothek 510 ff. 31–132ᵛ (Kurze's E1) has been relegated from a ninth-century dating to a 'tenth- eleventh-century' one by the late Professor Bernhard Bischoff: *Lorsch im Spiegel seiner Handschriften* (Munich, 1974), 77 n. 83 and 120–1. Kurze did not see all of the manuscripts, relying on collations, made for him by various friends, of the Italian and British

in several respects still is, one hundred years after it first saw the light of day, it is probably overdue for replacement.

Some of the long-standing and still-current assumptions concerning the processes of composition and the intentions of the compilers of the text are also due for renewed critical scrutiny. These require some preliminary consideration here, as they have a bearing on the relationship between *ARF* and the Revised Version of it (hereinafter *Rev.*). The fact that most of the assessments of the compositional history and authorial purposes of the work stem from pronouncements made by Leopold Ranke in 1854 would seem to suggest either that his judgments are surprisingly free from error or that they have not been seriously reconsidered.[3] Essentially, he argued in respect of the entries for the years 741 to 795 that the compiler of *ARF* was so well informed in a wide range of areas, and yet so discreet on such matters as military defeats and conspiracies, that his work must have had some kind of official backing; indeed, that it was essentially a court composition, produced with the specific intention of moulding public opinion. The idea of a composition of that period having so overtly propagandistic a purpose must now seem rather anachronistic. How it could have achieved such an effect was hardly considered, and the evidence for its manuscript transmission would in any case mark it out as a dismal failure, if that had truly been its primary function. That it reflected a particular view of the events that were selected for inclusion is a far more acceptable verdict on the nature of the contents. Whether that was the viewpoint of a single person, or of an institution or of a group of individuals, influential or otherwise, or even of a Frankish ruler, remains open to argument – of which there has been perhaps too little in recent decades.[4]

Ranke also contributed to the formation of what has become a virtual consensus on the history of the composition of the work. From his and other nineteenth-century scholars' arguments, it remains accepted that a 'first author

ones in particular. Not all of these are comprehensive or exact. The apparatus of the edition also suffers from certain odd editorial ideas, such as the false premise of an *Ur*-chronicle, which Kurze called the '*Annales Ripuarienses,*' underlying some of the minor annals.

3 L. Ranke, 'Zur Kritik fränkisch-deutscher Reichsannalisten,' *Abhandlungen der Preussischen Akademie der Wissenschaften zu Berlin* (1854), 415–35. For a survey of the, mainly German, late nineteenth- and early twentieth-century literature on the annals, see Wattenbach-Levison, *Deutschlands Geschichtsquellen im Mittelalter*, vol. 2, ed. H. Löwe (Weimar, 1953), 247–57, 260–5.

4 As with the arguments over the identity of the author or authors of the *Chronicle* of Fredegar, this may reflect intellectual exhaustion in an essentially Franco-German debate of the late nineteenth/early twentiethth centuries, that seemed increasingly intractable. F.L. Ganshof, 'L'historiographie dans la monarchie franque sous les Mérovingiens et les Carolingiens,' *Settimane* 17 (1970): 631–750, comments, 'Nous croyons que l'on ne peut dans ce domaine arriver à des certitudes' (at 675), on the problems of the composition of *ARF* and *Rev.*

compiled *ARF* between 787 and 793 on the basis of older annals and the continuations of Fredegar.'[5] A second author is thought to have taken over, writing
the annals of the years 795 to 807 on a year-by-year basis. A third author is then
believed to have carried on the annual entry-making during the period from 808
to 829, at which point the text ends. While there was some disagreement over
the possible identities of the presumed three authors, the basic compositional
pattern thus outlined has not occasioned much serious debate for several
decades. The lack of scholarly interest in *ARF* in both its versions may be seen,
for example, in their virtual absence from Donald Bullough's 1970 survey of
recent work on the reign of Charlemagne and its sources.[6] This inertia has to be
a reflection of tacit agreement that the old certainties do not need to be
reviewed. But even those wedded to belief in the historian's task as being the
making of bricks to embed in a mighty wall of truth ought to find such a lack of
weathering rather peculiar.

   Recently, in a finely argued book, Matthias Becher was led to question,
among other things, the contemporary nature of *ARF*'s account of the oaths
taken by Tassilo III of Bavaria and his trial. He sees the annalist's treatment as
being essentially retrospective and the product of the changed political circumstances of the period after 790.[7] There are indeed yet other grounds for suspecting that the annal for 788 marks an important break in *ARF*. Up to and including
the entry for that year, the compiler makes frequent use of the word *tunc* (then)
in bridging sections of his narrative. In itself this usage may be thought to have
a retrospective rather than a contemporary flavour.[8] It disappears completely
from the annals with the end of the 788 entry. This is the most obvious but not
the only stylistic change that may be seen between the pre-789 section and that
which follows. Thus, for example, in *ARF* (though not in *Rev.*) all references to
the ruler are relatively elaborate, employing such formulae as *Domnus Carolus
gloriosus rex* and *Domnus Carolus benignissimus rex*, in the entries up to 788,
but after that the simpler 'rex' becomes standard.[9] Although Kurze's attempt to

---

5 B.W. Scholz, *Carolingian Chronicles* (Ann Arbor, 1970), 5 (quoted here) gives a useful short
   summary of the orthodox view.
6 D. Bullough, '*Europae Pater* Charlemagne and His Achievements in the Light of Recent
   Scholarship,' *English Historical Review* 85 (1970), 59–105, who notes, 'The problem of the
   place of origin of those "Revised Annals" is still very much where Bloch left it in 1901' (p.
   69). Even the most recent survey of Carolingian historiography, by Matthew Innes and Rosamond McKitterick (see n. 28, below), while having one intriguing suggestion to offer about
   Rev., omits any discussion of *ARF*.
7 M. Becher, *Eid und Herrschaft: Untersuchungen zum Herrscherethos Karls des Grossen* (Sigmaringen, 1993).
8 It also appears in the 'Lorsch Annals' as a bridging phrase up to and including the entry for
   791 (ed. G.H. Pertz, MGH SS [in folio] 1: 22–39), and in *ARF* s.a. 814 and 815.
9 Both examples to be found in *ARF* s.a. 769, ed. Kurze, 28.

use the differences in the manuscript transmission of *ARF* as the principal tool in uncovering its compositional history has not fully stood the test of time, idiosyncratic features of some of the manuscripts may still provide guidance.[10] Thus, his lost MS A1 from Lorsch, which ended its text of *ARF* with the entry for 788, may indeed represent a significant testimony to its textual history.[11]

While 788 marks a stylistic divide, it is also quite clear that the entries for 789 to 792 represent a later, and relatively brief, record of the events of those years. In several of the entries of *ARF*, which as usual centre on royal activities, the king is neither named nor given his title. The (implied) personal pronoun 'he' in the main verb is the only point of reference to the subject. In other words, it is the last-named reference to the monarch in a previous entry that indicates unambiguously who is being mentioned. Such a procedure seems intrinsically unlikely if the annals in question were being composed on a yearly basis. What we have, therefore, is continuous narrative spanning several years, written up at possibly no more than one time.[12] This phenomenon can be seen clearly in *ARF* in the entries for the years 781, 789, 790, 791, 792. Taken in conjunction with Becher's analysis of the ideological content of the account of Tassilo's oaths, it looks as if a case should be made for seeing a major act of compilation, covering the events of the years 741 to 788, as taking place after 790. If annual court-based composition of annals did occur, it is thus unlikely to have commenced before 793/4, and it does not have to be associated directly or at all with the compilation of the 741-to-788 section of *ARF* as we now have it. The latter section could also have been produced in a quite different centre and annexed at a subsequent point, when it would have been necessary to provide the brief and surprisingly laconic bridging section to cover the years 789 to 792.[13] The very slightness of the contents of most of this section might suggest that it was not written up as close to the events it describes as *ca* 793/4, when it would have been possible to recall from memory alone much fuller details of

---

10 F. Kurze, 'Über die fränkischen Reichsannalen und ihre Überarbeitung,' *Neues Archiv* 19 (1894): 295–329; 20 (1895): 9–49; and 21 (1896): 9–82. For criticism, see H. Wibel, *Beiträge zur Kritik der Annales regni Francorum und der Annales quae dicuntur Einhardi* (Strasbourg, 1902). There is a debate between the two in *Neues Archiv* 28 (1903), with a contribution by Manitius.

11 Henricus Canisius, *Antiquae lectiones ... tomus tertius* (Ingolstadt, 1603), 187–217, derives its text of the annals from a manuscript 'in Bavarica bibliotheca' (in Munich?) copied from a very old codex from Lorsch.

12 E.g. in *Rev.* the entry for 778 continues in this way directly from that for 777, as does the entry for 780 from that for 779. See, too, *Rev.* entries for 781, 782, 783, 785, 801.

13 The lost Lorsch MS (see n. 11, above) testifies to this problem, and to the fact that it contained a free standing text of the annals, ending in 788 and not linked to the later *ARF* tradition, by using a short continuation in the form of the 789-to-793 entries from the so-called Lorsch Annals. On the latter see Bullough, '*Europae Pater*,' 65.

such recent occurrences.[14] Comparison between the 790 entry in *ARF* and its equivalent in the 'Lorsch annals' is instructive in this regard: while the former confines itself to the brief and negative statement 'In sequenti vero anno nullum fecit iter,' the latter mentions both the reception of an Avar embassy and the despatch of an army to Bavaria.[15]

This uncertainty over the precise status of the pre-789 section of *ARF* as printed in Kurze's edition is accentuated when comparison is made with the so-called *Annales Mettenses priores* [hereinafter *AMP*].[16] Following Hoffmann's study of this text, it is now widely accepted that this compilation of earlier annal materials was put together around 802, and given a partly original continuation for the years 803 to 805, before returning fully to the orthodox text of *ARF* for its account of 806 to 829.[17] There is a final original section relating to the events of 830/1. Interestingly, however, its relationship to *ARF* varies rather more than such a view suggests. From the accession of Charlemagne in 768 (and the end of the text of the Continuations of Fredegar) up to the year 789, the text of *AMP* is largely dependent on *ARF* for its contents, but rarely literally and exclusively so. The narrative of *ARF* is generally followed, but not exactly.[18] There are several close parallels in the vocabulary, but the grammar can differ markedly. Additional details and pieces of information not to be seen in *ARF* can be found in *AMP*. Then, for much of its entries for the years 789 to 791, *AMP* is clearly independent of *ARF*, both textually and in its content. For 792 and 793, it returns to the previous state of close but not slavish reliance, before entering into a relationship of almost total fidelity for its account of the rest of the 790s. It is thus perhaps misleading to think of *AMP* as basically an independent work up to its entry for 805, with a subsequent direct borrowing of *ARF* for the period 806 to 829 serving just as a bridge to a final continuation that was written around 831. The direct borrowing from *ARF* in fact comes in two parts: 794 to 801 and 806 to 829.

The implications of all this are various. For the earlier section there must be allowed the possibility that the compiler of *AMP* was using a different version

---

14 The entry for 791 is larger in scale than the others in this section, though sharing the character-istics just outlined of a retrospective annal. It is also one of the entries that is most markedly different from its equivalent for the same year in the text of *Rev*.

15 *ARF* s.a. 790, ed. Kurze, 86; *Annales Laureshamenses*, ed. Pertz, 22–39.

16 B. von Simson, ed., MGH SRG [10] (1905).

17 H. Hoffmann, *Untersuchungen zur karolingischen Annalistik* (Bonn, 1958), 9–61. There are sections of *ARF* worked in with original or otherwise unidentified materials in the entries for 803, 804, and 805.

18 The decision of the editor, Bernhard von Simson, to put all sections of *AMP* that have any relationship to *ARF* into a common small typeface conceals the variations in the degree and nature of the dependence.

from that now found in the manuscripts of *ARF*, which he or she followed as faithfully for the pre-789 entries as in those for the 790s.[19] Alternatively, it might be argued that the greater fidelity to the model displayed in the latter section reflected the specially privileged nature of that part of the text covering the period 794 to 801. This is harder to understand, but may reflect a view that it carried particular authority, owing to its place of composition or authorship. However, it might also be suggested that the similarity of the relationship between the texts of *AMP* and *ARF* for both the periods 794 to 801 and 806 to 829 could best be explained by arguing that the whole *AMP* compilation should be dated to *ca* 831.[20] By this interpretation the original form of the work, as it related to the period 768 to 830, would consist of the following components: (1) either a rewritten form of the text of *ARF* up to 788/9 or a close following of an alternative version of it; (2) the text of *ARF* as we now know it for the years 794–801 and 806–29; (3) sections of material from other sources used to fill in lacunae relating to the years 789–93 and 802–5; (4) an original account relating to 830 and early 831.[21] While incorporating borrowings from other sources, identifiable or not, the section of *AMP* relating to the reign of Charlemagne might also in such a view qualify as another revised version of *ARF*.

It is perhaps no coincidence that both *AMP* and the Revised Version of the *Annales regni Francorum* change their relationship to *ARF* with the annal for 801. In the case of *AMP*, as already seen, this is to launch into a section of new material. With *Rev.*, the work itself comes to an end. In the extant manuscripts, other than one that is truncated at the entry for 749, the text of *Rev.* then leads into what is regarded as the mainstream of *ARF* for the years 801–29.[22] Some of the implications of this are discussed further below, but it has long been felt, not least because of what has been thought about the relationship to *Rev.* of Einhard's *Vita Karoli* and the work of 'Poeta Saxo' (writing *ca* 888/91), that in its

---

19 Janet Nelson, 'Gender and Genre in Women Historians of the Early Middle Ages,' in *L'historiographie médievale en Europe*, ed . J.P. Genet et al. (Paris, 1991), 149–63, on women historians and compilers working in this period.

20 If the compiler were working around 802/3, it is perhaps perplexing that he or she had nothing at all to add from their own perspective, even if only drawn from memory, to the *ARF* account of the later 790s. See Hoffmann, *Untersuchungen,* 38–41.

21 For present purposes, the more complex but intriguing questions relating to the sources of *AMP* for the period from the later seventh century to 741 are ignored. On these see Hoffmann, *Untersuchungen,* 12–38, and W. Levison, 'Zu den Annales Mettenses,' in *Kritische Beiträge zur Geschichte des Mittelalters. Festschrift für Robert Holtzmann* (Berlin, 1933), 9–21.

22 MS Florence Bibl. Laurent. LXV, 35 (A2 in Kurze's edition); an eleventh-century codex of Eutropius, Orosius, Jordanes (*Romana* and *Getica*), Gregory of Tours' *Historiae,* and Einhard's *Vita Karoli,* in which the section of *Rev.* for 741 to 749 continues the *Liber Historiae Francorum*.

original form the Reviser's work ended with the entry for 801.[23] This does not necessarily imply that he (or she) actually wrote at that time.[24] It is equally possible that the Reviser's text of *ARF* ended with the entry for 801. For the compiler of *AMP*, if writing in the early 830s, the situation was slightly better, in that an extension or continuation of the text existed covering the period 806–29. However, for both authors or compilers there was an absolute lack of material in their source relating to the period from 802 to 805.[25] Further arguments will be advanced below to support the view that there was a further significant break in the compiling of the annals around the years 806/7. While it is not intended to undertake a full-scale study of *ARF* here, doubts clearly can be raised as to the continuing strength of the older certainties concerning its structure, purpose, and compositional history. But, from the above discussion, it is at least possible that: (1) the 741–88 section of *ARF* was in origin an independent annalistic compilation, prepared after 790; (2) the 794–801 and 806–29 annals were not continuous; and (3) *AMP* is intrinsically a compilation of the early 830s, although using some original material from a source or sources unknown to fill in the lacunae or supplement its primary dependence on *ARF* for the account of the reign of Charlemagne.

II

Most of the problems, recognized or not, afflicting the *Annales regni Francorum,* apply equally to *Rev.*, the set of annals once attributed to Einhard. Even by Kurze's day that attribution was in doubt, and he published the text in parallel to that of *ARF* under the heading *Annales quae dicuntur Einhardi.*[26] It is possible that some scholars might wish to revive the association between this text and Einhard, whose *Vita Karoli* is normally thought to be indebted to it, but for now it may be said that there is a consensus in attributing the work to a single author, and that no attempt has been made to argue that it was composed in stages, let alone on a year-by-year basis in the way that is normally assumed to

23 Louis Halphen, *Études critiques sur l'histoire de Charlemagne* (Paris, 1921), 3–15; in the case of Poeta Saxo, a close relationship between the two is clear for the years 772 to 801. Hermann Bloch in a review of Gabriel Monod's *Études critiques sur les sources de l'histoire carolingienne* (Paris, 1898) in the *Göttingische gelehrte Anzeigen,* 63 (1901): 876–97, suggested that the poet's manuscript was defective (p. 883). On Einhard, see below, p. 207.
24 See below, pp. 202 ff.
25 MS Munich clm 23618, a tenth-century codex from Salzburg (Kurze's E9) begins its text of *ARF* with the annal for 806, while the ninth-century MS Vatican Reginensis lat. 213 (Kurze's B3) ends its text (which is not accidentally truncated) of *ARF* with the entry for 806. Can these just be coincidences?
26 See Wattenbach-Levison, *Deutschlands Geschichtsquellen im Mittelalter,* 2: 253–6.

be the case with much of *ARF*.[27] The most recent comment on its date and purpose, while not seeking to identify its author, attributes responsibility for commissioning the work to the emperor Louis the Pious, and it is implied that it was
intended in part to be critical of his father.[28] Only if it is assumed that the military failures of subordinate commanders reflected adversely on Charlemagne
himself could it be said that *Rev.* was in any way critical of him. When it comes
to the person of the ruler and his own involvement in campaigns, the account of
the Revised Version is always highly laudatory. It may tell us more of the things
that went wrong than does *ARF* proper, but there are no intrinsic grounds for
regarding anything in the text as being in the slightest degree condemnatory of
its principal subject. Intriguing as the idea of such an anti-history commissioned by his son may be, no grounds have yet been given for thus interpreting
it, or even for dating it to the latter's reign.

The manuscripts have been considered to be of limited help in trying to
solve the fundamental problems of the origins, authorship, and original contents of both *ARF* and *Rev.*, as none of them approaches quite close enough in
date to the initial periods of composition. There also always seem to be various
stages of later 'editorial' involvement, not least in the way these texts have been
combined with others in the manuscripts, making it hard to be sure that we now
have them in their original form.[29] It is worth noting that such re-employment
of historical texts and the essential anonymity of these works are standard features of the Frankish historiographical tradition as it existed between the death
of Gregory of Tours in 594 and the 830s. During that period not a single historical work written or compiled in the Frankish kingdoms has any indication of
authorship. Even Einhard's *Vita Karoli* may have been anonymous in its original form, only receiving its attribution of authorship in Gerward and Walahfrid's editions of it, made in the 830s and 840s. Larger-scale compositions, such
as the so-called *Chronicle of Fredegar*, are reworkings, acknowledged and
otherwise, of earlier histories, to which are added original sections, in the form
of both interpolations and continuations. Most of the sets of annals, including
ARF and *AMP*, partake of the same character. Hardly any could be described as

27 The relationship between *Rev.* and Einhard's *Vita Karoli* is not close verbally, and there are
various points, as will be shown below, at which Einhard ignores or contradicts the testimony
of *Rev.*
28 Matthew Innes and Rosamond McKitterick, 'The Writing of History,' in *Carlingian Culture*,
ed. Rosamond McKitterick (Cambridge, 1994), 193–220, at 209, reviving a suggestion made
in Wattenbach-Levison, *Deutschlands Geschichtsquellen im Mittelalter*, 2: 256.
29 As mentioned above (see n. 11) the lost Lorsch MS may reflect an early state of the 741-to-
788 annals, but, apart from the contents, no indications have survived to help with even provisional dating of this codex.

being fully independent, and they generally use earlier or other contemporary sources with considerable freedom. Our own concern with establishing authoritative texts of individual works, and in trying to assign authorship, can obscure the character of Frankish historiography as it was actually practised in this lengthy period.

Five classes of manuscripts have been identified, embracing both versions of *ARF*.[30] The fifth of these, Class 'E' in Kurze's edition, is that representing the various manuscripts of the Revised Version. The earliest of these was thought to be MS Vienna Österreichische Nationalbibliothek 510 (= E1), which at the end of the nineteenth century was dated to the last part of the ninth century and was subsequently made out to be even earlier by relocation to a point 'no later than 850.'[31] However, reassessment at the hands of the late professor Bischoff has led to a redating to the tenth 'or even tenth/eleventh' centuries.[32] Some of the codices of other classes still retain their ninth-century dating, but the way that the annals can be seen to have been treated makes it difficult to draw firm conclusions as to their original form from the state in which they are to be found in the manuscript transmission. Thus, for example, MS Vatican Reginensis lat. 213 (= Kurze's B3), which was written in Rheims, contains a section of *ARF* covering the years from 791 to 806. This is, however, tacked on without break or any form of heading to a section of the 'Lorsch Annals,' covering the period from 768 to 790. This in turn had been appended without any division or indication of change of source to the so-called Chronicle of Fredegar and its Continuations up to 768.[33] In other words, in compiling this late ninth-century manuscript, or an exemplar from which it derived, a composite historiographical survey was created by adding two sections of late eighth- and early ninth-century annals onto the Fredegar corpus.

The manuscript tradition of the Revised Version of the annals gives clear indications that the work in the form we now have it has passed through a similar editorial process, affecting its basic structure. All of our evidence relating to

---

30 Kurze edition, ix–xv. For other manuscripts unknown to Kurze, see Hans Haefele's edition of Notker Balbulus, MGH SRG NS 12 (1959), xxvii–xli.

31 L. Halphen, ed., *Eginhard. Vie de Charlemagne*, 4th ed. (Paris, 1967), xv n.1, citing the authority of Tangl and Holder-Egger.

32 Bischoff, *Lorsch*, 120–1; his eagerly anticipated catalogue of ninth-century manuscripts (covering libraries in locations with names between the letters A and M) may contain further revisions.

33 The Continuations of Fredegar end on the last line of fol. 148ᵛ, and the section of Lorsch annals commence on the top line of folio 149ʳ without any heading. The transition to *ARF* on fol. 151ʳ is in mid-page, and there is no break at all in the text or indication of a change of source. The text of *ARF* in this manuscript ceases on line 8 of fol. 157ᵛ, and its ending with the 806 annal is thus not the product of any mutilation of the codex.

the structure of *Rev.* and the intentions of its author may be affected by subsequent ninth-century editorial alterations to its original form. For example, virtually all manuscripts of it include some or all of the text of the mainstream *ARF* for the years 801 to 827/9.[34] If, as is normally taken to be the case, the original Revised Version only ever extended up to the year 801, where differences in the content of the two versions cease to be found, or even up to the year 812, where minor stylistic distinctions can no longer be detected, then the addition of the entries for the years 801/13 to 829 must represent the action of a compiler; one that was probably made at a relatively early stage of the process of transmission, as no alternative form now exists.[35]

It is possible to form some idea of the time by which this process had taken place. Possibly all of the manuscripts containing the work also include a text of Einhard's *Vita Karoli*.[36] Some of these also enjoy a special relationship to Thegan's *Gesta Hludowici Imperatoris* (written *ca* 836/7). The characteristic structure of the contents of this group of manuscripts takes the following form: The first seven chapters of Thegan are followed by Einhard's *Vita Karoli*; then comes the Revised Version of *ARF* extending up to 829; and after this are found chapters 8 to 58 of Thegan.[37] In considering the manuscript tradition of Thegan, Ernst Tremp argued that this distinctive compilation, with its unique structuring of these works, was developed at Lorsch around the middle of the ninth century.[38] Accepting his reconstruction of the manuscript history of Thegan implies that the junction of the Revised Version of *ARF* with a section of the latter covering the period 802/13–829 had occurred by the time this distinctive Lorsch historiographical compilation had been put together in the mid-ninth century.

---

34 MS London, British Library add. 21,109 (mid-twelfth century, possibly from the monastery of Stavelot) ends the text of the annals with the entry for 827. The decision of Kurze to stop printing the parallel text of *Rev.* opposite that of *ARF* with their respective entries for the year 801 obscures the fact that none of the manuscripts stops here or at the year 812.

35 Kurze's E9 (his edition, xiv) is MS Munich Clm 23618 (tenth century; from Salzburg), which is badly damaged and consists of only forty folios, which contain just the annals for 806 to 821; in other words, just the later section, but with the distinctive stylistic changes associated with the 'E' class manuscripts in the text of the entries for 806 to 812 (where such minor variations cease).

36 It has not yet been possible to find an adequate account of MS Paris lat. 5942 (= E2), an apparently tenth-century codex from Bec.

37 MSS Paris BnF lat. 15, 425; Trier Stadtbibliothek 1286/43 (written at Prüm in 1084); Verdun Bibliotheque Municipale 3 (in which the text of the annals has given way to the chronicle of Sigebert of Gembloux and other later annals); London British Library add. MS 21,109.

38 E. Tremp, *Studien zu den Gesta Hludowici imperatoris des Trierer Chorbischofs Thegan* (Hanover, 1988), 150–200, for the manuscripts and his deductions.

We may wonder if the uniting of two previously distinct sections of annals, as just described, actually formed part of the wider process of putting together the Lorsch Einhard–Thegan–annals compilation. While all of the manuscripts of *Rev.* contain all or part of the later sections of *ARF* and, unless extremely lacunose, are found in association with a text of Einhard's *Vita Karoli*, they are not exclusively associated with the Lorsch compilation. The latter, for example, is notable for a small addition to the text of *Rev.* in the entry for the year 752, which is not to be found in other manuscripts of the work.[39] MS Vienna Öster-reichische Nationalbibliothek 510 (ff. 31–132^v), briefly discussed above, contains both *Rev.* and the *Vita Karoli*, and, although now forming part of a composite manuscript with later parts, shows no trace of material being sandwiched between sections of Thegan's work, the hallmark of this compilation.

Two of the manuscripts containing *Rev.* and Einhard's *Vita Karoli* also contain a text of Notker's *Gesta Karoli Magni* (written *ca* 883/4).[40] Although the start of its manuscript tradition is relatively far removed from the actual date of composition, it is notable that these two codices are regarded as the best representatives of the first two distinct classes of the text.[41] At the same time, as can be seen from the apparatus to Kurze's edition, they contain a closely interrelated text of the Revised Version of *ARF*. It can hardly be accidental that these two manuscripts are both so close to each other in terms of their text of *Rev.* and also contain Notker's *Gesta Karoli,* although the latter appears in two variant forms. This may imply that the association between Notker's work and *Rev.* was an early one, preceding the bifurcation in the textual form of the *Gesta Karoli*. At the same time as previously mentioned, both of these manuscripts contain a text of Einhard's *Vita Karoli*. The limited apparatus of the modern editions of the latter make it impossible to discover quickly to which class of the text these belonged, or to assess the degree of relationship between them. However, it remains possible that a similar affirmation of early association could be made in the case of *Rev.* and Einhard. Certainly the relationship between the annals and the *Vita* is identical in the two manuscripts, and Hae-

---

39 This records Charlemagne's presence at Lorsch at the dedication of the church of St Nazarius and the translation to the monastery of his body on 1 September in the year 774. This must have been wrongly entered into the text for 752 in the archetype of this group of manuscripts.

40 MSS Hanover XIII, 858 (first third of the twelfth century: 'aus einem der Hirsauer Reformk-löster': ed. Haefele, MGH SRG Nova Series 12, xxvii) and Munich Clm 17736 (twelfth century : 'aus St. Mang in Stadtamhof,' ed. Haefele, xxxi) – of the latter there are a further six copies of thirteenth- to fifteenth-century date: MSS Vienna 532 and 610; Mantua bibl. Estensis V D 12; Kassel hist. 5; London B.L. Arundel 242, and Munich Clm 569.

41 *Gesta*, ed. Haefele, xxvii–xliv.

fele, the editor of Notker, both accepted it and saw a possible origin for this particular compilation of Einhard–*Rev.* and the *Gesta Karoli* in the Abbey of St Gall and under Notker's own direction.[42] So, it may well be that Notker or whoever it was that put together this compilation involving his *Gesta Karoli*, Einhard's *Vita Karoli*, and the Revised Version of the annals, including the later sections, received the latter two works as a previously formed corpus. As noted, this is the way in which they are to be found in MS Vienna 510. However, this transmission is not connected with that of the text of Thegan. Thus, while it remains quite possible that it was at Lorsch that the combining of *Rev.* and the later sections of *ARF* first took place, it probably preceded, and was independent of, the formation of the distinctive compilation that included Thegan's *Gesta Hludowici*.

It may also be significant that within this Lorsch historiographical compilation, the version of Einhard's work primarily represented is that of text class A.[43] This, among other things, lacks the verse dedication to the emperor Louis the Pious written by his *bibliotecarius* Gerward. As the latter was formerly a monk of Lorsch and seems to have bequeathed his own books to that monastery in the time of abbot Eigilbert (856–64), it is possible at least to suggest that the Lorsch historiographical compilation was formed prior to the arrival of a text of Gerward's edition of Einhard. This might imply that this collection was made and given its distinctive shape at some point between the composition of Thegan's *Gesta Hludowici* in 836/7 and the reception of Gerward's library between 856 and 864. If this be thought too hypothetical, then the *termini* might be the composition of the *Gesta Hludowici* in 836/7 and that of Notker's *Gesta Karoli* in 883/4.

The above argument has proceeded on the supposition that *Rev.* indeed extended no further than 801 or 812, and that the entries for the years 802/13–829 belong intrinsically to the mainstream tradition of the original *ARF*.[44] It is, however, just as conceivable that the present text of the annals for 802 to 829 belongs on the trunk of *Rev.* (where it is certainly found in all extant manuscripts). This might mean that the main line of *ARF*, in however many compositional sections it may be thought to have consisted, ended *ca* 801, and in its present format, extending up to 829, it was *ARF* rather than *Rev.* that ben-

---

42 Ibid., xxviii; here following Kurze, 'Zur Überlieferung der karolingischen Reichsannalen,' *Neues Archiv* 28 (1903): 650, 661.

43 One of the MSS, London BL add. 21109, is thought to pertain to the C class; this looks more like an A class MS corrected against one of the C class: see Holder-Egger's edition, xxiv.

44 It would seem peculiar, from all else that can be said of the author(s) of *Rev.*, that he would have been content to do no more than copy *ARF* for the years 802 to 812 without making more than the most minute stylistic alterations.

efited from a later editorial exercise. Thus, what is now thought of as the
Revised Version would originally have been composed using the text of *ARF*,
whose entries only extended up to the year 801, with the intention that it should
serve as the first section of a new set of annals covering the period 802 to 829.
In due course this latter section of new material came to be added to the text of
ARF itself, thus extending it, too, up to the year 829. However, it was with the
Rev. text for 741 to 801 that the annals for 801 to 829 originally belonged.
There are a number of features of the text of both *Rev.* up to 801 and that of the
later annals for the years 802 to 829 that might support such a reconstruction.

Thus, there are a large number of cases in which the form of a name in the
Revised Version differing from the form used in the original *ARF* version continues in use in the later section: for example, *ARF* refers to the Auvergne as
'Alvernum' (s.a. 761) whilst *Rev.* calls its 'Arvenorum castella'[45] (ibid.), a use
mirrored in the reference to Warin as 'Arverni comes' (s.a. 819). *ARF* spells the
name of the bishop of Wurzburg as 'Burghardus' (s.a. 749), while *Rev.* makes it
'Burchardus.' This is the spelling also used in the later section for Count Bur-
chard (s.a. 807 and 811). While *ARF* uses the form 'Franci Austrasiorum' (s.a.
787), *Rev.* employs 'Franci orientales' (s.a. 778, 782, 785, 787), and this is the
usage to be found in the later section (s.a. 816, 819).[46] *ARF* refers three times to
'Gallias' (s.a. 794, 795, 796); in its more frequent use of this geographical term,
Rev. prefers the single form 'Gallia' (s.a. 756, 758, 770, 777, 782, 786, 794).
This is also the consistent usage of the later section (s.a. 801, 809, 813, 815,
817, 821). *Rev.* likes to use the word *aspera* in referring to a hard winter, for
example in the phrase 'hiemalis temporis asperitas' (s.a. 784; *ARF* makes no
reference to the weather here). This also appears in the later section as 'hiemis
asperitatem' (811) and 'hiems in tantum prolixa successit et aspera ...' (s.a.
821). *ARF* calls the river Main 'Mohin' (s.a. 793), where *Rev.* uses 'Moenus'
(s.a. 790, 793, 795), as does the later section (s.a. 826). *ARF* calls Mainz
'Mogontia civitas.' *Rev.* and the later section use 'Mogontiacum' (s.a. 770, 794,
795, 800, 813, 817, 826). Similarly, *ARF*'s 'Niumaga' for Nijmegen is replaced
by the more classical 'Noviomagus' in *Rev.* and is also the usage of the later
section (s.a. 771, 806, 808, 817, 821, 825). The Sorbs (*Sorabi*) only feature by
name in *Rev.* and the later section (s.a. 782, 806, 816, 822, etc.). The Abodrite
leader is called Thrasuco in *ARF*, but is known as Thrasco in *Rev.* and also in

---

45 NB where *ARF* uses *castrum*, *Rev.* tends to use *castellum* (though not in reference to Monte
    Cassino: for example, s.a. 746).

46 Also the usage of Walahfrid Strabo in the preface to his edition of Einhard's *Vita Karoli
    Magni* (840/9). In general the use of such terms as *Austrasii* and *Austrasia* seems to go out of
    fashion by the early ninth century, in favour of more pan-Frankish terminology, such as 'East-
    ern' and 'Western' Franks.

the later section (s.a. 798, 809, 817, 819). The Thuringians are called the 'Toringi' in *ARF*, but the 'Thuringi' in *Rev.* and in the later section (s.a. 782, 787, 822). Additionally, the region of Saxony called 'Transalbiana' (i.e., across the Elbe) is only mentioned in *Rev.* and in the later section (s.a. 785, 804, 817, 829).

It is also typical of the Reviser that he should refer to the Avars by the anachronistic but archaic name of 'Huns.' This is his constant practice, not paralleled at any point by the compiler(s) of *ARF* up to 801. It is also the way that the Avars are referred to in the later section, and likewise in Einhard's *Vita Karoli*. The king's name provides another such pointer. While *ARF* both refers to him frequently by name and calls him 'Carolus,' both *Rev.* and the later section are much more sparing in the use of his personal name, preferring to call him by his title of *rex*, and then *imperator*, but, when they do name him, they employ the spelling 'Karlus.'[47] Many other such examples could be given, even allowing for variations between different manuscripts and possible stylistic influences coming from later scribes rather than the original forms of the texts. Some of this could be explained in terms of a general revival in learning both in literary style and in the taste for classical forms, but there are other features that link the text of *Rev.* with that of the later section of *ARF*.

As well as in the employment of distinctive forms of personal and place-names, there is an interesting continuity both in literary style and in debts to classical authors between *Rev.* and the later section. One of the undoubted merits of the Kurze edition is the editor's sensitivity to possible literary debts in the text of the two versions of the annals.[48] The parallel passages given in the footnotes, taken from a variety of sources, are generally found to be convincing. The vocabulary and structure of the passages almost always seem to be sufficiently well mirrored in the text of the annals to allow that these are genuine borrowings or reminiscences, and at the same time they are sufficiently distinctive to rule out pure coincidence or common usage. A small but distinct group of authors emerges from this process, including Aulus Gellius, Caesar (*Bellum Gallicum* only), Florus, Justin, Livy, Quintus Curtius Rufus, Tacitus, and Velleius Paterculus. It is possible to be even more precise in the case of the authors of longer or multiple works. Thus, of the works of Tacitus, comparisons can be found only with the text of his *Annals* and, moreover, only with the first three books. Likewise, in the case of Livy, viable borrowings can be established

---

47 The only exception here being Kurze's E6 (the eleventh-century MS Hanover XIII, 858), which is variable, using all four forms: Karolus, Carolus, Carlus, and Karlus.

48 See the apparatus to the edition. M. Manitius, 'Einhards Werke und ihr Stil,' *Neues Archiv* 7 (1882): 517–58, made similar claims for Einhard, though only some have come to be accepted: see n. 53, below.

only from Books I and II and XXI to XXIII. Strikingly, these limitations can be shown to correspond exactly to what is known of the complex manuscript transmission of these works. In the ninth century the first six books of Tacitus's *Annals* circulated together. At the same time the first ten books of Livy were transmitted together, but entirely detached from Books XX to XXV. The borrowings that have been detected thus do not do violence to what is known of the manuscript transmission of the works concerned.

Virtually all of the texts concerned can be shown to have been available in the Carolingian Empire around the first half of the ninth century.[49] Caesar's *Bellum Gallicum* is represented by a mid-ninth-century manuscript written at Fleury; Florus features in a Lorsch library catalogue of the early ninth century; Justin's epitome of Pompeius Trogus is also known to have existed at Lorsch, not least in the form of a manuscript given by its former monk Gerward, the *Bibliotecarius* of the library of Louis the Pious; there was a manuscript of the first six books of Tacitus's *Annals* at Fulda by *ca* 850, and the lost archetype of Velleius Paterculus came from the monastery of Murbach and is recorded as having been written in an early Caroline minuscule.[50] Of Livy, Books XX to XXV were in Charlemagne's court library around 800, when a copy was made by a Tours scribe, and the Third Decade can also be found in a Corbie manuscript.[51] Corbie likewise possessed a manuscript of the First Decade, but in general the dissemination of Livy in ninth-century Francia appears to have been very limited.[52] Obviously, this list represents the random chances of survival, and not all of the earliest manuscripts of these works pre-date the presumed dates of writing of the annals, but the manuscript evidence, together with that of library catalogues and citations in the works of contemporary authors, makes it clear that these texts were available in the period under consideration. On the other hand, it also appears to be the case that such writings were far from widely distributed.[53] Indeed, no named author, certainly not Einhard, can be shown to have read all these works. They cannot, therefore, be taken to be no more than what an educated Carolingian with a taste for history should have been expected to have read. Thus, the existence of reminiscences of all of them

---

49 R. McKitterick, 'The Audience for Latin Historiography in the Early Middle Ages: Text Transmission and Manuscript Dissemination,' in *Historiographie im frühen Mittelalter,* ed . A. Scharer and G. Scheibelreiter (Vienna and Munich, 1994), 96–114.

50 *Texts and Transmission,* ed. L.D. Reynolds (Oxford, 1983), 35–6 (Caesar), 164–6 (Florus), 197–9 (Justin), 406–7 (Tacitus, *Annals* I-VI), 431–3 (Velleius Paterculus).

51 Ibid., 205–9 (Livy, decades 1 and 3).

52 D. Ganz, *Corbie in the Carolingian Renaissance* (Sigmaringen, 1990), 58–9 and 153–4.

53 For example, it seems that Florus, while known to Einhard, was never read by Lupus of Ferrières: *Texts and Transmission,* ed. Reynolds, 164 n. 1. There is a clear borrowing from Florus (detected by Manitius) in *VK* 30, p. 34 and n. 3.

in both *Rev.* and the later section is positive testimony for a close degree of relationship between the two. It is also evidence that the Reviser, whoever he may have been, was extremely well read, with access to an unusually good library or libraries.[54]

What is striking about the use of phrases and tags from classical authors in the annals is that, within the *ARF* tradition, this phenomenon is confined entirely to *Rev.* and to the later section, but only from the entry for the year 808 onwards. Moreover, most of the authors who can be detected in *Rev.* reappear in the later section. Thus, Livy, Tacitus, Quintus Curtius Rufus, Justin, Velleius Paterculus, Caesar, and Florus have all been detected in the 808-to-829 section of the annals. It is possible to go further than Kurze in picking out possible borrowings from classical sources, in that individual items of vocabulary can also suggest such debts. For example, such unusual words might include 'foedifragus' (s.a 775 and 798; both in *Rev.* only), which is classified by Lewis and Short as 'very rare' but which may be found in Aulus Gellius (XIX vii 6), and 'obnubilo' (s.a. 778; cf. Aulus Gellius I ii 5).[55]

It should be added that the use made of classical texts, in both the Revised Version and in the section of annals relating to the years 808–29, is similar in character, and is unostentatious whilst indicative of clear familiarity with these works. The phrases in question are usually short and, while close, are rarely exactly identical to the form they take in their original contexts. They are not overly numerous, and the borrowings from the various authors are scattered throughout the text. There is no sense of a concentration of such borrowings from a particular author at any one point. In other words, the Carolingian compiler is using language that has been absorbed into his own through his reading, and is in no sense carrying out a crude scissors-and-paste operation on the works of earlier historians to give an artificial elegance to his own writing.

This is rather different to Einhard's employment of the works of classical predecessors in his *Vita Karoli*, where, as is well known, citations are taken almost exclusively from Suetonius. Although there are some small borrowings from the lives of later emperors, the overwhelming debt is to the *Vita Augusti*, which is used almost as a structural framework around which the new work is built: the verbal borrowings from the *Life of Augustus* come almost entirely in the order in which they would have been found in the original. The lack of employment of most of the historical and other texts known to the Reviser, and

54 Such reading was not confined to classical historians. See *Eugippe: Vie de Saint Séverin*, ed. Philippe Régerat (Paris, 1991), 46 and n. 86, for a probable debt to the *Vita Severini*.
55 Described as 'very rare' by Lewis and Short, who otherwise only give examples from Cicero. This book of Gellius' work is one of those included in the MS copied from one once owned by Einhard: Reynolds, *Texts and Transmission*, 178.

the distinctive way in which Suetonius is used to give form and shape to the *Vita Karoli Magni*, do not necessarily prove that Einhard and the Reviser were not one and the same person, but they support doubts as to their being identical.[56] Different genres may require different techniques, and even different uses of language, but it must also be said, though, that the lack of any apparent indebtedness to the text of Suetonius in *Rev.* is also surprising.

There would thus seem to be some strong grounds for suspecting that there are authorial similarities between *Rev.* and the later section of annals, at least from 807/8 onwards. If the author of the one is not that of the other, then they must have enjoyed a very similar intellectual formation and had access to the same library. On the other hand, if Einhard drew upon the Revised Version of *ARF* in writing his *Vita Karoli*, as is usually thought, this would seem to indicate that *Rev.* and the later section of *ARF* were not at that time combined. There is not only the allegedly strong, albeit negative, argument that there are no verbal parallels between the *Vita Karoli* and the post-801 section of *ARF*, there is supposed to be at least one positive indicator to this lack of knowledge on Einhard's part.[57] In the *Vita* he refers to various celestial portents that presaged the emperor's death, including the appearance of spots on the face of the sun for a period of seven days.[58] Although Einhard locates it around 810, this is most likely to refer to an event described in the later section of *ARF* in the entry for 807, in a round-up of the astronomical highlights of that year: 'Nam et Stella Mercurii XVI Kal. Aprilis visa est in sole quasi parva macula, nigra tamen, paululum superius medio centro eiusdem sideris, quae a nobis octo dies conspicitur. Sed quando primum intravit vel exivit, nubibus impedientibus minime adnotare potuimus.'[59] Although Halphen assumed that Einhard drew on the annal, the differences in detail, in terms of the duration of the phenomenon and the explanation given for it, would seem to make this improbable.[60] That

---

56 There are numerous other differences that may be thought to be more telling: e.g., A. Klein-clausz, *Eginhard* (Paris, 1942), 238, draws attention to the lack of formal titles in referring to Charlemagne and an absence of the miraculous and the pious in *Rev.* as opposed to Einhard. See also further arguments advanced below.

57 The last point at which there are possible textual parallels between Einhard's *Vita Karoli* and *Rev.* come in the latter's entry for the year 799; ed. Kurze, 109.

58 Einhard, *VK* 32, p. 36; ed. Halphen, 88 and n. 4.

59 *ARF* s.a. 807, ed. Kurze, 123.

60 Halphen, *Eginhard*, 89 n. 4. While the datings for the various celestial events of 807 referred to in *ARF* can be confirmed, including one for a transit of the moon by Jupiter on 31 January, the explanation given in this source for the spot on the face of the Sun is astronomically impossible. With an eighty-eight-day rotation period around the Sun at distances from 70 to 46 million kilometres, such an eight-day long transit of the Sun by Mercury is quite inconceivable, but the Carolingian observers could not have known that.

Einhard remembered the event, which must have been of some note at the time, would seem a quite sufficient explanation.

The section in the 807 annal, previously mentioned, is very interesting, in that it shows that close watch was kept on the sky, probably at Aachen. Thus, for example, the transit of the Moon by Jupiter on 31 January will have been visible at Aachen only between 2:40 and 4:00 A.M. This was not something that could have been predicted, and its recording depended on empirical observation. It is clear that detailed records were kept, with precise information as to the timing and celestial locations of such events. It is probable, too, that these records were kept independently of the making of the annals, how and whenever that was done, as the observational program that appears to be involved was obviously quite intensive, while the references to the events in the annals are sporadic. The section on them in the entry for 807 is unusually detailed and lengthy, and it is important not to assume that only those mentioned in the annals were actually seen.[61] While unsuitable weather conditions might explain many eclipses not being observed, reports of them appear only in certain parts of the annals. Indeed, apart from a solar eclipse in 764, which is mentioned only in *Rev.*, such phenomena are recorded in the annals exclusively in the section beginning with the entry for 807.[62] Like the reappearance of verbal reminiscences of classical sources, this is another feature that seems to mark a significant divide in the annals in 807.[63]

It is not just in diverging from the information that may be found in this later section of *ARF* that Einhard shows himself independent of the annal tradition. The actual evidence for his debt to *Rev.* itself is hardly strong. At a number of points what he has to say is flatly contradicted by what may be read in *Rev.*, as, for example, over the time of year assigned to the conspiracy of Pippin the Hunchback in 792.[64] Likewise, the treatment of the final stage of the career of Carloman, the former mayor of the palace and brother of Pippin III, in the *Vita Karoli* is totally at variance with the account of it in *Rev.*[65] Similarly, there is a subtle but clear distinction in the two sources' presentation of the process whereby Pippin III was made king of the Franks in 751.[66] There are also signif-

61 Numerous other such events occurred – e.g. there were thirty-one solar and ninety-nine total or partial lunar eclipses potentially visible from Aachen between 741 and 829.
62 *ARF*, ed. Kurze, s.a. 807, 809 (lunar), 810, 812, 817 (lunar) 818, 820 (lunar), 824 (lunar) and 828 (lunar)
63 The entry for 808 is the last one in which the transitional formula *et inmutavit se numerus annorum in ...* appears. After this no such phrase is used to bridge from one year to the next. E class manuscripts never use it at all.
64 *Rev.*, s.a. 792, ed. Kurze, 91 (Summer); *VK* 20, p. 25 (Winter).
65 See below, p. 211.
66 *Rev.* s.a. 750, ed. Kurze 9: 'secundum Romani pontificis sanctionem Pippinus rex Francorum

icant differences in detail in their respective accounts of the Spanish campaign of 778 and the defeat of the rearguard at Roncesvalles. These are more to Einhard's credit than some of the others, in that he provides an even fuller version than *Rev.*, but there is little evidence to support belief in direct dependence. In general, verbal similarities between Einhard and *Rev.* are surprisingly few and brief. In virtually all cases these could be assigned to coincidence, or at best a distant memory of an account previously read but not to hand. While *Rev.* shares a manuscript transmission with one version of the *Vita Karoli*, this does not mean that the author of the latter knew the former. Grounds for certainty that Einhard actually had a text of *Rev.* are effectively non-existent. This is regrettable, in that had it been clear that he had *Rev.* but did not know the 807-to-829 section of the annals, then the date of composition of his *Vita Karoli*, debatable as it still might be, would provide a *terminus post quem* for the uniting of the two.[67]

Some of the differences between the text of *ARF* and that of the Revised Version are very well known, if not notorious. In particular the latter's inclusion of information concerning Frankish military reverses and also conspiracies against Charlemagne marks a major divergence from the principles of selection used by the compiler(s) of *ARF*.[68] Likewise the greater elegance of language of the Reviser, even when not changing or augmenting the information of *ARF*, is a constant and notable feature.

It is probably worth looking a little more closely for other significant areas of difference that may give further indications of the Reviser's purposes and milieu.[69] One marked difference is in the quantity and quality of the informa-

appellatus est et ad hiuius dignitatem honoris unctus sacra unctione manu sanctae memoriae Bonifatii ...'; Einhard, *Via Karoli* 3, ed. Holder-Egger, 5: 'Pippinus autem per auctoritatem Romani pontificis ex praefecto palatii rex constitutus ...' *Sanctio* and *auctoritas* are not synonymous, and why does Einhard omit reference to the unction? Einhard and *Rev.* coincide here only in mentioning a papal role in the process, not referred to in *ARF*.

67 For a recent attempt to revive an early dating, around 817/18, see Innes and McKitterick, 'The Writing of History,' 203–10.

68 For military reverses – none of which directly involved Charlemagne in person – compare the respective entries for the years 775, 778, 782, and 793. The D class of manuscripts of *ARF* do, however, include mention of the conspiracies of Hardrad (s.a. 788) and of Pippin the Hunchback (s.a. 792). The latter, though not the former, also appears in the *ARF* text of MS Vatican Reginensis lat. 213, otherwise a B class manuscript.

69 Some of the minor but marked differences between the two versions can be presented in the form of the following six categories, with examples:
  A. Additional minor details in information given by *Rev.* include the facts that the patrician Michael sent as envoy from the empress Irene was additionally named 'Ganglianos'; that Romo(a)ld was the elder son of Aregis, duke of the Beneventans (s.a. 786); that Salerno was a maritime city (s.a. 786); that Worad was Count of the Palace (s.a. 782).

tion given that relates to Italy. The Reviser provides much more detail on Franco-Byzantine relations in 787 to 788 and is in general highly informative

B. Cases where *Rev.* uses either a more correct or more classical form of a name: referring to Argenton, *ARF* calls it 'Argentomus,' while *Rev.* uses 'Argentomagus' (s.a. 766); for the Bardengau, *ARF* employs 'Bardengauwi,' while *Rev.* calls it 'Bardengoo' (s.a. 785) or 'Bardengoi' (s.a. 795); *ARF* calls Kostheim 'Cuffinstang,' as opposed to *Rev.*'s more credible 'Cuffestein villa' (s.a. 795); *ARF* gives 'Pampilona' for Pamplona, while *Rev.* uses the classical 'Pomp(a)elo' (s.a. 778); Trento is called 'Trianto' in *ARF* but 'vallis Tredentina' in *Rev.* In describing the monastery that Carloman built near Rome, *ARF* (s.a. 746) locates it 'in Serapte monte'; *Rev.* more elegantly and accurately places it 'in monte Soracti.' The former is close to the usage in 'The Life of Pope Sylvester' in the *Liber Pontificalis* (ed. Duchesne, 1: 170), but the latter is the correct classical form (cf. Pliny, *Hist. Nat.* VII. ii. 2).

C. Names the Revised Version seems to offer a better or more specific version of include Abuthaur for Abu Tahar, instead of *ARF*'s Abutaurus (s.a. 778). *ARF* refers to Fritzlar as 'Fricdislar,' while *Rev.* makes it 'Frideslar' (s.a. 773). In referring to the Great St Bernard, *ARF* uses the slightly clumsier 'Iuppiter mons,' for which *Rev.* employs 'mons iovis' (s.a. 773). The Weissgau is known as 'Waizzagawi' to *ARF* but 'Huettagoe' to *Rev.* (s.a. 784). It is notable that the Reviser has two marked characteristics in the use of place-names. If there is a Roman form, he uses that in preference to any modern variation. Thus, in the case of Argenton, it is credible that *ARF*'s 'Argentomus' is close to the name as actually employed in the late eighth century, while *Rev.*'s 'Argentomagus' is antiquarian, in that it retains the classical Roman form. On the other hand, for settlements and lands outside the former territories of Rome and where no classical form could be found in literary sources, the Reviser's versions often seem more exact or realistic. This is particularly the case with Germanic and Slavic toponyms and personal names. If a deduction were to be made from this, it might be that the author was himself a German speaker. *Rev.* also uses archaic or decorative forms, such as 'Britannia cismarina' (s.a. 786) and 'Brittonum provincia' (s.a. 799) for Brittany, and in general employs the more classical *limes* in preference to *ARF*'s *marca* when referring to the March. Where *ARF* uses *castrum*, *Rev.* tends to use *castellum*.

D. Places referred to in *Rev.* but not mentioned by name in *ARF* (or only in the later section) include 'Coriosolitarum regio' (around Corseult s.a. 786); Hesse, in the forms 'Hassi' (s.a. 774) and 'Hassiorum pagus' (s.a. 778); the monastery of the martyr Saint Erasmus in Rome and the church of Saint Laurence in Rome (both s.a. 799), which is further defined as being called 'ad Craticulum.'

E. Persons mentioned only in *Rev.* include Dragawit, king of the Wiltzi (s.a. 789), Elipandus metropolitan bishop of Toledo (s.a. 791), the Lombard abbot Fardulf of St-Denis (s.a. 792, 793); the *missus* Gottschalk (s.a. 798); the chamberlain Meginfred (s.a. 791); Pope Stephen III (768–72) (s.a. 772); Swanahild, the niece of duke Odo of the Bavarians; Count Theoderic, relative of Charlemagne and commander in a number of campaigns against the Saxons (s.a. 782, 791, 793); Theodore the Byzantine patrician in Sicily (s.a. 788).

F. Some other differences include the following: *ARF* uses *flumen* where *Rev.* prefers *fluvius*; Abbot Fulrad of St-Denis is given the rank of *capellanus* in *ARF*, where *Rev.* calls him 'presbyter' (s.a. 749 and 771); *Rev.* prefers the classical *legatus* to *ARF*'s more contemporary *missus*. The formula *Domino adiuvante* or *Domino auxiliante* is much favoured in the first section of *ARF* up to 789 (s.a. 755, 769, 773, 774, 775, 776, 778, 779, 783, 784, 788,

about Italian events in the 780s and 790s, and on the Papacy. This culminates in the relatively lengthy and detailed account of the attack on Pope Leo III in Rome in 799. The Reviser is also often more precise and accurate in giving events and names relating to Saxony and the Slavs.[70] This, and the detailed treatment of much of the fighting across the Rhine, has even led to the suggestion that the Reviser might himself have been a Saxon. If so, he would have been highly *deraciné*, as one of the few clearly distinguishing personal characteristics of this author is the markedly anti-Saxon tone of some of the narrative.[71] Another notable distinction between the two sets of annals is the amount of prominence and detailed discussion that the Reviser is prepared to give Bishop Felix of Urgell and the Adoptionist controversy in the 792 entry.[72]

One particularly instructive comparison concerns how *ARF* and *Rev.* deal with the way Carloman, the former mayor of the palace, intervened in Franco-Lombard–papal diplomacy in the year 753. For the compiler of *ARF* 'Carlomannus, monachus et germanus supradicti Pippini regis, per iussionem abbatis sui in Franciam venit, quasi ad conturbandam petitionem apostolicam.' The Reviser gives this information in characteristically more elegant fashion: 'Venit et Carlomannus frater regis iam monachus factus iussu abbatis sui, ut apud fratrem suum precibus Romani pontificis obsisteret.' He goes on, however, to provide an *apologia* in turn for both Carloman and the abbot of Monte Cassino: 'invitus tamen hoc fecisse putatur, quia nec ille abbatis sui iussa contempnere nec abbas ille praeceptis regis Langobardorum, qui ei hoc imperavit, audebat resistere.' Under monastic discipline Carloman could no more resist the command of his abbot than the latter could disobey the command of the Lombard king. With this it might also be worth noting the brief comment that

---

789), as are variations such as 'Domino largiente' (s.a. 789), 'opulante' (s.a. 788), 'protegente' (s.a. 788 twice) or 'volente' (s.a. 786), but none of these features in *Rev.* In referring to the first Saxon campaign *ARF* makes the Irminsul a shrine ('fanum'), where *Rev.* calls it an idol ('idolum') (s.a. 772). *ARF* makes Iburg a fortress ('castrum'), while *Rev.* calls it a 'mons' (s.a. 753). In referring to Lübbecke (between Minden and Osnabrück), *ARF* calls it 'Lidbach,' while *Rev.* employs the more Slavic-sounding 'Hlidbecki' (s.a. 775). *Rev.* refers by name to Mallorca and Minorca, stating once that these are what the islands are now ('nunc') called; this is also how they appear in the later section, while *ARF* refers to them only more generally as 'insulae Baleares' (s.a. 798, 799, 813).

70   See examples given in n. 69, above. It is possible these features suggest that *Rev.* was compiled when Frankish political and cultural hegemony were firmly established in Saxony, and greater knowledge of the western Slavs was available; late in the reign of Charlemagne at the earliest.

71   See the entries for the years 775 and 795, among others; e.g., 'perfidam ac foedifragam Saxonum gentem' (s.a. 775).

72   *ARF* and *Rev.* s.a. 792, ed. Kurze, 90–1.

the Reviser made about Carloman's decision to enter monastic life in Monte Cassino in 746. *ARF* describes how Carloman originally founded a monastery of his own 'in Serapte monte,' before moving on to become a monk of Monte Cassino. The Reviser, as well as improving the style and using the more classical 'Soracte' for *ARF*'s 'Serapte,' adds the comments that 'meliori consilio hoc loco dimisso,' and Carloman 'monachicum habitum suscepit' at Monte Cassino. He also characteristically adds that the latter was located 'in Samnio provincia.' The perceptions of the Reviser are here far more firmly monastic than those of *ARF*. Under obedience, what choice had Carloman in 753, and how could it not be wiser for him to submit to regular discipline in 746 rather than attempt to live a monastic life of his own devising? There is one further item of information in this particular story that is unique to the Reviser. *ARF* reports that Carloman died at Vienne in 755 in the custody of his sister-in-law. To this the Reviser adds that 'it is said' that his body was taken back to Monte Cassino for burial. It is worth noting that the version of these events in Einhard's *Vita Karoli* is quite different. Carloman is said, after 'several years' in his monastery on Mount Soracte, to have decided to change his location to the monastery of Monte Cassino in order to escape from the pressure to which he was being subjected by members of the Frankish nobility to involve him in current political events. Here he was said to have passed the rest of his life in monastic contemplation.[73] If Einhard did indeed have a copy of *Rev.*, he was here deliberately ignoring what it said in producing his sanitized and misleading account of Carloman's years in Italy.

Whatever Einhard's motives, the perspective of *Rev.* on these events is markedly that of an adherent of regular monasticism, as dubious as Bede of the value of independent self-founded aristocratic monasteries and unwilling to apportion blame to a monk, whatever his origin, acting on his abbot's orders. Perhaps this provides a rare clue to the kind of context in which *Rev.* was compiled. On the other hand, it has to be admitted that this episode is exceptional in illuminating a monastic outlook on the basically secular events that provides the bulk of *Rev.*'s narrative. A profile of the Reviser would have to take account of this feature, of his interest in the Adoptionist controversy, of the eastern Frankish nature of some of his place- and personal names, of the unusually full nature of his Italian and papal information, as well as that concerning several of the Saxon campaigns. Yet, as with virtually all of seventh-, eighth- and early ninth-century Frankish historiography, the doubt would have to remain as to how much of this reflected the chance availability of source material and how much the personal predilections and character of the compiler. His intellectual

73 Einhard, *VK* 2.

formation and reading, like that of the author of the 807 to 829 section of *ARF*, if they be not identical, remain perhaps the most distinctive features of authorial personality. They may also provide the best clues as to dating and location.

Drawing together the various questions here raised may not lead to a totally new profile for the compiler of *Rev.*, but it may be hoped to have cast some doubt on the overconfident sense of assurance with which both this text and *ARF* have been treated for much of this century. While longer and fuller study would be necessary to decide these issues, it may be suggested that the *ARF* tradition may be less linear than has been assumed. The 741-to-788 section may have been grafted on to it, rather than created to serve as its prologue. The 789-to-793 and 801-to-806 sections are not entirely secure mortaring of the gaps, and the 807-to-829 section has more in common at least with the intellectual milieu that produced *Rev.* than it has with that of the earlier parts of *ARF*. At the same time, *AMP* in its present form may be as much a product of the early 830s as of *ca* 802. All in all, these texts conform more to the pattern – seen elsewhere in eighth- and ninth-century Frankish historiography – of reuse and reworking of earlier materials for current purposes than that allowed by the older view of year by year court-based annal keeping. Certainly, it would not be sensible to feel that the texts of *ARF* and *Rev.* as we have them lead directly and in uncomplicated fashion just to a period of composition in the reign of Charlemagne.

11

Pirenne and Charlemagne

BERNARD S. BACHRACH

During the late 1920s and the early 1930s, the great Belgian historian Henri Pirenne published a series of key studies that were to form the basis for his exceptionally important and always controversial *Mohamet et Charlemagne*.[1] For more than a generation following the Second World War, scholars hotly debated what has come to be known as the Pirenne thesis.[2] Pirenne argued that there were essential continuities in the west between the later Roman Empire and its successor states during the fifth, sixth, and part of the seventh centuries.[3] Today we tend to refer to those states that replaced the Empire in the west as Romano-German kingdoms rather than as barbarian tribal polities. The change is due, in part, to the impetus provided for continuity by Pirenne's arguments and to the substantial body of scholarship that his work stimulated.[4] Indeed, our honoree has played a key role in this reconceptualization, and that is why I have chosen an aspect of the Pirenne thesis for discussion here.[5]

1 *Mohammed and Charlemagne*, trans. Bernard Mial (New York, 1939), and cited here in the form of the Meridian Books edition 1957, in which Jacques Pirenne provided a convenient list of the relevant articles (9–11).
2 *The Pirenne Thesis: Analysis, Criticism and Revision*, ed. Alfred F. Havighurst, 3d ed. (Lexington, Mass., 1976); Bryce D. Lyon, *The Origins of the Middle Ages: Pirenne's Challenge to Gibbon* (New York, 1972). The fundamental study of Pirenne's life and work remains Bryce D. Lyon, *Henri Pirenne: A Biographical and Intellectual History* (Ghent, 1972).
3 *Mohammed and Charlemagne*, 17–144.
4 Among those scholars who have argued for continuity, see Jean Durliat, *Les finances publiques de Diocletien aux Carolingiens (284–889)*, (Sigmaringen, 1990); and Karl-Ferdinand Werner, *Histoire de France: Les origines (avant l'an mil)* (Paris, 1984). My views were made clear in Bernard S. Bachrach, *Merovingian Military Organization (481–751)* (Minneapolis, 1972), 128, where I observe: 'As with many aspects of Merovingian life, the military organization recalls *Romania* and not *Germania*.'
5 See, for example, the collection of Walter Goffart's essays, *Rome's Fall and After* (London and Ronceverte,1989); and, more importantly, *Barbarians and Romans, A.D. 418–584: Techniques of Accommodation* (Princeton, 1980).

While stressing continuity into the seventh century, Pirenne took the position that the ancient world came to an end, and thus that the Middle Ages began, when the unity of Mediterranean society was destroyed by the Muslim conquests of the later seventh and eighth centuries. Pirenne argued passionately that Charlemagne's Empire represented something very new and very different from Rome's successor states. It was Pirenne's contention that the Carolingian Empire was 'purely an inland power' and 'for the first time in history the axis of Occidental civilization was displaced towards the North.'[6] Indeed, Pirenne contended: 'It is therefore strictly correct to say that without Mohammed Charlemagne would have been inconceivable.'[7] He concluded, 'The Carolingian empire, or rather, the empire of Charlemagne, was the scaffolding of the Middle Ages.'[8]

Pirenne's view of a radical break between the Merovingian and Carolingian worlds has stimulated sufficient research to place the proposition in serious doubt. The thesis that the Carolingian world marked the beginning of Medieval Europe found, and is continuing to find, little favour among scholars working in the later eighth, ninth, and tenth centuries. By contrast, his attempt to establish continuity from the later Empire to the Romano-German kingdoms has resulted, as noted above, in the abandonment of the traditional view of an abrupt rupture in the fifth century. As a consequence, many scholars now see continuity, even ironically economic continuity, from the later Roman Empire through the Romano-German kingdoms to Carolingian Europe.[9]

Pirenne's efforts also focused attention for two scholarly generations on patterns of trade and socio-economic trends rather than on individuals and ideas during the later Roman Empire and the early Middle Ages. Such a focus would appear to be an unfortunate but ineluctable by-product of economic history and aided substantially in the process of conditioning medievalists to concentrate on impersonal or, more accurately, depersonalized forces, institutions, structures, and *mentalités*. This *Tendenz* matured in an *Annales* scholarly milieu, which Pirenne himself did so much to establish.[10] The *Annales* brand of historiography, which focuses attention on economic and social trends in the *longue durée,* has as one of its invidious goals, and arguably as its primary purpose,

---

6 *Mohammed and Charlemagne*, 184–5.

7 Ibid, 234.

8 Ibid, 233–4.

9 See, for example, Durliat, *Les finances publiques*; Werner, *Histoire de France*; and Bernard S. Bachrach, *Fulk Nerra – the Neo Roman Consul: A Political Biography of the Angevin Count (987–1040)* (Berkeley–Los Angeles, 1993).

10 Bryce D. Lyon, 'Henri Pirenne and the Origins of *Annales* History,' *Annals of Scholarship* 1 (1980): 69–84.

'demythologizing' the role of the individual in history and thereby discrediting a biographical approach to the past.[11]

The victory of an anti-individual and pro–social science approach to history, championed by *Annales* and all too often propelled by a Marxist-materialist agenda, is exceptionally well demonstrated in a recent review article, 'The Carolingian Age and Its Place in the History of the Middle Ages,' by Richard Sullivan. In touring the scholarly horizon of the Carolingian world, Sullivan found it necessary to mention Charlemagne only three times in forty pages. In the first reference he quotes Pirenne, 'It is therefore strictly correct to say that without Mohammed Charlemagne would have been inconceivable.' The second mention is also a quotation, Robert Fossier's label of Charlemagne as 'un souverain antique.' The third reference gets to the heart of the matter and ostensibly satirizes pre–Second World War intellectuals who sought solace in troubled times in the idea of Charlemagne's Empire as 'the fountainhead of the European experience where presided one of Europe's few shared heroes.'[12]

The process of depersonalizing history and demythologizing heroes was aided greatly in the case of Charlemagne by the terrible effect that the disasters of the Second World War had on the confidence of European intellectuals. The man who may be seen as initiating the post–Second World War process of cutting the great Charles down to size was Heinrich Fichtenau, whose *Das karolingische Imperium: Soziale und geistige Problematik eines Grossreiches*, published in 1949, played a key role in greatly diminishing the scholarly image of Charlemagne held by modern scholars.[13] By the mid-1960s, nevertheless,

11 In general see G.C. Iggers, *New Directions in European Historiography* (Middletown, 1975), who tends to be sympathetic to the social-science approach; for the *Annales* school, see 43–79. As this brand of history has come under increasing criticism for dehumanizing the story of mankind, the 'princes of *Annales* (Georges Duby and Jacques Le Goff) recently announced that *we could do biography again* [my italics].' For this quotation, see Thomas F. X. Noble, 'From Brigandage to Justice: Charlemagne, 785–794,' in *Literacy, Politics, and Artistic Innovation in the Early Medieval West: Papers Delivered at 'A Symposium on Early Medieval Culture' Bryn Mawr College, Bryn Mawr, PA*, ed. Celia M. Chazelle (New York, 1992), 50. The fact that it was necessary for the current *Annales* priests (more apt I believe than 'princes') to speak out in justification of biography – incidentally, just as they each undertook potentially lucrative biographical projects – draws attention to the *ex cathedra* authority exercised in the French historical profession as well as the *de fide* nature of the long standing anti-biographical dogma.

12 *Speculum* 64 (1989): 169, 170–1, 172, respectively, for the quotations. I counted only mentions of Charlemagne in the text. For the influence of the so-called new history which arguably is neither new nor history see pp. 269–71, 297–304.

13 (Zürich, 1949). All citations below are to the revised edition of *Das karolingische Imperium* and its translation by Peter Munz: *The Carolingian Empire* (Oxford, 1957). The excellent introduction by Munz provides an important context for Fichtenau's views. Ganshof also was infected by this early post-war pessimism and contributed to undermining previous views of Charlemagne's reign. See below, n. 21.

the glimmerings of an effort to restore to Charlemagne some of the credit he had once enjoyed for helping to provide a certain unity to European culture was in train. The process of gradual and tentative rehabilitation was being carried out by the senior scholars who had survived the Second World War. In this spirit, a large international conference was held in 1965 at Aachen, 'conveniently linked to the eight-hundredth anniversary of his [Charlemagne's] "canonization."' Despite the drama of the occasion, Charlemagne was not to emerge with the grandeur of the pre-war emperor. Impersonal forces were to be found much more in the foreground than the role of the individual.[14] The continuing ambivalence regarding Charlemagne may perhaps be indicated by the fact that Fichtenau did not publish a contribution in *Karl der Grosse*. Yet, Bullough, who provided a faithful examination of the articles produced for the Charlemagne Festschrift, boldly, and I believe correctly, argued that Charlemagne deserves the characterization provided by the contemporary author of the *Paderborn Epic* and approved by Leonardo Bruni: 'Europae venerandus apex, pater optimus.'[15]

The new postwar generation of scholars, very much under the influence of the increasingly important *Annales* school, moved to the forefront in the 1970s. In this context, note must be taken of the international conference held in 1979 at Spoleto under the sponsorship of the Centro italiano de studi sull'alto medioevo. The two volumes of *Nascita dell'europa ed europa carolingia: Un'equazione da verificare*, which appeared in 1981, come to more than 1,000 pages. Of the twenty-two articles not a single one has Charlemagne, Charles the Great, Karl der Grosse, or Carolo Magno in the title. Indeed, not even the 'diminished' Charles or its variants is used.

In this essay I will briefly suggest that Charlemagne is an excellent symbol for representing the history of western civilization, of which medieval Europe, of course, is a fundamental part, and for refocusing scholarly attention on the individual. In addition, I will use the behaviour of Charlemagne, the paramount ruler in the west, as symbolic of continuity.

Through the greater part of his career, Charlemagne behaved fundamentally as the ruler of much of the western half of the Roman Empire, and this was so even before he was crowned on Christmas day, 800.[16] Such an observation is

14 *Karl der Grosse: Lebenswerk und Nachleben*, ed. W. Braunfels et al., 4 vols. (Düsseldorf, 1965–7). For the quotation, see the magisterial review article by Donald Bullough, '*Europae pater*: Charlemagne and His Achievement in Light of Recent Scholarship,' *English Historical Review* 85 (1970), 63.
15 '*Europae pater*,' 104–5.
16 It is not without some interest that little more than a generation before Charlemagne succeeded his father, Peppin I, in 768, a Roman in Italy named Tiberius Petasius had himself proclaimed

hardly pathbreaking. Almost twelve hundred years ago, Einhard, Charlemagne's contemporary and biographer, made a considerable effort to cast his
former patron as the thirteenth Caesar.[17] It is true that Charlemagne acquired
the imperial title *de manu papae*[18] rather than the more traditional *de ritu
exercitus*, which is to be found so often in the raising up of Roman emperors.[19]
But this 'innovation' was surely an appropriate ritual substitution for a devout
Christian whose father had previously been legitimized as *rex* by the hand of
Saint Boniface and the approval of the pope.[20] Arguably, in fact, Charlemagne
was the most effective and successful *imperator* in the west between Theodosius I and Napoleon, both in fact[21] and in legend.[22]

emperor. See *V. Gregorii II*, c. 23 (*Le Liber Pontificalis, texte, introduction et commentaire*,
ed. L. Duchesne, revised C. Vogel, 3 vols. [Paris, 1955–7]); and the discussions by H. Hubert,
'Étude sur la formation des états de l'église: Les papes Grégoire II, Grégoire III, Zacharie et
Étienne II et leurs relations avec les empereurs iconoclastes (726–757),' *Revue historique* 79
(1899): 13–14; August Schäfer, *Bedeutung der Päpst Gregor II. (715–731) und Gregor III.
(731–741) für die Gründung des Kirchenstaats* (Montjoie, 1913), 29-30. Earlier in the eighth
century there was at least one other attempt to establish an emperor in the west; see *V. Gregorii II*, c. 17.

17 *Éigenhard, Vie de Charlemagne*, ed. Louis Halphen (Paris, 1947), passim and xi, where
Halphen observes, 'sa *Vie de Charlemagne* apparaît souvent plus comme la treizième "vie des
Césars" que comme une oeuvre originale.' Cf. Matthew S. Kempshall, 'Some Ciceronian
Models for Einhard's Life of Charlemagne,' *Viator* 26 (1995): 11–37, who is correct in
emphasizing that Einhard was far more erudite and nuanced than Halphen allowed. However,
the Caesarian model of Charlemagne provided by Einhard remains.

18 The imperial coronation is truly an immense topic, but see the useful review of the problem by
Robert Folz, *The Coronation of Charlemagne*, trans. J.E. Anderson (London, 1974).

19 See *Flavius Cresconius Corippus, In laudem Iustini Augusti minoris Libri IV*, ed. and trans.
Avril Cameron (London, 1976), 161–2.

20 See Robert Folz, *The Concept of Empire in Western Europe from the Fifth to the Fourteenth
Century*, trans. Sheila Ann Ogilvie (London, 1969), 16–25, with the literature cited there; and,
more recently, Janet Nelson, 'Kingship and Empire,' in *The Cambridge History of Medieval
Political Thought*, ed. J.H. Burns (Cambridge, 1988), 211–39. Pirenne, *Mohammed and
Charlemagne*, 233, utilizes a careful selection of papal views of Charlemagne's coronation in
an effort to show that 'his Imperial title had no secular significance.'

21 See, for example, F.L. Ganshof, 'L'échec de Charlemagne,' *Académie des inscriptions et
belles lettres. Comptes rendus de séances* (1947), 248–54; and 'La fin du règne de Charlemagne: Une décomposition,' *Zeitschrift für Schweizerische Geschichte* 28 (1948), 533–52.
The highly negative and, indeed, pessimistic tone of these two very influential studies was
conditioned more by the Nazi horrors that devastated his post–First World War optimism and
the events of the war in which his native Belgium suffered greatly than by a balanced appreciation of Charlemagne's reign. Ganshof's later work has a more positive tone, and when I studied with him in 1963–4, his views on Charlemagne and his reign could not be characterized as
negative. F.L. Ganshof, *The Carolingians and the Frankish Monarchy*, trans. Janet Sond-
heimer (London, 1971), makes these two articles, cited above, available in English.

22 See, for example, Robert Folz, *Le souvenir et la legende de Charlemagne dans l'Empire ger-*

Charlemagne's imperial behaviour is evident from early in his reign. For example, from 774 onward he made it clear to all that he ruled more than one kingdom: he was styled in his *acta* as *rex Francorum et rex Langobardorum*.[23] In both ancient and medieval political thought the rule of more than one kingdom was the *sine qua non* for being considered an emperor.[24] In addition, Charlemagne created a kingdom, the *regnum Aquitanorum*, and by so doing, exercised an imperial prerogative.[25] Charlemagne's treatment of the coinage of the realm is yet another index of his imperial behaviour and orientation.[26] Indeed, in this latter context he had coins issued in the style of earlier emperors with his head adorned with a laurel wreath.[27]

Charlemagne acted in an imperial manner in a great many other ways. For example, he had great buildings constructed. This type of activity was regarded as essential to the imperial persona; Augustus, for instance, was said to have found Rome a city of brick and left it a city of marble, and Constantine had a new city built that he named for himself. In case the point of all his building projects was missed by less historically-minded or intellectually-oriented contemporaries, Charlemagne used imperial models for his own constructions.[28]

Charlemagne ruled the church as the emperors had before him. For example, he routinely appointed bishops and abbots, dominated the papacy, ordered the universalization of the liturgy, and legislated for the church in his capitularies.

manique médiéval (Paris, 1950); and Barton Sholod, *Charlemagne in Spain: The Cultural Legacy of Roncesvalles* (Geneva, 1966).

23 J.F. Böhmer and Engelbert Mühlbacher, *Regesta Imperii: Die Regesten des Kaiserreichs unter den Karolingern, 751–918*, vol. 1 (Innsbruck, 1908), 77 ff.

24 For the background, see Steven Fanning, 'Jerome's Concept of Empire,' in *Images of Empire*, ed. Loveday Alexander (Sheffield, 1991), 239–50; and Steven Fanning, 'Bede, *Imperium*, and the Bretwaldas,' *Speculum* 66 (1991): 1–22. Folz, *Concept of Empire in Western Europe*, 17, with regard to Charlemagne's adviser Alcuin.

25 Cf. Gustav Eiten, *Das Unterkönigtum im Reiche der Merowinger und Karolinger* (Heidelberg, 1907), who gathers the relevant data regarding sub-kingdoms.

26 Philip Grierson, 'Money and Coinage under Charlemagne,' in *Karl der Grosse: Lebenswerk und Nachleben*, 1: 501–36, is still the best survey of Charlemagne's coinage. See, in addition, the important study by Karl F. Morrison with the collaboration of Henry Grunthal, *Carolingian Coinage* (New York, 1967).

27 Maurice Prou, *Les monnaies carolingiennes: Catalogue des monnaies françaises de la bibliothéque nationale* (Paris, 1906), xi, contends that this was done only after the imperial coronation; Grierson, 'Money and Coinage,' 518–19, dates it to the period 806–14 and suggests a Constantinian coin was the model. This coin type surely appeared before Charlemagne's imperial title was recognized by the east Roman emperor. See also the important article by Harry A. Miskimin, 'Two Reforms of Charlemagne? Weights and Measures in the Middle Ages,' *Economic History Review*, 2d ser. 20 (1967): 35–52.

28 Fichtenau, *Carolingian Empire*, 67–9. See, in general, Kenneth Conant, *Carolingian and Romanesque Architecture, 800–1200*, 2d ed. (Harmondsworth, 1978).

Like Constantine at Nicaea in 325, Charlemagne presided at Frankfurt in 794 over the most important church council of his reign.[29] However, with regard to religion, Charlemagne went well beyond *imitatio*. As a distinguished scholar has observed, Charlemagne sought 'to obtain equality of rank with the rulers of the east by raising his own position and by discrediting theirs in the eyes of his contemporaries.'[30] It is now well recognized that the *Libri Carolini* provided a rather subtle opportunity for this effort on a grand scale.[31]

Let us put Charlemagne and his western Empire in historical perspective and look very briefly at the Romans in the 'good old days' of conquest and expansion that marked the late Republic and early Empire. This was a past that was reasonably well known, at least to Charlemagne's advisers and very probably to the ruler himself. In this context, it may be noted that for more than four centuries Rome made sacrifices of human and material resources in order to integrate Gaul and Britain into the Empire successfully.[32] In addition, a massive though unsuccessful attempt was made to make Free Germany an integral part of the Empire.[33]

It is not without some irony, in the context of the Pirenne thesis, that Constantine the Great, who served at the court of his father, Constantius Chlorus, in Britain, ostensibly won the imperial title with northern armies.[34] Charlemagne would appear never to have contemplated seriously the reconquest of Britain.[35] Indeed, the Carolingian court surely knew from Bede's *Ecclesiastical History* that the emperor Honorius had given this distant and troubled province autonomous status, as evidenced by its obligation for self-defence.[36] Neverthe-

---

29 In general see F.L. Ganshof, 'The Church and Royal Power in the Frankish Monarchy under Pippin III and Charlemagne,' in *Carolingians and the Frankish Monarchy*, 205–39; and, for Frankfurt, see Fichtenau, *Carolingian Empire*, 58.

30 Fichtenau, *Carolingian Empire*, 71, for the quotation and discussion of how Charlemagne used the *Libri Carolini*.

31 The basic work on the *Libri Carolini* remains a series of articles by Ann Freeman: 'Theodulf of Orleans and the *Libri Carolini*'; 'Further Studies in the *Libri Carolini* I and II'; 'Further Studies in the *Libri Carolini* III: The Marginal Notes in Vaticanus latinus 7207,' published in *Speculum* 32 (1957): 663–705; 40 (1965): 203–39; 46 (1971): 597–616. See also Walther Schmandt, *Studien zu den Libri Carolini* (Mainz, 1966). For Charlemagne's use of the *Libri Carolini* to advance his imperial agenda at the expense of the emperor in the east, see Noble, 'From Brigandage to Justice,' 61–3, and 74, n. 60, for additional literature.

32 Peter Salway, *Roman Britain* (Oxford, 1981).

33 A brief review of imperial policy with regard to 'Free Germany' is provided by Robin Seager, *Tiberius* (London, 1972), 44, 74–88, 93–4.

34 See, in general, A.H.M. Jones, *The Later Roman Empire: 284–602* (Norman, Okla., 1964), 1: 78–81.

35 J.M. Wallace-Hadrill, 'Charlemagne and England,' in *Karl der Grosse: Lebenswerk und Nachleben*, 1: 683–98.

36 Bede, *Historia Ecclesiastica* I 12: *Bede's Ecclesiastical History of the English People*, ed.

less, Charlemagne did work effectively with King Offa of Mercia, and thus revivified imperial mercantile interests in Britain that had undergirded, at least in part, Julius Caesar's efforts to bring the island under Rome's control more than eight centuries earlier.[37]

Whereas Charlemagne, like his late imperial predecessors, prudently avoided pouring his troops into Britain, he did, nevertheless, resuscitate the expansionist policy of Augustus and made massive gains in what was still Free Germany. The disaster of the *Teutoburger Schlacht*, where three imperial legions were annihilated in A.D. 9 by a group of German armies that had been combined under the command of Arminius, assured the halt of imperial eastward expansion beyond the Rhine.[38] Charlemagne, however, reversed the decision of the Teutoburger during a generation of brutal and deliberate warfare.[39] Indeed, the conduct of his Saxon campaigns surely would have been very well appreciated by Roman military experts.[40] As a result of these extended efforts, Saxony was thoroughly integrated into the western Empire.[41]

Bertram Colgrave and R.A.B. Mynors (Oxford, 1969). Shortly after the *Historia* was completed, copies were available in the *regnum Francorum* as a result of the efforts of Anglo-Saxon missionaries. See R.A.B. Mynors, 'Circulation of the Oldest Manuscripts,' in *The Moore Bede*, ed. Peter Hunter Blair, Early English Manuscripts in Facsimile 9 (Copenhagen, 1959), 33–4. The famous Moore Bede, the oldest extant copy of the *Historia*, was written in Northumbria *ca* 737 and is known to have been at Charlemagne's court no later than *ca* 800; how much before 800 cannot at present be ascertained. See Bernhard Bischoff, 'The Court Library of Charlemagne,' in *Manuscripts and Libraries in the Age of Charlemagne*, trans. and ed. Michael Gorman (Cambridge, 1993), 67–8. The Moore Bede was the father of manuscripts of the *Historia* in *Francia occidentalis*, while the MSS mentioned above as having been brought by missionaries, would appear to have fathered the *Francia orientalis* group.

37 In general, see Wallace-Hadrill, 'Charlemagne and England,' 683–98; Grierson, 'Money and Coinage,' 501–2, emphasizes the close connection between the coinage of Charlemagne and Offa.

38 With regard to Arminius' career, see Dieter Timpe, *Arminius-Studien* (Heidelberg, 1970); and, for Roman efforts, Seager, *Tiberius*, 44, 74–88, 93–4.

39 For the Saxon wars, see Karl Brandl, 'Karl des Grossens Sachsenkriege,' *Niedersächsisches Jahrbuch für Landesgeschichte* 10 (1933): 29–52, repr. in *Die Eingliederung der Sachsen in das Frankenreich*, ed. Walther Lammers (Darmstadt, 1970), 3–28; Martin Lintzel, 'Die Unterwerfung Sachsens durch Karl den Grossen und der sächsische Adel,' *Sachsen und Anhalt* 10 (1934): 30–70, repr. in Martin Lintzel, *Ausgewälte Schriften*, 2 vols. (Berlin, 1961),1: 96–127; and Louis Halphen, 'La conquête de la Saxe,' *Revue historique* 130 (1919): 252–78, and 132 (1919): 257–305, repr. in Louis Halphen, *Études critiques sur l'histoire de Charlemagne* (Paris, 1921), 145–218.

40 J. Brian Campbell, 'Teach Yourself How to Be a General,' *Journal of Roman Studies* 77 (1987): 13–29, provides a useful introduction to the rather neglected topic of Roman military experts.

41 Regarding the success of the Saxon wars, see Louis Halphen, *Charlemagne et l'empire carolingien* (Paris, 1949), 65–72.

Where Augustus had failed and left to Tiberius the humiliating task of establishing the imperial frontier on the Rhine, Charlemagne succeeded and extended western civilization to the Weser and beyond. The Carolingians arguably went all the way to the banks of the Elbe.[42] It would be a mistake to assume that Charlemagne was unaware that by conquering Free Germany he was making good an imperial initiative that had been stymied eight centuries earlier. Of course, it is copiously documented that the Carolingian court was very well aware of Suetonius' *Twelve Caesars*.[43] Far more important in the present context is Velleius Paterculus' *History*, which describes in considerable detail the Empire's offensive wars against the Germans during the first century A.D.[44] This text not only was available to the Carolingian court, but was considered to be of such importance that a copy was commissioned and made during the later eighth century.[45]

---

42 With regard to the Carolingian conquests, see the general background provided by Rosamund McKitterick, *The Frankish Kingdoms under the Carolingians, 751–987* (London, 1983), 41–76. With regard to bridging the Elbe, see L. Dralle, *Slaven an Havel und Spree* (Berlin, 1981), 94–5.

43 E.K. Rand, 'On the History of the *De Vita Caesarum* of Suetonius in the Early Middle Ages,' *Harvard Studies in Classical Philology* 37 (1926): 1–48; S.J. Tibbitts, 'Suetonius,' in *Texts and Transmission: A Survey of the Latin Classics*, ed. L.D. Reynolds, corr. ed. (Oxford, 1986), 399–404. See the discussion of the use of Suetonius by Einhard in Halphen, *Éigenhard, Vie de Charlemagne*, passim. The compelling argument by Kempshall, 'Some Ciceronian Models,' that Einhard's *Vita Karoli* was very much influenced by Cicero's works does not undermine the general point that Suetonius' *De vita Caesarum* was well known at the Carolingian court.

44 Regarding the sources for imperial operations in Germany, see Seager, *Tiberius*, 44, 74–88, 93–4. For information concerning Germany, see Velleius Paterculus *Hist.* II xcvii–cxxix, passim (*Vellei Paterculi Historiarum ad M. Vinicium Consulem Libri Duo*, ed. W.S. Watt [Leipzig, 1988]).

45 Basic here is *Velleius Paterculus: The Tiberian Narrataive (2.94–131)*, edited with an introduction and commentary by A.J. Woodman (Cambridge, 1977), who accepts an eighth-century date for the MS copy. Cf. L.D. Reynolds, 'Velleius Paterculus,' in *Texts and Transmission: A Survey of the Latin Classics*, ed. L.D. Reynolds, corr. ed. (Oxford, 1986), 431–3, who is willing to accept a late eighth-century date but also suggests the possibility of an early ninth-century date for this copy.

It is important to emphasize in the present context the pragmatic or perhaps even utilitarian aspect of Carolingian high culture. For example, Rhabanus Maurus, who was taught by Alcuin, edited Vegetius' *De re militari* for the emperor's grandson, Lothair, and indicated in the preface that he had included in the epitome only those matters that were of use 'tempore moderno.' He apparently excised everything else ruthlessly. For the surviving sensctions of the epitome, see *De procinctu romanae militiae*, ed. Ernst Dümmler in *Zeitschrift für deutsches Alterthum* 15 (1872), and p. 450, for the quotation.

For the importance of *imitatio* as practised by the Romans and interpreted by the Carolingians, see the insightful observations by Kempshall, 'Some Ciceronian Models for Einhard's Life of Charlemagne,' 32–3, with the literature cited there. How political leaders used and

The attention given above to Charlemagne's treaty with Offa and his Saxon campaigns is not intended to buttress Pirenne's argument for a radical change of focus in the west following the Islamic invasions. An emphasis on mercantile relations between the Carolingian Empire and peoples dwelling around the North Sea, and even along the shores of the Baltic during the period of Charlemagne's rule, would not be so intended either.[46] Rather, the purpose here is to emphasize that the northern and eastern parts of Europe, from the early Empire and even before, had been and continued to be legitimate theatres of imperial operation in both a military and a commercial sense.[47]

Moreover, like western Roman emperors before him, Charlemagne was not preoccupied by his policy in regard to relations with Britain, northern trade, or the conquest of Free Germany. He had a much broader view of imperial geography, and over the course of his lengthy reign he dedicated far greater resources in the direction of reunifying the western half of the Empire and placing it under his control than he dedicated to northern projects.

Charlemagne is known to have possessed three engraved table-top maps. The ones that depicted the city of Rome and the city of Constantinople need not detain us here but the third was a map of the entire world ('totius mundi descriptionem').[48] It may be surmised that these engraved maps were based upon texts available at Charlemagne's court, the well-known *Descriptio urbis Romae*, *Descriptio urbis Constantinopolis*, and the *Mappa Mundi* that had been commissioned by Emperor Theodosius II *ca* 435. The Theodosian map was of

continue to use 'literary' models of previous successful leaders to further their own policies is an important matter but well beyond the scope of this study.

46 Despite the fact that Richard Hodges, *Dark Age Economics: The Origins of Towns and Trade, A.D. 600–1000* (New York, 1982), provides a rather peculiar view of North Sea and Baltic trade, a careful reader nevertheless can grasp the relevant facts.

47 See, for example, Birgit Arrhenius, 'Connections between Scandinavia and the east Roman Empire in the Migration Period,' in *From the Baltic to the Black Sea: Studies in Medieval Archaeology*, ed. David Austin and Leslie Alcock (London, 1990), 118–37; S. Bolin, *Fynden av romerska mynt i det fria Germanien* (Lund, 1926); Henrik Jarl Hansen, 'Dankirke: Affluence in Late Iron Age Denmark,' in *The Birth of Europe: Archaeology and Social Development in the First Millennium A.D.*, ed. Klavs Ransborg (Rome, 1989), 123–8; O. Kyhlberg, 'Late Roman and Byzantine *solidi*,' in *Excavations at Helgö*, ed. A. Lundström and H. Clarke (Stockholm, 1986), 13–126; U. Näsman, *Glas och handel i senromersk tid och folkvandringstid:en studie kring glas fran Eketorp-II, Öland, Sverige* (Uppsala, 1984); U. Näsman, 'The Gates of Eketorp-II: To the Question of Roman Prototypes of the Öland Ring-Forts,' *The Birth of Europe: Archaeology and Social Development in the First Millennium A.D.*, ed. Klavs Randsborg (Rome, 1989), 129–39; and Joachim Werner, 'Zu den auf Öland und Gotland gefundenen byzantinischen Goldmünzen,' *Fornvännen* 44 (1949): 257–86. Note that Pirenne, *Mohammed and Charlemagne*, 237, recognizes that Rome traded with the north but does not grasp either the geographical breadth of this trade or its extent.

48 Einhard, *VK* c. 33.

exceptional military value because it included the measurement of distances between localities.[49] In the military context, it is well established that Charlemagne's armies, after thoroughly securing the southern parts of Gaul and not neglecting the gradual conquest of Free Germany, went on to reintegrate Pannonia, Illyria, parts of Moesia, much of Italy, and parts of Spain into the western Empire.[50]

The western half of the Roman Empire had based its military strength on its armies and not on its navies.[51] Charlemagne understood very well that the western Empire during his reign was no different. It was rumoured that on one occasion he observed to Byzantine envoys who were visiting at the Carolingian court: 'Oh, were it the case that the pond [i.e., the Mediterranean Sea] did not lie between us. For if it did not then perhaps we would either divide the wealth of the east equally between us or else we would hold it in common.'[52] Nevertheless, like previous emperors in the west, Charlemagne understood that it was necessary also to have a naval capacity.

I will leave aside here discussion of Charlemagne's riverine fleets, which were used to very good effect beyond the frontiers of the Empire.[53] I will even ignore the major effort expended by the Carolingians towards building a Rhine–Main–Danube canal, the construction of which failed because of exceptionally bad weather, but which was intended to project Carolingian military

49 O.A.W. Dilke, *Greek and Roman Maps* (Ithaca, N.Y., 1985), 166–82; and P.D.A. Harvey, *Medieval Maps* (Toronto, 1991), 7–37, provide useful introductions to this difficult topic.

50 Margaret Deanesly, *A History of Early Medieval Europe from 474 to 911* (London, 1969), 339–76; and McKitterick, *Frankish Kingdoms*, 41–76, provide useful surveys of Charlemagne's conquests.

51 Although the Mediterranean was undoubtedly an important, if not the central, geographical reality of the ancient world, the Roman Empire clearly focused its military power on its land-based armed forces and developed noteworthy naval capacity only to deal with specific problems. See, for example, Edward N. Luttwak, *The Grand Strategy of the Roman Empire from the First Century A.D. to the Third* (Baltimore, 1979), where the role of the blue-water navy in Roman strategy is correctly given little attention. For the Roman navy, in general, see Chester Starr, *The Roman Imperial Navy*, 2d ed. (Ithaca, 1960); and M. Reddé, *Mare Nostrum: Les infrastructures, les dispositif et l'histoire de la marine militaire sous l'empire romain* (Rome, 1986).

52 Notker, *Gesta Karoli* I 26, ed. and trans. R. Rau (Berlin, 1960). Cf. the interpretation of this rumour by Fichtenau, *Carolingian Empire*, 31. The use of the word 'gurgitulus' to describe the Mediterranean in this context is curious since *gurges, gurgitis*, has an ominous connotation, but making it into a diminutive surely results in its significance being reduced.

53 See John Haywood, *Dark Age Naval Power: A Reassessment of Frankish and Anglo-Saxon Seafaring Activity* (London and New York, 1991), 95–109; and cf. H. Sproemberg, 'Die Seepolitik Karls des Grossen,' in H. Sproemberg, *Beiträge zur belgisch-niederländerischen Geschichte* (Berlin, 1959), 1–29, who is very critical of Charlemagne's efforts in general.

power into the Black Sea and beyond, to Constantinople itself.[54] These important Carolingian operations will not be examined so that we may pay some attention to Charlemagne's blue-water navy. Well before the end of the eighth century, a Carolingian navy was operating in the western Mediterranean. For example, in 799 one of Charlemagne's fleets defeated a Muslim flotilla off the Balearics, while on the islands, that is, on land, a Carolingian military force overcame a Saracen army. As a result of this combined operation, Carolingian rule over the islands was secured. Charlemagne would appear to have accepted the submission of the Christian inhabitants of the Balearics prior to dispatching his fleet and the army it carried.[55]

During the next several years, Carolingian fleets in the Adriatic and the Mediterranean engaged both Byzantine and Muslim naval assets. In 800, Charlemagne planned an invasion of Sicily. Between 806 and 810, Carolingian ships engaged the Byzantines in the Adriatic with considerable success. Throughout the last decade of his reign, Charlemagne not only had fleets in the Mediterranean and the Adriatic, but ordered the fortification, or in most cases the refortification, of western Mediterranean ports from Rome to Barcelona. Carolingian fleets engaged Muslim naval assets off the coast of Corsica in 806, in 807 they won a victory off the coast of Sardinia, and in 813 another victory was won off the coast of Majorca.[56] Charlemagne clearly understood that a blue-water navy had a place in the Carolingian armamentarium.[57]

Although the Roman authorities in the east carped interminably about terminology, Charlemagne's supremacy in the west was recognized to be as thoroughly real as when Licinius acknowledged Constantine's elevation to the purple in 311.[58] Indeed, Charlemagne surely merited eastern recognition for having succeeded marvellously in restoring a great part of the western Empire to unified western imperial-Christian rule through his consistent and dogged military and naval operations for a period of more than forty years.[59]

54 The basic work on the technical aspects of the canal project remains Hans Hubert Hofmann, '*Fossa Carolina*: Versuch einer Zussammenschau,' in *Karl der Grosse: Lebenswerk und Nachleben*, 1: 437–53.
55 *ARF* and *Rev.* a. 799, ed. Friedrich Kurze, MGH SRG(1895).
56 For a brief survey see Haywood, *Dark Age Naval Power*, 113–15.
57 Pirenne, *Mohammed and Charlemagne*, 158–63, is aware of Charlemagne's naval operations but casts them unfairly as a failure by looking well beyond the emperor's efforts to those of his more distant successors.
58 Folz, *Concept of Empire*, 22–35, traces the machinations with regard to various forms of intitulation and the putative policies behind these variations. With regard to the Byzantine reaction, see George Ostrogorsky, *History of the Byzantine State*, trans. Joan Hussey (New Brunswick, N.J., 1957), 176, n. 3, who observes: 'before 812 the title of Basileus seldom appeared with the addition "Romaion," and after 812 seldom appeared without this.'
59 The Carolingians clearly were not considered barbarian upstarts by the east Roman emperors.

The great rulers of antiquity, like military theorists of more modern times, were very well aware of the dictum in one or another variation that 'war is merely the continuation of policy by other means.'[60] Charlemagne was no exception.[61] His most ambitious diplomatic initiatives were reserved for Harun al Rashid, whose caliphate dominated the erstwhile Persian Empire as well as several provinces of the eastern and western halves of the Roman Empire. Peppin had opened diplomatic relations with the Abbasid caliphate no later that 765. The success enjoyed by Charlemagne's ambassadors in negotiating with the government of the caliph should be seen as a continuation of Peppin's efforts. The 'protectorate' over the holy places in Jerusalem that was granted to Charlemagne by the caliph was praised by the religiously oriented writers of the Carolingian realm. However, the commercial and military results of Carolingian diplomacy were likely of far greater importance to the west.[62]

From the commercial perspective, it is essential to emphasize the overwhelming importance of Jewish merchants in the long-distance trade between east and west. Among these merchants, the Radanites, who likely made their western headquarters in the valley of the Rhône, were of great renown.[63] Ibn Kurradadhbah, an Abbasid governor in eastern Persia, reported on 'The Routes of the Jewish Merchants Called Radanites' and emphasized the great range of their experience. 'These merchants,' he says, 'speak Arabic, Persian, the languages of the Roman Empire, of the Franks, the Spanish, and the Slavs.' He

For example, in 781 the Empress Irene tried to arrange a marriage between her son, the Emperor Constantine VI, and Charlemagne's daughter, Rotroude. See Einhard, *VK* c. 19.

60 Carl von Clausewitz, *On War*, ed. and trans. Michael Howard and Peter Paret (Princeton, 1976), 128.

61 There are many examples of Charlemagne engaging in extensive diplomatic activities for the purpose of gaining his goal without having to go to war, but in the end resorting to military force because diplomacy had failed. One of the most often discussed of these diplomatic initiatives concerns Charlemagne's efforts to settle matters with the Lombard king, Desiderius. Concerning the negotiations, see, for example, Peter Classen, 'Karl der Grosse, das Papsttum und Byzanz: Die Begründung des karolingischen Kaisertums,' in *Karl der Grosse* 1: 548–9; Ottorino Bertolini, *Roma e i longobardi* (Rome, 1972), 117–18; and J.T. Hallenbach, *Pavia and Rome: The Lombard Monarchy in the Eighth Century* (Philadelphia, 1982), 137–61.

62 For useful treatments of Carolingian relations with the Abbasid caliphate see, for example, F. W. Buckler, *Harunu'l-Rashid and Charles the Great* (Cambridge, Mass., 1931); and Giosuè Musca, *Carlo Magno ed Harun al Rashid* (Bari, 1963), and the scholarly works cited in these studies. Much, however, still remains controversial.

63 The basic work remains J.J. Rabinowitz, *Jewish Merchant Adventurers: A Study of the Radanites* (London, 1948). See, in addition, Cecil Roth, 'Economic Life and Population Movements,' in *The World History of the Jewish People*, 2d ser., vol. 2: *Medieval Period–Dark Ages*, ed. Cecil Roth (London, 1966), 23 ff.; Walther Björkman, 'Karl und der Islam,' *Karl der Grosse*, 1: 672–82; and Bernard S. Bachrach, *Jewish Policy in Western Europe* (Minneapolis, 1977), 72–5.

notes that sometimes they 'ship out from Frankish territory on the Mediterranean Sea,' pass over the Suez land bridge, and sail into the Red Sea for al-Jar and Jidda, the ports for Medina and Mecca, respectively. At other times the Radanites take a different route when 'they leave the kingdom of the Franks and sail across the Mediterranean to Antioch' and then travel on the Euphrates to Baghdad. After transporting cargoes of 'eunuchs, female and males slaves, silken cloth, various kinds of furs, and swords' to these centres of Islamic society, the Radanites went on to 'Sind, India, and China' in order to pick up cargoes of 'musk, aloes, camphor, cinnamon, and various other goods from eastern lands' for sale in the Christian west.[64] These Radanites obviously flourished despite Muslim conquests in the Mediterranean basin and domination of the Persian Empire.

Charlemagne gave extensive privileges to Jewish merchants and obviously did not limit his support to the Radanites.[65] However, it is perhaps more important to emphasize that these trade relations, in so far as they concerned the east, depended upon the support of the caliph and his officials. It seems very likely therefore that the Carolingian legations, including Jewish diplomats, which were sent to the Abbasid court, played a primary role in securing these trade relations as well as in gaining access to the holy places for Christian pilgrims. In short, both Christian and Muslim governments had to be in accord regarding these trade matters for Jewish, and indeed any other, merchants to operate successfully.[66]

---

64 Ibn Kurradadhbah, *Le livre des routes et des royaumes*, ed. and trans. M.J. de Goeje (Leiden, 1889), 114 ff; for an English translation, see Bachrach, *Early Medieval Jewish Policy*, 72–3. It is of interest that Ibn Kurradadhbah also emphasizes Radanite contact with the Khazars: 'All of these routes are interconnected and links can be made over land ... Sometimes [merchants leaving the Frankish kingdom] take the route that passes on the other side of Byzantium and after crossing the country of the Slavs they arrive at Khmalij, the capital of the Khazars.' On the Khazars, see the ageing but still useful work of D.M. Dunlap, *The History of the Jewish Khazars* (Princeton, 1954). For recent observations on the chronology of the Khazar realm, see Constantin Zuckerman, 'On the Date of the Khazar's Conversion to Judaism and the Chronology of the Kings of the Rus Oleg and Igor,' *Revue des études Byzantines* 53 (1995): 237–70. Pirenne, *Mohammed and Charlemagne*, 158–9, is surely incorrect to believe that the Jews did not sail on the western Mediterranean.

65 Bachrach, *Early Medieval Jewish Policy*, 66–83. Note the observation of Pirenne, *Mohammed and Charlemagne*, 257, that in regard to Jews 'we are dealing with great merchants who were indispensable.'

66 Pirenne, *Mohammed and Charlemagne*, 255, argues, 'These Jews were men who actually lived by commerce, and apart from a few Venetians they were almost the only people who did so.' This conclusion depends upon the assumption that all mentions of international merchants in Charlemagne's documents refer to Jews or to their Christian employees. However, the texts that Pirenne cites (256–9) make clear that there were important Christian merchants as well.

It is clear that Jewish merchants, whether they were Radanites or uncon-
nected to any major commercial network, were professionals. As Pirenne himself argued, Jewish merchants embodied the true capitalist spirit.[67] Pirenne also
recognized the importance of the capitalist spirit displayed by Venetian, Christian merchants.[68] It seems very likely that the Venetians obtained their privileges to trade in the Muslim east as a result of Carolingian diplomatic initiatives
much in the same way that the Jews had benefited.[69] The political situation in
Benevento also lends itself to a similar interpretation.[70]

Charlemagne and his advisers appreciated not only the so-called capitalist
spirit but also the importance of a free market that supports such economic
activity.[71] In this context, Carolingian legislation regarding the so-called just
price is crucial. The just price was, in fact, the market price established through
free concourse between buyers and sellers. It is true that Charlemagne legislated against monopolistic practices such as hoarding as well as against other
restraints of trade.[72] However, such interventions in the free market are well

67 *Mohammed and Charlemagne*, 174, 253–9; Jewish merchants, he admits, 'were numerous
    everywhere.'
68 Ibid., 176–9.
69 It is clear that Charlemagne wanted to control both Venetian trade and Venice itself, but that
    the islanders tried with some success to maintain a degree of independence by endeavouring to
    play the Carolingians and the Byzantines off against one another. Cf. Pirenne, *Mohammed and
    Charlemagne*, 175–97, who does not seem to appreciate either the economic or the political
    underpinnings of Charlemagne's policy towards Venice. Rather he emphasizes the latter's
    close connections in the long term with Byzantium.
70 Cf. Pirenne, *Mohammed and Charlemagne*, 148, 180–2, 229–30.
71 The economic 'theory' that undergirds Pirenne's thinking is in need of elucidation if the role
    he attributes to various historical phenomena is to be understood. See, for example, the inter-
    esting, but very limited, effort by Louis A. Dow, 'The Rise of the City: Adam Smith versus
    Henri Pirenne,' *Review of Social Economy* 32 (1974): 170–85. The debate between Pirenne
    (for example, *Mohammed and Charlemagne*, 251–2, n. 2) and Alfons Dopsch (*Die Wirt-
    schaftsentwicklung der Karolingerzeit vornehmlich in Deutschland*, 2 vols. [3d ed. Weimar,
    1962]) often appears highly tendentious because neither scholar exposed the economic model
    with which he was working.
72 Kenneth S. Cahn, 'The Roman and Frankish Roots of the Just Price of Medieval Canon Law,'
    Studies in Medieval and Renaissance History 6 (1969): 3–52. The fact that Charlemagne
    found it necessary to legislate in order to assure that market forces operated freely surely per-
    mits the inference that there were sufficient numbers of merchants seeking to benefit from the
    manipulation of markets to require government intervention. Whether we classify these greedy
    merchants as rogue capitalists or give them some other appellation, it is clear that the profit
    motive remained strong in the Carolingian world. Cf. Pirenne, *Mohammed and Charlemagne*,
    251–2, regarding the anti-capitalist spirit of Charlemagne's legislation that putatively prohib-
    ited the taking of interest. Cf. Dopsch, *Die Wirtschaftsentwicklung der Karolingerzeit*, 2: 282,
    n. 2, who has the better of this argument.
       The notion of gift exchange frequently raised by medievalists in the unhealthy thrall of
    anthropologists is of no value here. See the critiques of these ideas by David Wilson, 'Trade

recognized as legitimate government prerogatives by modern economists as they had been by observers in the ancient world.[73] Charlemagne had a strong interest in lending the support of his government to long-distance capitalist trading ventures both in the Mediterranean and in the north, and he vigorously encouraged commerce throughout his Empire by sustaining the values of a free-market economy.[74]

In conclusion, it is important to emphasize that Charlemagne behaved consistently as the Christian-Roman emperor in the west both before and after he assumed the imperial title on Christmas day, 800. He worked diligently to bring under his direct control those territories that had escaped imperial rule during the preceding centuries. Carolingian armies and navies took control of the Balearic Islands and extended Christian-imperial domination of the Mediterranean coast of Spain beyond Barcelona.[75] Charlemagne would appear also to have dealt with the Muslim rulers of North Africa.[76] In an effort to impose Carolingian domination over the more inland areas of the Iberian peninsula, he led a major campaign to capture the great fortified city of Zaragossa.[77] When he realized that such operations did not enjoy the full support of the Christian inhabitants, it would appear that he arranged to work through King Alfonso II of Asturias. The latter commended himself to Charlemagne in a manner that

between England and Scandinavia and the Continent,' in *Untersuchungen zu Handel und Verkehr der vor- und frühgeschichtlichen Zeit in Mittel- und Nordeuropa*, ed. Kalus Düwel, Herbert Jankuhn, Harald Siems, and Dieter Timpe, vol. 3: *Der Handel des frühen Mittelalters* (Göttingen, 1985), 225–69; and Bernard S. Bachrach, 'Anthropology and Early Medieval History: Some Problems,' *Cithara* 34 (1994): 3–10.

73 Henry William Spiegel, *The Growth of Economic Thought*, 3d ed. (Durham and London, 1991), 9, for attacks on monopoly in the classical period; 34, for the illegality of 'rings and trusts'; and 37, for the rational-man model.

74 Cf. Hodges, *Dark Age Economics*, who, despite errors both in fact and conception, makes clear Charlemagne's interest in the advancement of trade. Despite the title of this book, Hodges is interested in northern Europe. A very useful critique of Hodges's work is provided by Wilson, 'Trade between England and Scandinavia and the Continent,' 225–69.

75 See Haywood, *Dark Age Naval Power*, 95–109; and cf. Sproemberg, 'Die Seepolitik Karls des Grossen,' 1–29. With regard to Carolingian operations in the south, see Bernard S. Bachrach, 'Military Organization in Aquitaine under the Early Carolingians,' *Speculum* 49 (1974): 1–33; repr. in *Armies and Politics in the Early Medieval West* (London, 1993) with the same pagination.

76 *ARF* a. 801; Einhard, *VK* c. 17, places these contacts within the framework of distributing alms to Christians in many parts of the Muslim world. Obviously, Charlemagne's efforts in these matters could not have been undertaken without the acquiescence of the Muslim authorities.

77 See the basic studies by Robert-Henri Bautier, 'La campagne de Charlemagne en Espagne (778),' *Bulletin de la Société des Sciences Lettres et Arts de Bayonne* 135 (1979): 1–51; and Michel Rouche, 'La défaite de Roncevaux,' ibid., 145–56, with the literature cited there.

may recall the so-called friendly kings who dealt with Rome during the Republic and early Empire.[78]

As noted above, Charlemagne reconquered Bavaria, Pannonia, Illyria, and parts of Moesia for the western Empire and strove to make his presence felt to the shores of the Black Sea. In Italy, Istria, and Sicily, Charlemagne actively sought to take control of east Roman assets. In this context, as we have seen, Venice was a major object of his attention. The pope clearly was no longer a subject of the emperor in the east but was a dependent of the western emperor, and thus came before Charlemagne for judgment in December 800.[79] Indeed, Charlemagne dominated the church in the western half of the Empire as he presided over the quashing of the Adoptionist heresy, a Spanish problem,[80] and used missionaries from Britain to press the conversion of Free Germany to Christianity.[81]

Charlemagne not only sought to drive the Muslims out of the western Mediterranean, but he worked to push the east Romans out of the western half of the Empire. These were efforts to gain control of assets that rightfully belonged to the western half of the Empire. The allotments found in the *divisio* of the Empire, which had been made according to the testament of Theodosius I in 395, were presumably evident to Charlemagne and his advisers from the *Mappa Mundi* of Theodosius II, which, as mentioned above, was available at the Carolingian court. Even if the *Mappa Mundi* were found to be insufficiently precise in this matter, then surely the information found in the *Notitia Dignitatum*, which was also available to Charlemagne, provided a sufficient supplement by which the Carolingians could ascertain what was properly a part of the western Empire.[82]

---

78 David C. Braund, *Rome and the Friendly King: The Character of Client Kingship* (New York, 1984). For the commendation of Alfonso to Charlemagne, Einhard, *VK* c. 16. While Einhard's language undoubtedly was influenced by Suetonius, it is perhaps somewhat more controversial to conclude that Charlemagne's relationship with Alfonso II was conditioned by the Carolingian ruler's view of proper imperial behaviour. Cf. Roger Collins, *Early Medieval Spain: Unity in Diversity, 400–1000* (London, 1983), 232–3.

79 Folz, *Concept of the Empire in Western Europe*, 16–25. For a detailed and nuanced examination of the sinuous road to papal rejection of east Roman control, see Thomas F.X. Noble, *The Republic of St. Peter: The Birth of the Papal State, 680–825* (Philadelphia, 1984).

80 Halphen, *Charlemagne et l'empire carolingien*, 216–17.

81 McKitterick, *Frankish Kingdoms*, 59–64.

82 Many of the administrative and geographical texts collectd by Charlemagne, including the *Notitia Dignitatum*, were copied into a new codex *ca* 825. It seems reasonable to suggest that these texts had been well used. Thus *ca* 825 a clean copy was made of the lot. Cf. J.J.G. Alexander, 'The Illustrated Manuscripts of the Notitia Dignitatum,' in *Aspects of the Notitia Dignitatum*, ed. R. Goodburn and P. Bartholomew (Oxford, 1976), 19, with the literature cited there.

In addition to trying to reclaim direct control of the western half of the Empire, Charlemagne meddled in what very properly were purely east Roman concerns. For example, he followed up his father's initiatives in negotiating with the caliph. Thus, as we have seen, he secured trading privileges for merchants who were based in the western half of the Empire and obtained a 'protectorate' of some kind over the Christians in the city of Jerusalem along with a guaranty that Christian pilgrims to the Holy Land would not be harassed.

Charlemagne's interests in England, the North Sea, and the Baltic are hardly evidence of a massive shift in western interests. These regions had been traditional areas of Roman economic exploitation even before the creation of the Empire. Finally, the Carolingian conquest of the greater part of Free Germany witnessed the making good of an imperial policy about which Charlemagne and his advisors were well informed, but which had failed almost eight centuries earlier.

Charlemagne was an ambitious and exceptionally successful west Roman emperor. By focusing upon Charlemagne, it has been possible to adumbrate his policies as an individual ruler and not have them lost in a survey over the *longue durée* that obscures what is of historical importance in order to chart economic and social trends. In Pirenne's famous dictum, Charlemagne was supposed to be inconceivable without Mohammed. When imperial policy is viewed over the long term, it seems rather as if Charlemagne is inconceivable without Constantine the Great and Theodosius I, who divided the Empire between east and west and put Christianity on the road to victory.

12

Lupus of Ferrières in His Carolingian Context

THOMAS F.X. NOBLE

I first encountered Lupus of Ferrières in an undergraduate class on medieval history, and I later met him again in a graduate course on the Carolingians. I knew of him pretty much what it seemed that everyone else did: he was a proto-humanist, a bibliophile, and an elegant Latin stylist. Lupus figured prominently in all accounts of the intellectual revival often called the 'Carolingian Renaissance.' It was Walter Goffart who introduced me to another Lupus. In carrying out various reading assignments in connection with my Carolingian history course, I encountered Goffart's *Le Mans Forgeries*.[1] There I read of Lupus as the author of letters to King Charles the Bald and others that were intended to recover some lost properties. As far as I then knew – and, obviously, I did not know very much – Lupus wrote letters only to borrow books and to show off his Ciceronian style. Goffart's brief remarks about Lupus' letters concerning the lost cell of St-Josse opened my eyes to new possibilities. Almost immediately I obtained Regenos's translation of Lupus' correspondence and, finding it fascinating reading, went right through it.[2] In those letters I encountered a person and a source that were far more interesting and important than any of my earlier reading had led me to suppose. I resolved to return one day to Lupus as a typical sort of Carolingian figure whose career is instructive, not because it is peculiar, but because it is, seen in its proper context, remarkably ordinary and, as such, wonderfully revealing of how lots of things worked and happened in the central decades of the ninth century. The brief and diverse reflections here offered on Lupus represent my attempt to keep that old resolution.

---

1 *The Le Mans Forgeries: A Chapter from the History of Church Property in the Ninth Century* (Cambridge, Mass., 1966), 3–6.
2 Graydon W. Regenos, trans., *The Letters of Lupus of Ferrières* (The Hague, 1966). Unless otherwise noted, translations of Lupus' letters cited in this essay are from this edition.

As is true of so many important Carolingian figures, Lupus' life and career are known only in part. Lupus' own letters, a few references in the *Gesta* of the bishops of Auxerre,[3] and scattered notices in other sources provide all that can be known. The first serious attempt to recover the details of Lupus' life was undertaken by Etienne Baluze in 1664,[4] and not much progress was made until F. Sprotte returned to the topic in 1880.[5] Ernst Dümmler, in notes accompanying his 1902 edition of Lupus' letters, and Léon Levillain, in studies preparatory to his own 1927–35 edition, uncovered a few new bits of information. Virtually nothing important has since been added to the basic outline of Lupus' life, although there have been substantial gains in the evaluation of his scholarly work.[6]

Lupus is thought to have been born around 805. The date of his death is generally agreed to have been 862, or slightly later, because nothing is heard from or about him after that year. His father was a Bavarian nobleman, Antelm, who may have migrated to the central region of Gaul after the fall of Duke Tassilo of Bavaria in 788. Lupus' mother, Frotildis, was a noble Frank, who seems to have originated in central Gaul. Lupus was undoubtedly born in this region. Antelm's brother, Angelelm, was bishop of Auxerre, and Lupus' own brother Heribold held that position as did, later on, Abbo, another of his brothers, who had earlier been abbot of St-Germain d'Auxerre. Lupus may also have been related to Archbishops Orsmar of Tours and Wenilo of Sens, Bishop Hilmerad of Amiens, and Abbots Marcward of Prüm and Otacher of Cormery. Given that at one time or another bishops of Bayeux, Chalons, Limoges, Sens, and Troyes had borne the name Lupus, it is a fair guess that our Lupus was marked out from the start for an ecclesiastical career.

---

3 MGH SS 13: 394–400, esp. 397–8.

4 *Beati Servati Lupi presbyteri et abbatis Ferrariensis O.S.B. Opera* (Paris, 1664). I have been able to consult only the second edition (Antwerp, 1710). The material on Lupus' life is to be found at 326–8.

5 *Biographie des Abtes Servatus Lupus von Ferrières nach den Quellen des neunten Jahrhunderts* (Regensburg, 1880).

6 For editions of Lupus' letters, see nn. 7 and 91, below. Summary accounts of Lupus' life may be found in Léon Levillian, 'Étude sur les lettres de Loup de Ferrières,' *Bibliothèque de l'école des chartes* 62 (1901): 447–54; Max Manitius, *Geschichte der lateinischen Literatur des Mittelalters*, 3 vols. (Munich, 1911–31), 2: 483–8; Emmanuel von Severus, *Lupus von Ferrières: Gestalt und Werk eines Vermittlers antiken Geistesgutes an das Mittelalter im 9. Jahrhundert*, Beiträge zur geschichte des alten Mönchtums und des Benediktinerordens 21 (Münster, 1940), 23–34; Eleanor Shipley Duckett, 'Lupus of Ferrières,' in her *Carolingian Portraits: A Study in the Ninth Century* (Ann Arbor, Mich., 1962), 161–201; John J. Contreni, 'Lupus of Ferrières,' *Dictionary of the Middle Ages*, ed. Joseph Strayer (New York, 1986), 7: 688; Hubert Mordek, 'Lupus von Ferrières,' *Lexikon des Mittelalters* (Munich 1993), 6: 15–16.

Lupus may have entered the monastery of Ferrières under Alcuin's pupil Adalbert, but Abbot Aldrich (821–9) was more important to Lupus' formation. In 828 or 829, Aldrich sent Lupus to Fulda 'to the venerable abbot Hrabanus, that he might introduce me to the study of the Holy Scriptures.'[7] Among his fellow students at Fulda were several men who would figure prominently in Lupus' life: Marcward and Eigil of Prüm, Gottschalk, Ado of Vienne, and, perhaps, Louis, who was subsequently abbot of St-Denis and chancellor to Charles the Bald.[8] While he was at Fulda, Lupus initiated an epistolary friendship with the hoary Einhard, and he twice visited the renowned scholar.[9]

At Fulda, Lupus found a world of scholarly intercourse which he can hardly have glimpsed in the western Frankish realm of his youth. Indeed, in his first letter to Einhard, Lupus says explicitly, 'in these days those who pursue an education are considered a burden to society.'[10] In part Lupus' words can be read as flattery. He has just praised the intellectual attainments of Charlemagne's generation and Einhard's own role in those accomplishments. But it was also true that the world of Lupus' adolescence and early manhood was one of civil strife, familial squabbling among the Carolingians, and early attacks by the Vikings. There were in those years impressive intellectual and artistic achievements, to be sure. But what was lacking was the central direction and focused leadership that, as John Contreni so persuasively emphasizes,[11] were central to the inauguration of the Carolingian intellectual revival in the last decades of the eighth century. In the very last letter in his collection – a letter which really cannot be dated securely – Lupus expressed joy that there was finally a bit of a surge in intellectual activity.[12] In Charlemagne's time, one speaks of court connections as central to intellectual life. In all the vast literature on Charlemagne's court, stress is always laid on the attraction of scholars, the collection of books, and the promotion of schooling.[13] When Michael Wallace-Hadrill characterized Charles the Bald as a 'Renaissance Prince,' he did so on the basis of that

---

7 Lupus, ep. 1: Loup de Ferrières, *Correspondence*, 2 vols., ed. Léon Levillain, Les Classiques de l'histoire de France au Moyen Âge (Paris, 1927–35), 1: 2–10, esp. 6, 8 (trans. Regenos, 2). Subsequent references to the letters use Levillain's numbering, followed by the volume and page numbers of his edition.

8 Levillain, 'Étude,' 448–9.

9 Epp. 1, 2, 4, 5, ed. Levillain, 1: 2–10, 10–12, 18–40, 40–50.

10 Ep. 1, ed. Levillain, 1: 4 (trans. Regenos, 2).

11 'The Carolingian Renaissance,' in *Renaissances before the Renaissance: Cultural Revivals of Late Antiquity and the Middle Ages*, ed. Warren Treadgold (Stanford, 1984), 59–74, esp. 59–61.

12 Ep. 133 (?862), ed. Levillain, 2: 218: 'Reviviscentem in his nostris regionibus sapientiam quosdam studiossime colere pergratum habeo.'

13 See, for example, Rosamond McKitterick, *The Frankish Kingdoms under the Carolingians, 751–987* (London, 1983), 140–68.

ruler's tastes, interests, and behaviour, not because he promoted a movement.[14] Lupus never enjoyed the kind of patronage, of enveloping support, that so deeply benefited the generation of his predecessors. Lupus' career illustrates that in later decades personal initiatives as well as personal connections were decisive. This, I think, is an important clue to reading those of his letters that sought to borrow or exchange books or to share information and ideas. I take those letters to be a sign of the times more than an indicator of particular ambitions and interests on Lupus' part.

In 836 Lupus returned to Ferrières. In a letter of 837 to a certain Altwin, a friend from the Fulda years, Lupus mentions his 'hearers,' which must mean students.[15] This suggests that, after long studies at Ferrières and Fulda, Lupus was appointed by his abbot, Odo, to teach. Since Lupus says of himself, 'A love of learning arose in me almost from my earliest childhood,'[16] it is reasonable to suppose that he was, from a very early stage, destined to become the schoolmaster at Ferrières. As to his teaching methods or interests, we have neither explicit statements by Lupus himself nor reminiscences by pupils. In fact, scholars have not been able to identify any pupils except Hieric of Auxerre.[17] No matter how intellectually significant Lupus has seemed to some modern authorities, he did not attract the kind of contemporary following that, say, Alcuin, Hrabanus, or Walafrid Strabo did. Ferrières was a medium-sized monastery, sheltering some seventy-two monks,[18] so its school cannot have been very large in any case.[19] And monastic education was addressed principally to the kinds of religious subjects that made good choir monks, not to the kinds of classical topics that made good scholars.[20] Thus, Lupus' direct or indirect influence on his times was undoubtedly very limited.

14 'A Carolingian Renaissance Prince: The Emperor Charles the Bald,' *Proceedings of the British Academy* 64 (1978): 155–84.

15 Ep. 9, ed. Levillain, 1: 72: 'auditoribus meis.' See von Severus, *Lupus*, 31 n. 3.

16 Ep. 1, ed. Levillain, 1: 4.

17 David Ganz, 'Conclusion: Visions of Carolingian Education, Past, Present, and Future,' in *'The Gentle Voices of Teachers': Aspects of Learning in the Carolingian Age*, ed. Richard E. Sullivan (Columbus, Ohio, 1995), 269.

18 Ep. 49, ed. Levillain, 1: 204, speaks of seventy-two monks at the time of Lupus' election as abbot.

19 For pertinent remarks on the size and character of monastic schools, see Heinrich Fichtenau, *Living in the Tenth Century: Mentalities and Social Orders*, trans. Patrick J. Geary (Chicago, 1991), 284–300.

20 I mean to draw an explicit contrast between the kinds of views represented by, on the one hand, Edward Kennard Rand, *Founders of the Middle Ages* (Cambridge, Mass., 1928) and, on the other, Detlef Illmer, *Formen der Erziehung und Wissensvermittlung in frühen Mittelalter: Quellenstudien zur Frage der Kontinuität des abendländischen Erziehungswesens*, Münchener Beiträge zur Mediävistik und Renaissance-Forschung 7 (Munich, 1971).

In addition to teaching, Lupus was burdened with a share in the administration of the monastery, perhaps owing to the occasional absence of the abbot.[21] When the abbot was present, Lupus seems to have served as his secretary. At any rate he wrote at least five letters for him.[22] In 836, with the help of unnamed friends, Lupus received an invitation to the court of Louis the Pious in Frankfurt.[23] A year later he was invited back, this time on the initiative of Judith, Louis's wife. She and Lupus both had East Frankish family connections, and while there is no evidence that they were directly related, it may be that he was a person whose interests she wished to promote, not least to attach him to the cause of her own son Charles.[24] It is worth noting that Lupus was conspicuously loyal to Charles throughout the remainder of his life. In 837, on the occasion of his invitation to the palace, Lupus wrote to a friend to say that 'she [Judith] has great influence, and many think that some high position is about to be conferred upon me.'[25] Lupus may have come to the attention of Judith and Louis through the powerful and influential Eberhard of Friuli, who was the husband of their daughter Gisela. When he was still a monk at Fulda, Lupus prepared for Eberhard a manuscript of Germanic laws, with illuminations and poems that may or may not be by his own hand.[26] As it turned out, Lupus' hopes were not realized at that moment and, in fact, he never received a court appointment. But when Louis the Pious died in the summer of 840, events were set in motion that led to Lupus' installation as abbot of Ferrières. Abbot Odo was unsure whom to support among Louis's surviving, and battling, sons, and he inclined towards Lothar.[27] By the autumn, Charles the Bald had assumed possession of the lands around Ferrières, and in late November he dismissed Odo and replaced him with Lupus.[28]

For the remaining twenty-plus years of his life, Lupus served energetically as the abbot of Ferrières.[29] Thanks to his correspondence and a few other scattered sources, Lupus' activities as abbot are quite well known to us. This is not

---

21 Ep. 10, ed. Levillain, 1: 80.
22 Epp. 14–18, ed. Levillain, 1: 90–102. Nos 14, 15, and 16 were sent to that Louis who was to become abbot of St-Denis and chancellor of Charles the Bald; no. 17 went to Bishop Jonas of Orléans; and no. 18 was addressed to Marcward and Sichard.
23 Ep. 11, ed. Levillain. 1: 84: 'annitentibus amicis.'
24 On Judith's background see Elizabeth Ward, 'Caesar's Wife: The Career of the Empress Judith, 819–829,' in *Charlemagne's Heir: New Perspectives on the Reign of Louis the Pious*, eds. Peter Godman and Roger Collins (Oxford, 1990), 208.
25 Ep. 11, ed. Levillain, 1: 84 (trans. Regenos, 28–9).
26 Von Severus, *Lupus*, 18–19.
27 Ep. 18, ed. Levillain, 1: 100–2.
28 Ep. 27, ed. Levillain, 1: 130. For additional details see ep. 24, 1: 118–20.
29 See, in general, the biographical accounts cited above, n. 6.

the place for a detailed account of all his doings, but as a way of illustrating the kinds of routine business that will have filled the careers of many Carolingian churchmen, a few high points may be noted. Lupus was a regular visitor to the royal court and he attended major meetings at Meersen in 847 and at Bonneuil in 855. He attended church councils at Germigny in 843, at Ver in 844, at Soissons in 853, at Moret sometime between 844 and 856, at Savonnières in 859, at Touzy in 860, and at Pîtres in 862. On several of these occasions he was assigned the task of writing the official records of the clerics in attendance. That Lupus functioned several times as spokesman for a significant segment of the West Frankish episcopate may have owed something to his reputation for learning and literary craftsmanship, but it also suggests that he enjoyed the confidence of his peers. Twice, Lupus was sent as a *missus* to Burgundy and, once, to Rome to Pope Leo IV. In 844 Lupus led out the troops dependent on his monastery and he was captured near Angoulême. His prompt and unexpected release from captivity near Toulouse may be what earned him the cognomen 'Servatus,' by which he has commonly been known since the late ninth century, even though he does not appear ever to have used the name himself.[30]

The most cursory reading of Lupus' correspondence would be enough to convince anyone that he was a conscientious abbot who looked out for the well-being of his monks and for the financial and administrative health of his monastery. One case, in particular, is especially revealing of the situation in which Lupus found himself and, I suspect, indicative, too, of what it meant to be a churchman in the turbulent decades in the middle of the ninth century. I refer to the long struggle by Ferrières to recover its confiscated cell of St-Josse (Sanctus Judocus) in the Pas-de-Calais.

The basic facts are these. Charlemagne gave the cell of St-Josse to Alcuin 'to provide hospitality to strangers,' and some years later Louis the Pious gave the cell to Ferrières so that its revenues, beyond those strictly necessary for alms, might support the monastic community. In the political turmoil following Louis's death in June 840, St-Josse passed into the hands of an otherwise unknown Rhuoding, and in November 840 Lupus, in what may have been one of his first acts as abbot, wrote to Lothar to ask him to return the cell to Ferrières.[31] The precise fate of St-Josse in the next few months is not known, but

---

30 His sobriquet may also have resulted from his recovery from a life-threatening illness in 836.

31 Ep. 19, ed. Levillain, 1: 102–4. In the following account I accept the chronology of Levillain. The notes accompanying the letters in his edition provide basic justifications for his dates, but a fuller account of his positions may be found in a series of articles in the *Bibliothèque de l'école des chartes*, 62 (1901): 445–509; 63 (1902): 69–118, 289–330, 537–86; 64 (1903): 259–83. All but the last of these were subsequently gathered together as *Étude sur les lettres de Loup de Ferrières* (Paris, 1902).

in May 841 Charles the Bald issued a document reinstating Ferrières' rightful possession.[32] Lupus says that his lost property was restored on the advice of Adalhard, an important public figure in the 840s in the West Frankish kingdom, and the uncle of Charles the Bald's wife, Ermentrude.[33] By early 844 Lupus was complaining to Charles and to various influential persons that St-Josse was in the hands of a Count Odulf. This Odulf had rallied the counts between the Meuse and Scheldt to Lothar in 840, and then switched sides and brought his followers over to Charles in 842.[34] Doubtless he got St-Josse as a reward. From the years between 844 and 847 (or possibly 851: the letters are difficult to date), we have thirteen letters by which Lupus sought to recover his lost cell.[35] Then, in 852, Lupus wrote to King Ethelwulf of Wessex, and to his chancellor Felix.[36] In both letters he signed as 'Abbot of St-Josse.' In the same year Lupus wrote to Archbishop Guigmund of York to say, among other things, that St-Josse had been returned to him.[37] In none of these letters does Lupus provide any details on how, or by whose influence, his property was recovered. In any case, it took some dozen years for Ferrières to gain satisfaction of its eminently just claims.

In general there is nothing especially interesting or unusual about a case involving a church that lost a piece of land and struggled hard to get it back. Medieval records are teeming with such cases. What is interesting about this particular case, however, is that Lupus' correspondence brings it into clear focus and perspective. The St-Josse case permits us to grasp many features of the behaviour of the mighty in the Carolingian world.

First, the letters give us a sharp sense of just what was at stake from a material point of view. In several of his letters pertaining to St-Josse, Lupus reveals the hardships that Ferrières was forced to endure because of the loss of its evidently very valuable cell. St-Josse provided clothing to Ferrières, and without its regular offerings, Lupus insists, the monks and servants were going about in tatters.[38] St-Josse was also expected to provide wax, fish, meat, cheese, and vegetables.[39] A lack of provisions, Lupus says, has forced him severely to cur-

32 *Recueil des actes de Charles II le Chauve*, ed. Georges Tessier (Paris, 1943), no. 3, 1: 9–12.

33 Ep. 32, ed. Levillain, 1: 148. On Adalhard see Janet L. Nelson, *Charles the Bald* (Burnt Mill, Harlow, 1992), 56, 70.

34 Nelson, *Charles the Bald*, 107, 121–5. On Odulf's rise to power, see Nithard, *Histoire des fils de Louis le Pieux*, 2.2, ed. Philippe Lauer, Les Classiques de l'histoire de France au Moyen Âge (Paris, 1964), 42.

35 Epp. 36, 42, 43, 45, 47, 48, 49, 57, 58, 59, 61, 65, 82, ed. Levillain, 1: 158–60, 174–8, 178–84, 186–92, 196–8, 198–202, 202–8, 220–4, 224–8, 228–30, 232–4, 238–42, 2: 66.

36 Epp. 84, 85, ed. Levillain, 2: 70–2, 72–4.

37 Ep. 86, ed. Levillain, 2: 74–6.

38 Epp. 42, 48, ed. Levillain, 1: 176, 200.

39 Epp. 42, 47, ed. Levillain, 1: 176, 198.

tail hospitality.[40] Lupus laments that his community has had to sell off its liturgical vessels and ecclesiastical ornaments in order to meet daily requirements.[41] In other letters Lupus complains of a severe shortage of grain.[42] This may or may not have been connected with the loss of St-Josse. Lupus complains that he 'lost everything' while on royal service in the disastrous Aquitanian campaign of 844, and that he lost ten horses when serving as an envoy in Burgundy.[43] More than once he complains that he lacks the wherewithal to attend meetings of the royal court.[44] Lupus pleads with correspondents to believe that in his efforts to recover St-Josse he is seeking, not luxury and extravagance, but mere survival.[45] The picture that emerges is of a Ferrières that was economically fragile and vulnerable. It is a fair guess that many Carolingian monasteries were in that precarious condition. St-Josse was valuable. It is easy to see why it would have been useful bait in royal attempts to catch supporters. And it is just as easy to see how devastating its loss was to Ferrières.

Second, the St-Josse case provides all sorts of clues as to how disputes were settled in ninth-century Francia. Lupus mobilized documents, saints, moral suasion, personal reputation, and political connections in his long-drawn-out battle to get back St-Josse. In order to open up these issues for scrutiny, it will be well to recall what was said above about Lupus' rise to the abbacy of Ferrières.

Lupus' family provided a number of churchmen to the archdiocese of Sens in the middle of the ninth century. Either through his family or through his own connections with Duke Eberhard of Friuli, Lupus effected some kind of a relationship with Empress Judith. On several occasions when Lupus was trying to persuade Charles the Bald to give him back St-Josse, he stressed to the king that the original gift of St-Josse to Ferrières had come about through Judith's generosity. Judith was, of course, Charles' mother. Lupus' family was obviously an important one, but it was not at the front rank of the 'Imperial Aristocracy.'[46] And Lupus, who never got a bishopric, never got one of the realm's truly great monasteries, and never got a court appointment, was not, perhaps, among the

---

40 Epp. 43, 45, ed. Levillain, 1: 180, 204.

41 Ep. 45, ed. Levillain, 1: 188.

42 Epp. 43, 45, ed. Levillain, 1: 180, 188.

43 Ep. 45, ed. Levillain, 1: 190.

44 Ep. 49, ed. Levillain, 1: 204–6.

45 Epp. 48, 49, ed. Levillain, 1: 200, 206.

46 I use this phrase in the customary way since the inception of the work of the 'Tellenbach School' more than a half-century ago. Two recent studies provide different, but complementary, accounts of the status and political activities of noble families: Gerd Althoff, *Verwandte, Freunde und Getreue: Zum politischen Stellenwert der Gruppenbildungen im frühen Mittelalter* (Darmstadt, 1990); Régine Le Jan, *Famille et pouvoir dans le monde franc (VIIᵉ–Xᵉ siècle): Essai d'anthropologie sociale* (Paris, 1995).

most important members of his family. His position was tenuous, as he knew. At least, that is how I take the letters in which Lupus expresses his deep concern at the blows to his reputation occasioned by his loss of St-Josse. Writing to Charles in mid-845 Lupus says, 'I am overwhelmingly dishonored because I have lost what other abbots have obtained by imperial munificence to strengthen religion, as if the lowliest and most worthless of all creatures.'[47] In a letter to Hincmar of Reims, Lupus expresses almost identical sentiments.[48] During or just after his period of captivity in Aquitaine in 844, Lupus was shocked to learn that rumours were abroad suggesting that Ferrières itself had been taken away from him and given to a certain Egilbert. Lupus protests that a great indignity has been inflicted on him in making him the equal of this lay-man.[49] It was undoubtedly humiliating to Lupus that he was esteemed lower than the layman Odulf for so many years.

As many scholars have pointed out, access to power, which in practical terms meant access to the king – *Königsnähe* – was the critical element in polit-ical and social success in the Carolingian world. The royal dynasty itself, nev-ertheless, had to reckon with the might of the very greatest aristocratic families in the Carolingian world. These families were not important because their members held duchies, counties, bishoprics, and abbacies. Rather, they held these offices because they were already important. Possession of secular or ecclesiastical office was a way of perpetuating power and of anchoring it in par-ticular localities that were often far removed from the original seat of that fam-ily's lands and offices. That is why these families are called 'imperial' aristocrats. They had interests all over the Carolingian world.[50] Families that were a rung or two down the social ladder – and I take Lupus' family to be one of these – tended to rise or fall either by marrying into a greater family or by securing preferments from the royal court.[51] Lupus and his clan were dangling from the fringes of real power. Lupus' entreaties concerning St-Josse got polite

47 Ep. 42, ed. Levillain, 1: 178 (trans. Regenos, 58).
48 Ep. 43, ed. Levillain, 1: 180–2.
49 Ep. 36, ed. Levillain, 1: 160.
50 For a brilliant discussion of how Carolingian political life really worked see Nelson, *Charles the Bald*, 41–74.
51 For several complimentary perspectives on these matters see: Hans K. Schulze, 'Reichsaristo-cratic, Stammesadel und fränkische Freiheit,' *Historische Zeitschrift* 227 (1978): 353–73; Anita Garreau-Jalabert, 'Sur les structures de parenté dans l'Europe médiévale,' *Annales: Économies Sociétés Civilisations*, 36 (1981): 1028–49; Régine Hennebicque (Le Jan), 'Struc-tures familiales et politiques au IXe siècle: En group familial de l'aristocratie franque,' *Revue historique* 265 (1981): 289–333; Josef Fleckenstein, 'Adel und Kriegertum und ihre Wandlung im Karolingerreich,' *Settimane* 27 (1981): 67–94; Hans–Werner Goetz, '"Nobilis": Der Adel im Selbstverständnis der Karolingerzeit,' *Vierteljahrschrift für Sozial- und Wirtschafts-geschichte* 70 (1983): 153–91.

hearings and at least twice, in 841 and again in about 852, and Charles gave the cell back to him. But Lupus was not so important that he could not be shunted aside in the political scrambles of the 840s. In one of Lupus' letters to Charles, there is a line whose cutting irony must have stung Lupus himself as he wrote it. He says, 'Fear not the mighty which you yourself have made and can humble whenever you wish.'[52] Such making and humbling is exactly what Lupus himself had to endure.

Family connections of the kind possessed by Lupus were important and useful but not necessarily decisive in accomplishing one's objectives in the ninth century. Personal connections were critical, too. In his campaign to recover St-Josse, Lupus sought the intercession of a considerable number of important people. In early 844 Lupus wrote to Hugh, an illegitimate son of Charlemagne and the abbot of St-Quentin, St-Bertin, and Lobbes. Lupus had not made Hugh's acquaintance, but insisted that he very much wished to do so. In writing to Hugh, Lupus dropped the name of Adalhard, perhaps to make his case seem more credible and worthy of support.[53] Four times Lupus wrote to Louis, a cousin of Charles', who was abbot of St-Denis and archchancellor to Charles the Bald.[54] Three times Lupus wrote to Archbishop Hincmar of Reims, whose importance and influence in the West Frankish realm grew greatly in the 840s and 850s.[55] In a letter to an unknown correspondent, whose assistance he requests, Lupus reveals that he had asked for the help of 'Lady Rh.'[56] He also, finally, called upon his old friend from the Fulda days, Marcward, now abbot of Prüm.[57] In the first of his letters to Abbot Louis, Lupus invoked 'friendship' as the reason why he expected some help. Friendship could have many meanings, and Lupus himself had many kinds of friends, ranging from powerful people at court to fellow scholars and churchmen around the Carolingian world. Friendships, carefully cultivated and prudently tended, represented one very effective means of getting things done.[58] Networks of friends, which often are distinguishable from networks of relatives,[59] made possible the kind of visibility and prominence that important people enjoyed and employed.

---

52 Ep. 31, ed. Levillain, 1: 144.

53 Ep. 32, ed. Levillain, 1: 146–50. On Hugh, see Nelson, *Charles the Bald*, 121.

54 Epp. 36, 45, 47, 82, ed. Levillain, 1: 158–60, 186–92, 196–8, 2: 66.

55 Epp. 43, 48, 59, ed. Levillain, 1: 178–84, 198–202, 228–30.

56 Ep. 61, ed Levillain, 1: 232–4.

57 Ep. 65, ed. Levillain, 1: 238–42.

58 Outstanding on the various kinds of groups to which people belonged is Althoff, *Verwandte, Freunde und Getreue*.

59 Contrast the view of Marc Bloch, *Feudal Society*, trans. L.A. Manyon (Chicago, 1961), 123–4: 'The general assumption seems to have been that there was no real friendship save between persons united by blood.'

But to talk in Lupus' case of bonds created by family and friendship is not at all to deny that formal, institutional structures existed too. Lupus speaks of discussions at the royal court. He himself went to the court to plead his case. One of his letters implies that a hearing of some sort was postponed because Odulf was ill.[60] Several times Lupus stresses that he has documents at his disposal to prove his claims.[61] Several important points are at issue here. First, it is clear from Lupus' willingness to advert to formal, public structures that it is an exaggeration to speak of the Carolingian state as a 'union of persons' that lacked regular institutional means of solving its problems.[62] Institutions and people must be seen in close and intricate relationships with each other. They are not alternative, but rather complimentary, modes of governing. Second, legal disputes were always, in Janet Nelson's words, resolved by 'social mechanisms as well as legal procedures.'[63] Political imperatives, personal connections, family connections, reputations, *Königsnähe*, documents, testimony, courts, and general Frankish assemblies all might play a role in any given dispute. There can be no doubt that the St-Josse case is illustrative of ninth-century dispute settlement, but until someone has worked exhaustively through Hübner's corpus of some 600 cases (257 from the ninth century alone) of Frankish judicial disputes and has tracked the cases through other kinds of sources, it will not be possible to state more than tentatively what our case actually does illustrate.[64] Third, there have been some interesting discussions lately of the place of writing in Carolingian government.[65] Lupus' case is a salutary warning that one must not press too hard a case for or against the significance of writing and of written instruments. Lupus clearly saw written documents as only one weapon in his arsenal, but he referred to them often enough, and with enough insistence and urgency, to make it clear that they were not an insignificant weapon. Again, one suspects that this is normal. Finally, and closely related to the previous point, it

---

60 Ep. 58, ed. Levillain, 1: 226.

61 Epp. 19, 32, 42, 49, ed. Levillain, 1: 102–4, 148, 176, 204.

62 The most recent argument on behalf of Theodor Mayer's old idea of the 'Personenverbandstaat,' is Johannes Fried, 'Der karolingische Herrschaftsverband im 9. Jahrhundert zwischen "Kirche" und "Königshaus,"' *Historische Zeitschrift* 235 (1982): 1–43. For critiques of this point of view see Nelson, 'Legislation and Consensus in the Reign of Charles the Bald,' in *Ideal and Reality in Frankish and Anglo-Saxon Society: Studies Presented to J. M. Wallace-Hadrill*, ed. Patrick Wormald (Oxford, 1983), 202–27; Althoff, *Verwandte*, ix–x, 1–14.

63 'Dispute Settlement in Carolingian West Francia,' in *The Settlement of Disputes in Early Medieval Europe*, ed. Wendy Davies and Paul Fouracre (Cambridge, 1986), 45–64 (the quotation is from p. 45).

64 Rudolf Hübner,*Gerichtsurkunden der fränkischen Zeit*, 2 vols. (Weimar, 1891–3).

65 The issues are pulled together superbly, with copious references, by Nelson, 'Literacy in Carolingian Government,' in *The Uses of Literacy in Early Mediaeval Europe*, ed. Rosamond McKitterick (Cambridge, 1990), 258–96.

seems never to have occurred to Lupus to prepare any forgeries, even though he
lived in a golden age of forgeries. There is much food for thought here. Lupus
seems to have thought that he had a good case and that he had perfectly valid
documents to help him make that case.[66] He did not need either to 'restore' lost
documents or to confect wholly new ones. He also saw himself working within
a web of relationships in which documents had only some persuasive and pro-
bative force. Perhaps forgery is the tool of the weak or, more emphatically, of
the weakly connected.

Another device employed by Lupus, as by his contemporaries generally, was
the gift. On one occasion Lupus sent Charles the Bald a book by Saint Augustine and some jewels.[67] Another time, in the midst of the St-Josse case, Lupus
complained to Abbot Louis that he lacked sufficient gifts for Charles.[68] During
his struggles, Lupus once asked for the help of Bishop Ebroin of Poitiers and to
show his appreciation he sent him an ivory comb.[69] As we have seen, Lupus
asked for assistance from Hincmar. To gain his ends, Lupus sent him ten pine
cones.[70] Lupus himself intervened with Charles on behalf of Ratbert of Corbie
and he expected a gift of fish in partial recompense.[71] To an old friend of his
youth, Odo of Corbie, Lupus once sent peaches.[72] Between 855 and 858 Lupus
wrote to Pope Benedict III to secure copies of some books in the papal
libraries.[73] I have a hunch that Lupus gained his familiarity with the papal collection during an earlier visit to Rome in 849 when Leo IV was pope. On that
occasion Lupus asked his friend Marcward to provide him with two linen gar-
ments and two blue robes so that he could present them to the pope.[74] Thus,
perhaps, did Lupus gain his admission ticket to the library. Gift-giving is an
immense subject whose early medieval dimensions would repay close study. I
merely mention in passing that Lupus gave gifts without reluctance or objection. He seems to have accepted the practice as a way of getting things done.
And his worry that he did not have a good enough gift for Charles suggests that
the right kinds of gifts could be efficacious indeed.

In addition to social, legal, and institutional means, Lupus employed religious ones in his efforts to regain St-Josse. He reminded Lothar in 840 that his
conduct was disrespectful to Saints Peter, Paul, and Mary, in whose names Fer-

66 Goffart, *The LeMans Forgeries*, 4–6, has some good words on this subject.
67 Ep. 124, ed. Levillain, 2: 190.
68 Ep. 45, ed. Levillain, 1: 188.
69 Ep. 23, ed. Levillain, 1: 114.
70 Ep. 108, ed. Levillain, 2: 146.
71 Ep. 52, ed. Levillain, 1: 214.
72 Ep. 106, ed. Levillain, 2: 140.
73 Ep. 100, ed. Levillain, 2: 120–4.
74 Ep. 77, ed. Levillain, 2: 20–2.

rières was dedicated.[75] Lupus asked Abbot Louis to remind Charles that his refusal to do justice threatened him with the loss of the favour of Saint Peter, the gatekeeper of heaven, and he told Charles himself this in a later letter. Lupus also reminded Charles that the monks of Ferrières regularly prayed for him but might be forced to cease doing so.[76] The implications of Lupus' remarks are twofold. On the one hand, the community is so impoverished that it cannot fulfil its liturgical duties. On the other hand, Charles's conduct threatened to place him beyond the efficacy of prayer. The force of Lupus' words on this account take on significance in light of the Memorial Books of the Carolingian world.[77] Kings and great aristocrats, and doubtless many lesser persons too, were eager to have their names entered on the prayer rolls of monastic communities. The constant prayers rendered on behalf of those whose names were entered joined those people to the religious communities and to one another. But they also, and just as importantly, joined the living with the dead, joined this world with the next, and helped to open the way into the next world for those here below. Lupus' references to Saint Peter take on real significance in this context. Lupus was inviting Charles the Bald to be mindful of the loss of his soul. Although I mention it last, I would not care to suggest that this was the least of the strategies used by Lupus to recover his lost cell.

Lupus' career and activities, then, reveal much about both him and his world. Substantial collections of letters, such as those of Boniface, Alcuin, Agobard, and Hrabanus Maurus – to mention only a few other prominent Carolingian figures – will inevitably reveal a great deal of valuable, detailed, and highly circumstantial information. Where Lupus' letters are concerned, they have usually been read for evidence of the career and interests of the humanist and bibliophile who is familiar to most people who have any acquaintance with medieval intellectual history. The Lupus we have been considering in these pages, however, is unlikely to be very well known at all. And yet, as I suggested at the outset, it is this 'situated' Lupus who can most help us to come to an understanding of the Carolingian world. Given that so many have said so much over so long a period of time about Lupus' scholarly work, there is no call here to attempt to add any new information to the dossier. But it may be possible to interrogate the information in that dossier on the basis of assumptions different

---

75 Ep. 19, ed. Levillain, 1: 104.
76 Epp. 45, 47, 57, ed. Levillain, 1: 188, 198, 222.
77 The most recent discussion of this now vast topic, with very good coverage of the literature, is Megan McLaughlin, *Consorting with Saints: Prayer for the Dead in Early Medieval France* (Ithaca, 1994). I think the author of this fine book exaggerates the 'associative' element in memorial prayer at the expense of the intercessory.

from those usually brought to the investigation. In other words, let us conclude by seeing if it is possible, or desirable, to situate Lupus' intellectual endeavours in different ways.

Lupus is primarily known for his letters, and these documents are most widely remembered for their allusions to, and citations of, classical authors. To them we shall return shortly. It is important to bear in mind that Lupus wrote a number of other texts that are typically Carolingian in their scope and interests. The first work to which Lupus turned his hand, done in concert with the Fulda monk Gerolf, was a correction of Hrabanus's commentary on *Numbers*.[78] Given that Lupus himself says that he went to Fulda to study the scriptures, this undertaking is hardly surprising.[79] We have already seen that, in his Fulda days, Lupus compiled a book of Germanic laws. Also while he was at Fulda, Lupus acceded to a request by Abbot Buno of Hersfeld to prepare a life of Saint Wigbert.[80] After his return to Ferrières, Lupus was asked by Waldo of Trier to write a life of Saint Maximinus.[81] At some point Lupus authored a commentary on the poetic meter of Boethius' *Consolation*.[82] During the logomachy over the ideas of Gottschalk of Orbais, Lupus wrote a theological treatise addressing predestination, free will, and redemption. To this treatise he added a collection of patristic proof-texts.[83] This essay and 'bibliography' are learned and interesting, but neither original nor of lasting significance. They show, like his letters on the same subjects to Gottschalk, Hincmar, and Charles,[84] that, in Levillain's words, Lupus knew how 'to tack between the parties.'[85] Three of Lupus' letters to Charles the Bald deserve to be included among the Carolingian *specula principum*.[86] They are distinctive in holding up both classical and Christian examples to the king and they stress the theme of 'common utility' more than is usual for Carolingian writing.[87] One sermon by Lupus is appar-

---

78 Manitius, *Geschichte*, 483.

79 Ep. 1, ed. Levillian, 1: 6–8.

80 Ep. 6, ed. Levillain, 1: 52–6; *Vita Wigberti*, MGH SRM 3: 71–82.

81 Ep. 13, ed. Levillain, 1: 88–90; *Vita Maximini*, MGH SS 15/1: 36–43.

82 Anicius Manlius Severinus Boethius, *Philisophiae Consolationis Libri Quinque*, ed. Rudolf Peiper (Lepizig, 1871), xxiv–xxix. Von Severus, *Lupus*, 13–19.

83 *Liber de tribus quaestionibus*, PL, 119: 619–48; *Collectaneum de tribus quaestionibus*, ibid., 647–66.

84 Epp., 80, 79, 78, ed. Levillain, 2: 42–54, 36–42, 22–36.

85 'Étude,' 451.

86 Epp. 31, 37, 42, ed. Levillain, 1: 140–6, 160–4, 174–8.

87 Von Severus, *Lupus*, 158–64; Hans Hubert Anton, *Fürstenspiegel und Herrscherethos in der Karolingerzeit*, Bonner historische Forschungen 32 (Bonn, 1967), 248–54.

ently extant,[88] though it seems that some poems long attributed to him are unlikely to be by his pen.[89]

Lupus displays a certain intellectual versatility but compared with, say, Theodulf of Orléans, his range appears limited indeed. As a theologian, Lupus seems solid and reliable, but not on a par with his old friend and chief opponent, Gottschalk. Certainly Lupus did not display the virtuosity exhibited by his contemporaries Paschasius Radbertus and Ratramnus in their writings on the eucharist. If Lupus' *specula* use classical examples, they nevertheless do so within an overall attempt to lay out a Christian ethic of rulership. That ethic did not seek to draw special advantages for the church as an institution, so in his writings on rulership Lupus was a bit different from other writers of his age, but not dramatically so. When Jonas of Orléans sent Lupus his *De cultu imaginum* for assessment, Lupus returned it without comment.[90]

Patient research by scholars in recent decades has established convincingly that the contemptuous judgments of earlier generations on the learning, originality, and importance of Carolingian thinkers were seriously flawed. Yet no amount of reassessment of Lupus, even when it is acknowledged that he wrote more than just letters, will move him into the front rank of Carolingian thinkers. The Carolingian Renaissance did not set out to produce geniuses. Its aim was to provide competent teachers. Lupus' writings show that he was that, and perhaps a little more besides.

Given the deplorable state of many of the texts with which Carolingianists must contend, it is astonishing that Lupus' letters have been edited seven times, including prestigious editions by the Monumenta, by the series Les Classiques de l'Histoire de France au Moyen Âge, and by the house of Teubner – an editorial ministration, incidentally, not accorded Lupus' other writings.[91] The reason

---

88 Wilhelm Levison, 'Eine Predigt des Lupus von Ferrières,' in *Kultur und Universalgeschichte: Walter Goetz zu seinem 60. Geburtstag dargebracht von Fachgenossen, Freunden and Schulern* (Leipzig, 1927), 3–14.

89 Von Severus, *Lupus,* 13–19.

90 Ep. 20, ed. Levillain, 1: 106.

91 The editions are those of: Papirius Masson (Paris, 1588), André Du Chesne (Paris, 1640), Etienne Baluze (Paris, 1664; 2d ed. Antwerp, 1710), G. Desdevises du Dezert (Paris, 1889), Ernst Dümmler (Berlin, 1902), Léon Levillain (Paris, 1927, 1935), Peter K. Marshall (Leipzig, 1984). Masson and Du Chesne both worked from the most important MS: Paris, BnF Lat. 2858, which contains only 127 of the 133 extant letters. Baluze used the same MS but procured a better edition. Desdevises du Dezert's edition differed from Baluze's in its attempt to place the letters in chronological order, but his edition of the letters themselves is inferior to Baluze's. Dümmler returned to the order of the letters in the Paris MS but he added six further letters from other MSS, achieved an excellent text, and equipped that text with numerous notes that mark an important advance in scholarship. Levillain, based on his extensive studies published between 1902 and 1904, produced an edition that once again eschewed MS order in

for this long-standing attention to Lupus' correspondence is easy to identify and is intimately connected to old, but dated and dispensable, ways of thinking about European intellectual history generally, and about early medieval intellectual history in particular.

Lupus' letters survive in one principal manuscript dating from the late ninth century and were without discernible readers or influence in the Middle Ages. As soon as his correspondence came to light in the sixteenth century, readers noticed Lupus' references to classical authors. This seemed unusual and intriguing in a 'Dark Age' author. It was Baluze who first authoritatively saw Lupus as a 'humanist,' and his judgment has persisted. Manitius maintained it,[92] as did Edward Kennard Rand, who called Lupus one of 'the great humanists of history.'[93] R.R. Bolgar designates Lupus 'the most active humanist of the ninth century,'[94] and M.L.W. Laistner speaks of Lupus' 'solitary pre-eminence in the field of humanistic studies.'[95] Until the end of the nineteenth century, the judgment that Lupus was a great humanist rested on his allegedly wide acquaintance with classical literature. Of Lupus, John Sandys said, 'A wide knowledge of Latin literature is displayed by his frequent references to Latin authors.'[96] Then, in 1891, Ludwig Traube discovered a manuscript of Valerius Maximus on which Lupus himself had done editorial work.[97] In 1910, Charles

favour of chronological order and that achieved a good text. Finally, Peter Marshall returned to MS order and improved on Dümmler's and Levillain's editions of the letters not in BnF 2858. There is a confusing element in the enumeration of the letters in the various editions. Dümmler and Marshall present 132 letters in the regular sequence, including nos 115 and 115bis. Levillain has 133, because he takes 115 as his 91 and 115bis as his 113. Yet Dümmler has, in a sense, 133, too, because he adds, as additional letter no. 6, a little epistolary treatise, *Quid sit ceroma*, which neither Levillain nor Marhall include. On this letter see Charles Henry Beeson, 'The Authorship of Quid sit Ceroma,' in *Classical and Medieval Studies in Honor of Edward Kennard Rand* (New York, 1938), 1–7; Franz Brunhölzl, *Histoire de la littérature latine du Moyen Âge, Tome 1: De Cassiodore à la fin de la Renaissance carolingienne*, trans. from the German by Henri Rochais (Louvain-la-Neuve, 1991), 233. The 133 letters represent 132 by Lupus and one by Einhard (no. 3). Among Lupus' letters are fifteen (in Levillain's enumeration nos 14–19, 26, 66, 81, 91–4, 98, 128) written by Lupus for other persons ranging from his abbot Odo, to Archbishop Wenilo of Sens, to Queen Ermintrude, to bishops gathered in synod.

92 *Geschichte*, 485; 'Lupus von Ferrières, ein Humanist des 9. Jahrhundert,' *Rheinisches Museum* 48 (1893): 313–20.

93 *Founders of the Middle Ages*, 103.

94 *The Classical Heritage and Its Beneficiaries* (Cambridge, 1954), 118.

95 *Thought and Letters in Western Europe, A.D. 500 to 900*, 2d ed. (Ithaca, 1957), 252.

96 John Sandys, *A History of Classical Scholarship*, 3 vols. (Cambridge, 1920), 1:489; cf. Brunhölzl, *Histoire de la littérature latine*, 229–33.

97 'Zu Valerius Maximus,' in his *Kleine Schriften*, ed. Samuel Brandt, vol. 3 of his *Vorlesungen und Abhandlungen*, ed. Franz Boll (Munich, 1965), 3–14.

Henry Beeson resolved to track down all extant manuscripts which might reveal Lupus' actual work as either copyist or editor.[98] He eventually found eleven such manuscripts, and subsequent research has revealed at least nine more.[99] Lupus, then, was worthy of attention because he read and quoted classical authors and because he sought good manuscripts and tried constantly to achieve accurate texts. Lupus was, in short, a 'renaissance man.' In an academic and intellectual environment dominated by classicists, Lupus had some claim to a place, albeit an inconspicuous one. This extraordinarily narrow view of the Western intellectual tradition made it almost impossible to evaluate figures who did not conform to the classicists' model of what constituted legitimate intellectual endeavour and seriously distorted any possibility of understanding a figure such as Lupus.

The conventional understanding of Lupus' work rests in the first place on his numerous citations of, or allusions to, classical writers. Painstaking research has tended to show, however, that Lupus knew fewer classical authors than was once thought, and that many of his citations were actually taken at second hand from grammarians and commentators, such as Priscian and Servius, or even from Christian writers, such as Augustine or Isidore.[100] This is not at all surprising when it is remembered that Lupus was a teacher and that his primary responsibilities would have revolved around inculcating in his pupils a basic command of the Latin language. The grammatical works that played a critical role in transmitting a knowledge of Latin were full of examples drawn from many classical authors, and any teacher who devoted a lot of his time to working through those texts with students would have had in mind many quotations. In the end, it appears that Lupus can be credited with a knowledge of Cicero that was rare, perhaps unrivalled, in his age.[101] But to claim for him a wide knowledge of classical letters is erroneous.

Another perspective on Lupus' classical quotations and allusions can be derived by comparing them with his use of the Bible and of Christian authors.

98 *Lupus of Ferrières as a Scribe and Text Critic: A Study of His Autograph Copy of Cicero's* De Oratore, Mediaeval Academy Publications 4 (Cambridge, Mass., 1930).

99 E. Pellegrin, 'Les manuscrits de Loup de Ferrières: À propos de manuscrit Orléans 162 (139) corrigé de sa main,' *Bibliothèque de l'école des chartes*, 115 (1957/8): 5–31; Robert Gariépy, 'Lupus of Ferrières: Carolingian Scribe and Text Critic,' *Mediaeval Studies* 30 (1968): 93–4; Bernhard Bischoff, 'Paleographie und frühmittelalterliche Klassikerüberlieferung,' *Settimane* 22 (1974): 59–86.

100 Gariépy, *Lupus of Ferrières and the Classics* (Darien, Conn., 1967); idem, 'Lupus of Ferrières' Knowledge of Classical Latin Literature,' in *Hommages à André Boutemy*, Collection Latomus 145 (Brussells, 1976), 152–8; Marshall, 'The Learning of Servatus Lupus: Some Additions,' *Mediaeval Studies* 41 (1979): 514–23.

101 Gariépy, *Lupus and the Classics*, 36–42; Marshall, 'Learning of Servatus Lupus,' 515.

The excellent index in Marshall's edition of Lupus' letters permits some basic insights into Lupus' reading. Lupus cites twenty-three classical writers at first or second hand. Cicero is cited 22 times, from twelve different works; Vergil, 16 times; and Aulus Gellius, 7 times. All told, Lupus cites classical works 99 times. Lupus also cites seventeen patristic authors a total of 72 times. Augustine, cited 17 times from nine works, is the most frequent. By far, however, the greatest number of references in Lupus' writings come from the Bible. The Psalms alone are cited 45 times, which is about what one would expect from a Benedictine monk. Lupus cites twenty-three books of the Old Testament a total of 133 times, and he cites seventeen New Testament books no fewer than 115 times. Lupus' religious references outnumber his classical ones more than three to one. Quite rightly does John Contreni say that what united all Carolingian scholars, in spite of their different interests, was 'the absolute centrality of the Bible in their intellectual life.'[102]

It is well known that the typical Carolingian attitude towards classical literature was distinctly ambivalent.[103] Generally classical texts were school texts, that is, they were propaedeutic to the study of the Bible and of the major expositors of the biblical corpus. Thus, Lupus has usually seemed different because he professed that classical texts were to be enjoyed for themselves and on their own terms: 'It is quite apparent to me that knowledge should be sought for its own sake.'[104] It is crucial to bear in mind three qualifications to that statement. First, Lupus made that claim in a letter to Einhard in which he was blatantly attempting to curry favour with the old man of letters. He was indulging in a bit of flattery and self-promotion. Second, in what was probably his very last letter, Lupus says that all knowledge comes from God, that God will provide a knowledge of the liberal arts, that the fear of the Lord is true wisdom, and that true wisdom will lead to a virtuous life.[105] Third, that last letter squares nicely with the overall range of Lupus' letters in a way that the first letter to Einhard does not. Many of Lupus' letters develop Christian themes at some length, but not a single letter works out anything that could legitimately be called a classical theme. Lupus requested classical texts, but he sought Christian ones, too. It is a matter of perspective, then, and a just perspective makes Lupus the literary humanist a little harder to see.

One can only admire the meticulous work of those scholars who have identified the manuscripts on which Lupus himself actually worked. But even if

102 'The Pursuit of Knowledge in Carolingian Europe,' in 'Gentle Voices of Teachers,' 110.
103 Giles Brown, 'The Carolingian Renaissance,' in Carolingian Culture: Emulation and Innovation, ed. Rosamond McKitterick (Cambridge, 1994), 38–9.
104 Ep. 1, ed. Levillain, 1: 6 (trans. Regenos, 2).
105 Ep. 133, ed. Levillain, 2: 216–22.

their labours have brought it about that Lupus is today seen more as a scribe and text critic than as a literary humanist, there is still room for a bit more modification of the traditional judgment. Lupus was by no means the only figure in the Carolingian period who was interested in collating manuscripts and in securing accurate texts. The whole Carolingian program enunciated in the *Admonitio generalis* of 789 and in Charlemagne's letter *On the Cultivation of Letters* was premised on securing, copying, and disseminating correct texts.[106] Theodulf of Orleans produced an extraordinary edition of the Bible that, in Contreni's words, is a 'true work of critical editorial scholarship.'[107] At both Laon and Corbie, John Contreni[108] and David Ganz[109] have been able to identify some of the masters who worked on some of the books that once constituted part of the library collections in those places. Other Carolingian libraries remain to be reconstituted, and the individual labours of other Carolingian masters remain to be reconstructed. It is perfectly clear nevertheless that Lupus' efforts were commendable but not unique. He was a man of his time.

This judgment of Lupus' scholarship is perhaps a fitting conclusion also for the brief review of the abbot's life that has been offered here. Lupus of Ferrières worked to some degree in isolation and lacked the grand patronage that a number of his predecessors and successors enjoyed. He was a teacher who seems to have mastered the basic Carolingian educational program, but who did not have a decisive impact on his own times. Much of what he was able to accomplish was possible only because of the various social and familial networks of which he was an integral member. He was, in a variety of ways, an important man, but not a figure at the very front rank. He commanded a purer Latin style than almost anyone else in his age, but his intellectual interests were fairly typical. Lupus is interesting and important to the student of the Carolingians, not because he is peculiar but because he is representative of persons, programs, and possibilities that are often hard to see and difficult to interpret.

106 I hold with the general interpretation of Josef Fleckenstein, *Die Bildungsreform Karls des Grossen als Verwicklichung der norma rectitudinis* (Bigge-Ruhr, 1953), against the stimulating but quirky Ludwig Edelstein, *Eruditio et Sapientia: Weltbild und Erziehung in der Karolingerzeit. Untersuchungen zu Alcuins Briefen* (Freiburg im Breisgau, 1965). The latter work contains (169–218) an assessment of Lupus' letters along lines which I cannot accept. For Charlemagne's documents, see *Capitularia Regum Francorum* 1: 58–9, 78, no. 22 (Admonitio), no. 29 (Epistola de litteris colendis), ed. A. Boretius, MGH LL Capitularia 1 (1883).

107 'Carolingian Biblical Studies,' in *Carolingian Essays*, ed. Uta Renate Blumenthal (Washington, D.C., 1983), 78.

108 *The Cathedral School of Laon from 850 to 930: Its Masters and Manuscripts*, Münchener Beiträge zur Mediävistik und Renaissance-Forschung 29 (Munich, 1978).

109 *Corbie in the Carolingian Renaissance*, Beihefte der Francia 20 (Sigmaringen, 1990).

13

What Was Carolingian Monasticism?
The Plan of St Gall and the
History of Monasticism

RICHARD E. SULLIVAN

Walter Goffart's career as a historian has been exemplary in so many different ways that it is difficult to decide what particular note to sound in order to pay him a proper tribute; perhaps if that question were opened for discussion among his peers, a consensus would soon emerge. In my view, he has repeatedly demonstrated an outstanding gift for wringing from opaque documents fresh but credible insights into what happened in the past. I think, for example, of what he mined that no one else had previously detected from Roman fiscal records or forged Carolingian legal texts or early medieval chronicles. Much of his wizardry has stemmed from his imaginative formulation of questions which he asked of the sources, and his integrity in managing the treacherous interface between what is asked of sources and what they actually say in response.

For this reason it seems appropriate to offer as a contribution to a volume in his honour an exercise in source criticism that will seek to emulate – but is not likely to equal – his prowess in that realm. This essay will examine a single document from the Carolingian age, a drawing known as the 'Plan of St Gall,' in search of assistance in defining a conceptual matrix within which Carolingian monasticism can be described and explained more fruitfully than has been, or is now, the case. The line of inquiry that will be pursued is not the result of a sudden illumination, such as befell Saint Paul or Martin Luther. Rather, it is the product of prolonged reflection on concerns that began to take shape fifty years ago, when a study of Carolingian missionary activity required a serious engagement with Carolingian monasticism. The questions that have so long been a

Versions of this essay were read at a meeting of the Delaware Valley Medieval Association held at Millersville State University on 12 October 1992, and at a convocation at Maryville College, Maryville, Tennessee, on 19 April 1994. I am grateful for suggestions made by members of both audiences. And I am especially indebted to Elizabeth Sullivan Hogg for her skill at exploiting the computer to reconstruct a modern version of the Plan of St Gall that is as ingenious as the original.

preoccupation are fairly simple: What was the essence, the distinctive characteristic, the defining quality of Carolingian monasticism that warrants treating it in its own right? What, if anything, constituted the inner dynamism that explains the change in monasticism during the period extending from the eighth to the tenth century? In brief, what was Carolingian monasticism?

II

Undoubtedly some readers will ask why anyone who has pondered so long over such issues has not turned to where any sensible person seeking understanding about the past turns – to the works of modern scholars who have studied Carolingian monasticism. Certainly there has been no lack of scholarly discourse on the subject.[1] But even a modest sampling of that vast outpouring raises serious doubts about whether historians of Carolingian monastic life have even addressed these questions, let alone answered them. With some justice it can be said that the treatment of monasticism is one of the weaker components of an otherwise impressive scholarly enterprise devoted to the history of the Carolingian era.

This harsh indictment needs fuller demonstration than can be given here, but a few observations will serve to support its validity. One would be hard-pressed to recommend to inquiring readers a brief essay of synthesis that would provide a holistic overview of the essential and unique quality of Carolingian monasticism.[2] Further inquiry suggests that the problem is rooted in the mainstream of scholarly enterprise from which syntheses conventionally draw their substance.

1 A useful, although somewhat outdated, guide to the basic literature on Carolingian monasticism is Giles Constable, *Medieval Monasticism: A Select Bibliography*, Toronto Medieval Bibliographies 6 (Toronto, 1976). More recent, but less comprehensive, are the bibliographies in Arnold Angenendt, *Das Frühmittelalter: Die abendländische Christenheit von 400 bis 900* (Stuttgart, Berlin, and Cologne, 1990), 482–3; and *The New Cambridge Medieval History*, vol. 2: *c.700–c.900*, ed. Rosamond McKitterick (Cambridge, 1995), 995–1002.

2 See, for example, Jean Leclercq, 'Le monachisme du haut Moyen Âge (VIIIᵉ–Xᵉ siècles),' in *Théologie de la vie monastique: Études sur la tradition patristique*, Théologie: Études publiées sous la direction de la Faculté de Théologie S.J. de Lyon-Fourvière 49 (Paris, 1961), 437–45; Réginald Grégoire, 'Il monachesimo carolingio dopo Benedetto d'Aniane (†821),' *Studia Monastica* 24 (1982): 349–80; F. Büll, 'Die Klöster Franken bis zum IX. Jahrhundert,' *Studien und Mitteilungen zur Geschichte des Benediktiner-Ordens und seiner Zweige* 104 (1993): 9–40; Josef Semmler, 'Le monachisme occidental du VIIIᵉ au XIᵉ siècle: Formation et réformation,' *Revue bénédictine* 103 (1993): 68–89; Otto Gerhard Oexle, 'Les moines d'occident et la vie politique et sociale dans le haut Moyen Âge,' *Revue bénédictine* 103 (1993): 255–72; and Mayke de Jong, 'Carolingian Monasticism: The Power of Prayer,' in *New Cambridge Medieval History*, 2: 622–53.

A review of general histories of medieval monasticism[3] and standard manuals of Carolingian church history[4] reveals why those trying to say something significant about Carolingian monasticism in brief terms find it so difficult. Beyond comments on the attempt by the Carolingian rulers to turn the monastic establishment into an instrument supportive of their power, and on the official effort to impose a uniform rule on the monastic establishment, these treatments

3 Philibert Schmitz, *Histoire de l'Ordre de Saint-Benoît*, vols. 1 and 2, 2d ed., rev. and enlarged (Maredsous, 1948–9); Patrice Cousin, *Précis d'histoire monastique*, La vie de l'église (Paris, n.d.); Lowrie J. Daly, *Benedictine Monasticism: Its Formation and Development through the 12th Century* (New York, 1965); David Knowles, *From Pachomius to Ignatius: A Study in the Constitutional History of the Religious Orders* (Oxford, 1966); George Zarnecki, *The Monastic Achievement* (New York, 1972); Karl Suso Frank, *Grundzüge der Geschichte des christlichen Mönchtums*, Grundzüge 25 (Darmstadt, 1975; English translation: *With Great Liberty: A Short History of Christian Monasticism and Religious Orders*, trans. Joseph T. Lienhard, Cistercian Studies Series 104 [Kalamazoo, Mich., 1993]); Edward Wynne, *Traditional Catholic Religious Orders* (New Brunswick, N.J., 1988); C.H. Lawrence, *Medieval Monasticism: Forms of Religious Life in Western Europe in the Middle Ages*, 2d ed. (London and New York, 1989); and Ludovicus Milis, *Angelic Monks and Earthly Men: Monasticism and Its Meaning to Medieval Society* (Woodbridge, U.K., and Rochester, N.Y., 1992).
4 Albert Hauck, *Kirchengeschichte Deutschlands*, 8th. ed., 5 vols. (Berlin and Leipzig, 1954), vols. 1 and 2; Hans von Schubert, *Geschichte der christlichen Kirche im Frühmittelalter* (Tübingen, 1921; repr. 1962); Émile Amann, *L'époque carolingienne*, Histoire de l'église 6 (Paris, 1947); Gert Haendler, *Geschichte des Frühmittelalters und der Germanenmission*, Die Kirche in ihrer Geschichte 2/E (Göttingen and Zürich, 1961); *Handbuch der Kirchengeschichte*, ed. Hubert Jedin, vol. 3: Friedrich Kempf, Hans-Georg Beck, Eugen Ewig, and Josef Andreas Jungmann, *Die mittelalterliche Kirche*, Part 1, *Vom kirchlichen Frühmittelalter zur gregorianischen Reform* (Freiburg, Basel, and Vienna, 1966; English translation: *Handbook of Church History*, ed. Jedin and Joseph Dolan, vol. 3: Friedrich Kempf, Hans-Georg Beck, Eugen Ewig, and Josef Andreas Jungmann, *The Church in the Age of Feudalism*, trans. Anselm Biggs [London and New York, 1969]); David Knowles with Dmitri Obolensky, *The Middle Ages*, The Christian Centuries 2 (New York, 1968); Rosamond McKitterick, *The Frankish Church and the Carolingian Reforms, 789–895*, Royal Historical Society Studies in History (London, 1977); J.M. Wallace-Hadrill, *The Frankish Church*, Oxford History of the Christian Church (Oxford, 1983); Pierre-Patrick Verbraken, *Les premiers siècles: Du collège apostolique à l'empire carolingien*, 2d ed. (Paris, 1984); Gert Haendler, *Die lateinische Kirche im Zeitalter der Karolinger*, Kirchengeschichte in Einzeldarstellungen, ed. Gert Haendler, Kurt Meier, and Joachim Rogge, 1/7 (Berlin, 1985); Jacques Paul, *L'église et la culture en occident, IXᵉ–XIIᵉ siècles*, 2 vols., Nouvelle Clio, l'histoire et ses problèmes 15, 15bis (Paris, 1986); *Histoire de la France religieuse*, ed. Jacques Le Goff and René Rémond, vol. 1: *Des dieux de la Gaule à la papauté d'Avignon (des origines aux XIVᵉ siècle)*, ed. Jacques Le Goff (Paris, 1988), 169–281; Angenendt, *Das Frühmittelalter*, 233–460, especially 401–19; and *Histoire du christianisme du origines à nos jours*, ed. J.-M. Mayeur, C. and L. Petri, A. Vancez, and M. Venard, vol. 4: G. Gagion, P. Riché, and A. Vauchez, *Evêques, moines et empereurs (610–1054)* (Paris, 1993).

are haphazard, disjointed, shaped by a conceptual framework defined by other aspects of Carolingian history, and devoid of coherence.

Even the works of specialized scholars who have laboured patiently with the sources in search of bits and pieces of information about Carolingian monasticism from which to draw a composite picture of what it really was have not served well. Although they have treated Carolingian monasticism from almost every conceivable angle, their efforts have failed to produce a convincing picture of what constituted its fundamental and essential features.[5] Everything considered, it appears that the foxes have had the upper hand over the hedgehogs in this particular field of Carolingian scholarship.[6]

5 The point might be illustrated by a close scrutiny of the scholarly contribution of Josef Semmler, who in a series of works published over the last four decades has established himself as the leading authority on Carolingian monasticism. These works include: 'Zur Überlieferung der monastischen Gesetzgebung Ludwigs des Frommen,' *Deutsches Archiv für Erforschung des Mittelalters* 16 (1960): 309–88; 'Les statuts d'Adalhard de Corbie de l'an 822,' *Le Moyen Âge* 68 (1962): 91–123, 233–69 (with A.E. Verhulst); 'Die Beschlüsse des Aachener Konzils im Jahre 816,' *Zeitschrift für Kirchengeschichte* 74 (1963): 15–82; 'Karl der Grosse und das fränkische Mönchtum,' in *Karl der Grosse: Lebenswerk und Nachleben,* ed. Wolfgang Braunfels, vol. 2: *Das geistige Leben,* ed. Bernhard Bischoff, 2d ed. (Düsseldorf, 1966), 255–89; 'Episcopi potestas und karolingische Klosterpolitik,' in *Mönchtum, Episkopat und Adel zur Gründungzeit des Klosters Reichenau,* ed. Arno Borst, Vorträge und Forschungen 20 (Sigmaringen, 1974), 305–95; 'Pippin III. und die fränkischen Klöster,' *Francia* 3 (1975): 88–146; 'Mönche und Kanoniker im Frankenreich Pippins III. und Karls des Grossen,' in *Untersuchungen zu Kloster und Stift,* Veröffentlichungen des Max-Planck-Instituts für Geschichte 68 (Göttingen, 1980), 78–111; 'Benedictus II: Una regula – una consuetudo,' in *Benedictine Culture, 750–1050,* ed. W. Lourdaux and D. Verhelst, Medievalia Loveniensia, Series 1, Studia 11 (Leuven, 1983), 1–49; 'Le souverain occidental et les communautés religieuses du IXe au début du XIe siècle,' *Byzantion* 61 (1991): 44–70; 'Benediktinische Reform und kaiserliches Privileg: Zur Frage des institutionellen Zusammenschlusses der Kloster um Benedikt von Aniane,' in *Institutionen und Geschichte; Theoretische Aspekte und mittelalterliche Befunde,* ed. Gert Melville, Norm und Struktur 1 (Cologne, 1992), 259–93; and 'Le monachisme occidentale du VIIIe au XIe siècle: Formation et réformation,' *Revue bénédictine* 103 (1993): 68–89. Each study in itself is a gem, reflecting a thorough mastery of the sources, sound judgment in assessing their value, and a firm grasp of the context within which Carolingian monastic history unfolded. Yet most of them are occasional pieces, often prepared to fit collections and structured to contribute to the illumination of themes other than monasticism. For this reason they lack connectedness with each other, and consequently any overall coherence.

6 The limitations on Carolingian scholarship devoted to monasticism have been revealed by the inadequacies of the one major study purportedly treating the subject, Jean Décarreaux, *Moines et monastères à l'époque de Charlemagne* (Paris, 1980), a work marred by an eccentric organization and a narrow thematic focus. Because of the chronological arrangement of his work, Décarreaux' readers are forced to return to his earlier study, *Les moines et la civilisation en Occident: Des invasions à Charlemagne* (Paris, 1962; English translation: *Monks and Civilization: From the Barbarian Invasions to the Reign of Charlemagne,* trans. Charlotte Haldane [London, 1964]), in search of what happened in the monastic world during the eighth century.

Perhaps, in focusing on what may be defined as church history in the conventional sense of that genre, we are looking in the wrong place for a better understanding of the fundamental configuration of Carolingian monasticism. Since the object of the monastic experience has always been a quest for spiritual perfection, it follows that the history of Carolingian spirituality might provide the answers that church histories have failed to supply. Alas, that is not the case. As Rosamond McKitterick observed, 'the history of the development of Carolingian religious sensibility has yet to be written.'[7] Proof of this observation is evident in recent histories of medieval spirituality, which are uniformly tentative, even evasive, on the essence of being a Christian during the Carolingian age.[8] These studies would not have helped Charlemagne in answering the poignant question he posed to his bishops, abbots, and counts in a capitulary dated 811: 'Are we really Christians?'[9] They tell even less about what it meant to be a monk in Charlemagne's world.

Perhaps this situation is changing. Chiefly as a consequence of conceptual and methodological stimuli provided by historians of mentalities and popular culture, and by practitioners of social history and the 'new cultural history,' there are signs that a new day may be at hand in the investigation of Carolingian spirituality.[10] However, it appears unlikely that these new approaches will

---

What they will find there is hardly worth the effort in terms of contributing to a holistic picture of Carolingian monasticism. In search of light on eighth-century monasticism, their time could be better spent with Friedrich Prinz, *Frühes Mönchtum im Frankenreich: Kultur and Gesellschaft in Gallien, den Rheinlanden und Bayern am Beispiel der monastischen Entwicklung (4. bis 8. Jahrhundert)*, 2d ed. (Munich, 1988), but unfortunately Prinz stops his inquiry before reaching the heart of the Carolingian age. Given the scholary stature of its particpants, the collaborative effort that emerged from an early Settimane at Spoleto on early medieval monasticism did not produce as much insight into Carolingian monasticism as might have been expected; see *Il monachesimo nell' alto medioevo e la formazione della civiltà occidentale*, *Settimane* 4 (Spoleto, 1957).

7 McKitterick, *Frankish Church*, 158, n. 5.

8 See, for example, Jean Leclercq, François Vandenbroucke, and Louis Bouyer, *La spiritualité du Moyen Âge*, Histoire de spiritualité 2 (Paris, 1961; English translation: *The Spirituality of the Middle Ages*, A History of Spirituality 2 [New York, 1982]); Léopold Genicot, *La spiritualité médiévale* (Paris, 1971); André Vauchez, *La spiritualité du Moyen Âge occidental: VIIIᵉ-XIIᵉ siècles*, Collection SUP (Paris, 1975); English translation: *The Spirituality of the Medieval West: From the Eighth to the Twelfth Century*, trans. Colette Friedlander, Cistercian Studies Series 145 [Kalamazoo, Mich., 1993]); *Christian Spirituality: Origins to the Twelfth Century*, ed. Bernard McGinn, John Meyendorff, and Jean Leclercq, World Spirituality 16 (London, 1987); and Jean Chélini, *L'aube du Moyen Âge: Naissance de la chrétienté occidentale: La vie religieuse des laïcs dans l'Europe carolingienne (750–900)* (Paris, 1991).

9 *Capitularia*, no. 71, c. 9, ed. Alfred Boretius, MGH LL, Capitularia Regum Francorum (Hanover, 1883), 1: 161.

10 Examples of new ways of treating new themes related to Carolingian spirituality are illustrated

throw much light on Carolingian monasticism. They have focused attention chiefly on popular religion and lay piety, arenas which currently seem more socially relevant, and even more politically correct, and thus more appealing, than does the monastic religious experience driven by an ethos at once world-denying and élitist.[11] Moreover, in the main, these studies reflecting a new orientation in the approach to early medieval spirituality embrace an era far longer

by the following studies: Jean-Louis Flandrin, *Le temps d'embrasser, aux origines de la morale sexuelle occidentale, VIe–XIe siècles* (Paris, 1963); J.-C. Poulin, *L'idéal de la sainteté dans l'Aquitaine carolingienne* (Quebec, 1975); Pierre J. Payer, *Sex and the Penitentials: The Development of a Sexual Code, 550–1150* (Toronto, 1984); *Histoire des saints et de la sainteté chrétienne*, vol. 4: *Les voies nouvelles de la sainteté, 605–814*, ed. Pierre Riché; vol. 5: *Les saintetés dans les empires rivaux, 815–1053*, ed. Pierre Riché (Paris, 1986); *Segni e riti nella chiesa altomedievale occidentale*, 2 vols., *Settimane* 33 (Spoleto, 1987); Yvette Duval, *Auprès des saints corps et âme: L'inhumation 'ad sanctos' dans la chrétienté d'orient et d'occident du IIIe au VIIe siècle* (Paris, 1988); *Santi e demoni nell' alto medioevo occidentale (secoli V–XI)*, 2 vols., *Settimane* 36 (Spoleto, 1989); Frederick S. Paxton, *Christianizing Death: The Creation of a Ritual Process in Early Medieval Europe* (Ithaca, N.Y., 1990); Thomas Head, *Hagiography and the Cult of Saints: The Diocese of Orléans, 800–1200*, Cambridge Studies in Medieval Life and Thought 4 (Cambridge, 1990); Valerie I. J. Flint, *The Rise of Magic in Early Medieval Europe* (Princeton, N.J., 1991); *Les fonctions des saintes dans l'monde occidental (IIIe–XIIIe siècle): Actes du colloque organisé par l'École française de Rome avec le concours de l'Université de Rome 'La Sapienza,' Rome, 27–29 octobre 1988*, Collection de l'École française de Rome 149 (Rome, 1991); and James C. Russell, *The Germanization of Early Medieval Christianity: A Sociohistorical Approach to Religious Transformation* (New York and Oxford, 1994). For some comments on the impact of these new approaches on Carolingian historiography, see Richard E. Sullivan, 'Introduction: Factors Shaping Carolingian Studies,' in *'The Gentle Voices of Teachers': Aspects of Learning in the Carolingian Age*, ed. Sullivan (Columbus, Ohio, 1995), 24–8.

11 Some of the promise and the problems associated with these areas of research are highlighted in the following works: Raoul Manselli, *La religione popolare nel medioevo (sec. VI–XII)*, Corsi universitari (Turin, 1974); Manselli, *La religion populaire au Moyen Âge: Problèmes de méthode et d'histoire*, Conférence Albert-le-Grand (Montreal, 1975); *La religion populaire dans l'occident chrétien: Approches historiques*, ed. Bernard Plongeron, Bibliothèque Beauchesne: Religions, société, politique 2 (Paris, 1976); *La piété populaire au Moyen Âge. Actes du 99e Congrès national des sociétés savants, Besançon 1974, Philologie et histoire jusqu' à 1610* (Paris, 1977); Oronzo Giordano, *Religiosità popolare nell' alto medioevo* (Bari, 1979); E. Delaruelle, *La piété populaire au Moyen Âge* (Turin, 1980); John Van Engen, 'The Christian Middle Ages as an Historiographical Problem,' *American Historical Review* 91 (1986): 519–52; Michel Lauwers, '"Religion populaire," culture folklorique, mentalités: Notes sur une anthropologie culturelle du Moyen Âge,' *Revue d'histoire ecclésiastique* 82 (1987): 221–58; André Vauchez, *Les laïcs au Moyen Âge: Pratiques et experiences* (Paris, 1987); and Rudi Künzel, 'Paganisme, syncrétisme et culture religieuse populaire au haut Moyen Âge: Réflexions de méthode,' *Annales: Économies, sociétés, civilisations* 47 (1992): 1055–69. Efforts to approach the Carolingian spiritual experience from this perspective are exemplified by the following: *Cristianizzazione ed organizzazione ecclesiastica delle compagne nell'alto medioevo: Espansione e resistenze*, 2 vols., *Settimane* 28 (Spoleto, 1982); *Histoire de la France religieuse*, ed. Le Goff and Rémond, 1: 417–95; Chélini, *L'aube du Moyen Âge*; Russell, *Ger-*

than has been conventionally defined as the Carolingian age. As a consequence, what they have to say about spirituality and its place in the monastic world can hardly be made exclusive to the Carolingian world.

Whether one looks to essays of synthesis, histories of monasticism, general church histories, studies devoted specifically to Carolingian monasticism, or treatments of early medieval spirituality, a single impression emerges: their authors appear anxious to avoid Carolingian monasticism. They seem reluctant to leave behind the exhilarating world of late antiquity, with its heroic desert fathers, its prodigious 'athletes of Christ,' its renowned rule-makers, and its holy men and women whose careers have caused almost as much stir in recent times as they did in their own. And they give the impression of being anxious to get beyond Carolingian times to the heady era of monastic renewal at Cluny and Citeaux and its impact in reshaping the ethos of the entire society of the High Middle Ages, with only an obligatory glance at the dreary chasm separating two heroic ages in monastic history.

What lies at the root of this apparent inability to make sense out of Carolingian monasticism? Perhaps Carolingianists are impaired by the deep-seated bias in the modern and postmodern mentality that sees monasticism as an aberrant response to the human condition, incapable by definition of adding anything constructive to the development of civilization. Perhaps the treatment of Carolingian monasticism has been diminished by structuralist approaches to the past that have cast doubt on the distinctiveness of many phenomena once called 'Carolingian.' Indeed, much has happened recently in the study of late antiquity and the early Middle Ages to challenge the role long attributed to Charlemagne as *Europae pater*[12] and to focus attention instead on developments in the eighth and ninth centuries that reflect continuity rather than disjunction. It has become increasingly difficult to avoid the conclusion that the only thing 'Carolingian' was a dynasty whose great failure was that it could only produce 'event' history which had no impact on societal structures in 'la longue durée.' In brief, perhaps there was no such thing as 'Carolingian' monasticism about which meaningful history can be written.[13]

---

manization of Early Medieval Christianity; and Julia M.H. Smith, 'Religion and Lay Society,' in *New Cambridge Medieval History*, 2: 654–78.

12 The nomenclature used by a contemporary of Charlemagne; see D.A. Bullough, '*Europae Pater*: Charlemagne and His Achievements in the Light of Recent Scholarship,' *English Historical Review* 85 (1970): 59–105.

13 For remarks on the place of the Carolingian age in the historical continuum and on the impact of modern ideological and methodological movements on Carolingian historiography, see Richard E. Sullivan, 'The Carolingian Age: Reflections on Its Place in the History of the Middle Ages,' *Speculum* 64 (1989): 267–306; and Sullivan, 'Factors Shaping Carolingian Studies,' 1–50.

But these questionable explanations of the constraints that afflict the study of Carolingian monasticism seem hardly worth pursuing in the light of another consideration that is conceptual in nature. For a long time, the treatment of all aspects of Carolingian history has been given shape and direction by an approach defined by the success or failure of a program of *renovatio* undertaken by the royal dynasty and its small circle of counsellors. This approach has meant that the history of virtually every aspect of Carolingian civilization has been plotted along a trajectory marked off by critical stages related to the effort to 'correct' society: the displacement of the 'do-nothing' Merovingian kings, under whose rule the Frankish world had sunk to 'a state of barbarousness' requiring renewal;[14] the setting of the stage for rebirth through the efforts of Charles Martel and Pepin III to establish order and muster the material and human resources required to rebuild the social and moral order; the proclamation of the program of *renovatio* and its vigourous enactment by Charlemagne, Louis the Pious, and Charles the Bald;[15] and finally the descent into a second 'dark age,' marked by the ascendancy of everything contrary to the reforming spirit.[16]

When applied to the investigation of monasticism, the 'renaissance' approach led to an examination in what might be called a reactive mode. Most aspects of monastic activity have been treated in terms of how individual monks, particular monastic houses, and the monastic establishment in general responded to the official reforming policy. At the epicentre of the Carolingian monastic experience cast in this renewal mode stood the official effort led by Benedict of Aniane to reform the monastic world. In a sense, the legislation

14   As Walafrid Strabo put it in his prologue to Einhard's biography of Charlemagne; see *Éginhard, Vie de Charlemagne*, ed. and trans. Louis Halphen, 3d ed., rev. and corrected, Les classiques de l'histoire de France au Moyen Âge (Paris, 1947), 106.

15   A salubrious development in recent Carolingian historiography has been a sharing out of credit for 'renewing' society to others than Charlemagne. The long struggle to give Louis his due as a constructive force culminated recently with the publication of a rich collection of studies whose title somewhat ungraciously capitalizes on his father's name but whose content serves 'des grossen Kaisers kleiner Sohn' with distinction; see *Charlemagne's Heir: New Perspectives on the Reign of Louis the Pious (814–840)*, ed. Peter Godman and Roger Collins (Oxford, 1990). The role of Charles the Bald has been put in relief by *Charles the Bald, Court and Kingdom*, ed. Margaret T. Gibson and Janet L. Nelson, 2d ed. (Aldershot, 1990); and Janet L. Nelson, *Charles the Bald*, The Medieval World (London and New York, 1992).

16   Recent interpretations of the tenth century make it increasingly difficult to accept the onset of a new 'dark age' at the end of the ninth century; see, for example, Heinrich Fichtenau, *Lebensordnungen des 10. Jahrhunderts: Studien über Denkart und Existenz im einstigen Karolingerreich*, 2 vols. (Stuttgart, 1984; English translation: *Living in the Tenth Century: Mentalities and Social Orders*, trans. Patrick J. Geary [Chicago and New York, 1991]); and *Il secolo di ferro: Mito e realtà dal secolo X*, 2 vols., *Settimane* 38 (Spoleto, 1991).

enacted at the councils of Aachen in 816 and 817 has defined what Carolingian monasticism was all about: it was about the effort of the royal establishment to impose *una regula et una consuetudo*, unity of structure and conformity in practice, on the entire monastic establishment.[17]

The exploration of Carolingian monastic history in a context defined by an official program of reform pursued by the Carolingian power establishment has expanded our understanding of the involvement of monks and monasteries in one particular strand of Carolingian history, the so-called Carolingian 'renaissance.' But for those concerned with monasticism *per se*, the cost has been high on two counts.

First, the treatment of monasticism within an explanatory paradigm focused on a renewal movement that ultimately fell far short of its ambitious goals has left a negative picture of Carolingian monasticism. Monastic life in that era has emerged as a directionless enterprise, buffeted by royal, episcopal, and aristocratic manipulation; mismanaged by greedy lay abbots; overburdened with wealth and worldly concerns; befuddled by a tentative comprehension of the ascetic ideal; and unfairly saddled with a major responsibility to devise an educational and spiritual program fit, not for a community of saints, but for unlettered, quasi-pagan, morally inert barbarians.[18] Each of these afflictions was in

17 The point is made with special force by Semmler, 'Benedictus II: Una regula-una consuetudo,' in *Benedictine Culture*, ed. Lourdaux and Verhelst, 1–49. For the synodal acts, see 'Legislatio Aquisgranensis,' ed. J. Semmler, in *Corpus Consuetudinum Monasticarum*, ed. Kassius Hallinger, vol. 1: *Initia Consuetudinis Benedictinae: Consuetudines Saeculi Octavi et Noni* (Siegburg, 1963), 432–81.

18 The negative tone suggested here is illustrated by works such as the following: Karl Voigt, *Die karolingische Klosterpolitik und die Niedergang des westfränkischen Königtums: Laienäbte und Klosterinhaber*, Kirchenrechtliche Abhandlungen 90–91 (Stuttgart, 1917; repr. Amsterdam, 1965); T.P. McLaughlin, *Le très ancien droit monastique de l'Occident: Étude sur le développement général du monachisme et ses rapports avec l'église seculière et le monde laïque de saint Benoît de Nursie à saint Benoît d'Aniane* (Ligugé and Paris, 1935); Lorenz Weinrich, *Wala, Graf, Mönch und Rebell: Die Biographie eines Karolingers*, Historische Studien 386 (Lübeck, 1963); Friedrich Prinz, *Klerus und Krieg in früheren Mittelalter: Untersuchungen zur Rolle der Kirche beim Aufbau der Königsherrschaft*, Monographien zur Geschichte des Mittelalters 2 (Stuttgart, 1971); Joachim Wollasch, *Mönchtum des Mittelalters zwischen Kirche und Welt*, Münstersche Mittelalter-Schriften 7 (Munich, 1972); Arnold Angenendt, *Monachi peregrini. Studien zu Pirmin und den monastischen Vorstellungen des frühen Mittelalters* (Münster, 1972); Ludolf Kuchenbuch, *Bäuerliche Gesellschaft und Klosterherrschaft im 9. Jahrhundert: Studien zur Sozialstruktur der Familie der Abtei Prüm*, Vierteljahrschrift für Sozial- und Wirtschaftsgeschichte, Beihefte 66 (Wiesbaden, 1978); Franz J. Felten, *Äbte und Laienäbte im Frankenreich: Studie zum Verhältnis von Staat und Kirche im früheren Mittelalter*, Monographien zur Geschichte des Mittelalters 20 (Stuttgart, 1980); Karl Suso Frank, 'Vom Kloster als schola dominici servitii zum Kloster als servitium imperii,' *Studien und Mitteilungen zur Geschichte des Benediktiner-Ordens und seiner Zweige*

some way a by-product of a failed 'renaissance,' the demands of which were beyond the resources of the monastic establishment that lacked any self-propelling dynamism derived from its own historical experience and its fundamental and unique character.[19]

Second, the persistent reading of the Carolingian monastic experience as a response to an officially defined and instituted reform program that sought to impose unity on a badly divided society has cut monastic scholarship off from a fructifying impulse that has energized much of recent Carolingian scholarship. The long search for the common institutional and ideological elements, which were once presumed to give Carolingian civilization its unique configuration,

91 (1980): 80–97; G. Moyse, 'Monachisme et réglementation monastique en Gaul avant Benoît d'Aniane,' in *Sous la règle de saint Benoît: Structures monastiques et sociétés en France, du Moyen Âge à l'époque moderne: Actes du Colloque tenu à l'Abbaye bénédictine Sainte-Marie de Paris, 23–25 octobre 1980*, ed. J. Dubois (Paris, 1982), 3–19; Fred Schwind, 'Zu karolingerzeitlichen Klöstern als Wirtschaftsorganismen und Stätten handwerklicher Tätigkeit,' in *Institutionen. Kultur und Gesellschaft im Mittelalter: Festschrift für Josef Fleckenstein zu seinem 65. Geburtstag*, ed. Lutz Fenske, Werner Rösner, and Thomas Zotz (Sigmaringen, 1984), 101–23; Brigitte Kasten, *Adalhard von Corbie: Die Biographie eines karolingischen Politikers und Klostervorstehers*, Studia humaniora 3 (Düsseldorf, 1985); Alain Dierkens, *Abbayes et chapitres entre Sambre et Meuse (VIIe–XIe siècles): Contribution à l'histoire religieuse des campagnes du haut Moyen Âge*, Beihefte der Francia 14 (Sigmaringen, 1985); Herbert Zielinski, 'Die Kloster- und Kirchengründungen der Karolinger,' in *Beiträge zu Geschichte und Struktur der mittelalterlichen Germania Sacra*, ed. Irene Cruzius, Veröffentlichungen des Max-Planck-Instituts für Geschichte 93, Studien zu Germania Sacra 17 (Göttingen, 1989), 95–134; *Herrschaft und Kirche: Beiträge zur Entstehung und Wirkungsweise episkopaler und monastischer Organisationsformen*, ed. Friedrich Prinz, Monographien zur Geschichte des Mittelalters 33 (Stuttgart, 1988), 147–296, 297–343, 345–85 (studies by Franz J. Felten, Ludolf Kuchenbuch, and Dieter Hägermann); Jean-Pierre Devroey, '"Ad utilitatem monasterii": Mobiles et préoccupations de gestion dans l'économie monastique du monde franc,' *Revue bénédictine* 103 (1993): 224–40; and Oexle, 'Les moines d'occident,' 255–72.

19 One historian recently put the point this way: 'Le monachisme a déjà une longue histoire au moment où les rois francs soumettent à leur authorité la plus grande partie de l'Europe occidentale. Aussi la vie monastique est-elle, dans l'Empire, autant un héritage du passé que le fruit de la renaissance carolingienne': see Paul, *L'église et la culture en occident*, 1: 103. For some sobering reflections on the limitations of the renaissance concept as a heuristic tool, see Janet Nelson, 'On the Limits of the Carolingian Renaissance,' in *Renaissance and Renewal in Christian History*, ed. Derek Baker, Studies in Church History 14 (Oxford, 1977), 51–69 (repr. in Nelson, *Politics and Ritual in Early Medieval Europe* [London, 1986], 49–68); Anita Guerreau-Jalabert, 'La "Renaissance carolingienne": Modèles culturels, usages linguistiques et structures sociales,' *Bibliothèque de l'École des chartes* 139 (1981). 5–35; and Carol Heitz, 'Renaissances éphémères du haut Moyen Âge (VIIe–XIe siècles),' in *De Tertullien aux Mozarabes: Mélanges offerts à Jacques Fontaine à l'occasion de son 70e anniversaire, par ses élèves, amis et collègues*, ed. Louis Holtz, Jean-Claude Fredouille, and Marie Hélène Jullien, 2 vols., Collection des études augustiniennes, série Moyen-Âge et temps modernes 26 (Paris, 1992), 2: 129–40.

has ironically discovered just the opposite. Instead of finding a society whose fundamental features were marked by shared, common, unifying institutions, practices, and ideas which touched the lives of all in a decisive way, modern scholars have revealed a world characterized by marked diversity in every facet of life. Cultural plurality now seems much more characteristic of the Carolingian period than does cultural unity. Until the Carolingian monastic world can be placed in that context of cultural diversity and its accompanying tensions, it is unlikely that modern scholars will be able to understand it fully.[20]

These reflections on the historiography of Carolingian monasticism lead to one conclusion: the investigation of that subject has been constrained by a conceptual paradigm that has demonstrable limitations. What is needed is a new conceptual approach capable of evoking new questions about that phenomenon that would give more coherent shape to the evidence available about Carolingian monastic history. The only corrective is to return to the sources in search of a more fruitful hermeneutical tool.

III

As already noted, attention here will focus on a single source in the form of a sketch measuring about 30 3/4 inches by 44 3/16 inches (78 cm by 112 cm) traced out in red ink on a surface made up of five separate pieces of parchment sewn together.[21] Figure 1 represents a modernized version of that 'map.' According to a transmittal letter inscribed on the upper border of the manuscript, the sketch represents 'the layout of monastic buildings' sent by an unidentified figure to his 'sweetest son' Gozbert, abbot of St Gall from 816 to

20 On this point, see Sullivan, 'The Carolingian Age,' *Speculum* 64 (1989): 287–97. The studies included in *Monastische Reformen im 9. und 10. Jahrhundert*, ed. Raymund Kottje and Helmut Maurer, Vorträge und Forschungen 38 (Sigmaringen, 1989), suggest some new approaches to the idea of reform as applied to Carolingian monasticism. That something may be amiss in the prevailing conceptual approach to the study of the Carolingian age was hinted at in the papers presented at a Spoleto Settimane in 1979 and published under the title *Nascita dell'-Europa et Europa carolingia: Un'equazione da verificare*, 2 vols., *Settimane* 27 (Spoleto, 1981).

21 Now preserved as St Gall, Stiftsbibliothek, MS 1092. There are three fundamental studies which not only summarize the major thrust of earlier scholarship, but also provide admirable summaries of the present *état de question* with respect to the Plan; they are: Walter Horn and Ernest Born, *The Plan of St. Gall: A Study of the Architecture and Economy of, and Life in a Paradigmatic Carolingian Monastery*, 3 vols., University of California Studies in the History of Art 19 (Berkeley, Los Angeles, and London, 1979); Konrad Hecht, *Der St. Galler Klosterplan* (Sigmaringen, 1983); and Werner Jacobsen, *Der Klosterplan von St. Gallen und die karolingishe Architektur: Entwicklung und Wandel von Form und Bedeutung im fränkischen Kirchenbau zwischen 751 und 840* (Berlin, 1992).

262   Richard E. Sullivan

837, to be used as its recipient saw fit.[22] It is now agreed, chiefly on paleographical grounds, that the drawing was prepared at the monastery of Reichenau,[23] perhaps shortly before 830, at the time when Gozbert was making plans for a major building program at St Gall. Although many scholars have argued that the Plan was designed and sent at the instigation of Haito, who served concurrently as bishop of Basel (802-823) and abbot of Reichenau (806–23) and was a prominent figure in the political and ecclesiastical affairs of the Carolingian world, the Plan's author remains problematic.[24] The Plan outlines forty separate buildings and their inner compartments, as well as open spaces for gardens and a cemetery. To aid in interpreting the sketch, two different Reichenau scribes provided 340 precise, often highly technical, inscriptions indicating the function of most of the buildings and their individual chambers, and providing identifications of the furniture and equipment in them.[25]

Since it became a subject of serious scholarly concern in the middle of the nineteenth century, the Plan of St Gall has evoked a huge outpouring of scholarship concerned with many problematic aspects of the sketch.[26] One of these issues will be the focus of our exploration: What did the designer of the Plan intend the sketch to be?

Building on previous conjectures about the origin of the Plan, Walter Horn and Ernest Born argued that the Plan was a copy of an official architectural statement inspired by the ideals of Benedict of Aniane and worked out at the court of Louis the Pious in connection with two synods concerned with monastic reform held at Aachen in 816 and 817. That official plan was intended to serve as a paradigmatic guide for all monastic construction in the Carolingian

22 Horn and Born, *Plan of St. Gall*, 1: 9, for the text and translation of the transmittal letter. As we shall see below, that translation has been challenged.
23 Bernhard Bischoff, 'Die Entstehung des Klosterplanes in paläographischer Sicht,' in *Studien zum St. Galler Klosterplan*, ed. Johannes Duft, Mitteilungen zur vaterländischen Geschichte 42 (St Gallen, 1962), 67–78 (repr. in Bischoff, *Mittelalterliche Studien: Ausgewählte Aufsätze zur Schriftkunde und Literaturgeschichte*, 3 vols. [Stuttgart, 1966–81], 1: 41–9).
24 The case for Haito's role is presented by Horn and Born, *Plan of St. Gall*, 1: 11–12. The case against Haito's authorship is summed up by Jacobsen, *Klosterplan von St. Gallen*, 327–8.
25 Horn and Born, *Plan of St. Gall*, 3: 1–88, for a catalogue of all these inscriptions accompanied by a translation into English.
26 Good overviews of that scholarship and the major problems associated with the interpretation of the Plan are provided by Johannes Duft, 'Aus der Geschichte der Klosterplans und seiner Erforschung,' in *Studien zum St. Galler Klosterplan*, ed. Duft, 33–56; Horn and Born, *Plan of St. Gall*, 1: 1–125; Alfons Zettler, 'Der St. Galler Klosterplan: Überlegungen zu seiner Herkunft und Entstehung,' in *Charlemagne's Heir*, ed. Godman and Collins, 655–87; and Jacobsen, *Klosterplan von St. Gallen*, 15–33, 321–32. Comprehensive bibliographies of modern literature are provided by Horn and Born, *Plan of St. Gall*, 3: 167–200; and Jacobsen, *Klosterplan von St. Gallen*, 335–73.

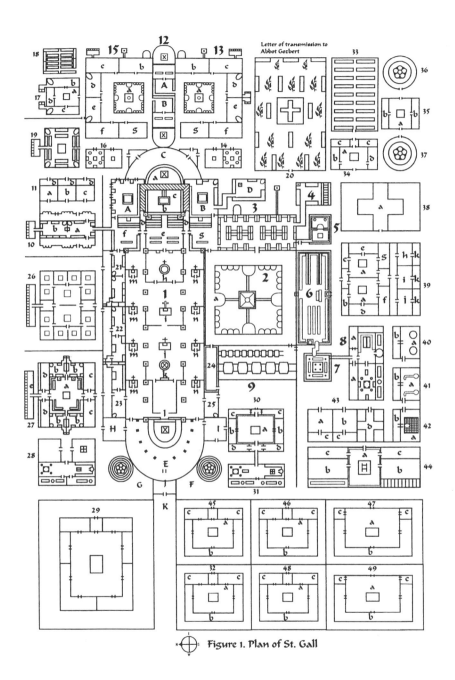

Figure 1. Plan of St. Gall

KEY TO FIGURE 1

1. MAIN CHURCH
A. Scriptorium with Library (above)
B. Sacristy with Vestry (above)
C. East Atrium (Paradise)
D. Room for Baking Communion Bread and Pressing Holy Oil
E. West Atrium (Paradise) with Roof
F. South Tower with altar to St Gabriel at top
G. North Tower with altar to St Michael at top
H. North Porch
I. South Porch
J. West Porch
K. Access Road
a. East Apse with altar to St Paul
b. Main Altar dedicated to Mary and St Gall
c. Sarcophagus
d. Entrance and Exit to Passage to Crypt (below Main Altar)
e. Choir with steps to Main Altar; altars of St Benedict and St Columban on either side; passage under steps to crypt
f. North Transept Chapel, with altar of Sts Philip and James
g. South Transept Chapel, with altar of St Andrew
h. Pulpit
i. Altar of the Holy Cross
j. Altar of John the Baptist and John the Evangelist
k Baptismal Font
l. West Apse with Choir and Altar of St Peter
m. North Aisle with altars of St Stephen, St Martin, the Holy Innocents, and Sts Lucia and Cecilia
n. South Aisle with altars of St Lawrence, St Mauritius, St Sebastian, and Sts Agatha and Agnes
2. CLOISTER YARD with arcades
a. Gallery for meetings
3. MONKS' DORMITORY WITH WARMING-ROOM (below)
4. MONKS' PRIVY
5. MONKS' LAUNDRY AND BATH HOUSE
6. MONKS' REFECTORY WITH VESTIARY (above)

7. MONKS' KITCHEN
8. MONKS' BAKE AND BREW HOUSE, with servants quarters (a)
9. MONKS' CELLAR WITH LARDER (above)
10. ABBOT'S HOUSE
a. Sitting Room with fireplace
b. Bedroom with fireplace and privy
11. ABBOT'S KITCHEN (c), CELLAR (b), BATH (a) and SERVANTS' ROOMS (d)
12. SECOND CHURCH
A. Chapel for Novitiate
B. Chapel for Infirmary
13. NOVITIATE
a. Novices' Cloister Yard
b. Novices' Warming Room with Furnace and Smoke Stack
c. Novices' Dormitory with Privy
d. Novices' Sick Room with Fireplace and Privy
e. Quarters for Master of Novices with Fireplace and Privy
f. Novices' Refectory
g. Store Room
14. KITCHEN AND BATH FOR NOVICES
15. INFIRMARY
a. Infirmary Cloister Yard
b. Infirmary Warming Room with Furnace and Smoke Stack
c. Infirmary Dormitory with Privy
d. Sitting Room for the Ill with Fireplace and Privy
e. Quarters for Master of Infirmary with Fireplace and Privy
f. Infirmary Refectory
g. Store Room
16. KITCHEN AND BATH FOR INFIRMARY
17. PHYSICIANS' HOUSE
a. Central Chamber with Open Hearth
b. Physicians' Bedroom with Fireplace and Privy
c. Chamber for Critically Ill with Fireplace and Privy
d. Pharmacy

18. MEDICINAL HERB GARDEN
19. BLOOD-LETTING HOUSE
20. CEMETERY AND ORCHARD with graves and trees
21. LODGING FOR VISITING MONKS with Fireplaces and Privy
22. LODGING OF MASTER OF THE EXTERNAL SCHOOL with Fireplace and Privy
23. LODGING OF PORTER with Fireplace and Privy
24. PARLOUR FOR MONKS' VISITORS
25. LODGING OF MASTER OF THE HOSPICE FOR PILGRIMS AND PAUPERS with Fireplace
26. EXTERNAL SCHOOL (2 central study halls with 12 student rooms and privy)
27. HOUSE FOR DISTINGUISHED VISITORS
 a. Central chamber with open hearth and dining tables
 b. Bedrooms with fireplaces and privies
 c. Servants' quarters
 d. Horse stalls
 e. Privy
28. KITCHEN, BAKE AND BREW HOUSE FOR DISTINGUISHED GUESTS
29. QUARTERS FOR RETINUE OF DISTINGUSIHED GUESTS (?)
30. HOSPICE FOR PILGRIMS AND PAUPERS
 a. Central chamber with open hearth
 b. Dormitories
 c. Servants' quarters
 d. Cellar and supply room
31. KITCHEN AND BAKE HOUSE FOR HOSPICE FOR PILGRIMS AND PAUPERS
32. HOUSE FOR SERVANTS FROM OUTLYING ESTATES OR ACCOMPANYING VISITORS
 a. Central chamber with open hearth
 b. Stalls for animals
 c. Sleeping quarters
33. MONKS' VEGETABLE GARDEN (with 18 planting beds)
34. GARDENER'S HOUSE
 a. Central chamber with open hearth
 b. Gardener's bedroom with fireplace
 c. Servants' quarters
 d. Tool and seed room
35. FOWLKEEPERS' HOUSE
 a. Central chamber with open hearth
 b. Keepers' bedrooms
36. GOOSE HOUSE
37. CHICHEN HOUSE

38. GRANARY with threshing floor (a)
39. COLLECTIVE WORKSHOP AND ANNEX
 a. Work spaces with central hearths
 b. Shoe makers
 c. Saddlers
 d. Sword makers
 e. Shield makers
 f. Wood turners
 g. Leather workers
 h. Fullers
 i. Blacksmiths
 j. Goldsmiths
 k. Sleeping quarters
40. MILL HOUSE
 a. Mill stones
 b. Living quarters
41. MORTAR HOUSE
 a. Mortars
 b. Living quarters
42. DRYING KILN HOUSE
 a. Furnace
 b. Living quarters
43. HOUSE FOR COOPERS AND WHEELWRIGHTS
 a. Coopers' workshop
 b. Wheelwrights' workshop
 c. Servants' quarters
 d. Granary for monks brewery and bakery
44. BARN FOR HORSES AND OXEN AND THEIR KEEPERS
 a. Central chamber with open hearth
 b. Stalls with hayloft above
 c. Keepers' sleeping quarters
45. BARN FOR SHEEP AND SHEPHERDS
 a. Central chamber with open hearth
 b. Sheep folds
 c. Keepers' sleeping quarters
46. BARN FOR GOATS AND GOATHERDS
 a. Central chamber with open hearth
 b. Stables
 c. Keepers' sleeping quarters
47. BARN FOR COWS AND COWHERDS
 a. Central chamber with open hearth
 b. Stables
 c. Keepers' sleeping quarters
48. BARN FOR SWINE AND SWINEHERDS
 a. Central chamber with open hearth
 b. Pens
 c. Keepers' sleeping quarters
49. BARN FOR BROOD MARES AND COLTS AND THEIR KEEPERS
 a. Central chamber with open hearth
 b. Stables
 c. Keepers' sleeping quarters

Empire. It represented 'a statement of policy drawn up on the highest levels of political and ecclesiastical administration and conceived within the framework of a monastic reform movement whose overriding preoccupation was to establish unity (*unitas*) where life had been controlled by disparate traditions (*diversitas*), to put "a single rule" (*una regula, una consuetudo*) in place of the mixed tradition (*regula mixta*).' Without being able to ascertain the exact process, Horn and Born surmised that a copy of the Aachen archetype somehow got to Reichenau, perhaps through the agency of Abbot Haito, who participated in the Aachen synods. There, perhaps around 820, still another copy was traced and inscribed for Abbot Gozbert of St Gall.[27]

Given the long-standing predisposition among Carolingianists to see all things Carolingian in terms of the thrust towards unity and conformity generated by a reforming movement, the interpretation of the Plan proposed by Horn and Born has had immense appeal. However, an impressive array of authorities have raised serious objections to its validity. They have questioned Horn's reading of the transmission letter on the Plan,[28] proved that the Plan was not a tracing of some other document,[29] raised doubts about the alleged correspondence between the Aachen legislation concerning monastic reform and features of the design of the Plan,[30] asked for concrete evidence proving that a paradigmatic architectural plan for an ideal monastery ever existed,[31] and sought proof that other monastic complexes built after 816–17 followed an official master plan

27 Horn and Born, *Plan of St. Gall*, 1: 1–53, for this explanation; the quotation is at p. 52.
28 Paul Meyvaert, 'Life at the Monastery,' *University Publishing* (Summer, 1980): 18–19, and (Winter, 1981): 25, 31; Adalbert de Vogüé, 'Le Plan de Saint-Gall, copie d'un document officiel? Une lecture de la lettre à Gozbert,' *Revue bénédictine* 94 (1984): 295–314; Warren Sanderson, 'The Plan of St. Gall Reconsidered,' *Speculum* 60 (1985): 615–23; and Lawrence Nees, 'The Plan of St. Gall and the Theory of the Program of Carolingian Art,' *Gesta* 25 (1986): 2.
29 Norbert Stachura, 'Der Plan von St. Gallen: Ein Original?' *Architectura* 8 (1978): 184–6; Stachura, 'Der Plan von St. Gallen: Der Westabschluss der Klosterkirche und seine Varianten,' *Architectura* 10 (1980): 33–7; Adalbert de Vogüé, 'L'originalité du Plan de Saint-Gall: Une confirmation,' *Revue bénédictine* 97 (1987): 87–9; and especially Jacobsen, *Klosterplan von St. Gallen*, 35–78.
30 Edgar Lehmann, 'Die Architektur zur Zeit Karls des Grossen,' in *Karl der Grosse*, ed. Braunfels, vol. 3: *Karolingische Kunst*, ed. Braunfels and Hermann Schnitzler (Düsseldorf, 1965), 301–19; Edward A. Segal, 'The Plan of Saint Gall and the Monastic Reform Councils of 816 and 817,' *Cuyahoga Review* 1 (1983): 57–71; Nees, 'Plan of St. Gall,' 4–8; and Hecht, *St. Galler Klosterplan*, 158–81.
31 Richard E. Sullivan, '*Schola Dominici Servitii*: Carolingian Style,' *Catholic Historical Review* 67 (1981): 421–32; Nees, 'Plan of St. Gall,' 3; Jacobsen, *Klosterplan von St. Gallen*, 243–59, 305–20.

reflected in the Plan of St Gall.[32] In short, while the study of Horn and Born may constitute 'the most stupendous monument ever erected to a ghost'[33] and represent 'one of the heroic enterprises of architectural history'[34] which must 'be the essential point of departure for future research,'[35] its explanation of the Plan's intention cannot be accepted as the final word. The issue remains open.

Perhaps the Plan is paradigmatic in a sense other than as an official building program to be applied everywhere in the Frankish realm. Could it have been the handiwork of some imaginative soul seeking to provide a menu of options from which abbots and their patrons might select when they decided to build or renovate a monastery? Perhaps the Plan is something akin to a master design fabricated in a modern architectural school for a comprehensive shopping mall from which builders and investors anywhere may select elements that can be combined to create a complex suited to local needs and resources. Certain aspects of the Carolingian cultural ambience suggest such a possibility. There is abundant evidence that Carolingian artists, including building designers, were accustomed to borrowing a bit here and a bit there in order to arrive at a final version of their artistic creations.[36] The Carolingian literary record is rich in *florilegia* consisting of selections from diverse sources intended to offer something useful

32 Jacobsen, *Klosterplan von St. Gallen*, passim. Other criticisms of the interpretation of Horn and Born were expressed by Rosamond McKitterick, 'Monastic Elevations,' *Times Literary Supplement*, 26 Dec. 1980, 1470; David Parsons, 'Consistency and the St. Gallen Plan: A Review Article,' *Archaeological Journal* 138 (1981): 259–65; and E. C. Fernie, 'The Plan of St. Gall,' *The Burlington Magazine* 124 (1982): 97–9. Horn and Born remained firm in their position despite all of this criticism; see Horn and Born, 'The Medieval Monastery as a Setting for the Production of Manuscripts,' *Journal of the Walters Art Gallery* 44 (1986): 16–47, especially 17–19.

33 J.M. Wallace-Hadrill, 'The Ghost Goes West,' *New York Review of Books* 27/17 (6 Nov. 1980): 46.

34 Spiro Kostov, Review of Horn and Born, *Plan of St. Gall*, in *Art Bulletin* 63 (1981): 318.

35 Nees, 'Plan of St. Gall,' 1.

36 This point becomes abundantly clear when one looks at treatments of Carolingian art and architecture; see, for example, Adolph Goldschmidt, *Die Elfenbeinskulpturen*, vols. 1 and 2: *Aus der Zeit der karolingischen und sächsischen Kaiser, VIII.–XII. Jahrhundert*, ed. P.G. Hübner and D. Homburger (Berlin, 1914–26; repr. 1969); Wilhlem Koehler, *Die karolingischen Miniaturen*, 5 vols. (Berlin, 1930–82); Jean Hubert, Jean Porcher, and Wolfgang F. Volbach, *L'empire carolingien* (Paris, 1968; English translation: *The Carolingian Renaissance*, trans. James Emmons, Stuart Gilbert, and Robert Allen, The Arts of Mankind [New York, 1970]); Wolfgang Braunfels, *Der Welt der Karolinger und ihre Kunst*, Kunstgeschichte in Einzeldarstellungen (Munich, 1968); C.R. Dodwell, *Painting in Europe, 800–1200* (Harmondsworth, 1971); Florentine Mütherich and James E. Gaehde, *Carolingian Painting* (New York, 1976); Wolfgang F. Volbach, *Elfenbeinarbeiten der Spätantike und des frühen Mittelalters*, 3d ed. (Mainz, 1976); Kenneth John Conant, *Carolingian and Romanesque Architecture, 800 to 1200*, 2d ed., rev., The Pelican History of Art (Harmondsworth, 1979; repr. 1987); Carol

to different audiences facing a variety of circumstances. In short, the Plan of St Gall might be a visual analogue to numerous literary texts fashioned for an age that prized encyclopedic compendia from which guidance could be drawn to assist in the effort to renew Christian society.[37] However, such an interpretation is extremely tenuous. The structures laid out on the Plan are too tightly integrated in scale, positioning, and function to permit one to think that its author envisaged their disjunction into components that could be mixed to create a variety of architectural complexes.[38] Beyond that, there is no evidence that anyone outside St Gall utilized any part of the Plan as a model for the construction or renovation of a monastic complex.[39]

In seeking to discern the intentions of the creator of the Plan of St Gall one must not overlook another possibility: perhaps the Plan was developed to serve as a guide for an actual building project. Recent studies of the Plan in the light of archaeological evidence, particularly that coming from St Gall and Reichenau, lend support to this possibility. That evidence shows significant correspondence between the ground plan of the church outlined on the Plan and the basilica that was actually built at St Gall by Abbot Gozbert between 830 and 835. Moreover, the Plan reflects basic elements incorporated in the church built by Abbot Haito at Reichenau between 806 and 816. It therefore seems highly possible that the Plan was drawn at Reichenau to serve Gozbert as he laid plans for his new church at St Gall. The Plan was modelled on the design used for Haito's church, but it incorporated ideas that were finding expression in other churches being built in the Carolingian world around 830 in a climate marked by an abatement of the reforming zeal prevailing in 816 and 817.[40]

Heitz, *L'architecture religieuse carolingienne: Les formes et leurs fonctions* (Paris, 1980); Carol Heitz and Jean Roubier, *Gallia Praeromanica: Die Kunst der merowingischen, karolingischen und frühromanischen Epoche in Frankreich* (Vienna, 1982); Marcel Durliat, *Des barbares à l'an mil* (Paris, 1985); and Carol Heitz, *La France pré-romane: Archéologie et architecture religieuse du haut Moyen Âge du IVe siècle à l'an mil* (Paris, 1987).

37 On Carolingian *florilegia*, see McKitterick, *Frankish Church*, 155–83. Such collections even existed in the monastic world; for prime examples, see *Codex Regularum Monasticarum et Canonicarum ... collectus olim a S. Benedicto Anianensis Abbate*, PL 103, cols. 393–702; and *Sancti Benedicti Abbatis Anianensis Concordia Regularum*, ibid., cols. 703–1380.

38 Especially persuasive on this point is Hecht, *St. Galler Klosterplan*, 102–40.

39 The effort made by Carolyn Marino Malone and Walter Horn, 'The Plan of St. Gall and Its Effect on Later Monastic Planning: Tradition and Change,' in Horn and Born, *Plan of St. Gall*, 2: 315–59, to show the impact of the Plan on later monastic architecture is not very convincing; see the comments of Nees, 'Plan of St. Gall,' 1, on this point. The meticulous study of many Carolingian church buildings by Jacobsen, *Klosterplan von St. Gallen*, passim, reveals that specific elements of the main church sketched on the Plan were reflected in other contemporary structures but provides no evidence that those architectural concepts and forms were derived from the Plan.

40 The case for the Plan as an actual building plan was summed up by Konrad Hecht, 'Der St.

While the evidence that the Plan of St Gall was conceived as a guide to an actual construction program lends an element of concreteness to its otherwise disembodied outline, it still leaves unanswered the fundamental question posed earlier. Presuming that he hoped that his imagined monastic establishment might be transformed from a flat sketch to real structures, what did the creator of the Plan intend his complex of buildings to say to contemporaries about monastic life? Perhaps that riddle can be resolved only if we step aside from the erudite scholarship that it has evoked to look again at the Plan itself in some detail.

IV

If one looks at figure 1, one thing leaps out immediately: the Plan envisages an inner space whose purpose is to separate the holy men from the outside. At the heart of that enclosure is the main church (**1**; hereafter all numbers and letters in parentheses refer to fig. 1), a double-apsed basilica 300 feet in length with a nave 40 feet wide flanked by side aisles each 20 feet wide.[41] A crossing

Galler Klosterplan – Schema oder Bauplan?' *Abhandlungen der Braunschweigischen Wissenschaftlichen Gesellschaft* 17 (1965): 165–206. The results of the excavations conducted at St Gall in 1964–67 were published by Hans Rudolf Sennhauser, 'Das Münster des Abtes Gozbert (816–837) und seine Ausmalung unter Hartmut (Proabbas 841, Abt 872–883),' *Unserere Kunstdenkmäler* 34 (1983): 152–67; a summary of Sennhauser's findings is provided by Horn and Born, *Plan of St. Gall* 2: 358–9. For further discussions of the Plan and the actual building program of Gozbert, see Thomas Puttfarken, 'Ein neuer Vorschlag zum St. Galler Klosterplan: Die originalen Massinschriften,' *Frühmittelalterliche Studien* 2 (1968), 79–95; Malone and Horn, 'The Plan of St. Gall and Its Affect on Later Monastic Planning,' in Horn and Born, *Plan of St. Gall*, 2: 319–32; Hecht, *St. Galler Klosterplan*, 314–47; and Jacobsen, *Klosterplan von St. Gallen*, 149–90, 322–3. On building activity at Reichenau in the ninth century, see Emil Reisser, *Die frühe Baugeschichte des Münsters zu Reichenau*, ed. Hans Erich Kubach, Forschungen der deutschen Kunstgeschichte 37 (Berlin, 1960); *Die Abtei Reichenau: Neue Beiträge zur Geschichte und Kultur des Inselklosters*, ed. Helmut Maurer (Sigmaringen, 1974); and Alfons Zettler, *Die frühen Klosterbauten der Reichenau: Ausgrabungen, Schriftquellen, St. Galler Klosterplan*, Archäologie und Geschichte. Freiburger Forschungen zum ersten Jahrtausend in Südwestdeutschland 3 (Sigmaringen, 1988). Especially useful in locating the Plan of St Gall in the general architectural setting of its day are Carol Heitz, 'L'architecture carolingienne à la lumière de la réforme religieuse: État générale des recherches depuis l'exposition d'Aix-la-Chapelle 1965,' and Werner Jacobsen, 'Benedikt von Aniane und die Architektur unter Ludwig dem Frommen zwischen 814 and 830,' both in *Atti del XXIV Congresso internazionale di storia dell'arte*, vol. 1: *Riforma religiosa e arti nell'epoca carolingia*, ed. Alfred A. Schmid (Bologna, 1983), 5–14, 15–22; and Jacobsen, 'Allgemeine Tendenzen im Kirchenbau unter Ludwig dem Frommen,' in *Charlemagne's Heir*, ed. Godman and Collins, 641–54.

41 While I am fully aware that scholars do not agree on the scale used in the Plan and how to translate its measurements into meaningful modern equivalents, the measurements used in my description are those proposed by Horn and Born, *Plan of St. Gall*, passim.

transept provides space for a 'choir for the psalmodists' ('chorus psellantium,' according to its inscription) (**1e**). East of the choir, elevated by seven steps, is the main altar of the basilica dedicated to Mary and Saint Gall (**1b**), whose crypt lies under the main altar. There are two passages to the crypt: one for the monks leads from the choir down through an opening in the steps to the main altar; the other for lay visitors consists of a U-shaped covered passageway opening on either side of the choir onto the church's side aisles (**1d**). On either side of the main altar and extending around the east apse and its altar (**1a**) are wall benches where the monks were to be seated during divine services. The north and south arms of the transept provide space for separate chapels, each with its own elevated altar and wall benches (**1f, 1g**). The west apse houses an elevated altar facing out onto a second choir (**1l**). Surrounding the west apse of the church is an atrium (**1E**) partly covered by a roof supported by columns and flanked by twin towers, each housing an altar at its top (**1F, 1G**). Three porches (**1H, 1I, 1J**) give access to this atrium, and thus to the main church. A matching atrium on the east (**1C**) is open to the sky but has no access to the main church. The nave and side aisles are partitioned into discrete spaces which provide the setting for several altars serving the religious needs of the community (the Plan provides for nineteen altars in the main basilica). Lying east of the transept and on either side of the main altar are two two-storeyed annexes, one housing (**1A**) a scriptorium with a library above, and the other (**1B**) a sacristy with a vestry above. The sacristy is connected by a passage to a building (**1D**) intended for preparing eucharistic bread and holy oil.

Against the church's south wall, the Plan's designer laid out a space where the monks would spend most of their time. This complex features an open courtyard (**2**) measuring about 100 feet on each side and surrounded by arcaded galleries. According to its inscription, the north gallery (**2a**) provides a place where the monks could gather to deliberate on matters of common concern.[42] The cloister yard and its galleries are enclosed by three two-storeyed structures. On the east is a building (**3**) whose upper storey houses a dormitory with seventy-seven beds, carefully depicted on the Plan; a door from there opens into the transept of the main church. Its ground floor provides a warming-room with its own furnace and smokestack; here when the weather was inclement the monks could gather during the intervals between daytime prayer services to warm themselves, socialize, or read. Connected to the dormitory/warming-room structure are a privy (**4**) with nine seats and a bathhouse and laundry (**5**).

---

42 Horn and Born, *Plan of St. Gall*, 3: 81: 'Hinc pia consilium pertract[et] turba salubre.' It is difficult to believe that this space would have sufficed to meet the provision set forth in the Rule of Saint Benedict that the abbot should call all the monks together to consult with them on matters of great importance to the community; see *La règle de Saint Benoit*, c. 3, ed. Jean

On the south side of the cloister square is a building (**6**) whose ground floor is designated as a refectory with tables for as many as 120 diners at a single sitting; above the refectory is a vestiary, where the monks' clothing was stored. The refectory is connected by passageways to separate structures, designated as a kitchen (**7**) and a combined brewery and bakery (**8**). West of the cloister yard is a structure (**9**) with a cellar for storing beer and wine on the ground floor (fourteen casks with a capacity of perhaps 50,000 gallons are shown on the Plan) and a larder above.

Close scrutiny of the sector of the Plan just described (roughly one-quarter of the total area of the complex) leaves no doubt that the space involved was intended to be an area set apart. Here was a reserved space within which could be constituted a 'dominici schola servitii.'[43] Here was located everything needed to unite the holy men in a closely bonded community whose members could perform in a structured way the *opus Dei* which assured their individual and collective progress towards holiness: to pray and contemplate; to be instructed; to labour at cooking, cleaning, doing laundry, serving tables, copying manuscripts; to eat and sleep a little; to answer to nature's implacable demands. Here the Plan's designer expressed visually what Saint Benedict commanded in writing: 'The monastery should, if possible, be arranged so that all necessary things ... may be within the enclosure, so that the monks may not be compelled to wander outside it, for that is not at all expedient for their souls.'[44]

However, the observant viewer of the church/cloister complex will already have noted that that inner space is not totally sealed off. It has windows opening out in several directions. For example, presuming that the Plan might have become an actual monastery, monks entering the east transept of the main church from their cloister would have noted the passage out of the north arm of the transept leading to a space containing two buildings. One (**10**) is a two-storeyed house for the abbot. The lower floor, flanked on two sides by arcaded porches, is partitioned into a sitting-room (**10a**) and a bedroom with eight beds (**10b**); the second floor contains a solarium and storage rooms. The other building (**11**) provides a kitchen, cellar, and bathhouse with servants' quarters to serve the abbot's house. From a variety of sources, it is clear that this facility represents more than living quarters for the abbot. It is a link to the outer world where he and his officers meet and deal with dignitaries from beyond the pale on matters of crucial importance to the existence of the community. The Plan

Neuville, trans. Adalbert de Vogüé, 6 vols., Sources chrétiennes 181-6, Série des Textes Monastiques d'Occident 34–9 (Paris, 1971), 1: 452–4 (hereinafter *RB*).

43 *RB*, Prologue, 1: 422.

44 *RB*, c. 66, 2: 600; English translation from *The Rule of Saint Benedict*, ed. and trans. Justin McCann (London, 1952), 153.

expresses visually what many written sources confirm: that Carolingian abbots were, indeed should be, both of and not of the enclosed community.[45]

But that is not the only opening to the outside. Had the structures envisaged on the Plan ever been realized, then a monk looking eastward out of one of the windows of the scriptorium or the library (**1A**) would have seen a complex of buildings that also had something to do with other worlds. There the creator of the Plan outlined separate facilities clustered around a second church building (**12**) to serve the needs of two special groups. One comprised the novices, including both adults who had come 'knocking' for admission to the community and 'young boys' whose parents or guardians had committed them to a monastic career.[46] The Plan provides the novices with a separate chapel (**12A**) opening onto an enclosed yard (**13a**), where, according to its inscription, 'the oblates live with the novices.'[47] Surrounding the cloister yard are a warming-hall, a dormitory with perhaps twenty beds and an attached privy, a sick room, an apartment for the master of the novices, a refectory, and a storeroom (**13b, c, d, e, f, g**). Standing separately is a structure housing a kitchen and a bath for the novices (**14**). Exactly duplicating the facilities for the novices is a complex serving the ill ('[Fra]tribus infirmis ... locus') with its own chapel (**12B**) and cloister yard (**15a**) and surrounded by chambers inscribed as a warming-room, a dormitory with a privy, a room for the critically ill, an apartment for the master of the infirmary, a refectory, and a storage room (**15b, c, d, e, f, g**). The infirmary has its own kitchen and bath (**16**). Lying north of the infirmary complex are two additional structures devoted to health care. One is a physicians' house (**17**) containing a main hall, a heated bedroom, a heated emergency room ('cubibulum [*sic*] ualde infirmorum'), and a pharmacy (**17a, b, c, d**) which depended for some of its raw materials on a medicinal herb garden (**18**), whose planting beds are carefully labelled. Close by the physicians' quarters is a building for blood-letting (**19**), apparently the chief form of preventive medicine. Also nearby is the cemetery (**20**). Growing over the graves is an orchard where, according to the Plan's inscriptions, thirteen different kinds of trees were to be planted.

45 For descriptions of the role of the Carolingian abbot, see Felten, *Äbte und Laienäbte,* passim: and Felten, 'Herrschaft des Abtes,' in *Herrschaft und Kirche,* ed. Prinz, 147–296. The matter of a separate residence and eating facilities for abbots was a cause of contention at the time the Plan was drawn up. The Benedictine Rule provided for such an arrangement; see *RB* c. 53, 2: 610–16. At the Aachen synod of 816 a failed effort was made to end such arrangements for the abbot; for a discussion of this attempt with the relevant texts, see Hecht, *St. Galler Kloster-plan,* 168–70.

46 *RB,* cc. 58 and 59, 2: 626–34, discusses the handling of anyone who 'veniens perseveraverit pulsans' and 'puer minori aetate.'

47 Horn and Born, *Plan of St. Gall,* 3: 55: 'Hoc claustro oblati pulsantib[us] adsociantur.'

In brief, most of the eastern segment of the Plan is reserved for a special function linking the inside and the outside realms. There the Plan's creator plotted out what in modern jargon might be called a 'loop' marking the flow of the human element out of which the holy community was to be formed and sustained. He was trying to say visually that those living the monastic life must be mindful of how the process leading from the sinful terrestrial world through the novices' quarters into the monks' church and cloister should be organized and managed. No less important should be care for the passage back out of the cloister through the infirmary and the cemetery on to the extraterrestrial spheres.

The Plan shows still other windows drawing those in the inner sanctum towards the outside world – and the world towards the cloister. Again imagining that what was sketched on the Plan became a reality, then a monk walking west from the scriptorium (**1A**) across the north transept (**1f**) could have proceeded through a series of chambers built against the north wall of the church intended for functions that point beyond the sacred precinct: a lodging for visiting monks (**21**); quarters of the master of the external school (**22**), where instruction is provided for a non-monastic clientele; the lodging for the porter (**23**); and a porch (**1H**) that gives access to the church and to the facilities for guests. Or had a perambulating monk left the monks' cloister yard (**2**) at its northwest corner, he would have passed first into a parlour (**24**) where monks on the inside received visitors from the outside and where the washing of the feet of the poor took place as the Rule commanded.[48] Next comes the apartment of the master of the hospice for pilgrims and paupers (**25**). Then there is a porch (**1I**) which gives access to the main church and to the yard of the hospice for pilgrims and paupers. Finally, at the west end of the church is a third porch (**1J**) opening onto a road (**1K**) whose inscription reads: 'This is the road of access to the church in which all folk may worship that they may leave rejoicing.'[49] Although a detailed examination of the interior of the main church shows that a large portion of it is screened off for the exclusive use of the monks, the Plan's designer opens a significant part of the structure for lay worship: attending masses (particularly at altars **1i** and **1j**), receiving baptism (at **1k**), hearing sermons preached from the church's main pulpit (**1h**), joining processions, and visiting the crypt of Saint Gall by way of a passage opening onto the side aisles of the church (**1d**).[50]

48 *RB*, c. 53, 2: 610–16.
49 Horn and Born, *Plan of St. Gall*, 3: 17: 'Omnibus ad scm turbis petet haec uia templum quo sua uota ferant unde hilantes redeant.'
50 Ibid., 1: 127–212, for a detailed description of the internal arrangement of the church.

V

It certainly seems plausible to think that in creating all of these openings to the outside the Plan's creator was trying to say something about the relationship between the monastic community and the outside world. But what kind of world? There are strong reasons to believe that he was not thinking of some remote, hypothetical, imaginary world filled with unspeakable evils that would inevitably corrupt all who became engaged with it in any way. Rather, the Plan defines an environment in which on any given day there was likely to be present within a limited space and interacting intimately with the holy men a mix of people representing the ninth-century world in a microcosm – females excepted.

There would have been present the visiting monks who slept in their special quarters (**21**) but ate with the other monks in the main refectory (**6**) and joined in the celebration of the monastic liturgical office. Always present would be youngsters – perhaps as many as forty-eight – occupying the building serving as the external school (**26**), most of them undoubtedly male scions of the nobility whose upbringing had not totally acclimated them to the austere regime expected of monks. Given the amplitude of space provided for the reception of distinguished guests, the creator of the Plan must have anticipated and applauded the constant presence of representatives of the *potentes*,[51] including emperors, their power-wielding *missi*, great nobles, and ecclesiastical potentates. The jewel in this hospitality suite is a guest house (**27**) measuring 55 feet by 67 1/2 feet and featuring a common room with a central hearth vented through the roof (**27a**) and four two-bedded sleeping chambers, each with its own corner fireplace and privy (**27b**). In addition to the biggest communal privy (**27e**) on the Plan, the visitors' guest house has lean-to chambers for servants (**27c**) and stalls for horses (**27d**). There is also a separate structure to serve as a kitchen, bakery, and brew house (**28**). Erasures by a twelfth-century scribe searching for space to finish a work he had begun to copy on the back of the parchment have obscured the exact shape of the structure occupying the northwest corner of the Plan, obliterating its descriptive inscriptions; it appears, nevertheless, that the creator of the Plan envisaged a large building (**29**) to accommodate the armed retinues of visiting dignitaries as well as their retainers and their horses, perhaps as many as forty men and thirty horses.[52] The Plan's designer assumed that these aristocratic outsiders would come in contact with

---

51 Ibid., 1: 155–65, estimates that one-fifth of the total area of the Plan was reserved to serve visiting dignitaries and their retinues.

52 For discussions of the circumstances surrounding the erasure of this part of the manuscript and of the structure's function, see ibid., 2: 166–7, 3: 74; and Hecht, *St. Galler Klosterplan*, 125–8.

the monks – in the abbot's house (**10**), in the main refectory (**6**),[53] in the parlour where visitors greeted their monk-relatives (**24**), and at one of the many altars in the great church to which the laity had access.

The Plan's creator provided for the presence within the monastic precincts of an even greater representation of laymen of lower status. A special building (**30**) with its own kitchen and bakery (**31**) is provided for the greeting and care of the pilgrims and the poor who came expecting hospitality and alms, as Saint Benedict had commanded.[54] Another building (**32**) is designated as 'the hall of the serfs who come with the services,' an inscription that has been interpreted to mean quarters for serfs belonging to the monastery's external *familia,* who had come to the monastery from a distance to render service or to bring provisions.[55] Along the entire south and most of the west sides of the Plan, its designer sketched in service buildings providing not only work stations, but also living quarters for members of the inner *familia* of the projected monastery. The Plan's inscriptions indicate that some of these dependants were to be skilled artisans: the gardeners with their own house (**34**); the shoemakers, saddlers, shield and sword makers, woodworkers, leather workers, fullers, blacksmiths, and goldsmiths to be housed in the great collective workshop and its annex (**39**); the coopers and wheelwrights living in their own building (**43**); and those serving the mill (**40**), the mortar (**41**), and the drying kiln (**42**). And a sizeable contingent of workers charged with the care of fowls and animals were to live in separate quarters, such as the house of the fowl-keepers (**35**), or in the barns housing horses and oxen (**44**), sheep (**45**), goats (**46**), cows (**47**), swine (**48**), and mares and foals (**49**). The Plan also makes provisions for quartering servants in the service unit attached to the abbot's house (**11**), in the house for distinguished guests (**27**), and in the hospice for pilgrims and paupers (**30**). Modern estimates of the number of laymen in the inner *familia* of the community envisaged on the Plan range from 80 to 150, numbers equalling or exceeding the 90 to 110 monks that could be accommodated in facilities laid out on the Plan. A full complement of guests might have added another 115 laymen pre-

---

53 The monastic reformers made a concerted effort at the synods of Aachen in 816 and 817 to exclude laymen from the monks' refectory but with far from total success; see Hecht, *St. Galler Klosterplan,* 168–9, which provides the key texts on this issue.

54 *RB,* c. 53, 2: 614.

55 Horn and Born, *Plan of St. Gall,* 3: 78: 'Dom[us] familiae quae cum servitio aduenerit.' On the function of the building, see ibid., 2: 165–6; and Hecht, *St. Galler Klosterplan,* 124–5. Some idea of the extent of St Gall's properties and the size of the dependent population attached to these lands is provided by Rolf Sprandel, *Das Kloster St. Gallen in der Verfassung des karolingisches Reiches,* Forschungen zur oberrheinischen Landesgeschichte 7 (Freiburg, 1958).

sent at the monastery on any particular day.[56] The hypothetical St Gall was not a place for monks only!

The designer of the Plan must have been aware that the presence of such diverse groups constantly pressing in on the inner sanctum held rich potential for distraction. There would be occasions when, as Benedict of Nursia had anticipated, one of the visiting monks was found to be 'exacting and depraved,' thereby managing to 'disturb the monastery by exorbitant wants.'[57] According to the Monk of St Gall in his biography of Charlemagne, the emperor himself had to reprimand the high-born students of the external school for neglecting the pursuit of knowledge to indulge in 'time-wasting follies and in the childish sport of fine living and idleness.'[58] Perhaps there is good reason for the fence around the external school.[59] Saint Benedict also warned that artisans could become 'puffed up' because of their skills and were not above price gouging.[60] It is not difficult to imagine what likely happened as night deepened in the northwest segment of the compound (**27, 28, 29**) after the distinguished guests and their retainers had drawn on the resources of their brewhouse sufficient times (why else so many seats in the guest house *necessarium*?). It is likely that the conviviality of the noble laity was matched among the artisans and animal keepers gathered around the central hearths in the great collective workshop (**39**) to sample the latest product purloined from the nearby monastic brewhouse (**8**) or from the prodigious treasure stored in the cloister cellar (**9**). Presuming that 'the throng of pilgrims [found] friendly reception' in the hospice for pilgrims and paupers (**30**), as its inscription indicated should be the case, the scene very likely became animated even in that quarter when the newly arrived

56 For these estimates, see Horn and Born, *Plan of St.Gall*, 1: 342–5; 2: 139–75; and Hecht, *St. Galler Klosterplan*, 140–57.

57 *RB*, c. 61, 2: 636–8; English translations from *Rule of Saint Benedict*, ed. and trans. McCann, 139.

58 *Notkeri Balbvli Gesta Karoli Magni Imperatoris*, Bk. 1, c. 3, ed. Hans F. Haefele, MGH SRG, new ser., 12 (Berlin, 1959; repr. Munich, 1980), 4–5; English translation from *Einhard and Notker the Stammerer: Two Lives of Charlemagne*, trans. Lewis Thorpe (Harmondsworth, 1969), 95–6.

59 There are problems associated with designating this structure (**26**) as an 'external school' devoted to the education of students not destined for monastic life. Its inscriptions indicate only that it was intended as a 'school.' The problem lies in the enactment of the Aachen synod of 817 prohibiting the education of anyone in a monastery who was not committed to monastic life. That prohibition led Hecht, *St. Galler Klosterplan*, 128–32, 173–5, to argue that the facility we have designated as the 'External School' was in fact a school for oblates. A thorough review of this issue is provided by M.M. Hildebrandt, *The External School in Carolingian Society*, Education and Society in the Middle Ages and Renaissance 1 (Leiden, New York, and Cologne, 1992), 72–107.

60 *RB* c. 57, 2: 624.

outsiders began to regale each other with tales of their travels and their misfortunes.[61] Already, by the time for compline, the *chorus psellentium* probably had to contend with sounds not noted in their liturgical books; perhaps the revelry still sounded across the complex when the monks arose at 2:00 A.M. for the first service of the day.

Even without assuming a worst-case scenario rooted in the debauched habits of the worldly, one can hardly avoid the fact that the Plan deliberately sets a stage upon which the holy men, supposedly occupied with contemplation and prayer, would in the course of normal affairs be subjected to a wide range of activities that had little to do with the *opus Dei* in the traditional sense. The Plan's author must have realized that monks would need to re-examine their understanding of *apatheia* as a consequence of their awareness of the kind of momentous negotiations occurring in the abbot's house (**10**) that allowed Abbot Gozbert to gain immunity for the monastery from the authority of the bishop of Constance.[62] Monks would have had their perception of human activity expanded by the tales of high adventure in the great outside world that passed from the hospice of pilgrims (**30**) into the monks' cloister (**2**).[63] Only the most obtuse designer with no sense of reality could have thought that monks could have remained oblivious to the hammering, sawing, grinding, arguing, and swearing that went on in the workshops and the stables lying just south and west of the monks' cloister. Who could have imagined any monk so far up

---

61 Horn and Born, *Plan of St. Gall*, 3: 70: 'Hic peregrinorum la[et]etur turba recepta.' The night habits of the laity were well known in monastic circles, as is obvious from the following passage written by Hildemar of Corvey in his *Expositio Regulae Sancti Benedicti*, c. 65, in *Vita et Regula SS. P. Benedicti, una cum Expositione Regulae a Hildemaro tradita*, ed. Rupertus Mittermüller (Regensburg, 1880), 611: 'quia dormitorium, ubi monachi suscipi debent, habetur separatum a laicorum cubiculo, i.e., ubi laici jacent, eo quod laici possunt stare usque mediam noctem et loqui et jocari, et monachi non debent, sed magis silentium habere et orare.'

62 The details of that struggle are outlined in Theodor Mayer, 'Konstanz und St. Gallen in der Frühzeit,' *Schweizerische Zeitschrift für Geschichte* 2 (1952): 473–524; and Sprandel, *Kloster St. Gallen*, 28–56.

63 A sample of the kind of travel tales that monks might have heard is provided by an account entitled *Hodoeporicon*, written about 786 by Huneberc (or Hugeburc), a nun at Heidenheim, recording what she claimed to have heard from an English monk, Willibald, later bishop of Eichstätt, about his travels undertaken between 722 and 729. For the Latin text of this account, see *Vitae Willibaldi et Wynnebaldi auctore sanctimoniale Heidenheimensis*, ed. O. Holder-Egger, MGH SS 15/1 (Hanover, 1887), 86–106 (English translation in C.H. Talbot, *The Anglo-Saxon Missionaries in Germany* [London, 1954], 152–77; repr. with changes in *Soldiers of Christ: Saints and Saints' Lives from Antiquity and the Early Middle Ages*, ed. Thomas F.X. Noble and Thomas Head [University Park, Pa., 1995], 143–64). One could undoubtedly buttress this point about the leakage of news of the outside world into the monastic confines by an analysis of the kinds of information that found a way into monastic chronicles and annals.

Jacob's ladder that he would not have noticed the constant coming and going of
the wagon trains which filled the granaries (**38, 43d**) and the monks' cellar and
larder (**9**), and supplied the workshops with the materials that put food in his
mouth, clothing on his back, and a roof over his head?

Given the numerous occasions for distraction from the pursuit of holiness
that leap out from the Plan, one must ask why its author arranged things in a
fashion seemingly so contrary to the ascetic ideal. One suspects that he saw in
what we have called distractions a means of educating the monks. By providing
a setting for monkish encounters with numerous 'outsiders,' the Plan's author
was seeking to give a new dimension to the *vita contemplativa*. He was concerned with how holy people related to the workaday world. It is easy to dis-
miss this matter by saying that the worldly presence involved nothing more
than providing the material needs of the holy men. But that is not the point. The
Plan reflects a concern with giving structure, order, and proportion to that
dimension of monastic life. It says that to be a monk involves coping with
worldly people and activity; being holy is defined by how this involvement was
managed. This is another way of saying the Plan was designed by someone
thinking about those relationships in terms of redefining monasticism. And that
person was seeking to express himself in an idiom different from the formulae
about the evils of the world that were a standard feature of conventional ascetic
discourse.

The Plan has another fascinating feature. Its designer leaves no doubt that
the monks in his projected community would live not only in the presence of
diverse human beings, but also surrounded by a considerable number of animals great and small. Again, it is easy enough to explain that feature of the Plan
by the community's need for meat, cheese, milk, leather, wool, draught animals, and warhorses. But why was the care of the animals and fowls required to
meet these needs located literally up against the walls of the monks' sacred
space? Perhaps the author of the Plan was thinking of a different kind of monkish contact with the world than that involving human beings. We all know from
encounters with acquaintances who keep pets that associations with these creatures can have a powerful effect on how their keepers perceive the cosmos.
Would Carolingian monks have been any different? I suspect that one could
muster evidence from written texts and the visual arts to prove that they were
not.[64] Would not monks have been 'educated' by the antics of kids, lambs,

64 Sedulius Scottus' poem on a gelded sheep comes to mind; the Latin text with an English translation can be found in Peter Godman, *Poetry of the Carolingian Renaissance* (London, 1985),
292–301. For another translation, see *Sedulius Scottus, On Christian Rulers and the Poems*,
trans. Edward Gerard Doyle, Medieval and Renaissance Texts and Studies 17 (Binghampton,
N.Y, 1983), 140–3. Even more revealing is the empathetic treatment of animals rendered in

piglets, colts, and calves? Would not what must have taken place within easy view from the cloister to require a place for brood mares and foals (**49**) and sows and piglets (**48**) have sent the monks a message not found in their psalters? At times the cacophony emanating from the coops for fowls (**36, 37**) and the barns (**44, 45, 46, 47, 48, 49**) must have competed with the psalmody marking lauds and prime. And on occasion, especially when the wind blew from the southwest, the odor of sanctity surrounding the church and cloister probably had a special fragrance. All of this involves real creatures, not the phantasmogoric beasts that monks encountered in the Book of Revelation or when their *lectio divina* introduced them to the temptations of Saint Antony.[65] The Plan's creator must have had something in mind in bringing monks and animals into close communion. I suspect that he made animal life an integral part of his monastic complex because of a conviction that the quest for spiritual perfection would not be complete unless the monk became engaged with the realm of nature represented by the animals living in the compound.[66]

Close scrutiny of the Plan leads one to think that its author had in mind still another order of interaction between the monastic community and the world, this one touching the realms of ideas and techniques. In providing for so many altars in the church, the Plan's designer must have envisioned a spiritual out-

the drawings in the Utrecht Psalter; see, for example, E.T. Dewald, *The Illustrations of the Utrecht Psalter*, Illuminated Manuscripts of the Middle Ages (Princeton, London, and Leipzig, n.d.), Plates 3 (fol. 2^v), 7 (fol. 4^v), 14 (fol. 8^v), 15 (fol. 9^r), 17 (fol. 11^r), 19 (fol. 12^r), 20 (fol. 13^r), 26 (fol. 16^r), 33 (fol. 20^v), 39 (fol. 24^v), 45 (fol. 28^r), 46 (fol. 28^v), 47 (fol. 29^r), 52 (fol. 32^r), 53 (fol. 32^v), 54 (fol. 33^r), 57 (fol. 35^r), 59 (fol. 36^r), 60 (fol. 36^v), 62 (fol. 37^v), 67 (fol. 41^v), 68 (fol. 42^r), 71 (fol. 44^r), 72 (fol. 45^r), 73 (fol. 46^v), 74 (fol. 47^r), 78 (fol. 49^v), 79 (fol. 50^r), 92 (fol. 57^v). 95 (fol. 59^v), 125 (fol. 80^r), 126 (fol. 80^v), 129 (fol. 82^v), 132 (fol. 84^r), 136 (fol. 86^r), and 137 (fol. 87^v) (folio references are to Codex 32, Utrecht, Bibliotheek der Rijksuniversiteit). A more recent facsimile edition of the Psalter was not available for this study, *Utrecht-Psalter: Vollständige Faksimile-Ausgabe im Originalformat der Handschrift 32 der Rijksuniversiteit te Utrecht: Kommentar*, ed. Koert van der Horst and Jacobus H. A. Engelbregt, Codices selecti phototypice impressi 75 (Graz, 1984).

65 See *St. Athanasius, The Life of Saint Antony*, cc. 9, 52, 53, trans. Robert T. Meyer, Ancient Christian Writers 10 (Westminster, Md., 1950), 27–8, 64, 65.

66 Perhaps the same point could be made about the trees and plants which the author of the Plan envisioned as growing in the cemetery orchard (**20**) and the herb and vegetable gardens (**18, 33**). Some sense of the feelings evoked in the Carolingian world by flowers, trees, and vegetables can be derived from Walahfrid Strabo's poem *De cultura hortorum*, ed. Ernst Dümmler, MGH, Poetae 2 (Berlin, 1884), 335–50 (English translation as *Walahfrid Strabo, Hortulus*, trans. Raef Payne, Hunt Facsimile Series 2 [Pittsburgh, Penn., 1966], 24–65); or from Sedulius Scottus' poem recounting a debate between a rose and a lily, text and translation in Godman, *Poetry of the Carolingian Renaissance*, 282–5 (for another translation, see *Sedulius Scottus*, trans. Doyle, 171–2). Significant insights on this theme are provided by *L'ambiente vegetale nell'alto medioevo*, 2 vols., *Settimane* 37 (Spoleto, 1990).

reach to other monasteries and to the lay world: these altars provided a setting where masses could be offered for the souls of the members of St Gall's prayer brotherhood that was developing rapidly in the ninth century.[67] What is known about the evolution of the library and scriptorium of St Gall in the early ninth century suggests that, when the author of the Plan sketched in those facilities, he was projecting space for the production and the collection of books that would embrace both sacred and secular learning and for the execution of documents dealing with all kinds of profane matters relevant to the operation of a monastery.[68] The curriculum that evolved at St Gall during the ninth century for the training of novices and external students embraced the entire range of disciplines undergirding Carolingian education.[69] The Plan reflects none of the

67 For treatments of the St Gall prayer brotherhood, see Johanne Autenrieth, 'Das St. Galler Verbrüderungsbuch: Möglichkeiten und Grenzen paläographischer Bestimmung,' *Frühmittelalterliche Studien* 9 (1975): 215–25; Karl Schmid, 'Zum Quellenwert der Verbrüderungsbücher von St. Gallen und Reichenau,' *Deutsches Archiv für Erforschung des Mittelalters* 41 (1985): 345–89; *Subsidia Sangallensia I: Materialien und Untersuchungen zu den Verbrüderungsbüchern und zu den älteren Urkunden des Stiftsarchivs St. Gallen*, ed. Michael Borgolte, Dieter Geuenich, and Karl Schmid, St. Galler Kultur und Geschichte 16 (St Gallen, 1986), 13–283; and Dieter Geuenich, 'The St. Gall Confraternity of Prayer,' in *The Culture of the Abbey of St. Gall: An Overview*, ed. James C. King and Werner Vogler (Stuttgart and Zurich, 1991), 29–38. The study of the texts relating to these brotherhoods in recent years marks one of the most important developments in the study of Carolingian monasticism; for a guide to the basic literature on the challenge and the potential of this field of study, see Oexle, 'Les moines d'occident,' 255, n. 2.
68 For general overviews of the scriptorium and library at St Gall, see J.M. Clark, *The Abbey of St Gall as a Centre of Literature and Art* (Cambridge, 1926); Émile Lesne, *Histoire de la propriété ecclésiastique en France*, vol. 4: *Les livres, 'scriptoria' et bibliothèques du commencement du VIIIe siècle à la fin du XIIe siècle*, Mémoires et travaux publiés par des professeurs des facultés catholiques de Lille 46 (Lille, 1938; repr. New York, 1964), 300–17, 736–60; Bernice M. Kaczynski, *Greek in the Carolingian Age: The St. Gall Manuscripts*, Speculum Anniversary Monographs 13 (Cambridge, Mass., 1988); and Horn and Born, 'The Medieval Monastery as a Setting for the Production of Manuscripts,' *Journal of the Walters Art Gallery* 44 (1986): 16–47. For the content of the library, see the ninth-century library catalogues published by Paul Lehmann, *Mittelalterliche Bibliothekskataloge Deutschlands und der Schweiz*, 2 vols. (Munich, 1918–28), 1: 55–148; descriptions of the manuscripts produced at St Gall can be found in Albert Bruckner, *Scriptoria Medii Aevi Helvetica. Denkmäler schweizerischen Schreibkunst des Mittelalters*, vols. 2 and 3: *Schreibschulen der Diözese Konstanz: St. Gallen* (Geneva, 1936–8). Ample proof of the production of documents dealing with worldly affairs in the St Gall scriptorium can be found in the monastery's surviving charters; see *Urkundenbuch der Abtei Sanct Gallen*, Pt. 1: *700–840*; Pt. 2: *840–920*, ed. Hermann Wartmann (Zürich, 1863, 1866; repr. Frankfurt am Main, 1981); Rosamond McKitterick, *The Carolingians and the Written World* (Cambridge, 1989), 77–126, provides an illuminating treatment of the significance of these charters in terms of the monastery's connection with the outside world.
69 For brief comments on the school at St Gall see Lesne, *Histoire de la propriété ecclésiastique en France*, vol. 5: *Les écoles de la fin du VIIIe siècle à la fin du XIIe siècle*, Mémoires et

suspicion one discerns in some circles of the Carolingian world, especially monastic, that secular learning was dangerous to the soul.[70] Just as in so many other ways, it invites reaching out to, and taking in of, the world culturally.

Perhaps the Plan's creator even deserves credit as a precursor of a long succession of advocates of the redemptive power of technology. He highlights the importance of incorporating the most advanced technology into monastic life. The plantings chosen for the gardens and the orchard,[71] the health facilities, the number and location of the privies and baths,[72] the heating devices,[73] the brewing and baking equipment,[74] and the mechanical devices in the mill, the mortar, and the kiln, all of them very likely water-driven,[75] leave no doubt that the latest technology related to healing, sanitation, heating, food preparation, horticulture, milling, and metalworking was necessary in providing the proper environment for 'a school for the service of the Lord.' Indeed, the Plan's designer may have been in the vanguard of these developments. Structural features of the main basilica, such as the double choirs, the crypt, the compartmentalized transept, the annexes on either side of the east choir, the western closure, and the twin towers, reflect its author's awareness of, and eagerness to utilize, current developments in architecture.[76] The internal layout of the church is closely

travaux publiés par des professeurs des facultés catholiques de Lille 50 (Lille, 1940), 394–413; L.M. de Rijk, 'On the Curriculum of the Arts of the Trivium at St. Gall from 850–c.1000,' *Vivarium* 1 (1963): 35–86; and Hildebrandt, *The External School*, passim. For illuminating discussions of St Gall as a cultural centre in the ninth century, see Clark, *The Abbey of St Gall*; *Notker der Dichter und seine geistige Welt*, ed. Wolfram von den Steinen, 2 vols. (Bern, 1948); Walter Berschin, *Eremus und Insula: St. Gallen und Reichenau im Mittelalter: Modell einer lateinischen Literaturlandschaft* (Wiesbaden, 1987); and *The Culture of the Abbey of St. Gall: An Overview*, ed. King and Vogler.

70 On this issue see John J. Contreni, 'Inharmonius Harmony: Education in the Carolingian World,' *The Annals of Scholarship: Metastudies of the Humanities and Social Sciences* 1 (1980): 81–96 (repr. in Contreni, *Carolingian Learning, Masters and Manuscripts*, Variorum Collected Studies Series CS363 [Aldershot, England, 1992], chap. 4); and Roberto Giacone, 'Giustificazione degli "Studia liberalia" dalla sacralizzazione alcuiniana all'immanentismo di Giovanni Scoto Eriugena,' in *Civiltà del Piemonte: Studi in onore di Renzo Gandolfo nel suo settantacinquesimo compleanno*, ed. Gianrenzo P. Clivio and Riccardo Massono (Turin, 1975), 823–32.

71 Wolfgang Sörrensen, 'Gärten und Pflanzen im Klosterplan,' in *Studien zum St. Galler Klosterplan*, ed. Duft, 193–277.

72 Horn and Born, *Plan of St. Gall*, 2: 301–13; and Hecht, *St. Galler Klosterplan*, 141–57.

73 Horn and Born, *Plan of St. Gall*, 2: 117–39.

74 Ibid., 2: 249–64.

75 Ibid., 2: 225–48; and Walter Horn, 'Waterpower and the Plan of St. Gall,' *Journal of Medieval History* 1 (1975): 219–58.

76 On this complicated matter, see Horn and Born, *Plan of St. Gall*, 1: 187–239; and especially Jacobsen, *Klosterplan von St. Galler*, 107–48, 191–320, where a close comparison made

attuned to the cutting edge of Carolingian liturgical developments.[77] Although the type of the structure that the author of the Plan envisioned for the various guest and service buildings will probably always remain problematic, strong cases have been made to support the conjecture that those buildings were intended to represent a technologically creative adaptation of forms of house construction prevailing in the ninth century.[78]

This impressive evidence of responsiveness to the way things were and should be done in the ninth-century cultural and technological world adds up to a single conclusion: The Plan of St Gall did not envision an austere 'cave' hidden away in a desert and consciously devoid of any concession to the human side of existence. Its creator made sure that no one would say of his 'Utopia'[79] what the Monk of St Gall said about the real monastery of St Gall in the late eighth century: that it was 'the poorest and most austere place in the whole empire.'[80] The Plan proclaims that monks should dwell in a 'city' where everything that the contemporary world possessed in terms of sustaining earthly existence and promoting human well-being could be put to use in nurturing the spirit. Such a 'city' was possible only if there was ongoing interaction between the cloister and the world in the arena of ideas and techniques.

VI

Having completed our scrutiny of the Plan of St Gall, can we draw any conclusions about the question that prompted our inquiry: What was the author of the Plan trying to say to anyone who reflected on the arrangement and the purposes

between the basilica proposed on the Plan and other Carolingian churches that have been excavated shows that the Plan's church reflected main currents in contemporary church architecture. Jacobsen, ibid., 35–78, 149–90, also reviews the evidence indicating that the creator of the Plan experimented with different forms before completing his sketch of the church.

77 See Carol Heitz, *Recherches sur les rapports entre architecture et liturgie à l'époque carolingienne* (Paris, 1963); Heitz, 'More romana: Problèmes d'architecture et liturgie carolingiennes,' in *Roma e l'età carolingia: Atti delle giornate di studio, 3–8 maggio 1976*, A cura dell'Istituto di storia dell'arte dell'Università de Roma (Rome, 1976), 27–37; Heitz, *L'architecture religieuse carolingienne*, 108–17, 254–60; and Jacobsen, *Klosterplan von St. Galler*, 239–59, 305–20.

78 Walter Horn argued that these buildings were to be modelled on a multipurpose pole house that had evolved over several centuries in Germanic northern Europe; see Horn and Born, *Plan of St. Gall*, 2: 3–116. Konrad Hecht argued for a house model derived from Roman peasant houses; see Hecht, *St. Galler Klosterplan*, 221–45.

79 The term is borrowed from Wolfgang Braunfels, *Monasteries of Western Europe: The Architecture of the Orders*, trans. Alastair Laing (London, 1972), 37–46.

80 *Notkeri Balbvli*, Bk. 2, c. 12, ed. Haefele, 72: '... ad cellam Sancti Galli, qui cunctis locis

of the structures he laid out on a fairly constricted surface that Walter Horn proposes measured 640 feet by 480 feet?[81] Our examination has provided compelling reason to think that the Plan, a completely unique 'text' which has no equivalent for several centuries before and after its creation, represents a pioneering statement expressed visually addressing the relationship between the cloister and the world in terms of defining what monastic life was. The Plan proclaims that whatever is fashioned as a monastic establishment must be arranged in a way that at once separates and links these two realms in a context that is terrestrial and human. The central message of the Plan is a call to all concerned to seek ways to give order and structure to a space within which the sacred and the profane *must* intersect so that each might sustain the other.

If the Plan of St Gall is a statement about the relationship between the cloister and the world, then it may provide the crucial clue to the deeper issue that modern scholarship has not satisfactorily resolved. It may be the smoking gun pointing to the essential characteristic of Carolingian monasticism that provided that institution with its distinctive quality and its unique dynamism. The Plan says that the central force driving Carolingian monasticism and shaping its institutional agendum was the quest for a solution to an unresolved problem that had always been inherent in the pursuit of the ascetic ideal. Carolingian monasticism was all about finding a place for the cloister in the terrestrial setting that would allow those in the cloister to progress in their search for spiritual perfection, while at the same time taking into account and making mutually fruitful the inevitable encounter between the two spheres.

This clue as to what Carolingian monasticism was all about is given added credence, perhaps even validated, by a brief reflection on the larger temporal framework within which western monasticism evolved. A case can be made that in traversing western monastic history between 350 and 1100, one encounters two contrasting concepts of the nature of monastic life and of the place of monasticism in the economy of salvation and in Christian society.

Prior to the Carolingian age, a monastery was perceived as an isolated enclave outside the larger Christian community, an island where individuals worked their way towards perfection, free from relationships with the mainland world, which was irreparably corrupt and inevitably corrupting. Such a vision of the fundamental nature of the monastery found expression in different insti-

imperii latissimi pauperior visa est et angustior.' This description was proffered to explain why Pepin the Hunchback was sentenced to imprisonment at St Gall because of his involvement in a revolt against Charlemagne in 792.

81 Since the Plan contains no indication of the location or the form of its outer boundaries, the question of the total area of the complex which the Plan's author had in mind must remain open.

tutional forms: the desert *lavra*; the Pachomian boot camp; the place made magical by the bones of a holy person; Cassiodorus' institute of advanced studies; the transient camp of the Irish *peregrinus* with his evanescent following of spiritual groupies; Saint Benedict's 'school for the service of the Lord.' But these models shared a common characteristic: each gathering of the holy stood alone, needing nothing from other gatherings or from society at large in order to pursue the strenuous business of opening conduits to the divine through which grace flowed into select individuals who had established their eligibility by severing all ties with the world. From the perspective of western monastic history *in toto*, the period from 350 to 700 perhaps can be described as an age when the quest for spiritual perfection was perceived and organized on an autarchic principle.

Beyond the Carolingian age, say, by about 1000, one encounters a monastic world that differs both in perception and in reality. Except for a few hermits seeking to return to the old autarchic ascetic ideals, most monks now collectively constituted a distinctive *ordo* discharging a special role vital to the spiritual condition and the salvation not only of individual monks, but of the total Christian community. The bonds knitting together the members of the *ordo* of monks were consciously articulated: a common constitution, a monarchically structured system of monastic governance, a standard regimen of activity, a uniform pattern of worship, a shared mode of interacting with ecclesiastical and political authorities, and a consistent message to the entire Christian community mapping out the path towards a richer spiritual life and salvation. Borrowing again from the language of political economy, monasticism had been collectivized and socialized.

How, when, and under what circumstances did that passage from one kind of monasticism to the other occur? Unless one subscribes to a 'big bang' theory of societal transformation, one must posit some process working in a discrete time frame to bring about the observed metamorphosis. The time seems obvious enough: the Carolingian age was the decisive period in the revolutionary transition from autarchic to collectivized, socialized monasticism. The Plan of St Gall provides a crucial clue to the process. The transition involved a conscious search for mechanisms that would allow monks to bond with one another as a distinctive component in the Christian community while at the same time permit them to define a collective role that would link them with the total society operating in an earthly, human context. An essential corollary to the realization of these ends was a reformulation of the traditionally negative ascetic view of the world in ways that envisaged positive consequences flowing from interaction between the cloister and the world. It was the creative effort, generated within the monastic world itself rather than imposed from outside, to realize these ends that made Carolingian monasticism unique and dynamic.

VII

It would be naïve to assume that a conceptual paradigm derived from a reading of a single 'text' and from what some may judge a bit of chronological legerdemain would win instant acceptance. The approach suggested here will be viable only if it can meet the test of the evidence contained in Carolingian sources relative to monasticism. Perhaps this essay can serve as a call to that challenge. It is a plea for a collaborative, interdisciplinary reassessment of the record pertaining to Carolingian monasticism aimed at testing a hypothesis that can be stated in these terms: The dynamic force shaping Carolingian monasticism was a conscious effort to recast in theory and in practice the traditional ascetic ideal in ways that would simultaneously allow all monks to identify with one another as a distinctive *ordo* dedicated to the quest for spiritual perfection and would define a role for that *ordo* in terms that allowed its members to turn to mutual benefit the inevitable interactions that must link the cloister and the world.[82]

Although it would be folly to predict the outcome of a scholarly campaign energized by such a hypothesis, I sense that it would produce an enriched and more accurate picture of Carolingian monasticism. This presentiment derives chiefly from some recent reflections on the role of Carolingian monks in the educational, literary, and artistic activities of the eighth and ninth centuries.[83] I had long been content to follow the lead of such luminaries as Erna Patzelt,

---

82 After I had developed this hypothesis on the basis of my interpretation of the Plan of St Gall, I read the stimulating essay by Oexle, 'Les moines d'occident,' 255–72, which, in assessing the crucial dimension of Carolingian monasticism, strikes a note similiar to my argument. Oexle's argument emboldens me to think that my hypothesis would find support not only in the *Libri memoriales* upon which Oexle relies heavily, but also in such texts as the capitularies and conciliar enactments concerning monasticism, hagiographical texts, liturgical texts, and especially in commentaries on monastic life. Among the commentaries that seem rich in expanding our insight into the fundamental nature of Carolingian monasticism if approached from a new perspective are those of Adalhard of Corvey, Haito of Reichenau in the so-called statutes of Murbach, Hildemar of Corvey, and Smaragdus of St Mihiel; see the following: *Statuta seu Brevia Adalhardi abbatis Corbiensis*, ed. J. Semmler, in *Corpus Consuetudinum Monasticarum*, ed. Hallinger, 1: 355–422 (English translation: 'The Customs of Corbie. Consuetudines Corbeiensis,' trans. Charles W. Jones, in Horn and Born, *Plan of St. Gall*, 3: 91–120); 'Actuum praeliminorum Synodi I. Aquisgranensis commentationes sive Statuta Murbacensis,' ed. J. Semmler, in *Corpus Consuetudinum Monasticarum*, ed. Hallinger, 1: 441–50; Hildemar, *Expositio Regulae Sancti Benedictini*, ed. Mittermüller; and *Smaragdi abbatis Expositio in Regulam S. Benedicti*, ed. Alfredus Spannagel and Pius Engelbert, in *Coprus Consuetudinum Monasticarum*, ed. Hallinger, vol. 8 (Siegburg, 1974).

83 These reflections arose in connection with editing a volume devoted to Carolingian learning; see '*The Gentle Voices of Teachers*,' ed. Sullivan. And they were nurtured by the stimulating essays in *Carolingian Culture: Emulation and Innovation*, ed. Rosamond McKitterick (Cambridge, 1994), and in *New Cambridge Medieval History*, vol. 2.

Max Laistner, Walter Ullmann, Pierre Riché, and Wolfgang Braunfels in approaching monastic cultural activities as responses to Charlemagne's program of educational and religious *renovatio*. Such an approach told me a great deal about Carolingian culture but not much about the essential character of Carolingian monasticism. However, when I began to review the evidence from the perspective of the hypothesis outlined above, a different picture suggested itself. Increasingly I began to sense that it was an impulse from within the monastic world, and not an imposed cultural mandate, that gave shape and direction to monastic cultural activity. Perhaps, during the Carolingian age, monastic leaders, abetted by secular and episcopal figures, began to see that the nurture of cultural activity could be a powerful instrument in the cause of reshaping monasticism, that is, in the cause of collectivizing and socializing monasticism. Perhaps to arrive at that conviction required no great leap of consciousness; the efficacy of learning as an instrument of personal spiritual advancement was well ingrained in the autarchic monastic world. All that was needed was to extend learning's function to serve the ends that would promote the collectivization and socialization of monasticism. What was dynamic and distinctive about the Carolingian age was that the leap was made not only in consciousness, but also in action. Mastering a common language, writing and speaking according to standard grammatical rules, reading and singing the monastic office from uniform texts, seeking spiritual sustenance from a common storehouse of tradition, exchanging reactions to the texts bearing that tradition, correcting each other's views on the interpretation of these texts, creating and sharing common visual symbols, all served to knit the entire society of monks together and to generate cultural artefacts that made palpable the monks' collective presence in the world. Cultural endeavours also served to develop essential skills promoting the socialization of monasticism. Such activities prepared monks to serve teaching, pastoral, missionary, and administrative roles, all vital functions permitting monks to claim a share in the correction and ultimate salvation of all society as partners with other agencies in the secular world. The Carolingian record is replete with evidence that cultural enterprises did provide the kinds of windows to the world that the designer of the Plan of St Gall built into his imagined monastery. In short, both Carolingian cultural life and Carolingian monasticism were given distinctive shape by individuals seeking to use thought and expression as a means of allowing monks to bond with one another and of articulating a role for monks that linked their enterprise in a fructifying way with the secular realm.[84]

---

84 In retrospect I sense that the study of Carolingian cultural life might have taken a different
   shape had scholars paid more serious attention to Jean Leclercq's effort to define '*monastic*

Perhaps comparable results would emerge if our hypothesis were applied to other aspects of Carolingian monasticism. Would a re-examination of the involvement of monastic communities in political life take on dimensions larger and more complex than mere secular manipulation if that involvement were approached in terms of an effort of the monastic establishment to fix its position as an *ordo* with a unique role in the governance of God's people? Would the concern for the management of monastic property become more than an unholy enterprise engaged in by cowled entrepreneurs seeking to ward off worldly corporate raiders while simultaneously enriching themselves if that concern were approached in terms of achieving monastic identity and of anchoring the monastic community permanently in the material world? Would monastic explorations of ecclesiology turn out to be something other than a defensive ploy to stand off the power moves of ministerial kings and magisterial bishops if those explorations were examined in the light of the effort to find a role for the *vita contemplativa* in the larger entity called the *ecclesia,* which embraced the entire *societas christiana*? Would the accomplishments of a constellation of amazingly productive abbots assume a different complexion if they were judged by their efforts to coalesce their colleagues and their minions into a collective force with a precise role in their world rather than by their performance as craven seekers of favours from the power establishment and self-satisfied 'fat cats,' basking in their worldly success?

Only time and effort can answer these queries that are really much more complex than they seem in their asking. In the meantime, let us hope that our brief engagement with the Plan of St Gall has in some small way suggested what Walter Goffart has so often reminded us: An effort to make the old texts sing a new song often opens the mind to new perspectives on the past as it actually was.

culture' as set forth in his *L'amour des lettres et le désir de Dieu: Introduction aux autours monastiques du Moyen Âge* (Paris, 1957) (English translation: *The Love of Learning and the Desire for God: A Study of Monastic Culture*, trans. Catharine Misrahi, 3d ed. [New York, 1982; repr. 1988]).

14

The *Chronicle* of Claudius of Turin

MICHAEL IDOMIR ALLEN

Claudius of Turin (d. *ca* 827) claims notice in most considerations of Carolingian literature, theology, and heresy. He enjoys the reputation of a fierce and articulate enemy of icons and pilgrimage. The received view of Claudius the rebel often masks his contemporary prominence as a teacher and exegete.[1] Yet it was precisely Claudius' renown as a teacher and the reputation of his didactic writings that ensured his fame as a heretic. The mouthpiece, as much as the message, made for scandal and opposition. Doubts remain as to the purport of Claudius' dissent as bishop of Turin, but literary outrage flared against him and deeply coloured his historical reputation.[2] Modern scholars have judged the contemporary reaction effective enough to push the bishop's writings into a

I should like to thank Lucy K. Pick for wise counsel, and the Michigan Society of Fellows at the University of Michigan, for research support that facilitated this essay.

1 In general, C. Leonardi, 'Claudius v. Turin,' *Lexikon des Mittelalters*, vol. 2 (Munich, 1983), cols. 2132–3 (with bibliography); M. Manitius, *Geschichte der lateinischen Literatur des Mittelalters* (Munich, 1911–31), 1: 390–6 (without mention of the *Chronicle*); of special importance for this essay, M. Ferrari, 'Note su Claudio di Torino, "Episcopus ab ecclesia damnatus,"' *Italia medioevale e umanistica* 16 (1973): 291-308, at 291–3. Notwithstanding Ferrari's beguiling epithet, Claudius died at most 'damned by his own judgment'; he was variously attacked, but never officially condemned: Walahfrid Strabo, *Libellus de exordiis et incrementis*, in *Capitularia Regum Francorum*, ed. A. Boretius and V. Krause, MGH Capitularia 2/3 (1897), 483, ll. 6–7 ('suo iudicio damnatus'). A further useful study appeared after this essay went to press: Michael Gorman, 'The Commentary on Genesis of Claudius of Turin and Biblical Studies under Louis the Pious,' *Speculum* 72 (1997): 279–329.

2 The key respondents were the Irish scholar Dungal (in 827) and Bishop Jonas of Orléans (in 840!), both eminent and harsh opponents. See the valuable study by A. Boureau, 'Les théologiens carolingiens devant les images religieuses: La conjecture de 825,' in *Nicée II, 787–1987: Douze siècles d'images religieuses*, ed. F. Boespflug and N. Lossky (Paris, 1987), 247–62.

penumbra of suspicion and anonymity.[3] The evidence is not conclusive, and Claudius' *Chronicle* offers at least one case where the reaction conspicuously failed. A critical edition of the work remains a desideratum, but fresh insights into Claudius' life and afterlife emerge from considering the available printed text, the manuscripts, the form, and the content of his *Chronicle*.[4]

According to his later detractors, Claudius came to Francia from Spain in the train of the Adoptionist heretic, Bishop Felix of Urgel, sometime before 800.[5] Claudius' handwriting points to his Visigothic background and elementary training in Spain. On his own testimony, his education included no formal course in secular letters, which agrees with his sometimes faulty Latin diction and rare use of classical borrowings. Claudius emphasized his time of study at Lyon during the cultural revival fostered there by Archbishop Leidrad at the beginning of the ninth century. Then and later, Claudius' principal focus was Scripture and its patristic commentators. It was from Lyon that Louis the Pious summoned the Visigothic priest to the court of his Aquitainian sub-kingdom, where Claudius soon enjoyed official credit. He cut a profile as a lecturer on the Bible, and Louis the Pious himself commanded him to set down his oral expositions as finished commentary.[6] Other patrons also pressed him to write. The earliest manuscript of his *Commentary on Genesis*, a work dedicated to an outside patron, Abbot Dructeramnus, features both autograph corrections by Claudius in Visigothic script and a *subscriptio* placing him at the palace at Chasseneuil, near Poitiers, in 811.[7] In addition to his commentaries on Matthew

---

3 Notably, M.L.W. Laistner, *Thought and Letters in Western Europe, A.D. 500 to 900*, 2d ed. (Ithaca, N.Y., 1957), 302. In this vein, MS. Düsseldorf, Universitätsbibl., B 3, with an abbreviation of Claudius' *Commentary on Genesis* copied in the 820s, consigns the author to oblivion: D.A. Bullough and A.L.H. Corrêa, 'Texts, Chant, and the Chapel of Louis the Pious,' in *Charlemagne's Heir: New Perspectives on the Reign of Louis the Pious (814–840)*, ed. P. Godman and R. Collins (Oxford, 1990), 498 and n. 29; cf. D. Ganz, *Corbie in the Carolingian Renaissance*, Beihefte der Francia 20 (Sigmaringen, 1990), 55.

4 A new edition of Claudius' *Chronicle* is in preparation for the CCCM by M.I. Allen.

5 Manitius, *Geschichte* 1: 390–6; B. Simson, *Jahrbücher des fränkischen Reiches unter Ludwig dem Frommen* , vol. 2 (Leipzig, 1876), 245–51.

6 Claudius, Ep. 6: *Epistolae Karolini Aevi*, ed. E. Dümmler, MGH Epistola 4 (1895), 601, ll. 29–34. Like other Carolingian exegetes, Claudius worked chiefly by excerpting and harmonizing patristic authorities: J.J. Contreni, 'Carolingian Biblical Studies,' in *Carolingian Essays: Andrew W. Mellon Lectures in Early Christian Studies*, ed. U.-R. Blumenthal (Washington, D.C., 1983), 85–8.

7 J. Vezin, 'Le commentaire sur la Genèse de Claude de Turin, un cas singulier de transmission des textes wisigothiques dans la Gaule carolingienne,' in *L'Europe heritière de l'Espagne wisigothique*, ed. J. Fontaine and C. Pellistrandi, Collection de la Casa de Velázquez 35 (Madrid, 1992), 223–9. Vezin discusses Lyon as a Visigothic *foyer de culture* and Claudius' corrections in MS Paris, BN, lat. 9575. Cf. Gorman, 'Commentary,' 295–6.

and sundry Pauline epistles, Claudius covered the first books of the Old Testament in a program of exegetical works.[8] He was the most admired and prolific Carolingian commentator on the Bible in the interval between Alcuin's death (d. 804) and the emergence of Hrabanus Maurus in the 820s.[9]

Claudius, a protégé of the imperial heir, securely weathered the change of regime that followed Charlemagne's death. His work as a teacher and commentator continued unabated, and in 814, the first year of the new reign, the court lecturer on Scripture penned at least one of the paired sections that form his *Chronicle*.[10] The work shows Claudius at the height of his reputation not long before his promotion by Louis the Pious to bishop of Turin in *ca* 816.

None the less, the *Chronicle* figures today among Claudius' least-studied writings. In 1657, the French antiquarian Philippe Labbe published two fragments of the text, which remain widely accessible thanks to the reprint in Migne's *Patrologia Latina*.[11] In 1895, Ernst Dümmler, an influential editor of Claudius, assayed the printed fragments and the three extant manuscripts of the *Chronicle*, but concluded mistakenly that the 'scanty chronological writing on the six ages of the world down to 814' was by another author.[12] He accordingly excluded the letter-preface to the *Chronicle* from his MGH edition of Claudius' *Epistolae*, and set a question mark over the work, which some scholars rightly disregarded.[13] In 1973, Mirella Ferrari restored the attribution of the text to Claudius of Turin, and laid the basis for further study by discussing the manuscripts and editing the letter-preface.[14] Her contribution stands on its merits, but stops short of attempting to address the contours and contents of Claudius' complete work.

---

8 I.M. Douglas, 'The Commentary on the Book of Ruth by Claudius of Turin,' *Sacris Erudiri* 22 (1974–5): 295–6. Claudius' commentaries are listed by F. Stegmüller, *Repertorium Biblicum Medii Aevi*, vol. 2 (1950): 242–9. The program discerned by Douglas perhaps anticipates the full commentary of Scripture envisaged by Helisachar in the 820s; cf. B. Bischoff, 'Die Bibliothek im Dienste der Schule,' in *Mittelalterliche Studien* 3 (Stuttgart, 1981): 232–3.

9 Manitius, *Geschichte* 1: 392, n. 2. Others neglect Claudius' contribution: for one, E.A. Matter, 'Exegesis and Christian Education: The Carolingian Model,' in *Schools of Thought in the Christian Tradition,* ed. P. Henry (Philadelphia, 1984), 90–105.

10 See below, n. 16.

11 *Novae Bibliothecae Manuscriptorum Librorum*, vol. 1 (Paris, 1657), 309–15; repr.in *PL* 104, cols. 917–26.

12 E. Dümmler, 'Über Leben und Lehre des Bischofs Claudius von Turin,' *Sitzungsberichte der königlich-preussischen Akademie der Wissenschaften zu Berlin* 1895, Pt. 1, 442. Cf. below, n. 28.

13 Notably, A.D. von den Brincken, who assessed the text of Labbe's fragments in her *Studien zur lateinischen Weltchronistik bis in das Zeitalter Ottos von Freising* (Düsseldorf, 1957), 117–18.

14 Ferrari, 'Note,' 301–8.

Beyond the letter-preface edited by Ferrari, Claudius' *Chronicle* comprises two distinct parts. The second of these has long been known from the fragments printed by Labbe. In this section, Claudius offers a rapid survey of the Six Ages of the World as conceived and presented in Bede's *De temporum ratione*, especially in the long chapter known as the *Greater Chronicle*.[15] Yet Claudius, unlike his more wide-ranging model, trains his sights relentlessly on Old Testament biblical data, which he uses to anchor the Six Ages and their sacred milestones on a scale of years reckoned from the Creation of the World to the Incarnation. The emphasis is on spans of time and datings, rather than interpreting events. Claudius' personal contribution to the composition is his effort to fit various Old Testament datings according to the Hebrew lunar calendar into the prevailing Christian system based on the Roman solar year (as presented by Bede). The resulting text abounds in sums and complex calendrical conversions, hence the tag 'reckoning section' which will distinguish it here. Its last calculation, keyed to the year of Charlemagne's death, dates Claudius' figurings to 814.[16]

In manuscripts of the complete *Chronicle*, Claudius' reckonings on the Six Ages take second place to a more lively 'display section' that features both diagram and text. The display consists of a series of verso–recto openings used as frames for a left-to-right progression of inscribed genealogical roundels accompanied by discursive exposition.[17] The result is a commentated genealogical tree from Adam to Emanuel whose textual component includes patristic extracts and occasional borrowings from the reckoning section that now figures spatially as the tailpiece, though it is textually prior.

The complete package begins with a letter-preface to the priest Ado from *Claudius peccator*, the epithet used by Claudius until his ordination as bishop.[18] The finished *Chronicle* therefore dates to the period between 814 and *ca* 816. Its combined sections suggest that Claudius now taught a range of material to a varied audience at the court. Diagrams and computations are the stock-in-trade of elementary instruction. Their use in the *Chronicle* mirrors how the text originated and flourished as a basic instructional tool.

---

15 On the Six Ages and Bede, von den Brincken, *Studien*, 91–2, 110–11; also R. Schmidt, 'Aetates mundi: Die Weltalter als Gliederungsprinzip der Geschichte,' *Zeitschrift für Kirchengeschichte* 67 (1956): 288–317, esp. 289–90.

16 *Chron.*, pt. 2, *PL* 104, 924D: '... colliguntur omnes anni a conditione mundi usque ad praesentem annum, qui est incarnationis Domini nostri Iesu Christi 814, quo piae recordationis et bonae semper memoriae Carolus gloriosus princeps ex hoc migrauit mortali saeculo, et ei pius princeps sanctae Dei Ecclesiae catholicae Ludouicus successit imperio, anni 4766.'

17 Cf. Ferrari, 'Note,' 303–4.

18 This Ado is probably not to be identified with the homonymous archbishop of Vienne (860–75). For *peccator*, Epp. 1–4, MGH Epistolae 4, 590–7. Cf. Ferrari, 'Note,' 302.

The extant witnesses of the *Chronicle* resist the clear-cut summary of content and form given above. A review of the evidence will clarify not only the work's structure, but also important features of the transmission.[19]

The earliest extant copy of the *Chronicle* is preserved in MS Paris, BnF, lat. 5001, fols. 1^r–8^v.[20] The codex groups elements from three separate, early manuscripts, whose dry-point ruling, content, and script visibly differ. The present *recueil factice* of four booklets measures 170 x 128mm and is bound in eighteenth-century covers stamped with the French royal blazon. The pertinent details are as follows:

Booklet I, fols. 1–8. 24 long lines, justification 145 x 95mm; begins in red, *Incipit prefatio in cronica Claudii*, then 'Quia igitur fautore Deo ...'; expl. '... regnauit mensibus tribus.' The text corresponds exactly to Labbe's first fragment (PL 104, 917C–924B). The script is from eastern France, saec. ix$^{3/4}$. The quaternion contains corrections in Tironian shorthand and bears the early quire mark 'G' at the base of fol. 8^v.

Booklet II, fols. 9–16. 25 long lines, justification 153 x 87mm; inc. '... adimitur quod ante luna deficit ...'; expl. 'Reliquum sextae aetatis Deo soli patet.' The text is Bede, *De temporibus* 12–22,[21] in a script, and with Tironian notes, as in booklet I.

Booklet III, fols. 17–24. 24 long lines, justification 142 x 94mm; with three texts in the script of booklet I: (1) the complete *Cronica regum Francorum* (Tiliana) to A.D. 855, probably the copy from which Jean de Tillet published the text in 1639 (fols. 17^r–19^v); (2) an aborted copy of the *Sententiae phylosophorum* of 'Caecilius Balbulus' (fols. 20^r–22^r); and (3) a copy of the well-known *Versus cuiusdam Scothi de AB* (fols. 23^r–24^r).[22] Two later hands (saec. x/xi) have written a genealogy of French kings after

19 I studied the Paris MS *in situ* and the Monza MS from a microfilm kindly supplied by Professor Mirella Ferrari. My observations on the Madrid manuscript build on Ferrari's account and on brief study of a microfilm received after this essay was in press. The present survey updates Ferrari on many points, but does not entirely replace her discussion.

20 Cf. Ferrari, 'Note,' 302–3. I wish to thank Professor Jean Vezin for discussing the codex with me.

21 Ed. C.W. Jones and T. Mommsen, CCSL 123C, 598–611. The variants in the Paris MS share the readings in Mommsen's apparatus for *P*, Città del Vaticano, BAV, Pal. lat. 1448 (Trier, A.D. 810); e.g., fol. 13^v, ll. 8–11, equals *P* at *De temporibus* 21, 606, l. 4.

22 On the *Cronica regum Francorum*, B.C. Barker-Benfield, 'A Ninth-Century Manuscript from Fleury: *Cato de senectute cum Macrobio*,' in *Medieval Learning and Literature. Essays Presented to Richard William Hunt*, ed. J.J.G. Alexander and M. Gibson (Oxford, 1976), 159, n. 4. On this copy of the *Versus de alphabeto*, B. Bishoff, 'Bannita: 1. Syllaba, 2. Littera,' in *Mittelalterliche Studien* 3: 247 ('aus dem dritten Viertel des IX. Jahrhunderts ... aus dem östlichen Frankreich'). Bischoff's dating and localization, though directed at the *Versus*, apply equally to the preceding texts.

the *Sententiae* breaks off (fols. 22^r–22^v).[23] The quaternion bears the early quire mark 'F' on the otherwise blank fol. 24^v.

Booklet IV, fols. 25–29, a binion with an extraneous singleton (fol. 28) on a stub. Binion: 24 lines in two columns, justification 139 x 97mm; with a complete copy of the *Notitia Galliarum* (fols. 25^r–27^v, 29^r), then *Voces uariae animalium* ('Ouis balat ... aes tinnit'; fol. 29^v). Singleton: 25 long lines, justification 148 x 90mm; with an unidentified six-line fragment of verse (fol. 28^r and an excerpt from Macrobius, *In somnium Scipionis* (fol. 28^{r-v}).[24] The binion and the singleton are each by different French hands, saec. ix^2.

From these details, a number of points are immediately clear. First, based on layout and content, booklet IV is a patchwork originally unrelated to the preceding group. Second, the first three booklets share a common chronographical theme, similar layout, and uniform script (eastern France, saec. ix$^{3/4}$); booklets I and II also contain Tironian notes by the same hand (no later than saec. x–xi); thus all three were together at an early date. Third, booklet III formerly stood before booklet I as quire 'F' to quire 'G,' without leaving a place for the display section of our *Chronicle*. Since Labbe published precisely the text contained by 'G' as well as a second authentic fragment, the manuscript must once have followed 'G' with a quire 'H' that originally contained the balance of the reckoning section. The span of text missing in Labbe's print suggests that 'H' had already lost its two outer bifolia by Labbe's day; the two inner bifolia have since disappeared.[25] Claudius' *Chronicle* thus circulated early (saec. ix$^{3/4}$) in a partial version limited to the reckoning section. The fully elaborated pairing of diagrams and calculation required generous spacing for the display section. The diminutive pages of this manuscript could not accommodate the sprawling genealogy, so the copyist omitted it. The incipit shows that he copied from the

23 A change of hand occurs after the entry on Childeric III, the last Merovingian. A second writer then begins with Arnulf; he terms Louis II, 'the Do-Nothing' (*nihil fecit*), and Charles III, 'the Stupid' (*stultus*), on fol. 22^v; and he ends with Robert II (996–1031). An eleventh-century hand adds a tailpiece on Henry I (1031–60), ending '... prout potest regnum Franciae gubernat.'
24 Barker-Benfield, 'Ninth-Century Manuscript,' 159, n. 4.
25 The missing text in Labbe equals two sets of four pages in the format of 'G.' For possibly related *membra disiecta*, see M. Mostert, *The Library of Fleury: A Provisional List of Manuscripts*, Middeleeuwse Studies en Bronnen 3 (Hilversum, 1989), no. BF1052. However, BF1052 has no letters of Lupus of Ferrières. Also, both BF1052 and BF1152 (Paris, BnF, lat. 8488A) have been linked to MS '000' from the Carmelite Library of Clermont-Ferrand (purchased for the Colbert collection in 1690) by C. Couderc, *Catalogue général des manuscrits des bibliothèques publiques de France: Départements* 14 (Paris, 1890), XVII, no. 34; XXI, no. 78.

complete *Chronicle*; the rubric names the author, something only possible if the abbreviator knew of *Claudius peccator* from the letter-preface to Ado.

The full, combined text of the *Chronicle* is transmitted in MS Madrid, BN, 9605 (285 x 197mm, justification 237 x 160mm; southern France, A.D. 1026), fols. 103^r-111^r, 112^r-116^v.[26] Here, the divide between the sections is explicitly articulated. At the top of fol. 111^v, the rubric *Explicit prima aedicio Claudii de sex aetatibus* trails the display section; the reckoning section begins at the head of fol. 112^r with the tag *Claudius iterum Adoni presbitero sermonem dirigit in Christo*. Both rubrics are peculiar to the manuscript. They name Claudius, but serve, in fact, to bracket a verso page of additions. An interpolator has filled the divide between Claudius' sections with apposite patristic extracts on the calendar date of Jesus' Passion (fol. 111^v).[27] The same individual probably also appended the string of like-minded calculations and chronological notes (fols. 115^r-116^v) that follow Claudius' reckoning section and conclude with a dating to A.D. 854 and a mention of Charles the Bald as reigning king (840–77).[28] In the surviving Provençal copy, the scribe, Arnulf, has added a colophon that dates his transcription to 1026.[29]

The interpolator of 854 shared Claudius' fascination with dates. His additions between the two parts of the *Chronicle* stabilized the work's layout, and situate his model close to Claudius' original. The layout of the display section posed strict limitations. The need to set genealogical frames across whole open-

26 Cf. Ferrari, 'Note,' 304–5. For detailed description, but with little on the Claudius portion, see A. Cordoliani, 'Un autre manuscrit de comput ecclésiastique mal connu de la Bibliothèque Nationale de Madrid,' *Revista de Archivos, Bibliotecas y Museos* 61 (1955): 435–81, esp. 481.

27 These additions are not identified in Ferrari's summary descriptions, nor are they explained. Yet her reports of the verso's incipit ('Victorinus homo Aquitanus invitatus a sancto Hilario ...') and explicit ('... pro uniuersis solis et lunae concordat cursus') point to Gennadius of Marseille, *De uiris inlustribus*, 89 (on *Victorius'* paschal tables), and to Bede, *De tempore ratione*, 47 (on the Passion); cf. respectively E.C. Richardson, ed., *Texte und Untersuchungen zur Geschichte der altchristlichen Literatur* 14/1 (Leipzig, 1896), 92, ll. 21–2; C.W. Jones and T. Mommsen, eds., CCSL 123B, 428–31, ll. 23–85.

28 Ferrari identifies the additions (from Julian of Toledo and Isidore of Seville); she then transcribes the entire tailpiece. It equates the beginning of the A.D. era with the year 5325 *ab inicio mundi*, which is without parallel; cf. von den Brincken, *Studien*, table 4. However, the transmission is suspect, since the next clause makes 854 the fortieth (*quadragesimum*) year of Charles the Bald's reign. Failing to distinguish interpolator from author, Dümmler used the mention of 854 to deny the authorship of Claudius of Turin (d. *ca* 827); cf. Ferrari, 'Note,' 301.

29 In the full colophon, Arnulf mentions the death in 1026 (the year used for trial computistical exercises early in the codex) of Adalax *comitissa*, whom Ferrari identifies as the wife of William I of Provence. Cf. no. 1432 in *Colophons de manuscrits occidentaux des origines au XVIe siècle*, by the Benedictines of Bouveret, 6 vols., Spicilegii Friburgensis Subsidia 2–7 (Fribourg, 1965–82), 1: 177.

ings made the letter-preface a doubly functional device: it not only introduced the work, but also filled space so as to wedge the ensuing genealogy onto an opening-sized frame. In the Madrid manuscript, an originally blank page precedes the *Chronicle*, which suggests that Arnulf, a skilful copyist, took care to safeguard a particular *mise-en-page*.[30] The letter-preface to Ado appears on a recto (fol. 103^r), while the display section begins, as it must, across a full opening (fols. 103^v–104^r). Claudius completed his work by joining the reckoning section as a tailpiece to the genealogical tree. The joint occurred after a blank verso that followed the sequence of opening-sized frames. Like Claudius' letter-preface, the additions inserted (fol. 111^v) after the display section of the Madrid manuscript wedge the beginning of the reckoning section onto the next recto (fol. 112^r). The interpolations first responded to, and then anchored, Claudius' arrangement of the text. Arnulf's copy mirrors Claudius' joining of the sections: the added material blocks out the 'empty' verso between the authentic parts.[31] The Madrid codex physically recalls both its ancestor of 854 and Claudius' finished work.

The complete *Chronicle* shows Claudius remarkably generous with parchment.[32] The genealogical tree was inherently wasteful and left valuable blanks that almost begged to be filled.[33] This invitation was met with verve in the third extant manuscript containing the full text: Monza, Bibl. Capit., c-9/69 (330 x 235mm, justification 250 x 170mm; northern Italy, saec. x^1), fols. 66ra–83vb.[34] The Monza copy shares the relatively large physical size and the effort to safeguard layout of the Madrid codex. A preceding column (fol. 67rb) is left blank to ensure that the display section will begin, as it should, across an opening (fols. 67^v–68^r). However, the genealogical commentary suffers from displacements, interpolations, and consequent disturbance of its original plan.

Within the Monza codex, Claudius' *Chronicle* figures as a distinct element in the so-called *Liber tertius* (fols. 19rb–86^v). This 'third book' is a subsection of a longer program of basic school texts, copied in the same hand and taken mostly from the works of Isidore of Seville. The 'book' begins with its own

---

30 In mentioning this blank, Ferrari emphasizes the artistic unity of the codex: 'Note,' 304 and n. 2; likewise, Cordoliani, 'Un autre manuscrit,' p. 436. The blank is purposive.

31 The manuscripts of the *Chronicle* of Eusebius-Jerome offer another, more elaborate example of how a complex layout tends to preserve itself. See R. Helm, Introduction to *Die Chronik des Hieronymus*, 3d ed. reprint, Griechische Christliche Schriftsteller 47 (Berlin, 1984), XXI–XXVII.

32 Yet in 815 he also bemoans his poverty: Ep. 2, MGH Epistolae 4, 595, l. 14.

33 Ferrari's 'scorie depositate dai lettori,' less common in the Madrid copy: 'Note,' 306.

34 Cf. Ferrari, 'Note,' 305–7. More generally on the codex, A. Belloni and M. Ferrari, *La biblioteca capitolare di Monza*, Medioevo e Umanesimo 21 (Padua, 1974), 54–6.

index of content (fols. 19rb–20rb), and combines sundry computistical, astronomical, and chronographical materials.[35] Claudius' *Chronicle* coincides with a series of indexed entries because its display section is now disordered at points and interspersed with additions. The letter-preface (fol. 66$^{ra–vb}$) ends with two bits of commentary (fols. 66vb–67ra) that should conclude the first genealogical frame. This particular opening presents the *prima saeculi aetas* (fols. 67^v–68^r), and properly ends with a pair of excerpts on Mathusala and Enoch, as occurs in the Madrid manuscript. Here, however, these texts have a distinct index entry and stand separated from the initial frame by the liminary blank column (fol. 67rb).[36]

The copyist of the Monza text remained careful to avoid homogenizing the varied content of a difficult exemplar. In the above example, the final commentary on the first opening in the model had, it seems, overflowed and forced a backward removal of text to avoid spoiling the next frame, which begins the *secunda saeculi aetas*.[37] The Monza scribe accepted what he found, and silently recopied the displaced texts, without understanding what had happened. His model elsewhere distinguished spurious additions by script or placement, for he carried these distinctions into his transcription via differential headings, layout, and indexing. The most considerable intrusions appear in the later openings of the Monza copy, and the longest comprises two chapters taken verbatim from Bede's *Lesser Chronicle* (fols. 75^r-76^r).[38] One curious addition etymologizes various book-related technical terms.[39] Others group and translate Hebrew personal names featured in Claudius' genealogy, with occasional blanks after uninterpreted entries.[40] The blanks suggest that the scribe found

---

35 Cf. B. Bischoff, 'Die europäische Verbreitung der Werke Isidors von Sevilla,' in *Mittelalterliche Studien* 1 (1966): 190–1.

36 The incipit/explicit of the excerpts ('Famosa quaesito ... esse iungendos') match Ferrari's citations from the conclusion of the first frame in the Madrid manuscript: 'Note,' 304 (fol. 104^v); see below, p. 303 and nn. 73 and 74. The index to the *Liber tertius* points to the texts jointly as the 'Questio de Matusala' (fol. 20ra).

37 Fols. 68^v–69^r in the Monza MS.

38 Bede, *De temporibus* 21–2, CCSL 123C, 606–11 (on the Fifth and Sixth Ages); cf. below, p. 309 and n. 108. The text differs from the overlapping fragment in Paris, BnF, lat. 5001, here the readings follow Mommsen's text at *De temporibus* 21, 606, l. 4; cf. above n. 21. This variance makes it unnecessary to consider further the coincidental presence of bits from *De temporibus* in connection with Claudius (cf. Ferrari, 'Note,' 306), who cites rather from Bede's *De temporum ratione*.

39 Fol. 74^v: 'Codex dicitur a cortice arborum ...'

40 Fols. 73$^{r–v}$: 'Incipiunt nomina patrum priorum qualiter in Latinum dicantur' (presented in order of chronological appearance in the Bible); likewise, fol. 74^v: '... nomina prophetarum ...' Blanks appear, for instance, on fol. 73^v, after Obed and Bathsheba ('Bersabe'). The inspiration

these notes incomplete in his model. Together, the intrusions eloquently document the use of Claudius' *Chronicle* as a learning tool long after his death.

While the origin of the additions is uncertain and probably multiple, one such dates and roughly places an ancestor of the Monza text. The addition gives a dating to the current year as a closing tag to the last genealogical frame: the year is A.D. 837, or 'the twenty-third of the imperial reign of Louis the Pious.'[41] The specific regnal formula establishes that the text, although surviving in an Italian copy, was being actively studied in Francia in 837.[42] Otherwise, Lothar I, crowned co-emperor in 824 and sequestered in his northern Italian *regnum* from 830, would figure in the formula.[43] The dating is significant because it documents the use of Claudius' *Chronicle* in a space and at a time when the clouds enveloping the author's reputation were supposedly at their darkest. Moreover, the presence of the formula in a northern Italian descendant establishes that Claudius' work continued to circulate in Carolingian channels of learning.

The assorted intrusions bear witness to the dynamism of the text, but they also upset the layout of the display section. In the Monza codex, the genealogical tree sprawls over eleven frames (fols. 67^v-78^r) in contrast to the eight required in the Madrid manuscript. The bulkiest of the intrusions, the extract from Bede's *Lesser Chronicle*, pushes a long tract of genealogical comment from the framework of openings into an interval of plain columns (fols. 78va-79rb) which precedes the reckoning section.[44] Nevertheless, the Monza manuscript preserves the complete text, and gives a reliable impression of what Claudius intended.

Claudius launched the finished combination of parts from the court by *ca* 816. On the manuscript evidence, the *Chronicle* was studied and perhaps copied in Francia in 837 and 854, and still survives in a roughly contemporary

is clearly Isidore of Seville (cf. *Etymologiae* VII, 6–8), who skips Obed and Bathsheba in his roster of *nomina*. Isidore is the star of the Monza codex (cf. above, nn. 34 and 35), but the intrusions in Claudius may predate the present codicological mix.

41 Fol. 77^v: 'De initio mundi usque in natale Domini anni secundum Hebraicam ueritatem III milia DCCCCLII et deinde usque nunc qui est annus imperii Hludoici XXmus IIItus anni DCCCXXXVII qui fiunt insimul IIII milia DCCLXXXVIIII; et secundum LXX interpretum translationem ...'

42 Ferrari prefers to situate the text 'in una scuola dell'Italia settentrionale nel secondo quarto del secolo IX,' perhaps owing to the Italian recensions of Isidore that precede the *Liber tertius* in the Monza manuscript: 'Note,' 305–6.

43 After 829, Louis the Pious dropped Lothar's name from offical documents issued north of the Alps. Cf. P. Depreux, 'Empereur, Empereur associé et Pape au temps de Louis le Pieux,' *Revue Belge de Philologie et d'Histoire* 70 (1992): 901–5 and notes.

44 See below, p. 309 and n. 110.

repackaging. The work prospered in a supposedly hostile ninth-century Francia. Claudius had struck a chord.

In his letter-preface, Claudius attributes his 'risky venture' of publishing the 'little book' on the 'years and generations from the world's beginning' to a request from Ado.[45] He is quick, however, to distinguish motives of his own for taking up the subject. A sermon falsely attributed to Augustine was, he says, 'being read in church to the populace.' This sermon consigned Adam to Hell for a full 5,228 years, that is, the entire span 'from the Creation to the Passion' according to Eusebius and the Septuagint.[46] Claudius, a keen student of Augustine, insists on the sermon's obviously false attribution. [47] Adam, he protests, did not give names to creation or father sons from Hell. However, a much deeper error remains. Claudius calculates a maximum of 3,986 years from the Creation to the Passion, based on Jerome's Vulgate translation of Hebrew Scripture. He therefore proposes to set out a chronology in accord with 'Hebrew authority.' Unusually, Claudius does not avow until late in the reckoning section his heavy debt to Bede,[48] whose revised year-keeping he adopts.[49] Here, he invokes Augustine and his principle of preferring the Hebrew original (knowable to Claudius through the Vulgate) where it conflicts with the Septuagint. Yet he takes the actual phraseology from Bede's *De temporum ratione* (hereinafter, *DTR*).[50] Claudius speaks in terms of the Bible, but relies constantly on Bede, and others, for the substance of his arguments. To expound sacred time, the professor of Scripture deploys the scissors-and-paste method of

45   I follow Ferrari's *editio princeps* of the letter-preface ('Note,' 307–8), but read 'Periculosum me opus facere iubes ...' for her 'Periculo summe opus ...' (l. 3); cf. ibid., 304 and 306.

46   The sermon remains unidentified. For the figure of 5228 years, based on the Septuagint, Helm, *Die Chronik des Hieronymus*, 174, ll. 1–5.

47   On Claudius and Augustine, J.C. Cavadini, 'Claudius of Turin and the Augustinian Tradition,' in *Proceedings of the PMR* [Patristic, Mediaeval and Renaissance] *Conference*, vol. 11 (Villanova, 1986), 43–50.

48   This near silence on sources contrasts with Claudius' usual fanfare in his exegetical dedications and, sometimes, in the ensuing margins. See Contreni, 'Carolingian Biblical Studies,' 80–2 and notes. On the method of excerpts, see above, n. 6.

49   Claudius' 3,986 years (expressed as 'non plus quam ...') combines the conventional age of Jesus (thirty-three and a half) at the Passion and Bede's calculation of 3,952 years from Creation to the Incarnation; for the former figure, see the consensus of the *compotiste* convoked in 809: *Epistolae uariorum*, no. 42, MGH Epistolae 4, 565, ¶ 3 ('XXXIII semis annos'). Later, Claudius appears to fix the Passion to A.D. 31; see below, n. 128. Bede likewise dates the Passion to 3984: *De temporum ratione* 66, CCSL 123B, 496, ¶ 274 (this edition cited hereinafter by page, then paragraph or line). Bede's pivotal influence is plain from the underlying correction to 3,952 years; cf. von den Brincken, *Studien*, 110–11; below, pp. 310–11 and n. 117.

50   Letter-preface to Ado, ed. Ferrari, 'Note,' 308, ll. 26–39; cf. Bede, *DTR* 66, 467, ¶ 19. Ferrari's apparatus cites only Augustine, *De ciuitate Dei* 15, 13.

Carolingian exegesis. The result reflects Claudius' interests and scholarly technique; it also responded to contemporary concerns.

Claudius' scriptural commentaries take up many vexed questions relating to biblical 'years and generations.' The commentaries also include solutions identical to some adduced in the *Chronicle*. Ado's request did not catch the master unprepared. Claudius could draw on a store of set excerpts and preconfigured argument. He states in the letter-preface to his contemporary *Commentary on Galatians* (*ca* 815) that he actually possessed a cache of patristic extracts ready to be worked into commentary.[51] When Claudius read and excerpted sources, he did so with an eye to useful discussions of biblical chronology. He lived in a cultural milieu newly preoccupied with temporal and calendrical issues, at least to judge from a gathering of time-reckoners (*compotiste*) convoked in 809. The surviving *capitula* of questions and answers make for a dismal comment on prevailing expert knowledge. The respondents failed at first to agree on the 'number of years from the world's beginning to the Incarnation,' and only belatedly settled on 'trusting the number of the Hebrew Truth,' in other words, Bede's Vulgate-based chronology.[52] In this exegetical and cultural ambience, Claudius had occasion and reason to sort through the issues he addressed in the *Chronicle*. When Ado requested the 'little book,' there was a dossier waiting. Literally and metaphorically, Claudius framed the elements provided by Bede and others into a vivid and wanted solution.

The display section of the *Chronicle* deftly marshals the relevant evidence on biblical 'years and generations.'[53] Its key is the genealogy of Christ as separately traced by the evangelists Matthew (1, 1–16) and Luke (3, 23–38). The paired genealogies focus the resulting chronology on pivotal biblical figures.[54]

---

51 Ep. 3, MGH Epistolae 4, 597, ll. 5–7: '... multa in manibus nostris tenentur excerpta ...' Compare the prologue to Claudius' *Commentary on Matthew* (A.D. 815): Ep. 2, ibid., 595, ll. 15–16: '... quaedam [excerpta] minus ordinata ... quaedam ... non fuerunt in tabellis excepta uel scedulis digesta ...'

52 For the capitula, see *Epistolae uariorum*, no. 42, MGH Epistolae 4, 565–6, here ¶ 4. For additional background, see A. Borst, *The Ordering of Time: From the Ancient Computus to the Modern Computer*, trans. A. Winnard (Chicago, 1993), 43–5 and 142 (n. 72); idem, 'Alkuin und die Enzyklopädie von 809,' in *Science in Western and Eastern Civilization in Carolingian Times*, ed. P.L. Butzer and D. Lohrmann (Basel, 1993), 53–78, esp. 70–1.

53 The Monza MS gives the text used here for the display section (*Chron.*, pt. 1) and supplements and sometimes corrects the version of the reckoning section (*Chron.*, pt. 2) given by the Paris MS and Labbe's fragments (in *PL* 104); these sources I cite hereinafter as Monza, Paris, and *PL* 104, respectively.

54 The *Chronicle* disregards non-sacred ancient history apart from a mention of Ninus and Semiramis: pt. 2, *PL* 104, 920D. This secular correlate to Abraham's birth figures in a longer verbatim citation from Bede, *DTR* 66, 470, ¶ 38. It constitutes an exception in Claudius, *pace* von

The teleological perspective makes ancient sacred chronology immediately relevant to Christian believers, and sets off the exegetical tangents that Claudius follows. The enterprise depends on the chain of generational roundels that mark time's advance. To uphold the structure, Claudius is obliged by the New Testament genealogies and the uneven terrain of Hebrew Truth to harmonize biblical variance.

Matthew and Luke thread quite different routes to arrive at the Incarnation.[55] Luke presents a full lineage, ascending from Jesus, via David, to Adam and God, whereas Matthew maps a direct descent from David. Before David, the Bible allows a single possible line, which any writer – Luke, Bede, or Claudius – must follow. From David on, the Gospel genealogies part ways before intersecting at Joseph, the husband of Mary and 'father' of Jesus. The divergence raises questions of fact and symbolism, but practical necessity now makes Matthew the only workable guide for the chronologist because Luke traces an undatable subsidiary line from David via Nathan. Matthew charts the descent from David via Solomon and the kings of Judah, whose regnal dates mark time's advance, not unlike the dated generational sequence found in Genesis. Claudius begins his work by tracking and commenting on the obligatory line from Adam to David. He then makes a fork to accommodate both Gospel genealogies. The descent traced by Luke veers to the bottom of the frames, while Claudius focuses above on Matthew's datable sequence, until Nebuchadnezzar ends the royalty. At this point, Claudius abandons his stepwise tally of years, since others – namely, Bede – have provided a reliable count of the Fifth Age to the Incarnation.[56] Claudius prolongs the twin genealogical branches until they join, and comments on how and why the branches differ, and how they converge in Joseph and Jesus. The display section thus maps the chain stretching from Adam to Emmanuel with notes on its links, segments, offshoots, and detours.

This combination of chronology and genealogy permits a general treatment of interwoven questions. The genius of the exploit lies in the overall fusion rather than the particular solutions, which stem from standard authorities. To harmonize the variant Gospel lineages, Claudius incorporates, for example, nearly all the genealogical exegesis given in Bede's *Commentary on Luke*,

---

den Brincken, *Studien*, 117. Other stray secular intrusions in Monza stem from Bede's *Lesser Chronicle* (*De temporibus*); these I ignore. See above, n. 38.

55 *Pace* Claudius, this genealogical conundrum, like many questions raised in the *Chronicle*, has no satisfactory solution. For a sketch of the basic issues, with patristic background, see *The Jerome Biblical Commentary*, ed. R.E. Brown, J.A. Fitzmyer, R.E. Murphy, 2 vols. in 1 (Englewood Cliffs, 1968), 2: 66 (43, 18) and 129 (44, 52).

56 See below, pp. 310–11.

which provides the biggest units and the longest collective parcel of comment from any source.[57] Sheer quantity underscores the importance of genealogy to the *Chronicle*.

Claudius lays out the fundamental content according to a simple formula. The main line of roundels occupies the upper register. Each roundel sets off a name plus *genuit*, and from it a thick trunk leads rightward to the next entry. A term in years – the patriarch's age at fathering his named successor, or a regnal period – stands above the roundel, with a further tag noting the 'year since the Flood' in the second and third *aetates*, or, later, the 'year of Fourth Age.'[58] Just above and outside the penned frame, Claudius labels all dated roundels with the total 'years from the World's Creation.' Other roundels, naming secondary off-spring and lineages, at points stand in the upper register, but usually hang on subsidiary limbs that snake around or through the block of commentary. The display section presents a segmented visual arc from Creation to the Incarnation. It remaps into diagram and added comment the raw material of the reckoning section. The genealogy from Adam to Emanuel, however novel in itself, is also a graphical transposition of the parallel between the First Adam and the Second, Jesus, established at the start of part two.[59] The display section visually enacts much of the post-fixed numerical *canevas*.

The main line from Adam to Jesus dominates by its placement or numerical superstructure. This sequence offers Claudius many possible targets for comment. He declares one topic he will emphasize by slicing the chain according to the Six Ages. The first frame of the genealogy treats the *prima saeculi aetas*, from Adam to Lamech, father of Noah.[60] Nine generations progress across the frame, each member tagged with his age and the aggregate *anni a conditione mundi* (hereinafter, *a.c.m.*) upon fathering his successor. The diagram recapitulates the data supplied in part two of the *Chronicle*, based on Bede and Genesis 5, with the improvement that here Claudius reports temporal progress uniformly in *a.c.m.*, instead of dating relative to Adam's lifetime (*anni uitae Adam*), or since his death (*anno post mortem Adam*).[61] The change sets the First Age and the ensuing ones under a common standard. The *a.c.m.* figures coincide with Bede's indications in *DTR*.[62] Down the left edge, and then across,

---

57 Bede, *Commentary on Luke* (ad 3, 23–38), ed. D. Hurst, CCSL 70, 87–93, ll. 2689–913; Claudius omits only ll. 2786–7 and ll. 2796–815.

58 These indications take the form '*N.* anno uitae suae ... genuit *N.* (anno post diluuium ...)' or 'Anno quartae aetatis ... *N.* regnauit annis ...'

59 Based on the calendrical 'coincidence' of Adam's creation and the Crucifixion on 23 March; cf. Bede, *DTR* 66, 464–5, ¶ 9. See below, pp. 313–14 and n. 128.

60 Monza, fols. 67ᵛ–68ʳ.

61 Cf. *Chron.*, pt. 2, *PL* 104, 918D–919B.

62 *DTR* 66, 465–6, ¶ 10–18.

Claudius also charts the doomed bloodline from Adam through Cain to Naamah (cf. Gen. 4, 17–22).

The commentary fitted to the diagram begins, exceptionally, with a remark by Claudius himself noteworthy for its ethical reach:

> This is Adam, the first created, from whose extracted rib woman was formed. This was done by almighty God's eternal and unchanging plan, so that man should embrace in woman a part of his own body, and not consider different from himself what he knows to be formed from himself.[63]

The second part of this formulation resonated enough for the words to reappear in Hrabanus Maurus' *Commentary on Matthew* of ca A.D. 821.[64] Hrabanus freely mined Claudius' earlier *Commentary on Matthew* (A.D. 815) for his own work on the gospel, without avowing the debt.[65] Here, the textual agreement between Hrabanus' commentary and the *Chronicle* points to Claudius' repeated use of his library of prepared slips to piece together different works of exegesis.[66] In the display section, it is, however, comparatively rare to find original exegetical statements. The preliminary descriptions of each age normally follow a set pattern of borrowing, all unacknowledged. After the brief exordium in his own voice, Claudius begins the usual formula of anonymous excerpts. He first copies the relevant lines from Bede's chapter 'De hebdomada aetatum saeculi' (in *DTR*), which matches each day of Creation with a corresponding Age of the World.[67] Claudius then adds the matching text from Bede's subsequent survey of the Six Ages at the start of the *Greater Chronicle*, which names each span of years and explains each period's allegorical counterpart in the Ages of Man.[68] This pattern recurs for all Six Ages. What Claudius adds to this formula reflects his particular concerns.

For the First Age, Claudius begins by expounding Bede's allegory in relation to the adjoining diagram. The 'division of light from dark' has been

---

63 Monza, fol. 67ᵛ: 'Hic est Adam protoplaustus ex cuius detracta costa fabricata est femina. Omnipotentis Dei actum aeterno et immutabili consilio ut portionem sui corporis uir amplecteretur in femina nec a se putaret esse diuersum quod de se cognosceret fabricatum.'

64 Hrabanus, *Commentary on Matthew*, PL 107, 1017C ('Omnipotentis ... fabricatum'). I follow the dating by E. Dümmler, MGH Epistolae 4, 388.

65 J.B. Hablitzel, 'Hrabanus Maurus und Klaudius von Turin,' *Historisches Jahrbuch* 38 (1917): 538–52.

66 Cf. above, n. 51. The text of Claudius' *Commentary on Matthew* remains unedited.

67 Bede, *DTR* 10, 310–12; on which see C.W. Jones, ed., *Bedae Opera de temporibus* (Cambridge, Mass., 1943), 345.

68 *DTR* 66, 463–4, ¶ 1–8. For both parallels, with the days of Creation and the Ages of Man, Bede follows Augustine.

equated with the 'separation of God's sons from the seed of iniquity,' which stands visible in the depicted progeny of Cain.[69] Claudius elaborates with arguments already made in his *Commentary on Genesis* (A.D. 811):

The posterity of Adam through the polluted murderer Cain is ended by the number eleven, which signifies sin. This numerical place is held by a woman [that is, Naamah], since from this sex began the sin through which we all die. In this posterity there is a foreshadowing of all evil.[70]

The observation, built on a snippet of Augustine, looks to the adjacent mapping of Cain's offspring which ends with the woman Naamah, the eleventh name in the biblical series (Gen. 4, 17–22). The explanation shows Claudius returning to his stock of excerpts. As often happens, the commentary abruptly swerves onto other topics. Claudius presents Augustine's long account of the necessity and consequences of consanguineous marriage in the first human family.[71] He then explains the advanced ages at which the early fathers generated their canonical successors. Here, again, he uses bits from Augustine already presented in the *Commentary on Genesis*.[72] By this point, the Monza manuscript's loosely written first opening is full, and two further excerpts that belong, and figure here in the Madrid codex, have been bumped into the void that precedes the frame. In dialogue with the overhead roundels, Claudius introduces his set reworking of Jerome's 'famous question' on whether Mathusala survived the Flood.[73] The frame then properly ends with Bede's explanation, from the *Commentary on Luke*, of Enoch's direct ascent to God by virtue of his 'sabbatical,' or seventh, position in the series from Adam to Jesus.[74] Together, this first

---

69 Bede, *DTR* 10, 310, ll. 4–9 ('... separatis Dei filiis a semine nequitiae ...').

70 Monza, fol. 67ᵛ, which to start follows Claudius, *Commentary on Genesis*, *PL* 50 (under the name of Eucherius of Lyon), 923D: 'Progenies ergo ex Adam per Cain, sceleratum homicidam, undenario numero finitur, quo peccatum significatur; et ipse numerus femina clauditur, a quo sexu initium factum est peccati, per quod omnes morimur'; with the added tail-piece: 'In qua progenie totius maliciae praesagium fuit.' The source of the shared text, to which Claudius adds *homicidam*, is Augustine, *De ciuitate Dei* 15, 20, ed. B. Dombart and A. Kalb, CCSL 48, 485, ll. 132–5.

71 Augustine, *De ciuitate Dei* 15, 16, CCSL 48, 476–7, ll. 1–45.

72 The *Chronicle* uses Augustine, *De ciuitate Dei* 15, 15, CCSL 48, 476, ll. 63–70 and 84–7. These lines appear in a longer, continuous citation in the *Commentary on Genesis*, *PL* 50, 923B.

73 The same version occurs in Claudius' *Commentary on Genesis*, *PL* 50, 924A–B; based on Jerome, *Questions on Genesis* (ad 5, 25–7), ed. P. de Lagarde, CCSL 72, 8–9.

74 Bede, *Commentary on Luke* (ad 3, 37), CCSL 70, 90–1, ll. 2814–26. Cf. Gen. 5, 24.

patchwork of commentary illustrates Claudius' varied interests – from society to numerical symbolism – and how he used and reused his store of materials in various works. The result is disjoint, but it responds both to 'famous' and peculiar questions that Claudius reads into the matching segment of genealogy.

The *secunda saeculi aetas* occupies the next two and a half Monza openings. The age runs from the Flood to Abraham and matches the first in the number of generations. Here, however, Claudius lavishes attention both on the progress of the primary genealogy and on the various subsidiary lineages that peopled the earth after the Flood. The first frame stands as two discrete, but related pages. The diagram begins at the top left with Noah linked by three spokes, in clockwise order, to Shem, Ham, and Japhet; the sons and grandsons of Japhet proliferate in descending and transverse spurs; the opposite page maps the progeny of Ham.[75] The next opening resumes the genealogical progress: above, it advances from Shem to Terah, Abraham's father, while pendant limbs name the wider progeny of Shem and, later, the agnates of Peleg, who lived when God disunited human speech and scattered the peoples at the Tower of Babel.[76] A final page maps the ancillary offspring of Terah down to Rebecca, the wife of Isaac.[77]

The numerical superstructure labels the roundel for Noah with the following tag: 'In 1656 *a.c.m.*, the Flood came in the first month, on the seventeenth day of the month. This was for Noah the 600th year of his life; for Shem, his son, the ninety-eighth.'[78] The figure 1,656 years merely repeats Bede's total, while the ages of Noah and Shem depend on statements found in Genesis.[79] The named month, however, is incorrect. The source for the error is the reckoning section, where Claudius also begins the Flood 'in the first month,' even though both Genesis and Bede name 'the second.'[80] The original mistake invalidates a calendrical discussion in the reckoning section; here, it amounts to a minor blemish. More generally, the error highlights the limitations of Claudius' method: his working notes were sometimes seriously inaccurate, and self-citation canonized defects. Claudius intends to restate fixed solutions, and succeeds at the cost of compounding some mistakes. Yet for the balance of the Second

75 Monza, fols. 68ᵛ–69ʳ.
76 Ibid., fols. 69ᵛ–70ʳ.
77 Ibid., fol. 70ᵛ.
78 Ibid., fol. 68ᵛ: 'Anno a conditione mundi mille DCLVI uenit diluuium mense primo septima decima die mensis qui erat annus uitae sue Noe DC, Sem uero filii eius XCVIII.' Cf. *Chron.*, pt. 2, *PL* 104, 919B–C and 920A.
79 Cf. Bede, *DTR* 66, 467, ll. 128–9; Gen. 7, 11; 11, 10.
80 See below, pp. 315–16 and nn. 134–5. The dating to the 'first month' is elsewhere unknown. In his *Commentary on Genesis*, Claudius sets the Flood's beginning *mense secundo*: *PL* 50, 925C.

Age, he copies the reckoned *anni post diluuium* from part two into the labelling of part one, and the results square neatly with Bede's *DTR*.[81]

Beneath the tree of names and numbers, Claudius supplies an intricate, relatively coherent discussion of the Second Age and its ramified genealogies. He begins with the usual characterization based on Bede.[82] The commentary then focuses on the various peoples founded by the sons of Noah, starting with Japhet (Gen. 10, 2–5), then Ham (Gen. 10, 6.7.13–20), and on the next opening, Shem (Gen. 10, 21–3). What slowly emerges is a 'table of nations.' Claudius again draws from the same materials used in his *Commentary on Genesis*; the excerpts feature identical reductions and omissions *vis-à-vis* the patristic sources.[83] Frechulf of Lisieux, who wrote a *World History* in the mid-820s, also set out a table of nations and likewise drew on the useful, if sometimes flawed, summaries in Claudius' *Commentary on Genesis*.[84] The biblical 'origins' of peoples invited different Carolingian writers to dilate on a phenomenon that obviously fascinated them. Claudius had assembled, and repeats in his *Chronicle*, information that contemporaries valued. The name of Peleg, which 'means division,' in memory of Babel, prompts him at this point to consider linguistic diversity, which shows a remarkable harmony amidst dizzying ethnic fracture.[85] He borrows the lesson from *DTR*, but alters Bede's telling of how precisely Latin serves as one language for many peoples. Instead of making it the shared tongue of diverse regions of Italy, Claudius updates the example:

Latin, though one language, is linguistic mistress to many peoples (*gentes*), like the famous and noble ones of our time: the Franks, the Gauls, the Italians (or Romans), the Lombards; and the Spanish, the Africans, the Asturians, and the Basques.[86]

---

81 Cf. *Chron.*, pt. 2, *PL* 104, 920A–C; Bede, *DTR* 66, 467–70, ¶ 21–37.

82 *DTR* 10, 310, ll. 9–15; *DTR* 66, 463, ¶ 3.

83 Monza, fols. 68ᵛ–69ᵛ: an arrangement of bits and pieces from the *Commentary on Genesis*, *PL* 50, 937C–941B. The original sources are Jerome, *Questions on Genesis*, and Augustine, *City of God*.

84 Frechulf of Lisieux, *Histories* I, 1, 27, *PL* 106, 934A–935B; cf. Claudius, *Commentary on Genesis*, *PL* 50, 937C–D, 938B–D. For an improved edition of Frechulf, with analysis of Claudius and his sources, see M.I. Allen, 'History in the Carolingian Renewal: Frechulf of Lisieux (fl. 830), His Work and Influence,' PhD diss. (University of Toronto, 1994), 246–54; the full critical text is to appear in the CCCM. For one flaw in Claudius, accepted by Frechulf but deceptively emended in *PL* 106, see idem, 'Bede and Frechulf at Medieval St. Gallen,' in *Beda Venerabilis: Historian, Monk and Northumbrian*, ed. L.A.J.R. Houwen and A.A. MacDonald, Mediaevalia Groningana 19 (Groningen, 1996), 74–5.

85 Monza, fol. 70ʳ.

86 Ibid.: 'Verbi gratia, cum una sit Latina lingua, attamen gentes infra se continent [*intellege* continet; cf. Madrid, fol. 107ʳ: gentes infra continet] multas, ut sunt insignes et nobiles nostro

306   Michael Idomir Allen

How Claudius groups these 'famous peoples' reveals the patterns of cultural communion he recognized. The Franks, of course, come first, heading the peoples they actually controlled down to the Lombards of Italy. The next grouping, a sketch of ninth-century Latinate Iberia, remarkably distinguishes North Africans resettled on the peninsula; and no less striking, Claudius, himself a *Hispanus*, marks Asturians as a separate brand of peninsular folk.[87] For a learned Frankish subject, this roster of *gentes* set fresh meaning to Augustine's remark, cited to conclude the aforesaid table of nations, and now repeated to cap the comments on peoples and tongues: '... the number of *gentes* has increased far more than the number of languages.'[88] The Franks were part of this increase, and their adopted Latin culture impinged powerfully on all the 'famous peoples' named.[89] Claudius deftly implicates his world in the *Chronicle*'s account of peoples and tongues.[90] His comments on the age conclude

tempore: Franci, Galli, Itali, qui et Romani, Largobardi [*sic*], et Hispani, Afri, Astures, atque Vascones.' See Bede, *DTR* 66, 469, ¶ 26, used in extenso, but updated at ll. 191–4, where Bede cites Arnobius Rhetor (*ca* A.D. 300): 'Verbi gratia, cum una lingua Latina sit, sub una lingua diuersae sunt patriae Bruttiorum, Lucanorum, Apulorum, Calabrorum, Picentum, Tuscorum, et his atque huiusmodi similia si dicamus.'

87 For learned Africans settled in Merida and Valencia in *ca* 570, see P. Riché, *Education and Culture in the Barbarian West*, trans. J.J. Contreni (Columbia, 1978), 298–9; for a consideration of the vexed topic of eighth-century immigration from Africa, see L. Vázquez de Parga, 'Los documentos sobre las presuras del obispo Odoario de Lugo,' *Hispania* 10 (1950): 635–80.

Frankish sources other than Claudius refer to *Hispani* without distinction. In Mozarabic texts, the label *Asturiensis* acquired a distinct edge during the Adoptionist Controversy, the backdrop, if not the cause, of Claudius' move to Francia. The Adoptionist camp, led by Elipandus of Toledo, identified its key domestic opponent as 'Beatus nefandus *Asturiensis* presbiter' (referring to Beatus of Liébana) and pointed accusingly to the 'fines *Asturienses*': *Opera Elipandi*, ed. J. Gil, in *Corpus Scriptorum Muzarabicorum*, vol. 1 (Madrid, 1973), p. 81, no. 3, l. 39; p. 82, no. 4, ¶ 1, ll. 2–3. On regional factors in the Adoptionist episode, see J.C. Cavadini, *The Last Christology of the West: Adoptionism in Spain and Gaul, 785–820* (Philadelphia, 1993), 147, n. 14; also W. Heil, 'Der Adoptianismus, Alkuin und Spanien,' in *Karl der Grosse: Lebenswerk und Nachleben*, vol. 2: *Das geistige Leben*, ed. B. Bischoff (Düsseldorf, 1965), 94–155. Claudius' awareness of Iberia allays doubts as to his Spanish background; cf. Gorman, 'Commentary,' 279, n. 4.

88 Monza, fol. 69^v and, again, fol. 70^r; following the *Commentary on Genesis*, PL 50, 941B. The ultimate source is Augustine, *De ciuitate Dei* XVI 6, CCSL 48, 507, ll. 48–9.

89 The connections are plain except, perhaps, for the Asturians. See Einhard, *VK* 16, p. 19, ll. 3–6; also W. Levison, 'A Letter of Alcuin to Beatus of Liébana,' in *England and the Continent in the Eighth Century* (Oxford, 1946), Appendix 11, 314–23.

90 Cf. A. Borst, *Der Turmbau von Babel: Geschichte der Meinungen über Ursprung und Vielfalt der Sprachen*, vol. 2, pt. 1 (Stuttgart, 1958), 504–5, and passim, for background and context. Borst considers only Claudius' *Commentary on Genesis* and the printed fragments of his *Chronicle*, and comes to different conclusions. In general, but with no reference to Claudius,

with remarks on the lesser offspring of Terah through Nahor (Gen. 22, 20–2) and the descendant peoples.[91] By a fresh ethno-linguistic example and a repetition of Augustine, Claudius linked past and present, and made ancient lore distinctly relevant to contemporaries.

The *tertia saeculi aetas* runs from Abraham to the establishment of David as king.[92] The primary genealogy halts with Jacob to allow a graphical roster of the house of Israel as it entered Egypt.[93] When the genealogical main line resumes, Claudius omits the accustomed numerical superstructure between Judah and David.[94] The reason is hinted at in the commentary, but only fully clarified in part two. After a tract from Augustine on Jacob's descent into Egypt,[95] Claudius' commentary cites from his own chronological discussion of Israel's bondage. A fuller version appears, not only in part two, but also in the contemporary *Commentary on Galatians* (A.D. 815). For the display section, Claudius simply extracts a list of numbers and a tedious calculation that eventually dates the Crossing of the Red Sea: 'If anyone doubts these things and has no knowledge of calculating the sum of years, let him add from Jacob's entry into Egypt ...'[96] The laborious exercise is important because it places the Crossing in 2453 *a.c.m.* and also because it illustrates how the Bible sometimes obviates the need for detailed figuring. Saint Paul, whom Claudius quotes to

---

see E. Zöllner, *Die politische Stellung der Völker im Frankenreich*, Veröffentlichungen des Instituts für österreichische Geschichtsforschung 13 (Vienna, 1950).

91 Monza, fol. 70ᵛ, including the Syrians and the Chaldeans. The text, again, follows Claudius, *Commentary on Genesis*, *PL* 50, 974A–B ('De Melcha ... uocati sunt'). The *Chronicle* follows the autograph MS of the *Commentary* (Paris, BnF, lat 9575, fol. 67ᵛ), reading 'uocabulo nuncupatus,' against 'uocabulo priuatur' in *PL* 50, 974B. Cf. Jerome, *Questions on Genesis* (ad 5, 25–7), CCSL 72, 27–8 (with 'nuncupatur').

92 Monza, fols. 71ʳ–73ᵛ.

93 For two pages in Monza, fols. 71ᵛ–72ᵛ.

94 Monza, fol. 73ʳ–ᵛ.

95 Augustine, *De ciuitate Dei* 16, 40, CCSL 48, 545–6. The chapter discusses how Jacob entered Egypt 'with seventy-five souls.' Cf. Gen. 46, 27 (LXX) and Acts 7, 14.

96 Monza, fol. 72ᵛ: 'Si quis ista dubitat uel calculandi non habet scientiam, sumat annos ab introitu Iacob ...' The complete comment ('Manserunt filii Israel ... anni II milia CCCC LIII') rehearses *Chron.*, pt. 2, Monza, fol. 81ʳᵃ; the matching lines in *PL* 104, 921C–D, end in '2451,' based on Paris, fol. 5ᵛ, which corrects 'LIII' to 'LI' by erasure. The extended text in part two reappears verbatim, minus the absolute datings, in Claudius' *Commentary on Galatians*, *PL* 104, 872C–873C; cf. *Chron.*, pt. 2, *PL* 104, 921C–922B ('Manserunt ... peragerent seruitutem'). The text starts independently, then copies Alcuin, *Questions on Genesis*, no. 168, *PL* 100, 537B–538A. Claudius' note reacts to the mention of '430 years' in Gal. 3, 17. In *Chron.*, pt. 1, the comment builds on the date for Jacob's descent into Egypt, stated in the Isaac label, Monza, fol. 71r: 'Isaac .. genuit Iacob, qui ... descendit in Aegyptum ... a conditione mundi II milia CCXXXVIII'; cf. *Chron.*, pt. 2, *PL* 104, 921A–B; Bede, *DTR* 66, 471, ¶ 43.

confirm his arithmetic, states that 430 years (Gal. 3, 17) elapsed from the Promise to Abraham, an established point of reference, to the Crossing of the Red Sea.[97] By implication, the complex calculation is superfluous since the result is knowable by simpler means. Claudius merely applies this lesson when he drops the overhead count of years from Judah to David, as he explains at this point in the reckoning section:

... I see that we need not delay counting the sum of years ... because the *historia* of the Book of Kings bears manifest witness: 'And it came to pass in the four hundred and eightieth year *after the exit of the sons of Israel from Egypt*, in the fourth year of King Solomon's rule over Israel, in the month of Zif (which is the second month), he began to build the Lord's House' (1 Kings 6, 1; my emphasis).[98]

Accordingly, after Claudius dates the Crossing from Egypt, both parts of the *Chronicle* abandon the stepwise count of years for the remainder of the Third Age.[99] The verse from Kings establishes the terminus of the epoch with a minimum of mathematical effort. The display section dispenses with datings virtually without justification because Claudius envisaged the *Chronicle* as a whole and consigned such mechanics to the reckoning section.[100] What also emerges from comparing both parts of the text is that Claudius resorts to numbers only when he finds them necessary. He aims for an accurate report of 'years and generations,' but it suits his purpose to bypass routine counting where the Bible permits. Claudius' *Chronicle* does not aspire to rehash every detail of Bede's chronology or any other.

This impression deepens with the divided genealogy that begins with David in the Fourth Age. The numbers that Claudius fits to the roundels on David and Solomon even show a hint of arithmetical independence. Whereas Bede begins the age in 2890 *a.c.m.*, Claudius makes the year 2889.[101] In the reckoning section, he equates the Third Age with 941 years, which he silently combines in part one with 1948 *a.c.m.*, the dating he shares with Bede for Abraham's birth,

97 For the year of the Promise to Abraham, *Chron.*, pt. 2, *PL* 104, 920D.
98 *Chron.*, pt. 2, *PL* 104, 923B–C, with revised punctuation and emendation to *uideo* ('I see ...') from *uidetur*, based on the consensus of Monza, fol. 81vb, and Paris, fol. 7^v. Claudius formulates and applies the shortcut on his own; cf. Bede, *DTR* 66, 476, ll. 404–5.
99 Cf. *Chron.*, pt. 2, *PL* 104, 921D–923C.
100 In Monza, the register for commentary in part one is now covered (fol. 73^r–v) with spurious additions until the end of the Third Age: first, Bede, *De temporibus* 19 ('De tertia aetate'), CCSL 123C, 603–4, ll. 8–23 ('Moyses ... exoritur'); then, translated Hebrew proper names. Hereafter, the copy, while complete, is progessively bloated with clutter.
101 Monza, fol. 74r: 'Primo anno regni Dauid impleret ann. II milia DCCCLXXXVIIII ...' Cf. Bede, *DTR* 66, 475, l. 389 (dating the end of Saul's reign to 2890).

to reach 2889.[102] Claudius carries his mistake into the label on Solomon,[103] but then takes the easier, if inconsistent course of using Bede's figures for the rest of the Fourth Age.[104] The distinctive commentary focuses from the start on the genealogical bifurcation. Claudius begins with excerpts from Bede's *Commentary on Luke*, meant to unfold the cardinal message of Gospel harmony and complementarity.[105] Claudius then must address a major difficulty posed by the numerical backdrop. The genealogy in Matthew (1, 8) skips from Joram to Ozias, thereby omitting four biblical rulers – Ahaziah, Queen Athalia, Joash, and Amaziah – whom Bede names and dates in *DTR*. Adapting Bede, Claudius merges Athalia's six-year reign and the single year of her son, Ahaziah, and then patches the resulting triad of kings into the Gospel lineage.[106] He recuts the chronistic cloth to produce a workable, dated sequence. This adaptation paves the way below for Jerome's comments on the 'three kings in the middle, whom the Evangelist here skips.' The exposition explains that Matthew envisaged a series of forty-two generations and suppressed a triad of especially evil kings to achieve this.[107] The Monza copy now intrudes two misplaced chapters from Bede's *Lesser Chronicle* (on the Fifth and Sixth Ages) between the genealogical strands.[108] The logic of context, however, suggests that Claudius here intended his reader to find the lengthy tract from Bede's *Commentary on Luke*, which the unsettled Monza text displaces into columns ahead of part two.[109] Building on Jerome, Claudius uses the Bedan tract on Luke to expound

102 For 941, *Chron.*, pt. 2, *PL* 104, 923C. Bede gives 942 in his précis of the Fourth Age: *DTR* 66, 463, ¶ 4. Where Claudius cites this in Monza, the figure has been corrected by erasure from 'DCCCCXLII' to 'DCCCCXLI' (fol. 71[r]). For 1948, *Chron.*, pt. 2, *PL* 104, 920C; Bede, *DTR* 66, 470, l. 227.

103 Monza, fol. 74[v]: 'Primo anno regni Salamonis impleti sunt anni a conditione mundi II milia DCCCC XXVIIII.' Cf. Bede, *DTR* 66, 475, l. 397 (dating the end of David's reign to 2930).

104 Monza, 74[v]–76[r]. Bede, *DTR* 66, 476–81, ¶ 89–142.

105 Monza, fol. 74[r]; copying Bede, *Commentary on Luke*, Prologue, CCSL 120, 8, ll. 147–57; then (ad 3, 31–2), 90, ll. 2788–95. The second, slightly reworked, passage from Bede reappears in Hrabanus, *Commentary on Matthew*, *PL* 107, 746C–D; cf. above, p. 302 and n. 65.

106 Monza, fol. 75[r–v], here 75[r] (above 'Azariam genuit'): 'In fine regni Azariae et Athaliae / anni a conditione mundi III milia LXXI / anni quartae aetatis CLXXXII / Azarias regnauit / anno I.' Cf. Bede, *DTR* 66, 477, ¶ 105–11. In contrast, the reckoning section lists Ahaziah and Athalia individually with their respective regnal periods: *PL* 104, 924A, to which Monza, fol. 82[rb], adds the cumulative years (e.g., 'CLXXXII' at Athalia) within the Fourth Age.

107 Monza, fol. 75[r] (just beneath the register of roundels): 'Certe quod secundum fidem hystoriae tres reges in medio fuerit, quos hic euangelista pretermisit ...' Claudius reworks Jerome, *Commentary on Matthew* (ad 1, 8–9), ed. D. Hurst and M. Adriaen, CCSL 77, 8–9, ll. 24–37 ('Verum quia euangelista ... ordine poneretur.').

108 Monza, fols. 75[r]–76[r].

109 Ibid., fols. 78[va]–79[rb].

the variant lengths of the Gospel genealogies and to address the mystical significance of the number forty-two (among others).[110] The comments are certainly authentic to Claudius' *Chronicle*, and fit by length and theme with the remainder of the Fourth Age. The extract continues the programmatic use of Bede's genealogical exegesis and lays a fresh accent on the Christ-centred trajectory of the diagram and text.

This focus dominates in the depiction and exposition of the Fifth Age. While Luke's genealogy hovers below, Claudius follows the letter of Matthew (1, 11–12) by inaugurating the age and the Babylonian Exile with Jechonias.[111] Both the reckoning section and Bede's *DTR* set two kings for this one, and then add Zedekiah, whose regime ends in the Destruction of the Temple.[112] The aforementioned extract from Bede's *Commentary on Luke*, which properly precedes the turn of the Fifth Age, accounts for the initial difference. As Bede says, Matthew has set 'Jechonias for two persons, that is, a father and a son, based on Chronicles.'[113] In accord with Bede's explanation, Claudius begins the age with the son who ruled only three months. In the numerical superstructure, he joins the eleven regnal years of Eliakim, the father, and thereby sets the end of the elongated reign in 3352 *a.c.m.*, when Jechonias is led captive to Babylon (cf. 2 Kings 36, 9–10).[114] The diagram silently abandons the usual date and epochal turning-point marked by the overthrow of the Babylonian puppet, Zedekiah, and by the Destruction of the Temple by Nebuchadnezzar.[115] The text of Matthew and the logic of the display section impose this adjustment. Claudius still nods to the normal milestone, which he accepts in the reckoning section, through a bland, disconnected tag on the eleven years of Zedekiah. More importantly, this sheepish note marks the end of the numerical superstructure.[116] Again, an explanation for this startling change comes only in the reckoning section. There, Claudius introduces a glowing encomium of Bede, who is richly, if tardily acknowledged, and he ends by positing the span of the

---

110 Bede, *Commentary on Luke* (ad 3, 38), CCSL 120, 91–3, ll. 2827–2913.

111 Monza, fol. 76[v].

112 *Chron.*, pt. 2, Monza, fol. 82[rb] (lacuna at *PL* 104, 924B). Cf. Bede, *DTR* 66, 481, ¶ 140–2.

113 Displaced in Monza to fol. 79[ra]: '... quia iuxta fidem Paralipomenon Iechonia pro duabus personis, patre scilicet et filio debeat conputari.' Bede, *Commentary on Luke*, CCSL 70, 92, ll. 2876–8. Bede offers an excuse rather than a solution; cf. 1 Chron. 3, 15–16.

114 Monza, fol. 76[v] (above 'Iechoniam [*sic*] genuit'): 'In fine regni Eliachim, anni a conditione mundi III milia CCC LII. / Heleachim, qui et Ioachim, regnauit annis XI.' Cf. Bede, *DTR* 66, 481, ¶ 140–1. 'Eliakim' (not used in *DTR*) occurs in *Chron.*, pt. 2, Monza, fol. 82[rb]: 'Heliachim, qui et Ioachim, filius Iosiae' (lacuna at *PL* 104, 924B); cf. 2 Kings 23, 34.

115 So, *Chron.*, pt. 2, *PL* 924C; and Bede, *DTR* 66, 481, ¶ 142.

116 Monza, fol. 76[v] (without a framing roundel): 'In fine regni Sedechiae anni a conditione mundi III milia CCCLXIII. / Sedechias regnauit annis XI.' Cf. Bede, *DTR* 66, 481, l. 566.

Fifth Age as set out in *DTR*. Bede's findings encompass the reports of Esdras, Maccabees, Josephus, and Julius Africanus.[117] His results invite Claudius to dispense with new reckonings for the Fifth Age, as he concludes: 'Whatever time remains until the Lord's coming in the flesh, I leave to the judgment of our predecessors (*maiorum nostrorum ... iudicio*) who wrote chronicles.'[118] This reasoning superficially justifies what happens in the display section. Thanks to Bede, Claudius need reckon no further; he drops the stepwise tally of years. Nevertheless, Matthew's genealogy bears the real credit for the change in substance and style: after Jechonias, as Claudius omits to observe, Matthew's series becomes undatable and even unattested in Hebrew Scripture.[119] The reprieve from counting, *maiorum iudicio*, is a sleight of hand. Claudius has configured the reckoning section with an eye to the non-workable non-content of the genealogical display. In the Fifth Age, Claudius must settle for the path, without the years, that leads to Jesus.

His distinctive commentary on the age makes a virtue of this necessity. The first words seize the crux of the remaining problem: 'Some rightly ask how Joseph could have two fathers from different lineages ...' Again, Claudius takes the query, its answer, and the lengthy mystical observations they trigger straight from Bede's *Commentary on Luke*.[120] The wide-ranging comment chaperons the visual progress of roundels until the separate lines of Luke and Matthew converge in 'Joseph, the husband of Mary, from whom the Christ was born.'[121]

117 *Chron.*, pt. 2, Monza, fol. 82[va–b] (incomplete at *PL* 104, 924B–C): 'Sanctae memoriae presbiter Beda, acer ingenio, suauis eloquio, utraque scientia, diuina scilicet atque humana, sufficienter inbutus ... in libro quem de temporibus edidit capitulo LXVI (qui praenotatur 'De sex huius saeculi aetatibus et septima uel octaua quietis uitaeque caelestis ...'), quintam aetatem saeculi, quae ab euersione coepit Hierusalem, quae facta est per Nabuchodonosor, et perseuerat usque ad aduentum Domini saluatoris in carne, ex libro Esdrae prophetae et historia libri Machabeorum et Iosippi atque Africani historiographi ... conprehendit annos DLXXXVIIII ...' This passage, and Claudius' willingness to follow Bede against Augustine (see below, p. 314 and n. 130), requires a revision of Cavadini's points that Augustine was Claudius' 'commentator of choice on *any* question' (my emphasis) and that other writers 'appear in Claudius' work with first names only, unadorned': Cavadini, 'Claudius of Turin,' 43.
118 *Chron.*, pt. 2, *PL* 104, 924D: 'Quicquid uero reliquum superest tempus usque ad aduentum Domini in carne maiorum nostrorum qui cronicas scripserunt iudicio derelinquo.' The *maiores* Bede and Jerome agree on the length of the Fifth Age: von den Brincken, *Studien*, 110.
119 Cf. *Jerome Biblical Commentary*, 2: 66 (43, 18).
120 Monza, fols. 76[v]–77[v], beginning: 'Merito mouet quomodo Ioseph duos patres ex diuersa prauorum (*intellege* proauorum) styrpe uenientes, unum quem Lucas, alterum quem Matthaeus commemorat, habere potuerit.' Bede, *Commentary on Luke* (ad 3, 23–4), CCSL 120, 87–90, ll. 2689–2785.
121 Monza, fol. 76[v]–78[r], here 78[r], second-to-last roundel: 'Ioseph uirum Mariae, de qua natus est Christus.'

Jesus is the telos of the genealogical display, and with the Incarnation, Claudius concludes his account of time at the dawn of the sixth and final age. He gives the usual descriptive formulae based on Bede's *DTR* above a central roundel on the Savior.[122] Then, as peroration to the entire multiform effort, he follows below with a lyrical, but chronologically attuned excerpt from Faustus of Riez (d. *ca* 495): 'To us a little one is born; to us a son is given' (Is. 9, 6). Receive the son of God in the final segment of the ages ...'[123] Christ, celebrated with various theological attributes, stands as the capstone to the summed 'years and generations.' Claudius, the biblical exegete, ends on sure, if not familiar, terrain. The subsequent unfolding of time was not his concern.

None the less, the display section of the *Chronicle* dialogues from end to end with wider circles of meaning which implicate the present: Claudius' reckonings, his sought-after exegesis, and, more generally, contemporary interest in peoples and temporal order. The *Chronicle* is not a disengaged trifle. Claudius means to impart relevant facts, exposition, and lessons. The reckoning section makes a special point of fitting elements of the past into the present.

Within the *Chronicle*, the reckoning section functions as both source and addendum to the genealogical display. How Claudius construed this verbal–numerical tailpiece emerges from its opening words: 'So, having just roughly displayed, with God's help, the years from the World's Creation here above, I shall now expound them a second time in a more detailed recapitulation.'[124] The incipit is decisive: 'Quia igitur fautore Deo annos a conditione mundi ...' Some years later, Claudius used identical terms to begin the second part of his *Questions on Kings* (*ca* 824), and thereby articulated a similar overall structure: 'Quia igitur iam fautore Deo in superioribus libris ...' As he explains in the latter case, the discussion here turns to 'bald literal questions' that will complement the preceding allegorical exegesis of Kings.[125] The distinctive, shared phraseology marks a parallel shift in content. Claudius arrayed both works according to the same two-part scheme. In the *Chronicle*, the 'lit-

---

122 Monza, fol. 78ʳ, final roundel: 'Iesus Christus, qui et Sother, Emmanuhel, Nobiscum Deus.' Above, Bede, *DTR* 10, 311, ll. 36–44; *DTR* 66, 464, ¶ 7–8.
123 Monza, fol. 78ʳ: 'Paruulus natus est nobis; filius datus est nobis. Accipe filium Dei in extrema parte saeculorum ...' Faustus of Riez, Ep. 7, ed. A. Engelbrecht, CSEL 21 (1891), 205, l. 19 to 206, l. 19. This excerpt occurs in none of the standard early medieval homiliaries.
124 *Chron.*, pt. 2, *PL* 104, 917C–D: 'Quia igitur fautore Deo annos a conditione mundi magna ex parte superius jam ostendimus, nunc eosdem denuo recapitulando latius exponemus.'
125 Ep.10, MGH Epistolae 4, 608, ll. 30–3: 'Quia igitur iam fautore Deo in superioribus libris quibusdam interrogationibus tuis satisfactum esse puto, frater karissime Theutmire, nunc autem quasdam questiones tuas in fine libri huius conectere studemus, quia superfluum michi uisum est, ut nudas littere questiones inter spiritales permiscere debuissem allegoriae flores.' Dümmler deceptively presents Claudius' prologue to the literal component of his *Questions*

eral' reckonings stand as a nuts-and-bolts justification and complement to the more 'spiritual' display section.

The few scholars who discuss Claudius' *Chronicle* have focused on Labbe's printed fragments and highlighted their dry chronological emphasis and indebtedness to Bede. In the reckoning section, Claudius spills much ink to compile numbers and intervals whose value only becomes fully clear in the genealogical display. His dry accounting, in keeping with the task at hand, dispenses with the niceties of metaphor and allegory.[126] The arrangement according to the Six Ages, the sacred focus, and the Vulgate-based datings easily give the impression of an impoverished caricature of Bede's *DTR* – the usual scholarly view of the *Chronicle*.[127] In this connection, it suffices to say that Claudius gives a highly stripped-down version of Bede's chronology with a few added errors. However, this observation ignores an equally important element of the reckoning section.

Claudius uses the second part of the *Chronicle*, not only to explain anew his count of years, but also to introduce fresh concerns. His chronological review spotlights dated or datable biblical events, which he struggles to situate within the round of the Christian solar year. From the start, this effort bulks large in the reckoning section, and it merits commensurate attention.

After promising a recount of years, Claudius begins with a seemingly extraneous excursus on dates. He lays the real foundation for his temporal musings by setting the Creation of Man and then Jesus' Passion and Resurrection into the Christian-Roman calendar:

So [after dating the creation of the sun and the firmament to the spring equinox, or 21 March] it follows, by veridical reckoning, that the first man, Adam, was [both] formed from the slime of the earth and fitted with a soul [two days later] on 23 March, on the seventeenth day of the moon. By my calculation, the Second Adam ... suffered on the same date [*eodem tempore*], but not on the same weekday [*eadem feria*], that is, on 23 March, and rose from the dead on 25 March.[128]

> on Kings as a distinct 'letter,' yet the significance of the verbal parallel hinges on its place *within* the single, longer context. Cf. Ferrari, 'Note,' 302. On the arrangement of the *Questions on Kings*, G. Italiani, *La tradizione esegetica nel commento ai Re de Claudio di Torino*, Quaderni dell'Istituto di Filologia Classica 'Giorgio Pasquali' dell'Università degli Studi di Firenze 3 (Florence, 1979), 16.

126 This part of the exercise consists often of naming step-wise periods (*anno uitae suae ... genuit, regnauit ... annis*) and running tallies of years within each age. See, for example, the version of Second Age as printed, reasonably accurately, in *PL* 104, 920A–C.

127 So, Dümmler, 'Über Leben und Lehre,' 442; von den Brincken, *Studien*, 117–18; and Borst, *Turmbau von Babel*, 505.

128 For simplicity, I translate Claudius' datings by Kalends, Ides, and Nones into the modern

Claudius thus reduces Bede's circumspect remarks on several much-debated points to a categorical pronouncement. Above all, the calendrical symmetry he asserts, and which anticipates the polar structure of the display section, breaks with an ancient, if shaky, consensus. The time-reckoners convoked in A.D. 809 could explain almost nothing, but they did know the tradition that dated the Passion and the Resurrection respectively to 25 and 27 March.[129] In the *DTR*, Bede took account of this view, upheld by Augustine among others, but finally suggested his own preference for another position – the one Claudius brashly adopts.[130] The resulting calendrical symmetry, hinging on 23 March, fixes the start and the end of Claudius' *Chronicle*. But more important, its synergy of dates hammers pivotal moments of human history – Man's Creation and

equivalents. Monza, fol. 79[rb–va]: 'Et ita ratione deducta decimo Kl. Apriles luna XVIIma inuenitur protoplaustus Adam ex terrae limo esse formatus pariter atque animatus. Secundum hanc nostram supputationem, secundus Adam, id est Christus, Dei filius, ... eodem tempore, sed non eadem feria, id est Xo Kl. Apriles, inuenitur *fuisse passum et VIII* resurrexisse a mortuis.' The equivalent passage in *PL* 104 (917D–918C) derives from Paris, fol. 1[r], both of which omit *fuisse passum et VIII* in the final clause. Von den Brincken noticed the odd date that results for the Resurrection (23 March), but confused her report (naming the *Kreuzigung*): *Studien*, 117 and n. 145. Along with other bits from the cited passage, the wrong dating of the Resurrection to 23 March reappears exclusively, in Migne's PL, in the *Ennarationes in Matthaeum* now often ascribed to Geoffrey Babion, schoolmaster of Angers (1096 to 1110); cf. Migne, *PL* 162 (under the name of Anselm of Laon), 1493A: 'Iuxta hanc computationem inuenimus etiam eo tempore, id est *decimo Kalendas Aprilis*, Dei Filium *resurrexisse* a mortuis, quo tempore, id est decimo Kalendas Aprilis, protoplastum Adam inuenimus esse formatum ex limo terrae.' There has clearly been contact between the flawed Paris text and 'Geoffrey'; on whom, see B. Smalley, 'Some Gospel Comentaries of the Early Twelfth Century,' in *Recherches de théologie ancienne et médiévale* 45 (1978): 147–80. Claudius' 'calculation' reflects the date for 'Easter' in A.D. 31 according to Bede; cf. *Circulus paschalis*, ed. C.W. Jones, CCSL 123C, 551 (at 'DLXIII,' the cyclical equivalent to A.D. 31).

129 *Epistolae uariorum*, no. 42, MGH Epistolae 4, 565, ¶ 2. The *compotiste* fail when asked to reckon these dates from the world's beginning. Whether they knew it or not, the *computus* cannot reconcile the traditional dates for the Passion or the Creation within any of the standard cosmic chronological schemes (Bede's included). On its limitations, see von den Brincken, *Studien*, 112 and 166–71.

130 With circumspection, Bede, *DTR* 6, 290–5, ¶ 6 (on the Creation), with commentary by Jones, *Bedae Opera de temporibus*, 337–8; and *DTR* 47, 432, ll. 98–123 (the Passion and Resurrection). Then, more plainly, *si non uerior sentientia uincit*, *DTR* 66, 464–5, ¶ 9 (Passion on 23 March; Resurrection on 25 March). Claudius is guided by this passage, but demurs when Bede sets Adam's Creation and Jesus' Passion 'on one and the same weekday' (*una eademque ebdomadis die*). The latter passage from *DTR* 66, ignored by most medieval authors, also appears verbatim in Ado of Vienne, *Chronicon, PL* 123, 24A; cf. von den Brincken, *Studien*, 127, who evidently missed the Bedan source. It is noteworthy that Claudius disregards the view of Augustine, so often his favourite authority, expressed, for instance, in *De ciuitate Dei* 18, 54, CCSL 48, 655, ll. 45–6.

Redemption through the Passion – into the recurring timetable of the Christian present.

In addition to counting years, Claudius launches a tandem project to memorialize biblical events in terms of the prevailing fixed calendar.[131] To do this, he means to shun inferior traditions and to establish truths based on Scripture and his own 'veridical' and 'cogent' reckonings.[132] His confidence bubbles with a mix of condescension and paranoia:

If anyone perchance less learned in the study of Holy Writ should hazard to doubt this work, let him turn to ... the Hebrew Truth ... and desist from condemning me ... And if anyone perchance should stubbornly persist in [doubting], let him go to the Jews, the enemies of the church, and look in their books ...

After this slap at detractors and a fresh invocation of Augustine's praise for the Hebrew original, Claudius sets about counting up the biblical record and converting a select stock of dates.[133]

The task of mapping 'years and generations' defines the ensuing string of dated biblical events. Claudius must await the Flood to find quarry and to launch his first proprietary effort to pinpoint anniversary dates on the prevailing solar calendar. He begins by falling victim to fancy, or inattention, and distorts the underlying biblical report:

... and the Flood came in Noah's 600th year. Noah went into the ark, according to lunar dates, 'in the *first* month, on the seventeenth day of the month,' and according to solar dates, on 5 April, on the seventeenth day of the moon (which the Hebrews, counting months by the moon rather than the sun, call the seventeenth day of the *first* month), on a Saturday (which we call the Sabbath); and on that very day the Flood came. It was God's marvelous verdict that the human race, which began in Adam on the seventeenth day of the moon, should incur at the Flood, on the seventeenth day of the moon, the punishment of death for not keeping God's command.[134]

131 Compare the relevant discussion of the ninth century in Borst, *Ordering of Time*, 43–7.

132 He uses the phrases *ratione ueridica* (*PL* 104, 917D) and *ratione deducta* (ibid., 917D and 920B).

133 *PL* 104, 918C–D. On Augustine, cf. above, p. 298 and n. 50.

134 Monza, fols. 79vb–80ra: '... et anno uitae illius DCmo uenit diluuium. Secundum dies lunares mense primo, XVIIma die mensis, secundum solares uero dies *nonas Apriles*, luna XVIIma (quem Hebrei, qui menses non a sole, sed a luna conputant, XVII diem uocauerunt primi mensis), feria VIIma (quam nos sabbatum nuncupamus) – ingressus est Noe in archa, et hac ipsa die uenit diluuium. Mirum omnipotentis Dei iudicium ut humanum genus, quod per Adam luna XVIIma accepit initium, in non custodiendo Dei praeceptum XVIIma in diluuium incurret mortis supplicium.' Among other errors, the equivalent passage in *PL* 104 (919B–C)

This mistaken, yet felicitous, symmetry ensures that Claudius never looks back. Had he bothered to recheck Genesis or Bede's *DTR*, he would have found that both specify 'the *second* month' for the Flood's coming.[135] Instead, Claudius seizes on the illusory coincidence of 'the *first* month, the seventeenth day ...' and invents a congenial parallelism.[136] Nevertheless, his real preoccupation lies elsewhere. The program is not to extend the Hebrew calendrical doublet, but to convert and project the lunar date for the coming of the Flood into the Christian solar calendar. In his remarks, Claudius is at pains to distinguish the different methods of dating, and what follows highlights his real object: converting the lunar date into the solar calendar via the *computus*. Claudius has fixed the year as 1656 *a.c.m.* He now arrays the derivative operands that produce a solar date for the event in question: it was a leap year; the January began on a Wednesday; the year numbered fourth in the Decemnoval Cycle; the epact was thus eleven; so the *neomenia* – 'that is, the start of the new moon and the beginning of the year according to the lunar months' – fell on 20 March. Therefore, the Flood came on 5 April, or should have according to the rules of *computus*.[137] Claudius, mistakenly satisfied with this result, pushes ahead to the end of the Flood, whose terminus is also given in Genesis and now accurately cited via Bede's *DTR*: 'On the first day of the Second Age, which is the twenty-seventh day of the second month, Noah left the ark.'[138] Claudius again lists the compu-tistical operands that combine to fix Noah's descent from the ark to 3 May. To finish, he consecrates the new anniversary dates by using them to calculate that

---

reads *Kalendis Aprilis*, based on *k. apl.* in Paris, fol. 2ʳ. Monza's *nonas Apriles* (5 April) is correct according to Claudius' subsequent computistical discussion. Bede accounts for the 'seventeenth day of the moon' at Adam's Creation in *DTR* 6, 290–5, ¶ 6; see Jones, *Bedae Opera de temporibus*, 337–8.

135 Gen. 7, 11. Bede, *DTR* 11, ll. 48–52; and *DTR* 66, 467, ll. 128–9.

136 Cf. above, pp. 313–14.

137 Monza, fol. 80ʳᵃ: '... impleti sunt anni a condicione mundi mille DCLVI. Eo enim anno quod diluuium fuit, annus bissextilis extitit. Et si more nostro conputarentur feriae uel kalendae, essent ipso anno kl. mensis Ian. feria IIII; et quia fuit annus cicli solaris quartus, et idcirco XI fuerunt in epacta, et XIIImo kl. Apriles fuit neomenia, id est nouae lunae principium et ipsius anni secundum menses lunares primi mensis initium.' Bede does not use *neomenia* in *DTR*; the term figures, with the meaning given here by Claudius, in Isidore of Seville, *Etymologiae* VI, 18, 10. For a brief account of the rules and jargon of medieval *computus*, see R.D. Ware, 'Medieval Chronology: Theory and Practice,' in *Medieval Studies: An Introduction*, 2d ed., ed. J.M. Powell (Syracuse, N.Y., 1992), 252–77, here 268–73.

138 Monza, fol. 80ʳᵃ: 'Secunda saeculi aetate prima huius die, que est *uicesima septima* dies mensis secundi, egressus est Noe de archa.' Bede, *DTR* 66, 467, ll. 145–6; cf. Gen. 8, 14. The allure of the figure seventeen has affected the text of *PL* 104 (919D); it reads *decima septima* for *uicesima septima* in Paris, fol. 2ᵛ.

Noah spent a 'solar year and four weeks in the ark.'[139] However misguided, this was time-keeping that brought a distant sacred watershed vividly into the calendrical present.

It was also time-keeping grounded in copy errors, wishful thinking, and a mating of problematical *a.c.m.* datings and basically sound computistical rules. The *computus*, defined by Bede in *DTR*, worked for its purpose of dating of Easter *within* the Christian era, but reckoning 'from the beginning' was quite another matter, even with 'correct' data.[140] On various grounds, Claudius inevitably failed to determine 'true' dates for ancient biblical happenings. What matters, however, are his intentions.

For the first two ages, the reckoning section allots equal space to calendrical discussion and strictly chronological counting.[141] In subsequent ages, the relative need, or rather the simple possibility, to address either concern varies, but Claudius hunts as much for dates as mere years. Hence his treatment of the Exodus: 'Since we have arrived at this point by investigating the years and ages from the world's beginning, let us now keenly investigate the date of the very first Passover celebrated in the time of the Old Testament.' Where it once sufficed to name the operands and the result, Claudius now verbally works through his arithmetic to prove that the first Passover occurred on Monday, 12 April 2453 *a.c.m.*[142] He follows indications in Exodus to conclude, for example, that the Hebrews arrived at Mount Sinai on 27 May (cf. Ex 19, 1) and there received the Law on the 31st (cf. Ex 19, 16). He quotes Bede's *DTR* to fix a date, Sunday, 20 March, in the second year of the wanderings, for Moses's consecration of the Tabernacle.[143] The use of 'historical' *computus* briefly reappears at the start of the Fifth Age. Here, Claudius dates Jerusalem's capture to 23 June, and the ensuing destruction of Solomon's Temple to 28 July.[144] Within a chronology compiled for other use, Claudius lights on key moments of Hebrew history, and repossesses them for his own time via the *computus* and the solar calendar.

---

139 *PL* 104, 919D–920A. Here, Claudius contradicts Bede's finding, based on the elapsed interval of lunar months, that Noah spent a 'complete solar year' in the ark: *DTR* 11, 315, ll. 48–51.

140 See above, n. 129.

141 *PL* 104, 918D–920C.

142 *PL* 104, 922B–923A. Claudius 'shows his work' in a way that would edify a modern teacher of maths.

143 Ibid., 923A–B. Bede, *DTR* 66, 471, ll. 282–4.

144 Monza, fol. 82[rb–va] (lacks at *PL* 104, 924B). Claudius quotes from Bede, *DTR* 66, 481, ll. 566–7; he uses, but does not name the year set by Bede, 3363 *a.c.m.*. Claudius also chooses dates among variant reports in the Vulgate: for the capture, Jer. 39, 2: 'undecimo autem anno Sedeciae mense quarto quinta mensis aperta est ciuitas' (vs. 4 Kings 25, 3, and Jer. 52, 6: '*nona* mensis'); for the destruction, Jer. 52, 12: 'in mense autem quinto decima mensis ...' (vs. 4 Kings 25, 8: '*septima* die').

At this point, the encomium of Bede obviates the need to count years that cease to match the genealogical steps towards Christ.[145] Claudius simply names the Bedan tally for the Fifth Age and fixes the Incarnation in 3952 *a.c.m.* To justify this shortcut and the aggregate result, Claudius resorts to a final computistical flurry. Bede's years to the Incarnation combine with the current year, A.D. 814, to give a cosmic total of 4766 *a.c.m.* Based on this terminus, a few lines of figuring establish that the year's computistical operands and the actual 'course of the moon in the present year' coincide.[146] The present thus corroborates the completed chronological scheme, and the *computus* forms a bridge between the prevailing calendrical cycles and the past 'scientific' projections used by Claudius to plot sacred dates.

The reckoning section closes with a profession of ignorance as to the time remaining for the 'present mortal world.' On this point, Claudius had 'learned nothing from his reading,' and declined to speculate against the Gospel dictum: 'Of that day and hour no one knows'...'[147] Nevertheless, his finished *Chronicle* imparted some lessons that were new and many others revitalized through their fresh arrangement.

Claudius mapped the 'years and generations' of early sacred time and, where possible, connected key biblical events to the recurring cycle of the Christian solar calendar. He provided a usable framework of cosmic reference and set its milestones, however imperfectly, within the round of days, months, and remembrances known to his readers. By drawing pivotal moments of sin, elation, and punishment into view, and often into the calendar, Claudius attempted to make a place for ancient sacred events on the landscape of the 'New Israel' of the Franks. The choice of happenings and their significance was no matter of a mere personal feeling. As Claudius saw it, science, in the form of the *computus*, applied to the divinely intended, sometimes datable biblical record. From abstract chronistic knowledge, there came practical truths and lessons, and the *computus* itself allowed the creation of so many dated prods to

---

145 See above, pp. 310–11 and nn. 117–18.

146 *PL* 104, 924D–925A: '... colliguntur omnes anni a conditione mundi usque ad praesentem annum, qui est incarnationis Domini nostri Iesu Christi 814, ... anni 4766. Sed ut apertius appareat quod dicimus, computa eosdem annos ...'

147 Matt. 24, 36. *PL* 104, 925B–926A. The ensuing conclusion (complete in Monza, fols. 83ra-vb; broken off in *PL* 104, at 926B) copies Bede's warnings about the unknown remainder of the Sixth Age: *DTR* 67, 536-7, ll. 11–60 ('Caeterum cunctis ... a nuptiis'). Bede's arguments and new Hebrew-Truth chronology had quelled apocalyptic fears about A.D. 800, the worrisome 6000th year in the world-era of Eusebius-Jerome: von den Brincken, *Studien*, 107–8. Claudius shares Bede's caution, but there is no hint of anxiety about A.D. 800. Cf. R. Landes, 'Sur les traces du Millennium: La "Via Negativa" (2^e partie),' *Le Moyen Âge* 99 (1993): 1–26, esp. 12–13 (on the 'terrors' of A.D. 800).

reflection. These prods were Claudius' distinctive contribution. In both its parts, his *Chronicle* is not an 'effort towards orientation in world history,'[148] but an essentially theological venture pitched to the exegetical, temporal, ethical, and even ethno-linguistic preoccupations of Carolingian readers.

The two-part *Chronicle* offers a novel and sometimes provocatively unconventional treatment of enduring questions and points of interest. Its transmission shows that Claudius' written teaching remained a valued resource. Even one useful work, among many such by the suspect bishop of Turin, posed a threat, at least to some. To scholarly adversaries, usefulness alone justified and even required the attacks on Claudius' teaching and memory that continued long after his death. But attacks did not cancel what Claudius the teacher had wrought. Nor did they quash the genius and lessons of his 'little book' on the 'years and generations from the world's beginning.'

---

148 H. Löwe, ed., Wattenbach-Levison, *Deutschlands Geschichtsquellen im Mittelalter: Vorzeit und Karolinger*, Hefte 2 (Weimar, 1953), 259 ('Streben nach einer Orientierung in der Weltgeschichte').

15

Monks and Canons in Carolingian Gaul: The Case of Rigrannus of Le Mans

GILES CONSTABLE

The document with which this essay is concerned was first published by Éti-enne Baluze in the appendix to his edition of the Carolingian capitularies.[1] He took it 'Ex veteri codice bibliothecae Colbertinae,' according to a marginal note, but it cannot be located among the manuscripts from Colbert's library now in the Bibliothèque nationale.[2] The incipit is not among those in the cata-logues at the Bibliothèque nationale, the Institut de recherche et d'histoire des textes, or the Hill Monastic Microfilm Library. Unless further information comes to light, therefore, the text stands by itself and must be studied on the basis of internal evidence.

The document was written, on the face of it, at Le Mans shortly after the pontificate of Robert, who was bishop from 859 until 883.[3] It is concerned with a young man named Rigrannus, whose father, Robert, died after being taken

1 Étienne Baluze, *Capitularia regum Francorum* (Paris, 1677; 2d ed., Paris, 1780), 2: 1476–80; repr. in Giovanni Domenico Mansi, *Sacrorum conciliorum nova et amplissima collectio*, new ed., 18B (Paris, 1902), 1476–80, and *PL* 129: 1263A–8B. I am indebted to members of the medieval seminar at the Institute for Advanced Study in 1995–6, with whom I discussed this document, and to Paul Dutton, Paul Meyvaert, Hubert Mordek, and Thomas Noble, who made some helpful suggestions, especially concerning the putative author and the type of work.The case is discussed briefly in an article by Janet L. Nelson, 'Parents, Children, and the Church in the Earlier Middle Ages,' in *The Church and Childhood*, ed. Diana Wood, Studies in Church History 31 (Oxford, 1994), 113.

2 Several of Colbert's manuscripts with texts from Le Mans, to which Baluze had access, have subsequently disappeared, according to Philippe Lemaître. This information was kindly sup-plied by Dominique Iogna-Prat, who consulted with the authorities at the Bibliothèque natio-nale. Hubert Mordek, in a letter dated 26 January 1996, wrote that this text is found in no known manuscript of Carolingian capitularies but may have come from the lost final folios of MS Paris, BnF, Lat. 4637, which ends with a letter of Bishop Lambert of Le Mans.

3 *Gallia christiana* 14 (Paris, 1856), 361–3; *Actus pontificum Cenomannis in urbe degentium*, ed. G. Busson and A. Ledru, Archives historiques du Maine 2 (Le Mans, 1901), 336–9, and Louis Duchesne, *Fastes épiscopaux de l'ancienne Gaule*, 2d ed., 2 (Paris, 1910), 314–17.

captive by the Northmen, probably during their attacks on Le Mans in 865 and 866.[4] As a child Rigrannus was dedicated to God by his father in the monastery of Cormery in the diocese of Tours, and he may have been born about 860. After his father's death he was given by his uncle, a priest named Urso, to Bishop Robert and the church of Le Mans, and was raised and educated in an unnamed monastery. Mindful of his father's promise, however, he decided to become a monk, against the wishes of both his master and his uncle, who wanted Rigrannus to succeed him. Finally, when he was eighteen years old, that is, in the late 870s, he became a monk, and five years later received the five minor orders and was ordained a subdeacon. Two years after that, however, when his uncle Urso died, he left the monastery and returned to the life of a secular canon. This situation had lasted for seven years when the work was written, apparently in the early 890s.

There is no serious reason to doubt the authenticity of the document aside from the fact that it deals with a question that was of less concern in the ninth century than in the eleventh and twelfth. It is hard to see, however, why a writer at that time would have placed the episode in a period that had no relevance to the later reform of the church. It might also be a contemporary forgery. Le Mans was a notorious centre of forgery in the ninth century, especially during the pontificate of Robert, as the recipient of this Festschrift has shown in his book on *The Le Mans Forgeries*,[5] but these were primarily concerned with episcopal property, which figures in this document only in a passing reference to an unnamed monastery 'of the same bishop.' Baluze clearly believed that it was authentic, and its inclusion in the appendix of his edition of the Carolingian capitularies and his description of the manuscript as 'old' (that is, for him, early medieval) both count in its favour. Baluze was not infallible in his judgments on medieval documents, as his involvement in the affair of the *Histoire généalogique de la maison d'Auvergne* shows,[6] but he was an experienced scholar with an extensive knowledge of medieval texts and manuscripts.

---

4 Hincmar of Rheims, *Annales Bertiniani*, s.a. 865, ed. Georg Waitz, MGH SRG (1883), 80, 84; trans. Janet Nelson (Manchester and New York, 1991), 128, 135; *Actus pontificum Cenomannis*, 338 and n. 2; and Walther Vogel, *Die Normannen und das fränkische Reich bis zur Gründung der Normandie (799–911)*, Heidelberger Abhandlungen zur mittleren und neueren Geschichte 14 (Heidelberg, 1906), 210. There were other attacks on Le Mans in 844 and in the late ninth century, and Robert may have been captured at some other time. In the *Gallia christiana* 14: 363BC, Robert is erroneously identified with the bishop of the same name.

5 Walter Goffart, *The Le Mans Forgeries: A Chapter from the History of Church Property in the Ninth Century*, Harvard Historical Studies 76 (Cambridge, Mass., 1966), who dated the forgeries under Bishop Robert, probably after 862/3 (146–7), and stressed their concern with ecclesiastical property, and especially episcopal monasteries.

6 Albert Giry, *Manuel de diplomatique* (Paris, 1894), 881–3.

The literary style is characteristic of Carolingian writers and shows a command of both classical and biblical terminology. *Altitonans iudex, lethea unda,* and *avernus* suggest a classical training, and the reference to 'illi qui deridebant uocem loquentis in exhortationem et consolationem uersi sunt' combines words and phrases from at least three biblical passages. The use of *canonici* for clerics generally (which will be discussed later) is also characteristically Carolingian. The author was probably a monk, and, to judge from his skill as a writer, he doubtless wrote other works, which some reader of this essay may be able to identify. The text may indeed have been written as part of a larger work, but it is self-standing in its present form and seems to constitute a brief tract designed to publicize the case of Rigrannus.[7]

The Latin text in the appendix to this essay is reprinted from Baluze's edition, with some normalization of the spelling, capitalization, and punctuation and with three textual emendations, one by Baluze, who proposed adding *tamen* in the passage describing Urso's reaction to the news that Rigrannus wanted to become a monk, and two by me: (1) *Patris* for *patri* in the sentence concerning the dedication of Rigrannus to Cormery. He may have made a vow to his father (as *patri* implies), but the references to 'a patre,' 'propositum patris,' and 'uotum patris' show that his father made the commitment, as was normal in cases of oblation. (2) *Socios* for *socius* at the end of the main body of the text, where *socius* in the nominative singular (unless it is an archaic accusative plural, which would again show the writer's classicizing style) is grammatically impossible. The sentence still presents some problems, which the translation presented here only partially solves.[8]

The holy church strives daily by various summonses to induce not only those who scorn the world but also, what is [a] greater [task], those whom worldly activity makes prosperous, to seek the lot of the elect and the beatitude of eternal life, in order that both the diversity of good deeds may multiply them here [in this world] and the difference of varied recompense may adorn them there [in the other world]. In the same way, on the other

7 Paul Dutton, in a letter dated 7 January 1996, wrote that 'The work directly fits no specific Carolingian genre, since it has elements of sermon, narrative, and hagiography in it.' Hubert Mordek, in his letter of 26 January, wrote that 'Bei aller Differenz im Thematischen erinnert mich der Bericht vom Genre her weitläufig an Hinkmar von Reims' De Villa Noviliaco.'

8 In the text, *v* and *j* have been replaced by *u* and *i*. *Despectus, antiquis, denuos,* and *soepissime* are silently corrected. In the translation, to avoid confusion, the terms *qui, ille, se, eum,* etc., to which the referents are not always clear in English, have occasionally been replaced by a proper name or by 'the boy,' 'the youth,' 'the priest,' 'the bishop,' etc. *Urbs* and *ciuitas* have been translated, respectively, as 'town' and 'city,' though they both refer to Le Mans. My colleague G.W. Bowersock assisted with two passages, and the editor of this volume made some helpful suggestions.

side, the ancient enemy never ceases to snatch pious people in order to know that those whom he cannot have as partners in glory will at least be companions with him in punishment. For since from the earliest time there have been in the three orders, that is, of lay men, canons, and monks, those who have tried with the divinely given spirit of understanding to examine and undertake more noble deeds, the Devil strives most greatly to catch those whom he encouraged at an early age to subject themselves beyond the Lord's precepts, so that rejoicing he may cast them as much more deeply into the depths as he once grieved that they had escaped his bloody jaws. The evangelical and apostolic texts teach how damnable it is for these people to leave their holy undertaking and confirm that just as they are wounded by serpentine poisons they may be reformed again by their remedies. For since there is a suitable cure for each person in accordance with the severity of the infection, and the doctors of the church, authorized by the thundering judge on high, permit hidden faults to be exposed in one way and open faults to be abolished in another, greater solicitude and care should be used for people who after the nobler devotion relapse again to the secular habit and become apostates. This most evil transgression is at present found beyond measure among both sexes and has involved many wavering people in changes and has led them by darkened lights from the proper path. This avoidable type [of transgression] stands in the open, and for this reason some of the assembly of good and bad Catholics reprove the evil and others defend it, in such a way that although they cannot render totally harmless those who are sunk in such a crime, they none the less try to show them to be innocent by lying speeches either through denying or concealing the deed or in some other way. For this reason, and because the case of many people is already more serious than that of one, it remains to bring into the open the controversy over this matter that has recently emerged in our region, so that when the truth is known the judgment of truthful people may be observed and muddled falsity may disappear.

For there was a certain very noble priest named Urso in the city of Le Mans who wanted one of his nephews to be his successor. And when he sought the opinion concerning this matter of the bishop of this town, that is, the venerable Robert, he not only gave his assent to Urso's request but also took care to ask that it should be fully done, since he thought the boy would both promote the interest of the church owing to his good family and receive the immortality of his soul more pleasantly by living and serving the institutions of the church. The aforesaid priest therefore hastened to complete this business, and together with his brother Wanilo he offered the aforesaid nephew, whose name was Rigrannus, to the lord bishop and his church in order that he might deserve to receive the honour of clerical status from him and his congregation. After this holy deed was nobly done at the time of Easter, the lord bishop again instructed the priest, who received the boy as a spiritual son, to serve as his tutor and guardian of his body and soul and to provide nourishment, so that after a suitable education in divine and human services, he could return to the bishop. The priest gladly obeyed the order of his lord and received the boy. And since he knew that there was no means of [teaching] letters at his house, he sent the boy to a certain monastery of the same bishop, where the monastic order flourished, so that he might be instructed and trained there in sacred letters. The boy was therefore received in the monastery and entrusted to a master, and when he had worked at scholastic disciplines for many days, he began at a certain time to be vexed by a serious weakness of his body. And while he was frequently tormented by such attacks, and a severe malady of his intestines and insides irremediably afflicted him, and no medical art offered a cure, the master began to wonder how and why the disturbance of such an infirmity afflicted the youth, and he asked him why he suffered so many and such bad things. When he had been questioned for a long time and gave no clear answer, one day, when he was bearing sharper pains and lay almost dead, scarcely breathing with a feeble breath, he finally confessed that in former years he had been dedicated to God by his father in the monastery of Cormery and on this account God would now kill him by his great infirmity following the vow of [to?] his father, and he therefore expected to suffer such great afflictions. When the master heard this he was silent within himself and asked him, after the boy's strength was restored and he had a chance to question him, whether the things he had heard from him at the time of his illness were fantasies. He affirmed that they were true, however, and showed how this had come about. He also said that he wanted to be a monk in order to free the souls of himself and his father from the danger of the vow. His aforementioned father Robert had indeed already expired. He had been captured by the Northmen and had so died worn out by their punishments. The youth therefore gradually came to believe that he should submit his neck to the light yoke of Christ (cf. Matthew 11.30) and fulfil the intention of his father. But the master denied that this could be done, 'because,' he said, 'you did not come here in order to be made a monk, and you did not receive the tonsure for that reason, nor did your relations give their assent to these words.' While the boy persevered in his assertion, however, and in his defence of his unfulfillable request, it happened that his uncle Urso, who had received him with fatherly affection, came to the monastery for the sake of a visit. While food was being prepared and they were talking together, the youth undertook among other things to reveal to his uncle the desire of his intention, and the travail that he suffered and the vow of his father. When the priest heard these things, he was very concerned and disturbed [but] did not dare to contradict what he was unwilling to urge. But he at last unwillingly agreed that the petitioner should do what he asked. And his habit was immediately changed; he put on a cowl; and he fell at his uncle's feet and kissed them. So from that day both the master who refused and those who 'laughed to scorn' (Matthew 9.24; Luke 8.53; etc.) 'the voice of one that spoke' (Numbers 7.89; Ezechiel 2.1) were turned into 'exhortation and comfort' (1 Corinthians 14.3). The bishop was meanwhile at that time far from the city, performing the work of preaching and confirmation wherever it was needed throughout the province. When he returned and was not far from the town, however, he summoned the aforesaid youth's master, who was also the abbot of the monastery, in order to find out what was going on with regard to the monks and the monastery. But after he learned everything, he last of all asked about the disciple. The abbot answered these questions and explained everything that had been done. When the bishop heard this, he was surprised and, hastening on, came to the city, wanting to know the form of the incredible thing he had heard; and he summoned the abbot and novice and some of the brothers. When they were in his presence, with a crowd of clerics and lay men standing all around, for it was time to celebrate mass, since the feast of the purification of the Virgin was at hand, he said in amazement to the novice, 'I recently left you a canon, brother Rigrannus, and now I see you in a cowl. Tell me therefore why you did this, or who forced or advised you.' But Rigrannus replied, 'I did this at the advice or suggestion of no one but only at the desire and prompting of my own spirit.' He therefore recounted to all the listeners everything that has been said above. He also added that he had seen a marvellous dream of which the meaning was that he should leave the world and take up the monastic life. But since the bishop and others who were present still did not believe it, he earnestly entreated him as his duty required to say whether these things were true. But the youth confirmed with an oath that he had said nothing falsely. On this account the venerable bishop was saddened, and his whole congregation grieved as if they had lost the solace and support of their church, and they questioned among themselves and were amazed that such prudence could appear in a youth, especially since he had already reached the more dangerous age. For he was, they thought, eighteen years old. The venerable bishop asked again, however, whether he intended to persevere all his days in the monastic order. But when he affirmed this and bore witness in the presence of everyone, the lord bishop gave him his blessing and granted the monastic place and order that he requested. After this was finished, when his uncle Urso heard what the bishop had done, for he was not present at the time because he was ill in another place, he and his other relations took it badly that their nephew was lost to the world and acquired for God. He sent to fetch him. And when he stood before him, he addressed him angrily and senselessly in this way: 'What have you done, wretch? Why do you want to be a monk? Why have you chosen one small loaf of bread rather than a hundred and a little wine rather than goblets to be drained in abundance? Why do you want to be satisfied with a pig-like life of beans and vegetables? Where will be the pleasures of the meats that you have rejected, the sweetness of drinks, the enjoyment of dogs and hawks, the voluptuous touch of women?' When he therefore saw that the youth's spirit resisted this and perceived that his replies were not those of a youth but had the strength of age, he added much more evil things, so that he even sent pimps to arouse him, and he also stirred up the other uncles, that is Lethardus, Wanilo, and many other relations, who said to the youth, 'Why do you want to dishonour us? Our family has had no business with poor men and beggars. The world has prospered for us; quantities of gold and silver and precious stones were ours. For us shining arms gleamed; horses preened themselves with gilded bridles and arched necks.

And you have spurned all these things?' Evil men said this, men who should have roused him to better things, men who living grandly wanted to be submerged in the waters of forgetfulness rather than to be washed in the fountain of salvation with those who have been freed and be praised after the works of mercies by the freeing effect of piety, saying 'We have passed through fire and through water; and thou hast brought us out into a refreshment' (Psalm 65.12). But the young man's spirit remained unbroken, and he wished to keep what he had begun and kept his orders and feelings according to the rule with the others in the monastery, so that his relations could not recall him for five years. But when among these things they stirred up all sorts of madness against the master, accusing him and demanding the disciple, the rash master did not fail to give up his charge. They received their nephew and kept him at home, always in the form of a monk. But after they had kept him for eight days and more, still entreating vigorously, they sent him back to the monastery, when the disciple begged and they consented. When the time came to receive the first ecclesiastical grades, however, the deception of the uncles was heard, and the venerable bishop sent to the priest saying that he should now assent to what he had previously agreed to, as we said above, but from which he had subsequently withdrawn his agreement, that the monk might receive the ecclesiastical grades in the same habit. After dissembling for a long time, therefore, the uncle finally sent to the lord bishop saying that he should do what reason and authority required. And this was done, and the young man received the blessings of the five ranks, and he remained and persevered willingly in the holy way of life. Two years later Urso suddenly and unexpectedly died. And when he was nearing his end, he summoned the aforesaid monk, his nephew. And when he was beside him, he was at pains to tell him about the glory of the world that he was leaving and did not give up his original purpose that his nephew should return to the canonical life, and he advised him, and most greatly by all the things he could have, in order to excite his mind by cupidity and useless glory. And so he died. And he accomplished dead what he could not accomplish alive. From that day the subdeacon began to depart from his early wish, therefore, and to join in way of life and spirit with his uncles Lethardus and Amarricus, by whose advice and cunning he was carried headlong, and they became priests against the law (cf. Sophonias 3.4), usurping the duty of the bishop. For they shut the young man up in a certain chamber, where without the judgment of the venerable bishop and priests they removed his monastic vestment and clothed him in an alb. And he was thus restored to a secular way of life. And they heaped blame on the master and lord bishop for their good deeds. For empty cunning led them with blinded eyes into the ruin of the snare (cf. Osee 9.8). For seven years they dared to do this violence, so that although it was evil it became much more damnable the longer it was known and persisted. Because the longer a good lasts the further it falls if it collapses. In the same way the more an evil grows the heavier the punishment to which it is subject. Hell wishes to receive those who pursue such things and, neglecting the consequences of penance, desire to have useless companions.

The witness of this thing is every order of this church, each of which according to its duty can prove that it happened in this way.

The purpose of the document, as stated in the introductory paragraph, was to publicize the case of Rigrannus as an example of the men and women 'who after the nobler devotion [that is, to the monastic life] relapse again to the secular habit and become apostates.' The author distinguished at several points in his narrative between monks and canons, who differed in tonsure, clothing, and way of life. Rigrannus' master (though himself a monk and, as it turns out, abbot of the monastery where Rigrannus was educated) at first refused his request to become a monk because he had not been tonsured or come to the monastery for that purpose. After he became a monk, Rigrannus observed the 'ordines suos et affectus regulares in monasterio' and kept the *figura monachi* (presumably the monastic habit and tonsure) when he left the monastery for eight days, and he was ordained 'sub ipso habitu.' Only after he left the monastery permanently, giving up his wish to be a monk and joining his uncles in spirit and way of life, was his monastic habit removed, and he was clothed in an alb, the visible sign of his new status. The author recognized the superiority of the monastic calling, but his primary purpose was neither to praise monks nor to condemn canons and secular clerics, aside from the satirical view of their worldly life embodied in the expostulations addressed to Rigrannus by his uncles and relations. Indeed, the writer accepted without question their distress, and that of Bishop Robert and the cathedral clergy, at Rigrannus' decision to become a monk. His fault lay not in being a canon but in returning to 'the secular habit' after having undertaken 'the nobler devotion.' The text is thus concerned more with the issue of transfer from one form of life to another than with the debate over the respective superiority of monks and canons, which was not in doubt.[9]

The author concentrates entirely on the transfer made when Rigrannus was a grown man and pays no attention either to his dedication as a boy to Cormery, which is described three times as a *uotum* and twice as a *propositum*, or to the apparent failure of the abbot of Cormery to lay claim to him, though he was clearly a good catch. Neither his relations nor the bishop seem to have considered the commitment binding, and only Rigrannus himself took it seriously. Although the text says that he was dedicated 'in monasterio quod uocatur Cormaricus,' the vow may have been taken in private, without witnesses or a ceremony of oblation, which were normally considered necessary, as in the cases of

---

9 On the general lack of practical distinctions between monks, clerics, and lay men in the early Middle Ages, see Franz Felten, *Äbte und Laienäbte im Frankenreich*, Monographien zur Geschichte des Mittelalters 20 (Stuttgart, 1980), 97.

Gottschalk and Lembert of Schienen, who claimed that his oblation was not binding because he had not been formally offered by his father and blessed by the abbot.[10]

The term *canonicus* was used here as equivalent to *clericus*. It is uncertain whether the author drew any distinction between canons as members of a cathedral chapter or collegiate church and other clerics, but the reference in the introductory paragraph to the three orders of lay men, canons, and monks shows that non-monastic clerics were called 'canons.' Charlemagne in the *Admonitio generalis* referred to the *clericatus* 'which we call the canonical life' and decreed that 'those clerics who present themselves as monks in dress and name, and are not' should be corrected 'so that they may be either real monks or real canons;'[11] and there were many references in the acts of Carolingian councils to the monastic and canonical orders and to canons in the sense of clerics.[12] The distinction was less clear in fact, however, than in theory. The council of Mainz in 813 ordered bishops to ascertain for each monastery 'how many canons each abbot has in his monastery and fully to provide equally for both. If they wish to be made monks, they should live regularly; if not, they should live fully canonically.'[13] Amalarius of Metz, who died about 850, said that the church consisted of monks who lived a contemplative life, canons who lived an active life, and those who lead a mixed life of contemplation and action, to

---

10 On oblation, see Mayke de Jong, *In Samuel's Image: Child Oblation in the Early Medieval West* (Leiden, New York, and Cologne, 1996), who discussed the cases of Gottschalk (77–91) and Lambert (91–9) and stressed the irrevocability of parental vows of oblation (168).

11 Charlemagne, Cap. 22.73, 77: *Capitularia Regum Francorum* 1: 60, ed. A. Boretius, MGH LL Capitularia 1 (1883); cf. Cap. 33.1 and 137 ('unicuique ordini, canonicorum uidelicet, monachorum et laicorum'), ibid., 92 and 274. On the *ordo canonicus* in the early Middle Ages, see Charles Dereine, 'Chanoines,' *Dictionnaire d'histoire et de géographie ecclésiastiques* 12 (Paris, 1953), 359, who said that the term was first used at the council of Autun in 670, but that canons were in fact not distinguished from the rest of the clergy; Josef Siegwart, *Die Chorherren- und Chorfrauengemeinschaften in der deutschsprachigen Schweiz vom 6. Jahrhundert bis 1160 mit einem Überblick über die deutsche Kanonikerreform des 10. und 11. Jh.* (Fribourg, 1962), 6, 30, 40; and, more generally, on the concept of orders in the early Middle Ages, my *Three Studies in Medieval Religious and Social Thought* (Cambridge, 1994), esp. 267–79.

12 Paris (829), can. 46: *Concilia Aevi Karolini*, ed. A. Werminghoff, MGH LL Concilia 2.1 (1906), 640; Sens (843/5) ('cum concilio fratrum nostrorum, canonicorum uidelicet et monachorum, necnon et fidelium laicorum'); Mainz (847), can. 12; Soissons (853), cap. 1: *Die Konzilien der karolingischen Teilreiche*, ed. W. Hartmann, MGH LL Concilia 3 (1984), 58, 168, 285. Druthmar of Corbie, who died in 1046, compared monks and canons to the Pharisees and Sadducees in his *Expositio in Matthaeum* 54, in *PL* 106: 1443A, saying 'et sicut inter nos sunt monachi et canonici, et tamen de una gente Francorum sunt, similiter erant apud ipsos.'

13 Mainz (813), can. 21: MGH LL Concilia 2.1: 267.

whom he gave no name;[14] and Alcuin in a letter to Arno of Salzburg referred to a third grade of those whose way of life was above that of canons and below that of monks.[15]

The priest Urso, Rigrannus' uncle, was probably a canon and member of the cathedral chapter. He referred to the bishop as his *senior* and gave Rigrannus to the bishop and his church 'in order that he might deserve to receive the honour of clerical status from him and his congregation.' They expected Rigrannus to return after being educated in the monastery, and when he became a monk, 'the venerable bishop was saddened and his whole congregation grieved as if they had lost the solace and support of their church.' Urso persisted to his dying day in his wish that Rigrannus 'should return to the canonical life,' and he secured by his death (or more likely, perhaps, his testament) what he had not achieved during his life. Urso's brothers Lethardus and Amarricus were also priests, though not necessarily members of the cathedral clergy. Another brother, Wanilo, was probably a lay man, as was Rigrannus' deceased father, Robert, and there are references to 'many other relations.' The text thus gives a picture of a wealthy urban family that owed much of its influence to clerical positions, which it was determined to keep in the family. Urso is called 'ualde nobilis,' but it is impossible to establish his precise social position, aside from the boasting about wealth, dogs, hawks, arms, and horses, which imply a way of life compatible with that of the secular aristocracy, and, apparently, not incompatible with that of canons. There was clearly no sense that it was an honour for the family for Rigrannus to become a monk.[16]

Bishop Robert is sympathetically portrayed as trying to carry out his duty both to the cathedral chapter and to Rigrannus, whom he allowed to become a monk in spite of his own and the clergy's desires and interest, and as performing his episcopal responsibilities throughout his diocese.[17] There are two references to the episcopal *ministerium*, one when Robert urged Rigrannus to tell the

14 Amalarius of Metz, *Codex expositionis* 2.11.5, in his *Opera liturgica omnia*, ed. Jean-Michel Hanssens, 1, Studi e testi 138 (Vatican City, 1948), 273.

15 Alcuin, Ep. 258, *Epistolae Karolini Aeui* 2, ed. E. Dümmler, MGH Epistolae 4 (1895), 416. See Otto Gerhard Oexle, *Forschungen zu monastischen und geistlichen Gemeinschaften im westfränkischen Bereich*, Münstersche Mittelalter-Schriften 31 (Munich, 1978), 131–3.

16 In this respect the case has some parallels with that of the seventh-century saint Rusticula, or Marcia, abbess of Arles, who was put in a monastery by the archbishop of Arles and whose mother tried to lure her back by promises of wealth and luxury: *Vita Rusticulae*, 5, ed. Bruno Krusch, MGH SRM 4 (1902), 342. See De Jong, *In Samuel's Image*, 205.

17 On the diocesan responsibilities of bishops in the tenth century, with references to other works, see Joseph H. Lynch, *Godparents and Kinship in Early Medieval Europe* (Princeton, 1986), 330–1, and Gerd Tellenbach, *The Church in Western Europe from the Tenth to the Early Twelfth Century*, trans. Timothy Reuter (Cambridge, 1993), 32.

truth 'ex suo ministerio' and the other when Rigrannus' uncles Lethard and Amarricus were said to have usurped the 'ministerium episcopi' by removing Rigrannus' monastic habit and clothing him in an alb 'without the judgment of the venerable bishop and priests.' The term is translated here as 'duty,' but it conveys some of the later concept of 'office,' as it does in the final sentence, where each order was called upon to show the truth of the story 'secundum suum ministerium.'[18]

The treatment of Rigrannus is also on the whole sympathetic, and the blame for his apostasy is laid primarily on his uncles and relations. As a child he was the object of his family's desires and ambitions: first, of his father, who (for unspecified reasons) wanted him to enter the monastery of Cormery and, after his father's death, of his uncle Urso, who gave ('obtulit') him to the bishop and his church. The bishop then commended ('commendauit') him to Urso, who received him 'as a spiritual son'[19] and treated him 'with fatherly affection' and who in turn entrusted him to a master in a local monastery, where Rigrannus first emerged as a character in his own right and decided to become a monk.[20] He stuck to his determination in spite of the opposition of his master, his uncle, the bishop, and the cathedral clergy. Finally, supported by a dream confirming that he must leave the world,[21] he was allowed to enter a monastery, perhaps Cormery.[22] In spite of the pleas of his relations, who presented a vivid picture of the pleasures of life in the world, Rigrannus remained true to his vocation until the death of Urso, whose heir he presumably was. He may have tired of the monastic life, or, more likely, have been persuaded by the attractions of secular life and the arguments of his uncles, who assisted his departure from the monastery. Such cases were not rare, among both men and women, according

18 On the term *ministerium*, see J.F. Niermeyer, *Mediae Latinitatis lexicon minus* (Leiden, 1976), 687–90, who lists twenty-four distinct meanings.

19 On spiritual kinship, which was usually established at baptism in the early Middle Ages, see Arnold Angenendt, *Kaiserherrschaft und Königstaufe: Kaiser, Könige und Päpste als geistliche Patrone in der abendländischen Missionsgeschichte*, Arbeiten zur Frühmittelalter-forschung 15 (Berlin, 1984), 97–105, and Lynch, *Godparents*, 169–92 and 285–339, esp. 304–32, on godparents and religious instruction. On the commendation of boys to protectors for the purpose of education, see De Jong, *In Samuel's Image*, 199.

20 The monastery, of which the name is unknown, was probably small, since the master was also abbot.

21 On dreams in Carolingian society, see Maria Wittmer-Butsch, *Zur Bedeutung von Schlaf und Traum im Mittelalter*, Medium Aevum Quotidianum, Sonderband 1 (Krems, 1990), esp. 103–15, on the generally negative valuation put on dreams in the early Middle Ages, citing the council of Paris in 829, can. 69, on *somniatorum coniectores* in MGH LL Concilia 2.1: 669, and Paul Edward Dutton, *The Politics of Dreaming in the Carolingian Empire* (Lincoln and London, 1994).

22 The text simply says that the bishop 'concessit locum et ordinem monasticum quem petebat.'

to the author, who wrote this account to warn others of the fate awaiting such apostates if they failed to repent.[23] Transfers from one type of religious community to another, with or without the permission of the superior, were common in the Middle Ages, and the possibility for monks was foreseen in the rule of Benedict, but it is unusual to find so well-documented a case for the Carolingian period, and it throws some interesting light on the attitudes towards both monks and canons at that time.

Appendix

Sicut cotidie sancta ecclesia ad sortem electorum atque beatitudinem perpetuae uitae capessendam diuersis euocationibus, non solum despectos seculi, sed etiam eos, quod maius est, quos mundialis actio perfloridos facit, adtrahere decertat, ut illos hic et diuersitas bonorum actuum multi-
5 plicet et illic dissimilitas retributionis uariae ornet, ita e contrario antiquus hostis pios indesinenter subripere non cessat, ut quos consortes non potest habere in gloria, saltim socios secum cognoscat in poena. Nam cum in tribus ordinibus, id est, laicorum, canonicorum, monachorumque, non desint qui a primaevo tempore nobiliora acta perscrutari atque aggredi ten-
10 tarint dato diuinitus intelligibili animo, eos maxime insidiari nititur quos in iuuenili aetate creuerit se ultro dominicis praeceptis mancipasse, ut tanto profundius ad ima gaudens proiciat quanto a suis cruentis faucibus semel euasisse dolebat, quorum deuiatio a proposito sancto quam damnabilis esse censeatur euangelica et apostolica documenta edocent, suisque medi-
15 caminibus ut denuo reformentur, qualiter serpentinis uenenis sauciantur, corroborant. Cum enim unicuique modus correctionis secundum grauitatem contagii conueniat, idque a doctoribus ecclesiae sanciri permissum sit data auctoritate altitonantis iudicis, ut aliter obtecta detegantur, aliter aperta deleantur, in his etiam qui post deuotionem nobiliorem ad secularem
20 iterum habitum dilabuntur atque apostatae efficiuntur maior sollicitudo et cura adhibenda esse decernitur. Quae praeuaricatio pessima in utroque

23 Smaragdus, in the early ninth century, wrote in his commentary on the passage in the Rule of Benedict concerning the return of oblates to the world that 'he had seen that in this way young men leave the monastery, give up the service of God for earthly things, and love the world ... Although this rarely occurred at that time, we however know that now it is done very frequently': Smaragdus, *Expositio in regulam s. Benedicti* LIX, 6, ed. A. Spannagel and P. Engelbert, Corpus consuetudinum monasticarum 8 (Siegburg, 1974), 300–1. See De Jong, *In Samuel's Image*, 73 and 224.

sexu modernis temporibus supra modum inuenitur, plurimosque uacil-
lantes suis uolubilitatibus implicare et deperire a recto tramite obfuscatis
luminibus inlisit. Sed quia hoc deuitabile genus in promptu stare uidetur, ac
25   propter hoc in coetu bonorum malorumque catholicorum pars sit in
redargutione, pars in defensione mali, ita ut eos quos in tali facinore
depressos, dum non possunt innocuos facere in toto, suis mendosis sermo-
cinationibus aut per abnegationem aut dissimulationem actus uel per aliquam occasionem innocentes conantur ostendere, sitque iam grauior casus
30   multorum quam unius, restat de hac ipsa controuersia quae modo nostris in
partibus excreuit aliquid ad medium deducere, quatinus cognita ueritate
iudicium obseruetur ueracium, et falsitas confusa euanescat.

Quidam namque sacerdos nomine Urso ualde nobilis fuit Cenomannis
ciuitate, qui unum ex suis nepotibus superstitem esse uolebat. Cumque
35   super hac re consultum ipsius urbis episcopi, uidelicet uenerabilis Rotberti,
peteret, non solum suae petitioni assensum praebuit, uerum etiam omni-
modo id agendum exhortare curauit, reputans in puero et ecclesiae utilitatem pro genere spectabili profuturam et immortalitatem animae dulcius
uiuendo atque ecclesiae instituta militando recepturam. Praedictus itaque
40   sacerdos hoc negotium adimplere festinans, adhibito secum fratre suo
nomine Wanilone, obtulit supradictum nepotem cognomine Rigrannum
domno episcopo ecclesiaeque eius, ut ab eo et ipsius congregatione honorem clericatus suscipere mereretur. Quod cum factum diebus sanctum
paschae fuisset nobiliter, denuo domnus episcopus praefato auunculo, qui
45   eum in spiritalis filii uicem susceperat, commendauit, ut tutor custosque
corporis et animae eius fieret ac nutrimenta praeberet, quatinus post edoca-
tionem aptum diuinis et humanis seruitiis ei reddere posset. Qui imperium
sui senioris libenter obtemperans, recepit puerum. Cumque apud se non
esse copiam litterarum cognosceret, misit eum in quoddam monasterium
50   ipsius episcopi, ubi ordo monasticus uigebat, ut illic instrueretur sacris litteris et erudiretur. Ergo susceptus puer in monasterio, traditusque magistro,
cum per plures dies scholasticis disciplinis operam dedisset, quodam tempore coepit fatigari languore graui corporis. Itaque dum saepissime talibus
impulsionibus cruciaretur, dirusque dolor intestinarum ac uiscerum inre-
55   mediabiliter eum uexaret, nulla arte medicinali medelam praebente, ob-
tupescere coepit magister quae et cur agitatio tantae infirmitatis
adolescentem infligeret, sciscitansque ab eo quam ob causam tot et talia
inuisa pateretur. Qui cum diutine interrogaretur et nullum certum responsum dedisset, quadam die acriores sustinens cruciatus, ut pene exanimis
60   iaceret, uix languido hanelitu flante, tandem confessus est se a patre Deo
deuotum fuisse in annis prioribus in monasterio quod uocatur Cormaricus,

propterea quod dominus se ipsum iam emortuum pro euentu nimiae infirmitatis patris[a] post uotum reddidisset, ac ideo sperare se pati tam grauia.
Quo audito, magister tacitus intra se requirebat ei recepto robore, cum tem-
65 pus inquisitionis adesset, si fuissent insania quae ab eo audierat hora infirmitatis. Ille autem adfirmabat uera esse, docebatque ordinem rei. Dicebat
etiam uelle se esse monachum, ut ipsius et patris anima a periculo uoti lib-
eraretur. Siquidem pater eius supra memoratus, uidelicet Rohtbertus, iam
humanis rebus excesserat. Deciderat enim in capturam Norcomannorum,
70 et sic eorum poenis attritus interierat. Itaque paulatim adolescens informa-
batur ut collum sub leui iugo Christi submitteret[1] atque propositum patris
expleret. Sed magister id fieri posse negabat dicens: Quia nequaquam huc
uenisti ut monachus efficereris, nec ideo tonsuram accepisti, sed nec parentes tui his sermonibus adquiescent. Perseuerante autem illo in adfirma-
75 tione et defensione rei quae petebatur non fiendae, contigit ut auunculus
eius, qui eum paterno affectu susceperat, uidelicet Urso, declinaret in
monasterium causa uisitationis. Quod cum edilia praepararentur et inuicem
confabularentur, inter caetera orsus est adolescens auunculo ostendere uol-
untatem propositi, laboremque quem patiebatur, ac uotum patris. His audi-
80 tis sacerdos non minime anxius grauiter ferebat, non[b] minime contradicere
audebat quod exhortari nolebat. Consensit tamen nolens diu petenti ut fac-
eret quod poscebat. Statimque mutato habitu induit cucullam, ac cadens ad
pedes auunculi, osculatus est illos. Sic ab illo die et magister qui denega-
bat, et illi qui *deridebant*[2] *uocem loquentis*,[3] in *exhortationem et consola-*
85 *tionem*[4] uersi sunt. Interea illis diebus episcopus a ciuitate longius
recesserat, exercens opus praedicationis et confirmationis per prouinciam
locis necessariis. Cum autem reuerteretur et esset non longe ab urbe,
uocauit magistrum supra memorati adolescentis, qui et abbas monasterii
erat, ut sciret quae agerentur circa monachos et monasterium. Postquam
90 uero cuncta cognouit, nouissime de discipulo interrogauit. Quibus interrogationibus responsum dedit abbas, atque omnia quae facta fuerant enunti-
auit. Quo audito, domnus episcopus admiratus, concitus in eundo usque ad
ciuitatem peruenit, scire uolens quam speciem haberet res audita, sed
incredibilis, iussitque abbatem et nouitium uocare et quosdam ex fratribus.

a   patri Baluze
b   tamen *add. in marg.* Baluze

1   Cf. Matthew 11.30
2   Matthew 9.24; Luke 8.53; etc.
3   Numbers 7.89; Ezechiel 2.1
4   1 Corinthians 14.3

95 Cumque coram eo assisterent, stante circum circa omni caterua clericorum
laicorumque, erat enim hora ad celebrandum missarum solemnia, quia fes-
tiuitas purificationis sanctae Mariae instabat, ait stupefactus ad iamdictum
nouitium: Nuper te, frater Rigranne, canonicum dimisi, et modo cuculla-
tum uideo. Dic ergo nobis cur hoc fecisti, uel quis coegit, aut consilium
100 dedit. At ille respondit: Nullius consilio uel suggestione, sed sola uoluntate
et sponsione proprii animi, a me hoc actum est. Retulit itaque audientibus
omnibus cuncta superius dicta. Addebat etiam somnium mirabile se
uidisse, cuius interpretatio talis erat, ut seculum dimitteret, et uitam monas-
ticam teneret. Adhuc autem non credente episcopo, nec caeteris adtenden-
105 tibus, adiurauit eum ex suo ministerio terribiliter ut profiteretur si uera
essent. Ipse uero confirmabat cum iureiurando nihil mendose locutum se
esse. Quamobrem uenerabilis episcopus moestus et omnis congregatio eius
dolebant quasi ablatum solatium adiutoriumque ecclesiae suae traditum,
sciscitantes etiam inter se admirando quae tanta prudentia in adolescente
110 posset apparere, praesertim cum in periculosiori aetate iam peruenerat.
Erat enim, ut aestimabatur, decem et octo annorum. Iterum autem uenerabilis episcopus perquisiuit si cunctis diebus destinasset perseuerare in
ordine monastico. Illo uero adfirmante et contestante coram omnibus, dedit
ei benedictionem domnus episcopus, concessitque locum et ordinem
115 monasticum quem petebat. His ita transactis, cum audisset praefatus auunculus, uidelicet Urso, rem actam ab episcopo, non enim fuerat tunc prae-
sens, quia infirmatus quodam loco iacebat, grauiter accepit cum caeteris
parentibus quod nepos eorum perditus esset seculo et adquisitus Deo. Misit
ad arcersiendum eum. Cumque ante eum adstitisset, cum omni ira et men-
120 tis insania ita ad eum locutus est: Quid fecisti, miser? Quare monachus
esse uoluisti? Cur elegisti unum paruum panem pro numero centenario et
parum uinum pro calicibus epotandis usque ad satietatem? Quamobrem
uita porcorum in leguminibus et horto ut sufficiens tibi esses uoluisti? Ubi
erunt deliciae carnium quas dimisisti, suauitas potionum, delectatio canum
125 accipitrumque, tactus uoluptuosus mulierum? Cum ergo animum adolescentis contra haec fortiter resistere uidisset et responsa non iuuenilis sed
robore senilis cerneret, addebat multo sceleratiora, ita ut etiam lenones
immitteret qui eum prouocarent, necnon etiam concitauit caeteros auuncu-
los, scilicet Lethardum, Wanilonem, et multos alios parentes, qui et dice-
130 bant ei: Cur nos degenerare uoluisti? Opus progeniei nostrae cum
pauperibus et mendicis non fuit. Nobis floruit mundus, copia auri et argenti
lapidumque apud nos fuit. Nobis arma fulgida resplenduerunt, equi auratis
oris et torto collo arriserunt. Et tu omnia ista spreuisti? Haec dicebant sce-
lestes, qui eum ad meliora excitare debuerant, qui magis pompatice

135 uiuentes demergi letheas in undas uolunt quam cum liberatis fonte salutari
    ablui et piissimo liberatori effectu decantari post ueniarum laborem,
    dicendo, *Transiuimus per ignem et aquam, et eduxisti nos in refrigerium.*[5]
    Sed animus iuuenis inuictus permansit, cupiens obseruare quod coeperat,
    ita ut per quinque annos eum reuocare non possent, ordines suos et affectus
140 regulares in monasterio cum caeteris custodiens. Porro inter haec, cum
    omnem bacchationem super iamdictum magistrum exagitarent, culpando
    illum, et requirendo discipulum, festinus magister reddere commendatum
    non neglexit. Qui recipientes nepotem, retinuerunt apud se semper figuram
    monachi habentem. Post retentionem uero octo dierum et amplius, rursus
145 ualde obsecrantes remiserunt eum in monasterium, deprecante discipulo, et
    illis consentientibus. Cum autem tempus accipiendi primos gradus ecclesi-
    asticos pertransiret, audita circumuentione auunculorum uenerabilis epis-
    copus misit ad praedictum sacerdotem, ut quod prius concesserat, sicut
    diximus, et postea a consensu longius se retraxerat, iam tunc assentaretur,
150 ut gradus ecclesiasticos sub ipso habitu monachus susciperet. Ergo diu dis-
    simulante illo, nouissime mandauit domno episcopo ut faceret quod ratio et
    auctoritas commendabat. Quod et factum est, acceptque benedictiones
    quinque graduum, degens et perseuerans uoluntarie in sanctam conuersa-
    tionem. Igitur expletis postea annis duobus, superuenit repentina dies
155 adimprouisus finis uitae Ursonis. Cumque ad exitum urgueretur, uocauit
    praedictum monachum nepotem suum. Ipso uero adsistente coram eo,
    ammonere curauit de gloria mundi quam relinquebat, non dimittens inten-
    tionem quam semper habuerat ut ad canonicam uitam reuerteretur, dato
    consilio, et rebus maxime omnibus quae habere potuerat, ut eius mentem
160 ad cupidiciam et inanem gloriam excitaret. Atque ita obiit. Impleuitque
    mortuus quod explere nequiuerat uiuus. Ex illa ergo die a pristina uoluntate
    subdiaconus coepit esse alienus, iunctus conuersatione et animo auunculis
    suis, Lethardo scilicet et Amarrico, quorum consilio et ingenio totus fertur
    in praeceps, fiuntque ipsi sacerdotes *contra legem,*[6] arripiendo ministerium
165 episcopi. Nam incluserunt eum in quodam coenaculo, ubi sine iudicio uen-
    erabilis episcopi et sacerdotum exuendo illum uestem monasticam,
    induerunt albis. Atque ita ad secularem conuersationem reuersus est.
    Omnemque delictum super magistrum et domnum episcopum con-
    gesserunt pro benefactis. Ipsos enim uana uersutio contenebratis oculis
170 grauiter ad ruinam laquei subduxit.[7] Qui per septem annos hanc uiolentiam
    timuerunt facere, ut multo damnabilior fieret longius uentilata et patrata,

5 Psalm 65.12
6 Cf. Sophonias 3.4
7 Cf. Osee 9.8

etiamsi malum esset. Quia quanto plus aliquod bonum perdurauerit, tanto, si ceciderit, profundius ruit. Similiter et malum quanto amplius succreuerit, tanto grauiori poenae subiacebit. Quos talia sectantes, neglecto fructu
175 poenitentiae, inanes socios[c] habere cupiunt atque auernus suscipere desiderat.

Huius rei testis est omnis ordo ipsius ecclesiae, qui unusquisque secundum suum ministerium probare potest ita factum esse.

c   socius Baluze

16

Jews, Pilgrimage, and the Christian Cult of Saints: Benjamin of Tudela and His Contemporaries

JOSEPH SHATZMILLER

It is almost impossible to imagine a study of pilgrimage in the medieval West which will not make reference to the 'Guide for the Pilgrim to Saint James of Compostella.'[1] The 'Guide' is the last of five treatises which constitute *The Book of Saint James (Liber Sancti Jacobi)*, known also as the *Codex Calixtinus* and preserved in the Cathedral of Compostella: in all probability it was composed around the year 1140 (or, more exactly, 1139) by Aimery Picaud of Parthenay-le-Vieux, a French cleric originating from the Poitou or the neighbouring Saintonge. Having in mind French pilgrims, the 'Guide' delineates four different itineraries the pilgrims could follow in order to reach the Pyrenean city Puenta de la Reina, from which one road, the 'Camino Frances,' led to the much-admired shrine. Printed in Spain over one hundred years ago, the 'Guide' has been edited, translated and commented upon on several occasions since 1938 by Ms Jeanne Vielliard. I was lucky enough to acquire the fifth edition – that of the year 1978 – which seems to be the most recent one.[2]

Going over the 'Guide' at my leisure, I was sensitive to Aimery Picaud's digressions and his care to inform the users of his book about secondary sanctuaries they were to visit, regions and rivers they were to cross, and the people of different cultures they were to meet. In a somewhat oblique manner, these digressions bring to mind those of Benjamin of Tudela – a younger contemporary of Aimery. This famous Jewish traveller set out for a trip to the Middle

---

1 See, for example, the authoritative repertoire by Jean Richard, *Les récits de voyages et de pèlerinages* (Brepols, 1981) (= L. Genicot [Dir.], *Typologie des sources du Moyen Âge*, Fasc. 38 [= A-I7]), 15–16; or, on the other hand, the popular, well-illustrated *Compostelle, le grand chemin* by Xavier Barral Altet (Paris, 1993), 47–76 and passim.

2 Jeanne Vielliard, *Le Guide du pèlerin de Saint Jacques de Compostelle* (Macon, 1978). In the extended introduction – on which I rely – there is a description of the manuscripts of the treatise, as well as its former editions.

East around the year 1165 and was back in Spain in 1173.[3] His report, written in Hebrew, is rightly considered one of the most important sources for the history of Mediterranean Jews of the time, even if scholars are not always ready to accept all of his information at face value.[4] Benjamin drew the attention of readers to all kinds of attractions, Jewish and non-Jewish, and enumerated for each locality its leading Jewish inhabitants. He also estimated, numerically, the size of the Jewish community in each locality. Why is the size of communities a concern? What was the purpose of his long trip, and why did he care to record his experiences? Much ink has already been spilled in an effort to untangle these mysteries. With the Guide to Compostella in mind, I arrived at much narrower problematics. Did Benjamin look for a 'Jewish Compostella'? And, if he did, why would he do so? Where did he expect to find it?

II

What motivated Benjamin's trip is not only the most important issue to explore, but in many ways also the most interesting. Pilgrims, then as now, undertook their travels for a variety of reasons: some looked for adventure or wished to explore unknown regions. Others were penitents who wished to repent sins, or individuals suffering from an illness in search of a miraculous cure.[5] Professor

3 For the different printings of Benjamin's itinerary, see M. Steinschneider, *Jüdishe Schriften zur Geographie Palästinas x–xix jahrhundert* (Hildesheim, 1971), 8–10. Two critical editions are of importance: *Itinerary of Benjamin of Tudela*, ed. and trans. A. Asher, 2 vols. (London, 1840-1). A more reliable edition and translation is that of Marcus Nathan Adler, *The Itinerary of Benjamin of Tudela – Critical Text, Translation, and Commentary* (London, 1907, repr. New York, s.d.). E.N. Adler published partial translations of the itineraries of Benjamin and others in his *Jewish Travelers in the Middle Ages* (London, 1930, repr. New York, 1987). In order to accommodate non–Hebrew-readers, I make reference to this book when possible. Although E.N. Adler has much praise in his Introduction for J.D. Eisenstein's *Treasury of Itineraries* (New York, 1926) (Hebrew), students should be warned not to rely on the texts published in it: the editor permitted himself to 'ameliorate' some texts. A much more reliable 'Treasury' is that of Abraham Ya'ari, *Travels in Palestine* (Tel Aviv, 1976) (Hebrew).
4 Cf., for example, Cezare Coalfemina, 'L'itinerario pugliese di Biniamino da Tudela,' *Archivio storico pugliese* 28 (1975), 81–100; Joshua Prawer, *The History of the Jews in the Latin Kingdom of Jerusalem* (Oxford, 1988), 191–206; A. Arce, 'El sepulcro de David en un texto de Benjamin de Tudela,' *Sefarad* 23 (1963): 105–15.
5 For a taxonomy of reasons to undertake pilgrimage, see: Edmond René Laband, 'Recherches sur les pèlerins dans l'Europe des XIe et XIIe siècles,' in *Cahiers de civilisation médiévale* 1 (Paris, 1958): 159–69, 339–47. There is an abundant literature about travel and pilgrimage in the Middle Ages. Here I shall mention just a few works: Margaret Wade Labarge, *Medieval Travelers* (London, 1982); Norbert Ohler, *The Medieval Traveler* (Woodbridge, 1989); Raymond Oursel, *Les pèlerins du Moyen Âge* (Paris, 1983); and, most importantly, Pierre André Sigal, *Les marcheurs de Dieu* (Paris, 1974).

Joshua Prawer is certainly right when he states that 'Judaism never knew indulgence and the cult of holy places as these developed in Christianity.'[6] However, the contrast is a matter of degree of involvement, of intensity, and of relative commitment, not of principled objection. In fact, Jews did practise a cult of the saints and engaged in pilgrimages to holy shrines where 'righteous individuals' (*Sadiqim* in Hebrew) were buried. Recent research has brought to light dozens of shrines in today's Iraq as well as in Morocco.[7] More than a thousand years ago, in the middle of the tenth century, a non-rabbinic Jew and leading member of the Karaite sect, Sahl ben Mazliah, severely condemned Jews for their devotion to holy shrines. Making precise reference to the cult around the grave of R. Yose the Galilean, Sahl states the following:[8]

And how should I let these goings-on pass in silence when several of the practices of idolatry are to be found among some of Israel? They sit at the tombs, they sleep in the clefts of the rocks and they supplicate the dead saying: 'Rabbi Yose the Galilean, pray, heal me, or give me a belly [i.e., make me pregnant],' and they light candles on the tombs of the *Sadiqim*, and burn before them incense and they bind clumps[?] on the palm tree of the *Sadiqim*, and make there their vows and they appeal to them and ask them to give them what they desire.

The Jews, probably Rabbinites, not Karaites, against whom Sahl targeted his critique, were living in the Middle East, that is, Iraq, Syria, Palestine, or Egypt of today. It is doubtful that he knew very much about Jews in western Europe, all Rabbinites. To this day no evidence has been discovered concerning Jewish holy shrines in Europe. Rather, in an indirect manner, some evidence leads to the conclusion that such shrines did not exist. For example, Benjamin's – probably a younger – contemporary, the famous Eliezer of Worms (1165–1230), who was very much interested in penance, indicated to his fellow Jews ways to repentance.[9] In several short penitentials that came from his pen, Eliezer catalogued, as the Christian penitentials do, the variety of possible crimes and sins,

6 Joshua Prawer, *The History of the Jews in the Latin Kingdom of Jerusalem* (Oxford, 1988), 129.
7 Pilgrimages to Jewish holy shrines take place nowadays as well; cf., for example, Ben Jacob's book cited in n. 33, below. I have not had access to S.S. Benaïm, *Le pélèrinage juif des lieux saints au Moroc*, published in Casablanca. I have consulted, however, the very authoritative investigation of Issachar Ben Ami, *Admiration of Saints among Moroccan Jews* (Jerusalem, 1984) (Hebrew). For a cult of a living saint in contemporary Israel, see E. Alfasi, *Baba Sali, Our Holy Teacher, His Life, Piety, and Miracles* (New York, 1986).
8 The translation is by Prawer, *Jews in the Latin Kingdom*, 172.
9 For a list of Eliezer's works, including several still in manuscript, see Ivan G. Marcus, *Piety and Society: The Jewish Pietists of Medieval Germany* (Leiden, 1981), 178–9.

assessing the relative importance of their gravity and, most importantly, explaining means for their expiation. Dietary restrictions, sexual abstinence, and even physical punishment (lashing) made up his repertoire. However, in no case are pilgrimages to holy shrines prescribed. The closest we come to this is the case of a convicted murderer who must wander for years around Jewish communities and endure humiliation and reprobation. Let us note, Jewish communities, and not Jewish shrines. In all probability shrines did not exist at that time in the medieval West.

III

This apparent absence would have become more conspicuous in the twelfth and thirteenth centuries, the great centuries of the European cult of saints. Rosalind and Christopher Brooke, in their book about popular religion in the Middle Ages, state: 'there was a remarkable concentration of interest in relics, translations and rebuilding of shrines and churches about them between the late tenth and thirteenth centuries.'[10] Ample evidence exists to show that Jews knew about this Christian veneration of relics and that they were indeed challenged by it. Thus in a collection of some two thousand Hebrew short exempla written in Germany around the year 1200, two such challenges by Christians are recorded.[11] The first tells the story of a tunic (Hebrew: *Halouk*) that miraculously would not catch fire. It belonged to none other than Christ himself. Jews were challenged to explain the miracle. 'Isn't there saintlyhood in the tunic,' asked the clerics of the Jews. It took a Jewish sage to demonstrate the flammability of the cloth: he did it after washing it with strong vinegar and with another chemical, probably soap (*Borit* in Hebrew).[12] The other exemplum is about a Jewish mother frightened for her sick child. A Gentile women offers her some virtuous water brought from Jerusalem from the holy sepulcher, and assures her that 'some Gentiles were given to drink and were cured.' But the Jewish woman, learning about the origin of the cure, refuses to employ it. For the authors of the exemplum, her behaviour was to be praised. 'This,' they say,

10 Rosalind and Christopher Brook, *Popular Religion in the Middle Ages: Western Europe, 1000–1300* (London, 1984), 39. For a similar assessment, cf. Barbara Abou-El-Haj, *The Medieval Cult of Saints* (Cambridge, 1994), 7–33, esp. 13 ff.
11 The book was edited on several occasions. Today scholars use either the edition based on the Parma MS. or the Bologna MS. For the first, see the Margolioth edition cited in n. 12, below; for the latter, see Jehuda Wistinetzki, *Das Buch der Frommen* (Berlin, 1891; repr. Frankfurt-am-Main, 1924) (Hebrew).
12 Reuven Margalioth, *Sefer Hasidim she-Hibber Rabenu Yehudah he-Hasid* (Jerusalem, 1964) (Hebrew), 531, n. 1014. For a similar story in Christian hagiography, see P.A. Sigal, *L'homme et le miracle dans la France médievale, XIe–XIIe siècle* (Paris, 1985), 119.

'is what the Bible enjoins us [to do] – "with all thy soul ... thou shall love the Lord thy God"!'[13] Christian hagiography of the same years refers to a Jewish woman who wished to heal her ailing leg with the help of water from the shrine of Thomas Becket, to the great dismay of the buried saint. The bucket she held exploded and the holy water it contained spilled.[14]

Another Christian source tells the story of a Jew of Oxford mocking a Christian procession in which the relics of a local saint, Saint Frideswide, were carried with great ceremony (possibly around 1180) to a more prominent shrine. The Jew Deulecresse, son of Moses of Wallingford, who lived in the neighbourhood, showed great contempt to the procession. Professor Cecil Roth summed up the incident with the following words: 'He would pretend to limp, and then walk freely or else clench his fingers as though with palsy and then open them again, and afterwards inform the bystanders that these miracles were quite as genuine as any wrought by the saint.' He also told participants in the procession 'that they might as well let him have their alms instead of presenting them to the church.' *The Acta Sanctorum*, which is the source of this story, adds that the young man committed suicide that same day.[15]

The challenge of the Christian cult of saints can be inferred not only by such daily street scenes, but also through Hebrew religious polemicists of the time. Around the year 1240, a French Jewish polemicist was rather ironic and light-hearted about the cult. Indeed, he said, one can believe that these 'relics make the blind see again, [the paralysed] walk and [the mute] talk' – all this, he adds, 'because this is the way God convinces those who have little faith in him.'[16] Less aloof and rather belligerent is another, anonymous, Jewish polemicist, writing around 1270, for whom the cult of relics is futile. The author, who knew about the cult of Saint James, argues that, if the true messenger of God refused burning incense in his honour (as in the Bible, Judges 13:17), why would one burn incense to 'dead bones.'[17] A contemporary of his, the anonymous author of the *Liber Nizzahon Vetus* ('ancient book of victory' or 'of polemics'), went a step further: 'This is how the heretics [Christians] should be refuted with regard

13 Wistinetzki, *Buch der Frommen*, exemplum no. 1352 (332–3).
14 On the cult of the relics of Saint Thomas Becket in Canterbury see, e.g., D.J. Hall, *English Mediaeval Pilgrimage* (London, 1965), 130–65; Ronald C. Finucane, *Miracles and Pilgrims: Popular Beliefs in Medieval England* (London, 1977), 121–6.
15 Cecil Roth, *The Jews of Medieval Oxford* (Oxford, 1951), 6. The Latin text was edited by Ad Neubauer in 'Notes on the Jews in Oxford,' in *Collectanea: Second Series*, ed. Montagu Burrows (Oxford, 1890), 282–3.
16 *Sepher Joseph Hamekané*, ed. Judah Rosenthal (Jerusalem, 1970) (Hebrew), 82, n. 85.
17 Judah Rosenthal, 'Pirqué Vikkuah' (Chapters in Controversies), in *Salo Wittmayer Baron Jubilee Volume*, eds. S. Lieberman and A. Hyman, 3 vols. (New York, 1974), 3: (Hebrew section), 395, n. 98.

to their practice of taking the bones of the dead as holy relics: The fact is that God has declared them impure ... Thus they are themselves impure and they also impart impurity on others.' To strengthen his point, he quite unexpectedly added the following: 'Indeed, even the bones of Abraham, Isaac, Jacob and all righteous men convey impurity just like those of other men, for scripture makes no qualification here ... and although everyone knows that the patriarchs lie in a cave at Hebron, no nation can enter there. Why is that so? It must be for the reason I have indicated.'[18] Around the year 1170 relics of a certain Christian lad, Pons Richard (in my reconstruction of the name), were venerated in Paris. The allegation must have been that he had been slain by the Jews. A community delegation who met with King Louis VII was relieved to hear that the monarch did not believe in the allegation or in the miracles attributed to the popular saint.[19] In a less polemical context, three Jewish doctors of southern France were asked to certify medical miracles performed by Saint Dauphine of Puimichel. Their testimonies were included in the proceedings of her canonization in 1363.[20]

As if to counter such challenges of the Christian cult of saints and relics, Jews boasted about miracles that occurred in the framework of their own religion. Peter the Chanter reports on a competition between Jews and Christians at Rheims which occurred probably when he pursued his studies in that city (he moved to Paris in 1173). Rheims was at that time hit with a drought, and a Christian procession – relics in hand – failed to bring deliverance. The Jews of the city then suggested bringing out the scrolls of the Torah, and even promised (we have to take Peter's word for it) to convert to Christianity if not successful.[21] A similar drought occurred in the Holy Land some forty or fifty years later, around the year 1210; a group of rabbis of French and English origin who happened to be there caused it to rain by engaging in prayer, and thus demonstrated, our author insists, the superiority of the Jewish religion. The source for this story is a collection of short historical accounts composed not later than 1300 and attached to the famous sixteenth-century Hebrew chronicle by Salomon ibn Verga called *Shevet Yehuda*.[22] The collection, which recounts about three dozen events, reports several miraculous incidents. Thus, in 1205,

18 *The Jewish–Christian Debate in the High Middle Ages: A Critical Edition of Nizzahon Vetus*, ed. and trans. David Berger (Philadelphia, 1979), 225, n. 240.

19 A.M. Haberman, *The Persecutions of Germany and France* (Jerusalem, 1946) (Hebrew), 144.

20 *Enquête pour le procès de canonisation de Dauphine de Puimichel, comtesse d'Ariano*, ed. Jacques Cambell (Turin, 1978), 412, 421, 433.

21 John W. Baldwin, *Masters, Princes, and Merchants*, 2 vols. (Princeton, 1970), 1: 328; 2: 219.

22 *Sefer Shevet Judah (The Scepter of Judah) of Salomon ibn Verga*, ed. A. Shohat (Jerusalem, 1946), 147. About the migration (*aliyah*) of these rabbis, cf. E. Kanarfogel, 'The Aliyah of "Three Hundred Rabbis" in 1211: Tosafist Attitudes toward Settling the Land of Israel,' *Jewish Quarterly Review* 76 (1986): 191–215.

when King Peter of Aragon returned from Rome, Jews participating in the *adventus* had to carry the scrolls of the Torah outdoors. It happened to be a rainy day and they were concerned that the holy scripture might be damaged by the water. A miracle occurred, the sky brightening at the very moment the scrolls were carried outside.[23] Another extraordinary event occurred when the coffin with the relics of the great sage Maimonides was transferred from Egypt to Palestine. Pirates who attacked the ship wished to throw the coffin into the sea, yet thirty of them were unable to lift the coffin – recognizing that 'God's man' lay therein.[24] Years before, when the third Lateran Council was convoked in 1179, alarmed Jews engaged in a public fast for three days. The fast was successful, and nothing but good came from the priestly convocation.[25]

Finally, echoes of an eager quest for miracles can be detected from a Hebrew report of a tragic event in 1171 in Blois, Champagne, where thirty-eight Jews were put to the stake for allegedly killing a Christian child. Three of the condemned Jews escaped from the fire and claimed a miracle occurred, but were slaughtered by the mob. Our Hebrew report also makes the point that the women and men at the stake engaged in singing hymns which, by the beauty of the melody, enchanted the Christian bystanders.[26]

IV

Benjamin was thus operating within a universe of miracles and saint cults. The question we must raise now is whether his intent was to produce a list of Jewish holy shrines in the Middle East. Although scholars who have been ready to entertain such a possibility (Prawer, Reiner, Graboïs)[27] have not endorsed it, in my opinion this hypothesis deserves renewed consideration. The best way to carry out the examination is, first, to look at reports of other Jewish travellers of the age of the crusades (Professor Prawer enumerates ten of them, including Benjamin)[28] and see to what extent they can or cannot help sustain this possibility. Most important of these reports is that of Petahia of Ratisbone, who

---

23 *Sefer Shevet Judah*, 147.

24 Ibid.

25 Ibid., 146.

26 Haberman, *Persecutions*, 125.

27 Prawer, *Jews in the Latin Kingdom*, 128–250; Elchanan Reiner, 'Pilgrims and Pilgrimage to Eretz Yisrael, 1099–1517' (unpublished PhD dissertation, Jerusalem, 1988), 37–8; Aryeh Graboïs, 'Travel and Pilgrimage to Eretz Israel in the Twelfth and Thirteenth Centuries' (in Hebrew), in *Proceedings of the Ninth World Congress of Jewish Studies* Division B, 1 (Jerusalem, 1988): 63–70.

28 Prawer, *Jews in the Latin Kingdom*, 169–250. This section of Prawer's book was published first in Hebrew, under the title 'Hebrew Itineraries of the Crusader Period,' in *Cathedra for the History of Eretz Israel and Its Yishuv* (Jerusalem 1986), 40: 31–62; 41: 65–90.

reached the Middle East after crossing southern Russia and the Caucasus.[29] Petahia first visited the Mesopotamian valley and then went on to explore Palestine. An almost exact contemporary of Benjamin, he was a member of the circle of Pietists (*Hasidim* in Hebrew) who assembled the exempla we made reference to previously; in fact his report was edited, and unfortunately also censored, by Judah Hasid, the leading personality in this group of Pietists. Of great importance is the fact that Petahia is clear and unequivocal concerning the purpose of his travels. He was looking for holy shrines. As he himself testifies, Samuel ben Ali, leader of Mesopotamian Jewry, equipped him with an introductory letter enjoining each community to indicate to the traveller all graves of holy men in and around their locality.[30] His exploration was crowned with success – dozens of shrines were discovered and properly catalogued.

Petahia, like Benjamin, though less so, embellished his report with anecdotes that at times had little to do with his original undertaking. Other Hebrew reports, written at the end of the twelfth and during the thirteenth centuries, were more to the point and did not provide much more than 'dry' lists of localities and the shrines that could be seen there.[31] Some of these localities were visited by Benjamin as well. However, unlike the authors of those lists, neither Benjamin nor Petahia had the land of Israel as his exclusive destiny, or even the final one. Petahia, as we have just seen, spent the first part of his journey in Mesopotamia, while Benjamin left for the eastern region after criss-crossing what was then the Latin Kingdom of Jerusalem. In fact, as we shall see in a moment, it was not in the Holy Land that both travellers found the most important Jewish shrines, but rather in Mesopotamia. One curious shrine, a coffin hanging over the Tigris River, was observed by both. It contained the relics of the prophet Daniel. Our travellers knew the story of competition and controversy, even aggressive confrontation, between Jews living on opposite sides of the Tigris.[32] As in rivalries over relics in Christian society, each community wished to have the relics in its possession because of the prosperity they

---

29 *Die Rundreise des R. Petachia aus Regensburg*, ed. L. Grünhut (Jerusalem, 1904) (Hebrew). Abraham David of Jerusalem has recently published a new edition, which I have yet to see, based on a newly discovered MS.

30 Ibid., 12, 18. For an English translation, cf. Adler, *Jewish Travelers*, 73.

31 Regarding 'itineraries' that do not contain much more than lists of holy shrines, see Prawer, *Jews in the Latin Kingdom*, 176–91, 215–21, 230–50.

32 For Petahia's report, see *Rundreise*, ed. Grünhut, 20–1, and Adler, *Jewish Travelers*, 79–80. For Benjamin's report, see Adler, *Itinerary of Benjamin*, 52 (English section) and 49 (Hebrew section). Regarding similar competition between cities over relics in Christian society, see Aron Gurevich, *Medieval Popular Culture: Problems of Belief and Perception*, trans. J.M. Bak and P.A. Hollingsworth (Cambridge, 1988), 39–41; Finucane, *Miracles and Pilgrims*, 29–30; Patrick J. Geary, *Furta Sacra: Theft of Relics in the Central Middle Ages* (Princeton, 1978; rev. 1990).

brought to the inhabitants. At first a compromise was reached (the informant is Benjamin), according to which the coffin annually changed hands. However, the 'Great Sultan' of Persia, on a visit to the place, imposed another solution: the coffin, encased in a container made of glass, was hung over the middle of the river. As late as 1624 a Jewish traveller reported seeing this unique 'hanging' shrine.[33]

Among the dozens of shrines shown to our travellers, one was outstanding in its privileged status – the shrine of the prophet Ezekiel.[34] Much of its importance probably had to do with its proximity to the city of Baghdad, the greatest Jewish metropolis of the time. Our reporters write about mass pilgrimages to the shrine at the beginning of each Jewish new year, or during the feast of tabernacles, according to Petahia. Petahia estimated that sixty to eighty thousand Jewish pilgrims, including their supreme leadership, would camp in the fields that surrounded the complex of buildings which constituted the shrine. The promise of healing miracles also attracted Moslem pilgrims who were on their way to Mecca. Although our reporters knew about other important shrines, it would seem that Ezekiel's was the principal one – a Jewish equivalent to the shrine of Saint James of Compostella. That this was well known, at least in the Middle East, can perhaps be deduced from the fact that Maimonides, acting as judge of Jews in Egypt, had to deal with a complicated marriage case where the father of the bride vowed a contribution 'To our master Ezekiel.'[35]

But did not the great distances to be travelled make shrines such as this irrelevant to Westerners? Is it realistic to imagine western European Jewish pilgrims visiting a shrine near Baghdad? The latter question can be answered, without hesitation, with an unqualified yes. Europeans of the age of the crusades, and even of the century that preceded 1096, became great travellers. Christian pilgrims – 'globe-trotters' would be a more contemporary term – not only made their way to Compostella or Rome, but landed in their thousands on the shores of the Latin Kingdom of Jerusalem, coming from Sicily, Italian port cities, Flanders, England, and Norway, not to mention France and Germany. Jews took part in the vogue of travel, and even distinguished themselves at it. Geniza documentation, explored by S.D. Goitein and others, as well as European rabbinic exchanges of letters in the twelfth century, show Jewish merchants taking part in commercial expeditions that extended over thousands of miles.[36] One of

33 Abraham Ben Jacob, *Holy Shrines in Babylonia* (Jerusalem, 1973) (Hebrew), 126.
34 For Petahia's references to the Shrine of Ezekiel, see *Rundreise,* ed. Grünhut, 13–17, and Adler, *Jewish Travelers,* 74–6. For Bejamin's description, see Adler, *Itinerary of Benjamin,* 43–5 (English section), 43–5 (Hebrew section).
35 *Responsa* of R. Moses b. Maimon (Hebrew and Judeo-Arabic), ed. and trans. Jehoshua Blau, 4 vols. (Jerusalem, 1986), 1: 431, no. 238.
36 Cf. I.A. Agus, *The Heroic Age of Franco-German Jewry* (New York, 1969), 23–51; S.D. Goitein, *A Mediterranean Society* (Berkeley, 1967), 1: 42–59, 273–352.

these Geniza merchants, Abraham ben Yiju, whose career was followed recently by Professor Amitav Gosh, was a twelfth-century North African Jew who reached the city of Aden on the Red Sea, and then went beyond it and settled for many years in Mangalore, a port in southwestern India. Then, towards the end of his life, he joined his family in Sicily.[37] Other Geniza documents introduce us to travellers who arrived at Cairo from southern France, Normandy, and Slavonia.[38] At the academy of R. Jacob Tam, in the very small city of Ramerupt in Champagne, one could encounter, around 1150, students from today's Ukraine, Austria, or Hungary;[39] while, in contemporary Toledo, at the centre of Iberia, the historian Abraham ibn Daud met students from Russia.[40]

Jewish travelling became so common that at times it became cumbersome and generated restrictive legislation, both internal and external. Thus European rabbinic authorities looked for ways to combat absenteeism by imposing a maximum period of time in which the husband could engage in voyages, as well as a minimum period between trips when he was expected to attend to his wife and children.[41] As for external, non-Jewish restrictive legislation, there was a case in the early years of the thirteenth century in the port city of Marseilles where it was enacted that no more than four Jews could embark on a boat which was destined for the Middle East.[42]

V

Pilgrims and travellers had to worry about hospitality when planning the itineraries they were to follow.[43] To date, our knowledge about this aspect of travelling is quite limited. For Jews, who had dietary laws and other demands of religious life (for example, not spending Saturday or holy days on a travelling

37 Amitav Gosh, *In an Antique Land: History in the Guise of a Traveller's Tale* (New York, 1992).

38 The most recent discovery of such an introductory letter is to be found in Norman Golb and Omeljan Pritsak, *Khazarian Hebrew Documents of the Tenth Century* (Ithaca, 1982). Professor Golb has dealt with such introductory letters in several important publications; for example, his *Les Juifs de Rouen au Moyen Âge: Portrait d'une culture oubliée* (Rouen, 1985), 51–70.

39 E.E. Urbach, *The Tosaphists: Their History, Writings, and Methods*, 4th. enlarged ed, 2 vols. (Jerusalem, 1980) (Hebrew), 1: 212–16.

40 Gerson D. Cohen, ed. and trans., *The Book of Tradition by Abraham ibn Daud* (Philadelphia, 1967), English section, 92–3.

41 Louis Finkelstein, *Jewish Self-Government in the Middle Ages* (Philadelphia, 1924, repr. New York, 1964), 169–70.

42 Cf. Raoul Busquet and Régine Pernoud, *Histoire du commerce de Marseille* (Paris, 1949), 1: 291.

43 For the different patterns of hospitality, see, for example, Pierre Maravale, *Lieux saints et pèlerinages d'Orient* (Paris, 1985), 167–9, 211–12; Sigal, *Les marcheurs de Dieu*, 68–72.

boat), hospitality while travelling would present serious difficulties. Their co-religionists, who were expected to offer hospitality, were not always at ease with the number of guests they had to entertain. It is true that, around 1160, Joseph Kimhi, an Andalusian Jew established in Narbonne, boasts about Jewish hospitality and claims that one would entertain a wandering brethren for an unlimited period.[44] It is equally true that some fifty years later a Geniza private message written in the port city of Alexandria and destined for Cairo, contains a complaint about a deluge of strangers who turn to the local Jewish community for help – 'As if we did not have enough beggars of our own.'[45]

This last remark brings us back, for the last time, to Benjamin and his interest in the size of the Jewish communities along the way. Chateaubriand, by the way, in his 'Itinerary from Paris to Jerusalem,' was somewhat dismayed that all that interested Benjamin in a momentous city like Corinth in Greece was the fact that it harboured 300 Jews.[46] However, Benjamin, in my opinion, concerned with the problem of hospitality, had to inquire about numbers and record the names of the leaders to whom one may turn for help. If pilgrims knew that the small city of Lunel, near Montpellier, harboured 300 Jews (individuals, and not heads of families as is sometimes claimed),[47] they could assess the potential for finding hospitality within the city. Although Benjamin does not provide us with the explanation that I have just suggested, it is not mere accident that the penultimate sentence of his book, in praise of the Jews of northern France, concludes with the following remark: 'They are charitable and hospitable to all travellers.'[48]

Even if we subscribe to the hypothesis that Benjamin was mainly concerned with pilgrimage and holy shrines, we have to repeat that his itinerary is not presented as a travellers' logbook, nor as a mere listing of holy graves. Benjamin tried to do more than that. He wanted to draw attention to monuments – in Rome and Constantinople for example – that a traveller should not miss. He extended his geography, and included in it regions that he obviously did not visit. There is no doubt that this makes a more fascinating story, yet it blurs the picture and impedes modern observers from understanding why he undertook his trip in the first place.

---

44 *The Book of the Covenant of Joseph Kimhi*, ed. Frank Talmage (Toronto, 1972), 33.

45 Quoted in Prawer, *Jews in the Latin Kingdom*, 79–80.

46 *Itinéraire de Paris a Jerusalem par F. De Chateaubriand,* ed. M.A. De Pontmartin (Paris, 1881), 149.

47 In 1295 Lunel's Jewry numbered forty-eight houses (*foci*), out of which twenty were abandoned. If we count five individuals per household, we reach the number 240, quite close to the 300 mentioned by Benjamin. For Lunel in 1295, see F. Maillard, 'Une enquête sur Lunel et Rochefort en 1295,' *Annales du Midi* 73 (1961): 45–81.

48 Adler, *Itinerary of Benjamin*, 81 (English section), 73 (Hebrew section).

17

The Trojan Origins of the French and the Brothers Jean du Tillet

ELIZABETH A.R. BROWN

For more than a millennium, myths explaining the origins of peoples fascinated, consoled, inspired, and promoted rivalry among the Europeans whose earliest beginnings they purported to describe. The myths took a variety of forms, which can be divided, roughly, into the triad biblical, Homeric–Vergilian, and Germanic–Scandinavian.[1] Myths based on the Bible flowed from the Tower of Babel and Noah's Ark. Trojan roots took pride of place in those inspired by Homer and Vergil. The chief figures in the German myths

My interest in the Trojan myth and the French has over the years been stimulated not only by Walter Goffart, but also by Gabrielle M. Spiegel, Susan Reynolds, and Romila Thapar, to whom I extend warm thanks. For her generous guidance to bibliography concerning Maximilian I, I am grateful to Paula Sutter Fichtner; I am similarly grateful to Charles Lohr for help with Beatus Rhenanus. For his expert responses to questions concerning Tatian and Otfrid of Weissenberg, I thank David Ganz. Thanks, too, to James K. Farge for help with the Du Tillet family, and to him, Ursula Baurmeister, and André Jammes for advice on Jean de Gaigny. Research for this paper was supported in part by a grant from the International Research and Exchanges Board (IREX), with funds provided by the National Endowment for the Humanities, the United States Information Agency, and the United States Department of State (Title VII). The following abbreviations are used: AN – Paris, Archives nationales; BnF – Paris, Bibliothèque nationale de France.

1   Susan Reynolds offers a useful analysis in 'Medieval *Origines Gentium* and the Community of the Realm,' *History* 68 (1983): 375-90; rprt. in eadem, *Ideas and Solidarities of the Medieval Laity*, Collected Studies Series (Aldershot, 1995), no. II. The popularity of myths explaining the origins of entire peoples seems to me to have endured (in France at least) far longer than she suggests. Although in the sixteenth century some French historians drew sharp distinctions between Franks and Gauls, others believed that the two peoples were soon intermingled, and some argued that the Franks were descendants of emigrant Gauls. See below for the stances of the brothers Du Tillet, and also Arlette Jouanna, 'La quête des origines dans l'historiographie française de la fin du XVᵉ siècle et du début du XVIᵉ,' in *La France de la fin du XVᵉ siècle: renouveau et apogée. Économie – Pouvoirs – Arts – Culture et Conscience nationales. Colloque international du Centre National de la Recherche Scientifique. Tours, Centre d'Études*

were Mannus and that 'womb of peoples,' the isle of Scanza. These myths prompted inventive elaboration and combination. Although it had its rivals, the myth that most appealed to the French was the story of their descent from the Trojans: that they were sprung from those who followed a descendant of Priam to settle near the Meotidian Marshes (where they came to be known as Franks), and who then, after many years and countless adventures, crossed the Rhine into Gaul, which, from their name, was later christened France.[2]

The appearance, spread, and elaboration of myths of origin in Europe – and especially France – have inspired numerous learned studies. So, too, have the ends, conscious and unconscious, which the myths served. Walter Goffart's work in analysing, editing, and fostering the edition of early texts has notably advanced understanding of the early fortunes of the European myths of descent.[3] More remains to be done, and later authors need to be examined with the same care that he has devoted to early ones. So inventively were the myths elaborated, so widely were they propounded (and in such a variety of media), so

Supérieures de la Renaissance, 3–6 octobre 1983, ed. Bernard Chevalier and Philippe Contamine (Paris, 1985), 301-11, at 306-7; eadem, 'Histoire et polémique en France dans la deuxième moitié du XVIème siècle,' Storia della storiographia/Histoire de l'historiographie/History of Historiography/Geschichte der Geschichtsschreibung 2 (1982): 57–76. Arno Borst's monumental study Der Turmbau von Babel: Geschichte der Meinungen über Ursprung und Vielfalt der Sprachen und Völker, 4 vols. in 6 (Stuttgart, 1957–63), provides an indispensable introduction to the full panoply of myths of origin. Since his focus is primarily on language, however, he does not deal with many historians (including the Du Tillet brothers) who studied the origins of the French.

2   R.E. Asher provides a comprehensive guide to bibliography in 'Myth, Legend and History in Renaissance France,' Studi francesi 39 (13th year, fasc. 3) (Sept.–Dec. 1969): 409–19. Also useful is Amnon Lindner's introductory survey in 'Ex mala parentela bona sequi seu oriri non potest; The Troyan [sic] Ancestry of the Kings of France and the Opus Davidicum of Johannes Angelus de Legonissa,' Bibliothèque d'Humanisme et Renaissance: Travaux et documents 40 (1978): 497–512, esp. 497–502. Still stimulating for its comments on Roman sources is the paper of Pierre-Nicolas Bonamy, 'Recherches sur l'historien Timagénes,' Mémoires de litterature, tirez des Registres de l'Academie royale des Inscriptions et Belles Lettres. Depuis l'année M. DCCXXXIV. jusques & compris l'année M. DCCXXXVII. 13 (Paris, 1740): 35–49 (delivered on 9 April 1734).

3   I think here, inter alia, of Walter Goffart's study 'The Fredegar Problem Reconsidered,' Speculum 38 (1963): 206–41, and, more recently, 'The Supposedly "Frankish" Tables of Nations: An Edition and Study,' Frühmittelalterliche Studien: Jahrbuch des Instituts für Frühmittelalterforschung der Universität Münster 17 (1983): 98–130; and The Narrators of Barbarian History (A.D. 550–800): Jordanes, Gregory of Tours, Bede, and Paul the Deacon (Princeton, 1988), 87–93 (Jordanes and Scanza), 12, 125–6 (the Fredegar chronicle and the Trojan origin of the Franks), 426 (Fredegar and Paul the Deacon). Michael Idomir Allen prepared a study of Frechulf of Lisieux under Walter Goffart's direction: 'History in the Carolingian Renewal: Frechulf of Lisieux (fl. 830), his Work and Influence' (PhD diss.; University of Toronto, Toronto, 1994), and he will shortly publish a new edition of Frechulf's Chronicle.

acrimoniously were they attacked and defended, that many aspects of the story of their adoption, elaboration, diffusion, and utilization are still obscure. Comprehensive surveys of the myths are both tantalizing and frustrating, since each of the authors who adopted and embroidered the myth he took as his own evidently did so for specific reasons and as the result of specific influences, which must be separated if the distinctive contribution of the author (whether historian, poet, or artist) is to be known. Such investigation can illuminate the ways in which ideas passed from one thinker to another, the media in which they were disseminated, and the geographical area within which they circulated. But it also poses problems, since failing to identify a source on which the author drew will necessarily credit that author with inventiveness he did not possess. Responsible generalizations and straightforward statements are exceedingly difficult to formulate – even about a single individual.

The same problems and opportunities confront those interested in the erratic process of demythification that after many centuries led Vico to search for 'the public ground of [the myths'] truth' and their significance as 'conceits of nations.'[4] The story of why, how, and when the myths began to be questioned, and were then scorned, and finally rejected, is fully as complex as that of their flowering – arguably more so, given the appearance of printing and the resulting speed with which texts old and new could be disseminated and (in the case of newly created works) revised. Far more evidence, manuscript as well as printed, survives for the period of the myths' rejection than for that of their creation. This makes it easier to chart subtle changes in the ideas of individuals and groups, and the curious interaction of reason and myth within individuals and the societies in which they lived.

Here I should like to offer to a cherished colleague, master of barbarian history (with whom for years I have debated the merits of *reditus ad codices*, which I believe as essential for studying the sixteenth century as for investigating the fifth), some reflections on the process by which, in the sixteenth century, the French began to repudiate the notion of Trojan origins and sought their roots in the forests of Germany. I shall concentrate on two brothers, both named Jean du Tillet, and the part they played before their deaths in 1570 in persuading their compatriots of the folly and irrationality of claiming Trojan descent. In analysing their work, I shall not propose that they made any significantly origi-

4   Giambattista Vico, *Principi di scienza nuova* (1744 ed.), in *Opere*, 2 vols., ed. Andrea Battistini (Milan, 1990), 1: 495 (Bk 1, section 2, *Degli Elementi*, III.125); and 1: 500 (ibid., XVI. 149–50). See also ibid., 1: 803–4 (Bk 2, section 11, *Geografia poetica*, ch. 2, *Corollario della venuta d'Enea in Italia*, 771–3) where Vico attempts to determine when the myth of Rome's Trojan origins was invented. For background, see H.J. Erasmus, *The Origins of Rome in Historiography from Petrarch to Perizonius*, Bibliotheca Classica Vangorcumiana 11 (Assen, 1962).

nal contribution to the rejection of the Trojan myth. Rather, I shall argue that they drew their inspiration and many of the facts they presented from the writings of a group of creative German humanists. These scholars (and most notably Heinrich Bebel [1472–1518],[5] Count Hermann of Neuenar [1492–1530],[6] and Beatus Rhenanus [1485–1547]),[7] refused to follow their fellow Germans (particularly Trithemius [1462–1516] and his invented chroniclers Hunibald and Megenfrid) in catering to the whims of the ambitious Maximilian I, eager to establish his Trojan origins.[8] Nor was Beatus Rhenanus

5   In an oration addressed to Maximilian, *De ejus atque Germaniæ laudibus* (published in 1504), Bebel praised Germany for being the birthplace of the Gauls, and the site of 'sincera Nobilitas Principum'; in a supplementary letter to a colleague which was published the same year Bebel endorsed Tacitus' declaration that the Germans were autochthonous and denounced French claims to Trojan origin: *Schardius Redivivus Sive Rerum Germanicarum Scriptores Varii, Olim a D. Simone Schardio, In IV. Tomos collecti, hactenus diu desiderati*, ed. Hieronymus Thomas, 4 vols. in 1 (Giessen, 1673), 1: 100, 105–7.

6   Little seems to be known about Hermann, count of Neuenar (in the archbishopric of Cologne, near Bonn), although the list of his publications shows that he was interested in medieval history and in 1519 addressed the imperial electoral college on behalf of Charles V: Jacques Le Long, *Bibliotheque historique de la France; Contenant le Catalogue de tous les Ouvrages tant imprimez que manuscrits, qui traitent de l'Histoire de ce Roïaume, ou qui y ont rapport: Avec des Notes critiques & historiques*, 2 vols. (Paris, 1719), 1: 300–1, no. 6450; Louis Moréri, *Le Grand Dictionnaire Historique, ou Le Mélange curieux de l'Histoire sacrée et profane ...*, new ed., ed. Claude-Pierre Goujet and Étienne-François Drouet, 10 vols. (Paris, 1759), 6: 56; and the British Library's Catalogue of printed books. Soon after Charles V's election as emperor, Count Hermann dedicated to him his treatise *De origine et sedibvs priscorvm Franc[orum]*, dated at Cologne on the kalends of February; the work was first published in *Vvitichindi Saxonis Rervm ab Henrico et Ottone I Impp. Gestarum Libri III, unà cum alijs quibusdam raris & antehac non lectis diuersorum autorum historijs, ab Anno salutis D. CCC. usque ad præsentem ætatem: quorum catalogus proxima patebit pagina. Huc accessit rerum scitum dignarum copiosus index* (Basel, 1532), 99–105; rprt. in *Historiæ Francorvm Scriptores coætanei, Ab ipsivs gentis origine, ad Pipinvm vsqve Regem. Quorum Plurimi nunc primùm ex Variis Codicibus MSS. in Lucem prodeunt: alij vero auctiores & emendatiores. Cvm Epistolis Regvm, Reginarvm, Pontificvm, Ducum, Comitum, Abbatum, & aliis veteribus Rerum Francicarum Monumentis*, 5 vols., ed. André and François Duchesne (Paris, 1636–49) 1: 172–5. Bodin criticized Count Hermann's essay, but still recommended it to readers, in his *Methodvs, ad facilem historiarvm cognitionem* (Paris, 1566), 242, 454.

7   On Beatus Rhenanus, see John F. D'Amico, *Theory and Practice in Renaissance Textual Criticism: Beatus Rhenanus between Conjecture and History* (Berkeley, 1988); for his edition of Tacitus, Walter Allen, Jr, 'Beatus Rhenanus, Editor of Tacitus and Livy,' *Speculum* 12 (1937): 382–5. George Huppert, *The Idea of Perfect History: Historical Erudition and Historical Philosophy in Renaissance France* (Urbana, 1970), 77-8, seems to me to underestimate the extent of Beatus Rhenanus' influence and the speed with which his ideas were accepted in France.

8   Paul Joachimsen, *Geschichtsauffassung und Geschichtsschreibung in Deutschland unter dem Einfluss des Humanismus*, Beiträge zur Kulturgeschichte des Mittelalters und der Renaissance 6 (Leipzig and Berlin, 1910), 50–7, 196–219. His analysis has been amplified by Alphons

long taken in by the fabulous writings attributed to Berosus and Manetho that Annius of Viterbo (*ca* 1432–1502) invented, which were widely endorsed, used by Jean Lemaire de Belges (1473–1516?), and published in Paris in 1512 under the patronage of Guillaume Petit (or Parvy), confessor to Louis XII, and then to Francis I.[9] Instead, these German scholars explored (and edited) ancient writ-

Lhotsky, 'Apis Colonna: Fabeln und Theorien über die Abkunft der Habsburger. Ein Exkurs zur Cronica Austrie des Thomas Ebendorfer,' *Mitteilungen des Instituts für österreichische Geschichtsforschung* 58 (1949): 193–230, rprt. in idem, *Das Haus Habsburg*, vol. 2 of his *Aufsätze und Vorträge* (Munich, 1971); and by Anna Coreth, 'Dynastisch-politische Ideen Kaiser Maximilian I. (Zwei Sudien.),' *Mitteilungen des Österreichischen Staatsarchivs* 3 (*Leo Santifaller – Festschrift*) (1950): 81–105, esp. 81–92. See also the comments of Bernard Guenée, *Histoire et culture historique dans l'Occident médiéval*, Collection historique (Paris, 1980), 144, 147. Marie Tanner considers Maximilian's ambitions in *The Last Descendant of Aeneas: The Hapsburgs and the Mythic Image of the Emperor* (New Haven, 1993), esp. 3–130; remarkably, although she treats Hunibald, she does not discuss Trithemius and his relations with Maximilian (nb. esp. 75, 103). Noel L. Brann's admiration for Trithemius' spirituality leads him, I think, to minimize the abbot's chicanery: see *The Abbot Trithemius (1462–1516): The Renaissance of Monastic Humanism*, Studies in the History of Christian Thought 24 (Leiden, 1981), esp. 96–7, 240, 308, 326; note, too (cf. 96, 121), that, in one of the two Compendia on the origin of the Franks which he published in 1515, Trithemius claimed already to have written the three volumes from which he said the Compendia were drawn (*Compendium siue Breuiarium primi volvminis Annalivm sive Historiarvm de origine regum et gentis Francorvm ad reverendissimvm in Christo patrem et principem dominum Laurentium Episcopum vuirtzpurgensem orientalisque Francie ducem Ioannis Tritemij Abbatis* [Mainz, 1515], 1v; see also Sigismund [Dullinger], *Trithemivs svi. ipsivs vindex: siue Steganographiæ admodvm reverendi, doctissimi, atque ingeniosissimi viri Ioannis Trithemii, primo Spanheimensis, ac postea S. Iacobi in Svbvrbano Herbipolensi Abbatis meritissimi, Apologetica defensio. Ex ipso ferè Trithemio collecta, & publici Iuris facta* [Ingolstadt, 1616], 11–12). For the dedication of the edition of the *Compendium* published in Paris in 1539, to the chancellor of France, Guillaume Poyet, who had acted as Jean du Tillet the elder's lawyer for almost a decade in the 1520s, see n. 63, below.

9   Beatus Rhenanus' studies with Lefèvre d'Étaples may account for his eventual rejection of the writings of Berosus forged by Annius of Viterbo, since Lefèvre was one of the first to denounce Berosus (in 1506, when Beatus Rhenanus was in Paris): D'Amico, *Theory and Practice*, 29–30, 43–5, 56–7 (Beatus Rhenanus' use of Berosus in his *Commentariolus* on Tacitus, published in 1519), 123–4 (Beatus Rhenanus' failure to cite Berosus in the *Castigationes* of 1533), 178–9 (Annius and Trithemius), 196–7 (Beatus Rhenanus' rejection of Berosus in his *Rerum Germanicarum Libri tres*, of 1531). On Lefèvre and Annius, see C. R. Ligota, 'Annius of Viterbo and Historical Method,' *Journal of the Warburg and Courtauld Institutes* 50 (1987): 44–56, at 44, esp. n. 2; on Annius, E.N. Tigerstedt, 'Ioannes Anniuus and *Graecia Mendax*,' in *Classical, Mediaeval, and Renaissance Studies in Honor of Berthold Louis Ullman*, ed. Charles Henderson, Jr, 2 vols. (Rome, 1964), 1: 293–310; and Roland Crahay, 'Réflexions sur le faux historique: le cas d'Annius de Viterbe,' *Académie royale de Belgique. Bulletin de la classe des lettres et des sciences morales et politiques*, 5th ser., no. 69 (1983): 241–67. Although each was generally careful to use reliable sources, Bebel, Johannes Aventinus (1477–1534), and Andreas Althamer (1498–1564) (who was much admired by the older

ings in order to discover the first authentic traces of the inhabitants of Germany, including the Franks – writings that included no reference to Priam, or even Pharamund, the legendary first king of the Franks. Having analysed the Greek and Roman sources, they fearlessly proclaimed the iconoclastic conclusions they drew from the antique classics.[10]

This is not to suggest that the two Du Tillet brothers were either uncreative or uninterested in sources and authenticity. They were. The younger brother was an avid seeker after manuscripts, and a thoughtful, punctilious, and principled editor of texts patristic and legal. The older brother was a pioneer in inventorying and utilizing documents and registers housed in royal administrative repositories. In these respects both made original contributions towards advancing critical investigation of the past. Yet as concerned the earliest history of the French, they were important because they endorsed the Germans' publications, and through their own writings spread their ideas. Thanks in no small part to the brothers Du Tillet, by 1570 (the year of their death), it had become unfashionable among the learned, orthodox Catholic élite to continue espousing the pop-

Jean du Tillet) cited and seem to have accepted Annius' Berosus: Frank L. Borchardt, *German Antiquity in Renaissance Myth* (Baltimore, 1971), 112–13, 166; Gerald Strauss, *Historian in an Age of Crisis: The Life and Work of Johannes Aventinus, 1477–1534* (Cambridge, Mass., 1963), 121–2; and for Bebel and Althamer, *Schardius Redivivus*, 1: 1–37, esp. 4–6 (Althamer's *Libellus* on Tacitus' *Germania*), 117–34, at 102 (Bebel's *Oratio ad Maximilianum*), 130–1 (Bebel's *De laude, antiquitate, imperio, victoriis rebusque gestis Veterum Germanorum*, where he acknowledges that the book of Manethon, also Annius' creation, was considered by many *corruptus*).

10 Jacques Ridé provides an impressive comprehensive survey of German authors, in *L'image du Germain dans la pensée et la littérature allemandes de la redécouverte de Tacite à la fin du XVIᵉᵐᵉ siècle (Contribution à l'étude de la genèse d'un mythe)*, 3 vols. (Lille and Paris, 1977). Still useful as a complement to Ridé's monumental work is Joachimsen's pioneering study *Geschichtsauffassung*, and the eminently reliable survey by Borchardt, *German Antiquity*. Donald R. Kelley noted the effect of German scholarship on French thinkers in general, and in particular on the jurists Andrea Alciato and Charles du Moulin, the humanist Jacques Lefèvre d'Étables, the historian Vincent de la Loupe, and the older (although not the younger) Jean du Tillet: *Foundations of Modern Historical Scholarship: Language, Law, and History in the French Renaissance* (New York, 1970), 93, 97, 154, 201–3, 210, 213, 229–31, 292. Du Moulin, who cited Hunibald and Berosus, waxed enthusiastic about the Germans but used them uncritically: see Asher, 'Myth,' 412. Marc Fumaroli presents an interesting discussion of the German humanists and notes their influence on French scholars, in 'Aux origines de la connaissance historique du Moyen Âge: humanisme, réforme et gallicanisme au XVIᵉ siècle,' *XVIIᵉ siècle* 114/115 (1977): 5–29, although I think that the widespread dissemination of printed texts was far more important than the reformed religion in spreading disrespect for the notion of Trojan origins. Kelley (*Foundations*, 201–2; cf., however, 229) likewise links support of Germanic roots with dedication to the reformed religion. Arlette Jouanna has pointed to the influence exercised by German scholars on certain French writers, in 'Quête des origines,' 307 (Paolo Emili), and in 'Mythes d'origine et ordre social dans les *Recherches de la*

ular myth that, not long before, King Louis XII had cherished. By the time they wrote, the political atmosphere had changed. Gone were the constraints that earlier in the century kept Nicole Gilles (d. 1503), Robert Gaguin (1433–1501), and Paolo Emili (d. 1529) from openly denouncing the Trojan myth and that led Jean Lemaire de Belges to endorse, embroider, and capitalize on it.[11] These pressures no longer existed, perhaps in part because imperial dedication to the legend had become an object of derision.[12] Francis I's own imperial ambitions may have made him more willing to accept the notion that the Franks were originally Germans.[13] More important, I think, were the intellectual acumen and respect for scholarship of a ruler who took pride in the appellation 'father of arts and letters.' This meant that Francis I was prepared – or that the leading scholars in France assumed he would be – to recognize the futility of attempting to determine whatever earlier, pre-Germanic history the Franks as a people may have had.

Each Jean du Tillet has occasionally been hailed as a pioneer in Germanifying (and de-Trojanizing) French history.[14] Most often, however, their contribu-

France,' in *Étienne Pasquier et ses* Recherches de la France, Cahiers V.L. Saulnier 8 (Paris, 1991), 105–19 (Étienne Pasquier). See as well the following note.

11 Particularly useful for their political perspective are Roland Crahay's comments on Louis XII and Jean Lemaire de Belges in 'Réflexions sur le faux historique,' 260–2; and also those of Lindner, 'Ex mala parentela,' 501–2. It was as 'Indiciaire et Historiographe stipendié' of Maximilian I's daughter Marguerite, duchess of Savoy and countess of Burgundy, and her ward and nephew Charles of Spain that Lemaire de Belges dedicated to Marguerite the first volume of his *Illustrations de Gaule: Œuvres de Jean Lemaire de Belges*, ed. Auguste-Jean Stecher, 4 vols. (Louvain, 1882–91), 1: 9–11. In *A Contribution to the Study of Jean Lemaire de Belges: A Critical Study of Bio-bibliographical Data, Including a Transcript of Various Unpublished Works* (New York, 1936), Kathleen Miriam Munn discusses Lemaire's patrons (2–3), and the critics of his work (4–37). Colette Beaune sees Lemaire as an innovative and creative revitalizer and reinterpreter of the Trojan myth, in *Naissance de la nation France,* Bibliothèque des histoires (Paris, 1985), 28–30, 35–7 (trans. as *The Birth of an Ideology: Myths and Symbols of Nation in Late-Medieval France*, trans. Susan Ross Huston, ed. Fredric L. Cheyette [Berkeley, 1991], 340–5); she does not discuss his patrons or their possible influence on his idea.

12 Even Maximilian harbored doubts regarding Trithemius' good faith and Hunibald's authenticity: Joseph Chmel, *Die Handschriften der k.k. Hofbibliothek in Wien, im Interesse der Geschichte, besonders der österreichischen*, 2 vols. (Vienna, 1840–1), 1: 312–20 (esp. the marginal notations in MS 9045*, and Trithemius' letters to the Emperor in 1513). See the excellent discussion of Trithemius and his forgeries, in Klaus Arnold, *Johannes Trithemius (1462–1516)*, Quellen und Forschungen zur Geschichte des Bistums und Hochstifts Würzburg 23 (Würzburg, 1971), 171–9.

13 See the comments of Karl Ferdinand Werner, *Les origines (avant l'an mil)*, vol. 1 of *Histoire de France*, ed. Jean Favier (Paris, 1984), 38.

14 Although my reading of the evidence sometimes differs from his, particularly as regards the importance of the younger Jean in discrediting the Trojan myth, I cannot emphasize enough

tions have received less attention than those of their more famous (and slightly younger) contemporaries. Among these are the historians Bernard de Girard, seigneur du Haillan (1535?–1610), François de Belleforest (1530–1583), and Nicolas Vignier (1530–1596); the polemicist François Hotman (1524–1590); the witty and perceptive historical essayist Étienne Pasquier (1529–1615); and the theorist Jean Bodin (1530–1596). Nor has the nature of their achievement – the sources on which they drew, the uses to which they put them, the influence their ideas exerted – been closely studied, or fully appreciated. Their failure to attract serious scholarly notice may result in part from the undramatic, matter-of-fact, non-argumentative way in which they presented their conclusions. Far more important, however, the works most relevant to the question of France's origins, although written much earlier, were not published until some years after they died, and thus after works of Du Haillan, Belleforest, Vignier, Hotman, Pasquier, and Bodin had been printed (the first book of Pasquier's *Recherches* in 1560, the key writings of the others in the 1570s). The elder Jean treated the origins of the French in the first recension of his *Recueil des Roys*, completed in the early 1550s, and then revised and presented to Charles IX in 1566. The work was not generally available until the second recension was published in two pirated editions in 1578, and two years later, in 1580, in an edition overseen by the *greffier*'s second son and literary executor, Helie. Still, in manuscript, it circulated among Du Tillet's intellectual peers and heirs.[15] As

the importance of Donald Kelley's pioneering research on the two Du Tillet brothers: see *Foundations*, 210, 215–38, although note 160 (the older Jean as 'one of the king's archivists'), 221 (Helie du Tillet as lord of La Bussière [which in fact came to the elder Jean through his marriage to Jeanne Brinon]; and as *greffier civil* [an office purchased for Seraphin du Tillet in 1519]), 229 (the older Jean as 'probably the first French scholar to reject outright the Trojan theory'); in his book Kelley reworked material he first presented in 'Jean du Tillet, Archivist and Antiquary,' *Journal of Modern History* 38 (1966): 337-54. In the introduction to their edition and translation of Hotman's *Francogallia*, Ralph E. Giesey and John Hearsey McMillan Salmon state that the *greffier* Du Tillet adopted the idea that the French were German in origin in the 1550s, and comment that the notion of the Germanic origin of the French was spread in the writings of Beatus Rhenanus; they suggest that Du Tillet's ideas may have influenced 'his friend' Pasquier: *Francogallia by François Hotman*, Cambridge Studies in the History and Theory of Politics (Cambridge, 1972), 21–3. They note the older Jean's conflict with Hotman over the issue of Francis II's minority, although they do not suggest (as I believe) that the senior Jean's ideas about the Franks' Germanic origin influenced Hotman; nor do they consider the likely influence of the younger Jean on both the elder Jean and on Hotman. Jouanna ('Quête des origines,' 307) remarks that in 1539 'l'historien Du Tillet' (in fact, the younger Jean) declared that the Franks came from Germany.

15 Elizabeth A.R. Brown, *'Franks, Burgundians, and Aquitanians' and the Royal Coronation Ceremony in France*, Transactions of the American Philosophical Society 82[7] (Philadelphia, 1992), 5–6; Francoys de Belleforest, *Les Chroniqves et Annales de France dez l'origine des Francoys, et leur venüe és Gaules. Faictes iadis briefuement par Nicole Gilles secretaire du*

to the younger Jean, a very brief statement of his views on French origins and the Trojan myth was published as the preamble to an outline sketch of French history in 1539 and often reprinted, in Latin and French, but the full version of his Chronicle, including a long preamble, first appeared as an appendix to the edition of his brother's works in 1580. This has led historians to underestimate the impact of their ideas on their contemporaries, who knew them (particularly in the case of the *Recueil des Roys*) through manuscript copies of their works, as well as through personal contacts with them.[16]

Who were the brothers Du Tillet? What – and why – did they write? How did they come to know the work of the German humanists? What prompted them to take the positions they did regarding the origins of the French? In attempting to suggest answers to these questions, I shall begin by sketching the brothers' careers. Then I shall turn to their ideas regarding Trojan origins, commencing with the younger Jean and then looking at the elder, in each case attempting to identify their sources. In dealing with the younger Jean, I shall consider briefly the work of Paolo Emili, since it was in a supplement to the ten books of his History that the younger Jean's ideas about the Trojan origins of the French first appeared.

The Brothers Jean du Tillet

The two Jeans were from the Angoumois, the second and fifth sons of Helie du Tillet and Mathurine Petiton. Helie and other members of his family served Francis, duke of Angoulême, and his mother, Louise of Savoy, before Francis became king of France on 1 January 1515; a week later the new king named Helie vice-president of the Chambre des comptes of Paris, an office he held

---

Roy, iusqu'au Roy Charles huictiesme, & depuis additionnées par Denis Sauuage, iusqu'au Roy Françoys second. A present Reueuëes corrigées & augmentées selon la verité des reg-istres, & pancartes anciennes, & suyuant la foy des vieux exemplaires, contenantes L'histoire vniuerselle de France, dez Pharamond, iusqu'au Roy Charles neuuiesme regnant àpresent ... Auec les Genealogies, & Effigies des Roys au plus pres du naturel, Et vne table alphabetique, ordonnée par lieux communs (Paris, 1573), fol. 3ᵛ. For English analogues, see H.R. Woudhuy-sen, *Sir Philip Sidney and the Circulation of Manuscripts, 1558–1640* (Oxford, 1996).

16 George Huppert, for example, presents 'the Catholic Du Tillet [the *greffier civil*]' as '*con-firm[ing]* the findings of the heretic Dr. Hotman' (italics mine), although the elder Jean du Tillet's ideas had been set down in the early 1550s and may well have been known to Hotman: *Idea of Perfect History*, 81. Similarly, a century ago Augustin Thierry viewed Hotman as an innovator, attributing to him the creation of a 'système' 'sans le secours d'aucun ouvrage de seconde main,' and noting that the scholarly works of Fauchet and Du Tillet were published after his had appeared: *Récits des temps mérovingiens précédés de Considérations sur l'his-toire de France*, 5th ed. (Paris, 1851), 26. In a generally accurate and eminently useful article

until his death in April 1526. The elder Jean was born sometime between 1495 and 1502 (the approximate birth dates, respectively, of Helie and Mathurine's second and fourth children, both sons, Seraphin and Pierre).[17] The second Jean, the last son, was a decade or so younger than the elder Jean,[18] and was probably no more than twenty-eight in 1538.[19] In that year, in a letter accompanying the young man's first publication, Jacques Bogard termed him *adolescens* and assured readers that the Carthusian Godefroy Tilmann (a learned champion of orthodoxy and opponent of Luther) had reviewed Du Tillet's work, thus rein-

published in 1969, Asher ('Myth,' 412) implied that the elder Du Tillet's ideas were influenced by those of Pasquier, rather than the reverse.

17 Elizabeth A.R. Brown, 'Le greffe civil du Parlement de Paris au XVIe siècle: Jean du Tillet et les registres des plaidoiries,' *Bibliothèque de l'École des chartes* 153 (1995): 325–72, esp. 335–7, 339 n. 35. The eldest child, Anne, married Pierre Regnier (doctor of laws and lieutenant of the seneschalsy of Poitou) on 11 December 1508: BnF, Cabinet de d'Hozier 320 (fr. 31201), Dossier 8890 (Tillet), fol. 9[v]. This date is given as 11 November 1508, in the genealogy of the family, based on one compiled by d'Hozier, in Jean-Baptiste-Pierre-Jullien de Courcelles, *Histoire généalogique et héraldique des pairs de France, des grands dignitaires de la Couronne, des principales familles nobles du Royaume, et des maisons princières de l'Europe, précédée de la généalogie de la maison de France*, 12 vols. (Paris, 1822–33) 3: 7 (separately paginated section on the Du Tillet).

18 Discussing the deaths of the older and younger Jean du Tillet in 1570, and remarking on the many similarities between them, Scevole de Sainte-Marthe asserted that they 'n'estoient gueres plus aagez l'vn que l'autre,' doubtless because he did not know when they were born: *Eloges des hommes illvstres, qvi depvis vn siecle ont flevry en France dans la profession des Lettres*, trans. Guillaume Colletet (Paris, 1644), 202; followed in *Gallia Christiana ...*, ed. Denis de Sainte-Marthe et al., 16 vols. (Paris, 1715–1865), 8: 1649 ('nec adeo multum ætate dispares'). For the dates of their deaths (the elder Jean on 2 October 1570, the younger on 19 November 1570), see the genealogy in Courcelles, *Histoire généalogique* 3: 7, 9. The only detailed study of the younger Jean's life contains little information about his activities before his appointment as bishop of Saint-Brieuc in 1553: l'Abbé Daniel, 'Étude sur Jean du Tillet, évêque de Saint-Brieuc (1553–64),' *Mémoires de la Société archéologique et historique des Côtes-du-Nord,* 2d ser., 4[2] (1890–1): 215–23. For his service as bishop of Meaux, see Auguste Allou, *Chronique des évêques de Meaux suivie d'un état de l'ancien diocèse et du diocèse actuel* (Meaux, 1875), 82–4. For his publications, see Cuthbert Hamilton Turner, 'Jean du Tillet: A Neglected Scholar of the Sixteenth Century,' in *The Bodleian Manuscript of Jerome's Version of the Chronicle of Eusebius Reproduced in Collotype*, ed. John Knight Fotheringham (Oxford, 1905), 48–63 (Appendix 5), and idem, 'The Bibliography of Jean du Tillet,' *Journal of Theological Studies* 12 (no. 45) (1910): 128–33.

19 In October 1531 Jean was still a minor: BnF, Chérin 196 (fr. 31758), no. 3878 (Du Tillet de Montramé), fol. 3[r-v] (reference to a decree of the Grands Jours of Angoulême dated 25 October 1531, in which Mathurine Petiton is identified as guardian of her minor children Louis, Jean, and Anne). According to various genealogies, the younger Anne was married to a minor noble of the Angoumois (David des Andrieux, lord of Gademoulins) in September 1532, but she need not have attained her majority to do so: BnF, Dossiers bleus 634 (fr. 30179), fol. 103[v], a genealogy prepared by Victor Le Gris, sieur de Teuville, with the aid of the Du Tillet

forcing his implication that Du Tillet was not mature enough to be a fully trust-worthy scholar.[20]

The two Jeans' oldest brother, Seraphin, had followed his father to Paris and held various royal financial posts until, in 1519, he acquired by purchase the office of *greffier civil* (chief civil clerk) of the Parlement of Paris. During these years the elder Jean and his younger brother, Pierre, were studying law at the University of Poitiers, and Pierre attended the University of Toulouse as well. Pierre obtained his doctorate from Poitiers in 1518, and in 1520 he and Jean sued the regents of the university in hopes of becoming regents themselves. Jean soon withdrew from the proceedings; his fortunes lay elsewhere. In 1521 he was an *avocat* licensed to practise before the Parlement of Paris. In that year, pressed by his father, Seraphin resigned in Jean's favour the office of *greffier civil* of the Parlement, but then baulked at relinquishing the post.[21] Nine years

family, which was published in 1701; BnF, Cabinet de d'Hozier 320 (fr. 31201), Dossier 8890 (Tillet), fols. 12ᵛ–13ʳ; and Courcelles, *Histoire généalogique* 3: 8.

20 *D. Paciani Barcilonæ integerrimi quondam Episcopi Parænesis ad Pœnitentiam. Altera eius-dem de Baptismo. Eiusdem Epistolæ duæ ad Sympronianum Nouatianum. Accessit his tracta-tus eiusdem Sancti, aduersus Nouatianos. Hæ Beati viri Christianæ lucubrationes, nunc primùm in lucem exeunt Lector pie, etiam si ab authore ante annos mille editæ sint* (Paris: Charlotte Guillard, 1538); Pacian's works are printed 'ex principe Tiliana editione,' in *PL* 13: 1051–94; on the edition, see Elizabeth A.R. Brown, *Jean du Tillet and the French Wars of Religion: Five Tracts, 1562–1569*, Medieval and Renaissance Texts and Studies 108 (Bing-hamton, 1994), 39–40 n. 88. The undated letter at the end of Du Tillet's edition, addressed to 'the pious reader,' is signed 'Iacobus Boïgardus.' His comments concerning the edition show that he was collaborating with Charlotte Guillard in producing the book, an aspect of the career of Jacques Bogard, Charlotte's nephew, apparently unknown to Philippe Renouard, who discusses Bogard in his *Répertoire des imprimeurs parisiens, libraires, fondeurs de car-actères et correcteurs d'imprimerie depuis l'introduction de l'Imprimerie à Paris (1470) jusqu'à la fin du seizième siècle ...*, ed. Jeanne Veyrin-Forrer and Brigitte Moreau (Paris, 1965), 40; see also 111–12, 189–90 (Charlotte Guillard and her sisters, and Guillaume Des Boys); on Charlotte, see Beatrice Beech, 'Charlotte Guillard: A Sixteenth-Century Busi-ness Woman,' *Renaissance Quarterly* 36 (1983): 345–67. Bogard succeeded his sister-in-law Edmée Tousan (widow of Conrad Neobar) as *libraire-imprimeur* in 1541; on Neobar, see Renouard, *Répertoire*, 322; in 1540, Neobar published the younger Du Tillet's edition (in Greek) of the Apostolic Canons and decrees of the early councils (Turner, 'Jean du Tillet,' 50). In 1548 Bogard brought out Du Tillet's edition of Ansegius' and Benedict the Deacon's collections of capitularies: Turner, 'Jean du Tillet,' 52. In 1550 Charlotte Guillard and her brother-in-law Guillaume Des Boys (husband of her sister Michelle) published Du Tillet's edi-tion of the sixteen books of Theodosius' Constitutions: ibid., 53–4. In 1538 Charlotte Guillard published Godefroy Tilmann's translation of Georgius Pachymeres' *Paraphrasis in decem epistolas B. Dyonisii Areopagitæ*, whose title declares that Tilmann's preface 'esse possit vice apologiæ pro libris B. Dionysii Areopagitæ adversus calumnias Laurentii Vallæ, Martini Lutheri et Des. Erasmi.'

21 Brown, 'Greffe civil,' 331–2, 339–40, 342–3.

of litigation and negotiation ensued before Jean was actually received as *greffier*, on 3 September 1530.[22]

During the forty years he served as *greffier civil*, the elder Jean du Tillet elevated the importance of the office and amassed a fortune for himself and his family. He also did a prodigious amount of historical research and writing. Some of his work was undertaken to support specific royal policies. Later, as religious conflict threatened, and then engulfed, France, he wrote a number of polemical works defending orthodoxy and obedience. But from the 1530s until his death, the projects that chiefly absorbed his energies were works in which he aimed to explain the growth and development of the kingdom of France and its institutions, and in so doing serve the king. As *greffier civil*, Du Tillet naturally had access to the civil archives of the Parlement of Paris. Francis I, probably in the early 1540s, gave him entry to the Trésor des chartes, commanding him to oversee the preparation of registers containing copies of its contents.[23] The king also ordered Du Tillet to compile a collection of royal laws and ordonnances, and he authorized him to search for the edicts 'wherever they might be found.'[24] After his accession in 1547, Henry II renewed and expanded his father's commissions. Du Tillet put the authorizations to good use, and he worked in numerous repositories, ecclesiastical as well as secular.[25] He soon

22 Ibid., 342–4, 347–65.

23 The royal mandate survives only in copies in two chancery registers, the first (BnF, fr. 5503, fols. 212^v–14^r) prepared towards the end of Francis I's reign for the royal secretary Cosme Clausse, the second (BnF, n. a. fr. 20256, fols. 55^v–57^r) completed *ca* 1570–1 for Clausse's son Pierre, who was also a royal secretary. Cosme Clausse himself copied the mandate (which is undated) and six other acts dated between 1542 and 1546 at the end of his formulary, which contains no later letters. The copy of the mandate in Pierre Clausse's manual, curiously, is dated at Saint-Germain-en-Laye on 12 May 1562, which is a whim of Clausse's copyist but has confused many scholars, some of whom have assumed that Francis II (1559–60) issued it. See Elizabeth A.R. Brown, 'Jean du Tillet, François Ier, and the *Trésor des chartes*,' in *Histoire d'archives: Recueil d'articles offert à Lucie Favier par ses collègues et amis* (Paris, 1997), 237–47. I discuss these formularies in another context, in 'Sodomy, Honor, Treason, and Exile: Four Documents Concerning the Dinteville Affair (1538–1539),' in *Sociétés et idéologies des temps modernes: Hommage à Arlette Jouanna*, ed. J. Fouilheron, Guy Le Thiec, H. Michel (Montpellier, 1996), 511–32.

24 AN, X^{1a} 1560, fol. 474^v (26 August 1547, referring to a royal letter of 2 July 1547); see Hélène Michaud, *La grande chancellerie et les écritures royales au seizième siècle (1515–1589)*, Mémoires et documents publiés par la Société de l'Ecole des chartes 17 (Paris, 1967), 384 n. 4; and *Catalogue des actes de Henri II*, Institut de France, Académie des sciences morales et politiques, Collection des ordonnances des rois de France (Paris, 1979–), 1: 175 no. 608.

25 In the dedication of the *Recueil des ordonnances* to Henry II, Du Tillet said that he had used documents 'tires par vostre ordonnance de voz tresor des chartres[,] parlement, chambre des comptes, eglises et autres plusieurs endroictz': BnF, fr. 17294, fols. 214^r-16^r, at 215^v (a copy

produced a spectacular harvest, in the form of three *Recueils* ('Collections'), which he presented to the king. The first was a compilation of ordonnances. The second, offered to the king in February 1558, was a survey of relations between France and England from 1066 to the present, which contained analytical inventories of the sources Du Tillet had used. So, too, did the third and most important *Recueil*, which Du Tillet completed and presented to the king between mid-1553 and early 1555. This 'Collection,' the *Recueil des Roys de France*, treated the history of the royal house and royal institutions, and it was here that Du Tillet first set out his ideas regarding the origins of the French. Despite his other interests, Du Tillet laboured on this *Recueil* for most of his remaining years, and he offered a greatly expanded and revised recension of the work to Charles IX in 1566.[26] In the new version, the chapter on the origins of the French was far longer than – although not essentially different from – the chapter written in the early 1550s. Here, however, it was given pride of place as the initial chapter of the *Recueil*.

The younger Jean du Tillet was probably born no earlier than 1510. He was just a child when his father moved from the Angoumois to Paris in 1515. Nothing is known of his formative years, aside from the fact that he and Emard de Ranconnet, a native of Bordeaux and future *conseiller* of the Parlement of Paris, were fellow students, perhaps at the Collège de Périgord in Toulouse, where Ranconnet is known to have studied in 1526.[27] Wherever he was edu-

corrected by Du Tillet). For Du Tillet's work in the library of the chapter of Beauvais, see Brown, *'Franks, Burgundians,'* 19–30.

26 On the version of the *Recueil des Roys* presented to Charles IX, see Elizabeth A.R. Brown and Myra Dickman Orth, 'Jean du Tillet et les illustrations du grand *Recueil des Rois*,' *Revue de l'Art* 115 (1997): 8–24. Not long before his death, Du Tillet gave the king an elegantly bound copy of his final work, the *Recueil des honneurs et rangs des grands*, a book on precedence composed largely of texts: BnF, fr. 5784. The free-standing columns on the luxurious binding suggest that the work must have been presented in 1568 or thereabouts, since Charles IX was still using intertwined columns as his device in November 1567: Brown, *Jean du Tillet and the French Wars of Religion*, 62, esp. n. 142.

27 See the dedication to Ranconnet that Du Tillet wrote for his *XXVIIII Titvli ex corpore Vlpiani* (Paris: Guillaume Morel, 1549), fol. A 2ʳ⁻ᵛ (dated 1 December 1549; 'propter veterem nostram studiorum coniunctionem'); in it, Du Tillet noted that he had shown Ranconnet the manuscript he was editing five years earlier. In dedicating his edition of the Theodosian Code to Jean Bertrand (who soon replaced Pierre Lizet as first president of the Parlement of Paris), Du Tillet declared that he was doing so because Ranconnet, 'my fellow-student since we were boys,' had assured him that Bertrand would appreciate it: *E libris Constitvtionum Theodosii A. Libri priores Octo, longè meliores quàm adhuc circumferebantur: sed ab Alarico rege Gotthorum ita deminuti, vt vix decima pars in his hodie appareat eorum, quæ in Theodosiano codice continebantur. Posteriores octo integri, nunc primùm post .M. annos in lucem reuocati a Io. Tilio Engolism. Dicati Io. Bertrando .V.C. Curiæ Parisiorum præsidi, & ab interiori consilio Henrici .II. Galliæ regis optimi maximi* (Paris, 1550) ; the dedication to Bertrand is dated 21

cated, and by whom, Du Tillet became an expert in the history of the Roman and canon law.[28] Like his elder brother Louis (the fourth of the Du Tillet brothers), the younger Jean entered the church, and both he and Louis became canons of Angoulême and held curacies in the Angoumois, Louis at Claix and Jean at Champniers.[29] Between 1534 and 1538, Louis fell under Calvin's spell

November 1549 (in Paris), the preface to readers (referring to Bertrand as president of the Parlement de Paris and stating that he 'voluit' the publication) is dated 17 April 1550 (also in Paris). On the work, see Turner, 'Jean du Tillet,' 53–4 (although note that the copy of the work at the BnF [classmark F 45213] [whose quires are not bound in proper order] in fact contains the preface to the reader). See Turner, 'Bibliography,' 130, for Jean du Tillet's loan to Ranconnet of a fifteenth-century manuscript of Æschylus (BnF, fr. 2789). On the careers of Ranconnet and Bertrand, see Édouard Maugis, *Histoire du Parlement de Paris de l'avènement des rois Valois à la mort d'Henri IV*, 3 vols. (Paris, 1913–16), 1: 230–2, 3: 150, 189, 191–2; Philippe Tamizey de Larroque, 'Un grand homme oublié: le Président de Ranconnet,' *Revue des questions historiques* 10 (1871): 230–45; and on Bertrand and Lizet, Jacques-Auguste de Thou, *Historiarum sui temporis libri CXXXVIII.*, ed. Thomas Carte, 7 vols. (London, 1733), 1: 217–18 Bk VI, ch. 12); and L. Douët d'Arcq, 'Prisée de la bibliothèque du président Lizet, en 1554,' *Bibliothèque de l'École des chartes* 37 (1876): 358–80, esp. 358–64. For the relationship between Du Tillet and Ranconnet, see also Paul Frédéric Girard, 'Le manuscrit des *Gromatici* de l'évêque Jean du Tillet,' in *Mélanges Fitting, LXXVe anniversaire de M. le Professeur Hermann Fitting*, 2 vols. (Montpellier, 1907–8), 2: 235–86, esp. 265–9 (discussing the copy Ranconnet made of the *Gromatici*, of which Du Tillet brought back a manuscript copy from Rome in 1553).

28 Shortly after the younger Jean's death, Pierre Pithou cited Du Tillet's edition of the Theodosian Code, termed him 'antiquæ eruditionis hominem,' and recalled the knowledge of legal manuscripts Du Tillet had displayed when they were involved in discussions 'de veterum Iurisconsultorum reliquiis.' See Pithou's *Mosaycarvm et Romanarvm Legvm Collatio, ex integris Papiniani, Pauli, Vlpiani, Gaij, Modestini, aliorumque veterum Iuris auctorum libris ante tempora Iustiniani Imp. desumpta. Eivsdem Imp. Ivstiniani Nouellæ Constitutiones III. Ivliani Antecessoris CP. Dictatum de Consiliarijs. Eivsdem Ivliani Collectio de contutoribus* (Basle, 1574), 71; Pithou's dedication to Christophle de Thou is dated 1 October 1572. As Turner has shown, Pithou used the manuscript of Ulpian that served as the basis of Du Tillet's edition of 1549: Turner, 'Jean du Tillet,' 58, 63 n. 1.

29 See Elizabeth A.R. Brown, 'La Renaudie se venge: l'autre face de la conjuration d'Amboise,' in *Complots et conjurations dans l'Europe moderne. Colloque international organisé par l'École française de Rome, l'Institut de recherches sur les civilisations de l'Occident moderne de l'Université Paris-Sorbonne et le Dipartimento di storia moderna e contemporanea dell'Università degli Studi di Pisa. Rome, 30 septembre – 2 octobre 1993*, ed. Yves-Marie Bercé and Elena Fasano Guarini, Collection de l'École française de Rome 220 (Rome, 1996), 451–74. Louis was a canon of Angoulême in 1528 (when he was, at most, twenty-two): AN, X1A 4885, fol. 221v; n. 19 above. According to the genealogy in Courcelles, *Histoire généalogique* 3: 7, Jean was a canon in 1533, which may be the case, although this genealogy, like others, says that Louis was younger than Jean; Jean appears as canon of Angoulême, and agent of the elder Jean, in an act dated 28 April 1541, for which see AN, Minutier Central VIII/61, fols. 9v–12v, at 10r. In a work published four years before his death, Jean referred to Champniers as 'ma paroisse de Chaniers en engoumois, la premiere eglise que i'ay seruie des

and followed him to Strasbourg and Switzerland. The younger Jean may well have known Calvin and either helped him gain access to the manuscript of the *Libri Carolini* on which a decade later Jean based his edition, or showed him notes he had made from the manuscript.[30] The younger Jean apparently spent the 1530s indulging his love of manuscripts, books, and historical research, and becoming a scholar. His first book, written when he was very young ('fort ieune'), in 1536 or 1537, was an outline Chronicle, in French, of the reigns and deeds of the kings of France; it was here that he first mocked the notion that the French were descended from the Trojans. His first publication was an edition that appeared in 1538. He seems likely to have spent as much time in Paris as in Champniers or Angoulême – although he later claimed to have been devoted to his first parishioners.

In Paris the young Du Tillet gained the attention of the theologian, scholar, and royal chaplain (*ecclesiasta*) Jean de Gaigny, who was an ideal mentor for a

---

ma ieunesse': *Du Symbole des Apostres, & des douze articles de la foy* (Paris, 1566), fol. A 2ᵛ. As part of a campaign directed against the Du Barry family in the Angoumois, the elder Jean manoeuvred the younger one into claiming the cure of Champniers in 1539 or thereabouts; the Parlement of Dijon pronounced for the Du Tillet and against Jean du Barry, lord of La Renaudie, on 20 October 1546: Brown, 'La Renaudie,' 457–64. The younger Jean must have been about thirty-six in 1546, which seems a bit old to qualify as 'jeune.' This suggests that he was installed at Champniers before the Parlement issued its final decree.

30 See Brown, 'La Renaudie,' 459–60, and also my *Jean du Tillet and the French Wars of Religion*, 3–5, 10, 38–41. There (ibid., 39–40 n. 88), I referred to Dr Al Wolters' work on Calvin's allusions to the *Libri Carolini* in 1547, two years before Du Tillet's edition appeared; I stated that Calvin was 'unlikely to have learned of the *Libri*' through the younger Jean du Tillet, because of the lapse of time – nine years – between 1538, when the relationship between the Du Tillet and Calvin was broken, and 1547, when Calvin apparently began citing the *Libri*. Professor James R. Payton, Jr, who is continuing Dr Wolters' work, challenged this assumption, and Dr Ann Freeman and Dr Paul Meyvaert have convincingly proposed (noting the errors in Calvin's references) that, in citing the *Libri*, the reformer was relying on hurried notes he had taken some years before – quite possibly before the breach between him and the Du Tillet brothers. They note that Calvin was in Paris in the summer of 1536, when he could have been in contact with the younger Jean du Tillet: Abel Lefranc, *La jeunesse de Calvin* (Paris, 1888), 190–1, 204–10. The manuscript of the *Libri* that Du Tillet used for his edition had passed from Reims to Laon, and it is unclear where (and when) Du Tillet worked on it, although scholars often borrowed manuscripts from ecclesiastical libraries – and retained them, especially when, like Jean de Gaigny, they had royal authority for their research. Before 1536, Du Tillet could have seen and used the manuscript either in Laon or Paris, perhaps, as will be seen, in Gaigny's *Gymnasium*. It seems to me more likely that Calvin was using notes given him by Du Tillet than that Du Tillet somehow arranged for Calvin to see the manuscript; it is even more unlikely, that Calvin himself managed to view it without assistance. See now, James R. Payton, Jr, 'Calvin and the *Libri Carolini*,' *The Sixteenth Century Journal* 28 (1997): 465–80.

fledgling scholar.[31] Gaigny had won the king's favour in 1536 and soon gained Francis I's support for his plans to unearth and publish forgotten manuscripts – as well as royal authorization to enter all libraries in the kingdom to copy any books he judged 'profitable for the republic of letters and the advancement of the empire of philology.' Relying on this letter, Gaigny immediately began visiting the libraries of the monasteries and chapters he encountered on his travels with the king. He soon discovered some hundred texts – which prompted Francis I to decide that such precious works should be published, to ensure their preservation.[32] Gaigny utilized the king's charge not only to copy, but also to collect manuscripts. According to the younger Jean du Tillet, Gaigny gathered in his *Gymnasium* in Paris copies of old theological works, which came from numerous libraries in France. The use to which the texts were to be put was fully in line with the king's purposes, since, Du Tillet said, Gaigny intended them to be published to combat heretics, particularly 'the insane Luther and his

31 On Gaigny, see James K. Farge, *Biographical Register of Paris Doctors of Theology,*
    1500–1536 (Toronto, 1980), 177–83 n. 199; and André Jammes, 'Un bibliophile à découvrir,'
    Bulletin du bibliophile (1996): 36–81; I am grateful to Professor Farge for supplying me with
    information concerning Gaigny which he has discovered since 1980, and to M. Jammes for
    sending me a copy of his illuminating article. To judge from the titles and dedications of his
    books, Gaigny became first almoner to the king between 1538 and 1540. Farge (ibid., 181)
    dates to 1536 the edition of Avitus and Claudius Marius Victor that was the first work which
    Gaigny dedicated to the king, although it seems likely to me that it actually appeared in 1537.
    Gaigny's dedication is dated at Lyon on the ides of March 1536, which (according to the new
    style of dating) would have been 15 March 1537, two weeks before Easter Day.
32 *Primasii vticensis in Africa Episcopi, in omnes D. Pauli epistolas commentarij perbreues ac*
    docti, ante annos mille ab autore editi (Cologne: Iohannes Cymnicus, 1538); Charlotte Guil-
    lard published another edition in Paris in 1543. A French translation by Gaigny appeared in
    1540: *Briefve et Frvctvevse Exposition sus les Epistres Sainct Paul aux Romains & Hebreux,*
    par Primasius, Iadis disciple de sainct Augustin: translatées de Latin en langue vulgaire
    Francoyse, par Iehan de Gaigny, docteur & premier aulmosnier du treschrestien Roy de
    France, Francoys premier du nom, par le commandement dudict Seigneur (Paris, 1540); the
    manuscript presentation copy is BnF, fr. 935. In the Latin, the dedication reads: 'Huius ego
    tam egregiæ sponsionis tuæ accepto in pignus diplomate publico, quo uniuersas mihi patere
    regni tui librarias iuberes, atque inde quotquot e re philologiæ uiderentur monimenta,
    describendi potestatem faceres, cœpi omnium cœnobiorum, quæ iter in comitatu tuo facienti
    occurrerunt, librarias uerrere: unde quum centum prope non inferioris notæ uolumina e tene-
    bris uindicassem ...' The sense of Gaigny's translation is slightly different: 'De laquelle tienne
    promesse incontinent ordonnas mestre depeschees letres patentes, par lesquelles commandoys
    mestre par toutes libraries publicques faicte ouuerture pour dicelles transcrire quelz liures ver-
    roye estre au proufict de la republicque literaire & accession de lempire de Philologie. Par-
    quoy executant ton royal vouloir commencay a fouiller & fueilleter toutes les libraries des
    monasteres & chapitres, lesquelz suiuant ta compaignie se sont offerts en chemin [*sic*]. Dont
    apres auoir vendicque des tenebres sans linteruention de ta maieste perpetuelle [*sic*] plusieurs

cohorts' – a goal with which Jean du Tillet surely sympathized, given his brother Louis' recent escape from Calvin's clutches.[33]

Du Tillet seems to have been welcomed in Gaigny's *Gymnasium*, and to have found there the manuscript of the first text he edited and published, the works of Pacian (saint and fourth-century bishop of Barcelona), which appeared in 1538. It is not surprising that he dedicated the edition to Jean de Gaigny, who surely inspired and fostered Du Tillet's love of manuscripts – and, as will be seen, may well have helped Du Tillet find a publisher for his summary Chronicle. Gaigny may also have helped Du Tillet obtain royal authorization, similar to his own, that permitted the younger scholar to search for manuscripts in all the kingdom's libraries – a mandate which, like Gaigny, Du Tillet used to enlarge his own library as well as discover texts to publish.[34]

Du Tillet's forays into the kingdom's libraries bore fruit as rich as Gaigny's. In the 1540s he published editions of numerous legal and ecclesiastical texts, including Ulpian, the Theodosian Code, Ansegisus and Benedict the Deacon, the Salic Law, and the *Libri Carolini*.[35] He dedicated the books to an array of luminaries, including, in 1540, Cardinal François de Tournon (one of the king's most influential councillors, then at the apogee of his power);[36] at the end of the decade, two leading officials of the Parlement of Paris; in 1554, Cardinal Charles of Lorraine, archbishop of Reims; and, in 1568, Pope Pius V. During these years, his career steadily advanced, doubtless at least in part because the older Jean supported him. After the accession of Henry II in 1547, his brother helped him obtain the post of prothonotary to Charles of Lorraine, archbishop

antiens liures de marcque non petite': BnF, lat. 935, fol. 2ᵛ. The French edition of 1540 reads (fol. A. iij.ᵛ)'se sont offerts en mon chemin,' and 'des tenebres (qui estoient, sans l'interuention de ta maiesté, perpetuelles).'

33 'ita tu vnus ad communem studiosorum vsum vndecunque potes, exemplaria veteris illius theologiæ corrogas ex omnibus propè Galliæ bibliothecis, quæ in tuum hoc Gymnasium Parisiense conuehas in exempla plurima transfusurus. Probè enim nosti quam strenuè depugnarint aduersus acerrimos ecclesiæ Christi hostes, hæreticos. Quare recta tecum mihi hæc videre eximie vir reputasse, qui istiusmodi veteres Theologos reuincendis elidendisque insani Lutheri cum sua synogoga dogmatibus apprimè conducibiles curas in apertam lucem edi: in quibus vnus hic est S. Pacianus Barcilonensis episcopus. Hic quanta fide conflixerit aduersus Nouatianos, fidelis sui gregis tutor: abundè testabuntur hæc, quae sub gratiosi nominis vmbra, primi emittimus': *D. Paciani Barcilonæ*, Du Tillet's dedication to Gaigny.

34 'perlustratis Francisci I permissu coenobiorum ac aliorum locorum toto regno celebrium, cum adhuc integrae essent, bibliothecis, atque inde peculiari sibi instructo librorum veluti penu copioso, ex quibus pleraque in utroque genere venerandae antiquitatis monumenta publico dedit': de Thou, *Historiarum ... libri* 2: 808 (Bk XLVII, ch. 22).

35 Turner, 'Jean du Tillet,' 49–57; idem, 'Bibliography,' 128–30.

36 See the excellent introduction by Michel François, ed., to *Correspondance du cardinal François de Tournon, 1521–1562, recueillie, publiée et annotée*, Bibliothèque de l'École des Hautes Études, Sciences historiques et philologiques 290 (Paris, 1946), 8–9, 21; and idem, *Le*

of Reims. In 1550 he became one of Catherine de Medicis' six almoners, in 1553 bishop of Saint-Brieuc, and in 1564 bishop of Meaux.[37] After 1558, in keeping with his episcopal status, he turned from scholarly edition to writing treatises (all but one in French) upholding orthodoxy and attacking the Huguenots.[38]

The Younger Jean du Tillet and the Myth of Trojan Origins

The younger Jean's contribution to the destruction of the Trojan myth was made in the preface to his first book: his succinct outline history of the world. Like this Chronicle, Du Tillet's preface survives in two versions – both of which reject the myth of Trojan origins.[39] One is far shorter than the second. It is in Latin, the other in French. The Latin version appeared in print in 1539, as

Cardinal François de Tournon, homme d'état, diplomate, mécène et humaniste (1489–1562), Bibliothèque des Écoles françaises d'Athènes et de Rome 173 (Paris, 1951), esp. 175–93.

37 The story of the elder Jean du Tillet's initially reluctant alliance with the Guise in 1547 (which enabled him to install his brother as the archbishop's prothonotary) is recounted by the Du Tillet's nephew Louis Regnier, lord of La Planche, in his 'Histoire de l'estat de France tant de la république que de la religion sous le règne de François II,' in *Choix de chroniques et mémoires sur l'histoire de France [XVIe siècle] avec notices biographiques*, ed. J.A.C. Buchon, Panthéon littéraire, Littérature française, Histoire (Paris, 1836), 202–421, at 309–10, quoted in Pierre Bayle, *Dictionnaire historique et critique*, new ed., 16 vols. (Paris, 1820), 14: 157–9 n. 15. Gaigny may also have helped the younger Jean gain favour with the Guise. He was on good terms with Cardinal Jean of Lorraine, who resigned the archbishopric of Reims to his nephew Charles in 1538, and held the sees of Lyon, Albi, Agen, and Nantes at the time of his death in 1550: see Gaigny's dedication to Francis I of his edition of *Christiana et docta diui alchimi Auiti Viennensis archiepiscopi, & Claudij Marij Victoris Oratoris Massilensis, poëmata, aliaque non pœnitenda* (Lyon, 1537), [5]ᵛ; and note that Gaigny dedicated to the Cardinal his commentary on the epistles of Paul, published in 1538 and again in 1539, as well as the expanded edition that he published in 1543. For Du Tillet's service as the queen-mother's almoner, see *Lettres de Catherine de Medicis*, ed. Hector de la Ferrière et al., 11 vols., Collection de documents inédits sur l'histoire de France (Paris, 1880–1943), 10: 528. When the younger Jean was named bishop of Saint-Brieuc in 1553, the *greffier* advanced 3893 l. 19 s. t. required to obtain the bulls necessary for his installation: AN, 405 AP 2, a copy dated 13 March 1651, of the division of property left by Jean du Tillet and Jeanne Brinon among their children on 3 September 1571, fol. 17ʳ; the act is analysed in BnF, Chérin 196 (fr. 31758), no. 3878 (Tillet – Du Tillet de Montramé), fols. 5ᵛ–6ʳ. For the expenses connected with the exchange of one bishopric for another, see the letter written by Jean de Langeac, bishop of Avranches (who was trying to obtain Limoges) to François II de Dinteville, bishop of Auxerre and ambassador to Rome, on 8 June 1532, in BnF, Duchesne 97bis, fol. 268ʳ⁻ᵛ; for Jean de Langeac (who entered Limoges, finally, on 22 June 1533), see *Gallia Christiana*, 2: 539, 11: 497.

38 Brown, *Jean du Tillet and the French Wars of Religion*, 14–15 esp. nn. 30–1.

39 Du Tillet had nothing to do with the French translation of the Latin condensation that was first published in 1539; I shall comment on it below.

an appendix to the ten books of Paolo Emili's History of France through the reign of Charles VIII that Michel Vascosan published in Paris.[40] There the work is entitled simply 'Chronicle of the Kings of France, Extended with Greatest Diligence to the Present Times.'[41] The longer French version of the preface (and Chronicle) was not printed until ten years after Du Tillet's death, when, in 1580, Jaques du Puys published it as an appendix to the first authorized edition of the *greffier* Du Tillet's *Recueil des Roys* and *Recueil des honneurs et rangs des grands*.[42] The volume's title describes the work, grandiosely, as an 'Abridged Chronicle of Everything that Has Happened, in War and Otherwise, between Kings and Princes, Republics and Foreign Potentates.' Within the volume it is designated, more modestly and accurately, as an 'Abridged Chronicle of the Political and Military Deeds and Actions of the Kings of France.'[43]

40 *Pavli Aemilii Veronensis, historici clarissimi, de rebus gestis Francorum, ad Christianissi-mum Galliarum Regem Franciscvm Valesium eius nominis primum, libri Decem. Additum est de Regibvs item Francorum Chronicon, ad hæc vsque tempora studiosissimè deductum, cum rerum maximè insignium indice copiosissimo* (Paris, 1539). The privilege of publishing the work for two years was granted to Vascosan (identified rather pretentiously as *chalcographus*) by the Parlement, and was signed by Du Tillet's brother, the *greffier civil*. The copy of this work in BnF, Rés. Fol. L[35]. 23 (2), is the presentation volume, which was kept in the royal library at Fontainebleau. It contains a handsomely decorated armorial frontispiece, painted on parchment; illuminated initials adorn the dedication and the commencement of each book. On the edition, see Ruth Mortimer (with Philip Hofer and William A. Jackson) *Harvard College Library, Department of Printing and Graphic Arts, Catalogue of Books and Manuscripts. Part I: French 16th Century Books*, 2 vols. (Cambridge, Mass., 1964), 1: 241–2 no. 197. The first edition of Emili's History (consisting of the first four books) appeared in 1517.
41 The title page preceding the Chronicle contains the same title (*De Regibus ... deductum*). The separate edition of the Chronicle that Vascosan brought out in 1548 was entitled simply *Chronicon de Regibvs Francorvm, a Pharamvndo vsqve ad Henricvm II.*
42 Jean du Tillet, *Recveil des Roys de France, Levrs Couronne et Maison, Ensemble, le Reng des Grands de France, par Iean du Tillet, Sieur de la Bussiere, Protonotaire & Secretaire du Roy, Greffier de son Parlement. Plvs, Vne Chronique abbregée contenant tout ce qui est aduenu, tant en fait de Guerre, qu'autrement, entre les Roys & Princes, Republiques & Potentats estrangers: Par M. I. du Tillet, Euesques de Meaux freres* (Paris, [1579]–80); this edition was reprinted in 1586 and 1587. From 1580 until 1618 (the date of the last edition of the *greffier*'s writings) the Chronicle appeared in regularly updated versions in the different editions of the *greffier*'s works. For the various editions and their titles, see Brown, *Jean du Tillet and the French Wars of Religion*, 184–5.
43 *Chroniqve abbregee des faicts et gestes politiqves et militaires des Roys de France par Reverend Pere en Diev Maistre Iehan du Tillet Euesque de Meaulx.* Here and later I cite the 1580 ed., where the address to the reader and the preface precede the text of the Chronicle. In the ed. of 1607 (rprt. in 1618), the address and preface are printed in error as pp. [1]33–6, sandwiched between Du Tillet's dedication of his *Recueil des Angloys* to Henry II and the text of this *Recueil*. The address to the reader, which defends epitomes and tries to justify the genre, proclaims the utility of such works for those serving the king. Filled with platitudes, it contains no statement that permits it to be dated; Du Tillet may well have written it in 1536 or 1537.

The complex history of Du Tillet's Chronicle is illuminated by a preface written by 'the Printer' (*L'Imprimeur*) for the French translation of the short Latin version that Galiot du Pré published in Paris in 1549.[44] It contains information that Du Tillet had given about the work, which, more than a decade after writing it, Du Tillet thought needed revision and improvement. The printer began by confessing that he himself had commissioned a translation (and expansion) of the only version of Du Tillet's work that he knew: the Latin Chronicle published in 1539. This was undertaken without Du Tillet's knowledge or consent, and most of this commissioned text (up to the reign of Louis XI) had been set in type before the printer actually came into contact with Du Tillet. Only then did he learn that, twelve or thirteen years earlier, Du Tillet had composed a longer and fuller work in French, which had been condensed, edited, and turned into Latin to accompany Paolo Emili's History. The printer regretted that he was not publishing the original Chronicle, but he was consoled by the misgivings Du Tillet expressed about it. The major flaw, Du Tillet said, lay in the sources he had used. These, he told the printer, were 'only common and vulgar histories, for the most part filled with fables and lies,' and in trying to avoid their errors he had introduced many himself. Since then he had collected a wealth of notes, charters, documents, and authentic evidence, and, further, age had improved his judgment.[45] Hence he hoped to produce a new and improved edition of the entire work, and the printer hinted that, when this happened, he might publish the book – although he still emphasized that the work he was bringing out had its own value and utility.

These comments suggest that the long preface to the Chronicle published in French in 1580 is the original one he wrote in 1536 or 1537. At this remove,

---

44 *La Chronique des Roys de France, puis Pharamond iusques au Roy Henry, second du nom, selon la computation des ans, iusques en l'an mil cinq cens quarante & neuf* (Paris, 1549); the introduction, which precedes the text and is entitled 'L'Imprimeur,' was probably written, not by Du Pré, but rather by the printer René Avril. Du Pré's exclusive five-year privilege was dated 9 July 1549 and signed by Saint Germain; the work was reprinted in 1550. The printer does not mention Du Tillet by name, although he says that the author is 'assez congnu, encores qu'il n'ait iamais voulu y estre nommé & intitulé.' This is curious since, as will be seen, Du Tillet was identified as the author of the Chronicle when it first appeared in 1539.

45 'Et lors estoit l'Autheur aydé seulement des hystoires communes & vulgaires, la plus part fabuleuses et mensongieres, qui en les fuyant luy auroyent faict faire plusieurs faultes, lesquelles apres il a recongnues, & espere amender pour commodité plus grande qu'il a de present d'vn bon nombre d'extraictz, chartres, monumens, & anciennetez authentiques, que par le temps & diligence depuis il a peu recueillir & voir, aussi auec meilleure congnoissance d'affaires que l'aage doit auoir gaignée': *Chronique des Roys de France* (1549 ed.), fol. A ij^v. Du Tillet also confessed that he had been too occupied to correct the various Latin editions; he admitted that the complexities of the work had caused the printer of the first edition to make many mistakes.

this cannot be proven,[46] but evidence in the long preface supports this hypothesis. It is found in the last of the author's three remarks about the Salic laws, a text that the younger Jean edited and published between 1549 and 1557, most likely in 1550.[47] After declaring, first, that the laws are mentioned in a gloss to the Decretum and in the *liure des Feudes*, and, second, that Nicolas of Cusa wrote that he had read them (particularly the clause 'which we observe in France, "that women cannot succeed to the crown"'), the author finally announces, 'I myself have seen some chapters of them' – 'quelques chapitres.'[48] Now Du

46 Le Long's indication that the Dupuy possessed a manuscript copy of the Chronicle, with additions from other histories, is misleading, as are other of his statements regarding Du Tillet's Chronicle: *Bibliotheque historique*, 1: 304 no. 6489*. The book owned by the Dupuy (BnF, Dupuy 679) is an interleaved copy of the printed Chronicle published in 1580, which contains Antoine Favreau's notations and continuation (from 1552 [fol. 529^r] through 1624 [fol. 629^v]); curiously, the manuscript foliation begins with the numbers 33 and 34 (assigned to the first two pages, which are blank); thus the printed title page is numbered 35. The notations are taken from such historians as Claude Fauchet, Papire Masson, and Nicolas Vignier.

47 The edition of various Frankish legal texts and codes, including the *Lex Salica emendata*, was published without the name of editor or publisher, and without place or date: Karl August Eckhardt, ed., *Pactus Legis Salicae*, MGH Leges Nationum Germanicorum 4.1 (1962), 1: xxvii–xxviii (and also xiv–xv, xviii–xx, for the manuscripts used by Du Tillet); also in idem, ed., *Pactus Legis Salicae*, Germanenrechte Neue Folge, Westgermanisches Recht (Göttingen, 1954), 40–1; and see also idem, ed., *Lex Salica. 100 Titel-Text*, Germanenrechte Neue Folge, Westgermanisches Recht (Weimar, 1953), 13, 70–4; J.H. Hessels, with H. Kern, ed., *Lex Salica: The Ten Texts with the Glosses and the Lex Emendata* (London, 1880), v, xvii–xxi; J.M. Pardessus, ed., *Loi salique ou Recueil contenant les anciennes rédactions de cette loi et le texte connu sous le nom de* Lex emendata, *avec des notes et des dissertations* (Paris, 1843), ii–iii, xxvi–xxx, 265, 267; Turner, 'Jean du Tillet,' 52 (noting the book's physical resemblance to Du Tillet's edition of Ansegisus' and Benedict the Deacon's collections of Capitularies, which Jacques Bogard published in Paris in 1549; on Bogard's involvement with Du Tillet's ed. of Pacian, published in 1538, see n. 20 above). In 1573 the collection of laws was reprinted by Jaques du Puy, who seven years later published the first authorized edition of the elder Jean's *Recueils* and the younger Jean's Chronicle.

48 'En quelque sorte que ce soit, les loix faites par eux, furent nommées *Saliques*. desquelles est fait mention en vne glose du Decret, & au liure des Feudes, le Cardinal Cusan escrit les auoir leuës, & mesmement l'article que nous tenons en France, *Que les femmes ne peuuent succeder à la Couronne*. I'en ay aussi veu quelques chapitres': preface to the Chronicle. For the prohibition against female inheritance, see ch. 59, *De alodis*, of the *Pactus Legis Salicae* (editions as in n. 47, above). For the legal manuscripts owned by Nicolas of Cusa, many of which reflect his study of secular law at Padua, see Gerd Heinz-Mohr, and Willehad Paul Eckert, *Das Werk des Nicolaus Cusanus. Eine bibliophile Einführung*, Zeugnisse der Buchkunst, Drittes Buch (Cologne, 1963), 142–4; for his interest in manuscripts and the classics, Ludwig Pralle, *Die Wiederentdeckung des Tacitus. Ein Beitrag zur Geistesgeschichte Fuldas und zur Biographie des jungen Cusanus*, Quellen und Abhandlungen zur Geschichte der Abtei und der Diözese Fulda 17 (Fulda, 1952), 65–8, 91–101. For the *Libri feudorum*, see *Consuetudines feudorum*, ed. Karl Lehmann and Karl August Eckhardt, Bibliotheca Rerum Historicarum,

Tillet would hardly have made such a statement after he had gained access to a complete manuscript of the laws, which had happened by the beginning of October 1549[49] – much less after he had edited them. Nor would anyone acquainted with Du Tillet's work have written this in his name after his death. Indeed, it is surprising that the editor of the Chronicle did not suppress the remark before entrusting the preface to Jaques du Puys for publication in 1580. Thus there seems no question that Du Tillet himself composed the long preface, and that it is the one he wrote in 1536 or 1537. Here I shall refer to him as author of the preface, in which there is no reference whatsoever to the Trojans.

The preface opens with Du Tillet's declaration that, in view of the nature of 'the small summary' of French history he is offering, he will not present a long discussion of the origins of the ancient *Gaulois*. This question he promises to treat elsewhere, and to present for scholarly judgment many passages from the Greek authors who had written most of what was known, who had heard about the *Gaulois* from their neighbours the Galatians (*les Galates*). This testimony, in any case, posed problems, since the Greeks designated as *Celtes* most inhabitants of Germany. Thus, before the time of the Romans there were no texts, Greek or Latin, on which to found a 'good judgment' regarding the nation that later became known for its use of arms. Du Tillet then used Caesar's tripartite division to describe Gaul, and noted that the Romans had made it a province before the advent of the Franks (*Franques*). It was they, Du Tillet said, who established the kingdom that endures to this day, 'for their successors, this name and crown of France.' As to the Franks, he declared it 'marvellously difficult to determine whence they came and to find reliable information about their origins, since everything written about them before imperial times is full of fables and lies invented *ad libitum*.'[50] When Tacitus described the peoples of Germany, Du Tillet declares, he did not mention the Franks, although they were doubtless living there. No more did any other ancient book, and the passage in the letters of Cicero that is often cited simply names them – and this, in any case, may well be a corrupt reading. What can be known is that when the Goths, the Vandals, and other barbarian nations rose in different places against the Roman Empire, the Franks were settled near the Rhine, and little by little occu-

---

Neudrucke 1 (Aalen, 1971), 160, l. 10, (*Das langobardische Lehnrecht*, ch. XXIX ['De filiis natis de matrimonio ad morganaticam contracto']).

49 Eckhardt, *Pactus Legis Salicae*, as cited in n. 47, above.

50 'Il est merueilleusement difficile de dire au vray, d'où ils sortirent, & auoir certain tesmoignage de leur commencement: d'autant que tout ce qui s'en trouue par escrit, deuant le temps des Empereurs, est plein de fables & mensonges controuuées à plaisir.' Cf. n. 45, above ('hystoires communes & vulgaires, la plus part fabuleuses et mensongieres').

pied Holland and Frisia, and then, despite the Romans, passed into Gaul. Du Tillet cited Vopiscus to show that Aurelian captured three hundred of them, and Maximian's panegyric to demonstrate that Probus drove them to a spot whence they escaped in a few ships to traverse Greece and a part of Asia before returning home through the Straits of Gibraltar. Then, invoking Eutropius, Jerome, Agathias, and Procopius, Du Tillet gave a thumbnail history of the little that could be known of the Franks, mentioning Constantine the Great's execution of two of their kings, their alliance with Julian the Apostate, and their passage into Gaul some forty years after the reign of Arcadius and Honorius, when they still controlled the area east of the Rhine, which was thenceforth known as Franconia. Meroveus was their leader – or king – and he came to an agreement with the Romans and fought against Attila under Aetius. For a time the Franks alternated between being friends and (more often) enemies of the Romans. Then, under Justinian, they concluded a treaty that permitted them to live in Gaul. Most of the Franks lived near the River Sal, and, for whatever reason, their laws were called Salic – which prompted the reflections on the Salic laws that I have just discussed. For the moment, Du Tillet confessed, all he could discover, beyond the few references to the Salic law that he cited, was that the Emperor Conrad entitled himself Salic because he was of the ancient house of the French. Noting that the names of the first kings of France were German, and the language currently in use corrupt Latin or *Romain*, Du Tillet then passed to the question (in his opinion difficult) of the language spoken earlier in Gaul. Here he cited Julius Caesar, Strabo, and Tacitus, whose testimony had convinced him that no single language was used throughout Gaul. Because of the many German words and usages still found in France (of which he offered examples), Du Tillet proposed that in the parts of Gaul near Italy and Germany, a tongue like German was used. He ended by presenting the German roots and analysing the meanings of the different names borne by Frankish kings, from Pharamund (*'Vvaarmund*, homme veritable') and Meroveus (*'Meieruuig*, par dessus les autres en reputation') to Frederick (*'Fridenreich*, paisible, ou qui a puissance de donner paix').

The brief Latin preamble to the condensed version of Du Tillet's Chronicle published in 1539 is very different from the French, emphasizing, as it does, the Franks, not the Gauls. It, too, however, makes clear the author's belief in the German origin of the French, and his lack of concern for or interest in any more remote roots. Here Du Tillet proclaimed that 'the people of the Franks, [sprung] from the German nobility, coming to Gaul founded their kingdom.' They were so great in spirit and virtuous that they never encountered any people whom they did not attack fiercely in war or, if provoked, did not repel with great honour. They conquered Gaul, with which almost all nations of the world contended, not for empire and glory, but for safety and life. They were the first people to rule over Germany, which neither the Romans nor any other powerful people could either tame or conquer. Du Tillet alluded to the Trojans only as a means of further elevating the Franks. 'There is,' he continued, 'no flourishing and noble kingdom or principate in Europe which does not now boast that its blood comes from the Franks, and flaunt the insignia of the lilies – just as long ago everyone who was most noble proudly claimed a Trojan origin.' Having thus cavalierly dismissed the search for Trojan descent as pretentious and outmoded, Du Tillet announced that he was purposely omitting the kings whom Berosus commemorated because he wished to record nothing that has not been handed down in uncorrupted testimony of past deeds. He declared it his chief aim to reveal in as clear and logical order as possible the absolute truth (*verissima*), which he had garnered from huge tomes and old fables, among which the truth lay scattered and dispersed. Thus he proclaimed that the Franks, having been ruled by dukes (or 'little kings' [*Reguli*]), had as their first and most powerful king Pharamund.[51] This having been established, the Chronicle begins, with Pharamund's reign assigned just a single entry, the establishment of the Salic law in 423.[52]

Du Tillet's condensed preface and Chronicle appeared as an annex to the first complete edition of Paolo Emili's History of France. Emili had died in 1529 before finishing the tenth and last book (ending in 1490), which Daniel Zavarisius of Verona (who described himself as Emili's *propinquus*) completed from Emili's notes in Italy, and which Pierre Danès forwarded to the publisher,

51 'Francorum gens è Germanica nobilitate in Galliam veniens, regnum condidit: quæ tanta fuit animi magnitudine & virtute, vt nullus vsquam populus fuerit, quem ferociter bello non appetierit, aut lacessita, magna cum laude non repulerit. Gallias enim debellauit, cum quibus non pro Imperio & gloria, sed pro salute atque vita omnes fere orbis nationes armis contenderunt. Ea prima toti pariter Germaniæ imperauit: quam neque Romani, neque alii quantumuis potentes, non modò domare, sed nec vincere potuerunt. Nullum porrò in Europa florens ac nobile regnum est, vel principatus, qui non vt olim à Troianis originem duccre nobilissimus quisque gloriabatur, ita à Francis sanguinem trahere se iactet, & Liliorum insignia circumferat. Reges quos Berosus ordine commemorat, sciens prætermitto, nolens quicquam literis mandare, quod non incorruptis rerum gestarum monumentis sit traditum. In primis enim operam dedi, & id maximè studui, vt quæ adhuc immensis voluminibus & veteribus fabulis dispersa iactabantur, ea paucis & certo ordine comprehensa, verissimáque, quantum fieri potuit, in lucem emitterem. Franci igitur, quibus Duces antea, aut, si mauis, Reguli imperitabant, Pharamundum primum Regem potentissimum habuerunt.' This text appears on the reverse of the title page of the Chronicle.
52 'Lex Salica hoc tempore condita fuit.' In contrast, there are seven entries for Pharamund's reign (some of them, admittedly, repetitive) in the French chronicle that was published in 1580.

Michel Vascosan, in Paris.[53] Danès had once been Jean de Gaigny's teacher, and it may well have been through Gaigny, via Danès, that Vascosan learned of Du Tillet's Compendium.[54] There seems no doubt that Du Tillet was responsible for condensing his Chronicle and turning it into Latin. Not only did Du Tillet indicate in 1549 that he felt responsible for the work by apologizing for the deficiencies of the first edition and his failure to correct subsequent ones. Equally important, although Du Tillet's name appeared on no title page in the edition of 1539, he received full credit for the work in Vascosan's dedication of the book to Francis I. There Vascosan described Du Tillet as 'commendable no less for the integrity of his manners and life than for his knowledge of eloquence and of both Latin and French literature.' Du Tillet, Vascosan said, had written the Chronicle 'with great effort, the greatest care, and much vigilance, basing it on French and Latin authors, and particularly Emili.' The Chronicle would be useful, Vascosan declared, because reading a summary in advance would make it easier to understand and remember a detailed history and appreciate its rhetoric.[55]

Du Tillet's work indeed attracted lavish praise, most remarkably in Jean Bodin's *Methodus* of 1566.[56] The work was reprinted with Emili's History in

53 In his dedication to Francis I, Vascosan described Danès as 'viro cum morum candore amabili, tum verò vtriusque linguæ cognitione admirando': Emili, *De rebus gestis ... Libri decem*, fol. A iii[r]. Zavarisius explained his role in completing Emili's unfinished tenth book in his address to the reader at the end of the book: ibid., fol. 248[r].

54 Gaigny referred to Danès as 'præceptor meus linguarum iuxta ac bonarum disciplinarum peritissimus,' in the address to readers that he wrote for his *Psalmi Davidici septvaginta qvinqve, in lyricos versvs, servata ecclesiasticæ versionis ueritate & Hebræorum uarietate, redacti* (Paris, 1547), fol. [* ij][v]. Explaining the approach he had used in versifying the psalms of David and distinguishing it from those taken by the two Germans and single Frenchman (Marc-Antoine Flaminio) who had turned the psalms into verse, Gaigny said that he had shown his own work to Cardinal Jean du Bellay, to the poet Salmon Macrin, and to Pierre Danès two years before Flaminio's renditions had appeared (they were published in 1545), and that Du Bellay and Macrin had encouraged him to publish his translations despite the existence of the others.

55 'Porrò quoniam ad historiæ faciliorem intellectum, & memoriæ subsidium, aduertenda etiam orationis ornamenta, denique ad rerum certitudinem conducit summatim prius legere historiam obseruata in primis temporum ratione, adiecimus Chronicon de rebus gestis Francorum, magno studio, summa cura, multísque vigiliis cum ex gallicis latinisque aliis scriptoribus, tum ex Aemilio maxime desumptum, à Iohanne Tilio viro non minus ob morum ac vitæ integritatem, quàm ob fecundiæ & literaturæ vtriusque peritiam commendabili': Emili, *De rebus gestis ... Libri decem*, fol. A iii[r].

56 Advising readers to start out with summaries before turning to longer works, Bodin declared, 'consimiliter de historia Francorum iudico, quam Io. Tillius breuissime complexus est vno libello. hunc igitur prius legendum putem quam Paulum Æmilium: & Xiphilinum, quam Dionem': *Methodvs*, 23; see also 454 (where he recommends the Chronicle – and also

1543, 1544, 1548, 1550, 1551 (and in Basel in 1569 and 1601), and as a separate volume in 1548.[57] As has been seen, in 1549 Galiot du Pré brought out a French translation.[58] The surest proof of the translation's popularity is its publication in pirated editions in Rouen in 1551 and 1552.[59] Du Pré, in high dudgeon, obtained a royal prohibition and privilege (for six years) on 15 June 1552, and in 1553 published what was to be his last edition of the work.[60] Two cheap

Trithemius' *Compendium*!). Bodin's publisher Martin Le Jeune was the son-in-law of Jacques Bogard (who supervised publication of Du Tillet's edition of Pacian in 1538); he took over management of Bogard's establishment in 1549: Renouard, *Répertoire*, 40, 231, and see above, n. 20, and the accompanying text. Le Long praised both the short and long versions, in *Bibliotheque historique*, 1: 304 no. 6489*. His assessment is based in part on that of Scevole de Sainte-Marthe, in his *Eloges*, 201 ('Et quoy que cet ouurage ne soit qu'vne espece de Chronique abregée, si est-ce que l'on peut dire auec raison qu'il n'y manque rien de ce que l'on peut souhaitter, & que c'est en son genre vne piece parfaite').

57 The edition of 1543 was issued with a new privilege, dated 1 December 1543; Vascosan published it both for himself and Galiot du Pré. In 1550, Vascosan joined to Emili's History and Du Tillet's Chronicle (to which he added entries for Francis I's reign) Arnold Ferron's continuation of Emili's History to the reign of Henry II. Sixtus Henricpetrus published Emili, Ferron, and Du Tillet (continued to 1569), at Basel in 1569; in 1601 Jacobus and Sebastian Henricpetrus brought out a similar edition, which included Jacobus Henricpetrus' continuation of Emili's and Ferron's narrative to the reign of Henry IV and of Du Tillet's Chronicle to 1600.

58 This edition included catalogues of popes and emperors and four conventional and thoroughly ordinary 'portraits' purporting to represent Pharamund, Francis I, Saint Peter, and Charlemagne. In the translation of the preface, 'la maison de France' was substituted for 'the people of the Franks' (*Francorum gens*) as the agent that, sprung from the German nobility, established a kingdom in Gaul (here, *es Gaules*). The translator rendered *Franci* as *Françoys* rather than *Francs*, thus diminishing the distance and difference between the early invaders and the current inhabitants of France. An added phrase emphasized that the conquerors had established their rule 'over this country' – as well as 'over Germany,' and an added sentence declared that no one before had ravaged 'that country' (*ce pays là*), 'which until the present day is found in subjection only to the line of France' – leaving it unclear whether 'that country' was Gaul or Germany. 'Hunibald and the others' replace 'Berosus' as the authors who listed the 'old kings' (here 'old French kings' [*les vieulx Roys, Françoys*]) who could not be authenticated 'by antique monuments and reliable histories.'

59 The publisher, Martin Le Mesgissier, altered the first and most important part of the title to read, *La Chronique des Roys de France, Et des cas memorables aduenuz depuis Pharamond, iusques au Roy Henry second du nom, selon l'ordre du temps & supputation des ans continuez, iusques en l'an mil cinq centz cinquante & vn* (BnF, 8° L[35]. 48A); the Chronicle was printed by Jehan Petit. A privilege dated 18 April 1551, after Easter, appears on the reverse of the title page. In 1992 Le Megissier's edition of 1552 was missing at the BnF (8° L[35]. 48B).

60 *La Chronique des Roys de France, puis Pharamond iusques au Roy Henry, second du nom, selon la computation des ans iusques en l'an mil cinq cens cinquante & trois*, followed by a Catalogue of popes from Saint Peter to Julius III, and of emperors from Octavian to Charles V (BnF, 8° L[35]. 48C). The privilege of 9 July 1549 is printed on the reverse of the title page, and followed by the royal letter of 15 June 1552.

imitations, published in 1556 in Rouen, and in 1557 in Lyon, testify to the reputation Du Tillet's Chronicle had acquired, but suggest that the volumes' editors were less interested in accuracy than Du Tillet's earlier publishers, since both editions began by declaring that 'the French, sprung from the Trojans (as the historians say),' had left the destroyed city to settle in the west.[61] In 1575 the Parisian printer Jean d'Ongoys received the exclusive right (for six years) to publish Du Pré's French version, but in the event Ongoys brought out just a single edition, illustrated with a stylized, imaginary portrait of each king.[62] Finally, in 1580, Jaques Du Puy resurrected and published Du Tillet's original French Chronicle, continued here to 1550. Until 1618, the date of the last edition of the *greffier*'s works, it regularly appeared, continually updated, as a supplement to his *Recueils* and other writings.

As the history of the publication of Du Tillet's Chronicle shows, even before the appearance of the full preface in 1580 the abbreviated preamble had disseminated to a wide audience the notions that searching for Trojan origins was both futile and silly, that the Franks sprang from the nobility of Germany, and that such fabulous sources as Berosus were to be rejected in favour of authentic memorials of the past. Du Tillet was not responsible for the French translation of 1549, but the replacement of Berosus with 'Hunibauld & les autres' did not change the thrust of what he wished to convey – although it does suggest that by 1549 the French were thought more likely to recognize the folly of Trithemius' creation than the stupidity of Annius of Viterbo's. It is ironic (but indicative of the work's wide appeal and reception) that, when Trithemius' *Compendium* was published in Paris in 1539, it was dedicated to Guillaume Poyet, who had faithfully represented the elder Jean du Tillet in at least two suits in the 1520s.[63]

61 'Les Francoys Issus des Troyens, ainsi que dient les historiens, sen vindrent apres la destruction de Troye': *Brefues narrations des Actes et Faictz Memorables, aduenus depuis Pharamond, premier Roy des François, tant en France, Espagne, Engleterre, que Normendie Selon l'ordre du temps & supputation des ans, distinctement continuées iusques à lan mil cinq cens cinquante & six* (Rouen, 1556); *Les Faits Memorables, advenvs depvis Pharamond, premier Roy des François, tant en France, Espagne, Angleterre, qu'Italie, selon l'ordre des annees, iusques à l'an 1557* (Lyon, 1557).
62 *La Chroniqve des Roys de France, Pvis Pharamond, ivsqves av Roy Henry, troisiesme, selon la computation des ans, iusques en l'an mil cinq cens soixante & quinze, auec l'effigie de chacun Roy, representee au plus pres du naturel* ... (Paris, 1575) (BnF, 8º L35. 48D). In the same year, Ongoys brought out his own Chronicle 'of the Facts, Deeds, and illustrious Lives of the Kings of France,' which contained the same series of portraits, first employed in Lyon in 1546 by Balthazar Arnoullet, and reused in numerous albums and histories of the kings of France: Mortimer, *Harvard College Library... Catalogue*, 1: 239–40 no. 194, 256–7 no. 208, and 2: 614–15 no. 501.
63 *Compendium siue Breuiarivm primi volvminis Annalium sive historiarvm, de origine Regum &*

According to the preface to the French translation of 1549, Du Tillet had acknowledged apologetically having used 'only common and vulgar histories, for the most part filled with fables and lies.' This echoed the declaration in the short Latin version of 1539 that Du Tillet had had to work with huge old tomes, filled with fables. Both these declarations exaggerate. In the longer version, remember, he cited a range of reliable authorities, from Caesar and Tacitus to Flavius Vopiscus and Jerome. In the 1530s these sources were readily available. German scholars had been using them for decades, and Emili cited some of them. Du Tillet's statements suggest, rather, an inclination to impress his readers by magnifying the challenges he had faced.

Vascosan offered a different, but rather vague, assessment in 1539. Lauding Du Tillet's work, the publisher declared that the Chronicle was based on French and Latin works, and particularly Emili's History. No more than Du Tillet's deprecatory statement is Vascosan's fully accurate – particularly if he is read as suggesting that Du Tillet's position on Trojan origins follows Emili's. I shall discuss Emili's position more fully elsewhere. Suffice it to say here that, although Emili did not endorse the Trojan myth, and although he hinted pointedly to his readers that he did not believe a word of it, he commenced his History with a full recitation of the traditional account. Du Tillet, in contrast, would have no part of the story. Further, the solidest piece of documentary evidence that Emili offered was a letter of Cicero which Emili mistakenly interpreted as containing a reference to the Franks. In contrast, in his long preface, Du Tillet minimized the significance of Cicero's epistle and suggested that its text might be corrupt. So, although Du Tillet was certainly familiar with Emili's work and profited from it, neither version of his preface repeated what was found in Emili's introduction to his History.

The Du Tillet Brothers' Sources

What sources, then, did the younger Jean du Tillet consult for his Chronicle? Unquestionably, he must have wrestled with medieval chronicles, the fabrications of Annius and Trithemius, and the recent histories that paid homage to French traditions and indulged the fancies of noble and princely patrons. But he also had easily available to him guides to the reliable sources. I have not been able to trace each of his citations to an intermediary secondary source, and he doubtless read ancient and medieval sources that were simply mentioned in

gentis Francorum, ad reverendissimum in Christo patrem & principem dominum Laurentium Episcopum Wirtzpurgensem, orientalisque Franciæ ducem Ioannis Tritemii Abbatis (Paris, 1539); the dedication was written by François Morin, who addressed Poyet as chancellor and praised his learning. For Du Tillet's relations with Poyet, see Brown, 'Greffe civil,' 331.

books he had read. However, it seems to me exceedingly likely that, in preparing the two prefaces to his Chronicle, he was inspired by the works of three German writers. First, Heinrich Bebel, who composed an Oration to King Maximilian, 'In Praise of Him and Germany,' a supplementary letter, 'Demonstrating that the Germans are Indigenous,' and a treatise, 'Concerning the Praise, Antiquity, Empire, Victories, and Deeds of the Old Germans.'[64] In each of these works Bebel called into question or denounced outright the myth of the Franks' Trojan origins; in the last one he derided Berosus' Hunnus, and the notion that the Germans came from Scythia. He mocked the work of Robert Gaguin and Enea Silvio Piccolomini, and although he offered no detailed solution to the problem of Frankish origins himself, he insisted on their German roots and cited a host of ancient authorities whom he had explored. Most important, he devoted an entire chapter of his treatise to demonstrating the tradition of German liberty, and another to establishing that the Germans were 'most noble [*nobilissimi*].' He declared that almost all the most illustrious families of Italy, recognizing the nobility of the Germans, wanted to trace their own nobility back to German roots. As to the ancient Romans, they were cutthroats and robbers (*latrones et prædones*), and those who fled from Troy were traitors (*proditores*). In the ancient Germans, in contrast, resided true nobility (*sincera nobilitas*); they possessed renown of lineage and the virtue of most humble men (*natalium claritudo, virtus hominum humilimorum*). Such words as Bebel's might well have led Du Tillet to declare that the people of the Franks (*Francorum gens*) was sprung from German nobility, and, substituting 'Franks' for 'Germans,' to proclaim that all the noblest yearned to trace their origin to the Franks rather than, as once was the case, to the Trojans.

The second source that I think Du Tillet likely (and the translator of 1549 – and, as will be seen, the older Jean du Tillet – virtually certain) to have known is the short work 'On the Origin and Abodes of the Early Franks,' which Count Hermann of Neuenar dedicated to Charles V not long after his accession in 1519. This treatise was published with a collection of other sources relating to German history, ranging from Widukind to Wimpfeling, in Basel in 1532.[65] The essay is less didactic and far wittier than Bebel's work. Count Hermann's chief aim was to inspire the new emperor, but his desire to discredit Abbot Trithemius and Hunibald moved him virtually as strongly. In the dedication to his work, he emphasized German liberty (and the freedom of speech this should

---

64 For Bebel's work, see nn. 5 and 9, above.

65 For Hermann's work, in *Vvitichindi Saxonis Rervm*, see n. 6, above. At the end of the dedication (ibid., 102), Hermann wished for the Emperor, 'ut imperium tuum fausto omine inchoatum, optimo felicissimoque fine concludat.'

entail); he mentioned the tripartite division of Gaul, the virtue of the Germans. He stressed particularly the nobility of all Germany, which he said stemmed from the Franks. Echoing Bebel's sentiments, he derided those who sought their roots in Rome. 'If they only knew that there was no nobility in Italy that the Germans had not brought there, they would not look for water from a rivulet and disregard its source,' he announced. The princes of Austria, Burgundy, Brabant, and Holland were all descended, he said, from the Franks.[66] In the body of the work, he devoted his efforts chiefly to attacking Hunibald. He did invoke some authorities, accusing Gregory of Tours, Regino of Prüm, and Sigebert of Gembloux of accepting the Trojan myth (and Gregory and Sigebert of deriving the Franks' name from *libertas*); he cited Tacitus, Trebellius Pollio, Procopius, and the Salian and Ripuarian laws.[67] But his chief purpose was to drive home two points. First, that the Germans were indigenous and not Trojans. Second, that only desire for glory led people to try to create ancient roots for themselves. In poking fun at the story of the flight from Troy, he commented cynically, 'if indeed the Trojan War ever occurred – which for quite persuasive reasons Dio Prusensis denies, relying on the sacred history of the Egyptians.' Here he was invoking an author who was rarely cited (although Jean Lemaire de Belges had, understandably, devoted considerable attention to refuting his ideas). To Dio, the senior Jean du Tillet would appeal in the second recension of his *Recueil des Roys* in (curiously) questioning the existence of Troy itself, not simply the Trojan War.[68]

66 'Ex hac nimirum gente [Francorum] tanquam ex equo Troiano totius Germaniæ nobilitas prosilijt; neque enim altius suos auos numerat ulla insignis familia: quum primum ad Ansgisum Maioremdomus uentum est, ibi uelut ad ancoram sacram hæretur. Nec nos mouet quorundam stultitia, suam originem ad Ro. referentium, qui si scirent nullam in Italia nobilitatem esse, quam non Germani eò aduexerint, non haurirent aquam è riuulis, ipso fonte contempto. Iam satis constat, maiores tuos Austriæ, Burgundiæ, Brabantiæ, Hollandiæque principes è Francorum sanguine fuisse propagatos, neque hoc augustum nomen tuum fortuito obuenisse tibi putaueris, quandoquidem hæreditaria quadam successione id in te deriuatum scirc dcbcs': ibid., 101; the passage is accompanied by the marginal note: *Nobilitas omnis à Francis.*

67 Agrippa von Nettesheim attacked the same writers as did Bebel (in the same order), in his *De Incertitudine & Vanitate Scientiarum & Artium, atque excellentia Verbi Dei, declamatio* (Paris, 1531), fol. 23[r]. The work was written between 1524 and 1526, and it seems to me possible that Agrippa knew Bebel's work. On Agrippa, see Charles G. Nauert, Jr, *Agrippa and the Crisis of Renaissance Thought,* Illinois Studies in the Social Sciences 55 (Urbana, 1965), esp. 81, 98–9.

68 'si Troianum bellum fuisse aliquando (quod pulcherrimis rationibus negat Dion Prusensis, sacra Ægyptiorum fultus historia)': Hermann, in *Vvitichindi Saxonis Rervm* (see n. 6, above), 103. In his eleventh Discourse, Dio Cocceianus (or Chrysostom) (40–*ca* 112) contested the

It is the third source that seems most clearly to have influenced the younger Jean du Tillet – as it surely did the older. This is Beatus Rhenanus' magisterial work *Three Books of German Matters*, dedicated to Charles V's brother Ferdinand, king of Bohemia and Hungary, in 1531, published by Froben in Basel in that year, and republished in 1551.[69] The parallels between the works of Beatus Rhenanus and the younger Jean du Tillet are striking. They cite the same sources, and often the same passages.[70] Beatus Rhenanus refers to the Franks as *nobilissima gens*;[71] he attacks Berosus as well as (and more often than) Hunibald;[72] he spends an entire chapter debunking the relevance to the Franks of Cicero's reference in his letter to *Francones*.[73] In a passage that, as will be seen, seems to have impressed the older Du Tillet, Beatus Rhenanus, investigating the language spoken by the 'old Franks,' called attention to the manuscript of a German translation of the Gospels that he had discovered at Freising; he gave numerous excerpts from it, and cited other examples of liturgical books that had been translated into German.[74]

fact that the Greeks had captured Troy; his *Oratio ad Ilienses Ilii captivitatem non fuisse* was published in Paris, first by Felix Baligault in 1494, and shortly afterwards by Antoine Denidel for Robert de Gourmont: Marie-Léontine-Catherine Pellechet, *Catalogue général des incunables des bibliothèques publiques de France*, 3 vols., Ministère de l'Instruction publique et des beaux-arts (Paris, 1897–1909), 3: 158–9. Jean Lemaire de Belges devoted the final chapter of the second book of his *Illustrations de Gaule et Singularitez de Troye* to a detailed refutation of Dio's position: *Œuvres* (see n. 11, above), 2: 236–44. See Du Tillet, *Recueil des Roys* (1580), 1 ('Si Troye fut [que Dion Prusensis a denié]'). Belleforest attacked Dio in his 'Diverses considerations svr l'origine des Francoys,' with which he prefaced his *Les grandes Annales, et histoire generale de France, des la venve des Francs en Gavle, ivsqves av Regne dv Roy Tres-Chrestien Henry III.*, 2 vols. (Paris, 1579), 1:A^r–v.

69 I have used for this paper the ed. of 1551, *Beati Rhenani Selestadiensis Rervm Germanicarvm Libri Tres, ab ipso avtore diligenter reuisi & emendati, addito memorabilium rerum Indice accuratissimo. Quibus præmissa est Vita Beati Rhenani, à Iohanne Sturmio eleganter conscripta* (Basel, 1551).
70 Note, e.g., Beatus Rhenanus' reference to the Panegyric to Maximinian (ibid., 29), to Flavius Vopiscus and the capture of 300 Franks (ibid., 32), to the murder of two Frankish kings (ibid., 31); to Julius Caesar and Tacitus on the languages that were spoken (ibid., 116); and his discussion of the River Sal (ibid., 131).
71 Ibid., 28; see also 39, 112 (*nobilissimum regnum*).
72 Ibid., 27 ('Neque enim Hunnibaldos & similes scriptores, si dijs placet, sequar, quorum somnijs nihil inanius'); 39, 191 192 (Berosus).
73 Ibid., 103–5.
74 On the manuscript of Otfrid von Weissenburg's work, see *Evangelienharmonie: Vollständige Faksimile-Ausgabe des Codex Vindobonensis 2687 der Österreichischen Nationalbibliothek*, ed. Hans Butzmann, Codices Selecti Phototypice Impressi 30 (Graz, 1972), esp. 13; and Natalia Daniel, *Handschriften des zehnten Jahrhunderts aus der Freisinger Dombibliothek: Studien über Schriftcharakter und Herkunft der nachkarolingischen und ottonischen Handschriften einer bayerischen Bibliothek*, Münchener Beiträge zur Mediävistik und Renaissance-

The Elder Jean du Tillet and the Myth of Trojan Origins

The writings of these and other learnedly iconoclastic German scholars were soon being read in France. The speed with which knowledge of their work spread is witnessed by the number of contemporary writers (including Beatus Rhenanus) cited by the opposing lawyers in 1535 in a suit between the *procureur général du roi* and the cathedral chapter of Toul over a jurisdictional issue involving the exact boundary between France and the Empire.[75] The royal lawyer Montholon cited a number of recent historians, relying most extensively on Paolo Emili. His opponent, Longueval, responded by producing a dazzling array of authorities, medieval and modern. The case was argued before the Parlement de Paris, where the *greffier civil* Jean du Tillet would certainly have heard, or heard of, the arguments that were exchanged. Whether he was already familiar with the German authors who were cited is unknown, but, like his younger brother, he came to know them and their works well in the following years.

Given the younger Jean du Tillet's attitude towards the Trojan myth, it is not surprising that his older brother rejected the legend. He did so first in the *Recueil des Roys* that he wrote for King Henry II and presented to him between 1553 and 1555.[76] This work opened with a dedication to the king and then presented a brief chapter describing the three royal houses of France, and setting forth and justifying the scope of the research whose fruits he was presenting. He entitled the introductory chapter, a bit grandiosely (and imprecisely), 'Genealogies and marriages of the kings, princes, and princesses, dowers of the queens and princesses of the house of France, during the rule of the third line, and of some houses founded by it.' What Du Tillet was actually doing in the first part of the book was presenting sketches of the reigns of individual kings and brief discussions of the princely houses that had sprung from the royal, commencing with Hugues Capet and ending with Henry II himself. In the second half of his work, he dealt with a range of topics concerning the monarchy and its officials, beginning with the 'tiltres, grandeur et excellence des Roys et

---

Forschung 11 (Munich, 1973), 63–5. On Beatus Rhenanus' discovery of the manuscript, see also D'Amico, *Theory and Practice*, 198–9.

75 Jean Rigault, 'La frontière de la Meuse: l'utilisation des sources historiques dans un procès devant le Parlement de Paris en 1535,' *Bibliothèque de l'École des chartes* 106 (1945–6): 80–99.

76 Several presentation copies and other manuscript copies of this work are found in the BnF: fr. 2854; fr. 18653; fr. 18654 (lacking inventories); also fr. 2050; and fr. 6491. Another, particularly carefully prepared, is in Saint Petersburg, National Library of Russia [hereinafter SP], Fr. F. v. IV, no. 8/1.

Royaulme de France,' and concluding with the 'cheualiers de l'ordre du Roy et estat de cheualerye.' Du Tillet appended to virtually every chapter an inventory listing the documents he had consulted, and these catalogues impressively reveal the extent of his research and his dedicated attention to documentary sources.

Since Du Tillet began his work at the accession of Hugues Capet in 987, he apparently felt that it would be inappropriate to treat the realm's earliest beginnings at the commencement of his work. He finally turned to the subject at the end of his survey of kings and princely houses, but the transition to the topical chapters of the second section was inept.

Du Tillet simply plunged in, beginning 'Pour clorre ce chapitre [dealing with Henry II], Nest a obmectre L'ancienne facon des francois, qui achaptoient leurs femmes ...' The chapter continued with a survey of marriage customs that ranged from ancient Greece and the Old Testament, to Germany and Merovingian France.[77] Here Du Tillet cited historians ancient and medieval, including Tacitus, Gregory of Tours, and Aimoin, as well as the Salic and Roman law – it was an impressive performance. But what logical connection Du Tillet thought this subject had with the list of five acts concerning Henry II which preceded the survey is hard to fathom, although it is perfectly true that, from the beginning, the kings of France (like their subjects) had married to produce successors. It is also true that the end of the first part in a sense responded to the topics he had announced for the initial chapter of his work: genealogies, marriages, and dowers.

The termination of the chapter and the transition to what followed was as awkward as the bridge between Henry II and marital rites. Du Tillet ended by announcing, 'Auant que passer oultre a la poursuyte de la maison de france, ne sera Impertinent parler de l'origine et nom des francois.' Perhaps not *impertinent*, but hardly what a reader expected. In any case, Du Tillet seized the opportunity to present a chapter entitled 'De lorigine et nom des Francois.' Here Du Tillet developed at some length his own ideas about the Franks' beginnings.

Du Tillet commences by declaring that those who had called the French true Germans by origin had more honoured them than those who linked them with Troy. Why? Because of the sterling character and desire for liberty that had once characterized Germany, and that would continue to do so if Germany were united (which affords him an opportunity to blame the division of religion for Germany's present condition). Expatiating on the Germans' love of freedom and their victories over the Romans, he concludes that 'this suffices to persuade France to acknowledge its beginning from Germany, since it can have no other that would be better.' This account of France's past, he says, is more likely to be

---

77 SP, Fr. F. v. IV, No. 8/1, fols. 115ᵛ–120ʳ.

true ('has a better appearance') than the other story, 'which on the face of it is filled with dreams and fables,' since it is based on authoritative sources (*histoires Receues*). Du Tillet gives no proof himself, but rather refers his readers to Beatus Rhenanus, and also to Althamer, the learned editor of and commentator on Tacitus' *Germania*.[78] He thus takes the question of French origins as settled and resolved, saying that, since Beatus Rhenanus and Althamer have presented the evidence 'faithfully and learnedly,' there is no reason to fill his *Recueil* with repetitions. Rather, Du Tillet eloquently advances the theory that the similarity of German customs and language to those of the French provides a pattern for analysing and understanding the effects of conquest on the conquered people, and the changes that occurred 'until the passage of time mixed the two peoples.'

Du Tillet's emphasis on the fusion of conquered and conqueror reveals his own irenic aspirations, which would be tested by the religious and social conflicts of the coming decades (and lead others to emphasize the animosities between the Gauls and Franks). But Du Tillet did not see the Germans as enemy or threat, and in the *Recueil* he proceeded to give a balanced analysis, based largely on Tacitus, of the ancient Germans' ways, arguing that the Salic and Gombettan laws revealed striking similarities between the Franks and Germans. Noting the presence of old German words in these Latin laws, he took up the subject of language and the presence of German in old manuscripts he had consulted. He cited particularly a volume that he (or his younger brother) had clearly seen in the cathedral library at Langres, which he described as 'a very old book of concordances of the four Gospels, with one page in Latin and the other a translation into the old German tongue, which the ancient French brought to Gaul when they conquered it.'[79] Thus he mimicked Beatus Rhenanus. Whereas the German scholar had learnedly invoked a manuscript of Otfrid von Weissenburg's concordance that he had found at Freising, Du Tillet,

78 SP, Fr. F. v. IV, no. 8/1, fols. 116^v–117^r ('Cecy suffise pour confirmer la france a aduouer son commancement de la Germanie, ne le pouuant auoir plus digne. Ceste part a meilleure apparence, que l'autre, qui d'elle mesmes paroist estre songee et fabuleuse, n'ayant conuenance aux histoires Receues, Lauctorite desquelles en plusieurs endroictz y Repugne, Ainsi que fidelement et doctement ont nagueres deduict Rhenan, et Althamer, dont Ie me passe, pour n'emplyr ce Recueil de Redictes'). Paul Joachimsen discusses the commentaries of Beatus Rhenanus (1519) and Andreas Althamer (1529, 1536), in 'Tacitus im deutschen Humanismus,' *Neue Jahrbücher für das klassische Altertum* 27 (1911): 697–717, at 708–13. In his second ed. of Tacitus' works, published in 1544 (Basel, 1544; 421–31), Beatus Rhenanus considerably expanded his commentary on the *Germania*, saying that he would have written at even greater length had it not been for the commentaries he had heard Andreas Althamer had composed; on the ed., see Maria Valenti, *Saggio di una bibliografia delle edizioni di Tacito nei secoli XV – XVII* (Rome, 1951), 8.

79 For this manuscript of Tatian's concordance, see Peter Ganz, 'MS. Junius 13 und die

nothing daunted, cited another similar concordance, this one by Tatian, that he himself knew. Having displayed his erudition, Du Tillet returned to his theme, announcing his belief that German continued to be used in France until the division of the Empire after the death of Louis the Pious.

Continuing his comparative survey of customs, Du Tillet briefly discussed marriage, a topic he had already considered exhaustively. Now, however, he ends his survey by declaring that he will treat further similarities between the French and Germans as he discusses different topics, 'pour confirmer l'opinion quilz sont originairement partys d'Allemaigne.' Having briefly sketched what he thought could be known of the Franks' movements within Germany, Du Tillet attempts to explain the emergence of the name Frank by hypothesizing that the German word signifying 'free' was simply adopted by a confederation formed by various people, to identify themselves and distinguish themselves from others; to buttress his hypothesis, he points to the Protestants' designation of themselves by this new name. He acknowledges that this explanation is the only one he can suggest to account for the sudden emergence of a people as strong as the Franks quickly showed themselves to be. Having said a few words about the conflicts between the Franks and the Romans, he again refers his readers to Beatus Rhenanus, who had assembled, he says, the relevant testimony of Greek and Roman writers. These writers all focused on Roman successes, he declares, whereas those of the Franks (which he believes were probably impressive enough) were never recorded. He rejects the testimony of such historians as Heligast, Clodomir, and Hunibald; to read them, he judges, is to spurn them and reveal them to be 'forgez a plaisir' (although he does not say when or by whom). Although he has just announced that the story of the Franks' conquest 'n'est de ma matiere,' he ends with praise of their victory: the occupation of Gaul and the lordships the Franks established there, acknowledged by all and lasting to the present, manifest the honour and profit that accrued to them from the wars with the Romans.[80] Du Tillet then passes to the first substantive topical chapter devoted to the rights and prerogatives of the kings of France, which (like the earlier ones centred on individual kings and

---

althochdeutsche Tatian-Übersetzung,' *Beiträge zur Geschichte der deutschen Sprach und Literatur* 91 (1969): 28–76, at 30. See also Achim Masser, with Elisabeth De Felip-Jaud, *Die lateinisch-althochdeutsche Tatianbilingue Stiftsbibliothek St. Gallen Cod. 56*, Studien zum Althochdeutschen 25 (Göttingen, 1994).

80 'Les auantaiges que les Romains eurent sur eulx, durans lesdictes guerres, n'ont este obmys par les hystoriens Grecs et Latins, et en a beaucoup assemble Rhenan, Dont le me deporte, parce que ce n'est de ma matiere. Ceulx des Francois (qui vray semblablement ne furent petitz) ont este oubliez, pource que de leur part en celle saison n'estoit Riens escript. Au Regard des Heligast, Clodomir, Hunibald, et semblables croniqueurs, leur Lecture les Reiecte et condanne, faisant cognoistre quilz sont forgez a plaisir. Toutesfois l'occupation des Gaules,

princely houses) has an inventory of sources, absent from Du Tillet's transitional chapters.

Du Tillet spent more than a decade revising and expanding his *Recueil des Roys*, and it is the new version, completed in 1566, that has come to be known through the many editions of it published between 1578 and 1618. Perhaps because the inventories of sources proved less appealing to his intended courtly audience than he had originally thought they would be, Du Tillet dropped them from the new *Recueil* (although they would be inserted as additions to relevant chapters of the second recension in the printed editions published in 1607 and 1618). He included large translated excerpts from the sources in his revised chapters, and he enlarged the scope of the volume considerably. In the second part, Du Tillet added additional chapters dedicated to royal officials who had not been discussed before; in the first part, he began with Meroveus rather than with Hugues Capet. This reorganization meant that Du Tillet could now comfortably begin at the beginning. Thus, following a dedication to Charles IX, he commenced by discussing the origins of the French, the names and surnames of the French, and the ancient laws of the French, before returning to the chapter that had opened the first recension, now retitled, more appropriately, 'Des couronne et maison de France.' The chapters on names and laws were composed for this edition, but the section on the origin of the French was cleverly adapted and edited from the transitional chapters Du Tillet had written for the earlier recension. These he revised and rearranged so that he could begin, not with marriage customs, but rather with the true German origin of the French; the analysis of marital practices he utilized later, when comparing the customs of the French and Germans.

Du Tillet expanded the chapter on the origins of the French, adding references to numerous authors (including Dio Prusensis, whom he would have done better to avoid), and polishing his narrative and sharpening his judgments. His messages, however, remain the same, even if his learning is more flamboyantly displayed. In one respect the chapter is far stronger. Du Tillet had decided to attack the Trojan myth outright, rather than to do so indirectly. The tack he took was general, emphasizing that all nations, 'to exalt themselves and make themselves feared, have invented false origins, which their descendents have believed and publicized.' He cited Ammianus Marcellinus' observation that some traced the Gauls back to the Trojans, others to sites near the German sea. The Burgundians (who Du Tillet says were true Vandals) claimed Roman descent, the Saxons Macedonian, whereas the Huns say they came from the

et seigneurie establye en Icelles par les francois confessees par tous, et durans Iusques a present, manifestent lhonneur et proufict leur estre ala fin demoure des guerres des Romains': SP, Fr. F. v. IV, no. 8/1, fol. 120ʳ.

devil. Du Tillet ringingly concludes, 'The prince of the world, reigning over idolaters, kept them in such shadows.'[81]

Neither Jean du Tillet, the older or the younger, produced a scholarly attack on the myth of Trojan origins that rivalled those launched by the German humanists. Yet they effectively spread to their compatriots the messages that the Germans first announced.[82] They represented a middle phase in the passage from acceptance of venerated tradition to scholarly investigation that would plumb the antique sources for reliable guides to what the Franks had actually been and what they became when they conquered Gaul. They effectively undermined the myths that had long been cherished, and it is difficult to see how and why the myths continued to exert the influence they did, until the writers of the 1560s and 1570s, following where the Du Tillet brothers had led, effectively demolished them. Much remained to be done. The question why the Trojan myth was invented was just beginning to be raised, and there still remained pockets of resistance, learned as well as sentimental. But the two Du Tillet brothers had done their part in advancing serious study of the distant origins of the French, based on the sources, narrative and documentary, that both brothers pioneered in investigating and presenting to their contemporaries.

81 'Les nations pour s'exalter & faire craindre, inuenterent des fausses origines, lesquelles leurs descendans creurent & publierent. Ammian Marcellin, auant que les François obtinssent la Gaule, recite que aucuns disoient les Gaulois estre descendus des Troyens: les autres, qu'ils estoient sortis des lieux proches de la mer Germanique. Ailleurs que les Bourguignons (qui estoyent vrais Wandales) se vantoient estre descendus des Romains. Les Saxons se glorifoient estre venus des Macedoniens: & Iornand dit, que les Hunnes mettoient en auant la façon par laquelle ils auoient esté engendrez des diables. Le prince du monde regnant sur les idolatres, les retenoit en telles tenebres': *Recueil des Roys*, 8 (1580 ed.), 6–7 (1607 ed). Citing Pliny, Tacitus, and philological evidence, Guillaume Paradin presents the Vandals (and Germans) as ancestors of the Burgundians in *De Antiqvo Statv Bvrgvndiæ Liber* (Lyon, 1542; with privilege dated 6 March 1537/8), 9-10.

82 Particularly important for the transmission of German ideas to France is Pierre Aquilon's study, 'La réception de l'humanisme allemand à Paris à travers la production imprimée (1480–1540),' in *XVIIIᵉ Colloque internationale de Tours. L'Humanisme allemand (1480–1540)*, Humanistische Bibliothek, Abhandlungen – Texte – Skripten, Reihe 1, Abhandlungen 38 (Munich and Paris, 1979), 45-80. I am grateful to Myra Dickman Orth for bringing this essay to my attention.

Notes on Contributors

Michael Idomir Allen has taught medieval Latin and Latin palaeography in the Department of Classics, University of Chicago, since 1996. He has written articles on the medieval tradition of Vegetius, the poetry of Henry of Avranches, and the library and scholars of late medieval St Gall. He is currently preparing editions of Frechulf of Lisieux's history and Claudius of Turin's chronicle. A monograph on Frechulf is to follow. He is the translator of two books: one on Einsiedeln Abbey by G. Holzherr, and one on the Carolingians by Pierre Riché.

Bernard S. Bachrach has taught history at the University of Minnesota for the last thirty years and is co-founder and editor of the journal *Medieval Prosopography*. He is the author of books on Merovingian military organization (1972), the Alans (1973), medieval Jewish policy (1977), the Angevin count Fulk Nerra (1993), and the Gundovald affair (1994), among others. Two volumes of his collected articles have recently been published by Variorum. He is currently completing a monograph tentatively entitled 'Early Carolingian Warfare: Prelude to Empire.' His next project is a military biography of Geoffrey Plantagenet.

Elizabeth A.R. Brown taught at Brooklyn College of the City University of New York from 1963 to 1992. She has published widely on the politics, ritual, and institutions of medieval and early modern France. Her books include *Customary Aids and Royal Finance in Capetian France: The Marriage Aid of Philip the Fair* (1992), *'Franks, Burgundians, and Aquitanians' and the Royal Coronation Ceremony in France* (1992), *The Lit de justice: Semantics, Ceremonial, and the Parlement of Paris, 1300–1600* (1994), and an edition of five tracts by Jean Du Tillet (1994). Two volumes of her collected essays have been published by Variorum.

Roger Collins has been a Fellow in the Institute for Advanced Studies in the Humanities, University of Edinburgh, since 1994. He is author of *Early Medieval Spain, 400–1000* (1983; 2nd ed., 1995), *The Arab Conquest of Spain, 710–797* (1989), *Early Medieval Europe, 300–1000* (London, 1991), *Law, Culture and Regionalism in Early Medieval Spain* (1992), and *Fredegar* (1996). He has also co-edited works on Frankish and Anglo-Saxon history. His most recent books are *The Oxford Archaeological Guide to Spain* (1998), and *Charlemagne*, also forthcoming in 1998.

Giles Constable is professor in the School of Historical Studies at the Institute for Advanced Study in Princeton. Before coming to Princeton in 1985, he taught history at Harvard University and, from 1977 to 1984, was director of Dumbarton Oaks in Washington, D.C. His chief field of research is medieval religious institutions, especially monasticism. In addition to editing several medieval texts, chief among them the letters of Peter the Venerable, he has written books on monastic tithes (1964) and, most recently, *The Reformation of the Twelfth Century* (1996). Several volumes of his collected studies have been published by Variorum.

Andrew Gillett is a research fellow at Macquarie University, Sydney. His interests include late antique and early medieval historiography and history, especially the roles of diplomacy and of religious and ethnic divisions. He has written articles on Olympiodorus of Thebes, Cassiodorus, and Jordanes, as well as on barbarian settlements, Gothic-imperial relations, the division of the western and eastern Empire, and the role of imperial capitals. A book on traditions of political communication and diplomacy in the fifth and sixth centuries is forthcoming. He is presently working on Arianism in the same period.

Martin Heinzelmann is a member of the Deutsches Historisches Institut, Paris, and an editor of the review *Francia*. He has written widely on social, ecclesiastical, and prosopographical aspects of Gallic history from the fourth to the ninth centuries. He is the author of *Bischofsherrschaft in Gallien* (1976), *Les Vies anciennes de sainte Geneviève de Paris* (1986), and *Gregor von Tours, Zehn Bücher Geschichte* (1994). He is also a co-director of the research project 'Les sources hagiographiques narratives composées en Gaule avant l'an mil (SHG).'

Edward James has taught at University College Dublin and at the University of York, where he was Director of the Centre for Medieval Studies from 1990 to 1995. Since 1995 he has been professor of medieval history at the University of Reading. He has written widely on the history and archaeology of the early Franks and has published a translation of Gregory of Tours' *Life of the Fathers* (1991). Since 1986 he has edited *Foundation: The International Review of Science Fiction* and he was one of the founding editors of *Early Medieval Europe*. His most recent books are *The Franks* (1988) and *Science Fiction in the Twentieth Century* (1994). His next book, *Britain in the First Millennium*, is in press.

Steven Muhlberger teaches history at Nipissing University in North Bay. He is the author of *The Fifth-Century Chroniclers: Prosper, Hydatius, and the Gallic Chronicler of 452* (1990) and has written articles on Eugippius, the Gallic chronicler of 452, and the Copenhagen continuator of Prosper. He has also published work on his other interest, the place of democracy in world history, and has developed on-line resources for medieval studies.

Alexander Callander Murray is a member of the Department of History and Centre for Medieval Studies, University of Toronto. He is the author of *Germanic Kinship Structure: Studies in Law and Society in Late Antiquity and the Early Middle Ages* (1983) and has written articles on Merovingian administration and office-holding, and on the dating of *Beowulf*. He is presently completing a collection of sources on late Roman and Frankish Gaul. A monograph on public order in the Merovingian kingdom is in preparation.

Janet L. Nelson is the director of the Centre for Late Antique and Medieval Studies at King's College London, where she has taught since 1970. She is the author of *Charles the Bald* (1992); the translator of *The Annals of St-Bertin* (1991); and co-editor of papers on Charles the Bald (1989) and Alfred (1997). Two volumes of her articles have been published by Hambledon. Her work continues to focus on earlier medieval rulership, but in recent years she has become increasingly interested in gender and women's history. She is currently co-editing *Rituals of Power in Early Medieval Europe* (1998) and preparing a study of earlier medieval political thought.

Thomas F.X. Noble has taught in the Department of History, University of Virginia, since 1980. His publications focus on the papacy, early medieval Italy, and the Carolingians. He is the author of *The Republic of St. Peter: The Birth of the Papal State, 680–825* (1984), and co-editor of *Soldiers of Christ: Saints and Saints' Lives from Late Antiquity and the Early Middle Ages* (1994) and *Religion, Culture and Society in the Early Middle Ages: Studies in Honor of Richard E. Sullivan* (1997). He is presently completing a book on Carolingian polemics about sacred art.

Susan Reynolds, who lives in London, is an Emeritus Fellow of Lady Margaret Hall, Oxford, and a Senior Fellow of the Institute of Historical Research, London. She has written three books, all published by Oxford: *An Introduction to the History of English Medieval Towns* (1977); *Kingdoms and Communities in Western Europe, 900–1300* (1984); and *Fiefs and Vassals: The Medieval Evidence Reinterpreted* (1994). A collection of her articles has been published under the title *Ideas and Solidarities of the Medieval Laity: England and Western Europe* (1995).

Joseph Shatzmiller taught for over twenty years in the Department of History, University of Toronto. Since 1993 he has been the Smart Family Professor of Judaic Studies in the Department of History, Duke University. His interests are Jewish history in the Middle Ages, medieval medicine, travelers, and justice. He is the author of *Shylock Reconsidered: Jews, Moneylending and Medieval Society* (1989) and *Jews, Medicine, and Medieval Society* (1994), among other titles. A monograph with the provisional title 'Justice et injustice au Moyen Âge: le pròces de Robert de Mauvoisin, archevêque d'Aix en 1317' is in press.

Richard E. Sullivan is professor emeritus at Michigan State University, where he taught from 1954 until his retirement in 1989. He has authored and edited seven books dealing with church history, Charlemagne, Carolingian learning, and western civilization. He is the editor of *The Gentle Voices of Teachers: Aspects of Learning in the Carolingian Age* (1995). A collection of his articles has recently been published under the title *Christian Missionary Activity in the Early Middle Ages* (1994).

Chris Wickham is professor of early medieval history at the University of Birmingham, where he has taught since 1977, and editor of the journal *Past and Present*. His interests include the social history of Italy, 400–1250; oral and popular culture; legal history; history and archaeology; and the socio-economic history of the early Middle Ages. Among his books are *Early Medieval Italy* (1981), *The Mountains and the City* (1988), *Social Memory* (1992) with James Fentress, and *Comunità e clientele* (1995). Some of his articles are collected in *Land and Power* (1995). His most recent book, which is in press, is *Law, Custom and Community*.

Ian Wood is professor of early medieval history at the University of Leeds, where he has taught since 1976. Between 1993 and 1998, he was also co-ordinator of the European Science Foundation's programme on the Transformation of the Roman World. He is the author of *The Merovingian North Sea* (1983), *The Merovingian Kingdoms* (1994), and *Gregory of Tours* (1994), and has co-edited several collections of papers. He is currently finishing a translation and commentary on the prose works of Avitus of Vienne, with Danuta Shanzer, and a book on missionary hagiography from the fifth to eleventh centuries.